LOUISVILLE'S

Waterfront Park

A Riverfront Renaissance

ISBN 978-1-935497-32-5

Printed in Canada

Book design by Scott Stortz

Published by:

Waterfront Development Corporation
129 East River Road
Louisville, KY 40202
(502) 574-3768
Fax (502) 574-4111
www.louisvillewaterfront.com

in partnership with

Butler Books
P.O. Box 7311
Louisville, KY 40207
(502) 897-9393
Fax (502) 897-9797
www.butlerbooks.com

This book is dedicated to the Dreamers – those men and women

throughout our history who envisioned a better Louisville –

and then set their shoulders to the wheel to make it so.

LOUISVILLE'S
Waterfront Park

A Riverfront Renaissance

RICK BELL

BUTLER BOOKS
LOUISVILLE

Contents

Acknowledgments

Support for the research of this book and the establishment of a permanent archive of Waterfront Park's history was provided by the Waterfront Development Corporation. While the WDC staff was generous with their time and knowledge beyond belief, no restrictions were placed, or suggested, on materials used in the editorial voice of this publication. To David Karem, Mike Kimmel, Phyllis Williams, Marlene Grissom, Gary Pepper, Kelley Lewis, Ashley Cox and the rest of the staff go my thanks for their patience and hospitality. Theirs is an enviable unity and commitment to the mission of Waterfront Park, and everyone who visits the Park should recognize what these creative people have accomplished. My very special thanks go to Margaret Walker, who has been instrumental in organizing the visual images, mastering all computer tasks and performing yeoman's duty in proofreading the manuscript.

The Board of Directors of the Waterfront Development Corporation authorized the creation of this publication and the establishment of an archive concerning the creation of the Waterfront Park. Their unflinching support of the process of the park's development has been unwavering for more than twenty years. I especially appreciate the help for this publication provided by Nicole Walton, Rip Hatfield and Oliver Barber.

Finally, it is important to acknowledge and thank all the political leadership, both local and statewide, whose financial and organizational support have made Waterfront Park a reality. One political leader who deserves to be singled out is Mayor Jerry Abramson. His tenure in office – nearly in its entirety – coincides with the life of the Waterfront Park project. His continued support has been exemplary.

Joe Hardesty and the staff of the Kentucky Room in the Louisville Free Public Library opened the doors to the past with their strong collection of local newspapers on microfilm and incomparable vertical clipping files. James Holmberg, an old friend and former office mate, displayed his mastery of the remarkable collections of the Filson Historical Society. Robin Walker, Special Collections Assistant of the Filson, was a great help in locating and selecting some of the images in this book.

I greatly appreciated Colleen Wilson, of the National Society of the Sons of the American Revolution, located in Louisville, for introducing me to the society's archival resources. One of the most pleasant research surprises of the project was the discovery of the rich photographic collection at the Kentucky Historical Society in Frankfort. Some of its river photos are remarkable illustrations of the great age of steamboats.

The University of Louisville Photographic Archives is the visual treasure chest of Louisville heritage. Archivist Delinda Buie and Bill Carner again led me through their resources, especially the great Caufield and Shook Collection, which documented the industrial dumping grounds that was the waterfront for many years. Any photograph not given credit in a cutline has been drawn from the files of the Waterfront Development Corporation.

Old friends opened up their collections and shared their detailed knowledge of local river lore. Mike Maloney shared his Farrell family stories and archives, providing three great photos for the book. My thanks go to Cletus Blandford, Louisville's fireman-historian, for opening his files, and also for introducing me to the Robinson Crusoe of Towhead Island.

A maritime historian without equal, Leland R. Johnson, could not have been more generous with his encyclopedic understanding of river lore and written sources. Once again, I have depended on old friend Chuck Parrish for his wise counsel and editor's eye for inspection of early versions of the manuscript. Our most articulate river rat, Chuck Parrish is a fountain of knowledge of local history.

Once again it was a great pleasure to work with my publisher, Carol Butler. Her constant positive attitude buoys many a sagging spirit and her contributions to Louisville's heritage cannot be over emphasized. It is a deep regret that Bill Butler, founder of Butler Books, is not still around to read this book. Every writer picks out an audience for his work and I aimed my efforts at the late Bill Butler. I felt that if Bill would have been informed, amused or intrigued by a passage, I had reached my goal as a writer.

Work on this book began in February 1957, when my dad and I, as a twelve-year-old, went down to the old Fourth Street wharf to take pictures of the Life-Saving Station. That's when I decided I wanted to learn more about the Louisville waterfront.

Rick Bell

Introduction

Each generation has determined its own purpose for the land where the city of Louisville meets the river's edge. This book attempts to chronicle the waterfront's story from Revolutionary War military post to major American inland river port, and from industrial powerhouse to its current manifestation – the majestic Waterfront Park – honored and well-used by the citizens of Louisville.

Because of its location next to the Falls of the Ohio, Louisville's history is uniquely tied to river life, river commerce and river traditions. In the earliest days of the Waterfront Development Corporation, the agency charged with renovating Louisville's blighted waterfront, citizen forums were held to ask people what they wanted at the riverfront. At these 1988 public discussions, many individuals expressed their desire for a downtown park at the water's edge. A particular request was to "make the waterfront unique and indigenous to Louisville."

The Park Master Plan, the vision statement of the Waterfront Development Corporation, expressed clear priorities for its mission. "The Waterfront Master Plan is not conceived as a generic waterfront development project that merely facilitates activities next to the river. Rather, it is seen as an opportunity to respect the history and character of Louisville; to create a place where nature and the city meet in a way that is unique to this time and place."

This book examines aspects of the character of Louisville and its citizens, with an emphasis on those events, personalities and opportunities stimulated by the best harbor and steamboat landing on the Ohio River. With its long history as a center for transshipment of passengers and cargo around the Falls, Louisville hosted numerous visiting writers, artists, mountebanks,

politicians, heroes and villains and, fortunately, many left behind their impressions. The city has also been blessed for generations with a lively tradition of quality journalism, and has boasted some of America's most distinctive editorial voices. Contemporary readers will notice the highly individualized spelling and punctuation styles of the eighteenth and nineteenth centuries. Even the city's founder, George Rogers Clark, occasionally spelled the name of his former outpost "Lewisville."

A progression of activities, always thought by contemporaries as community improvements, transformed the Louisville waterfront from its mud-flats origin. When Beargrass Creek was moved during the 1850s it was hailed as the transformation of the city. In the early 1880s, with the installation of the Short-Line railroad trestle across the city's front door, Louisville's business community saw this as a grand advancement. A later group of civic boosters in the 1920s, who actively promoted the construction of docks, warehouses, salvage yards, asphalt plants, sand and gravel operations and other maritime industries, trumpeted the city's modernity and progressive industrial outlook. In the 1960s a new interstate highway running above the old elevated railroad track was declared essential to the city's continued economic welfare.

The historic barriers between the city and its waterfront – Beargrass Creek, the Short-Line Railroad and I-64 – served to alienate Louisvillians from their source, the Ohio River. Despite these barriers, the river continued to draw people to its shoreline to sit and quietly watch the river roll past them. When the vision of creating the Waterfront Park emerged in the mid-1980s, the Waterfront Development Corporation began a long and determined campaign that emphasized continuity of effort and persistent application of quality landscape design standards.

When Louisville was granted city status in 1828, the community chose as its first motto the Latin word "*Perseverando.*" The term meaning "by persevering" speaks volumes about Louisville's character. Hardened by periods of destructive flooding, citizens have repeatedly pulled together for the common good, and building the Waterfront Park became one of those community causes.

Now in 2011, and after twenty-five years of activity, the initial project as envisioned in the Master Plan is nearing completion, with only the paving of the Big Four Bridge walkway left to conclude. Waterfront Park will never be finished, as future generations will determine their purpose for the Louisville waterfront. But for at least awhile, at the beginning of the twenty-first century, a landscaped jewel lies at the river's edge at Louisville.

The Ohio River reaches its widest expanse at the natural barrier at the Falls. The river has carried travelers since ancient times including Native American hunters, French explorers, British colonists and American frontiersmen.

Louisville, Virginia
(1773-1792)

…I observed the little Island of about seven acres oposite to whare the Town of Lewisville now stands seldom or never was intirly covered by the water, I resolved to take possession and fortify which I did…dividing the Island among the Families for Gardens, these Families that followed me I now found to be of Real Service as they ware of little expence, and with the Invalids would keep possession of this Little post untill we should be able to Occupy the Main shore which happened in the Fall.

– George Rogers Clark - 1778

Most Louisvillians believe that George Rogers Clark and his band of American patriots were the first English-speaking party to establish the site of their hometown. But by the time Clark reached the Falls of the Ohio in 1778, many of the fundamental elements of town building, including the initial land surveys, establishment of legal ownership and published advertisements – the underlying steps in establishing a town on the frontier – had already been achieved.

Boasting topography unique among American inland rivers, including an imposing navigational barrier and the finest natural harbor on the Ohio River, the Falls of the Ohio invited settlement. Clark's use of the site during the American Revolution as a staging area for attacks on the British forts in the Illinois territory was a fortunate combination of need and opportunity. But others had come before Clark, and many others would follow.

Oyo, the Great River

Untold generations of Native Americans were intimately familiar with the Falls of the Ohio. The Ohio (from the Iroquoian word "Oyo", meaning "great" or "beautiful" river) was the major water transportation artery for the region's Shawnee, Delaware, Wyandot and other mid-continent inland tribes. As the river was normally at a very low stage during summer and fall months, the rocky Falls provided a predictable route for the enormous buffalo herds on their seasonal north-south migrations. Indian hunters since ancient times knew the strategic opportunity provided by the annual passage of these distinctively American beasts that were the economic and nutritional base for most of the region's native people.

French explorers, trappers, clerics and military parties had traveled the maritime highway they referred to as *La Belle Riviere* since at least 1749, when Pierre-Joseph Céloron de Blainville came down from Canada to explore and defend his nation's land claims. Their extensive trade agreements with the area's tribes legitimized French command of the central Ohio River Valley. Following their defeat in the French and Indian War, these original European visitors to the Falls lost claim on the area. Great Britain, and most especially the Virginia Colony, assumed ownership and control.

British agents were quick to investigate the new lands they had won. George Croghan was the first known English-speaking explorer to record his brief visit to the future site of Louisville's Waterfront Park. In his journal entry for June 1, 1765, Croghan recorded a laconic memorial, "We arrived within a mile of the Falls of the Ohio, where we encamped, after coming about fifty miles this day."

The following day he added, "early in the morning we

embarked, and passed the Falls. The river being very low we were obligated to lighten our boats, and pass on the north side of a little island, which lies in the middle of the river. In general what is called the Falls here, is no more than rapids; and in the least fresh, a bateau of any size may come and go on each side without any risk. This day we proceeded sixty miles…"

In the following year, Captain Thomas Hutchins, a British army officer and future geographer of the United States, visited the area and prepared a thorough study of the Ohio Valley. He drew an accurate map and left a studied written description of the Falls of the Ohio. It was the first detailed overview of the area provided by a qualified engineer or surveyor.

THE RAPIDS, IN A DRY SEASON, ARE DIFFICULT TO DESCEND WITH LOADED BOATS OR BARGES, WITHOUT A GOOD PILOT; IT WOULD BE ADVISABLE THEREFORE FOR THE BARGEMEN, IN SUCH SEASON, RATHER THAN RUN ANY RISK IN PASSING THEM, TO UNLOAD PART OF THEIR CARGOES, AND RESHIP IT WHEN THE BARGES HAVE GOT THROUGH

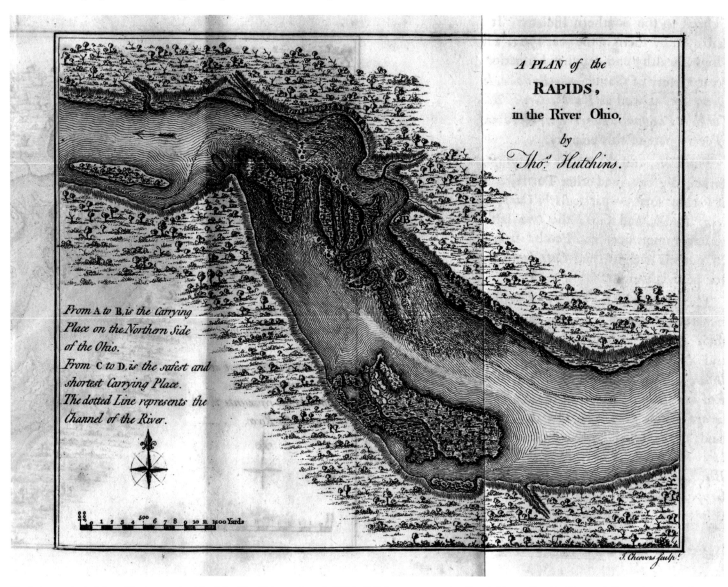

A PLAN of the RAPIDS, in the River Ohio, by Thos. Hutchins.

From A to B, is the Carrying Place on the Northern Side of the Ohio.
From C to D, is the safest and shortest Carrying Place.
The dotted Line represents the Channel of the River.

The first accurate depiction of the topography at the Falls of the Ohio was drawn in 1766 by British army cartographer Captain Thomas Hutchins. The map indicates the preferred passage through the dangerous rapids and shows Beargrass Creek when it still emptied into the river in what would become downtown Louisville. (Filson Historical Society)

THE RAPIDS. IT MAY, HOWEVER, BE PROPER TO OBSERVE THAT LOADED BOATS IN FRESHES HAVE BEEN EASILY ROWED AGAINST THE STREAM (UP THE RAPIDS), AND THAT OTHERS, BY MEANS ONLY OF A LONG SAIL, HAVE ASCENDED THEM.

Captain Hutchins' perceptive analysis provided a pattern for the first one hundred years of Louisville's history and its economic development. He correctly identified the dangers to boatmen trying to pass over the surging rapids with valuable cargoes, and he suggested the role of Falls Pilots, a calling which would develop into a uniquely Louisville profession.

Hutchins also recognized the area's prime economic opportunity, that of transshipping cargoes and passengers around the Falls by landing at the future site of Louisville and carrying their trade goods and furs to an area safely below the rapids. The two most eligible sites on the southern Ohio River shoreline would become Portland and Shippingport, the lower river locations essential to portage successfully around the Falls.

Hutchins also described the physical power of the river as it poured through a passage in the exposed shelf of Devonian limestone that created the barrier.

IN A DRY SEASON THE DESCENT OF THE RAPIDS, IN THE DISTANCE OF A MILE, IS ABOUT TWELVE OR FIFTEEN FEET, AND THE PASSAGE DOWN WOULD NOT BE DIFFICULT EXCEPT, PERHAPS, FOR THE FOLLOWING REASONS: TWO MILES ABOVE THEM THE RIVER IS DEEP AND THREE QUARTERS OF A MILE BROAD; BUT THE CHANNEL IS MUCH CONTRACTED AND DOES NOT EXCEED TWO HUNDRED AND FIFTY YARDS IN BREADTH (NEAR THREE-QUARTERS OF THE BED OF THE RIVER, ON THE SOUTHEASTERN SIDE OF IT, BEING FILLED WITH A FLAT LIMESTONE ROCK, SO THAT IN A DRY SEASON THERE IS SELDOM MORE THAN SIX OR EIGHT INCHES OF WATER), IT IS UPON THE NORTHERN SIDE OF THE RIVER, AND BEING CONFINED, AS ABOVE MENTIONED, THE DESCENDING WATERS TUMBLE OVER THE RAPIDS WITH A CONSIDERABLE DEGREE OF CELERITY AND FORCE. THE CHANNEL IS OF DIFFERENT DEPTHS, BUT NOWHERE, I THINK, LESS THAN FIVE FEET. IT IS CLEAR, AND UPON EACH SIDE OF IT ARE LARGE BROKEN ROCKS, A FEW INCHES UNDER WATER.

Both Croghan and Hutchins agreed that the series of rock ledges were more correctly termed rapids, rather than falls. In about two and one-half miles of river distance, the elevation of the river bed drops about twenty-six feet. When the river was filled from rains or snow melt, the passage over the Falls was relatively easy, even when ascending. What would come to be called the Upper River stretched from Pittsburgh to the head of the Falls at Louisville. The Lower River commences below the Falls at Portland and continues south and west until it reaches the Mississippi River at the future site of Cairo, Illinois.

Approximating the Ohio River's cascading rapids, the Water Feature in Waterfront Park recalls the stair-step rock ledges and shallow pools that characterized the natural Falls, where the river drops 26 feet in about 2.5 miles. The only natural navigational barrier between Pittsburgh and New Orleans, the Falls attracted American frontiersmen to its southern shore.

The British political system in the North American colonies extended the boundaries of the seaboard colonies westward to the Pacific Ocean. The Colony of Virginia created Fincastle County in 1772 to provide administrative authority over the large area south and west of the Kanawha River, south of the Ohio and north of the Carolina line.

In 1769, shortly after Hutchins' visit, two brothers, Hancock and Richard Taylor, explored the area around the Falls of the Ohio. The Taylors, like many other pioneer Virginians, did little more than observe, but they would have a lasting impact on Louisville's future. The Taylor family provided the names of streets, lakes, subdivisions and military installations for future Louisville maps.

After leaving the Falls and traveling down the Mississippi River, the Taylors returned to Virginia by passing through the Creek Indian nation. They and their descendants later returned to Kentucky and earned considerable notoriety. A son of Richard Taylor, General Zachary Taylor, would become the only Louisvillian to serve as President of the United States.

To compensate colonial soldiers and militia who successfully fought and won the French and Indian War, the British government provided land grants rather than cash payments. The land provided was located west of the Allegheny mountains and south of the Ohio River. While royal officials in London considered this British territory, the original inhabitants of the area strongly disagreed. Attempts to claim and defend the Fincastle County land grants would lead to the most bitter and protracted warfare between white men and red men ever experienced in America. Kentucky, "the dark and bloody ground," was too valuable to relinquish without a fight. Bitter struggles – both on battlefields and in courtrooms – would mark the first two decades of life at the Falls.

An Unlikely Partnership

If the Louisville story has a villain, the leading candidate for the role must be Dr. John Connolly of Pittsburgh. For his service as a surgeon's mate in the British army, Connolly was awarded a 2,000-acre land grant in December 1773 from a grateful Crown. Connolly was one of the most dependable British agents in America, serving the last royal governor of Virginia, Lord Dunmore. At the outbreak of the Revolution, Connolly was ordered to raise a regiment of Tories, form alliances with Indian tribes and conduct a merciless war against rebels west of the Alleghenies.

The hard Devonian shelf of limestone that nearly transects the Ohio River presented challenges to voyagers. Ordinarily too dry to allow boats safe passage above the sharp rocks, the Falls was only navigable during high water, usually in the late winter and early spring. Failing a rise in the river's depth, boats were compelled to land on the Kentucky shore and transport cargoes around the Falls.

To his original land grant, Connolly added an additional 2,000 acres purchased from Ensign Charles DeWarnsdorff. With his great knowledge of the western territories, Connolly chose the real estate that would become downtown Louisville and its West End, four thousand acres stretching from Preston Street west to Shawnee Park and from the Ohio River south to Broadway.

To finance his large land purchase from DeWarnsdorff, Connolly found a most unlikely business partner. Colonel John Campbell, also of Pittsburgh, was a successful merchant, fur trader and an American patriot. Campbell's investment resulted in an equal share in the prime four thousand acres of tree-covered land adjacent to the Falls of the Ohio. The most direct route linking upper and lower Ohio River ports traversed the Connolly-Campbell land, and the establishment of a town at this crucial pinch-point in navigation was predictable.

On July 8, 1773, another well-known local name made its first appearance at the Falls. Surveyor Thomas Bullitt was sent by Lord Dunmore to chart land grant claims in the Kentucky wilderness. Captain Bullitt and his surveying party established a base camp when they reached the natural harbor formed by the entrance of Beargrass Creek into the Ohio River. At that time, and for much of the city's formative history, the mouth of Beargrass Creek lay directly between what would become Third and Fourth Streets. Two hundred years in the future, in 1962, this spot would become the dock for the *Belle of Louisville* steamboat.

Bullitt's survey crew featured some very important players in Kentucky's history, including James Douglas, James Harrod, John Smith, James Sodousky, Isaac Hite, Abram Haptonstall, Ebenezer Severns, John Fitzpatrick and John Cowan. Although none of their survey maps survive, the basic layout of Louisville is the result of their efforts. However, since Colonel William Preston, the Surveyor of Fincastle County, had not named Bullitt an official deputy, he demanded that all the original surveys be repeated by his own assistants before he would recognize their legal validity.

Colonel Bullitt returned to Virginia and became involved in the early struggles of the American Revolution. Fully intending to return to the Falls, Bullitt died and passed his own land claims to a half-brother, Major William Bullitt. His sons Thomas and Cuthbert and nephew Alexander Scott Bullitt of Oxmoor were among the upper tier of local society for generations.

The unlikely partners, John Connolly and John Campbell, wasted little time in preparing a land sale in the proposed new town they called Falls of the Ohio. The April 7, 1774, edition of the *Virginia Gazette* in Williamsburg proclaimed the land at the head of the Falls as "formed by Nature as a temporary Magazine...for Produce and Merchandises." There were no known buyers for the promising location, and with Revolution looming, Indian warfare on the increase and political instability the rule, there would be none.

The fates of Connolly and Campbell were omens of a rocky start to town building at the Falls. During the earliest days of the American Revolution in 1775, John Connolly, the prime Tory agitator and instigator of violent resistance by his Indian allies, was captured by rebel forces in Maryland as he attempted to reach Lord Dunmore. He would remain a prisoner in American custody until 1781. Ironically, John Campbell, the ardent American patriot, was captured by the British after he left Louisville bound for Pittsburgh. He, too, would be imprisoned for the duration of the war, and, as time would demonstrate, a great many decisions would be complicated by Campbell's absence.

"This spot in the wilderness seemed a very Eden…"

To guarantee that claimants secured legally recognized land claims, Colonel William Preston sent his own party of twenty-six men to re-survey and validate the original Bullitt charts. James Douglas and Hancock Taylor returned to the Falls to lead two of three survey crews. Preston's assistant, John Floyd, brought another group, arriving at the Falls on May 29, 1774. Perhaps no single individual, save George Rogers Clark, had the lasting impact on the area's future as John Floyd. His energy, intelligence and natural leadership abilities made him a commanding presence, and his name would become identified with creeks, knobs, parks and a future county in Kentucky.

The surveyors camped on a small rocky island laying several hundred yards off the Kentucky shoreline, a site known at the time as Dunmore's Island. From this relatively secure location, Douglas surveyed the 4,000-acre claim of Dr. John Connolly, and John Floyd claimed his personal 1,000-acre plot in what was later known as St. Matthews.

Hancock Taylor carved out a 1,000-acre claim for William Preston, located just east of what would become First Street, and an additional 1,000 acres for himself. Part of his land, about six miles east of the Falls, would become Springfield, the childhood home and eventual burial ground of President Zachary Taylor. Shortly after completing his task, Hancock Taylor was killed by Indians near the mouth of the Kentucky River, gaining the unwelcome distinction of being one of the first white men slain in Kentucky.

To protect his land claims at the Falls, John Connolly dispatched his own party of five frontiersmen, led by Sanders "Sandy" Stewart. To Stewart falls the honor of being Louisville's earliest resident. In later years he remembered the pristine natural state of the Falls of the Ohio as he first saw them.

WITHOUT ANY INTERRUPTION FROM INDIANS WE LANDED ON THIS ISLAND JUNE 8, 1775. THE SCENERY AT THIS TIME WAS BEAUTIFUL, AND SUCH AS THE EYE OF CIVILIZED MAN EVER GAZED UPON. HERE WAS THE BROAD AND BEAUTIFUL OHIO, SWEEPING ON DOWN HER PEACEFUL SHORE IN SILENT GRANDEUR AND FLOWING ON FOR HUNDREDS OF MILES TO MINGLE HER WATERS WITH OLD OCEAN. THE ODORS OF THE WILD FLOWERS – THE HAWTHORN, THE HONEYSUCKLE, THE JESSAMINE, THE ROSE AND LILY; THE GREEN FOREST, WHERE THE AX WAS A STRANGER, ALL IN ITS NATIVE BEAUTY, FILLED UP THE BACKGROUND. THE FEATHERED TRIBE, FROM THE EAGLE TO THE LINNET, THE SEAGULL AND THE CRANE, SWEEPING OVER THE FALLS, TURNING UP THEIR SNOWY WINGS GLITTERING IN THE SUNLIGHT; THE BUFFALO, THE BEAR, THE DEER LYING UNDER THE TREES IN WARM WEATHER, PERFECTLY SERENE, AS THEY WERE STRANGERS TO THE SOUND OF THE RIFLE AND SO UNACQUAINTED WITH MAN THAT THEIR TAMENESS ASTONISHED ME. THIS SPOT IN THE WILDERNESS SEEMED A VERY EDEN; AND I HAD NO EVE TO BE TEMPTED BY THE SERPENT, I RESOLVED TO TAKE UP MYSELF HERE, AND NEVER FROM THIS ISLE DEPART. HERE I WILL BE BURIED.

Sandy Stewart made good his intention to stay at the Falls, and especially on Corn Island. John Filson, in his *Discovery, Settlement and Present State of Kentucke*, quotes Daniel Boone as saying that in 1777, Boonesborough, Harrodsburg and Logan's

Station contained all the white people in Kentucky, except for those at the Falls of the Ohio. A condition of Connolly's land claims was a requirement to clear and cultivate a portion of his land within two years. The probable purpose of Stewart's party was to accomplish this mission.

Although there is scant documentation of Sandy Stewart's life, he would be remembered as the "island ferryman" of Corn Island. He survived until the early 1830s and, even as an eighty-year-old man, earned his living by piloting a skiff between the main shore and his beloved island where visitors enjoyed fish fries, barbecues and other social events.

The Son of Virginia – The Sword of Kentucky

At last, the stage is set for the appearance of Louisville's founder, defender and great hero, George Rogers Clark. The second son of a remarkable frontier Virginia family, Clark received a fine education in a private academy taught by Donald Robertson, where he excelled in mathematics, natural sciences, history and geography (any review of the letters of George Rogers Clark will reveal he performed less well in the craft of spelling).

Raised a woodsman, Clark used his education to become a surveyor, one of many bright young Virginians like Washington, Jefferson and Floyd who saw pristine wildernesses and recognized their great potential.

Clark's ability to inspire confidence in the militia men who defended the Virginia frontier was

A bronze tribute to General George Rogers Clark, Louisville's founder, and one of the great heroes of the American Revolution, stands on the city's Belvedere. Clark made nearly every important decision concerning the town he named Louisville, and was the first person to advocate preserving an open public space on the waterfront.

manifested at an early age. In 1774, at the age of twenty-two, George Rogers Clark was already fighting the Shawnee during the brief conflict known as Lord Dunmore's War, and he was surveying for the Ohio Company in Kentucky. Shortly after the outbreak of the Revolution, he traveled to Williamsburg to successfully argue that Fincastle County should be reorganized as Kentucky County. He returned to the land west of Cumberland Gap and south of the Ohio River where he distinguished himself as a political and military leader. A master of both strategy and tactics, Clark formed a bold vision to defend the struggling stations on the Kentucky frontier from Indian attacks, and to strike a staggering blow to British forces in the Illinois Territory at the same time. No other American officer during the Revolutionary War led with the vigor, vision and audacity of George Rogers Clark. To accomplish his goals, Clark needed to recruit and equip a fighting force, and locate a secure base for his military campaigns.

George Rogers Clark chose the Falls of the Ohio to be his base. In later days, Clark stated, "…it would be absolutely necessary to have a post of Communication on the River between the Illinois and Kentucky and of course the Falls was the more Elligible spot as it would answer all those desirable purposes and in a great measure Protect the Navigation of the River as every Vessel would be obliged to stop some time at that place they would be always exposed to the Indians …I wrote to Colonel Bowman informed him of my Intention of fixing a Garrison at the Falls…"

Clark convinced Virginia's first republican governor, Patrick Henry, of the wisdom of attacking the British outposts of Vincennes, Cahokia and Kaskaskia in far western Illinois. Clark and Governor Henry agreed that plans for the operation must be kept in strict secrecy, believing that a volunteer militia force would be unwilling to undergo such a challenge if they knew the true mission. Clark recruited 150 volunteers – the Illinois Regiment – who navigated down the Ohio River under the assumption they were going to defend the early Bluegrass stations against Indian war parties, particularly the powerful Shawnee.

Attaching themselves to the military party preparing to depart Redstone, near Fort Pitt, were some fifteen to twenty civilian families. These eager pioneers were drawn by the promise of rich and available land being opened in Kentucky. Although Clark was initially skeptical about the presence of the civilians, they helped screen the true purpose of his campaign.

On May 27, 1778, the party landed its flatboats on the seventy-acre island outcropping of limestone and willow trees lying just off the Kentucky shoreline, where Clark began training his troops. The outcropping was easily defendable, having the river as a protective moat. Upon being informed of the party's true mission to invade the British forts, Lieutenant Colonel Clark was forced to capture and punish several men who waded ashore and attempted to desert. The civilian pioneers, led by Richard Chenoweth, began erecting a small stockade and planted a crop. After this crop ripened, Dunmore's Island became Corn Island.

I KNEW THAT MY CASE WAS DESPERATE, BUT THE MORE I REFLECTED ON MY WEAKNESS THE MORE I WAS PLEASED WITH THE ENTERPRISE; JOINED BY A FEW OF THE KENTUCKYANS, …I HAD ENCAMPED ON A SMALL ISLAND IN THE MIDDLE OF THE FALLS…ON THIS ISLAND I FIRST BEGAN TO DISCIPLINE MY LITTLE ARMY KNOWING THAT TO BE THE MOST ESSENTIAL POINT TOWARDS SUCCESS, MOST OF THEM DETERMINED TO FOLLOW ME, THE REST SEEING NO PROBABILITY OF MAKING THEIR ESCAPE I SOON GOT THAT SUBORDINATION AS I COULD WISH FOR; ABOUT TWENTY FAMILIES THAT HAD FOLLOWED ME MUCH AGAINST MY INCLINATION I FOUND NOW TO BE OF SERVICE TO ME IN GUARDING A BLOCK HOUSE THAT I HAD ERECTED ON THE ISLAND TO SECURE MY PROVISIONS.

After a month of preparation and training, Clark's grand invasion of the West was ready to commence.

...EVERY PREPARATION NOW MADE FOR OUR DEPARTURE AFTER SPENDING A DAY OF AMUSEMENT IN PARTING WITH OUR FRIENDS OF KENTUCKY THEY TO RETURN TO THE DEFENCE OF THEIR CUNTREY AND WE IN SERCH OF NEW ADVENTURES AND ON THE [BLANK IN MANUSCRIPT] OF JUNE 1778 WE LEFT OUR LITTLE ISLAND AND RUN ABOUT A MILE UP THE RIVER IN ORDER TO GAIN THE MAIN CHANNEL, AND SHOT THE FALL AT THE VERY MOMENT OF THE SUNS BEING IN A GREAT ECLIPSE WHICH CAUSED VARIOUS CONJECTURES AMONG THE SUPERSTITIOUS...

George Rogers Clark's adventurers made their dramatic departure westward and gained immortality in their capture, and re-capture, of Vincennes and the other British outposts. Thoroughly outmaneuvering his archenemy, Lieutenant Governor Henry Hamilton, the hated "hair-buyer" of the Kentucky frontier, George Rogers Clark seized control of an area that would become all or part of seven American states. His conquest of the Northwest Territory cowed his Indian enemies and gave the fledgling Kentucky forts a breathing space to build houses, plant crops and improve defenses.

When Clark and his men triumphantly returned to the Falls of the Ohio in 1779, the small frontier community they left behind had a new location and a new name.

Shortly after departing the Falls, Clark received the welcome news that France had formed an alliance with the United States to join the war against Great Britain. To salute King Louis XVI for his support for the American cause, Lieutenant Colonel George Rogers Clark sent back a message to the outpost on Corn Island that the location would henceforth be called Louisville. He also ordered that the settlers leave the temporary sanctuary of their island and move to the Kentucky mainland. Beginning in the winter of 1778-79 they selected a location near the river's edge and the future Twelfth Street. Here, under the able direction

The ill-fated King Louis XVI, Louisville's namesake, stands on the Courthouse Square at Sixth and Jefferson Streets, one of only two public lots that survived a sell-off of land by the town's earliest trustees. General Clark ordered the new town be named to honor France's monarch in appreciation of his nation's support against the British during the American Revolution.

of Richard Chenoweth, they erected a series of wooden houses joined together to form protective walls. Outside the gates of the structure, called Fort-on-Shore, the settlers began to build cabins, blacksmith shops and other essential improvements. They referred to this, the first Louisville neighborhood, as "White Home."

In April of 1779 legal procedures to establish the town of Louisville began when residents held a public meeting and elected seven trustees, including William Harrod, Richard Chenoweth, James Patton, Henry French, Edward Bulger, Simeon Moore and Marsham Brashears. They began the process, under the existing laws of Kentucky County, of dividing the land in an equitable manner by creating a map and conducting a public lottery for half-acre lots.

The opportunity to acquire free town lots was irresistible to land-hungry pioneers, and "adventurers" were immediately attracted to the area. Free land and Clark's dramatic victories in the West inspired confidence in the future of the new town of Louisville. The first trustee meeting detailed the process of dividing the land. It provided, "That each adventurer draw for only one lot by equal chance. That every such person be obligated to clear off the undergrowth and begin to cultivate part thereof by the 10th of June, and build thereon a good covered house, 16 feet by 20, by the 25 of December. That no person sell his lot to some person without one, but that it be given up to the trustees to dispose of to some new adventurer on pain of forfeiture thereof." The Virginia Assembly would grant three extensions of the time limit to build cabins because of the persistence of Indian attacks during the formative years of Louisville's history.

Urban Planning in Eighteenth-Century America

George Rogers Clark was involved in virtually every early decision concerning Louisville. He created a town plan, based on a gridiron pattern of cross streets meeting major thoroughfares at right angles. This pattern, referred to as the "Philadelphia plan" among colonists, was considered the only acceptable design of a new town. In the minds of early Americans, curving or meandering streets were reminiscent of a bucolic village. Early settlers believed every new town had the potential of becoming the next Philadelphia, and an orderly street pattern was considered a necessity.

Clark's 1779 plan of Louisville reveals that the military commander was also a visionary urban planner. The entire riverfront was to be considered public property, providing free

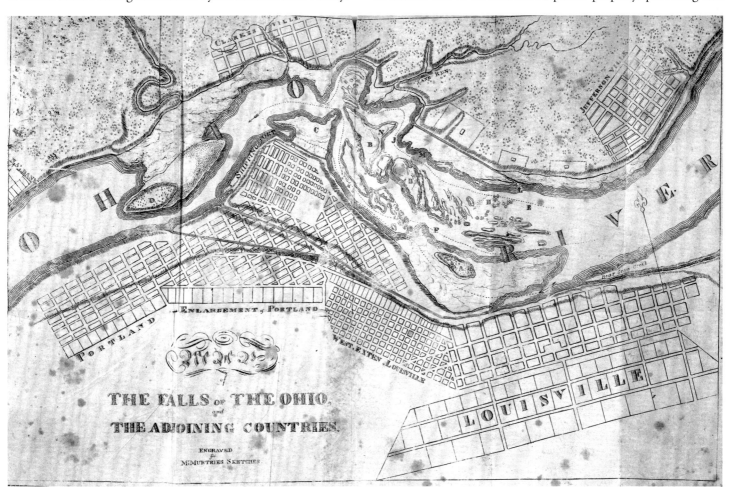

The first history of Louisville, written in 1819 by Dr. Henry McMurtrie, featured a detailed map of the town, with most of the features still familiar two hundred years later. The most significant difference was the relocation of Beargrass Creek from its original site between Third and Fourth Streets, to its Cut-Off two miles upstream. *(University of Louisville Photo Archives)*

and easy access to the water's edge. This was viewed as both an economic and social advantage, with free trade based on river traffic and transshipment around the Falls seen as essential. Clark also believed that good health was dependent upon providing breathing space for everyone. Even though the site was still densely covered with a thick forest, he envisioned a future when city streets and closely packed buildings would become the norm.

His primary streets, which ran east and west, paralleled the predominant profile of the river frontage of the Ohio. The riverfront was little more than a mud flat, with land rising quickly to the south to form a "second bank" on what would become Main Street. George Rogers Clark extended his town plan southward to include Market and Jefferson, broad east-west streets that moved back from the river. A series of numbered streets – First through Twelfth – ran downriver from the town's eastern border. Clark proposed undeveloped space be left as public property between Jefferson Street and Green Street, lying one-half block to its south. This strip of undeveloped land extended the entire width of the town, and was intended to supply an open common for public assembly and militia drill grounds, while also providing a shady area for social gatherings, barbecues and recreation.

La Barre Grasse

Running almost parallel to the banks of the Ohio River was a broad clear stream rising out of eight natural springs that drained the highlands east and south of Louisville. Almost eighty feet wide when it entered the Ohio, the stream was Beargrass Creek. Along with the Falls, it was the defining geographical feature that influenced Louisville's development.

There are several theories about the origin of the word Beargrass. Some believe that the pioneers saw bears eating the tall grasses that grew near the stream's edge. Others contend that a yucca plant, called Beargrass, was its inspiration. Captain Alfred Pirtle, a perceptive nineteenth-century historian, gave his reasoning for the Beargrass name as follows:

Since its difficult and expensive relocation in 1854, Beargrass Creek has emptied into the Ohio River well above Louisville and Towhead Island. This formerly pristine pioneer-era stream became an open sewage system for dozens of slaughterhouses and other heavy industries lining its shores in Butchertown.

THE FRENCH SAW THE CREEK THAT FELL INTO THE MAIN STREAM, DIRECTLY OPPOSITE THE HEAD OF THE ISLAND, THAT HERE DIVIDED THE RIVER. THEY HAD EARLY NOTED THE VERY HARD LAYER OF ROCK THAT EXTENDED ALMOST ALL THE WAY FROM ONE BANK OF THE RIVER TO THE OTHER, AND THAT IN A SEASON OF EXTREME LOW WATER IN THE FALL OF THE YEAR, THAT THIS LAYER OF ROCK FORMED A COMPLETE DAM, EXCEPT FOR A SMALL PASSAGEWAY NEAR THE RIGHT BANK, TO THE WATERS OF THE RIVER. THEY GAVE THIS REEF THE FRENCH NAME OF "LA BARRE GRASSE," IN ENGLISH, THE "BIG REEF," AND THE NAME NATURALLY BECAME ATTACHED TO THE SMALL STREAM ENTERING THE RIVER AT THE HEAD OF THE REEF. ENGLISHMEN, IN COURSE OF TIME, BECAME ACQUAINTED WITH THE NAVIGATION OF THE OHIO, LEARNING IN THEIR TURN, ITS FEATURES FROM THE FRENCH, BUT THEY CORRUPTED THE PURE FRENCH "BARRE GRASSE" INTO THE

Virginia vernacular of "Bar Grass," and in writing was given as Bear Grass.

The Falls, by crossing the path of the Ohio, broadened and slowed the great river's flow. The islands and rocks in the river directed the current back toward the Kentucky shore in a series of strong eddies. Beargrass Creek, entering the river diagonally from the east, was a welcoming port for slow-moving flatboats coming down the Ohio River.

Where Beargrass Creek joined the Ohio River, a narrow triangle was formed. As it stretched eastward, toward the source of the creek, the wedge of land lying between the two streams gradually widened. This area north of Beargrass Creek and adjacent to the Ohio River became known as the Point. Prior to naming the new town Louisville, in early letters and diaries the community at the Falls of the Ohio was often referred to as "Mouth of Beargrass." This spear point of land evolved through decades of usage, passing from a mud-flat trading camp to the site of Louisville's Waterfront Park and, in doing so, it provided a stage for the next twenty-two decades of American history.

As people gathered at the Falls of the Ohio, they banded together to face common threats to their survival and, together, they formed a society built on the river's edge.

"I am in a dangerous situation…"

John Floyd, like many of the earliest residents of Kentucky County, chose to erect a fortified station further east on the banks of Beargrass Creek, at a site located near today's Breckinridge Lane. John Floyd's early letters describe the trials he, his wife Jane Buchanan and their young sons would endure as Louisville pioneers.

Bear Grass 26 Nov 1779
I arrive here the 8th inst[ant] with all my family and stock safe and hearty. I have this day got a fine cabbin raised, and hope in a few days to have a shelter something better than a tent which we have laid in almost ten weeks. I should not have been quite so tedious in building but the first tree Bob cut down on the place lodged and slipped back on the stump and tore off his right foot, or at least all the skin and flesh from the ankle down. I have nothing to dress it and I am persuaded it must rot off what is left. I have no view now but to grub and maul which I think I can do with the greatest cheerfulness on so fine a tract of land.

I am in a dangerous situation, only five men: and the Indians killed or took a man from Bullit Lick and wounded another since I came here. My company all disappointed me in coming out, but I have no doubt of settlers enough from the falls, as many are preparing to join me here.

The brief mention of the slave Bob alludes to one of the first African-Americans in Louisville, and his loss meant additional manual labor for John Floyd and his few companions at Floyd's Station. As legal owner of the thousand-acre tract he had claimed during his 1774 explorations, Floyd was surprised, but not dismayed to discover that eleven families of squatters had already settled on his property. These were welcome additions to the defense of Floyd's fortified home and, together, this small band faced one of the most challenging trials in Louisville's founding years – the Hard Winter of 1779 and 1780. In letters, Floyd described the perilous conditions.

Bear Grass 19th Jany 1780
When I attempted to write in Dec. the ink froze in the pen and it is no better yet, as the snow has never melted off the south side of the cabbin since the first of last month….We have no prospect of

GETTING ANY LINEN WHICH WE SHALL SOON BE IN VERY GREAT WANT OF...

IF ANYONE COMES BY WATER I WISH WE COULD GET A LITTLE FLOUR BROUGHT DOWN AS IT WAS AS DEAR AS GOLD DUST – SINCE I WROTE YOU CORN HAS SOLD AT THE FALLS FOR 165 DOLLARS PER BUSHEL AND PEOPLE SEEM DESIROUS TO HAVE EVERY OTHER ARTICLE IN PROPORTION TO THAT. MONEY IS OF NO ACCOUNT HERE.

BEAR GRASS MAY 31ST 1780
HARDLY ONE WEEK PASS WITHOUT SOMEONE BEING SCALPED BETWEEN THIS AND THE FALLS AND I HAVE ALMOST GOT TOO COWARDLY TO TRAVEL ABOUT THE WOODS WITHOUT COMPANY.

DO ORDER CHARLES TO BRING ALL THE NET PROFITS OF THE CROP ETC, IN CLOTHING OR WE SHALL BE OBLIGED TO USE FIG LEAVES.

JEFFERSON 26TH APRIL 1781
OUR LITTLE SETTLEMENTS HERE ARE IN GREAT CONFUSION AND DISTRESS, OWING TO THE FREQUENT VISITS WE RECEIVE FROM OUR NEIGHBORS FROM THE WEST SIDE OF THE OHIO. FORTY SEVEN OF THE INHABITANTS OF THIS COUNTRY HAVE BEEN KILLED AND CAPTURED BY THEM SINCE THE FIRST OF JANUARY LAST, AND OTHERS BADLY WOUNDED.

"The Ohio is the most beautiful river on earth."

Thomas Jefferson, in his *Notes on Virginia*, wrote in 1782 that "the Ohio is the most beautiful river on earth." And although Jefferson never actually saw the Ohio or visited the area, his impact on life at the Falls was profound. He was Louisville's political patron and during his term of Virginia governor (1779-1781) helped the struggling community establish a permanent government. Louisville's original town charter, signed by Jefferson in May 1780, defined Louisville's political future and presented concerns of legal ownership:

Whereas, Sundry Inhabitants of the County of Kentucky have at great expense and hazard settled themselves on certain lands at the falls of Ohio said to be the property of John Connolly and have laid off a considerable part thereof into half-acre lots for a town, and having settled thereon have preferred petitions to this General Assembly to establish the said town – Be it therefore enacted that one thousand acres of land being the forfeited property of the said John Connolly adjoining the lands of John Campbell and Taylor be and the same is hereby vested in John Todd, Jr., Stephen Trigg, George Slaughter, John Floyd, William Pope, George Meriwether, Andrew Hines,

Governor Thomas Jefferson signed the original town charter when Clark's frontier military post officially became Louisville, Virginia in 1780. Jefferson County, named for the governor, was founded four months after Louisville's organization when Virginia's Fincastle County was subdivided into three counties.

James Sullivan and Marsham Brashears. Gent. Trustees to be by them or any four of them laid off into lots of a half-acre each, with convenient streets and public lots, which shall and the same is *hereby established a town by the name of Louisville*. And be it further enacted that after the said lands shall be laid off into lots and streets... Provided that nothing herein contained shall extend or injure the title of lands claimed by Jno. Campbell Gent. Or those persons whose lots have been laid off on his lands but that their titles be and remain suspended until the said Jno. Campbell shall be relieved from his captivity.

Four months after adoption of the town charter of 1780, Virginia's Kentucky County was split into three parts – Jefferson, Fayette and Lincoln, with Louisville named the administrative center of Jefferson County. On June 5, ninety-four citizens met and established a judiciary of six representatives who were empowered to elect magistrates "to regulate the many Villanys and bring to justice all offenders."

"…find out and encourage Boat-builders and good workmen…they shall have good wages in hard Money."

General George Rogers Clark's military boldness was unsurpassed, and his defense of frontier Kentucky was essential to the survival of the earliest forts and stations. A man of enormous vitality and strategic genius, during his Revolutionary War glory days, George Rogers Clark became known as the "Sword of Kentucky."

Despite Louisville's new political status, the Virginians in their flimsy stockade at Fort-on-Shore remained under constant threat of attack from their Indian enemies. This condition caused George Rogers Clark, now promoted to the rank of brigadier general of the Virginia militia, to improve his defensive capabilities. Increasing numbers of settlers arrived at the Falls in flatboats or by foot via the frontier highway called the Wilderness Road. This convenient path of immigration, and the attraction of Beargrass harbor, combined to funnel pioneers into Louisville, the westernmost outpost of Revolutionary America.

The Wilderness Road entered Kentucky at Cumberland Gap and passed through Harrodsburg on its route to the Falls. This route was favored by many pioneers because it was deemed safer than the downriver journey on the Ohio, where Indian attacks were common. The Wilderness Road, perhaps the most famous trail in America's early western expansion, terminated at the future site of Seventh Street. Here Clark ordered the erection of a permanent fortress, to be called Fort Nelson, in honor of Virginia's third governor.

The garrison at Louisville was strengthened by the addition of 150 militiamen under the command of Colonel George Slaughter. With the goal of establishing an impregnable fortress, land was selected north of Main Street and stretched from Sixth to Eighth Streets. It possessed strong outer walls fully capable of withstanding artillery assaults and contained over an acre of land. A ditch, eight feet deep and ten feet wide, was dug and filled with water to form a moat. Artillery pieces, including a brass six-pounder captured from Vincennes, were mounted on the walls. Fort Nelson, an intimidating stronghold to Native Americans, was never attacked during its existence.

General Clark, charged with Kentucky's defense, had established the main settlement at Louisville, but the Bluegrass stations remained in constant danger. Any hostile Indian or British force entering Kentucky needed to cross the Ohio River, and Clark devised an ingenious method of discouraging the nearly constant invasions. At a temporary shipyard located on Beargrass Creek, within protection of Fort Nelson, Clark commissioned the first warship ever built in the American West.

General Clark wrote to Joseph Lindsay in March 1782 to describe his plans.

WE ARE GOING TO BUILD ARMED BOATS…TO DISPUTE THE NAVIGATION OF THE OHIO EITHER UP OR DOWN…FIND OUT AND ENCOURAGE BOAT-BUILDERS AND GOOD WORKMEN TO REPAIR TO THIS PLACE IMMEDIATELY, THEY SHALL HAVE GOOD WAGES IN HARD MONEY. SHIP CARPENTERS…SHALL HAVE ALMOST WHAT WAGES [THEY] WILL ASK.

A man who would become an important player in Louisville's future worked as carpenter on the boat. Daniel Broadhead, Jr. was paid ten pounds to help build the Row Galley on the Point. General Clark provided a detailed description of the war vessel.

WE HAVE…A GALLEY ON THE STOCKS, THAT WILL BE FINISHED IN ABOUT TWENTY DAYS, THAT I THINK WILL DO BUSINESS. SHE IS SEVENTY THREE FEET KEEL, CALCULATED FOR NAVIGATION OF THE OHIO, TO HAVE FORTY SIX OARS (AND) ONE HUNDRED AND TWO MEN. ONE SIX, TWO FOURS, AND A TWO POUNDER IS HER PROPOSED METAL. WE HAVE GREAT DEPENDENCE ON THE CANNON YOU PROMISED US ARRIVING IN TIME. OPEN, SMALL BOATS WILL BY NO MEANS ANSWER THE PURPOSE OF CRUISING ON THE RIVER, AS THEY ARE LIABLE TO BE AMBUSCADED WHEN THEY COME NEAR THE SHORE, OR IN THE NARROW PARTS OF THE RIVER; BUT ON THE GALLEY, GUNNELS… PLAY ON HINGES AND RAISE HER SIDES SO HIGH THAT SHE CAN LAY WITHIN PISTOL SHOT OF THE SHORE WITHOUT THE LEAST DANGER.

The Row Galley patrolled the Ohio River between Louisville and the Licking River. Because it moved silently and without a regular schedule, Indian war parties were hesitant to be surprised when crossing the river into Kentucky. Its military career was brief, lasting only from March until September 1782, when it sank at the mouth of Beargrass Creek. It was the first of a great many boats to be built in Louisville.

A $4,091 Mortgage Alters Louisville's Waterfront Plans

The question of legal ownership of the land claimed by the adventurers of Louisville grew more crucial as residents began moving out of the fort and building cabins. The legal claims of ownership by Dr. John Connolly were dismissed by the Virginia Assembly in July 1780 and his land was escheated, or legally confiscated, because of his active support of the British cause. An escheating jury in Lexington, including frontiersman Daniel Boone, rendered a verdict that stripped Connolly of his lands at Louisville and denied him any compensation.

The greater dilemma came in the case of his partner, Colonel John Campbell. After he was freed from a British prison following the British surrender at Yorktown, Campbell returned to the Falls of Ohio to assert his legal claims. John Campbell, a genuine American patriot with powerful friends in the Virginia Assembly, had suffered greatly for his commitment to the rebel cause and had every legal right to the land he owned in partnership with Connolly. Town trustees ordered a new survey done to compensate Campbell for his loss of real estate in downtown Louisville, and he was awarded one thousand acres, nearly all the future West End, in partial payment.

In October 1784, the town trustees ordered that virtually all the riverfront and Green Street lots designated by George Rogers Clark as public property be auctioned and the proceeds used to pay John Campbell the full value of his mortgage on the Connolly lands. His cash settlement was $4,091, with an additional $753 given as an IOU. At that point, the only public property still owned by the town of Louisville was the court house square at Sixth and Jefferson Streets and a small pioneer graveyard at Twelfth and Jefferson. In this cemetery, most of the early pioneers of Louisville were buried. One hundred years later, this plot of land would be converted into Baxter Square, the city's first public park.

After his release, John Campbell made his home at the Falls and sought to develop the thousand acres he owned west of town. At the most northern point of Jefferson County, just at the end of the rapids, he established a new town. Originally called Anonymous when it was chartered by Virginia, Campbell renamed the place after himself. By 1806 Campbelltown would become much better known as Shippingport. At this place in 1783 he established a tobacco warehouse, which was the birthplace of Kentucky's large and lucrative tobacco industry.

John Campbell became politically active and was important as the Virginia county of Kentucky started the process of becoming a state in the new national union. Campbell represented Jefferson County in the first state convention in Danville in 1792 and was named a state senator in the first session of that legislative body.

Boats of every description plied the waters of the Ohio River, bringing new citizens, supplies and opportunities for early Louisvillians. Trade goods arriving in flatboats, broadhorns, rafts, barges and keelboats made the new town a thriving commercial center and major inland American riverport. *(Filson Historical Society – BOA.36)*

In 1798 he was named speaker of the Kentucky Senate and served as a trustee of Lexington's Transylvania Seminary.

The first meeting of Louisville's town trustees was held on February 27, 1781, with seven men named to serve on that board. Only one, Colonel John Floyd, was actually a resident of Jefferson County, as the rest were drawn from the more populous Bluegrass region. Of these seven original trustees, three were killed by Indians before the next meeting, held nearly two years later. At their first meeting, the trustees declared thirty feet be left on the bank of the Ohio as a common street. At their next meeting on June 4, 1783, they resolved that the first street running parallel with the river be called and known by the name of Water Street, the first officially named thoroughfare in Louisville.

The year 1783 witnessed several other significant local events. In April, Colonel John Floyd was ambushed and killed by Indians near his Beargrass Creek home. The small community keenly felt his loss, as most citizens viewed Floyd as a strong and capable leader. Twelve days after his death a son, also named John Floyd, was born. This child was taken by his mother back to her native Virginia, and years later he was elected governor of that state. His son, John B. Floyd, was also elected governor of Virginia and served as a brigadier general in the Confederate army.

Louisville, Virginia, Becomes Louisville, Kentucky

While Fort Nelson was highly defensible, life was still dangerous just outside its walls. For years, individuals or small parties were subject to devastating Indian attacks. In May 1786 a pioneer named Abraham Lincoln was attacked and killed in eastern Jefferson County. His son, Thomas, witnessed the event and passed the story along to his son, also named Abraham, who even as president remembered the cruel fate of his grandfather.

The last recorded attack in Jefferson County occurred in 1789, and the victims were among the first residents of Corn Island. The family of Richard Chenoweth, the builder of Fort-on-Shore and a mainstay of the pioneer community, was attacked and several were killed. His wife Margaret, severely wounded and scalped alive at the event remembered as the Chenoweth Massacre, survived. She must have been made of tough stuff, for Margaret Chenoweth survived for decades and delighted in removing her cap and showing children her bare head.

A happier occasion occurred in 1783 when Daniel Broadhead, Jr., the boatbuilding carpenter of the Row Galley, returned to Louisville. Broadhead travelled back to Philadelphia and transported a large load of commercial products over the Alleghenies to Pittsburgh by pack horse. From there, he filled a flatboat with the goods and drifted downriver to Louisville. On Main Street, he opened the town's first general store, filled with calicoes, wool hats, linens, dishes and a choice of groceries the Louisville pioneers could barely imagine. Overnight, local belles traded their linsey-woolsey dresses for factory cloth and men went from buckskin to printed waistcoats. Broadhead's store, where fine whiskey sold for fifteen dollars a half-pint and corn liquor for ten dollars a gallon, quickly became the focus of social life and provided a degree of refinement to pioneer Louisville. No longer would citizens like John Floyd beg his brother Charles for linens to replace their "fig leaves." A new era opened along with Broadhead's store, and life at the Falls slowly changed from primitive survival to progress.

The next step in the process would be political independence from Virginia, and 1792 would witness the transition from Louisville, Virginia, to Louisville, Kentucky.

Louisville's first two decades were filled with strife and challenges. The necessity of close cooperation created a local tradition of dependence upon one's neighbor and quick responses to danger. Despite all the progress made in this era, an opportunity to create a truly unique American urban landscape was damaged by the necessity of selling off George Rogers Clark's proposed public park lands. The city's first historian, Dr. Henry McMurtrie, bemoaned this decision in his 1819 book, *Sketches of Louisville and Its Environs*:

AS TO THE FLAGRANT WANT OF TASTE, EXHIBITED IN THE MODE OF IMPROVING THE BANKS OF THE RIVER NOTHING BUT THE GREAT VALUE OF THE GROUND CAN BE URGED AS AN EXCUSE. HAD THE FIRST, OR MAIN STREET, BEEN LAID OFF SO AS TO HAVE EXTENDED 90 FEET FROM THE BRINK OF THE SECOND BANK, FORMING AN AVENUE FRONT OF THE TOWN, AND HAD NO HOUSES BEEN PERMITTED TO EXIST NORTH OF THAT AVENUE THOSE TO THE SOUTH ALL FRONTING IT, AND OF COURSE THE RIVER, LOUISVILLE WOULD HAVE EXHIBITED A COUP D'OEIL, SURPASSED, IN POINT OF BEAUTY, BY FEW IN THE WORLD. AS IT IS, THE TOWN HAS TURNED ITS BACK UPON THE VARIED AND INTERESTING PROSPECT PRESENTED BY THE OHIO AND ITS FALLS, HERE AND THERE STUDDED WITH ISLANDS, A BEAUTIFUL AND VERDANT COUNTRY EXTENDING SIX MILES BEYOND IT, BOUNDED BY THE SILVER CREEK HILLS, WHOSE MAJESTIC TOPS, CROWNED WITH LEAFY HONOURS OF VARIED HUES, TERMINATE THE SCENE.

Nature's presence is re-introduced at the river's edge in an upland meadow in the Linear Park section of Waterfront Park. A triumph of landscape design, the Park reclaims the waterfront's potential as foreseen by General George Rogers Clark and Dr. Henry McMurtrie.

The Ohio River's shoreline is an ever-shifting environment where eddies, waves and floating materials scour the river banks. Erosion and periodic episodes of flooding make design of a riverfront park especially difficult and technically challenging.

Clinging to the River's Edge

(1793-1811)

> *Louis ville is the county town of Jefferson and is situated on the banks of Ohio. The situation is beautiful and I think this place may in time be of consequence although it's now an inconsiderable village. Louis ville has about 30 houses but there is not an Elegant Hous in the place. The Court Hous in the place is of stone and built with some taste. At this place I see a number of Indians from the Nations over the Ohio, Piankiashas Delawares and Wyantes. Notwithstanding Louis ville is the Landing place of all Boats bound to any place below the Falls in consequence of which there is a great resort of Company yet there is not a Tavern in the place that deserves a better name than Grog Shop. Louis ville is by Nature a beautiful place but the handy work of Man has instead of improving destroyed the works of Nature and made it a detestable place.*
>
> **– Moses Austin - 1781**

The dour description of early Louisville by traveler Moses Austin captures a verbal picture of life at the Falls shortly before Kentucky's statehood. His description of Indians in the streets and the town's stone courthouse is indicative of the community's transition from the eighteenth to the nineteenth century. Austin's "detestable place" was slowly acquiring a veneer of civilization, thanks largely to a greatly expanded amount of trade, using the maritime highway of the Ohio River.

Following statehood in 1792, Kentucky's new government began to relax the strong restrictions Virginia placed upon the self-governance of towns. Louisville's population had grown from 200 residents in 1790 upwards to 600 a decade later.

The emerging community required strong local government to establish and maintain order. In 1795 a legislative act allowed for enhanced local powers, and seven trustees were elected annually. They adopted fundamental public laws including: establishing penalties for racing or shooting in the town limits; regulating public springs and water sources; making and recording deeds of conveyance; appointing a street surveyor; cleaning ponds and other nuisances; building a public market house; preventing fires; regulating tippling houses (the low grog shops so despised by Austin); and maintaining the harbor in good order.

The trustees in 1797 created a public office unique to Louisville. The County Court appointed the first of many Falls pilots authorized to guide vessels over the rapids for a fee. Captain James Patton, one of the initial settlers on Corn Island, was chosen, the first of many Louisvillians over the next 140 years to serve in this critical role. It was a highly profitable career, demanding brave river men with intimate knowledge of the Falls and the river's eddies, chutes and moods. Louisville Falls Pilot, a profession predicted by Captain Thomas Hutchins in 1766, would become one of the city's most prestigious jobs.

Another memorable event was the appointment of Evan Williams as harbor master, with duties to keep the harbor and mouth of Beargrass Creek clean and free of nuisances. Williams is credited as being Kentucky's first distiller and, two hundred years later, a historical marker at the corner of Fourth and Main Streets would commemorate that fact.

In 1799 Congress passed an act declaring Louisville to be a point of entry into the United States and establishing a customs house on the wharf for shipments moving up the Mississippi and Ohio Rivers. New Orleans remained in possession of the French until the Louisiana Purchase of 1803, and Louisville was the first American town encountered by boatmen on their northern voyages. At the Port of Louisville, agents of the U.S. Treasury Department collected taxes due on goods being imported to America.

Louisville took the condition of its harbor, its main economic engine, very seriously. In November 1800, the trustees adopted the following act:

The daily life of boatmen, roustabouts and stevedores is graphically depicted in a series of WPA murals hanging in the halls of the Family Health Center – Portland. The paintings, done in 1935 by artist Henrick Martin Mayer, present a progression of river life in this former U.S. Marine Hospital facility.

AND BE IT FURTHER ENACTED, THAT THE HARBOR AT THE MOUTH OF BEARGRASS SHALL, AND IS HEREBY DECLARED TO BE UNDER THE DIRECTION OF THE SAID TRUSTEES, OR A MAJORITY OF THEM; AND THEY ARE HEREBY VESTED WITH FULL POWER AND AUTHORITY, FROM TIME TO TIME, TO PASS SUCH BY-LAWS AND MAKE SUCH REGULATIONS AS TO THEM MAY SEEM PROPER FOR THE CLEANING AND KEEPING THE SAID HARBOR IN GOOD ORDER, AND FOR THE LANDING AND MOORING OF BOATS THEREIN...

Clutter had begun to accumulate on Louisville's waterfront and in 1801 the town took action to remove a large stack of millstones left at the mouth of Beargrass. Orders were given to take these obstructions away from the creek's mouth and locate them above the river's high water mark.

"It was then a beautiful, clear stream of water"

Despite considerable progress in frontier urbanization, Louisville still retained much of its wilderness aspect. Huge trees covered most of the land and dense forests came right down to the river's edge. As the site of Louisville is primarily a level plain, a series of standing ponds and swampy areas became breeding grounds for malaria and other diseases.

Contemporary descriptions often comment on the presence of Beargrass Creek and the area known as the Point. Fifty years after migrating to Louisville, an old gentleman named Hugh Hayes recalled his earliest impressions of the waterfront.

I HAVE SEEN SO MUCH ABUSE HEAPED UPON OUR OLD CREEK, THE BEARGRASS, BY THE PAPERS THAT SOMETIMES I FEEL VEXED ABOUT IT. HAD YOU SEEN IT BEFORE THE HAND OF MAN DISFIGURED IT AND ITS SURROUNDINGS YOU WOULD NOT BLAME ME. THE CREEK IS FED BY HUNDREDS OF CRYSTAL SPRINGS FROM THE RICHEST LANDS IN THE COUNTRY. FIFTY YEARS AGO I SAW THIS CREEK. IT WAS THEN A BEAUTIFUL, CLEAR STREAM OF WATER. ITS MOUTH WAS AT THE FOOT OF THIRD

STREET AND WAS A HARBOR FOR FLATBOATS, &C AT SECOND
STREET WAS THE ONLY BRIDGE THAT CROSSED IT, TO THE FERRY
AND TO FULTON STREET. AT THAT TIME THE POINT WAS A
SOLID FOREST OF MONSTER TREES AND WILD GRAPEVINES, AND
THE EARTH WAS COVERED WITH GROUND IVY.

Beargrass Creek, although a beautiful stream and ideal natural harbor, presented difficulties for the growing town of Louisville. The stream ran almost parallel to the river bank from Third Street upriver to beyond Towhead Island, a distance of over two miles. This water course served as a barrier for traffic between Main Street and the Ohio River. It was not the last impediment for Louisvillians seeking the river's edge, but it was one of the most enduring and troublesome.

The trustees ordered a bridge over Beargrass Creek to be built at the end of Second Street in the year 1801. Asahel Linn and James Hunter offered a bid of $430 to design and build Louisville's first bridge, and it was a miserable failure. Faulty engineering or construction caused the superstructure to collapse into the stream and angry voices were raised as to the competence, or incompetence, of its builders.

We Proceeded Onward – From Louisville

In 1803 one of the stirring moments in American history happened at the mouth of Beargrass. It was here that Meriwether Lewis met William Clark to begin their epic journey of discovery to the Pacific Ocean. After President Thomas Jefferson negotiated the purchase of the vast Louisiana territory from France, he decided to send a party of American explorers to investigate the unknown lands between the Mississippi River and the Pacific Ocean.

Jefferson chose his personal secretary, a young Virginian named Meriwether Lewis, to lead the Corps of Discovery. Both agreed that a co-captain for the mission was desirable, and Lewis suggested a trusted friend with whom he had served in the U.S. Army. It is doubtful that anyone ever made a better choice for a partner and traveling companion. William Clark, the youngest brother of

While the initial 1803 meeting of Meriwether Lewis and William Clark is memorialized on the grounds of Indiana's Falls of the Ohio Interpretive Center, the explorers actually joined forces at the original entrance of Beargrass Creek, located at that time near Louisville's Third Street. There, Captain Clark's group of local recruits for the Corps of Discovery met Captain Lewis bringing supplies downstream from Pittsburgh prior to crossing over to the Indiana shore for training.

George Rogers Clark, was a Louisvillian with woodlands experience, and he possessed the Clark family trait of inspiring confidence in his command.

When Lewis extended an invitation to Clark to participate in the Corps, he also asked his Kentucky friend to recruit eligible young men capable of contributing to the long and difficult journey. William Clark, in a letter from Louisville dated July 24, 1803, eagerly agreed to the proposal with this response:

> DEAR LEWIS: I WROTE YOU IN ANSWER TO YOUR LETTER
> OF THE 1ST ULTO: BY THE LAST MAIL, THE CONTENTS OF
> WHICH AS I BEFORE INFORMED YOU WERE TRULY PLEASING
> TO ME AND SUCH AS I HEARTILY JOIN YOU IN. I AM ARRANGING
> MY MATTERS SO AS TO DETAIN BUT A SHORT TIME AFTER

YOUR ARRIVAL HERE, WELL CONVINCED OF THE NECESSITY OF GETTING AS FAR AS POSSIBLE UP THE (MISSOURI RIVER) THIS FALL TO ACCOMPLISH THE OBJECT AS LAID DOWN BY YOURSELF AND WHICH I HIGHLY APPROVE OF.

I HAVE TEMPORALLY ENGAGED SOME MEN FOR THE ENTERPRISE OF A DESCRIPTION CALCULATED TO WORK & GO THRO' THOSE LABOURS & FATIGUES WHICH WILL BE NECESSARY. SEVERAL YOUNG MEN (GENTLEMEN'S SONS) HAVE APPLYED TO ACCOMPANY US. AS THEY ARE NOT ACCUSTOMED TO LABOUR AND AS THAT IS A VERRY ESSENTIAL PART OF THE SERVICES REQUIRED OF THE PARTY, I AM CAUTIOUS IN GIVING THEM ANY ENCOURAGEMENT. THE NEWSPAPER ACCOUNTS SEEM TO CONFIRM THE REPORT OF WAR IN EUROPE AND THE SESSION OF LOUISIANA TO THE UNITED STATES AND AS I THINK IT POSSIBLE THAT A CONFIRMATION OF THE SESSION OF LOUISIANA MAY HAVE DETAINED YOU AT THE CITY LONGER THAN YOU EXPECTED, I HAVE ENCLOSED A LETTER TO YOU UNDER COVER TO MR. JEFFERSON. PRAY LET ME HEAR FROM YOU AS OFTEN AS POSSIBLE.

YR. WC.

This mission required tougher stuff than gentlemen's sons unused to hard physical labor. While Lewis gathered the boats, specialized equipment and stores needed for the journey in Pittsburgh, William Clark began recruiting qualified young men ready and willing to attempt the great journey. One of the first to volunteer was Charles Floyd, the nephew of Beargrass pioneer John Floyd. He was soon promoted to sergeant and proved to be one of the most dependable members of the Corps of Discovery, and their only fatality. One year and three days after enlisting, Charles Floyd died of a ruptured appendix near Sioux City, Iowa, at a place called Floyd's Bluff.

The Louisvillians William Clark and his slave York waited with other members of the proud fraternity remembered as "the nine young men from Kentucky" for the arrival of Meriwether

York, the slave of Captain William Clark, was an integral part of Lewis and Clark's Corps of Discovery. His statue, created by Louisvillian Ed Hamilton, stands on the Belvedere in Louisville, surrounded by a modern city unimaginable to the pioneers of nearby Fort Nelson.

Lewis. York would prove to be one of the most important members of the Corps and was an irresistible attraction to the native people he encountered. York was perhaps the first African-American to visit the northern plains, and his dark complexion, great strength and frolicsome behavior fascinated the Indians.

Louisville did not yet boast a newspaper, and the only published announcement of this epic journey appeared in Lexington's *Kentucky Gazette and General Advertiser*:

LOUISVILLE, OCTOBER 15. CAPTAIN LEWIS ARRIVED AT THIS PORT ON FRIDAY LAST. WE ARE INFORMED THAT HE HAD BROUGHT BARGES &C ON A NEW CONSTRUCTION, THAT CAN BE TAKEN IN PIECES, FOR THE PURPOSE OF PASSING CARRYING-PLACES; AND THAT HE AND CAPTAIN CLARK WILL START IN A FEW DAYS ON THEIR EXPEDITION TO THE WESTWARD.

It is probable they spent only a short time at the Louisville wharf as the entire force, with all their equipment, soon crossed over the river and through the Falls to temporary quarters at the primitive cabin of General George Rogers Clark in the Indiana Territory. There they spent about ten days training, packing and preparing to proceed onward. Their last mention in the *Kentucky Gazette* appeared on October 29, 1803.

LOUISVILLE. CAPTAIN CLARK AND MR. LEWIS LEFT THIS PLACE ON WEDNESDAY LAST, ON THE EXPEDITION TO THE WESTWARD. WE HAVE NOT BEEN ABLE TO ASCERTAIN WHAT LENGTH THIS ROUTE WILL EXTEND, AS WHEN IT WAS

FIRST SET ON FOOT BY THE PRESIDENT, THE LOUISIANA COUNTRY WAS NOT CEDED TO THE UNITED STATES AND IT IS LIKELY IT WILL BE CONSIDERABLY EXTENDED — THEY ARE TO RECEIVE FURTHER INSTRUCTIONS AT KAHOKIA. IT IS, HOWEVER, CERTAIN THAT THEY WILL ASCEND THE MAIN BRANCH OF THE MISSISSIPPI AS FAR AS POSSIBLE: AND IT IS PROBABLE THEY WILL THEN DIRECT THEIR COURSE TO THE MISSOURI, AND ASCEND IT…ABOUT 60 MEN WILL COMPLETE THE PARTY.

On Louisville's waterfront, Meriwether Lewis joined William Clark, and so began their great adventure. St. Louis has long claimed the honor as the starting place of the Corps of Discovery, but Louisville's riverfront deserves consideration as the true launching point.

A Gathering of Heroes

At the conclusion of the American Revolution, many victorious rebels decided to build new lives in the West. Louisville attracted a good share of the veterans who were honored members of the Continental Army. Captain George Gray, a neighbor and friend of Washington, raised, financed and led the Third Virginia Regiment. He commanded a boat when the desperate American army crossed the Delaware River and captured Trenton. Beside him in the boat was his first lieutenant and cousin, a young man named James Monroe.

Following the war, George Gray was awarded a 4,000-acre land grant and moved to Louisville with his twelve children and forty slaves. Captain Gray would live to be eighty-two years old and die in 1822. He is buried in a little-known cemetery on Louisville's Floyd Street between Oak and Ormsby, a part of his original farm. One of George Gray's sons, John Thompson Gray, would become the dominant force in economic development at the waterfront.

Another longtime survivor of the Revolution was Colonel Richard Taylor, who died at age eighty-four in 1829. Having first explored the area in 1769 with his brother Hancock, Taylor returned to Louisville in 1797, where he acquired 1,650 acres in Jefferson County, and an additional 10,000 acres elsewhere in Kentucky. On his 400-acre estate called Springfield, Taylor saw his wealth and influence grow. An owner of seven slaves in 1790, by 1810 he would claim thirty-seven on his tax records making Richard Taylor one of Jefferson County's largest slave-owners. President Washington appointed him collector of the Port of Louisville and he served in the state legislature.

Perhaps Louisville's most intriguing Revolutionary hero was Old Ben Duke. His obituary, printed in the March 10, 1856, edition of the *Louisville Daily Courier,* provides a respectful, even reverent, farewell to this remarkable man.

DEATH OF THE OLDEST INHABITANT

LOUISVILLE HAS LOST BY DEATH HER OLDEST INHABITANT. YESTERDAY DIED "OLD BEN DUKE," AS HE HAS BEEN STYLED FROM TIME IMMEMORIAL, AT THE AGE OF ONE HUNDRED AND TEN YEARS, EIGHT MONTHS AND THREE DAYS! THE DECEASED WAS A MAN OF COLOR, AND A NATIVE OF MARYLAND, FROM WHICH STATE HE EMIGRATED WHEN KENTUCKY WAS A COMPLETE WILDERNESS, AND OUR CITY BUT A MERE OUTPOST ON THE FRONTIER. ALL OF THOSE WHO WERE THEN RESIDING IN THIS SECTION OF THE STATE HAVE LONG SINCE PASSED AWAY, WITH THE FOREST, THE ABORIGINES, AND THE SAVAGE GRANDEURS OF UNTAMED NATURE. OLD BEN, HOWEVER, SURVIVED MORE THAN TWO GENERATIONS, AND WITNESSED THE PROGRESS OF LOUISVILLE FROM THE FELLING OF THE FIRST TREE IN BEAR GRASS VALLEY TO THE ATTAINMENT OF HER PRESENT COMMANDING POSITION AMONG THE CITIES OF THE NATION.

HE WAS MANY YEARS A RESIDENT OF VIRGINIA, AND AT THE AGE OF THIRTY ENTERED THE SERVICE

OF WASHINGTON, OF WHOM HE RETAINED THE
LIVELIEST RECOLLECTIONS; ALWAYS BEING HAPPY
WHEN HE COULD RELATE TO YOUNG LISTENERS THE
STORY OF HIS CAMPAIGNING WITH THE FATHER OF
THE COUNTRY. WITH REVOLUTIONARY INCIDENTS HE
WAS ABUNDANTLY SUPPLIED, AND OFTEN FOUGHT HIS
BATTLES O'ER, PROUD OF THE PART HE HAD TAKEN IN
FREEING THE COUNTRY, ALTHOUGH A MAN OF COLOR
HIMSELF.

SO PROTRACTED A LIFE COULD NOT, OF COURSE,
BE WITHOUT MANY AND STRANGE INCIDENTS. WE
HAVE HEARD HIM NARRATE THESE, AND ALWAYS WITH
THE GREATEST PLEASURE. BEN DUKE WAS ORIGINALLY
A SLAVE, BUT THE ENTIRE RACE OF HIS OWNERS HAS
BECOME EXTINCT, AND HE HAS BEEN A FREE MAN FOR A
LONG TIME. OF LATE YEARS HE SUSTAINED HIMSELF BY
SELLING WOOD, DRIVING A SMALL ONE HORSE WAGON
ABOUT THE CITY. HIS FEATURES WERE SOME WHAT OF
THE INDIAN CAST; HIS FORM MANLY AND IMPOSING,
ALTHOUGH SLIGHTLY BENT WITH AGE, AND HIS BEARD
AND HAIR VERY LONG AND WHITE.

THE FUNERAL SERVICES OF THIS OLD AND
ESTEEMED COLORED CITIZEN, WILL OCCUR ON TO-
MORROW (TUESDAY) AFTERNOON AT 3 O'CLOCK, FROM
THE GREEN STREET BAPTIST CHURCH, BETWEEN
FLOYD AND PRESTON.

"Louisville is most delightfully situated"

As the city grew more secure and wealth began to
accumulate, some prominent Louisvillians began to expand
their lifestyles by building large, and often imposing, homes
in the city. These owners prided themselves on their spacious
manicured grounds, with special status being reserved for
those living nearest to the river. A French immigrant, Michael
Lacassagne, fled the Reign of Terror and became Louisville's

first postmaster. On the northeast corner of Fifth and Main,
he built a large house facing the Ohio River. These estates
were terraced down from Main Street to Water Street at the
river's edge. The grounds were described as a rich carpet of
bluegrass, with fruit trees and abundant flowers. Before his
death in 1797 Lacassagne made a friend promise that his
magnificent trees would receive loving care.

Two new mansions were built on Main Street overlooking
the river in 1804, when brothers Thomas and Cuthbert Bullitt
moved to town. The nephews of Captain Thomas Bullitt, the
city's first surveyor, the brothers accumulated considerable
fortunes as merchants and land speculators. Cuthbert Bullitt
bought the home and grounds of Michael Lacassagne, and
his brother Thomas purchased the adjoining land at Sixth
and Main. A small lane, called Bullitt Street, separated their
property and ran down the hill to the river landing. The
street corresponds with the walking path which today leads
up from Main Street to the statue of George Rogers Clark on
the Belvedere. When Cuthbert Bullitt tired of his river view,
he could spend time at his country estate on a site that would
later be known as Central Park.

A very successful tobacco merchant, Richard Burge,
bought the property that originally hosted Fort Nelson at
the north end of Seventh Street. There he built an imposing
mansion, complete with a massive cupola on the roof, which
provided a magnificent view of the Falls and bustling wharf.
This building would remain standing even after the fateful
tornado of 1890 had destroyed all the buildings surrounding
it.

The most famous of Louisville's riverfront mansions was
located at the northwest corner of Second and Main Streets,
and its name would echo through the city's history. Dr.
William Craig Galt, the city's most respected early physician,
built his gracious home and made his riverside garden the

envy of the town. A dedicated botanist, Dr. Galt laid out a formal English garden in intricate formations and leafy walking paths. After a long and successful medical career, Dr. Galt sold his home and retired to his country estate. His property became the site of the city's finest early luxury inn, and a Louisville hotel named The Galt House has served visitors periodically since 1835.

In 1808 an English traveler named Fortescue Cumings viewed this impressive array of grand homes overlooking Louisville's waterfront, stretching from Second to Seventh Streets, and recorded his impressions:

> Louisville is most delightfully situated on an elevated plain to which the ascent from the creek and river is gradual, being just slope enough to admit of hanging gardens with terraces, which Dr. Gault at the upper and two Messrs. Bullits at the lower end of the town have availed themselves of, in laying out their gardens very handsomely and with taste. From the latter, the view both up and down the river is truly delightful. – Looking upwards a reach of five or six miles presents itself.

> Louisville consists of one principal and very handsome street, about half a mile long, tolerably compactly built, and the houses generally superior to any I have seen in the western country except for Lexington. Most are of handsome brick, and some are three stories, with a parapet wall on the top in the modern European taste, which in front gives them the appearance of having flat roofs.

> I had thought Cincinnati one of the most beautiful towns I had seen in America, but Louisville, which is almost as large, equals it in beauty, and in the opinion of many excels it.

"The prospect from the town is such that it would please even the eye of a Swiss."

Louisville's first wave of European immigrants came from France, people fleeing the terror of their Revolution. Many nobles, and French clerics like Flaget, Chabrat and Stephen Theodore Badin, had good reason to escape. Two brothers, John Anthony and Louis A. Tarascon, were the founders and proprietors of Shippingport, the former home of John Campbell. Their employee and future business partner James Berthoud also played an important role in the small town on the northwest peninsula of Jefferson County.

Berthoud's actual identity was Bon Hervé de Belisle, with the right to the title of Marquis de Saint-Pierre. His wife, Elizabeth, was *dame d'honneur* to Louis XVI's ill-fated Queen Marie Antoinette. Family tradition reports that he and his family escaped France with the assistance of his Swiss coachman named Jacques Berthoud. The Marquis and family were saved when the coachman secured a passport in his own name. Upon reaching America in 1794, the former Marquis adopted his loyal servant's name.

In September 1802 the firm of Tarascon, Junr., James Berthoud & Company was formed. A year later, Berthoud purchased forty-five acres of land, the site of Campbelltown, from Allan Campbell for $2,306.25. Because all goods and cargoes had to be carried (*porté* in French), they renamed the town Shippingport to emphasize its role in transshipment of materials. To their new Kentucky home they attracted additional French immigrant families, including the Berthouds, Offands, Schraders, Avalonds, Fouches and Cerfs. A lively French community began to coalesce at the Falls.

In 1808 Louisville's most famous Frenchman came and stayed only a few years, but his reputation became worldwide

John James Audubon's talents as a naturalist developed, while his career as a Louisville shop keeper floundered, during his brief residence in the area beginning in 1808. Passenger pigeons, once the most often seen birds at the Falls of the Ohio, were pictured by Audubon prior to their eventual extinction.

and he always viewed Louisville with affection and fond remembrance. John James Audubon, a mediocre shopkeeper with a wonderful artistic vision, moved with his new bride Lucy Bakewell to the Indian Queen Hotel to attempt a career as a merchant. Leaving most of his business responsibilities to his partner Jacques Rozier, Audubon indulged his passion for drawing pictures of the birds of the Falls. For sheer exuberance, Louisville would have no greater booster than Audubon, as he displayed in his autobiography written after he was rich, successful and famous.

LOUISVILLE IN KENTUCKY HAS ALWAYS BEEN A FAVORITE PLACE OF MINE. THE BEAUTY OF ITS SITUATION ON THE BANKS OF LA BELLE RIVIERE, JUST AT THE COMMENCEMENT OF THE FAMED RAPIDS, COMMONLY CALLED THE FALLS OF THE OHIO, HAD ATTRACTED MY NOTICE, AND WHEN I REMOVED TO IT, IMMEDIATELY AFTER MY MARRIAGE, I FOUND IT MORE AGREEABLE THAN EVER. THE PROSPECT FROM THE TOWN IS SUCH THAT IT WOULD PLEASE EVEN THE EYE OF A SWISS. IT EXTENDS ALONG THE RIVER FOR SEVEN OR EIGHT MILES, AND IS BOUNDED ON THE OPPOSITE SIDE BY A FINE RANGE OF LOW MOUNTAINS, KNOWN BY THE NAME OF THE SILVER HILLS. THE RUMBLING SOUND OF THE WATERS AS THEY TUMBLE OVER THE ROCK-PAVED BED OF THE RAPIDS IS AT ALL TIMES SOOTHING TO THE EAR. FISH AND GAME ARE ABUNDANT. BUT, ABOVE ALL, THE GENEROUS HOSPITALITY OF THE INHABITANTS, AND THE URBANITY OF THEIR MANNERS, HAD INDUCED ME TO FIX UPON IT AS A PLACE OF RESIDENCE; AND I DID SO WITH THE MORE PLEASURE WHEN I FOUND THAT MY WIFE WAS AS MUCH GRATIFIED AS MYSELF BY THE KIND ATTENTIONS WHICH WERE SHOWN TO US, UTTER STRANGERS AS WE WERE, ON OUR ARRIVAL.

WE LIVED FOR TWO YEARS AT LOUISVILLE, WHERE WE ENJOYED MANY OF THE BEST PLEASURES WHICH THIS LIFE CAN AFFORD; AND WHENEVER WE HAVE SINCE CHANCED TO PASS THAT WAY, WE HAVE FOUND THE KINDNESS OF OUR FORMER FRIENDS UNIMPAIRED.

DURING MY RESIDENCE AT LOUISVILLE, MUCH OF MY TIME WAS EMPLOYED IN MY EVER FAVORITE PURSUITS. I DREW AND NOTED THE HABITS OF EVERYTHING WHICH I PROCURED, AND MY COLLECTION WAS DAILY AUGMENTING, AS EVERY INDIVIDUAL WHO CARRIED A GUN ALWAYS SENT ME SUCH BIRDS OR QUADRUPEDS AS HE THOUGHT MIGHT PROVE USEFUL TO ME. MY PORTFOLIOS ALREADY CONTAINED UPWARDS OF TWO HUNDRED DRAWINGS. DR. W. C. GALT BEING A BOTANIST, WAS OFTEN CONSULTED BY ME.

"The whole neighborhood joined with one consent."

Perhaps it was the large number of veterans, or Louisville's own important role in the American Revolution, but the Fourth of July has always been embraced by its citizens as a special holiday deserving the most exuberant celebration. Audubon experienced this memorable Louisville Independence Day in 1809 on grounds that would become the Linear Park section of Waterfront Park.

Culture was coming to the Falls of the Ohio, and sometimes in unusual packages. The April 28, 1809, minutes of the town trustees meeting recorded an unexpected spectacle:

"RESOLVED, THAT THE PERSON NOW EXHIBITING AN ELEPHANT IN THIS TOWN BE AND HE IS HEREBY DIRECTED TO PAY TO ELISHA L. HALL COLLECTOR OF THE TOWN TAXES THE SUM OF TEN DOLLARS IT BEING A FINE IMPOSED BY AN ACT OF THE GENERAL ASSEMBLY IN THAT CASE MADE AND PROVIDED."

Theatrical and circus performances were strictly regulated and subject to high license fees. The ten dollars earned from the circus elephant was used to purchase five ladders for the town's volunteer firefighters.

Audubon Remembers Louisville's Independence Day

Beargrass Creek, which is one of the many beautiful streams of the highly cultivated and happy State of Kentucky, meanders through a deeply shaded growth of majestic beech woods, in which are interspersed various species of walnut, oak, elm, ash and other trees, extending on either side of its course. The spot on which I witnessed the celebration of an anniversary of the glorious Proclamation of our Independence is situated on its banks, near the city of Louisville. The woods spread their dense tufts toward the shores of the fair Ohio on the west, and over the gently rising grounds to the south and east. Every open spot forming a plantation was smiling in the luxuriance of a summer harvest. The farmer seemed to stand in admiration of the spectacle: the trees of his orchards bowed their branches, as if anxious to restore to their mother earth the fruit with which they were laden; the flocks leisurely ruminated as they lay on their grassy beds; and the genial warmth of the season seemed inclined to favour their response.

The free, single-hearted Kentuckian, bold, erect, and proud of his Virginian descent, had, as usual, made arrangements for celebrating the day of his country's Independence. The whole neighborhood joined with one consent. No personal invitation was required when every one was welcomed by his neighbour, and from the governor to the guider of the plough all met with light hearts and merry faces.

It was indeed a beautiful day; the bright sun rode in the clear blue heavens; the gentle breezes wafted around the odours of the gorgeous flowers; the little birds sang their sweetest songs in the woods, and the fluttering insects danced in the sunbeams.

A burst of music from violins, clarionets, and bugles, gave the welcome notice, and presently the whole assemblage seemed to be gracefully moving through the air. The "hunting-shirts" now joined in the dance, their fringed shirts keeping time with the gowns of the ladies, and the married people of either sex stepped in and mixed with their children. Every countenance beamed with joy, every heart leaped with gladness; no pride, no pomp, no affectation, were there; their spirits brightened as they continued their exhilarating exercise, and care and sorrow were flung to the winds. During each interval of rest, refreshments of all sorts were handed round, and while the fair one cooled her lips with the grateful juice of the melon, the hunter of Kentucky quenched his thirst with ample draughts of well-tempered punch.

Even a touring elephant was not the most dramatic event in life at the Falls. In October and November of 1811, there occurred, in quick succession, some of the most extraordinary events ever witnessed by Louisvillians. The Great Comet of 1811 blazed through the heavens and created a world-wide sensation, with observations reaching their peak in October. A great many people felt the event was an omen of dramatic changes, and perhaps it was.

The Battle of Tippecanoe, in northern Indiana, took place on November 7, with American forces under General William Henry Harrison crushing the Indian coalition led by Tecumseh. This event effectively ended Indian warfare east of the Mississippi River and launched Harrison on his path to the White House. Prior to the battle, many Native Americans saw the comet and believed it to be a forecast of doom and defeat.

In 1806 Judge Fortunatus Cosby purchased 3,000 acres, below and adjoining the Ohio River, from an heir of John Campbell, for $10,000. Judge Cosby, a son-in-law of ferry-owner Aaron Fontaine, was an important early Louisville jurist, and his purchase secured all of the original DeWarnsdorff land grant and most of Louisville's West End. The next year Cosby deeded one-third of his newly acquired land to Senator Henry Clay for "$1 dollar and other considerations," a settlement most people viewed as the payment of a large gambling debt.

In May 1811 Henry Clay accepted $45,000 and title to land in downtown Lexington from his friend, General William Lytle of Cincinnati. Lytle and his brother-in-law, Senator John Rowan, obtained the land with the idea of selling off enough property below the Falls to personally finance the building of a canal around the rapids. Lytle hired a young cousin of Rowan, Joshua Gill Barclay, to serve as his agent in the creation and sale of land in his new land development. Barclay personally chose the name Portland for the village, to emphasize its eligibility as a fine harbor and river port three miles west of Louisville.

William Lytle hired surveyor Alexander Ralston to take measurements and lay out streets and lots in his new town. Ralston had previously worked as a rodman for Pierre Charles L'Enfant and helped survey the site of Washington, D.C. Prior to working for Lytle, Ralston was deeply involved in the Burr Conspiracy, and was one of only three men indicted for, but not convicted, of treason. After leaving Portland, Alexander Ralston moved north and designed the distinctive circular town plan for Indianapolis.

On November 12, 1811, Ralston wrote to Lytle to report on his progress. "On Friday last we finished the plan of your Town as proposed by you. Mr. Barclay shewed me a sketch of the work which he tells me he has forwarded to you which will serve to guide you in your sites &c. Would it not be well to know whether you intend any buildings between Water Street and the river – and whether you intend that the whole shall be public ground or not – if public ground who will wharf it?"

From their earliest days, the primary concern of river towns was access and control of their wharf facilities. Lytle, an experienced land speculator and town proprietor, believed that for the common good, and to enhance development of his new community, the Portland wharf should be public space. Years later, when John Rowan took control of this property, he lost a bitter legal battle with the town trustees of Portland concerning his plans to hold the land as his private property. The Portland wharf is the only riverfront property in the entire 37 miles of the Ohio River contiguous to Jefferson County that has never been privately owned, and has always belonged to a local municipal government, either the Town of Portland or the City of Louisville.

"The roar of the escaping steam, then heard for the first time…"

Even as Ralston was busy with his preliminary survey of Portland, an even more significant event occurred just three miles to the east, at Beargrass harbor and the Louisville riverfront. In a twinkling, a new era was born when the steamboat *New Orleans*, commanded by Captain Nicholas Roosevelt, made its unannounced – and totally unexpected – appearance at Louisville. The event was described by J. H. B. Latrobe from personal interviews with his uncle Nicholas.

THE STAY AT CINCINNATI WAS BRIEF, ONLY LONG ENOUGH TO TAKE IN A SUPPLY OF WOOD FOR THE VOYAGE TO LOUISVILLE, WHICH WAS REACHED ON THE NIGHT OF THE FOURTH DAY AFTER LEAVING PITTSBURGH. IT WAS MIDNIGHT ON THE FIRST OF OCTOBER, 1811, THAT THE *NEW ORLEANS* DROPPED ANCHOR OPPOSITE THE TOWN. THERE WAS A BRILLIANT MOON. IT WAS AS LIGHT AS DAY ALMOST, AND NO ONE ON BOARD HAD RETIRED. THE

ROAR OF THE ESCAPING STEAM, THEN HEARD FOR THE FIRST TIME WHERE, NOW, ITS ECHOES ARE UNCEASING, ROUSED THE POPULATION, AND, LATE AS IT WAS, CROWDS CAME RUSHING TO THE BANK OF THE RIVER TO LEARN THE CAUSE OF THE UNWONTED UPROAR. A LETTER NOW BEFORE ME, WRITTEN BY ONE OF THOSE ON BOARD, AT THE TIME, RECORDS THE FACT — THAT THERE WERE THOSE WHO INSISTED THAT THE COMET OF 1811 HAD FALLEN INTO THE OHIO AND HAD PRODUCED THE HUBBUB!

Nicholas Roosevelt, an intrepid entrepreneur and adventurer, piloted a deep-keel steamboat owned by the Fulton-Livingston partnership to the Louisville shore from Pittsburgh. The business leaders of Louisville were quick to realize the potential for the new contraption. In early 1811, *Niles' Register* estimated that nearly 1,200 flatboats, barges and keelboats had passed over the Falls at Louisville in the previous year, usually bound for New Orleans with cargoes of corn, whiskey, tobacco and hemp. Only eleven keelboats, manned by hardy traders, made the backbreaking trip upstream against the current. The trip took four grueling months. With cargo holds filled with sugar, coffee, Havana cigars, Spanish lace and other exotic luxuries, upriver trips proved enormously profitable. The merchants of Louisville threw a congratulatory party for Roosevelt and his pregnant wife Lydia Latrobe Roosevelt, the daughter of U.S. Capitol architect Benjamin Henry Latrobe.

NOT TO BE OUTDONE IN HOSPITALITY, MR. ROOSEVELT INVITED HIS HOSTS TO DINE ON BOARD THE NEW ORLEANS, WHICH LAY ANCHORED OPPOSITE THE TOWN. THE COMPANY MET IN THE FORWARD OR GENTLEMEN'S CABIN, AND THE FEAST WAS AT ITS HEIGHT, WHEN SUDDENLY THERE WERE HEARD UNWONTED RUMBLINGS, ACCOMPANIED BY A VERY PERCEPTIBLE MOTION IN THE VESSEL. THE COMPANY HAD BUT ONE IDEA. THE NEW ORLEANS

HAD ESCAPED FROM HER ANCHOR, AND WAS DRIFTING TOWARD THE FALLS, TO THE CERTAIN DESTRUCTION OF ALL ON BOARD. THERE WAS AN INSTANT AND SIMULTANEOUS RUSH TO THE UPPER DECK, WHEN THE COMPANY FOUND, THAT, INSTEAD OF DRIFTING TOWARDS THE FALLS OF THE OHIO, THE NEW ORLEANS WAS MAKING GOOD HEADWAY UP THE RIVER AND WOULD SOON LEAVE LOUISVILLE IN THE DISTANCE DOWN STREAM. AS THE ENGINE WARMED TO ITS WORK, AND THE STEAM BLEW OFF AT THE SAFETY VALVE, THE SPEED INCREASED. MR. ROOSEVELT, OF COURSE, HAD PROVIDED THIS MODE OF CONVINCING HIS INCREDULOUS GUESTS, AND THEIR SURPRISE AND DELIGHT MAY READILY BE IMAGINED. AFTER GOING UP THE RIVER FOR A FEW MILES, THE *NEW ORLEANS* RETURNED TO HER ANCHORAGE.

Because the river level was low, Roosevelt was forced to wait three weeks for the river to rise enough to pass over the Falls unscathed. During that time Roosevelt made a return trip to Cincinnati and gave occasional rides for hire, the first instance of an excursion boat on the Ohio. As with George Rogers Clark passing over the Falls during an eclipse, the passage of the *New Orleans* over the Falls was equally dramatic. While crossing the Falls, Lydia Roosevelt gave birth to a new son. Just days later, as they cruised down the Ohio, they were struck by the first jolts of the great New Madrid earthquake, one of the most powerful geological events in human history.

Roosevelt's demonstration of cruising upriver under steam power was a tremendous success. Instead of taking four months to travel from New Orleans to Louisville, within a few years the same trip could be made in five days. Louisville historian George H. Yater best summarized the impact of the *New Orleans,* when he commented, "The river made Louisville a town, the steamboat made Louisville a city."

Steamboats have been an essential part of the Louisville waterfront since the first arrival of the *New Orleans* in 1811. The *Belle of Louisville*, America's oldest steam-powered sternwheeler, continues the long tradition of steamboats landing at the Louisville wharf. *(Photo courtesy of the Belle of Louisville)*

SHIP CHANDLERY AND
Boat Store.

SMITH & BUCKNER
WATER STREET, BETWEEN
FIFTH AND SIXTH,

Have on hand, and intend keeping constantly, a full supply of every thing in their line, for the accommodation of all who may favor them by calling on them. They have *Blocks, Hooks, Thimbles, Rigging, Ropes,* and *Twine* of the most usual sizes; *Glassware, Queensware,* fine and common *Cutlery* of almost every description used in boat supplies; imported and domestic liquors, groceries and provisions of equal quality of any in market. The above, with the addition of all things in season, such as fowls, venison, pickles, preserves, &c. &c. for the use of families or boat stores, will be disposed of on terms equal to any House in town.

Steamboats Turn a Town into a City

(1812-1828)

> *J. G. Barclay & Company have received by late arrivals an extensive assortment of groceries &c among which are:*
>
> *Best Havana coffee; N. Orleans sugar, in hogsheads, barrels and half barrels; imperial gunpowder and young hyson tea, in boxes; Teneriffe wine, in quarter casks; pepper, allspice, alum, copperas, logwood, indigo, madder, ginger; olive oil, in baskets; soft shell almonds; raisins, smoked herrings, Cod fish, in boxes; molasses in barrels; mackerel in barrels and half barrels; iron, assorted; iron spike rods; tin plates, in boxes; English blister and commons steel, cast steel, spades and shovels, coffee mills; Ohio superior flour, fresh; rice in casks, kegs, &c; QUEENSWARE, assorted, in casks, expressly for country sales; 10 boxes wool hats, best quality; domestic shirting and sheeting; pasteboards, post and fools' cap paper, printing and wrapping paper, blank books, assorted; cotton yarns, assorted, No. 5, 6 and 7: candle wick. Dutch lamps, beaver and other furs, upper and sole leather, skirting leather; candles, in boxes; bed cords and plough lines, wire sifters, manufactured tobacco, in kegs and boxes; segars, in barrels and boxes; chocolate, in boxes. ALSO 1000 barrels Kenhawa Salt*
>
> **— Louisville Public Advertiser - 1826**

As the epochal last months of 1811 passed, the next year produced a new war and new economic opportunities for Louisville. America's second war against Great Britain had been fanned by the passionate rhetoric of Senator Henry Clay and was tremendously popular in America's West. Frederick Geiger, a Marylander who moved to Jefferson County in 1790, took an active part in the war. In 1802 Geiger purchased a very large tract of land east of downtown Louisville and north of Beargrass Creek, becoming the largest single owner of land on the Point. Here he established a successful mill harnessing the power of the Beargrass and was granted a license to operate a ferry to Jeffersonville. Frederick Geiger responded quickly to a call for volunteers and raised a company of mounted riflemen to serve under Colonel Joseph Hamilton Daviess. His command distinguished themselves at the Battle of Tippecanoe and Geiger returned home a local hero.

The War of 1812 between the United States and Great Britain meant that imports of English manufactured goods like pottery, flatware, cotton cloth, boat rope and other familiar products were no longer available. As European trade goods disappeared from the shelves of general stores, American manufacturers took advantage of the opening to build factories, workshops, foundries and mills. Lexington eagerly adopted the cultivation of hemp and became a leader in the production of ropes for sailing ships and bagging and cord for cotton merchants. Cincinnati embraced the production of pottery, queensware, tools and pork production.

Louisville largely resisted the impulse to manufacture household products, but Paul Skidmore began a foundry in Shippingport in 1812 that would be taken over four years later by David Prentice and Thomas Bakewell, the brother of Lucy Audubon. With the emergence of the new steam technology, the Falls was poised to take advantage of its extensive forests, river frontage and available workforce.

The town fathers did not get around to officially naming Louisville's downtown streets until January 7, 1812, when the trustees voted to establish Main, Market, Jefferson, Green (now Liberty) and Chestnut. The next year a fledgling attempt to pave Main Street from Third to Sixth Streets proved unsuccessful. The local limestone used as pavement was soon crushed under the heavy iron-clad wheels of the numerous dray carts, hackney cabs and wagons. Bad roads would be the bane of Louisville's existence through much of its formative decades.

Hugh Hayes, writing years later, recalled, "Manufacturers received but poor encouragement here. They were looked upon as a part of the working class, who were not much respected by the aristocratic element which then predominated. In 1832 the writer of this article appealed to the richest land owner in the country for ground on which to erect a factory. This worthy, venerable gentleman frankly informed him that this was no place for workingmen, but "only a fit place for merchants and retired gentlemen to live in."

Louisville's true interest was in transshipping products made by someone else. A new type of businessman, the commission merchant, emerged as the economic and political leader of the community. While Louisville blossomed when steamboats ruled, the foundation for handling and marketing river-borne trade was already established. Historian Ben Casseday, in his 1852 history of Louisville, recalled the heyday of an American original, the Ohio River boatman.

These early attempts at navigation were soon succeeded by the constant and regular trips of the Barges. Perhaps the most stirring and exciting scenes of western adventure were connected with the voyages of these peculiar craft. The bargemen were a distinct class of people whose fearlessness of character, recklessness of habits and laxity of morals rendered them a marked people... In the earlier stages of this sort of navigation, their trips were dangerous, not only on account of the Indians whose hunting-grounds bounded their track on either side, but also because the shores of both rivers were infested with organized banditti, who sought every occasion to rob and murder the owners of these boats. Besides all this, the Spanish Government had forbidden the navigation of the lower Mississippi by the Americans, and thus, hedged in every way by danger, it became these boatmen to cultivate all the hardihood and wiliness of the Pioneer, while it led them also into the possession of that recklessness and independent freedom of manner, which even after the causes that produced it had ceased, still clung to and formed an integral part of the character of the Western Bargeman.

The boatmen were a wild and wooly bunch. Often the children of early settlers, they were young men drawn away from the family farm by the attraction of adventure, travel and cash payment for their work, something their fathers rarely experienced. Their unfettered freedom provided the chance to be loud, coarse, violent, fun-seeking and, as often as possible, on an alcoholic spree. In many ways the Ohio boatmen were the precursors of the Forty-Niners or cowboys on a trail drive.

A Portland Ferry Operator Changes Navigation History

The direction of American navigation changed again in 1815 when Henry Miller Shreve, owner of the ferryboat at the Portland wharf, took the first steamboat into war. Shreve began his career as a keelboatman on the Monongahela in 1807. In December 1814, Shreve piloted downriver the *Enterprise*, a seventy-five-ton capacity steamboat equipped with an oscillating cylinder engine designed by Daniel French. It was filled with a cargo of munitions and military supplies to aid the American army in New Orleans commanded by General Andrew Jackson.

When the *Enterprise* arrived in New Orleans, General

THE FACILITY AND CONVENIENCE OF THE PASSAGE, IN ASCENDING THE RIVERS, ARE SUCH AS TO GIVE A DECIDED PREFERENCE TO THIS MODE OF NAVIGATION, WHILE THE SIZE AND CONSTRUCTION OF THE BOAT ENTITLES IT TO ALL THE ADVANTAGES WHICH THE *AETNA* AND *VESUVIUS* HAVE IN VAIN TRIED TO MONOPOLIZE OVER THE FREE WATERS OF OUR COMMON COUNTRY.

The Falls of the Ohio was the home of a great source of maritime-related jobs, including ferry operators, pilots, crews, roustabouts, cargo clerks and boatbuilders. Local commercial fishermen gained an intimate understanding of dangers in all types of weather or river conditions and mastered the dangerous waters at the Falls.

Jackson commandeered the vessel and sent it on various scouting and delivery missions, marking the first time in world history a steam-powered vessel was used in warfare. Shreve commanded a cannon battery during the decisive American victory over the British on January 8, 1815, but it was his return trip home that made news.

In the June 1, 1815, edition of the Louisville *Western Courier* appeared an announcement that changed Louisville:

COMMUNICATION – ARRIVED IN THIS POINT, IN 25 DAYS FROM NEW-ORLEANS, THE STEAM-BOAT, *ENTERPRIZE*, CAPTAIN SHRIEVE. THE CELERITY AND SAFETY

Shreve's achievement of piloting a steamboat upriver to Louisville revolutionized western commerce and is the pivotal economic event in the history of the Falls communities. This practical demonstration of upriver navigation now meant that manufactured goods, passengers, information and capital could be cheaply transported upstream, as well as down. Two years later Shreve would create the flat-bottomed western steamboat with decks stacked one above the other, moving the engines up from a deep keel. This advancement provided the ideal craft for shallow water navigation and is the steamboat style most people recognize as the classic paddlewheeler.

Louisvillians quickly recognized the potential of steam navigation. The *Western Courier* proclaimed, "On Monday the 3d of July, was safely launched from her stocks, at the mouth of Beargrass into her destined element, the elegant new steamboat *Governor Shelby*, owned by Messrs. Gray, Gwathmey, Gretsinger and Ruble of this town. The *Governor Shelby* is intended as a regular trader between this place and New Orleans, is of 122 tons burden, and is thought by judges to be one of the handsomest models, which does great credit to her constructors, Messrs. Desmarie and McClary."

The Graveyard of the West

The broad area stretching south of Main Street, away from the river, provided a grand and eligible location for an expanding city, except that the area was festooned with stagnant ponds and marshy flats with very poor drainage. As long as the town crowded close to the river shoreline the ponds presented few problems, but when people began to move further inland, a dramatic increase in sickness became evident. Louisville acquired the reputation as an unhealthy, disease-ridden place. Cincinnati, Louisville's upriver commercial rival, continually complained of the tolls their merchants were forced to pay to transship cargoes around the Falls and newspapers in the Queen City labeled Louisville as "the Graveyard of the West," as travelers began to steer clear of the community.

Englishman Thomas Hulme shared his concerns during a brief visit in 1819. "Arrived at Louisville, Kentucky… Perceiving stagnant waters about the town, and an appearance of the house that we stopped at being infested with bugs, we resolved not to make any stay at Louisville, but got into our skiff and floated down the falls to Shippingport. We found it very rough floating, not to say dangerous."

Another public health concern was the growing numbers of itinerant boatmen landing at Louisville's wharf. These hardscrabble crews represented the most mobile members of American society and their lack of self-restraint was legendary. While on voyages the crewmen were exposed to semi-tropical diseases in the Deep South, freezing work conditions in the upper Mississippi valley and venereal diseases wherever they went. Steamboat captains did not run charity institutions, and if a crewman was too ill or injured to do his job, he was routinely set ashore at the first opportunity. Boatmen suffering from contagious diseases collapsed on the wharf and streets of Louisville and depended upon the kindness of strangers for care or treatment.

A growing number of boatmen arriving at the busy Louisville, Shippingport and Portland wharves needed medical treatment. Prominent Louisville citizens began a movement to provide a hospital for "the relief of persons who might, owing to the fatigue and exposure of long voyages, become sick or languish at the port of Louisville."

An epidemic of yellow fever gripped Louisville in 1817 and inspired two leading citizens, Cuthbert Bullitt and Thomas Prather, to donate seven acres for a hospital site. A hospital located at Chestnut Street, between Floyd and Preston, was authorized to treat boatmen and local citizens. The State of Kentucky appropriated $17,500 and the U.S. Government provided revenue from the Custom House in New Orleans to treat mariners. The town of Louisville allocated a levy of two percent of auction sales in the city.

The Louisville Marine Hospital opened its doors in 1822. This original hospital served river men until 1852, when the United States Marine Hospital in Portland opened. The downtown hospital became better known as Louisville General Hospital and served the public until it was demolished in 1914. The original Louisville Marine Hospital location still serves as the center of health care services for Louisville.

The Duty of Port Wardens

The growth of commercial activities on Louisville's waterfront demanded greater governmental control, and the office of port warden was created. The *Louisville Public Advertiser* described the job in its March 3, 1819, edition.

WE PUBLISH IN THIS DAY'S PAPER, THE ACT OF THE LAST SESSION OF THE LEGISLATURE OF KENTUCKY, AUTHORIZING THE APPOINTMENT OF PORT WARDENS WHERE SUCH OFFICERS MAY BE REQUISITE IN THIS STATE. THE UTILITY OF THIS MEASURE WILL BE APPRECIATED BY THOSE WHO ARE INTERESTED IN THE NAVIGATION OF

THE WESTERN WATERS. TO ESTABLISH THE CHARACTER OF A BOAT, OF ANY DESCRIPTION, IT WILL ONLY BE NECESSARY FOR THE OWNERS TO APPLY TO ONE OR MORE OF THE PORT WARDENS TO EXAMINE HER, AND TO CERTIFY HER CONDITION. THE CERTIFICATE THUS OBTAINED WILL TEND TO PREVENT THOSE DISPUTES, WHICH SO FREQUENTLY OCCUR BETWEEN THE MASTER AND SHIPPER, RELATIVE TO THE QUALITY AND CONDITION OF THE BOAT; AND THE RECORD THEREOF, BEING RECOGNIZED AS LEGAL EVIDENCE, WILL SERVE TO FACILITATE THE ATTAINMENT OF SPEEDY AND IMPARTIAL JUSTICE.

IT IS, ALSO, THE PROVINCE OF THE PORT WARDENS TO ATTEND TO, OR EXAMINE THE STOWAGE OF ANY BOAT, WHEN CALLED ON, EITHER BY THE MASTER OR THE SHIPPER OF GOODS. THE SAFETY OF A CARGO, NOT UNFREQUENTLY DEPENDS ON THE MANNER IN WHICH IT MAY BE STOWED AWAY.

Gray's Famous Warehouse

In 1819 Louisville's early skyline was dominated by a single structure located at the end of Third Street, just where Beargrass Creek met the Ohio River. The warehouse of John Thompson Gray was an imposing four-story building at the river's edge which served as the town's post office, commercial storage for the river trade and unofficial headquarters for

John Thompson Gray's imposing warehouse, post office and customs house dominated the early Louisville waterfront and was the center for commerce and communications. As indicated by a long list of newspaper advertisements, the Gray warehouse offered a vast number of services and products for sale, trade or storage. (Courtesy of the River's Institute at Hanover College)

John T. Gray,

Has for Sale,

Rolled and hoop iron,
Juniatta   do
4d. 6d. 8d. and 10d. cut nails,
8d. and 10d.   do brads,
Castings, assorted,
Buckley's black flint mill stones,
McDougle's Raccoon Burrs,
Tarred and white cordage,
Royal, super royal and medium printing paper,
Letter and common writing paper,
Wrapping and tea   do.
Barrels tanners' oil,
   "   Linseed do.
   "   New-Orleans rum,
   "   Whiskey, old,
   "   Mackerel, No. 3, fresh,
   "   Kenhawa salt,
Kegs allum,
   "   Madder,
   "   Pepper,
   "   Race ginger,
   "   Cloves,
   "   White lead, in oil,
   "   Powder, Trotter's and Warfield's & Co.
Shot, assorted,
Pig and bar lead,
8 by 10, 10 by 12, and 12 by 18 window glass,
Boxes glassware,
Alum salt, in bags.
August 24.   405—ow

John T. Gray,

Offers for sale, at his store in Louisville,

15,000 pounds bale rope, of the very best quality—*Also,*
     10,000 lbs. hemp yarns.
August 17.   403—ow

JUST RECEIVED,

Per Steam Boats Fayette and Henry Clay,
and for sale by

JOHN T. GRAY,

12 hogsheads New-Orleans sugar
40 barrels molasses
20   do   mackerel
2   do   French brandy
4 bales superior Louisiana cotton
     ALSO—*On hand for sale*
Imperial, super royal and royal printing paper
Wrapping paper
Writing   do   Nos. 1, 2 & 8
Blue tea   do
White and tarred cordage
Sickles
White lead in oil
Bar and pig lead
May 21   482—ow

John T. Gray

OFFERS FOR SALE,

At his Warehouse at the mouth of Beargrass, Louisville, Ky.
20,000 pounds of superior bale rope, made entirely of clean hemp, of the best quality.
May 28   484—ow

JUST RECEIVED,

And for sale by

John T. Gray,

50 barrels family flour
100   do   Kenhawa salt.
June 21   491—ow

---

maritime communication. The first story was built of heavy stone laid in hydraulic lime, with a solid floor of concrete to protect the structure during times of flooding. The upper stories were brick and strengthened by solid hewn columns of walnut placed at intervals, with the entire structure buttressed like a castle.

Gray, the son of Revolutionary War hero Captain George Gray, became Louisville postmaster in 1811, a position he would hold for twenty-two years. In 1825 Gray published a description of his job responsibilities. "I am authorized by the Post Office Department to receive proposals for carrying the mail, by steam boats, from Louisville to New Orleans, three times a week, to stop at all the principal intermediate towns on the river. Any person or persons wishing to undertake the transportation of the mail in this way, will hand their proposals to me, in writing. Those living at a distance will write by mail, directed to me, as postmaster. The proposal of one person shall not be seen by, or communicated with any other."

Gray's warehouse also served as the informal place of exchange among riverboat pilots and captains arriving at the wharf. Here they posted messages, recruited crew members, secured cargoes and swapped information about river conditions, including the location of ever-shifting sandbars, bank erosions or disabled boats they had seen.

In 1819 John Thompson Gray was present at the Louisville waterfront to welcome his cousin James Monroe on the first visit to the community by a U.S. president. Accompanying Monroe was General Andrew Jackson leading an official party, making an inspection of military posts in the West. The presidential tour arrived from Nashville in carriages and was officially greeted by George Gray, Monroe's commander during the Revolution. The President addressed an assembly of citizens by stating, "The kind reception given me by the citizens of Louisville affords me the highest satisfaction. To meet among them, many of my old friends, who sustained with exemplary gallantry and firmness the hardships and perils of the great struggle which secured to our country, its liberty, independence, and all the blessings which we now enjoy, and whose subsequent lives have so fully supported the character acquired on that great occasion, excites feelings which I shall not attempt to describe."

The following day the party was ferried over to Jeffersonville on the steamboat *Perseverance* to inspect a proposed site of a canal to bypass the Falls on the Indiana side. The presidential party left the next day by carriage to travel to Frankfort, and on their way stopped at Major Croghan's Locust Grove estate. Joining Monroe and Jackson for this leg of the journey was Lieutenant Zachary Taylor, a young Louisvillian beginning his career in the U.S. Army. For a brief period, three of the nation's first twelve presidents gathered together on the Louisville waterfront.

The Old Monarch and Mr. Louisville

A small newspaper advertisement in 1820 announced a new era at the Falls:

JOHN ROWAN & JAS. GUTHRIE WILL OCCUPY AS A LAW OFFICE AT LOUISVILLE, THE ROOM CONNECTED WITH THE EXCHANGE OFFICE OF WM. S. THOMAS, FIRST DOOR ABOVE THE UNION HALL. J. ROWAN WILL HENCEFORTH ATTEND THE JEFFERSON CIRCUIT COURT REGULARLY, AND MAY BE CONSULTED DURING THE TERMS OF THAT COURT AT THE AFORESAID OFFICE. JAMES GUTHRIE RESIDES AT THE HOTEL, AND WILL BE CONSTANTLY AT THE OFFICE, UNLESS WHEN ABSENT ON HIS CIRCUIT. — BUSINESS CONFIDED TO THAT OFFICE, WILL BE FAITHFULLY AND REGULARLY ATTENDED TO.

Few at the time could anticipate the impact young James Guthrie would have on Louisville. His partner, Senator John Rowan, had been his instructor of law in Bardstown and the ambitious Mr. Guthrie was well prepared for his move to the larger town of Louisville. He earned the honorific "Mr. Louisville," as over the next forty years James Guthrie would steer the business and legal affairs of the community more than anyone else in its history. He served as president of the Louisville-Portland Canal Company, promoter of the new Jefferson County Court House and president of the newly founded University of Louisville. While he earned national renown as the secretary of

the U.S. Treasury under Franklin Pierce, it was Guthrie's role as president of the Louisville and Nashville Railroad that left its greatest impact.

The law firm's senior partner was John Rowan, the majestic jurist and United States senator, known as "The Old Monarch." Rowan enjoyed a very successful practice in Bardstown and built his home, Federal Hill, on the town's edge. This house is believed to have been the inspiration for the song "My Old Kentucky Home," a sentimental air written by Rowan's young cousin, Stephen Collins Foster. Rowan also built an impressive townhouse on Fifth Street in Louisville, immediately opposite the front door of the new cathedral, and grew richer and more powerful with his efforts at the Falls.

Another of Rowan's cousins, Joshua Gill Barclay, had worked for his cousin and William Lytle in the establishment of the new town of Portland. After he left their employ, he developed into a successful businessman, lawyer and farmer. Barclay had the unusual distinction of being related to two of America's most beloved artists. He was the cousin of songwriter Stephen Collins Foster, a relationship he shared with John Rowan. He was also, for a brief time, John James Audubon's nephew by marriage. Barclay's short-lived first wife, Julia Berthoud, was the daughter of Lucy Bakewell Audubon's sister Eliza.

Joshua Barclay established a career as a commission merchant, where he purchased shipments arriving by steamboat and subdivided cargoes to distribute coffee, sugar, processed groceries and other commodities to individual general stores, hotels and merchants. Barclay family tradition says that Joshua was a vain man, and when he ballooned to over four hundred pounds, he left the city and retired to a farm in Trimble County.

In preparation of leaving town, Barclay offered the sale of his estate, Belle Vue. This farm complex was located east of the city and adjacent to the huge farm and mill of Frederick Geiger and his son Jacob. In the early 1820s, several large estates with impressive mansions were being built on the Point to enjoy the magnificent views of the Ohio River before it widened as it approached the Falls. Belle Vue was well named, and an 1824 advertisement provides a vivid picture of its complexity:

Vol. 6.

FOR SALE OR TO RENT, BELLE VUE,

The late residence of Mr. J. G. Barclay.

THIS agreeable and pleasantly situated country seat, on the bank of the Ohio, only one mile and a half above Louisville, adjoining Mr. Geiger's ferry, and immediately opposite Jeffersonville, has a convenient and neat dwelling house, kitchen, (adjoining to which is a well of excellent water,) ice house, milk house, smoke house, chicken house, stable and carriage house; an excellent garden, with a considerable quantity of grape vines and fruit trees in bearing; a beautiful grass lot in front of the dwelling house, in which a large number of choice fruit trees were planted last season, with other lots fit for cultivation or meadows. The whole comprising about 20 acres of land, all enclosed with post and rail fences in good order.

Gentlemen who have business to attend to in Louisville, and wish their families to reside in the country, are invited to call and see the premises; and persons wishing to attend to the culture of vegetables, for the supply of the Louisville market, would find this a very advantageous situation.

Mr. Geiger, who resides adjoining, will shew the premises. For terms, apply to

N. BERTHOUD.

Shippingport, Jan 10   549—ow

Twenty-first century visitors wishing to see the site of Belle Vue must travel east from the Tumbleweed restaurant in Waterfront Park and continue a short distance upstream. Adjacent to the site of Barclay's home is the only remaining example of an early Point mansion. The rear section of the Paget House was probably built around 1800, with a major front addition later added by Mrs. Margaret Paget. It is remarkable that this building has survived, as it has borne the brunt of every Ohio River flood and has frequently been covered to the

roof line. In addition to natural disasters, in 1839 it was the victim of an arson attempt.

POLICE COURT. HENRY JOHNSON, WM. QUINN AND JAMES DOUGLAS, THREE GENTLEMEN OF THE "FREE AND EASY" KIND, WERE INTRODUCED TO THE COURT BY MRS. PAGET. THIS WAS A PEACE-WARRANT. THE COMPLAINANT, WITHOUT REFERRING TO ANY PARTICULAR OFFENCE ON THE PART OF THE ACCUSED, IN WHICH EACH COULD BE RECOGNIZED AS HAVING TAKEN PART, GAVE A VERY BAD CHARACTER OF THEM GENERALLY. DOUGLAS AND QUINN SHE REPRESENTED AS YOUNG MEN OF VIOLENT PASSIONS, HAVING ON ONE OCCASION NEARLY RAZED HER HOUSE WITH COALS, AND AFTERWARDS CLEARED OUT WITH HER BED-CURTAINS.

Life on the Point could be tough, as later generations of residents would attest.

"…in the suppression of these, and other vices"

The city fathers were becoming weary of Louisville's growing reputation as a freewheeling riverport town and began to strengthen controls on local laws, as evidenced by this 1824 code:

BE IT ORDAINED BY THE TRUSTEES OF THE TOWN OF LOUISVILLE, THAT FROM AND AFTER THE FIRST DAY OF JULY, 1824, IF ANY PERSON OR PERSONS SHALL KEEP A BAUDY HOUSE, OR HOUSE OF ILL FAME AND PROSTITUTION, ON WATER STREET, MAIN STREET, MARKET STREET, JEFFERSON STREET, OR GREEN STREET, OR ON FIRST, SECOND, THIRD, FOURTH, FIFTH, SIXTH, SEVENTH, EIGHT, NINTH, OR TENTH CROSS STREETS, BETWEEN WATER AND GREEN STREET, EACH AND EVERY PERSON SO OFFENDING FOR THE SPACE OF SIX DAYS, SHALL BE SUBJECT TO A FINE OF TWENTY-DOLLARS, RECOVERABLE BY WARRANT, BEFORE A MAGISTRATE, IN THE NAME OF THE TRUSTEES OF LOUISVILLE.

A new civic campaign, led by Samuel Churchill, was launched to improve public morality. The *Louisville Public Advertiser*, just three days before Christmas 1824, carried the following news story:

WHEREAS, IT IS ADMITTED BY ALL GOOD MEN, THAT VICIOUS HABITS, ACQUIRED BY THE UNRESTRAINED PRACTICE OF INIQUITY, ARE ALWAYS DESTRUCTIVE TO THE PEACE, HAPPINESS AND SAFETY OF SOCIETY; AND WHEREAS, THE WANTON USE OF CLANDESTINE AND UNLAWFUL WEAPONS HAS BECOME NOTORIOUSLY PREVALENT IN THIS TOWN TO AN ALARMING EXTENT; AS, ALSO, THE PROFANATION OF THE HOLY SABBATH, BY CARRYING ON TRADE AND ENGAGING IN UNLAWFUL SPORTS, BOTH BY PEOPLE OF COLOR AND BY WHITES; AND AS TIPPLING SHOPS, AND OTHER HOUSES OF DANGEROUS TENDENCY, ARE GREATLY MULTIPLIED, TO THE ANNOYANCE OF THE WELL DISPOSED, BOTH ON THE SABBATH AND WEEK DAYS, TOGETHER WITH GAMBLING, DRUNKENNESS AND OTHER PRACTICES, SUBVERSIVE OF THE PEACE, COMFORT AND GOOD ORDER OF SOCIETY: IN ORDER, AS MUCH AS POSSIBLE, TO EXTIRPATE SUCH SCENES, AND TO ENCOURAGE THE EXECUTIVE AUTHORITY OF THIS PLACE IN THE REGULAR DISCHARGE OF THEIR DUTIES, IN THE SUPPRESSION OF THESE AND OTHER VICES, RUINOUS TO THE PUBLIC INTERESTS.

Louisville's social order, so long determined by Episcopalians and Presbyterians of Virginia origin, was being put to a test and would be further stressed in the days to come. The diary of William Owen, a traveling evangelist and early abolitionist, gives his impressions of life in Louisville in 1824 while waiting for his steamboat.

LOUISVILLE HAS ONE GOOD STREET PARALLEL WITH THE RIVER; THE OTHERS ARE SHORT, SOON LEADING TO FIELDS OR WOODS. IT CONTAINS ABOUT 4000 INHABITANTS AND HAS A HOSPITAL AND FOUR CHURCHES.

IT LIKEWISE SUPPORTS A THEATER DURING SOME MONTHS OF THE YEAR. A NUMBER OF HACKNEY COACHES PLY THE STREETS. THESE ARE THE FIRST WE HAVE SEEN WEST OF THE ALLYGHANA MOUNTAINS.

WE WALKED SOUTH TO THE OUTSKIRTS OF THE CITY, THROUGH NUMEROUS MUDDY CROSSINGS AND PUDDLES, OWING TO THE LATE RAIN. AS FAR AS THE CITY HAS BEEN LAID OUT, THE GROUND, AS YET UNOCCUPIED BY BUILDINGS, IS COVERED WITH GRASS AND THE STREETS MARKED OFF BY PALINGS; FURTHER ON STILL IS SURROUNDED BY WOODS. WE ASCENDED A GENTLE SLOPE WHICH EXTENDED OUR PROSPECT A LITTLE. THE CITY SEEMED TO BE SITUATED ON AN EXTENSIVE BOTTOM OF GOOD, THOUGH SANDY, SOIL. IT IS SURROUNDED BY A GREAT MANY POOLS AND MARSHES, WHICH RENDER THE SITUATION UNHEALTHY.

WE MET AN INHABITANT WHO SEEMED TO BE CONVERSANT WITH THE FOIBLES OF THE PLACE. HE TOLD US THAT AT THE POINT WHERE WE STOOD THE MAGISTRATE HAD DRAWN A LINE, BEYOND WHICH THE GAMBLERS AND LOOSE CHARACTERS WERE NOT PERMITTED TO RESIDE. HE SAID THAT A GOOD MANY INDIVIDUALS CAME HERE WHO RUINED THEIR HEALTH MUCH MORE BY THEIR DISSOLUTENESS THAN BY THE CLIMATE. HE GAVE US A VERY POOR IDEA OF THE MORALITY OF THE PLACE.

Pointed Out by the Finger of Nature

Many people believed that Louisville dragged its feet when it came to the long-anticipated construction of a boat canal and lock system to accommodate the safe passage around the Falls. Canal schemes had flourished on both sides of the Ohio River since 1804. Many accused Louisville of delaying the project so as not to diminish the transshipment trades. By 1825, public pressure to build the canal had reached its boiling point. Governor DeWitt Clinton of New York, the promoter and champion of the highly successful Erie Canal, came to Louisville, both to enhance his growing national political profile and to investigate the site of a proposed canal.

Upon examining the straight passage from Louisville's Tenth Street to the Shippingport harbor, Governor Clinton remarked that the route itself had been pointed out by the finger of nature. Speaking to supporters of the canal project, Clinton told the crowd:

> On this occasion, you will permit me to congratulate you on the bright prospects which open in this important section of our country. I mean the certainty of a canal around the Falls of the Ohio – a work which will remove the greatest obstacle to the navigation of that river, and which has been a long time contemplated, but never accomplished. In its completion a vast population is vastly interested. I have, during my stay among you, visited the localities of this contemplated operation, and read the reports of the engineer on the subject; and so far as I can judge, I have no hesitation in saying that, of its practicability, I entertain no doubt – of its economical execution, I have no doubt – of its usefulness, I am equally certain.

> The removal of this natural impediment, to a free transit on your great river, will be a precursor to all kinds of productive industry; and the expense avoided, the time saved, and the risk removed, will be so much gained, to the interests of agriculture and internal commerce. With your felicitous position on the Ohio, with the vast and flourishing regions around you, there is nothing necessary to secure and to extend the blessings you now enjoy, if enterprise and industry are put into requisition.

Despite optimistic assessments that the entire canal could be dug and operational in six months, a cold dose of reality hit when solid bedrock was discovered below the subsoil. It would require five years, and thousands of manual laborers, to dig out the two-mile-long canal and install the three sections of locks required to drop or raise a boat twenty-four feet in elevation from the upper to the lower Ohio River. The local sale of shares was insufficient to finance the entire project and the federal government stepped in as the major stockholder. The Portland Canal opened in December 1830, but in the five years it took to dig it, the width of the average American steamboat had outgrown the original dimensions of the canal. Despite the fact that the fifty-foot-wide canal could only accommodate one-third of the boats seeking passage, high tolls on the canal guaranteed a successful investment for all its backers.

Historian Richard C. Wade, in his classic study of western development, *The Urban Frontier*, recognized one of the long-term impacts of the Portland canal project.

> In the late twenties, however, the canal boom in the West brought a new group of transients to Pittsburgh, Cincinnati and Louisville. The construction of new waterways required large contingents of workers, and neighboring towns could provide only a small portion. Hence the new country was flooded with vagabond laborers who lived haphazardly and moved from job to job, staying in cities only when building was nearby. But at Louisville, the Portland Canal attracted large numbers of the unskilled who resided for several years. In 1827 nearly ten percent of the population found employment on the project. Though some settled down quickly, others remained floaters – working by day, drifting by night – a constant irritant to local officials.

THE IRREGULAR LIFE OF THE TRANSIENT POPULATION CENTERED UPON A FEW BLOCKS IN EACH CITY. USUALLY LOCATED NEAR THE WATERFRONT AND BUSINESS DISTRICTS, THESE SPOTS CONTAINED ROOMING HOUSES, CHEAP HOTELS, GROG-SHOPS AND TIPPLING HOUSES. SEALED OFF FROM THE REST OF TOWN ESPECIALLY AFTER DARK — THESE AREAS DEVELOPED HABITS AND PATTERNS OF THEIR OWN.

Welcoming the Nation's Guest

Despite growing social divisions, with society becoming split between the very wealthy and the working poor, there was one subject all Louisvillians agreed upon. When the "Nation's Guest" came to town, Louisville was prepared to do him honor.

The Marquis de Lafayette, the French nobleman who stood next to Washington in the hearts of Americans, made a grand farewell tour of the United States in 1825. His visit was scheduled well in advance, and Louisville, like every other American community, scrambled to do him proper honor. A grand barbecue was scheduled on the grounds of the Point just east of the wharf to allow the population a chance to see their aging hero. A triumphal arch was built over Beargrass Creek and painted by Louisville's leading theatrical producer, Mr. A. Drake, with one side featuring French and American flags and on the other "Welcome, Our Country's Friend." All surviving Revolutionary War veterans were invited as special guests.

To accommodate the expected large crowds, the trustees requested that toll roads be opened without charge and that businesses and schools close their doors for the great event. It was estimated that 10,000 people lined the streets to witness Lafayette's journey from the Portland wharf to downtown Louisville. The figure is remarkable in that Louisville's population barely exceeded 7,000, but the number was swelled by the people of Indiana and rural districts who flocked to town.

As civic celebrations go, it was a bust. On his way upriver

The arrival of the Marquis de Lafayette to Louisville was part of his grand tour of America in 1825. After greeting local men who had been his compatriots during the Revolution, Lafayette rode, in a driving rainstorm, through a town thronged with over 10,000 adoring citizens. At the time, Louisville boasted a population of about 7,000, but "the Nation's Guest" attracted visitors from the entire region.

to Portland, Lafayette's steamboat sank and his entire party was fortunate to reach a small island and safety. General Lafayette lost his wardrobe, including his red wig, as well as the tokens of esteem he had been given on his tour. He was picked up and brought to the Portland wharf where a formal service was prepared. The *Public Advertiser* of April 14, 1825, reported on his journey downtown while a driving rainstorm pelted the scene:

THE GENERAL WAS THEN PLACED IN AN OPEN CARRIAGE, DRAWN BY FOUR HORSES, ACCOMPANIED BY COLONEL ANDERSON, A REVOLUTIONARY OFFICER, WHO HAD ACTED

AS ONE OF HIS AIDES IN OUR STRUGGLE FOR FREEDOM, AND WAS ESCORTED TO TOWN…ON PASSING SHIPPINGPORT, THE STEAMBOATS IN PORT, EACH FIRED A NATIONAL SALUTE, AND ON REACHING LOUISVILLE, HE FOUND BETWEEN EIGHT AND TEN THOUSAND PERSONS, CROWDED ON THE SIDEWALKS OF MAIN STREET, ANXIOUSLY AWAITING HIS APPROACH. THE WINDOWS OF THE HOUSES WERE FILLED WITH LADIES, AND THE LITTLE MISSES OF MOST OF OUR SCHOOLS WERE ARRANGED ON THE SIDEWALKS, AND AS OUR VENERATED GUEST PASSED UP MAIN STREET, THEY BOWED, WAVED THEIR HANDKERCHIEFS, AND STREWED THE STREET WITH FLOWERS.

Unfortunately, the rains forced a cancellation of plans for the outdoor barbecue in the field next to Beargrass Creek. Had it been held, the triumphant visit by General Lafayette would have been the earliest community celebration on what future Louisvillians would recognize as Waterfront Park's Great Lawn.

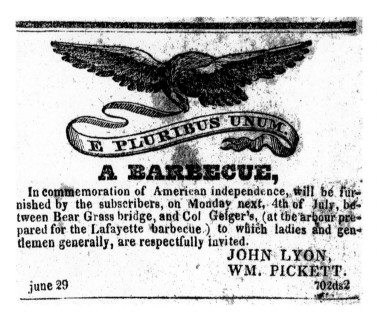

"…they have power to levy and collect a tax."

At the end of 1825, the town trustees passed a sweeping act to stabilize government's control over its public spaces. The town agreed that:

THEY AND THEIR SUCCESSORS IN OFFICE SHALL HAVE AUTHORITY TO PURCHASE AND HOLD REAL ESTATE FOR THE PURPOSE OF ERECTING AND KEEPING WHARVES, MARKET HOUSES, FIRE ENGINE HOUSES, WATCH HOUSES, AND OTHER PUBLIC BUILDINGS, FOR THE USE AND CONVENIENCE OF SAID TOWN, AND THAT THE PURCHASES ALREADY MADE BY SAID TRUSTEES OF THE SLIP OF GROUND BETWEEN WATER STREET AND THE LOW WATER MARK OF THE OHIO RIVER, FROM JAMES A. PEARCE AND JOHN ROWAN, BE AND THE SAME IS HEREBY CONFIRMED; AND THAT THEY HAVE POWER TO LEVY AND COLLECT A TAX NOT TO EXCEED THIRTY DOLLARS ON EACH EXCHANGE OR BROKER'S OFFICE IN SAID TOWN.

Just six months earlier, Louisville made an unusual bargain with attorney John Rowan and James A. Pearce, the son-in-law of General Jonathan Clark, for the land they owned just west of the main steamboat landing at Fourth Street. Being the legal owners of the riverfront property, Rowan and Pearce agreed to become equal partners with the trustees to jointly build and maintain a wharf on their land between Water Street and the Ohio River. The ground extended from John T. Gray's wharf to the western boundary of the town at Twelfth Street. Rowan agreed to allow building stone to be quarried from the bed of the Ohio River, the former limestone shelf surrounding Corn Island, for use on the wharf. Louisville promised to build and pave the wharf as quickly as possible and share the profits from wharf fees equally with the landowners. Private citizens, already wealthy, were set to become even more so as boats used their landing and paid hefty fees for the privilege.

The town of Louisville could grow no more, and local citizens began to appeal to the state legislature to take an unprecedented step and declare Louisville to be the Commonwealth's only first-class city. In 1828 the time was right for the transition.

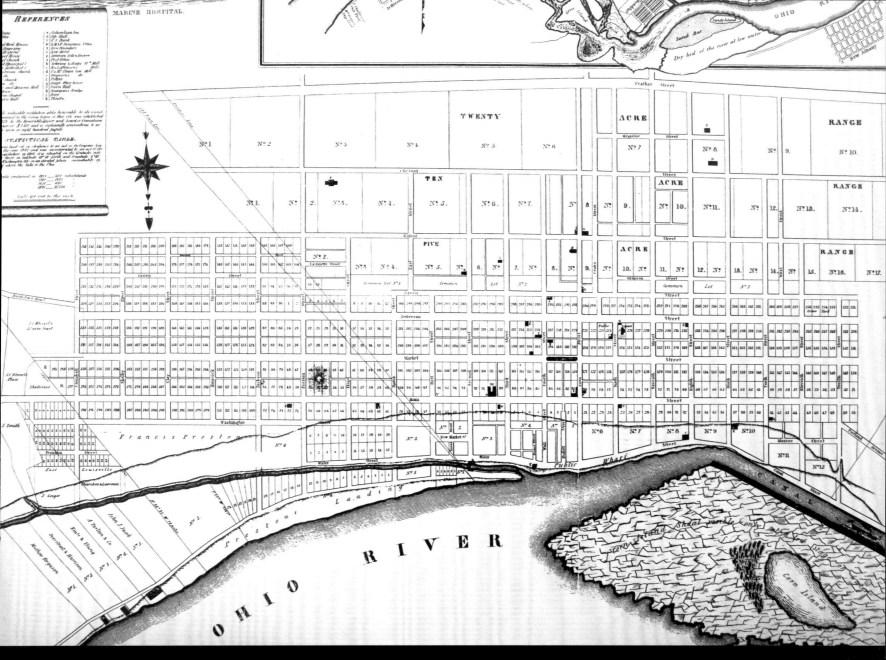

A detailed map of downtown Louisville, drawn in 1831 by city surveyor E.D. Hobbs, delineates Beargrass Creek's entrance into the Ohio River between Third and Fourth Streets. The wedge of land between the Ohio River and Beragrass Creek, called "The Point" from the earliest pioneer days, would be the site of the future Louisville Waterfront Park.

The new city of Louisville, as seen from Jeffersonville, Indiana, in 1840, shows Main Street slowly extending along the upper bank of the river. The harbor, full of various vessels including flatboats, steamboats and john boats, was well on its way to becoming one of America's premier inland ports. *(Filson Historical Society, PR750-0048)*

A Very Public Wharf

(1828-1850)

The landing at the time was thronged with steamers, and yet the incessant "boom, boom, boom," of the high-pressure engines, the shrill hiss of scalding steam, and the fitful port-song of the negro firemen rising ever and anon upon the breeze, gave notice of a constant augmentation to the number. Some, too, were getting underway, and their lower guards were thronged by emigrants with their household and agricultural utensils. Drays were rattling hither and thither over the rough pavement; Irish porters were cracking their whips and roaring forth alternate staves of blasphemy and song; clerks hurrying to and fro, with fluttering note-books, in all the fancied dignity of "brief authority;" hackney-coaches dashing down to the water's edge, apparently with no motive to the nervous man but noise; while at intervals, as if to fill up the pauses of the Babel, some incontinent steamer would hurl forth from the valves of her overcharged boilers one of those deafening, terrible blasts, echoing and re-echoing along the river-banks, and streets, and among the lofty buildings, till the very welkin rang again.

To one who has never visited the public wharves of the great cities of the West, it is no trivial task to convey an adequate idea of the spectacle they present.

– Edmund Flagg - 1838

Louisville had grown in population and sophistication since it received its town charter from Virginia in 1780 and, by 1828, people were demanding an improved form of local government. Demands for change came from working-class citizens, and when the Kentucky General Assembly authorized a vote for city status on February 13, 1828, a division between rich and poor became evident. Many wealthy Louisvillians voted against the measure that would raise their taxes and diminish their political power. With voting open to "all free white male citizens," and no requirement for land ownership, working men supported the measure, which passed by 250 votes.

With the end of the trustees, a tight-knit group primarily consisting of merchants and lawyers who frequently voted in their own self-interest, power went to the hands of a mayor and city council. Until 1837, mayors were elected annually for one-year terms and were allowed to succeed themselves in office. Community leader Frederick Kaye was elected to seven terms as mayor, but, during that time, the office was more advisory than administrative. Power rested in the hands of the city council with the community divided into five wards, each represented by two councilmen. The new charter expanded powers to authorize support of public schools, street paving and other civic improvements.

A provision required by the General Assembly was the adoption of an official city seal. A design was approved, reflecting the city's highest priority, its waterfront. The council decreed that the seal should be "a representation of a wharf with boxes and bales thereon – a steamboat approaching the wharf with the words 'The City of Louisville' engraved at the top of the seal." They also adopted an odd motto reading, "Industry and Punctuality," at a time when there were few manufacturers and no standardized timekeeping. Shortly afterwards, the official motto of Louisville was changed to *Perseverando*, a Latin word meaning "by persevering."

Shortly after the new charter was adopted, a letter to the *Louisville Public Advertiser*, written by "Senex," reflected a citizen's concern for the future:

The first city seal of Louisville displays a steamboat coming upstream, with cargo waiting on the wharf for transport. Louisville's initial motto, *"Perseverando,"* indicated the new city's determination to persevere through all challenges.

WHAT HAVE WE GAINED BY THE INCORPORATION OF OUR CITY? I AM READY TO ADMIT WE HAVE ATTAINED A MORE EFFECTUAL POLICE AND AN EXTENDED IMPROVEMENT OF OUR TOWN IN ITS WHARVES, ITS STREETS AND GENERAL GOVERNMENT, HIGHLY CONDUCTIVE TO THE COMFORTS OF BUSINESS. BUT IS THIS PHYSICAL IMPROVEMENT EVERY THING, OR EVEN THE GREATEST BOON, WHICH OUR CITY GOVERNMENT COULD CONFER ON ITS *SUBJECTS*, USING THE TERM IN NO DEGRADING SENSE? SHALL WE IN KENTUCKY NEVER RISE ABOVE THE CONTRACTED SCALE OF GOVERNMENT? IS THERE NOTHING BETTER IN MUNICIPAL LEGISLATION, THAN CUTTING DOWN STREETS AND FINING RIOTERS? WHEN SHALL WE LEARN AND PRACTICE THE LESSON, THAT THE GREATEST WISDOM OF GOVERNMENTS IS TO PREVENT CRIMES, RATHER THAN *PUNISH* THEM? TO IMPROVE THE MIND AND MORALS OF SOCIETY BEFORE ORNAMENTING OUR STREETS AND SQUARES? TO EFFECT THIS, WHAT IS SO NECESSARY AS A SYSTEM OF FREE SCHOOLS FOR *ALL* THE CHILDREN OF THE CITY? WHAT ELSE WILL SAVE A LARGE PORTION OF THE RISING GENERATION FROM MORAL AND INTELLECTUAL RUIN? WHEN SOCIETY DOES NOT EDUCATE ITS POORER AND MORE UNFORTUNATE SONS, TOO MANY BECOME THE ENEMIES OF THAT SOCIETY, AND BY A TERRIBLE REACTION AVENGE THEMSELVES BY DEPREDATIONS UPON THE PROPERTY AND PERSONS OF THEIR FELLOW CITIZENS.

Louisville was growing as an economic power, and in the seat of that power were the commission merchants of Main Street and the cargo capacity of the wharf. A writer for the *Louisville Focus* analyzed the economic impact of two important commodities that passed through Louisville hands in 1829:

THE PRINCIPAL DEALER IN THESE ARTICLES WAS CALLED ON PERSONALLY, AND THERE WAS OBTAINED FROM EACH, A STATEMENT OF THE QUANTITY ACTUALLY RECEIVED, DIRECT FROM NEW ORLEANS, AND SOLD BY THEM....

THERE WERE 4,064 HOGSHEADS OF SUGAR, AND 8,307 BAGS AND BARRELS OF COFFEE, RECEIVED AND SOLD IN THIS PLACE FROM 1ST JAN. 1828 TO 1ST JAN. 1829. ESTIMATING THE SUGAR AT 1000 LBS, FOR EACH HOGSHEAD, AND THE AVERAGE PRICE AT 8 1/2 CTS. PR. LB., IT WOULD AMOUNT TO 4,064,000 LBS. AND AT 8 ½ CTS. PR. LB. TO $345,440.00

ESTIMATING THE COFFEE AT 180 LBS. PR. BAG OR BARREL, AND THE AVERAGE PRICE AT 16 CTS. PR. LB, IT WOULD AMOUNT TO 1,494,260 LBS. WORTH $239,241.60

WHICH ADDED TO THE VALUE OF THE SUGAR MAKES $584,681.60

A large percentage of the taxes raised from these transactions went toward improving the wharf. An 1829 financial report to the council revealed that city receipts for the past year were greater than $36,600, with $265 coming from exhibitions of animals and other things, $2,036 from wharf fees and $1,425 earned from the operation of Gray's wharf and ferry.

Expenses named for operating the wharf included $2,300 for maintenance and $520 for the wharfmaster's salary (partly based on a percentage of the fees he collected from boats at the landing). The greatest expenses, $20,134, reflected the cost of construction and physical improvements to the wharf, with an additional $670 to purchase the small point of land at the tip of Beargrass.

"Industry and enterprize here find a certain reward. This is Louisville."

Caleb Atwater, a visitor to the city in 1829, recorded his very favorable impressions of Louisville and its citizens in his travel account, *Remarks Made on a Tour to Prairie du Chien:*

DURING HIGH WATERS, THIS PLACE RESEMBLES A SEAPORT, VESSELS CONTINUALLY ARRIVING AND DEPARTING. ALL IS LIFE, ACTIVITY AND MOTION. THE DRAYMAN IS CONSTANTLY EMPLOYED, AND ALL THE HACKNEY COACHES, FIFTY OR UPWARDS, ARE FILLED WITH PASSENGERS.

WHEN THE WATERS ARE LOW, IN SUMMER, THE STAGES ARE CROWDED WITH PASSENGERS COMING TO TOWN OR DEPARTING FROM IT; SO THAT IN ALL SEASONS OF THE YEAR,

The bustling Louisville wharf was a beehive of activity, as indicated in this 1905 photo of roustabouts loading cargo on the steamboat *Tell City*. With nothing but human muscle power and ingenuity, hundreds of tons of materials were routinely transferred to and from boats to waiting dray carts and local warehouses. Many visitors to the waterfront reported hearing the large crews of roustabouts, primarily African-American, sing while performing their laborious work. *(Kentucky Historical Society.1987ph04.65)*

THIS IS A BUSY, BUSTLING PLACE...AS THE WESTERN STATES FILL UP WITH INHABITANTS, THE TRADE OF THIS PLACE MUST INCREASE IN AMOUNT, AND IF IT SHOULD EVENTUALLY SURPASS THAT OF BALTIMORE OR PHILADELPHIA, NO ONE NEED BE SURPRIZED WHO WOULD TAKE THE TROUBLE TO EXAMINE THE MAP OF THE WESTERN STATES.

THE PRESENT INHABITANTS ARE THE MOST HOSPITABLE IN THE WESTERN STATES. A WORTHY MAN WILL NEVER WANT FRIENDS HERE, AND IT IS THE LAST PLACE IN THE WORLD FOR ONE OF AN OPPOSITE CHARACTER TO VISIT. THE CONSTANT INFLUX OF STRANGERS, HAS RENDERED THE PEOPLE HERE SHREWD OBSERVERS OF MEN. IF A BAD MAN, AN ACTIVE POLICE INSTANTLY DETECTS AND PUNISHES HIM FOR THE VERY FIRST OFFENCE. IF THE STRANGER BE A GOOD MAN, HE IS INSTANTLY TAKEN BY THE HAND, ALL HIS WISHES ARE CONSULTED AND HIS INTERESTS ADVANCED.

THERE ARE PROBABLY MORE EASE AND AFFLUENCE IN THIS PLACE THAN IN ANY WESTERN TOWN – THEIR HOUSES ARE SPLENDID, SUBSTANTIAL, AND RICHLY FURNISHED; AND I SAW MORE LARGE MIRRORS IN THEIR BEST ROOMS THAN I EVER SAW ANY WHERE ELSE. PAINTINGS AND MIRRORS ADORN THE WALLS, AND ALL THE FURNITURE IS SPLENDID AND COSTLY. MORE ATTENTION IS BESTOWED ON DRESS, AMONG THE YOUNG GENTLEMEN AND LADIES OF LOUISVILLE, THAN WITH THOSE OF CINCINNATI.

THE RECOLLECTION OF MY RECEPTION AT LOUISVILLE, WILL ALWAYS REMAIN WITH ME, WHILE MEMORY LASTS, AMONG THE MOST AGREEABLE ONES OF MY LIFE.

THE HOSPITALITY OF THIS PEOPLE CONSISTS NOT SOLELY IN FURNISHING THE GUEST WITH THE BEST OF EVERY THING, THE HOUSE AFFORDS, BUT ALL HIS INCLINATIONS ARE CONSULTED, (I MEAN VIRTUOUS ONES) AND EVERY ART, THOUGH, EXHAUSTED TO DO SO,

CAREFULLY CONCEALED FROM HIM. HE MAY SET HIS DAY AND HOUR TO LEAVE THEM, BUT BEFORE THEY ARRIVE, SOME NEW INDUCEMENT IS HELD OUT TO HIM, TO TARRY LONGER, AND FINALLY, HE WILL FIND IT ALMOST IMPOSSIBLE TO LEAVE THEM.

TO THE MAN OF FORTUNE – TO THE SCHOLAR AND MAN OF SCIENCE – TO THE MANUFACTURER AND THE INDUSTRIOUS MECHANIC, LOUISVILLE MAY BE RECOMMENDED AS A PLACE, WHERE AS MUCH HAPPINESS IS TO BE ATTAINED AS WOULD FALL TO HIS LOT ANY WHERE IN THE WORLD. INDUSTRY AND ENTERPRIZE HERE FIND A CERTAIN REWARD. THIS IS LOUISVILLE.

Not all visitors reacted so positively. America's favorite author, Washington Irving, left a brief, but critical assessment of Louisville in 1832.

ARRIVE AT LOUISVILLE HALF-PAST TWELVE – DINE AT THROGMORTON. QUAY OF CITY PRESENTS A MOTLEY SCENE – HUTS – STEAM-BOATS – CARRIAGES – HEAPS OF IRON – OF LEAD – LEATHER. &C

TAKE PLACES ON BOARD THE STEAMER *ILLINOIS* FROM LOUISVILLE – AFTER GOING ON BOARD WE RUN AGAINST POST – BREAK SOME OF THE MACHINERY AND HAVE TO REMAIN ALL NIGHT.

"The advocates of rail-roads will be delighted with this exhibition..."

Steam engines were the technological marvels that transformed Louisville. Many innovations saw their debut on the Louisville waterfront. One of America's earliest locomotive engines, built by Joseph Bruen of Lexington, was publicly demonstrated in March 1830 in front of Lawrence's Store at Fourth and Water Streets. Persons desiring to ride around the track in its one small car could do so for a quarter.

MINIATURE RAIL ROAD

WE WITNESSED LAST EVENING, WITH GREAT SATISFACTION, THE OPERATION OF MR. BRUEN'S MINIATURE LOCOMOTIVE ON A MINIATURE RAILROAD. THE STEAM CARRIAGE, WITH THE ENGINE, WEIGHS FROM 180 TO 200 POUNDS. THE SUPPLY OF WATER KEPT IN THE BOILER DOES NOT, PERHAPS, EXCEED THREE PINTS — THE CYLINDER IS $1\frac{1}{2}$ INCH IN DIAMETER — THE STROKE NOT QUITE 5 INCHES — AND THE WHEELS OF THE STEAM CARRIAGE ARE ABOUT ONE FOOT IN HEIGHT. THE ENGINE WORKS WITH GREAT RAPIDITY AND PRECISION, AND THE STEAM CARRIAGE DRAWS A LIGHT CAR, WITH ONE OR MORE PERSONS IN IT, AT THE RATE OF ABOUT THREE MILES AN HOUR — NOTWITHSTANDING THE FACT, THAT A PORTION OF THE MINIATURE RAILWAY ASCENDS, AT THE RATE OF 80 FEET PER MILE.

THE ADVOCATES OF RAILROADS WILL BE DELIGHTED WITH THIS EXHIBITION, AS IT AFFORDS PROOF THAT MUST BE CONSIDERED UNERRING, OF THE RECTITUDE OF THEIR VIEWS; AND WHICH CANNOT, WE BELIEVE, FAIL TO CONVINCE THE MOST SKEPTICAL OF THE SUPERIORITY OF RAILROADS OVER CANALS.

EVERY MAN WHO CAN SPARE THE TIME TO DO SO (AND A FEW MOMENTS WILL SUFFICE) OUGHT TO PAY THE INGENIOUS PROPRIETOR A VISIT. MONEY CANNOT BE BETTER SPENT IN ACQUIRING INFORMATION ON A SUBJECT SO VITALLY IMPORTANT TO THE FUTURE PROSPERITY OF OUR COUNTRY.

Prior to the construction of bridges across the Ohio, ferry boats made regular trips back and forth from Louisville to the Indiana port towns of Jeffersonville, Clarksville and New Albany. Rowboats and horse-driven ferries served until the first steam-powered transfer boats commenced in 1831. *(Kentucky Historical Society, 1987 ph1.6055)*

Steam power also impacted another important fact of Falls life. Since the city's founding, ferryboats crossed the Ohio to the Indiana shore and, prior to the construction of the first local bridge in 1870, all river crossings were accomplished by boat. The earliest ferries were skiffs propelled by oars, and in later days horse boats were developed. These were powered by a horse walking on a continuous treadmill to supply the motive power to small paddlewheels.

In 1831 a new and commodious steam-powered ferry began its regular runs from Gray's wharf to Jeffersonville. It contained a roomy cabin for passengers with a deck accommodating wagons, carriages, horses and other livestock. Its success was short-lived when, one month after starting service, the boiler exploded. Four persons were killed and several others seriously injured, and similar catastrophes were becoming commonplace as the number of steamboats on the western waters increased dramatically.

The average life of an American steamboat was between three and four years. They operated about 180 days a year, and accidents were commonplace, with burst boilers and engine fires common, as well as punctured wooden hulls from submerged trees, referred to as snags or sawyers. A small working boat of one hundred tons consumed about eighteen cords of wood during every twenty-four hours of service, with seven bushels of coal required to equal one cord.

By the late 1830s, a captain of an Ohio and upper Mississippi riverboat earned a salary of $150 a month, with the engineer paid about $125. A good clerk received $50 and the lowly firemen averaged about $25 a month. Some boats were designated as packets and maintained a routine commuter run between certain cities, so accommodations were regular and schedules dependable. A trip from Pittsburgh to Louisville cost about fifteen dollars and accommodations between Louisville and New Orleans were sixty dollars a trip. Passage on a steamboat averaged about three cents a mile, while land travel on a stage coach was at least twice

that cost. Boats heading downstream averaged between ten and twelve miles an hour, with six being a good speed for an upstream voyage. Deck passengers provided their own meals, which they prepared on a cooking stove provided for their use.

A few individuals did not think they needed a steamboat to head downstream from Louisville. The *Louisville Public Advertiser* of August 21, 1839, told a curious tale of a daring young man.

REUBEN BRYNUS, A YOUNG MAN OF THIS CITY, SWAM DOWN THE FALLS OF OHIO YESTERDAY, BY WHICH HAZARDOUS FEAT HE WON ONE HUNDRED DOLLARS. HE WORE AN ORDINARY LIFE-PRESERVER, AND A PAIR OF STOCKINET DRAWERS. THE RIVER IS QUITE LOW, THE CURRENT OVER THE FALLS EQUAL TO TEN KNOTS AN HOUR, AND IN THE LAST FOURTH OF THE DISTANCE, THE WATER WAS AS ROUGH AS THE SURFACE OF LAKE ERIE WHEN AGITATED BY A STRONG WIND. THE ATTEMPT WAS DARING IN THE EXTREME, AND THE SUCCESS OF BYRNUS PROVES THAT HE IS A MAN OF IRON NERVES.

SEVERAL GOOD SWIMMERS HAVE BEEN DROWNED IN ATTEMPTING TO SWIM ACROSS THE FALLS AT POINTS DEEMED FAVORABLE.

"…to open an iron store, mainly to sell nails."

By the late 1830s, many aspects of life in Louisville were changing. In that year, the Louisville Gas and Waterworks Company, chartered with capital of $1,200,000, began operation. Although the firm had the right to provide water service, this proposed mission was soon dropped. The firm also had limited banking privileges as a savings institution, but did not issue notes, and that aspect of the business was repealed in 1854.

The mission of the Louisville Gas Company was to manufacture and supply gas for streets, businesses and homes. One of the first gas manufacturing plants in the nation was

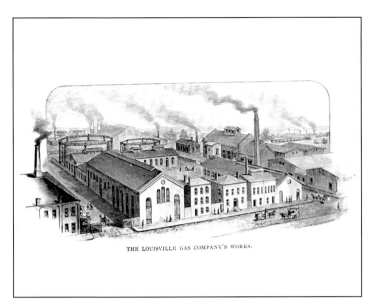

The Louisville Gas Company, beginning in 1839, was one of the first suppliers of gas for illumination in the nation. Their first plant to convert coal to natural gas was located on Beargrass Creek near the corner of Jackson and Washington Streets. Large fleets of barges brought vast amounts of coal up Beargrass Creek to be unloaded directly into the gas plant. *(University of Louisville Photographic Archives, P-00555)*

constructed on Beargrass Creek near the corner of Jackson and Washington Streets. Coal barges, primarily from the Pittsburgh area, were able to slip into the creek and deliver their loads of coal at the factory's door. The first home in Louisville was lighted by gas on Christmas Day of 1839.

The City of Louisville subscribed $200,000, which allowed the installation and operation of street gas lamps at the rate of $20 each. The area between First and Fifth Streets and Jefferson to Water Streets was selected as a test project to determine how many street lights would be needed to provide adequate illumination. It was determined that six lamps on each block was required, with that number doubled on Water Street to provide adequate night lighting for the wharf. The illumination of each lamp was to equal twelve sperm candles, and the time of operation was from the close of twilight to the dawn of the following day, except for bright, clear moonlit nights.

The following year saw the beginning of another Louisville institution. In 1840, a young manufacturer

named William B. Belknap came to Louisville "to open an iron store mainly to sell nails." Within a few years, Belknap was so successful he opened his own smelting operation at the Louisville Rolling Mill. Realizing that the city's constant traffic by dray carts moving cargoes between the Louisville and Portland wharfs provided an opportunity, Belknap began providing replacement wagon wheels, farrier supplies and harnesses. Future additions to the Belknap business included the production of farm implements and equipment, as well as nails, roofing and other building supplies for contractors. Belknap's firm, originally located at Third and Main Streets, flourished and grew with Louisville.

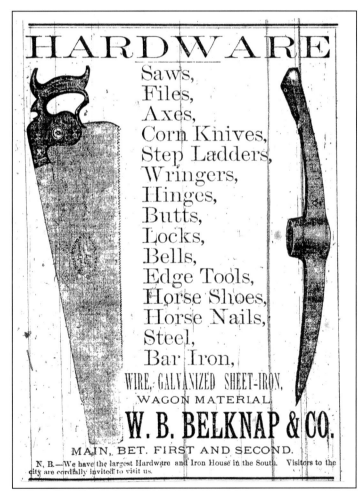

Belknap Hardware, a staple in Louisville business since 1840, began as a small Main Street store selling nails. Founder William B. Belknap established a great fortune by catering to the construction and transportation needs of a growing region and nation. After the Civil War, Belknap became the nation's largest hardware distributor, using the Louisville wharf as its primary shipping site.

"...the negroes were strung together precisely like so many fish upon a trot-line."

In the antebellum South, a polite fiction concerning the benevolent nature of "our peculiar institution" helped justify slavery. Although located in a slavery state, Louisville lacked the strong agricultural and industrial base that benefited from involuntary servitude. Most slaves in Louisville were household servants, or had a specialized trade like cobbler or barber. Poor white European immigrants, especially those from Ireland and Germany, began to flood the Ohio Valley and were happy to accept any wage-paying job. To avoid the considerable annual expenses of owning a slave – their purchase, housing, food, clothes and insurance – many local owners began selling their surplus labor. A trip to Garrison's Slave Pen, just opposite the Galt House Hotel at Second and Main Streets, followed by transport down the river to the Deep South and cotton field servitude was a bitter fate for many local African-Americans. During the 1850s, between 3,000 and 4,000 slaves were annually shipped south from Louisville.

Other white owners chose to put their slaves out for hire, and Louisville became known for its large number of workers rented out by their owners for a year to someone needing their labor. Typical jobs for hired slaves in Louisville included dray and hackney cab drivers, brick makers or roustabouts on steamboats. This status allowed a limited form of freedom, since the slave was not directly under the master's gaze and usually rented sleeping space and provided his own maintenance, thanks to an earned income. Some hired slaves were able to earn enough extra income to purchase theirs and their family's freedom. Diarist William Owen reported on an interview with a former slave while in Louisville:

A BLACK, WHO CUT MY FATHER'S HAIR THIS MORNING, SAID HE HAD BEEN FREE FOR 4 YEARS. HE HAD PAID $150 PER ANNUM TO HIS MASTER, TILL HE WAS ABLE TO SAVE $1,000 WHICH HE PAID FOR HIS FREEDOM. SINCE THEN HE HAS GIVEN $900 FOR HIS WIFE AND ONE CHILD. HE MUST HAVE WORKED VERY HARD TO ACCOMPLISH ALL THIS; INDEED HE TOLD US HE HAD WORKED NEARLY NIGHT AND DAY FOR YEARS.

Abraham Lincoln experienced a profoundly moving moment on the Louisville waterfront as he was leaving town to return to Illinois. Following a three-week visit with his friends, the Speed family of Farmington, Lincoln wrote an affectionate note to his hostess, Mary Speed, on September 27, 1841:

WE GOT ON BOARD THE STEAM BOAT *LEBANON*, IN THE LOCKS OF THE CANAL ABOUT 12.O'CLOCK M. ON THE DAY WE LEFT, AND REACHED ST. LOUIS THE NEXT MONDAY AT 8 P.M. NOTHING OF INTEREST HAPPENED DURING THE PASSAGE, EXCEPT THE VEXATIOUS DELAYS OCCASIONED BY THE SAND BARS BE THOUGHT INTERESTING. BY THE WAY, A FINE EXAMPLE WAS PRESENTED ON BOARD THE BOAT FOR CONTEMPLATING THE EFFECT OF CONDITION UPON HUMAN HAPPINESS. A GENTLEMAN HAD PURCHASED TWELVE NEGROES IN DIFFERENT PARTS OF KENTUCKY AND WAS TAKING THEM TO A FARM IN THE SOUTH. THEY WERE CHAINED SIX AND SIX TOGETHER. A SMALL IRON CLEVIS WAS AROUND THE LEFT WRIST OF EACH, AND THIS FASTENED TO THE MAIN CHAIN BY A SHORTER ONE AT A CONVENIENT DISTANCE FROM THE OTHERS; SO THAT THE NEGROES WERE STRUNG TOGETHER PRECISELY LIKE SO MANY FISH UPON A TROT-LINE. IN THIS CONDITION THEY WERE BEING SEPARATED FOREVER FROM THE SCENES OF THEIR CHILDHOOD, THEIR FRIENDS, THEIR FATHERS AND MOTHERS, AND BROTHERS AND SISTERS, AND MANY OF THEM, FROM THEIR WIVES AND CHILDREN, AND GOING INTO PERPETUAL SLAVERY WHERE THE LASH OF THE MASTER IS PROVERBIALLY MORE

RUTHLESS AND UNRELENTING THAN ANY OTHER WHERE; AND YET AMID ALL THESE DISTRESSING CIRCUMSTANCES, AS WE WOULD THINK THEM, THEY WERE THE MOST CHEERFUL AND APPARENTLY HAPPY CREATURES ON BOARD.

Others witnessed similar scenes and held their own interpretation. A popular column in the *Louisville Daily Journal*, called *Town Trifles*, captured such a moment on a Louisville street in 1855:

WE ARE NOT SQUEAMISH, NOR PARTICULARLY SENSITIVE ABOUT CERTAIN INCIDENTALS THAT MAKE OUR "PECULIAR INSTITUTION." BUT IT COMES NOW AND THEN TO OUR OBSERVATION, SIGHTS OF WHICH WE WOULD RATHER BE IN IGNORANCE. THESE, HOWEVER, ARE CHARGEABLE TO NOTHING INHERENT IN SLAVERY, BUT TO A GROSSNESS OF FEELING AND BRUTALITY OF DISPOSITION, CHARACTERISTIC OF SOME MEN, IN ALL CLASSES AND SOCIETIES. THIS INHUMANITY MARKS THE FACTORY OVERSEER IN THE NORTH, AS WELL AS THE SLAVE DRIVER IN THE SOUTH, AND WHEREVER OCCURRING DESERVES THE SEVEREST REPREHENSION. ON SATURDAY WE WITNESSED TWO SPECIMENS OF THIS NATURE, AND FROM THESE INFREQUENT ACTS, COME ALL THE TALES OF HORROR THAT AGITATE THE FANATICAL BOSOMS OF THE ABOLITIONISTS. PASSING DOWN MAIN STREET, WE SAW AN OLD GREY-HEADED MAN LEADING A NEGRO BY A STRING THAT WAS AROUND HIS NECK, AND HAND-CUFFS UPON HIS HANDS. ON ANOTHER STREET, SHORTLY AFTERWARDS, WE SAW A MAN CONDUCTING TWO NEGROES IRONED AT THE WRISTS. IT WAS NOT LONG, HOWEVER, BEFORE WE CASUALLY OBSERVED A PLEASING CONTRAST TO THE SCENE JUST NOTICED. DEFILING DOWN STREET WAS A PROCESSION OF SLAVES, MEN, WOMEN AND CHILDREN, ALL COMFORTABLY CLAD, AND HAPPY IN APPEARANCE — AND THE NEGRO ALWAYS MANIFESTS HIS HILARITY BY A BRISKNESS OF WALK —

WHILE BEHIND THEM FOLLOWED WAGONS WITH THEIR STOCK OF GOODS AND FURNITURE. THERE WAS NO ATTENDANT GUARD, NO IRONS, NO FETTERS, ALL FREE, ALL JOYOUS IN DEMEANOR. THESE WE DISCOVERED WERE THE PROPERTY OF A GENTLEMAN EMIGRATING FROM ONE OF THE UPPER COUNTIES, AND WHO WE KNOW IS LOVED AND REVERENCED BY HIS SLAVES, IN SUCH A MANNER AS IS ONLY BEGOTTEN BY THE INTIMATE AND INTERDEPENDENT RELATIONS OF MASTER AND SERVANT. THEY WERE ALL BOUND FOR THE FAR-WEST, AND THOUGH PERHAPS A REGRET MIGHT OCCASIONALLY STEAL INTO THEIR BOSOMS AT THE THOUGHT OF LEAVING THE "OLD KENTUCKY HOME," THE DEPARTURE WAS THE CAUSE OF AS POIGNANT SORROW TO THE OWNER AS TO HIS NEGROES.

The Intelligent Community

It is doubtful there ever was a true example of slaves "happy in appearance" making their way to board a steamboat headed south, but many people maintained the belief that slavery was both good and justified in Holy Scripture. A growing number of Louisvillians disagreed, and the *Louisville Public Advertiser* featured an article concerning a meeting of the Louisville Colonization Society, a local group of leading Whig party members who advocated manumission, or freeing of slaves, and the return to Africa of slaves set free by benevolent masters. Henry Clay led the American Colonization Society for three decades, and many of his supporters agreed with the Great Compromiser in the wisdom of sending freed slaves to the newly created African democratic state of Liberia.

The local society met on January 10, 1839, with the stated goal:

...TO DEVISE MEANS OF REVIVING THE DORMANT ENERGIES OF THE SOCIETY OF LOUISVILLE. WE DESIGN TO MAKE AN ARRANGEMENT WHICH WILL GIVE INTEREST AND PLEASURE TO OUR MEMBERS AND THE

African-Americans, both free and slave, provided the main source of laborers on the Louisville waterfront. Many slave owners found it more profitable to rent the services of their slaves to individuals and companies needing a ready source of workers. Hired slaves gained a measure of independence by receiving wages and providing their own room and board, and some saved enough money to buy their own freedom. (*Detail of WPA mural in Family Health Center – Portland*)

SUCH IS THE PECULIAR CONDITION OF THE ANOMALOUS CASTE OF OUR POPULATION UPON WHICH THIS SOCIETY DESIGNS TO ACT, THAT SO LONG AS HUMAN NATURE CONTINUES WHAT IT IS, WE CANNOT DO OTHERWISE THAN EXPECT FROM IT, ONE WAY OR OTHERS, SOME PORTENTOUS CONSEQUENCES. IT IS, INDEED, A STAGNANT POOL IN THE BOSOM OF THE LAND, FROM WHOSE PUTREFACTION, THOUGH, FOR A WHILE, SILENT AND UNOBSERVED, A NOXIOUS VERMIN WILL BE ENGENDERED THAT WILL EAT INTO AND DISFIGURE, IF IT DOES NOT FOUNDER, THE VESSEL OF THE REPUBLIC.

FOR THE CASTE, THEN, RELIGION PLEADS; HUMANITY IMPLORES, NATURE INVOKES, POLICY POINTS, AND SELF-PRESERVATION CALLS US TO ACTION, SUSTAINED BY OUR EFFORTS AND BY ALL THEIR SANCTIONS. THE OFFICERS OF THIS SOCIETY BEG YOUR ATTENTION.

Liberation was not easy, but the local Colonization effort, led by Presbyterian minister Reverend Alex Cowan, faced the challenges and kept their faith in the principle. A February 1849 article in the *Louisville Journal* updated supporters on the progress of their latest voyage to freedom.

INTELLIGENT COMMUNITY. JUDGE WILKESON OBSERVES: "ABOLITIONISTS HAVE TURNED THE CURRENT OF PUBLIC BENEVOLENCE INTO A PERFECTLY UNWHOLESOME CHANNEL, WHICH HAS ALREADY DISTURBED AND THREATENS TO DESTROY THE POLITICAL RELATIONS OF OUR COUNTRY. REGARDING COLONIZATION AS THE CONSERVATIVE PRINCIPLE, WHICH WILL SAVE OUR UNION AND ELEVATE THE COLORED MAN, I HAVE ACCEPTED AN AGENCY FROM THE AMERICAN COLONIZATION SOCIETY, FOR THE UNITED STATES, BELIEVING THAT MANY GOOD MEN WILL BE FOUND WILLING FREELY TO DEVOTE THEIR TIME AND INFLUENCE TO GIVE NEW LIFE AND ENERGY TO THE CAUSE."

MESSRS. EDITORS: I NOTICED IN YESTERDAY'S *JOURNAL* AN ARTICLE IN REFERENCE TO THE CHOLERA, HAVING "APPEARED ON BOARD OF THE BARK *LAURA*, THAT SAILED FROM NEW ORLEANS WITH 150 LIBERATED SLAVES FOR LIBERIA, SEVEN OF WHOM HAD DIED." YOU STATE THAT THEY ARE SOME OF THE LIBERATED SLAVES LATELY SENT OFF BY THE KENTUCKY COLONIZATION SOCIETY. WHILE I DEEPLY REGRET TO LEARN THAT THE *LAURA* HAS BEEN THUS VISITED, I REJOICE TO TELL YOU THAT THOSE WHO WENT FROM KENTUCKY TO EMBARK AT NEW ORLEANS FOR LIBERIA, LEFT THAT CITY BEFORE THE 150 ARRIVED THERE BY ORDER OF THE AMER. COLONEL SOCIETY ON ACCOUNT OF THE

CHOLERA, AND HAVE RETURNED TO KENTUCKY TO AWAIT FURTHER ORDERS TO LEAVE FOR LIBERIA.

The gap between slavery and freedom was made plain in an incident at the Louisville wharf in 1853, as reported by the *Daily Courier*:

SLAVE SET FREE – QUITE A GATHERING OF DARKIE DRAYMEN WAS SEEN IN FRONT OF THE STEAMER *SAM SNOWDEN*, AT THE UPPER WHARF LAST EVENING, WHO WERE WAVING THEIR HANDS TO ANOTHER DARKIE ON THE BOAT, AS SHE WAS LEAVING THE WHARF, AND SHOUTING AT THE TOP OF THEIR LUNGS, "GOOD BYE, NED," "FAREWELL, NED!" UPON INQUIRY WE ASCERTAINED THAT NED WAS A DRAYMAN, A SLAVE OF MISS SPEED, DAUGHTER OF JAMES SPEED, ESQ., WHO HAD SET NED FREE, AND HE WAS TAKING HIS DEPARTURE FOR CANADA.

Ned's former master, James Speed, Esq. would be called to Washington by his friend Abraham Lincoln to serve as attorney general in his administration. Ned was one of the first of many to gain emancipation through the efforts of James Speed, Esq.

Sharks, Green Turtles and Trappists

Many local traditions that would echo through the years were introduced during this time period. With many citizens originating in Maryland and tidewater Virginia, Louisville craved seafood, especially oysters. Barrels of freshwater oysters were on the first upriver voyage by Captain Henry Miller Shreve in 1815. Large numbers of commercial fishermen worked the waters of the Ohio River to produce catches for the local market houses, with fried fish sandwiched between slices of rye bread a favorite among German Catholics. In 1844 the Corn Island Exchange, Charles H. Feldbush's popular restaurant on the corner of Fifth and Water Streets, offered green turtle soup or steaks to hungry customers. Generations later, a KingFish restaurant located at nearly that exact site continued to serve most of these Louisville favorites.

A surprising variety of food products became available to Louisvillians with the expansion of the steamboat trade. Barrels of oysters and turtle steaks became regular offerings in local taverns and restaurants and were especially popular with residents from the seaboard states craving the familiar foods of their upbringing.

While the Louisville waterfront hosted visits by presidents, missionaries, authors and other celebrities, it also attracted a more sinister crowd. Prostitutes and streetwalkers, the "frail sisters of easy virtue" made it their home, as did the denizens of the low grog shops of O'Neill Alley. Counterfeiters, bunco artists, pickpockets and confidence men preyed upon green youngsters from the country and naïve travelers from everywhere.

The most notorious of all the slick players were the riverboat gamblers of lore. A profile of the card shark appeared in the March 30, 1844, edition of the *Daily Dime*:

THE SHARK.

Of all the pests that infect society, the accomplished gambler is the most subtle and dangerous. The robber and pirate are almost merciful when compared to him, for he not only robs his victim of his mo-

The Card Shark, as illustrated in an 1844 article in the *Louisville Daily Dime*, shows a typical riverboat gambler of the era. The transient nature of waterfront life was an open invitation to scores of gamblers, confidence men, counterfeiters and other criminals to prey upon an unsophisticated public.

THE SHARK

Of all the pests that infect society, the accomplished gambler is the most subtle and dangerous. The robber and the pirate are almost merciful when compared to him, for he not only robs his victim of his money, but in many cases with it, deprives him of character of honor, and happiness.

Our country, particularly the South-west, unfortunately has too many of those worse than drones roaming at large. They almost form a large and distinct class among us, but fortunately they are beginning to be distinguished by certain marks scarcely to be mistaken. A finished "hawk" (one of their many soubriquets) has generally a most pleasing and fashionable exterior — generally very well dressed, in fact, so well, that to many, adorning his person would seem his only occupation. But even in dress, there are many things to the experienced eye bespeak the gambler. For instance, though his garments are invariably made of the best materials, still they are fashioned rather outré. His hat is worn in a sort of jockey style, the leave being bent up a little behind, while an innumerable quantity of gold chains and diamond breast-pins grace his breast. The eye, however, tells the man, more perfectly than any other feature or point about one of these individuals — there is an affected sleepiness or listlessness, which will, if watched but for a moment or two, show itself, and prove to the observer that instead of being as it seems, it is both restless and watchful.

Apparently gamblers were not the only itinerants to affect a glittering display of personal adornment. Charles Dickens, the most noted author ever to visit Louisville, met and interviewed Big Jim Porter, the Kentucky Giant, on board a steamboat waiting to pass through the canal in 1842. Dickens seemed genuinely charmed by the Shippingport giant, but Porter later indicated he resented being summoned by Boz. A few years later, Archibald Prentice wrote of his interview with Porter and the giant's distaste for Dickens.

Among the lions of Louisville is Mr. James Porter, who stands seven feet eight inches in his stockings, the only man of his height I ever saw with a good head on his shoulders and good legs beneath him. He is much respected, and has been one of the councilmen of the city. He told

ME THAT LORD MORPETH CALLED UPON HIM AT HIS COFFEEHOUSE, AND THAT HE WAS MUCH PLEASED WITH HIS LORDSHIP'S PLAIN, UNPRETENDING MANNER. HE DID NOT LIKE DICKENS, WHO HAD SENT FOR HIM. "HE HAD A DOUBLE GOLD CHAIN OUTSIDE HIS WAISTCOAT," SAID PORTER, "AND SUCH BREAST-PINS, THAT I THOUGHT HE LOOKED LIKE ONE OF OUR RIVER GAMBLERS;" A CLASS OR PERSON WHO, IT SEEMS, PARTICULARLY AFFECT A SHOW OF JEWELERY.

More than cargoes and passengers traveled on the steamboats. News, music, popular culture and entertainment also passed up and down the Ohio River, making regular stops at Louisville. During the Mexican War, when many local soldiers were serving far away, people craved current information on the status of the conflict. Louisville boasted several newspapers, both English and German language, to feed the appetite for news. The *Louisville Courier* proudly boasted of its efforts to be the first to deliver the news in this 1848 announcements:

WE HAVE A TRUSTY MESSENGER AT PORTLAND WHO WILL BRING US OUR FILES OF SOUTHERN PAPERS IMMEDIATELY ON THE ARRIVAL OF BOATS AT THAT LANDING. WE DON'T THINK IT WILL TAKE HIM MORE THAN EIGHT AND THREE QUARTERS MINUTES TO MAKE THE RUN BETWEEN PORTLAND AND OUR OFFICE.

On December 23, 1848, an unusual group of immigrants reached the Louisville waterfront. When a large colony of Trappist monks arrived from France to establish a new monastery near Bardstown, they landed at the Louisville wharf in the dead of night with over twelve tons of farm equipment, religious materials, food supplies and even their wooden shoes. Abbot Eutropius, O.C.R., left a memorable description of his group's welcome to Louisville.

THE BOAT DID NOT ARRIVE UNTIL EVENING. BEING BOUND FOR PITTSBURGH, IT ONLY STOPPED TO LAND OUR COLONY AND BAGGAGE. THE DARKNESS OF THE NIGHT WAS SO THICK, THAT ONE COULD SCARCELY SEE TWO STEPS. IN A MOMENT WE WERE SURROUNDED BY STREET-WALKERS AND LOUNGERS, WHO SOUGHT NOTHING ELSE BUT PILLAGE. I FEARED THAT SOME OF OUR ARTICLES, WHICH WERE THROWN PELL-MELL ON THE DOCK, WOULD DISAPPEAR. TO OBVIATE THE DANGER, I GATHERED SOME DRY WOOD ALONG THE RIVER BANK. I PLACED ALL THE RELIGIOUS IN A CIRCLE AND MADE A LARGE FIRE IN THEIR MIDST. THEY MADE A GOOD GUARD, WHILE I WENT TO THE CITY TO FIND SOME DRAYS TO BRING OUR BAGGAGE TO THE WAREHOUSE.

More than religious missions landed at the wharf. It was a prime location for the introduction of dangerous diseases carried by passengers on the incoming boats. Cholera, the public's greatest fear, made its terrifying periodic appearances at the Louisville wharf. No one knew the cause of the disease, only its dreadful effect, and news stories in 1849 speculated on the current health care crisis.

- A FEW DEATHS HAVE OCCURRED ON THE STEAMBOATS THAT HAVE ARRIVED FROM BELOW. THE *LAFAYETTE* HAD ONLY ONE DEATH, BY CHOLERA — THE PERSON CAME ON BOARD SICK; THE *MAGNOLIA* HAD ALSO ONE DEATH; THE *NIAGARA*, FROM ST. LOUIS, HAD ONE DEATH; THE *DIADEM*, FROM ST. LOUIS, HAD TWO DEATHS. THE SECOND ENGINEER OF THE *PARIS*, FROM ST. LOUIS, WAS DYING WHEN THE BOAT LEFT THERE; AND THE *COLORADO*, FROM NASHVILLE, HAD ONE DEATH. ALL THE DEATHS ON STEAMBOATS WERE ON DECK.

- WE OBSERVE A DISPOSITION ON THE PART OF MANY TO

USE BRANDY AS A CHOLERA PREVENTIVE. WE REGRET THAT TO SEE SOME WHO HAVE NEVER USED IT RESORTING TO IT, UNDER A MISTAKEN IDEA THAT IT WILL PREPARE THE SYSTEM TO RESIST IT. IT RATHER PREPARES THE WAY FOR THE SPREAD OF THE DISEASE.

- CHOLERA – THE NUMBER OF CASES OF CHOLERA HAVE DIMINISHED SINCE LAST FRIDAY. MR. DANFORTH MARBLE DIED LAST EVENING AT THE LOUISVILLE HOTEL. MRS. GREY DIED IN STRADER'S ROW, ON SATURDAY. MR. PARKS, OF THE FIRM OF PARKS & MAYS, DIED YESTERDAY MORNING. A CHILD OF MR. REILLY, ON FIFTH STREET, DIED NIGHT BEFORE LAST, AND A SISTER-IN-LAW OF MR. FOWLER, ON WATER STREET, DIED ON SATURDAY. FOUR OR FIVE NEW CASES ARE YET UNDER TREATMENT. WE HAVE THE ASSURANCE OF A PHYSICIAN THAT THE WHOLE NUMBER OF CHOLERA DEATHS SINCE ITS FIRST APPEARANCE HERE DOES NOT EXCEED THIRTY.

- FRESH FISH ARE NOW CONSTANTLY EXPOSED FOR SALE IN OUR MARKETS. LET NO ONE BUY THEM WHILE WE HAVE ANY INDICATIONS OF CHOLERA AMONGST US. ARSENIC IS HARDLY MORE POISONOUS DURING THE PREVALENCE OF CHOLERA. NUMEROUS DEATHS FROM CHOLERA IN NEW ORLEANS WERE DIRECTLY TRACEABLE TO THE USE OF FRESH FISH. SHOULD NOT THE CITY COUNCIL PROHIBIT THE SALE OF FRESH FISH IN THE MARKET WHILE WE ARE THREATENED WITH THIS PESTILENCE?

"The scene was beautiful and stirring beyond description – the Louisville wharf for three or four hundred yards filled with a mass of people…"

It is not every day that a community gets to salute a native son en route to his inaugural. In February 1849, Louisville's Zachary Taylor was the popular Whig Party president-elect made famous by his Mexican War battlefield victories at Palo Alto, Monterrey and Buena Vista. The *Louisville Journal* detailed an affectionate welcome home for the president who grew to manhood at Springfield farm on the road to Brownsboro.

WHEN THE *COURTLAND* RETURNED, THE GENERAL WAS WAITING ON THE NEW ALBANY WHARF, AND HE IMMEDIATELY EMBARKED. THERE THE THREE BOATS DEPARTED FOR LOUISVILLE, AND TEN MINUTES AFTER WERE SEEN COMING OVER THE FALLS, THE *BOONE* LEADING, AND THE *COURTLAND* AND *OCEAN WAVE* LASHED TOGETHER. THE SCENE WAS BEAUTIFUL AND STIRRING BEYOND DESCRIPTION – THE LOUISVILLE WHARF FOR THREE OR FOUR HUNDRED YARDS FILLED WITH A MASS OF PEOPLE, SWAYING TO AND FRO, AND EVERY FACE BEAMING, AND THE THREE BOATS WITH THEIR LIVING MASSES MOVING MAJESTICALLY OVER THE FALLS. THE DAY WAS LIKE SPRING AND THE FACES OF THE DENSE, DARK MASS ON THE SHORE GLEAMED LIKE MIRRORS IN THE SUNLIGHT.

A BROAD ALLEY WAS FORMED IN THE CROWD BY THE MARSHALS, FROM THE SHORE TO THE UPPER EDGE OF WATER STREET….THE GENERAL APPEARED UPON THE DECK, AND A SHOUT ASCENDED SUCH AS HE HAD NOT HEARD SINCE THE MORNING OF BUENA VISTA. THE CONQUEROR WAS RETURNING, AFTER AN ABSENCE OF NINE YEARS, TO THE HOME OF HIS CHILDHOOD AND HIS EARLY MANHOOD, TO THE LAND OF HIS RELATIVES AND EARLY FRIENDS, COVERED WITH THE LAURELS OF MANY BRILLIANT FIELDS, AND CALLED BY THE VOICE OF HIS COUNTRYMEN TO THE FIRST POST IN THIS COUNTRY'S GIFT. THE GREAT, THE GOOD OLD MAN, FIRST IN WAR, FIRST IN PEACE, AND FIRST IN THE HEARTS OF HIS COUNTRYMEN, AFTER SO LONG AND SO EVENTFUL AN ABSENCE, IS ABOUT TO PRESS THE VERY GROUNDS ON WHICH HE HAD SO OFTEN SPORTED WITH HIS YOUTHFUL PLAYMATES; BY THE SIDE OF THE VERY WATERS IN WHOSE BOSOM HE HAD TRIED HIS YOUNG ARMS, UNTIL HE COULD SWIM FROM SHORE TO SHORE AT A SEASON WHEN NO OTHER DARED TO VENTURE. IT WAS A TRYING SCENE TO THE HERO, AND A TOUCHING ONE TO THE OBSERVER, AND NO WONDER THAT KENTUCKIANS BY THOUSANDS AND TENS OF THOUSANDS CROWDED THE LANDING WITH SUCH INTEREST, AND UTTERED SUCH A VOICE OF WELCOME.

IN RESPONSE TO A GRAND WELCOME, GENERAL TAYLOR REPLIED: IN VISITING MY NATIVE STATE – FOR ALTHOUGH I WAS NOT BORN WITHIN ITS TERRITORY I FEEL AS I WAS, IN AS MUCH AS MY RECOLLECTIONS OF BOYHOOD ARE ALL ASSOCIATED WITH THE SOIL OF KENTUCKY, AND ESPECIALLY THIS IMMEDIATE NEIGHBORHOOD – I COULD NOT BUT FEEL THE SYMPATHIES OF DAYS LONG GONE, REVIVE WITHIN ME. THESE EMOTIONS HAVE BEEN STRENGTHENED BY THE KINDNESS OF YOUR ADDRESS, AND, BY THE ENTHUSIASM OF THE RECEPTION I HAVE RECEIVED FROM THE CITIZENS OF LOUISVILLE.

AT A BANQUET HELD IN TAYLOR'S HONOR, THE USUAL ROUND OF PATRIOTIC TOASTS GAVE NEARLY EVERYONE PRESENT A CHANCE TO SALUTE GENERAL TAYLOR. COLONEL THOMAS ANDERSON REMARKED THAT HE WOULD OFFER A SENTIMENT, WHICH, HE WAS SURE, WOULD MEET WITH A WARM RECEPTION IN EVERY HEART PRESENT, AND OFFERED THE FOLLOWING: "CAPTAIN BRAGG – A LITTLE MORE GRAPE."

Every person present recognized the reference as a tribute to Zachary Taylor's cool leadership during the Battle of Buena Vista when he commanded a young artillery officer, Braxton Bragg, to fire more shrapnel at the enemy. Few expected that in slightly more than a decade, Louisville would prepare to send shrapnel toward the former Captain Bragg.

Less than two years later, President Taylor returned to the Louisville wharf en route to his burial at the family farm. Early November 1850 editions of the *Daily Journal* detailed the city's response to the death of its popular president.

WHEN THE WORDS WE ARE NOW WRITING SHALL MEET THE PUBLIC EYE, THE MORTAL REMAINS OF GEN. TAYLOR, LATE PRESIDENT OF THE UNITED STATES, WILL PROBABLY BE IN THIS CITY. LESS THAN TWO YEARS AGO, HE CAME AMONG US, ON HIS WAY TO THE IMPORTANT POINT TO WHICH THE VOICE OF HIS COUNTRY HAD CALLED HIM, AND HE WAS FOLLOWED BY A LONG RETINUE OF DISTINGUISHED MEN AND RECEIVED WITH SHOUTS, THE FIRING OF CANNON, THE WAVING OF FLAGS, THE GATHERING OF MULTITUDES, AND ALL OTHER POSSIBLE MANIFESTATIONS OF ADMIRATION AND LOVE, AND NOW ALL OF HIM THAT CAN PERISH RETURNS, ACCOMPANIED BY SILENT AND WEEPING FRIENDS, TO FIND A RESTING PLACE IN THE BURIAL GROUND OF HIS FATHERS.

WE UNDERSTAND THAT GEN. TAYLOR'S REMAINS ARE ACCOMPANIED BY COLONEL JOSEPH TAYLOR, THE BROTHER, AND COLONEL BLISS, THE SON-IN-LAW OF THE DECEASED. THE BODY IS TO BE BURIED IN THE CEMETERY OF THE TAYLOR FAMILY, ABOUT SEVEN MILES FROM THE CITY AND TWO MILES FROM THE FRANKFORT TURNPIKE ROAD.

THUS HAVE WE LOST FROM AMONG US THE LAST MELANCHOLY MEMENTO OF THE PRESENCE OF ZACHARY TAYLOR. WHO CAN FORGET THE DAY WHEN THAT MUCH-VENERATED FORM FIRST APPEARED IN OUR STREETS? IT SEEMS AS IF THE SHOUTS OF HIS ENTHUSIASTIC WELCOME WERE YET SOUNDING IN OUR EARS; AND NOW – AFTER SO BRIEF, SO TRANSIENT AN ENJOYMENT OF THE HIGHEST HONORS THAT MAN CAN CONFER – WHAT IS LEFT, BUT THE FUNERAL HEARSE, THE COFFIN, AND THE SHROUD? IT IS LIKE SOME BRIGHT, BUT FLEETING DREAM.

…WE HAVE HAD MANY MORE BRILLIANT PRESIDENTS, NEVER A MORE UPRIGHT ONE.

The fleeting dream of Taylor's presidency disappeared in the first year of the 1850s, the decade that brought untold strife and tension to Louisville, Kentucky. It was also the golden age of American ingenuity, and a phrase familiar to any nineteenth century Kentuckian, "The Palmy Days of Steamboating," was especially appropriate. "Palmy" in this sense referred to great profits, cash in hand, a dollar in your palm. The decade of the 1850s was the most contentious in local history, and the Louisville waterfront was the chief focus of controversy.

The decade of the 1850s saw the peak of waterfront activities in Louisville. As depicted in this 1852 engraving, steamboats line the wharf and people scurry to conduct their business. The stone bridge over Second Street, the first permanent bridge in the city, spanned Beargrass Creek and united the Point with the rest of Louisville. This view corresponds to looking westward while standing on the second floor porch at Joe's Crab Shack. *(Filson Historical Society)*

Engineering the Waterfront
(1851-1861)

In all large cities, the reservation of lawns or parks for the common use of the public is deemed as essential to the preservation of the public health as is the organism of the lungs to the vital existence of animal nature, or as light and heat to the germination and growth of the vegetable kingdom.

If then, this principle is true, (and who that examines the nature of vitality will doubt it?) how immeasurably important to the welfare of this community to provide a public lawn for the common benefit of our citizens, where they may resort at will to breathe the pure air of heaven!

Gentlemen of the Council, see ye to it!

— **Louisville Daily Courier - 1853**

Louisville's population growth had been steady in its earliest decades but, by 1850, the community was experiencing explosive increase. In 1790 there were barely 200 permanent residents at the Falls and that number tripled in the next decade. By 1827, and the elevation of Louisville to city status, over 7,000 citizens were counted. In 1830 the census revealed 10,341 Louisvillians, and by 1850 the number reached 42,194. Louisville was now the tenth largest city in the United States and ready for a new charter and new municipal powers.

The General Assembly provided legislation for a new charter for Louisville on March 24, 1851, allowing greater independence from state control. Under the original 1828 charter, a unicameral council with a very weak mayor was the order. Most new laws and initiatives came from council committees and, as the city grew in complexity, this system proved less effective.

The new City Charter of 1851 established a board of aldermen and a common council as the legislative wing and greater powers for the mayor who, as chief executive, had the power to veto council actions. Many city offices became elective and civic administration was provided by appointed officials or boards. Some, like the school board, were determined by popular election. A new poll tax of $1.50 for each free white male wishing to vote was now required.

The office of Falls Pilot, a part of Louisville government since 1797, was greatly strengthened because of the unprecedented amount of river traffic crossing over the rapids. Under a new pay rate, Falls Pilots could charge three dollars for each flatboat, ten dollars for boats under one hundred ton capacity and twenty dollars for those over two hundred tons. Anyone other than a boat's owner taking a vessel over the Falls was subject to a fine between twenty and fifty dollars. These fines were paid into the city treasury for the benefit of the university and the public schools of Louisville.

In April 1852 the federal government opened the modern U.S. Marine Hospital in Portland. The Marine Hospital Service of the U.S. Treasury Department levied a twenty cent monthly fee on each registered boatman, and this guaranteed four months of free medical care in one of their new hospitals on the Western Waters. Designed by architect Robert Mills, this hospital for ill and injured boatmen reflected the most modern design innovations

BRIDGE OVER BEARGRASS CREEK, LOUISVILLE.

The bridge over Jackson Street, with the Louisville Gas Works in the background, is typical of the spans over Beargrass Creek. There were five such bridges over the stream, each presenting an impediment to boats wishing to move up the stream to warehouses and factories in Louisville. Ironically, two centuries later when the popular Water Feature was installed in the Park, five bridges link the Festival Plaza with the Great Lawn. *(Filson Historical Society, BRI.43)*

in America, boasting central heating, interior water closets and a sophisticated ventilation system. Prior to the popular acceptance of the germ theory in the 1880s, the prevailing public sentiment was that fresh air was essential for good health and people suffered when trapped in tight and unventilated quarters.

The independent town of Portland, after much controversy, became the first major western expansion of Louisville's city limits in

September 1852 and, for the first time, all the original 4,000 acres belonging to John Connolly were united under a single municipal government. Louisville assumed Portland's assets, an improved public wharf, streets, town pumps, a new school and cemetery, and the city pledged perpetual maintenance of all. Portland and Louisville had attempted a merger in the 1830s to allow the Lexington and Ohio Railroad to link the Bluegrass area with a river port below the Falls, but that was only briefly successful. In 1837 America's first interurban ran down Main Street to the Portland Wharf, and Louisville boasted three miles of rail at a time when there were only twenty-three miles of track in the entire nation.

Bridging the Beargrass

With the great gains in river traffic, and local businesses demanding access to the streets, warehouses and railroads of the city, Louisville's waterfront was stymied by the barrier of Beargrass Creek running parallel along the northern edge of the city. For decades the city's answer was to build additional bridges across the stream, a policy lamented by a reporter for the *Louisville Democrat* in April 1852:

> BUT HERE WE ARE ON THE BRIDGE (LOCATED AT SECOND STREET); THIS IS THE FINEST BRIDGE OUR CITY CAN BOAST, AND ALTHOUGH NOT MORE THAN 60 OR 80 FEET LONG, AND NOT VERY HIGH, COST THE ENORMOUS SUM OF NINETEEN THOUSAND DOLLARS! YONDER, YOU CAN JUST SEE, ARE TWO MORE BRIDGES, ARCHED STONE, EACH COSTING ABOUT FIFTEEN THOUSAND DOLLARS. YOU THINK IT WOULD BE A GOOD IDEA TO LET THIS DITCH OF A BEARGRASS INTO THE RIVER ABOVE TOWN, DO YOU? WELL, THERE ARE A GOOD MANY IN TOWN WHO THINK SO TOO, BUT OUR COUNCILMEN HAVE HITHERTO SEEMED TO THINK THAT BUILDING BRIDGES WAS THE CHEAPEST.

The five bridges over Beargrass, located at Second, Third, Brook, Preston and Jackson Streets, were narrow and caused congested traffic jams. Because of their proximity to the river, they were covered with mud after flooding and required constant maintenance. Their low elevations made it difficult for boats to pass under and even small steamboats found their stacks too tall. Coal barges were pushed upstream as far as Preston Street to supply the Louisville Gas plant with fuel.

Many believed that the best resolution to the problems with Beargrass Creek was to remove the stream from the wharf area altogether. Increasingly, citizens argued that Beargrass Creek should be diverted to flow into the Ohio River two miles upstream from its original mouth at Third. The creek's channel could then be filled and the necessity of bridging the Creek eliminated. After years of discussion, a vote on the proposal was scheduled for March 27, 1853, and was reported by the *Louisville Daily Courier*:

> THE PRESENT CITY COUNCIL HOLDS ITS LAST SESSION TO-NIGHT. COMMITTEES OF ITS MEMBERS HAVE EXAMINED INTO THE DIFFERENT QUESTIONS THAT HAVE ARISEN WITH REGARD TO BEARGRASS CREEK — THE OPENING OF A NEW OUTLET TO THE RIVER, THE FILLING UP OF THE OLD CHANNEL THAT WILL BE LEFT USELESS, &C, &C THE WHOLE SUBJECT HAS BEEN TIME AND AGAIN PRESENTED AND DISCUSSED BEFORE BOTH BOARDS. ALL THE FACTS BEARING UPON IT HAVE BEEN DETAILED IN OFFICIAL REPORTS.

> IT IS A VERY COMMON OPINION AMONG WELL-INFORMED CITIZENS, THAT TIME ENOUGH HAS BEEN DEVOTED TO THIS MATTER ALREADY, BOTH IN COUNCIL AND OUT OF IT. IT IS MANIFESTLY PROPER, THEN, THAT THE SUBJECT SHOULD GO TO A VOTE IN EITHER BOARD. THE APPROPRIATION ASKED, WE BELIEVE, IS ONLY $30,000. *LET THIS BE MADE TONIGHT* AND LET OPERATIONS UPON THE NEW OUTLET BE COMMENCED AT ONCE.

> PROVISION HAS BEEN MADE FOR A PARTIAL EXTENSION OF THE PUBLIC WHARF. FARTHER EXTENSION WILL SOON BE NECESSARY. BEFORE THIS IS ATTEMPTED BEARGRASS SHOULD RECEIVE FULL ATTENTION, AND THEN PEOPLE WILL BE ABLE TO SEE MORE CLEARLY WHAT ADDITIONAL IMPROVEMENTS ALONG THE RIVER WILL BE NECESSARY.

The measure passed, and with it an aggressive new series of civic improvements was launched. In the next few years, new leadership and a bitter local controversy would put waterfront improvements at the center of Louisville's political conflicts.

Travelers arrived day and night at the active Louisville wharf and many climbed the steep slope from the river's edge to Main Street accommodations. During the 1850s, much of the social and economic life in Louisville focused on the waterfront and its steamboat-related industries.

"…scenes of mob law and violence."

But in this expansive era, other battles were being fought at the waterfront, and many of them were bloody and mean spirited. These were the Old West days on the Louisville waterfront and conflict was the norm. A great many people demanded access to the same small piece of real estate at the same time, and tensions between ethnic minorities and longtime residents, townspeople and steamboat crews, and steamboat crews with each other, became common occurrences.

Louisville Daily Journal, January 13, 1851 –

AFFRAY – Yesterday afternoon the steamer *Gulnare*, Captain Linn, arrived from below at the lower wharf in this city. On her arrival a drunken Irishman, who had been making a disturbance onboard, was put on shore by three or four of the crew in obedience to an order of the captain. These members of the crew were thereupon attacked by several Irishmen living in the vicinity, and, after a short fight, driven on board the boat which immediately moved to Strader's wharf. The Irishmen, joined by thirty or forty of their countrymen, followed, and when the boat landed, made another attack upon the crew with stones and brickbats but were finally beaten off. In the course of the last conflict, several firearms were discharged, but nobody was hurt except by stones and brickbats.

Louisville Daily Courier, December 10, 1852

A ROW ON THE WHARF – Yesterday evening the usual bustle of the wharf was very considerably diversified, and enlivened by the captains, clerks, bar keepers, cooks and crews promiscuously, of two steamboats engaging in a general row with each other. We could not ascertain the cause of the difficulty, or who "threw the first brick," but saw a bit of the

FIGHT. THE CAPTAIN OF THE *TWIN CITY* PITCHED INTO THE CAPTAIN OF THE *MCFADEN*, AND GAVE HIM A BLOODY NOSE, AND MAYHAP A PAIR OF BLACK EYES. HE WAS ABLY SECONDED BY TWO OR THREE MORE OF HIS CREW, WE COULDN'T TELL WHO, AND IN THE MELEE THAT ENSURED, THE CLERK OF THE *MCFADEN* GOT A LICK ON THE BACK AND GAVE A LICK BACK TO SOME ONE IN THE CROWD, WHEN BOTH FELL OVER A PILE OF IRON AND GOT SEPARATED. IT WAS A SORT OF RUNNING FIGHT ALL ROUND, AND WAS SOON ENDED BY THE INTERPOSITION OF SOME OF THE FRIENDS OF BOTH PARTIES WHO WERE PEACEFULLY INCLINED, AND WHAT BID FAIR AT ONE TIME TO BE A BLOODY BATTLE, WAS ENDED WITH BUT LITTLE BLOOD SHED. SEVERAL OF THE PARTIES HAD PISTOLS OUT, AND IN THE HANDS OF ONE MAN WE SAW A HUGE BUTCHER KNIFE.

Tensions between lifelong citizens and newly arriving immigrants was a hallmark of life in Louisville in the 1850s. During the digging of the Portland Canal in the late 1820s, Irish workmen had found employment with picks, shovels and wheelbarrows. Many of Portland's original Irish residents remained after the canal was completed and found work on the early railroads in the switch yards, engine houses and locomotives. By now, many men who started as day laborers had demonstrated their abilities and were being promoted to better jobs.

The Great Irish Potato Famine of the 1840s drove an entire generation of men and women from their homes. Desperate Irish families reached Louisville, and were welcomed by relatives who had made the journey years before, and were able to offer assistance.

The largest group of newcomers to the city came from Germany, where habits, language, traditions and dress were different, and a bit threatening, to lifelong residents. The *Louisville Daily Courier,* in August 1852, reported an unusual sight at the wharf:

> A PARTY OF 35 GERMAN EMIGRANTS ARRIVED HERE YESTERDAY ON THE *LADY FRANKLIN*, FROM THE SEABOARD, VIA CINCINNATI — THEY HAD A VAST PILE OF 'PLUNDER' IN PINE CHESTS, AND WERE QUITE UNIQUE IN THEIR DRESS, THE MEN WEARING BLACK VELVETEEN TIGHTS, AND HEAVY HORSE HIDE BOOTS. THEY DESIGN LOCATING IN THIS CITY.

Many of these new German immigrants were fleeing the chaos of the Revolution of 1848 in their native land. Some resisted mandatory conscription and others were the liberal idealists of their age. All sought the political and religious independence promised in America, and many came supplied with capital, technical skills, good educations and a heritage of hard work. They should have been received with open arms by native Louisvillians as grand additions to the community, except for one thing.

Almost all of the new wave of immigrants were Roman Catholics.

A national anti-Catholic backlash arose during this era as descendants of the early Protestant Americans felt their values threatened. Germans brought their tradition of Sunday afternoons at a pleasure garden, enjoying music, dancing, sausages and beer. These weekly assemblies ran counter to laws and community rules of morality, causing friction and a growing pattern of violence in Louisville. The Anti-Papist sentiment found a home in the expanding political movement called the American Party, better known as the Know-Nothings. A splinter group of the dying Whig Party, this reactionary political movement was taking hold in Louisville.

The Palmy Days of Steamboating

Louisville was a center of the Great Steamboat Era, and not just for its wharves, warehouses and canal. Many boats had been built and launched since Clark's Row Galley patrolled the Ohio. Major shipyards, on both sides of the river, created a lively industry for engineers, designers, finish carpenters, painters, master machinists, upholsterers, glazers and marine architects. The Point, with its broad flat land at the river's edge, became the site of boat-building activities, while sawmills powered by Beargrass Creek supplied much of the lumber. In 1839 the launch of a new boat, *Arrow*, was noticed in the *Public Advertiser*:

ON SATURDAY AFTERNOON THE NEW STEAMBOAT *ARROW*, BUILT BY MURRAY AT HIS SHIPYARD ABOVE THE SAWMILLS, WAS LAUNCHED IN GALLANT STYLE BEFORE A LARGE CONCOURSE OF DELIGHTED SPECTATORS. IT WAS ONE OF THE PRETTIEST THINGS OF THE KIND WE HAVE EVER SEEN. THE DAY WAS FINE – THE ASSEMBLY LARGE AND CHEERFUL – AND ALL THE ARRANGEMENTS WERE COMPLETE AND WELL CALCULATED TO GIVE THE BEST POSSIBLE EFFECT TO THE EXCITING SCENE. WE HAD FULL LEISURE TO EXAMINE HER BUILD, AND, AS FAR AS WE MAY BE COMPETENT TO JUDGE, WE MUST PRONOUNCE HER A MODEL OF SPEED, OF THE FIRST ORDER. SHE LOOKED LIKE A GRACEFUL SWAN UPON THE WATER; SCARCELY DRAWING 14 INCHES, THOUGH BUILT FOR 250 TONS BURDEN. HER MEASUREMENTS ARE 152 FEET LENGTH ON DECK, BREADTH OF BEAM 25.6, AND DEPTH OF HOLD 6 FEET. SHE WILL BE COMMANDED BY CAPTAIN MCCORD, PART OWNER; AND WAS BUILT IN 43 WORKING DAYS BY MR. MURRAY.

Captain Robeson DeHart was one of America's original steamboatmen, had served as a crewman on Robert Fulton's *North River Steamboat*, commonly called the *Clermont*, and later distinguished himself as a captain and pilot on the western waters. After a very long maritime career he was named inspector of hulls and port warden, and reported on the local boat building industry:

TO CAPTAIN R. DEHART, INSPECTOR OF HULLS AND PORT WARDEN, WE ARE INDEBTED FOR A LIST OF BOATS BUILT AT LOUISVILLE, NEW ALBANY AND JEFFERSONVILLE, DURING THE YEAR 1851. IT WILL BE SEEN THAT THERE WERE FOURTEEN BUILT ENTIRELY AT LOUISVILLE, FIVE AT JEFFERSONVILLE, AND FOURTEEN AT NEW ALBANY, MAKING IN ALL THIRTY-THREE BOATS, ADDED TO WHICH IS THE *SULTANA*, THE HULL OF WHICH WAS BUILT AT PADUCAH, AND THE ENGINES, CABIN, &C, AT LOUISVILLE, WHICH IS A GRAND TOTAL OF THIRTY-FOUR BOATS.

THE TONNAGE OF THE ABOVE BOATS – GOVERNMENT MEASUREMENT – IS 10,695 TONS. THE COST OF THE BOATS WAS FULLY $900,500. IN THE LIST IS INCLUDED SOME OF THE MOST SUPERB AND MAGNIFICENT BOATS EVER BUILT IN THE WORLD, WHICH IN POINT OF SPEED, DURABILITY AND BEAUTY, WILL DEFY COMPETITION. FIRST IN THE LIST STANDS THE GREAT *ECLIPSE*; THE GREATEST AND BEST BOAT EVER BUILT IN THE WEST. HER ENTIRE COST TO HER ENTERPRISING OWNERS CANNOT BE LESS THAN $120,000 – OUTFIT, AND EVERYTHING COMPLETE. AMONG THE OTHER SPLENDID BOATS THE *SOUTHERN BELLE* STANDS PROMINENT. SHE IS MOST GORGEOUSLY FURNISHED, HAS THE PRETTIEST CABIN, AND IS THOUGHT TO BE THE FASTEST BOAT EVER BUILT. SHE WAS BUILT FOR THE MOBILE TRADE AT A COST OF ABOUT $65,000.

Speed was the great goal of steamboats and their crews. Fast boats attracted busy travelers, post office contracts and boasting rights. Elaborate contests, sometimes planned and sometimes spontaneous, became a popular obsession. The most recent Great Steam Boat Race – subject of a thousand inexpensive lithographs

The Garvey Hotel, at the foot of Seventh Street, is shown in the 1870s. Hotels, taverns, boarding houses and inns serving the steamboat crews lined the streets near the Louisville waterfront. Some, like the Garvey, survived for decades by providing rooms, meals and drinks at reasonable prices. These boatmen hotels also served as communication exchanges among steamboat owners and operators. *(Kentucky Historical Society, 7jefa4)*

– became the national sport. People were amazed in 1866 to learn that the sleek new *Robt. E. Lee*, of New Albany and Portland, could cruise at seventeen miles per hour. At a time when distance was measured by how far a person could walk in a day, this was astounding speed and the very idea seized the imagination of a young nation.

The mouth of Beargrass Creek divided the city's available wharf space into two parts, making direct contact up and down the waterfront impossible and freight traffic expensive and difficult. Late in his life, historian Alfred Pirtle remembered the layout of the wharves of Louisville prior to the filling of Beargrass Creek.

Perhaps nothing is more responsible for spreading popular culture in America than Western steamboats and their crews. African-American rhythms blended with Irish and other European traditions to create new and distinctively American musical forms like jazz. The published sheet music of Stephen Foster was quickly disseminated from Pittsburgh to New Orleans, linking the nation together by songs shared by all Americans. *(Kentucky Historical Society, a6ken5)*

THE WHARF WAS ALWAYS LINED WITH BOATS FROM SECOND STREET DOWN TO SIXTH. BEARGRASS CREEK DIVIDED THE WHARF INTO TWO UNEQUAL PORTIONS, THAT ABOVE THE MOUTH OF THE CREEK, WAS CALLED STRADER'S WHARF, AND THAT BELOW, THE PUBLIC WHARF. IT WAS THE CUSTOM OF THE NEW ORLEANS BOATS, OWNED IN LOUISVILLE, TO LAND AT STRADER'S WHARF WHEN THERE WAS WATER FOR THEM TO ASCEND THE FALLS, FOR THOSE BOATS WERE TOO LARGE TO USE THE (THEN) CANAL LOCKS.

WATER STREET WAS LINED WITH STORES AND BOARDING HOUSES FROM THIRD STREET TO SIXTH. OVER ON THE POINT, OR THAT PART BEYOND THE CREEK, STOOD STRADER'S ROW, A NAME GIVEN TO A ROW OF THREE-STORY BRICK STORES, THAT OCCUPIED ALMOST ALL THE SPACE ON THE SOUTH SIDE OF FULTON STREET, FROM THIRD TO SECOND STREET, USED FOR COMMERCIAL PURPOSES. THIS DISAPPEARED WHEN THE CREEK WAS FILLED UP, SAY 1868-69, AND THE WHARF WAS RAISED TO ITS PRESENT HEIGHT.

WHEN THE WATER GOT UP SO THAT THE DRAYS COULD NOT CROSS THE BRIDGE AT THE FOOT OF THIRD STREET, A LINE OF FLAT-BOATS WAS LASHED TO THE WHARF BOAT AND TO EACH OTHER, AND CAME FAR ENOUGH UP THIRD STREET TO MEET STAGES RAISED ON PILES OF TIMBER, OVER WHICH THE TRAFFIC WAS CARRIED FROM THE SHORE TO THE WHARF BOAT.

Life on the Louisville wharf in the 1850s was often a wondrous spectacle, and contemporary newspaper accounts provide a picture of energy, activity and, sometimes, chaos:

Louisville Daily Courier, January 11, 1852

THIEF ON THE WHARF - Pat Lally, a broth of a boy, was caught stealing a pig of iron from the wharf last Saturday night. He says he was trotting along the levee and met the pig iron on the walk, and it got upon his shoulder and walked off with him. He was held to bail for his good behavior three months, in $300, cave.

Louisville Daily Courier, March 24, 1852

MAN DROWNED – Yesterday afternoon we witnessed one of those sad casualities that are of too common occurrence on our Western rivers. A laboring man from the city, a German we believe, who was in the act of rolling a barrel of pork from the upper wharf boat on to the steamer *S. F. J. Trabue,* fell overboard and was drowned. The barrel of pork first rolled from the staging, and in his endeavor to save the barrel, he lost his balance, and together with the pork fell into the river. The current was turbid and swift, and before any assistance could reach him he sunk forever.

Louisville Daily Courier, May 10, 1852

POLICE COURT – Jas. O'Bryan was arrested for drunkness and disorderly conduct. He had stripped himself on the wharf and was stark crazy, as well as naked, and had to be hauled off on a dray. The court to make an example of him as well as to endeavor to cure his complaint, held him to bail a month in $100.

Louisville Daily Courier, August 18, 1852

RIVER AND STEAMBOAT NEWS - The River was at a stand yesterday with 2 feet 8 inches water in the canal. The weather yesterday morning was rainy, but it cleared off quite warm in the evening.

Louisville Daily Courier, October 21, 1852

Loafer's retreat, or the dwellers under the Third Street bridge, has been swept away, not by the rearing waters of Beargrass, but by the ruthless grasp of the day police, headed by Kirkpatrick, who marched off five Tuesday, and seven yesterday. One poor fellow had to be hauled away on a dray, as he was dead – drunk.

Louisville Daily Courier, December 9, 1852

Business along the wharf yesterday was unusually active, being a great number of boats in port receiving and discharging freight. There were no less than eight arrivals from Pittsburgh, "the head of the hollow," and some five or six from New Orleans, including the *Eclipse* with 600 tons of groceries.

Louisville Daily Courier, January 19, 1853

POLICE COURT - David McKee and Sol. Paugh (paw) were arrested on the charge of passing several $2 counterfeit notes on Mr. J.A. Gray, in Strader's Row, and for having another counterfeit note in their possession. These chaps were passengers, or hands on the *Grand Prairie,* but had been on the *Mary Stephens.* The $2 bills were on the Southern Bank of Kentucky, and McKee, the note holder, had a $20 counterfeit in his possession on the Bank of Kentucky. He is rather a rough-looking, middle-sized chap with both hands crippled, his fingers being contracted.

Several negro converts were baptised yesterday, in the river, at the foot of Fourth Street. As usual, upon such occasions, there was a crowd to witness the ceremony.

"The condition of the streets defies description."

Travelers passing through Louisville were keen, and frequently critical, observers of life at the Falls. Virtually every visitor from Charles Dickens onward commented on the terrible condition of the city streets. Mrs. Frances Gage added her voice to the chorus

in a letter that was reprinted in the January 1, 1853, edition of the *Daily Courier:*

THE WAYS OF LOUISVILLE

We had heard of Louisville as a beautiful city. It may be, but we saw little else than its terrible streets, through which we went lurching along like a lumber cart on an old fashioned corduroy road through a swamp.

The condition of the streets defies

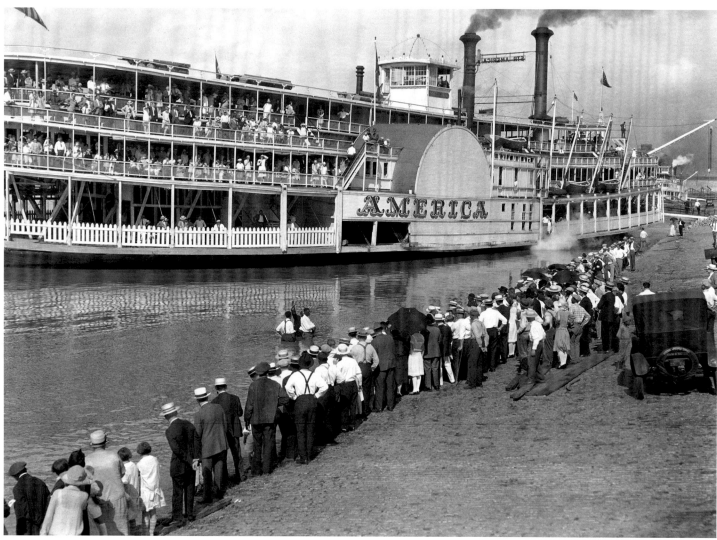

Full-immersion baptisms have a long local tradition on the Louisville levee. Even into the 1920s, ministers brought their congregations to the river's edge, where large groups of onlookers lined the shore and riverboats to watch the ceremonies. *(University of Louisville Photographic Archives, CS085419)*

DESCRIPTION. POOR, JADED-LOOKING HORSES, ALL SULKY SKIN AND BONE MULES, WITH ROUGH, SWEARING, HARD-FACED DRIVERS TRANSPORTING TOBACCO AND WHISKEY – WERE, TO ME, AS I LOOKED ON, ALL OF LOUISVILLE. THE PLANK ROAD FROM LOUISVILLE TO PORTLAND, WAS WORTHY OF A PATENT RIGHT FROM WASHINGTON. THE PLANKS HAVING BEEN, UNDOUBTEDLY, LATELY ENGAGED IN A ROW, HAD LAID THEMSELVES OUT ON THEIR OWN RESPONSIBILITY, MOST OF THEM HIGH AND DRY AT THE SIDES OF THE ROAD, UNTIL THE MUD, WHICH WAS FROM SIX TO EIGHTEEN INCHES IN DEPTH, ACCORDING TO CIRCUMSTANCES, SHOULD CONCLUDE TO ASSUME SOMEWHAT MORE OF CONSISTENCY, AND ALLOW THEM TO TAKE THEIR PLACE WITHOUT BEING WHOLLY ENGULFED.... BUT ALL THINGS WILL COME TO AN END, AND SO DID THIS HORRID RIDE, AND THE DRIVER SET US DOWN UPON THE PORTLAND WHARF, AND RECEIVED HIS DOLLAR WITH A GRIN OF SATISFACTION, AND DECLARING WITH A DECIDED EMPHASIS THAT IT WAS THE WORST ROAD HE EVER PUT HIS TEAM OVER IN ALL "HIS BORN DAYS."

An unidentified correspondent from the *New York Herald* shared his criticism for the local accommodations in another edition of the *Courier*:

I ARRIVED HERE LAST EVENING, IN THE TRAIN FROM FRANKFORT. THE RAILROAD NEEDS CONSIDERABLE MANAGEMENT TO MAKE IT RANK WITH OTHER ROADS OF THIS AGE. FIVE HOURS TO RUN SIXTY MILES IS NO RUN FOR A RAILROAD.

THE HOTELS HERE ARE OLD AND BEHIND THE AGE. THERE IS NOT A GOOD HOTEL IN THE CITY, THOUGH THE CHARGING IS EQUAL TO THE ST. NICHOLAS, THE ASTOR OR THE METROPOLITAN. THE HOUSES ARE POOR AND OLD FASHIONED – FOUR BEDS IN A ROOM,

WITH MANY OLD TIME ARRANGEMENTS.

IMPROVEMENTS ARE GOING ON IN EVERY DIRECTION AND THE PEOPLE SEEM FIRED WITH NEW ENERGY AND ENTERPRISE. THE OLD FASHIONED HOUSES ARE BEING TORN DOWN, AND NEW ONES OF MODERN STYLE ERECTED IN THEIR PLACES. THE STREETS ARE BEING REPAVED, AND ERE LONG THE CITY WILL BE MADE NEW.

Louisville's reputation as a place of commerce and sharp business practices did not escape the notice of a touring French writer, Marie Fortenay, in her 1855 book *The Other World*:

THE "DOLLAR" IS THE BASIS OF THE EXISTENCE IN THE UNITED STATES. BUT IF IT BE AN OBJECT OF PASSION AMONG MEN, IT IS SURELY THAT OF WORSHIP AMONG WOMEN.

LOUISVILLE IS THE CAPITAL OF KENTUCKY. THE INHABITANTS OF THAT STATE ARE RENOWNED FOR THEIR INDEPENDENT MANNERS, FOR THEIR SUPERB DISDAIN OF ALL ETIQUETTE, AND ALL CEREMONY BEFORE LADIES AND SOCIETY. THEY ARE ALSO CELEBRATED FOR THEIR BOASTFULNESS AND THEIR APLOMB IN ALL CIRCUMSTANCES. THEY ARE THE GASCONS OF THE UNITED STATES. THEIR INTELLIGENCE IS REMARKABLE CONCERNING ALL THINGS REFERRING TO BUSINESS. SOMETIMES EVEN THE VOICE OF THEIR INTEREST GOES SO FAR AS TO MAKE THEM SPEAK AS IF THEY WERE MEN OF GENIUS.

IT IS AT THE BAR OF LOUISVILLE WHERE I WENT TO HEAR THE PLEADINGS THAT I RECEIVED THE FOLLOWING AMERICAN DEFINITION OF THE WORD GENTLEMAN:

"Mr. Jones, do you say that the defendant is a gentleman? What do you mean by that?"

"I give that name, Judge, to all men who pay their bills the first time they are presented to them."

Louisville natives also joined in with their critical comments. On February 27, 1852, a concerned citizen expressed his opinion.

To the Editor of the *Louisville Courier*:

SIR – I wish to call the attention of the proper city authorities to the wretched and dilapidated state of Water Street, between Third and Fifth, and lower down, thereby expressing the wish of all tax-paying residents of said street. This street, besides being in conjunction with the wharf, one of the most lucrative resources of the city, is the main thoroughfare for heavy loaded vehicles, such as drays, &c, and needs the fostering care of the city authorities. But in the present state it is the "death" to drays and horses, besides the beautiful (?) impression the appearance of it makes upon strangers visiting our city. The alley between Wall and Bullitt Streets, needs repairing, also, to avoid the collection of water after rain. Very respectfully,

A TAX PAYER AND SUBSCRIBER

"The body of Henry Clay in a hearse, drawn by four white horses…"

America, and especially Kentucky, lost a monumental political leader with the death of Senator Henry Clay in 1852. Louisville had long been a Clay stronghold, with members of his Old Line Whigs dominating the political, financial and social hierarchy of the city. George D. Prentice, the firebrand editor of

O'Neill Alley, a warren of low-rent boarding houses and grog shops, was located between Third and Fourth Streets off old Water Street. This illustration, by local newspaper cartoonist Alexander Van Leshout, appeared in a collection of his works entitled "Odd Corners In Louisville" which provides views of often-overlooked details of downtown Louisville just after the turn of the twentieth century. *(University of Louisville Photographic Archives, OCL.37)*

the *Louisville Journal*, had originally been brought to Louisville to pen a campaign biography of Clay, and he stayed to be the dominant local journalist of his day. The Whigs, champions of internal improvements and high tariffs, were the sworn opposition to Andrew Jackson and the Democrats. Growing tension between Northern Whigs, with their emancipationists' views, and the Southern Whigs, defenders of slavery, tore the party without the unifying presence of Henry Clay.

The body of Henry Clay, accompanied by a committee of the U.S. Senate including General Sam Houston, arrived at the Louisville wharf on July 10, 1852. The cream of local Whiggery, including a promising young builder named James S. Speed, made up a welcoming committee with the sad duty of saying goodbye to their political hero. The corpse of Henry Clay had made a farewell tour coming down the Ohio River, and arrived in Louisville to proceed to the funeral in Lexington Cemetery.

ALL BUSINESS WAS SUSPENDED AT AN EARLY HOUR, AND THE ENTIRE CITY, ALONG THE ROUTE OF THE PROCESSION, WAS CLOTHED IN MOURNING DRAPERY. THE HEAVENS, AS IF PARTICIPATING IN THE GENERAL SORROW, WERE COVERED WITH CLOUDS, AND EVERYTHING BORE A SOMBER HUE.... THE PROCESSION PROCEEDED THROUGH THE CITY ACCORDING TO THE PUBLISHED PROGRAM, AND PASSED THE GALT HOUSE.

THE BODY OF HENRY CLAY IN A HEARSE, DRAWN BY FOUR WHITE HORSES, EACH LED BY GROOMS, WITH TWENTY-SIX PALL BEARERS.

DURING THE MOVING OF THE PROCESSION YESTERDAY, ALL THE BUSINESS HOUSES OF THE CITY WERE CLOSED, AND THE CITY PRESENTED SUCH AN APPEARANCE AS IT NEVER DID BEFORE. ALL THE PUBLIC HOUSES, BANKS, STORES AND DWELLINGS, ALONG THE LINE OF THE PROCESSION WERE SUITABLY AND TASTEFULLY DRAPED IN MOURNING, AND MAIN STREET, FROM END-TO-END, SEEMED TO BE DRESSED IN BLACK FROM THE ROOFS OF THE HOUSES TO THE PAVEMENT.

A Most Bitter Mayoral Contest

A flaw in the construction of the City Charter of 1851 left serious legal questions as to the manner of filling the office of mayor if a vacancy occurred before the completion of a full two-year term. The resulting controversy escalated into what would become, in essence, a full blown *coup d'état*, resulting in the expulsion from office of one of Louisville's most effective chief executives.

Immediately after adoption of the new charter, John Delph was elected mayor in April 1851 to serve a two-year term. In October, Delph resigned that position and the

General Council selected James S. Speed to serve as mayor "pro tem," an appointment Speed held until April 1852, when he ran for and was elected mayor. An article in the *Louisville Daily Courier* of May 1855 attempted to untangle a confusing series of events.

THAT AT THE GENERAL ELECTION FOR CITY OFFICERS, IN 1852, SPEED WAS VOTED FOR AND ENTERED UPON THE DUTIES OF THE OFFICE, AND CONTINUED TO ACT AS MAYOR UNTIL THE APRIL ELECTION OF 1855.

THAT IN APRIL, 1853 AND 1854, AT THE GENERAL ELECTION IN EACH YEAR THE PEOPLE VOTED FOR MAYOR, AND SPEED EACH TIME RECEIVED THE GREATEST NUMBER OF VOTES AND TOOK THE OATHS OF OFFICE.

THAT PREVIOUS TO THE ELECTION OF 1853, SPEED DECLARED HE WAS NO CANDIDATE, INASMUCH AS HE, BY THE ELECTION OF 1852, WAS ENTITLED TO HOLD THE OFFICE FOR TWO YEARS; THAT AFTER THE ELECTION IN 1853 THE GENERAL COUNCIL PASSED A RESOLUTION DECLARING THAT THERE WAS NO VACANCY IN THE OFFICE OF MAYOR, BECAUSE THE ELECTION IN 1852 FILLED THE OFFICE FOR TWO YEARS; THAT THIS RESOLUTION WAS HANDED TO SPEED FOR AFFIRMATION, BUT THAT HE NEVER RETURNED IT, NEITHER SIGNIFYING HIS APPROBATION NOR DISAPPROVAL.

James S. Speed became known as the city's Builder-Mayor and was the person most responsible for relocating Beargrass Creek upstream and improving Louisville's busy public wharves in the 1850s. A victim of religious prejudice, Mayor Speed was illegally ousted from office by a Know-Nothing City Council because he was a convert to Catholicism. *(Louisville Metro Archives)*

THAT AFTER THE ELECTION IN APRIL 1854, THE

GENERAL COUNCIL PASSED A RESOLUTION WHICH SPEED APPROVED, DECLARING THAT THERE WAS NO VACANCY, AS BY THE ELECTION OF 1853 SPEED WAS MAYOR UNTIL 1855; THAT AT THE APRIL ELECTION IN 1855, SPEED AND (JOHN) BARBEE WERE BOTH VOTED FOR THE OFFICE OF MAYOR, AND THAT BARBEE RECEIVED THE LARGEST VOTE; THAT HE HAD BEEN QUALIFIED, AND HAD BY RESOLUTIONS OF THE GENERAL COUNCIL HAD BEEN RECOGNIZED AS MAYOR, AND WAS NOW DISCHARGING THE DUTIES OF THE OFFICE.

A series of bitter court battles resulted in Speed being affirmed as the legal mayor, but Know-Nothing politics reared its head throughout the process. Mayor James S. Speed was represented by a prominent member of the board of aldermen, James Speed, Esq. of Farmington. The attorney Speed, destined to become Lincoln's attorney general, and the builder Speed, Louisville's embattled mayor, had more in common than their name and they worked together in an effective partnership during this difficult and confusing time.

John Barbee, the American Party candidate for mayor, ran on a platform stating no Catholic should be allowed to serve in public office. Chancery Court ruled that Speed was the legally elected mayor, but local elections in 1855 filled the common council, known locally as the Know-Nothing Lodge, with Barbee supporters who refused to accept the court's ruling. The Court of Appeals, now packed with Barbee's backers, overturned the previous decision and declared Barbee the winner.

James Stephens Speed deserved better. He had been born in 1811 on his father's farm, located nine miles south of Louisville on the Salt River Road (Dixie Highway), in an area later known as Shively. As a young man he moved to the city and began working with a contractor named Pickett, and they established a highly successful partnership.

As a young man, Speed was hired to build a church south of town, and there he met and wed Miss Julia Kearney. She was Catholic and he Protestant, and he made the decision to convert and raise his children in the Catholic faith. Although widely praised as Louisville's Builder-Mayor, James Speed became a target of the wrath for the Know-Nothings.

Unlike most of his predecessors in office, James S. Speed was a contractor, not a merchant or lawyer. He used his office to solve the city's problems, some small and others very large. The *Louisville Daily Courier*, and its editor Walter H. Haldeman, were originally supportive of Speed's policies of civic improvements:

THE BOULDER PAVEMENT – THE FIRST BOULDERING IN LOUISVILLE, AS HERETOFORE STATED, IS TO BE COMMENCED ON MAIN STREET BETWEEN THIRD AND FOURTH. WE FEEL ASSURED, FROM THE ENERGY DISPLAYED BY MAYOR SPEED, WHO IS GIVING THE WORK HIS CONSTANT SUPERVISION, THAT IT WILL BE THE BEST AND MOST DURABLE PAVING IN THE CITY.

Granite paving blocks, often misidentified as cobblestones, formed many of Louisville's busy streets and the wharf. An earlier paving material, limestone blocks cut from the Falls of the Ohio, proved to be an impractical building material due to its soft composition, which was quickly crushed into dust by heavily-laden dray carts with iron wheels.

ANOTHER GOOD MOVE – MAYOR SPEED HAS RECOMMENDED TO THE GENERAL COUNCIL THE NECESSITY OF PAVING THE WHARF WITH BOULDERS INSTEAD OF LIMESTONE.

Relocating the mouth of Beargrass Creek, and a vast program of wharf improvements, were the platform of Speed's policies. A thoughtful letter to the *Daily Courier* in February 1853, from a citizen signing himself B. F. A. (probably Benjamin Franklin Avery), summarized the controversial decisions faced by Louisville's leaders:

MY OBJECTIVE IS TO CALL THE ATTENTION OF OUR CITIZENS, AND ESPECIALLY OF OUR BUSINESS MEN, TO THE POLICY AND NECESSITY OF PROVIDING AMPLE WHARF ACCOMMODATIONS, NOT ONLY FOR THE PRESENT, BUT FOR THE PROSPECTIVE BUSINESS OF OUR CITY. THIS SUBJECT WAS LAID BEFORE OUR CITY LEGISLATORS BY OUR PRESENT MAYOR WITHOUT PRODUCING ANY ACTION ON THEIR PART, AND MY ATTENTION WAS A FEW DAYS AGO CALLED TO THE MATTER BY NOTICING THE "CONFUSION WORSE CONFOUNDED" THAT PREVAILED ALONG OUR CITY LANDING. THE *R. M. PATTON* WAS DISCHARGING A PART OF HER FREIGHT OF COTTON BALES AT THE LOWER WHARF (AND HERE LET ME SAY THIS COTTON TRADE IS JUST OPENING UPON US) WHILST THE *ECLIPSE* WAS POURING HER LARGE CARGO ALONG STRADER'S WHARF. BY THESE TWO STEAMERS ALONE A LARGE PORTION OF OUR LANDING WAS FILLED WITH FREIGHT, AND CONSEQUENTLY CRAMMED AND BLOCKED WITH DRAYS, A PERFECT LABYRINTH OF INEXTRICABLE CONFUSION, IN WHICH THE POOR ANIMALS CHAINED TO THE DRAYS ARE ALWAYS SURE TO COME OFF SECOND BEST.

EVERY MAN WHO FEELS AN INTEREST IN THE PROSPERITY OF OUR RAPIDLY IMPROVING CITY, SHOULD BE PREPARED TO ANSWER THE QUESTION, WHERE MUST BE OUR CITY WHARF WHEN OUR BUSINESSES HAVE INCREASED FOUR FOLD, OR PERHAPS TEN FOLD? MY REPLY WOULD BE, ADOPT THE PLAN OF MR. DRAKE, OR ANY OTHER ONE THAT WOULD EMBRACE THE FILLING UP OF THE PRESENT MOUTH OF BEARGRASS, AND THUS LAY THE FOUNDATION FOR A BROAD AND AMPLE STEAMBOAT LANDING, WHICH WILL BE EQUAL TO THE WANTS OF OUR COMMERCE WHEN LOUISVILLE SHALL NUMBER 200,000

INHABITANTS, AND HER COMMERCIAL AND MECHANICAL ENERGY BE SECOND TO NO CITY IN THE GREAT VALLEY OF THE MISSISSIPPI. WE SHOULD BE ABLE TO POINT THEM TO OUR WHARVES, TO OUR WAREHOUSES, TO OUR MERCHANTS, TO OUR MECHANICS, AND THROUGH OUR LIBERALITY AND ENTERPRISE IN ALL OUR TRANSACTIONS TO BID THEM WELCOME TO OUR CITY, AND THUS RETAIN THEIR CUSTOM. SHALL BEARGRASS BE FILLED UP? WHO WILL REPLY?

"It is high time that Louisville renovates herself…"

Other local voices were beginning to argue loudly for the presence of parks, or open spaces, in downtown Louisville. A letter-to-the-editor writer made his argument for a public square, a Louisville amenity missing since the original trustees sold off the public lots to satisfy the legal claims of John Campbell:

MITCHELL, THE GEOGRAPHER, IN SPEAKING OF LOUISVILLE, SAYS "IT IS REGULARLY LAID OUT; HER STREETS CROSSING EACH OTHER AT RIGHT ANGLES." AND THAT IS ABOUT ALL ANYBODY CAN SAY IN FAVOR OF HER APPEARANCE AT THE PRESENT TIME. SHE HAS NO PUBLIC SQUARE – NO "STREETS OF SHADY ELMS." – NONE OF THE PARADISEAN PROMENADES OF NEW HAVEN – NONE OF SUCH AVENUES AS ADORN PHILADELPHIA – SHE LACKS NOT A FEW ESSENTIALS TO HEALTH AND HAPPINESS, CONVENIENCE AND BEAUTY. LOUISVILLE HAS NEGLECTED MANY OPPORTUNITIES OF PURCHASING LAND FOR PUBLIC WALKS, AND YET IT MAY NOT BE TOO LATE TO OBTAIN GROUND SOMEWHERE WITHIN THE CORPORATION LIMITS.

WESTERNERS SHOULD VISIT NEW ENGLAND AND LEARN IN THE LAND OF THEIR FOREFATHERS HOW TO LAY OUT THEIR TOWNS. YANKEES HAVE AN EYE TO PHYSICAL ECONOMY AND RURAL BEAUTY. EVERY PLACE

ON THEIR SEASHORE AND IN THE INTERIOR, HAS A PUBLIC SQUARE, WHERE MORTALS MAY BREATHE THE BRACING AIR AND ENJOY THE SUNLIGHT OBSCURED ONLY BY THE LEAVES OF MAJESTIC ELMS OR NOBLE OAKS.

IT IS HIGH TIME THAT LOUISVILLE RENOVATE HERSELF, AND PRESENT A DIFFERENT ASPECT TO THE WORLD. WHEN THE "FALLS CITY" SHALL HAVE ASSUMED A PREPOSSESSING APPEARANCE AND MADE AMPLE ACCOMMODATIONS IN EVERY RESPECT FOR THE REST OF MANKIND, SHE MAY THEN EXPECT TO ELICIT THE ADMINISTRATION OF STRANGERS, AND DRAW MULTITUDES TO HER DESIRABLE SITE.

After a series of disastrous fires devastated many local businesses, on several occasions entire blocks of Main Street, a movement started to establish a public Water Works, with its prime mission to provide water for fire-fighting, rather than drinking or sanitation. Well water was considered superior, but the widely scattered public cisterns were inadequate to protect huge wooden warehouses filled with combustible materials like pork products, tallow and coal oil. The initial public vote to authorize the construction of a water company failed.

New railroads, especially James Guthrie's Louisville & Nashville, were coming into the city and all wanted access to the public landing and wharf. The agricultural richness of the Midwest and central Kentucky poured into the hands of Louisville merchants who were anxious to process, package and sell their products to consumers, some of them in far-off Europe. Mayor James S. Speed, in his annual message of 1853, announced the priorities of his administration:

THE MAYOR IS OF THE OPINION THAT THE PROSPECTS OF LOUISVILLE WERE NEVER BEFORE SO BRIGHT AND ENCOURAGING AS THEY ARE AT THIS TIME, AND IN ORDER THAT THOSE PROSPECTS MAY NOT BE BLIGHTED, HE RECOMMENDS A LIBERAL POLICY IN THE MATTER OF APPROPRIATIONS OF MONEY FOR OBJECTS OF UNDOUBTED PUBLIC UTILITY.

THE ORDINARY REVENUES HAVE BEEN AMPLE TO MEET THE ORDINARY EXPENDITURES, WHILST THE EXTRAORDINARY OR SINKING FUND REVENUE SHARE NOT ONLY MET THE CURRENT CHARGES THEREON; BUT PAID OFF THE BALANCE OF THE COST OF THE WHARF IMPROVEMENTS PURCHASED FROM STRADER & CO., AMOUNTING TO UPWARD OF $6,000; THE COST OF THE MARKET-HOUSE ERECTED BETWEEN TENTH AND ELEVENTH STREETS, ON MARKET STREET, UPWARDS OF $9,000; NEARLY $11,000 OF THE INDEBTEDNESS OF THE TOWN OF PORTLAND, PAID AFTER AND IN ACCORDANCE WITH THE ANNEXATION OF THAT TOWN TO THE CITY; AND $70,000 OF THE FUNDED DEBT OF THE CITY, CREATED PRIOR TO THE ADOPTION OF THE PRESENT CHARTER.

THE MAYOR LAMENTS THE FAILURE OF THE LATE EFFORT TO ESTABLISH WATER WORKS, AND RECOMMENDS ANOTHER TRIAL, ASSIGNING GOOD REASONS WHY LOUISVILLE SHOULD HAVE A SUPPLY OF RIVER WATER. AMONG HIS RECOMMENDATIONS ARE THE FOLLOWING — THAT A NEW ISSUE OF CITY BONDS BE MADE, FOR THE PURPOSE OF RAISING THE MEANS OF IMPROVING STREETS AND OTHER THOROUGHFARES; THAT THE PUBLIC LANDING BE EXTENDED, A NEW OUTLET FOR BEAR GRASS BE MADE AT THE EXTREME EASTERN LIMIT OF THE CITY, AND THE PRESENT CHANNEL OF THAT CREEK FROM THAT LIMIT TO THE RIVER BE FILLED UP...

THE MAYOR CONCLUDES HIS REMARKS UPON THE EXTENSION OF THE PUBLIC LANDING, WITH THE FOLLOWING PROPOSITIONS:

"I WOULD FURTHER RECOMMEND TO YOUR HONORABLE BODY, THAT THE CITY PURCHASE THE INTERESTS OF THE PERSONS WHO NOW OWN A PORTION OF OUR WHARF. THE INTEREST IN THE HEIRS OF THE LATE HON. JOHN ROWAN CAN BE PURCHASED FOR THE SUM OF $75,000, WHICH IS THE PRICE FIXED IN HIS WILL, TO BE PAID AT SUCH TIME AS THE CITY MAY DEEM PROPER, PROVIDED THE INTEREST BE REGULARLY PAID. THE INTEREST OF STRADER AND THOMPSON CAN ALSO BE PURCHASED UPON TIME AND FOR A REASONABLE PRICE. BY THIS ARRANGEMENT ALL FUTURE EXTENSION AND IMPROVEMENT OF THE WHARF WOULD ENSURE TO THE SOLE BENEFIT OF THE CITY, AND I CANNOT HESITATE ONE MOMENT TO ASSERT THAT THE INCREASED RECEIPTS FROM THE WHARF ALONE WOULD, IN THIRTY YEARS, PAY THE PRINCIPAL AND INTEREST OF THE SUM NECESSARY TO ACCOMPLISH THE OBJECT ABOVE PROPOSED."

IN CONNECTION WITH THIS SUBJECT (REPAIR OF COURTHOUSE) I WILL SUGGEST A NEW COURTHOUSE AND YARD BE CONVERTED INTO A PUBLIC PARK, OR THAT THE SAME BE SOLD AND THE PROCEEDS OF THE SALE APPROPRIATED TO THE PURCHASE OF GROUNDS IN SOME PORTION OF THE CITY TO BE DEDICATED TO A SIMILAR USE.

Reuben T. Durrett, future founder of The Filson Club, introduced an ordinance in the common council to purchase and extend the Louisville wharves. The mayor was authorized to issue bonds in the sum of $1,000 at 6 percent interest and running thirty years. Over $300,000 was committed to purchase the area east of Beargrass Creek known as Strader's Wharf and to improve existing waterfront property. An ambitious engineering project aimed to raise the wharves above flood stage from Third to Ninth Streets. New construction was authorized on land east of Preston Street to extend upriver towards the Point. The first major improvement of Louisville's waterfront was set to begin.

The Galt House Gains a Lighthouse

Other things in Louisville were improving also. The venerable old Galt House Hotel, located on the northeast corner of Second and Main, had been open since 1835 and was beginning to show its age. Isaiah Rogers, the nation's premier hotel architect, had moved to Louisville to partner with Henry Whitestone, and they hired one hundred workers to tear away old features and add new luster to the venerable establishment. A local painter, J. C. Miller, redecorated the entire facility.

Louisville's Main Street, looking eastward from Third to Second Streets was the heart of the city in the 1850s. The original Galt House Hotel (located at far right side of this 1863 engraving) was the center for social life in Louisville for decades. Originally built in 1835, the accommodations were upgraded and improved in 1854.

A February 1854 news account described the dramatic change to Louisville's skyline by the improvement program:

THE GALT HOUSE – THE IMPROVEMENTS TO THIS FAVORITE HOTEL ARE PROGRESSING WITH UNABATED VIGOR, AND WHEN ALL COMPLETED, IT WILL BE THE MOST COMPLETE AND COMFORTABLE HOTEL IN THE SOUTHWEST. THE MAIN STREET FRONT WILL BE SIX STORIES IN HEIGHT, SURMOUNTED BY A CUPOLA OF THE MODERN STYLE, ON WHICH WILL BE PLACED AN IMMENSE GLOBE, FROM THE TOP OF WHICH SPRINGS A MAST, AND AT THE HEAD OF THE MAST WILL BE SWUNG A LANTERN THAT WHEN LIGHTED AT NIGHT WILL BE VISIBLE FOR MILES AND MILES AROUND IN ALL DIRECTIONS. THE LANTERN WILL BE ELEVATED ABOUT 300 FEET FROM THE GROUND, AND WILL SERVE AS A BEACON TO BOATS ENTERING PORT.

Not all was contention and conflict on the Louisville waterfront. Riverboats delivered the world to Louisville's door and sometimes brought amusement, rather than commerce. A massive circus boat, the *Floating Palace*, operated up and down the inland rivers and was a frequent visitor to the Louisville wharf. Exotic attractions like the wild African animals, daredevil performers and colorful costumes were highlights, as was the giant circus boat itself. The main showboat was a three-story barge converted into a Big Top with a seating capacity of over 1,100. Pushed by a steamboat, the *Floating Palace* was accompanied by a large menagerie boat for the animals and another vessel for circus performers and ticket offices.

The circus owner and impresario, Van Amburgh, made his fame as an animal trainer working with tigers and other big cats and he proudly boasted the moniker "The Lion King." One hundred and fifty years after his appearance at the Louisville wharf, the Kentucky Center for the Arts would be built near the *Floating Palace's* old mooring spot. One of their most popular successes was a road company's production of a Broadway musical, also called "The Lion King."

A promotional message in the October 27, 1853, *Daily Courier* gives a brief picture of the showboat and its attractions:

VAN AMBURGH'S GREAT MENAGERIE

Despite the inclemency of the weather yesterday, the exhibitions of Van Amburgh's trained animals on board the *Floating Palace* were well attended, and gave unbounded satisfaction. We do not believe there was every before such a diversified collection of birds, beast and reptiles, as are in this famous menagerie. Noah in his Ark could not have equaled it.

The performance of the elephant, Tippoo Sultan, is very wonderful, and elicit the applause of all spectators. An hour or two

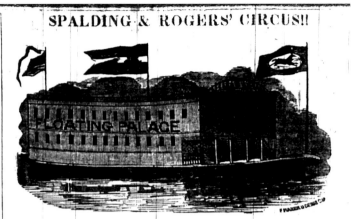

Van Amburg's *Floating Palace*, the grandest of all the traveling riverboat circus operations, was a regular caller at the Louisville wharf. Housing a massive floating Big Top, the three-story barge contained 1,100 seats and could accommodate trapeze artists flying from its rafters. Two companion boats, one for the performers and the other as an exotic animal menagerie, accompanied the *Floating Palace* on its cruises up and down the Ohio River (opposite page).

cannot be spent more pleasantly than in witnessing this interesting exhibition. The *Palace* is at the foot of Third Street, and prepared expressly for the comfortable accommodation of a large crowd, particularly for ladies. The menagerie comprises the choicest animals of two continents.

The *Floating Palace* would also introduce another distinctive element of Ohio River and steamboat lore, as detailed by an 1857 news article:

THE CALLIOPE – The steamer *Jas. Raymond*, of the *Floating Palace* concern, sports a sure enough Calliope on her hurricane deck to blow out music to the millions. It speaks in loud and very musical

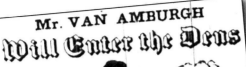

Mr. VAN AMBURGH
Will Enter the Dens

OF HIS TERRIFIC GROUP OF
LIONS, TIGERS, LEOPARDS

In the presence of the Audience, as he has done with
much *eclat* in Europe and America.

Van Amburgh's Trained Anim

Consist of two Numidian Lions, a Royal Beng
ger, Four African Leopards, Asiatic Lion and Lioness,
Black Tiger, and Brazilian Tiger.

NEW HOLLAND OSTRICHES,

Pair African Crowned Cranes, Pair Black Swans, White
Stork, Silver Pheasants, English Pheasants, Blue Cranes,
Pair White Angora Rabbits, Pair White Guinea Hens
from South Africa, Pair Large Turkish Rabbits, Ma-
caws, Parrots, Ichneumons, Badgers, and a

Colony of the Monkey Tribe!

An amusing Performance will be given by the

TRAINED ELEPHANT
With his Keeper. Also with the
PONIES AND THEIR MONKEY RIDERS.

At the conclusion of M
formance with the Lion
☞ For full particul
Bills, Lithographs &c.

RHINOCEROS,

OR, UNICORN OF HOLY WRIT!

Male Elephant Tippo Sultan, Arabian Pack Cam
White Lama, Zebu or Burmese Ox Nandi, African Z
bra, Canadian Elk, Chilian Alpacas,

10 Lions and Lionesses, Asiatic & African

Royal Bengal Tigers, Pair Brazilian Tigers, Royal
Tiger, 3 African Leopards, Kaffir Lioness and 3 R
Whelps, Pair Senegal Leopards, Black Tiger, 2 B
American Lions, Black Leopard, Four North Am
Panthers, Pair Spotted Hyenas, Striped Hyenas,
Wolves, 2 Grizzly Bears, Russian Brown Bear,
American Black Bear, White Coon from Siberia,

AND HIGHLY
TRAINED ANIMALS!

In their various stages of training and subjugation by
their great master and owner: others,

FEROCIOUS & TERRIFIC!

Fresh from their native fastness: with innumerable
specimens of the

RARE BIRDS THAT FLY IN THE AIR!

All to be seen for One Price of Admission
WILL EXHIBIT AT
LOUISVILLE, TUESDAY, OCTOBER 25,

AT 2 AND 6½ O'CLOCK, and also
Wednesday, Thursday, Friday and Saturday,
AT 10, 2 AND 6½ O'CLOCK.

☞ Mr. Van Amburgh's performances with the
Trained Animals at 3 and 8 o'clock only.
☞ Admission, 50 cents. Children and servants half
price.

☞ The Entertainments will be given between the
FOOT OF SECOND AND THIRD STREETS,

ABOARD THE FLOATING PALACE

TONES THAT CAN BE HEARD A MILE OR MORE. IN ITS SHAPE AND CONSTRUCTION IT RESEMBLES A HAND ORGAN, HARP OF A THOUSAND SCREAMS, AND A PIANO EIGHTY. THE MUSIC IS A COMBINATION OF ALL THESE INSTRUMENTS WITH A GOOD STRONG HISSING WHISTLE THROWN IN.

"Bloody Beargrass"

The city's decision to relocate and fill Beargrass Creek required a great deal of soul-searching and debate, but the actual construction of the project proved to be far more challenging. Perhaps the most compelling reason for removing Beargrass Creek from the center of town was the growing problem of pollution flowing down its formerly pristine waters. An area east of Louisville, formerly known as Uptown, was becoming the community of Butchertown. Huge commercial slaughter houses and pork-packing firms were built on the shores of Beargrass Creek to utilize the water supply and each used the stream as an open sewer. Effluvial materials flowed downstream and entered the Ohio River at Third Street, the same location hosting the grand showboats, luxury packet boats and incoming visitors to Louisville. This sewage, described in stomach-turning detail by contemporary observers, was a local scandal as news accounts attest.

Louisville Daily Courier, November 29, 1854

CERTAIN IT IS, HOWEVER, THAT 'BLOODY BEARGRASS' IS "SOME PUMPKINS," WHETHER WE CONSIDER IT HISTORICALLY, GEOGRAPHICALLY, OR ITS BANKS AS THE SEAT OF THE MANY IMMENSE PORK-PACKING ESTABLISHMENTS THAT HAVE GIVEN OUR CITY SO JUST A REPUTATION FOR ENTERPRISE, COMMERCIAL WEALTH AND PROSPERITY. FROM THESE, TOO, COMES THE SANGUINARY APPELLATION THAT THE STREAM WEARS DURING THE WINTER SEASON. INDEED, FOR MONTHS NOW WILL THE WATER PRESENT A DARK CRIMSON COLOR, INDICATING THE COPIOUS TORRENTS OF BLOOD FLOWING UPON ITS SURFACE FROM A HALF MILLION SLAUGHTERED HOGS. NEVER, SINCE THE DAYS OF THE OLD INDIAN WARFARE, WHEN OFTEN IN THIS VICINITY THE SHOUT AND YELLS OF THE TERRIFIC COMBATS THEN WAGED WERE HEARD IN THIS VICINITY, WAS PEACEFUL BEARGRASS STAINED BY BLOOD, UNTIL ENTERPRISE MARRED THE BEAUTY OF ITS SHADY SHORES, AND RENDERED A CLASSIC STREAM THE SEWER FOR ALL MANNER OF OFFAL. THE CREEK, HOWEVER, YIELDS PROFIT TO SOMEBODY, AND WE NOTICED A FEW DAYS AGO A METHOD FOR TURNING AN HONEST PENNY, ADOPTED BY A MAN WHO HAD LOCATED HIMSELF OPPOSITE THE LARGE PORKHOUSE OF JARVIS & CO. HE HAD ERECTED ACROSS THE STREAM TWO DAMS, AND WAS BUSILY ENGAGED IN SKIMMING OFF THE SURFACE OF THE WATER ALL THE OLEAGINOUS SUBSTANCES THAT COLLECTED UPON IT. THIS HE RENDERED IN A KETTLE OVER A FURNACE, PLACED UPON THE BANK, INTO LARD, FORMING, IN FACT, A TEMPORARY LARD-RENDERING ESTABLISHMENT. WE UNDERSTAND THAT IN THIS MANNER A GREAT DEAL OF WASTE MATERIAL FROM THE DIFFERENT PORT ESTABLISHMENTS IS SAVED, AND THAT IT INVARIABLY PROVIDES A SOURCE OF CONSIDERABLE PROFIT TO THE INDUSTRIOUS PERSON THUS ENGAGED.

Louisville Journal, March 5, 1857

T. R. SCOWDEN (CHIEF ENGINEER OF THE LOUISVILLE WATER COMPANY) EXPLAINED WHY HE DOESN'T PLAN TO DRAW LOUISVILLE'S WATER FROM THE CANAL. HE SAID ITS ENTRANCE LIES BELOW BEARGRASS CREEK.

...NOR COULD I SHUT MY EYES TO THE FACT THAT BEARGRASS CREEK DISGORGES THE ACCUMULATED FILTH OF ALL THE SLAUGHTERHOUSES, BUTCHER ESTABLISHMENTS, SOAP, GLUE AND CANDLE FACTORIES SITUATED UPON IT INTO THE RIVER ABOVE THE MOUTH OF THE INLET

PIPE, MAKING THE MOST DISGUSTING AND POISONOUS COMPOUND AND SOLUTION THAT THE IMAGINATION COULD POSSIBLY CONCEIVE, CONTAINING AND POLLUTING WITH DISEASE THE WHOLE SOURCE OF SUPPLY.

AT THE TIME I MADE THE EXAMINATIONS AND TOOK SOUNDINGS OF THE DEPTH OF WATER, THE RIVER WAS AT ITS VERY LOWEST STAGE, AND EVEN THEN THE NORTH SIDE OF WILLOW BAR WAS STREWN WITH DECAYING HOGS' LIVERS AND OTHER PUTRESCENT MATTER AND OFFAL FROM SLAUGHTER HOUSES; THE WATER WAS DISCOLORED WITH BLOOD AND SLIME FOR AT LEAST ONE HUNDRED FEET FROM THE SHORE. WHEN THE RIVER IS HIGHER, I AM TOLD THE WASHINGS AND IMPURITIES ARE CARRIED OUT STILL FURTHER INTO THE CHANNEL OF THE RIVER.

Efforts to alleviate the polluted Beargrass Creek were complicated by construction problems, some trivial, and others very serious. An unexpected labor dispute, characteristic of its era, occurred on All Saints Day of 1854:

YESTERDAY WAS ONE OF THE MOST INTERESTING FESTIVALS OF THE CATHOLIC CHURCH, AND WAS DULY CELEBRATED IN THIS CITY BY THE CLERGY AND COMMUNICANTS OF THAT NUMEROUS BODY OF RELIGIONISTS.

ALL SAINTS' DAY

IS ONE OF PECULIAR OBLIGATION, AND IS OBSERVED WITH GREAT SANCTITY BY THE PIOUS CATHOLICS. LABOR IS GENERALLY SUSPENDED, AND FASTING AND PRAYER MADE THE ORDER OF THE DAY. NEITHER PERSUASION NOR MONEY CAN LEAD ANY TO THE VIOLATION OF WHAT THEY ESTEEM WITH MOST BINDING VOWS; AND IT FREQUENTLY OCCURS THAT THIS PARDONABLE SPIRIT OF RELIGIOUS ENTHUSIASM LEADS TO THE GREATEST DEGREE OF INCONVENIENCE AMONG EMPLOYEES. IT

CAUSED, YESTERDAY, AN AMUSING CESSATION OF LABOR AT THE BEARGRASS CUT-OFF. THE DIGGERS AND SPADE MEN ARE ALL CATHOLICS, WHILE THE CARTERS ARE PROTESTANTS. IN THE MORNING THE LATTER APPEARED AS USUAL AT THE PLACE OF WORK, BUT THERE WAS NO ONE TO FILL THEIR CARTS. THIS PRODUCED NO LITTLE FEELING AMONG THEM, AS THEY FELT ALTOGETHER INDISPOSED TO LOSE A DAY'S WAGES ON ACCOUNT OF ANY IRISHMAN'S RELIGION. CHARITY SHOULD HAVE TAUGHT THEM A BETTER SPIRIT, BUT THE DIVINE LAW OF LOVE HAS BUT LITTLE INFLUENCE WHEN THERE IS AN INTERVENTION OF SORDID GAIN.

The digging project's first contractor abandoned the job after wasting fifteen thousand dollars and several months work. He was accused of submitting an unrealistically low bid and his failure was credited to his own "greedy folly." When work was renewed, the second contractor, and fifty of his one thousand men digging the Cut-Off trench, died from illnesses contracted during the project. The Beargrass Cut-Off, a mere five-eighths of a mile in length, cost $60,000 and was not completed until 1856 by the third and final contractor, John G. Lyon.

"…the Mayor of Louisville for all time to come."

Political pressure grew to resolve the legal question over the office of mayor of Louisville. Both James S. Speed and John Barbee claimed to be the legitimate claimant to the job, and the growing power of the Know-Nothings exerted strong arguments against Speed. The editorial voice of the *Daily Courier* attacked James Speed in their April 7, 1855, edition:

THE MAYORALTY

ACCORDING TO MR. SPEED'S INTERPRETATION OF THE CHARTER, HE IS THE MAYOR OF LOUISVILLE FOR ALL TIME TO COME. HIS TERM OF OFFICE NEVER CAN EXPIRE. LOUISVILLE IS UNDER THE RULE, NOT OF A MAYOR, BUT OF A DICTATOR.

We have no fault to find with Mr. Speed's discharge of his duties as Mayor; his efficiency or inefficiency as an officer has nothing to do with the matter at issue. The city is tired of this question of the indefinite term of office; it is quite time that we were beginning to know if we are ever to have a change in our Mayoralty, or if the city is to be under the rule of the present officer for the term of his natural life. The present is the time to decide this question.... For ourselves, we have no doubt but that his term of office is already expired, and the same opinion has been several times expressed by the best legal talent of the city. He has now served out two full terms, and he yet claims his seat, and he hopes to gain it more by the indifference of the voters than by any canvassing on the part of himself, or of his friends. The voters should remember that unless they do GO PROMPTLY TO THE POLLS AND VOTE FOR BARBEE, the question so long disputed may again be presented to them the next year, and the next, and the next. Let us settle this dispute now.

The mayoral term of John Barbee was a blight on Louisville's honor. During the gubernatorial election, held on August 6, 1855, Know-Nothing thugs denied naturalized citizens, especially in Irish and German neighborhoods, the right to vote. The resulting series of shootings, arson, riot and mayhem is remembered in Louisville history as "Bloody Monday." Fanned by the editorial comments of Haldeman and Prentice, the city reacted with unparalleled violence, resulting in the death of at least twenty-two individuals. The burning of an Irish tenement called Quinn's Row at Tenth and Main Streets was the scene of the greatest horrors. The following day, it was reported that 300 German families got on steamboats and departed Louisville for friendlier destinations.

Barbee's bigotry extended beyond the Catholics, he also assailed African-Americans living in Louisville. In January 1856, he submitted the following proposal to the Board of Aldermen:

TO THE GENERAL COUNCIL

GENTLEMEN: Complaints are becoming so frequent with regard to the great facilities our slaves have of escaping that it is absolutely necessary some prompt and active measures should be taken to remedy or, at least, to lessen the evil.

Our proximity to the free States, the many railroad communications between the Ohio River and Canada, and the easy intercourse which lawless or designing persons have with our slaves, render their escape, if they choose it, almost certain, and their recapture extremely doubtful; but the most crying evil is the great number of free negroes from other States who are allowed to settle among us, and who are either leagued with, or are the tools of base men, who, by every means in their power, engender and foster a spirit of rebellion in our slaves, rendering them discontented, and affording them every possible assistance to escape.

Our revised statutes provide for the infliction of penalties on free negroes emigrating to our State, but this law is never enforced. Many of the free negroes in our city are emigrants, and most of the slaves who escape do so by their advice and connivance.

If the General Council would pass an ordinance requiring the registry of free negroes, many of them would be compelled to leave, or become amenable to the laws; and the police would be better able to control the others, and prevent them having such

UNRESTRICTED COMPANIONSHIP WITH OUR SLAVES. I WOULD THEREFORE, MOST RESPECTFULLY RECOMMEND THE PASSAGE OF SUCH AN ORDINANCE. RESPECTFULLY,

JOHN BARBEE, Mayor

Barbee's draconian proposal failed. Following his illegal ouster as mayor, James Speed left the city and moved to Chicago. Even after he had departed, the *Daily Courier* continued to attack both Speed and others of his administration.

DEFALCATIONS AND SHORTCOMINGS

THAT THERE HAS BEEN SAD BUNGLING AND CARELESSNESS IN THE MANAGEMENT OF THE AFFAIRS OF THE CITY DURING THE PAST TWO OR THREE YEARS, HAS BEEN MADE PAINFULLY MANIFEST TO ALL WHO HAVE TAKEN THE TROUBLE TO INVESTIGATE THE MATTER. WHAT HAS BEEN THE EXTENT OF THE LOSSES INCURRED BY THE CITY WILL PROBABLY NEVER BE KNOWN, ALTHOUGH INVESTIGATIONS NOW IN PROGRESS, WHICH WE TRUST WILL BE MADE RIGIDLY AND THOROUGHLY, WILL, WHEN GIVEN TO THE PUBLIC, ASTONISH THOSE GOOD PEOPLE WHO HAVE BEEN DELUDING THEMSELVES WITH THE IDEA THAT THEIR PUBLIC SERVANTS HAVE BEEN FAITHFUL IN GUARDING THE CITY'S PROPERTY AND INTERESTS.

THE RECORDS OF THE GENERAL COUNCILS NOW SHOW THE FOLLOWING PERSONS TO BE DEFAULTERS TO THE CITY TO THE AMOUNTS ANNEXED. IF THESE RECORDS DO ANY OF THE PARTIES INJUSTICE, THEY SHOULD NOT PERMIT THEM TO REMAIN UNCORRECTED.

JAS. S. SPEED, LATE MAYOR, IS CHARGED WITH HAVING USED ILLEGALLY, SECRET SERVICE MONEY TO THE AMOUNT OF $1,200, FOR WHICH HE HAS NOT ACCOUNTED; WITH HAVING FROM THE BARDSTOWN TURNPIKE COMPANY $300, WHICH HE NEVER PAID OVER TO THE CITY TREASURER; AND WITH HAVING SOLD THE COPPER FROM THE ROOF OF THE COURT HOUSE AT 17 CENTS PER LB., WHEN 22 OR 24 CENTS COULD HAVE BEEN OBTAINED FOR IT; AND WITH USING $896.12 OF THE MONEY WHICH IS NOT ACCOUNTED FOR.

WM. HAMLET, LATE MARKET MASTER, IS CHARGED WITH BEING A DEFAULTER TO THE AMOUNT OF $1,588.

J. J. WHITE, MARKET MASTER, IS CHARGED WITH BEING A DEFAULTER TO THE AMOUNT OF $653.

After being accused of selling even the roof of the county courthouse, James S. Speed left Louisville. In his brief autobiography, Speed did not mention service as the mayor of the city, but he deserves the credit for resolving the lingering issues of Beargrass Creek, consolidation of the public wharf and improvements to the streets of Louisville.

Hog Ice, Frog Ice or Common Ice

Throughout the chaos that was Louisville during the mid-1850s, daily life at the waterfront continued to develop in interesting ways.

Louisville Daily Courier, January 24, 1852

THE ICE MERCHANTS WERE BUSY LAYING IN A HARVEST, FROM THE ICE IN FRONT OF WALL STREET, WHICH THEY WERE CUTTING OUT WITH SAWS.

Louisville Journal, January 5, 1856

THE ICE CROP IS QUITE ABUNDANT, AND MANY PERSONS ARE BUSY LAYING IN THE SUMMER SUPPLY IN ALL ITS VARIETIES. WE MAY EXPECT NEXT SEASON TO HAVE CHOICE OF EITHER HOG ICE, FROG ICE, OR COMMON ICE. HOG ICE IS PROCURED FROM BEARGRASS

CREEK, IN THE NEIGHBORHOOD OF THE PORK HOUSES; IT IS OF A DELICATE WINE COLOR, BUT IS TOO HIGHLY FLAVORED FOR OUR PALATE. THE FROG ICE IS FOUND IN THE PONDS BORDERING THE CITY; IT HAS A PALE GREENISH TINGE WITH OCCASIONAL STREAKS OF DUCKWEED; WE ARE NOT FOND OF IT AND SHALL LEAVE IT FOR THOSE WHO ALWAYS PUT IN A FEW DROPS OF THE "ARDENT" TO KILL THE ANIMALCULES. AS FOR COMMON ICE, IT IS GOT FROM THE RIVER AND IS TOO WELL KNOWN TO NEED DESCRIPTION. WE GIVE IT OUR PREFERENCE AND WISH THE GETTERS OF ALL SUCCESS.

The area north of Main Street was home to a great number of Louisvillians. Two children, William and Helen Hamilton are shown playing in front of their home at 138 North Third Street in1920. The children were part of the Farrell family, which provided three generations of crew members to the nearby Life-Saving Station #10. *(Photo courtesy of Michael Maloney)*

Louisville Daily Courier, August 28, 1854

THE STORM OF YESTERDAY - IMMENSE LOSS OF LIFE! - EIGHTEEN PERSONS KILLED

LOUISVILLE WAS VISITED YESTERDAY BY A STORM WHICH HAS LEFT TRACES OF ITS DESOLATING PROGRESS WHICH WILL LONG BE REMEMBERED IN THIS CITY. IT TORE THE ENTIRE ROOF FROM A ROW OF TWENTY-ONE BUILDINGS AND SPRINKLED ITS PATH WITH THE RUINS. THE GREATEST RANGE OF DESTRUCTION WAS IN THE SPACE BETWEEN EIGHTH AND EIGHTEENTH STREETS, EXTENDING FROM THE SUBURBS TO THE CITY TO THE RIVER.

THE FURY OF THE WHIRLWIND NEXT SWEPT THE HARBOR AND BLEW THE NEW STEAMERS *NEW MEMPHIS, W. W. FARMER,* AND THE *W. A. EACES* FROM THEIR MOORINGS, TOGETHER WITH A NUMBER OF EMPTY FLATBOATS, RAFTS, &C, ALL OF WHICH STRANDED ON THE FALLS, AND WERE MORE OR LESS INJURED. THE *NEW MEMPHIS,* A BOAT OF THE LARGEST CLASS, WAS ALMOST TOTALLY WRECKED. THE UPPER WORKS OR CABINS, WHICH WERE IN FRAME, AND NEARLY OCCUPIED, WERE SWEPT OFF THE TEXAS AND FORWARD PORTION OF THE CABIN BEING BLOWN 50 YARDS INTO THE RIVER, A COMPLETE WRECK. THE OTHER PORTIONS OF THE CABIN ARE SO SHATTERED AND OUT OF LINE THAT THE WHOLE STRUCTURE WILL HAVE TO BE REBUILT. THE BOAT STRUCK WITH SUCH FORCE AGAINST THE REEF OF ROCKS THAT HER SEAMS LEAKED, THE RUDDER POST WAS TWISTED, AND SHE LEAKED BADLY. THE ENTIRE DAMAGE CANNOT BE LESS THAN $8,000 TO THE CABIN.

Louisville Daily Courier, May 31, 1855

A CARGO OF LIVE MORMONS

YESTERDAY THE STEAMER *AMAZON* REACHED THIS PORT ON HER WAY TO ST. LOUIS, WITH A CARGO OF ABOUT SEVEN HUNDRED AND FIFTY MORMONS. THE BOAT, AFTER LIGHTENING HER CARGO, MAKING THE LIVE STOCK GO ASHORE, PROCEEDED OVER THE FALLS TO PORTLAND, WHERE THE MORMONS REJOINED HER. THE TRIBE EMIGRATED FROM THE NORTH OF ENGLAND, AND ARE ON THEIR WAY TO SALT LAKE CITY. THEY ARE A SINGULAR LOOKING SET, WITH THEIR QUAINT, OLD FASHIONED DRESSES AND THE WOMEN IN THEIR ODD, OLD, ROUND CROWNED CHECK BONNETS. THEY SHIPPED, OR ENGAGED PASSAGE, ON THE *AMAZON* AT PITTSBURGH, PAYING FULL PASSAGE FOR FIVE HUNDRED PERSONS TO ST. LOUIS, COUNTING TWO OF THEIR CHILDREN AS ONE WHOLE PERSON, MAKING THE AGGREGATE ABOUT SEVEN HUNDRED AND FIFTY SOULS.

Louisville Daily Courier, October 31, 1855

GREAT PROFIT ON WHISKEY

THE PRESENT PRICE OF RAW WHISKEY IN THIS CITY IS 34 CENTS PER GALLON, WHICH YIELDS AN ENORMOUS PROFIT TO THE DISTILLER. HE PAYS 30 CENTS PER BUSHEL FOR HIS CORN — NEW CORN — GRINDS OUT ABOUT 400 BUSHELS PER DIEM; WHICH MAKES UPWARDS OF 1,600 GALLONS OF NEW WHISKEY, OR RATHER MORE THAN FOUR GALLONS TO THE BUSHEL. THUS A BUSHEL OF CORN COSTING 30 CENTS YIELDS TO THE MANUFACTURER UPWARDS OF FOUR GALLONS OF WHISKEY, WHICH, AT 34 CENTS PER GALLON, AMOUNTS TO THE SNUG SUM OF $544 PER DAY. THE NET PROFIT ON THIS SINGLE DAY'S WORK OF CONVERTING CORN INTO WHISKEY, IS FULLY $250 OR UPWARDS OF $1,500 PER WEEK, PROVIDED THE WORK IS SUSPENDED ON SUNDAY.

Mr. Heigold Builds His Dream House

As the decade of the 1850s ended, a number of local

The home of Christian Heigold, built in 1857 on the Point, is covered with the builder's elaborate stone-carved tributes to George Washington and America. Better known in later years as the Heigold façade, this is a rare photo of the building while still intact. The Heigold façade would eventually find three different locations, all in close proximity to River Road. *(University of Louisville Photographic Archives, 1994-18-0618)*

controversies were being resolved. The community seemed to have stunned itself with the Bloody Monday fury, and as the Know-Nothings quickly lost steam to the growing Republican wing of the old Whig Party, a kind of community reconciliation began to take place.

An odd memorial to democratic ideals was created by a German immigrant named Christian Heigold. He brought to America the training and skill of a master stone carver and met financial success when he was hired to install the broad front steps of the Jefferson County Court House. Two years after Bloody Monday, Christian Heigold began building an impressive two-story brick home at 106 Marion Street in the Point. A *Louisville Commercial* article written in 1893 provided a respectful look back at the creation of a Louisville original:

CHARLES (SIC) HEIGOLD BUILDS HIS HOUSE
IN SOLID STONE

AN OLD HOUSE ON THE POINT, WHICH TOOK
SEVEN YEARS TO ADORN

CHARLES HEIGOLD'S WORK

ONE OF THE MOST REMARKABLE MONUMENTS TO THE MEMORY OF GEORGE WASHINGTON IS LOCATED IN THIS CITY.

A HOUSE BUILT BY CHARLES HEIGOLD, A STONE-CARVER, IN 1857, AND LOCATED ON THE "POINT," IS A STANDING MEMORIAL TO THE HERO. MR. HEIGOLD CUT AND CARVED ALL THE STONE AND BUILT THE HOUSE HIMSELF, THE LIKE OF WHICH CAN HARDLY BE FOUND ANYWHERE. ALTHOUGH THE BUILDER HAS BEEN DEAD FOR ABOUT THIRTY-TWO YEARS, THE WORK BY HIM STILL STANDS, A MARK OF HIS PATRIOTISM AND A MEMORIAL TO THE COUNTRY'S HERO. THE FRONT OF THE HOUSE IS OF STONE AND SO WELL BUILT THAT IT HAS WITHSTOOD THE RAVAGES OF STORMS AND FLOODS FOR THE LAST THIRTY-

SIX YEARS AND IS STILL IN FIRST-CLASS CONDITION. IT IS OCCUPIED AS THE HOME OF TWO OF CHARLES HEIGOLD'S CHILDREN, A SON-IN-LAW AND FIVE GRANDCHILDREN.

THE HOUSE IS LOCATED AT 106 MARION STREET, ON THE POINT. IT TOOK THE BUILDER SEVEN YEARS TO CARVE THE PICTURE, WREATHS AND DESIGNS WITH WHICH HE DECORATED THE FRONT. IT IS A TWO STORY AND ATTIC HOUSE. IN THE MIDDLE, NEAR THE TOP, HE CARVED A MEDALLION OF PRESIDENT BUCHANAN, AS ARE ALL THE REST OUT OF SOLID STONE. THE LIKENESSES OF THE PERSONS REPRESENTED IN HIS WORK ARE SAID TO BE VERY GOOD.

IMMEDIATELY OVER THE MAIN ENTRANCE AND ABOVE THE FRONT PORCH IS A LARGE SOLID STONE INTO WHICH IS CARVED THE LIKENESS OF GEORGE WASHINGTON. IN A WREATH IN THE LEFT CENTER IS HIS WIFE AND THE GODDESS OF LIBERTY ON THE RIGHT.

UNDER THESE ARE THE CANNON, BALLS, THE AMERICAN EMBLEM — AN EAGLE AND THE SHIELD, ALL NEATLY ARRANGED AND WELL BROUGHT OUT.

ABOVE THE CENTER-PIECES ARE THIRTEEN STARS AND BELOW THE WORDS "CONSTITUTION" AND "E. PLURIBUS UNUM," IN SOLID STONE.

Eventually, even the *Louisville Courier* began to express a greater tolerance for Catholic Louisvillians, whatever their place of origin. A March 2, 1859, editorial comment repudiated the Know-Nothing regime of John Barbee and signaled an end to ethnic and religious smears, and recognition of the growing contribution of the recent immigrants.

GOOD NEWS FOR MECHANICS

FOR THE LAST FOUR YEARS AN UNFORTUNATE

FACTION HAS LORDED IT OVER LOUISVILLE, AND BY THEIR PROSCRIPTIVE AND BIGOTED TACTICS, DRIVEN OFF MANY OF OUR MECHANICS AND STARVED OUT OTHERS. THE FOREIGN ARTISAN AND CATHOLICS HAVE NOT BEEN UPON AN EQUALITY WITH THE NATIVE AND THE PROTESTANT. AND, STRANGER THAN ALL, THE ARISTOCRATIC MECHANIC, THE WIELDER OF CAPITAL, AND THE BOSSER OF HANDS, HAS COME IN FOR THE LION'S SHARE OF THE JOBS THAT SMALLER CONTRACTORS WERE CONSIDERED IMPUDENT IN ASPIRING TO UNDERTAKE.

A CHANGE, HOWEVER, HAS COME OVER THE DREAMS OF THOSE POLITICAL EMPYRICS WHO THOUGHT THEY COULD MAKE A CITY'S POPULATION ACCORDING TO ORDER. THEY HAVE LEARNED THAT BOTH THE CATHOLIC AND THE FOREIGN ELEMENT ARE AS NECESSARY IN A GREAT CITY AS THE NATIVE AND PROTESTANT. THERE IS AN APPROPRIATE SPHERE FOR THE ACTION OF BOTH, AND THAT SPHERE CANNOT BE FILLED WITHOUT THEM. THE MONEY OF THE CATHOLIC IS AS GOOD TO BUY AND TO SELL WITH AS THAT OF A PROTESTANT, AND THE LABOR OF THE FOREIGNER AS NECESSARY, IN ITS PLACE, AS THAT OF THE NATIVE.

Tensions between Protestants and Catholics began to relax as people began to recognize their common interests. And when young Catholic men began courting young Methodist women, new bridges of understanding and acceptance were formed. To join the city's original Scotch-Irish and Virginian founders, immigrants from France, Ireland, Germany and Switzerland, along with African-Americans, both free and slave, brought their native languages, customs, skills and personalities to Louisville and created new American homes and institutions. The preservation and neighborly blending of these native attributes inspires the community's unique flavor and character.

A Post-Virginian Louisville Emerges

A news article in the May 5, 1861, edition of the *Daily Democrat* confirms the new international flavor of Louisville. Bullitt Street, a narrow alley between Fourth and Fifth Streets, led uphill to Main Street from the river's edge. A minor story about a house fire features a Scot, an Italian and a Frenchman, all new citizens to Louisville.

FIRE – ABOUT 1 O'CLOCK THIS MORNING, A HOUSE ON THE WEST SIDE OF BULLITT STREET, NEAR THE RIVER, WAS DISCOVERED TO BE ON FIRE. THE ALARM SOON BROUGHT ENGINES TO THE SPOT, BUT NOT HOWEVER, UNTIL THE INTERIOR OF THE BUILDING WAS CONSUMED. THE LOWER STORY WAS USED AS A BOX FACTORY, AND THE UPPER PART AS A DWELLING.

THE HOUSE AND ENTIRE CONTENTS WERE CONSUMED. ARGUS KECK, AND AN ITALIAN BY THE NAME OF JOHN REPPETTO, JUMPED FROM THE SECOND OR THIRD STORY WINDOW TO SAVE THEIR LIVES. NEITHER WERE SERIOUSLY HURT. REPPETTO AND FAMILY LOST EVERYTHING, INCLUDING A CONSIDERABLE AMOUNT OF MONEY. THE FIRE WAS DISCOVERED BY OFFICER JUNOT. THE TIMELY ARRIVAL OF THE FIRE ENGINES SAVED THE ADJOINING BUILDINGS.

The decade of the 1850s, the "Palmy Days of Steamboating" in Louisville, had prepared the city for its next great challenge. War was brewing, but the Falls City was beginning to grow stronger and more united. In 1865 – ten years after Bloody Monday – Louisville elected as its new mayor Philip Tomppert, a native of Germany.

Mooring rings in the Louisville wharf, a reminder of the city's origin as a riverport, were integral parts of the landing operations of steamboats and barges. Massive iron rings were embedded into the pavement at various heights to allow mooring at any stage of the river's elevation. *(Photo courtesy of Scott Nussbaum)*

War Comes to the City's Doorstep
(1861-1865)

In God's name, why do not our people awake to a sense of their danger? Why not fortify the city? Let the work commence immediately. Let every able-bodied man go at it. Stop all business; close all hotels, and send officers and soldiers to their camps. Be in earnest. Spades are trumps and let them be played boldly and vigorously.

— Louisville Daily Journal - 1862

Every military strategist since George Rogers Clark recognized Louisville as the defensive keystone to the Ohio River and its tributaries. Control the Falls and you control the river and all its traffic. The Ohio River, the only natural barrier between Union and Confederate states, was a grand prize and of vital importance in the early days of the War of the Rebellion or, as it is better remembered, the American Civil War.

At the outbreak of the war Louisville was a commercial city with strong ties to northern industries and a long tradition of loyalty to Whig political principles. Slave-owning Louisville and the rest of Kentucky were at growing odds, since city leaders viewed the Confederate cause as bad for business. James Guthrie, president of the L&N railroad, bent or broke all rules concerning shipments of supplies to southern states during their process of secession. Guthrie kept the tracks humming with every available locomotive and boxcar headed south, loaded with soon-to-be quarantined military and civilian merchandise. He ignored orders to cease shipments until all possible profit was wrung from the southern trade; then he reversed position and began fulfilling contracts for the federal government.

Kentucky had attempted to declare itself a neutral state, but that fiction was shattered when Confederate general Leonidas Polk invaded the Commonwealth and invested the small southwestern river town of Columbus. Two days later, a freshly minted Union general, Ulysses S. Grant, countered the invasion of neutral Kentucky by landing on the grounds of the U.S. Marine Hospital at Paducah. Sam Grant was still dressed in a civilian suit, since his newly ordered general's uniform had not yet been delivered. The Civil War had come to Kentucky.

Prior to the outbreak of hostilities, Louisville's leaders were being pressed with new challenges. A recently adopted Kentucky law made it illegal for any free African-American to remain in the state. The harsh application of the Free Negro Law was documented in the January 18, 1861, edition of the *Louisville Courier*:

IN THE POLICE COURT YESTERDAY, JACOB MITCHUM, A FREE NEGRO, WAS PRESENTED ON A FELONY WARRANT, ACCUSING HIM OF COMING TO THE STATE CONTRARY TO THE ACT PASSED BY THE LAST LEGISLATURE. IT APPEARED THAT JACOB LIVED BACK OF NEW ALBANY A SHORT DISTANCE, AND HAD COME TO PORTLAND TO SEE ABOUT GOING ON A BOAT. HE HAD NOT BEEN IN KENTUCKY MORE THAN HALF AN HOUR BEFORE HE WAS ARRESTED. HE WAS COMMITTED TO JAIL IN DEFAULT OF BAIL TO ANSWER A FELONY AT THE CIRCUIT COURT. THIS LAW IN REGARD TO FREE NEGROES FROM OTHER STATES TO COME HERE FOR

ANY PURPOSE WHATEVER, AND IF A FREE NEGRO OF THIS STATE CROSSES THE RIVER, HE CANNOT RETURN WITHOUT BEING GUILTY OF A FELONY. FREE NEGROES RESIDING IN FREE STATES, WHO MAY COME HERE ON BOATS, THOUGH ENGAGED ON THEM, ARE ALSO LIABLE TO BE PUNISHED FOR A FELONY. WE UNDERSTAND THAT IT IS THE INTENTION OF THE POLICE TO ENFORCE THE LAW TO THE VERY LETTER.

Pressures built as old friends and relatives took opposing views on the question of secession. States Rights Democrats maintained their privilege of withdrawing from the Union, while the recently elected Republican branch of the Whig Party disagreed. It was up to the newly inaugurated president of the United States, Kentuckian Abraham Lincoln, and his attorney general, James Speed of Farmington, to enforce the nation's laws.

But just prior to hostilities, Louisville gave itself one last chance to gather and celebrate the one event all could agreed on, the annual birthday salute to General George Washington. The Saturday morning edition of the *Daily Democrat* of February 23, 1861, described an exciting day in the city:

THE 22ND OF FEBRUARY, 1861, WAS A GALA DAY IN LOUISVILLE, AND THE SKY WAS AS SERENE, THE SUN AS BRILLIANT AND CHEERING AS THE MOST SANGUINE UNION MAN COULD WISH. THE PECULIAR CONDITION OF POLITICAL AFFAIRS, THE DANGERS THAT ENVIRON THE UNION, AND THE TREASON OF PARTISAN LEADERS, RENDERED THE OCCASION ONE OF INTENSE INTEREST. THE NATAL DAY OF GEORGE WASHINGTON WAS CHOSEN WITH PECULIAR APTITUDE FOR THE ELEVATION OF THE NATIONAL ENSIGN UPON OUR MAGNIFICENT COURT-HOUSE, AND EVERY CITIZEN, NO MATTER WHAT WERE HIS FORMER POLITICAL ASSOCIATIONS, WHO STILL REMAINED LOYAL TO THE FLAG OF HIS COUNTRY, COULD NOT BUT BE FILLED WITH PATRIOTIC EMOTIONS.

THE DEMONSTRATION WAS A GLORIOUS ONE — WORTHY OF THE METROPOLIS OF KENTUCKY. NOT LESS THAN 50,000 PERSONS PARTICIPATED IN THE DEMONSTRATION AT THE COURT-HOUSE, AND TESTIFIED THEIR LOYALTY TO THE STARS AND STRIPES.

THE ACTION OF THE COMMON COUNCIL IN THE MATTER IS FRESH IN EVERY MIND. THE CITY FATHERS MADE AN APPROPRIATION FOR THE PURPOSE OF PLACING THE FLAG OF THE UNION UPON THE COURT-HOUSE, AND VERY PROPERLY DELAYED THE CEREMONY UNTIL YESTERDAY, THAT IT MIGHT BE CONDUCTED WITH PECULIAR EMPHASIS.

THE MILITARY LOOKED AND BEHAVED MOST ADMIRABLY, AND MADE A VERY FAVORABLE IMPRESSION UPON THE PUBLIC. AS THE FIRST PUBLIC PARADE OF THE BATTALION, THE STATE GUARD HAVE EVERY REASON TO BE PROUD OF THEIR APPEARANCE AND PERFORMANCE. AFTER THE CEREMONIES THE BATTALION FOLLOWED THE PRESCRIBED LINE OF MARCH, AND WERE REVIEWED ON THE COMMON BACK OF BROADWAY, NEAR FLOYD STREET, BY GENERAL BUCKNER.

One year and three days later that same officer, Confederate General Simon Bolivar Buckner, surrendered Fort Donelson to his old Army friend, U.S. Grant, giving Buckner the dubious honor of being the first Confederate commander to surrender an army. He earned this humiliation when his two superior officers, General Gideon Pillow and General John B. Floyd, escaped the fort prior to its fall. Floyd, the former governor of Virginia and failed U.S. Secretary of War under James Buchanan, was the grandson of Beargrass pioneer John Floyd.

October 1861 saw Louisville threatened by invasion and the city woefully unprepared. Secretary of War Simon Cameron visited the city to meet with

An Ohio regiment of Union troops, serving as bodyguards for General Don Carlos Buell, is shown arriving at the Louisville wharf in time to hastily reinforce the city's defenses. This engraving from *Harper's Magazine* indicated the national significance of preserving Louisville, and Kentucky, as Union territory.

its temporary commanding officer, General William Tecumseh Sherman. After assessing the military situation in Louisville, Cameron sent the following telegram to President Lincoln: "Matters are in a much worse condition than I expected to find them. A large number of troops needed here immediately."

One week later, Louisvillians experienced a great sense of relief with the report of Union soldiers arriving in town. The *Daily Democrat* of October 23, 1861, trumpeted the good news:

ARRIVAL OF THE FLEET

CONTRARY TO GENERAL EXPECTATIONS THE FLEET OF BOATS, SIX IN NUMBER, BEARING THE BRIGADE OF PENNSYLVANIA TROOPS, ARRIVED AT OUR WHARF ABOUT FIVE O'CLOCK LAST EVENING. THE FLEET MADE A MAGNIFICENT APPEARANCE AS IT CAME DOWN THE RIVER FROM SIX MILE ISLAND. AT THAT POINT THE ENTIRE SIX FORMED IN LINE, ABREAST, AND STEAMED DOWN TOWARDS THE CITY IN THAT ORDER, TILL THEY ARRIVED AT THE FOOT OF WILLOW BAR, WHEN THEY BROKE LINE AND WHEELED AROUND TO THE CITY WHARF, LANDING AT THE FOOT OF FIFTH STREET. THE REPORT THAT THEY WERE IN SIGHT SOON SPREAD, AND THE WHARF WAS LINED WITH THOUSANDS OF PEOPLE, MOSTLY WOMEN AND CHILDREN.

THE FLEET CONSISTS OF THE FOLLOWING STEAMERS: *J. W. HAILMAN*, *CLARA POE*, *ARGONAUT*, *MODERATOR*, *SIR WM. WALLACE* AND *SILVER WAVE* — EACH BOAT CARRYING ABOUT 500 MEN. THIS BRIGADE IS COMPOSED OF SOME OF THE FINEST-LOOKING MEN WE HAVE SEEN ANYWHERE, ALL LARGE, HEALTHY, ABLE-BODIED MEN, IN EXCELLENT HEALTH AND FINE SPIRITS.

WE LEARN THAT THE OFFICERS OF THE BRIGADE WITH GEN. SHERMAN AND STAFF, PARTOOK OF A SUMPTUOUS ENTERTAINMENT SET FOR THEM BY CAPTAIN SILAS F. MILLER, THE WHOLE-SOULED HOST OF THE GALT HOUSE.

THE TROOPS REMAINED ON THE BOATS LAST NIGHT, AND WILL TAKE UP THEIR LINE OF MARCH THIS MORNING FOR THE NASHVILLE DEPOT, ON THEIR WAY TO SUCH DESTINATION AS GEN. SHERMAN MAY ASSIGN THEM.

As the army presence in Louisville increased, most military activities took place on, or near, the waterfront. The *Daily Democrat* reported on army routine on the Louisville wharf:

THE EIGHTEENTH REGULARS – THIS SPLENDID BODY OF MEN ARE AT PRESENT ON THE *TELEGRAPH NO. 3*, AT THE FOOT OF THIRD STREET. YESTERDAY AFTERNOON THEY MARCHED THROUGH THE CITY...AS THEY PASSED THEY EXCITED THE WARMEST APPROVAL FOR THEIR PRECISION IN STEP AND DRILL.

WE UNDERSTAND THAT AT FOUR O'CLOCK THIS AFTERNOON A DRESS PARADE WILL BE HELD BY THE 18TH ON THE LEVEE, AND THAT AT PARADE A SERGEANT WILL BE DEPOSED TO THE RANKS AND A PRIVATE PROMOTED TO HIS PLACE, AS A PUNISHMENT FOR SOME INFRACTION OF MILITARY LAW.

GENERAL NELSON'S BRIGADE HAS BEEN ENTIRELY RE-FURNISHED WITH COMFORTABLE CLOTHING, OVERCOATS, &C, AND ARE NOW READY FOR THE FIELD.

"...to sustain the reputation of Kentucky for a large-hearted hospitality."

In April 1862 the war turned truly deadly with the first major bloodbath experienced in the small Tennessee community of Pittsburgh Landing, or as it would become better known,

Shiloh. Two brutal days of battle left the army of General Grant reeling from casualties but in possession of the field of battle. The Union army of 65,000 men suffered more than 13,000 casualties including dead, wounded and missing in action. The Confederate army of 44,000 lost 10,700 men and its commander General Albert Sidney Johnston. It was Shiloh, more than any previous battle, which convinced Americans they were in for a long and deadly fight to the finish.

The inadequate and ill-supplied medical corps of the Union Army was unable to treat even a fraction of the wounded following the battle. Fortunately, Louisville was the headquarters for the Kentucky branch of the U.S. Sanitary Commission, a national benevolent society dedicated to helping soldiers and sailors receive adequate nutrition, medicines and supplies, humanitarian treatment and assistance with such routine tasks as letter-writing, reading to the wounded or comforting personal visits. The Louisville waterfront saw frantic efforts to locate and load relief boats with needed supplies.

Local newspapers reported the spirited response Louisvillians gave to the survivors of Shiloh:

Daily Democrat, April 15, 1862
THE SANITARY COMMISSION FOR THE DEPARTMENT OF KENTUCKY RESPECTFULLY AND GRATEFULLY ACKNOWLEDGES THE BENEFICENT CONTRIBUTIONS OF THE CITIZENS OF LOUISVILLE, OF VARIOUS PORTIONS OF KENTUCKY, AND OF SEVERAL PARTS OF INDIANA, FOR THE CARE, COMFORT AND RESTORATION OF THE WOUNDED AT PITTSBURGH LANDING, TENNESSEE. BY THE PROMPT MUNIFICENCE THAT RESPONDED TO THE APPEAL OF THE SANITARY COMMISSION WE WERE ENABLED TO SEND THE STEAMER *E. H. FAIRCHILD* OFF ON THURSDAY NIGHT ON HER MISSION OF MERCY AND LOVE, RICHLY FREIGHTED WITH AN ABUNDANCE OF THE

ARTICLES MOST NEEDED BY THE SUFFERING MARTYRS FOR THEIR COUNTRY'S SALVATION. IN REPRESENTING KENTUCKY IN THIS WORK, WE FELT THAT WE HAD A DOUBLE RESPONSIBILITY ENTRUSTED TO US. WE HAD NOT ONLY TO REPRESENT THE COMMON SYMPATHY OF AN ENLIGHTENED HUMANITY, BUT TO SUSTAIN THE REPUTATION OF KENTUCKY FOR A LARGE-HEARTED HOSPITALITY.

The U.S. Sanitary Commission was a cross between the U.S.O. and the Red Cross and it provided the pattern for the future development of both organizations. A letter to Louisvillians from their national executive secretary provided sensible advice to the public wanting to assist the soldiers. Thirty years later, the executive secretary would figure prominently in Louisville's plans for public parks.

THE SANITARY COMMISSION, AT THE REQUEST OF GENERAL HALLECK, COMMANDER-IN-CHIEF OF THE ARMIES OF THE UNITED STATES, MOST EARNESTLY ADVISES AGAINST THE PRACTICE OF SENDING PRESENTS TO SOLDIERS OF ARTICLES WHICH IT IS SUPPOSED WILL ADD TO THE CONVENIENCES OF THEIR CAMP LIFE.

THE HOSPITAL OF A REGIMENT IN THE FIELD SHOULD BE SUPPLIED WITH NOTHING BUT THE BAREST NECESSITIES FOR THE TEMPORARY TREATMENT OF THE SICK, WHO IN ALL SERIOUS CASES ARE REMOVED AS FAST AS POSSIBLE TO GENERAL HOSPITALS...

FRED. LAW OLMSTED, GENERAL SECRETARY

By September 1862 a full-scale invasion of Kentucky by two Confederate commands, led by General Braxton Bragg and General Kirby Smith, focused on capturing central Kentucky before proceeding to conquer Louisville. Martial law was declared and Colonel Henry Dent, provost-general, issued the following orders:

BILLIARD SALOONS, LIVERY STABLES, NEWSPAPER PRINTING OFFICES, BAKE HOUSES, DRUG STORES, BARBER SHOPS, BATH HOUSES, UNDERTAKERS, CIGAR ESTABLISHMENTS (CONNECTED WITH HOTELS), EATING HOUSES (IF BARS ARE ATTACHED THE LIQUORS MUST BE REMOVED AND THE PROPRIETOR MUST GIVE POSITIVE PLEDGE NOT TO SELL OR EVADE THIS ORDER DIRECTLY OR INDIRECTLY), CAN KEEP OPEN THEIR ESTABLISHMENTS AS USUAL.

WHOLESALE AND RETAIL GROCERIES ARE PERMITTED TO BE KEPT OPEN UNTIL 4 O'CLOCK P.M., BUT NO LIQUOR TO BE SOLD.

PROOF OF LOYALTY OF ALL PERSONS OVER 45 AND UNDER 18 YEARS OF AGE, AND WHO HAVE NOT ENROLLED THEMSELVES, WILL BE SUFFICIENT PASS THROUGHOUT THE CITY.

THE OATH OF ALLEGIANCE BEFORE ANY MAGISTRATE IS THE TEST OF LOYALTY REQUIRED.

In a letter to the editor of the *Louisville Daily Journal* on September 16, 1862, a concerned citizen sought to convince Louisvillians that their city was threatened and immediate preparations were needed:

THE PEOPLE OF LOUISVILLE DO NOT SEEM TO HAVE A JUST APPRECIATION OF THEIR PRESENT POSITION. THEY ARE INEXCUSABLY SUPINE AT A TIME WHEN REBEL CANNON ARE THUNDERING ALMOST ON THE VERY CONFINES OF OUR COUNTY...FRANKFORT IS IN POSSESSION OF THE INSURGENTS AND IS BEING FORTIFIED BY THEM; BRAGG'S ARMY IS AT GLASGOW SOME THIRTY MILES NEARER TO LOUISVILLE THAN BOWLING GREEN, WHERE BUELL'S FORCES ARE SAID TO BE CONCENTRATING, AND THE BLUE GRASS REGION IS OCCUPIED BY TWENTY THOUSAND

A panorama of the Louisville waterfront in 1862 shows the chaos that was a daily occurrence during the most threatening days of the Civil War in Louisville. Stacks of arms and formations of troops are mixed with civilian passengers rushing to steamboats for evacuation out of the city. *(Filson Historical Society.CIV11)*

ARMED AND DESPERATE MEN — REBELS, EACH ONE OF WHOM IS AN OFFICER, BECAUSE HE KNOWS WHAT HE IS AFTER, AND IS INTENTLY ENGAGED, SOUL AND BODY, IN ITS ATTAINMENT….HOW IS IT WITH LOUISVILLE? ARE HER PROMINENT MEN AND HER MILITARY COMMANDERS MAKING THE PROPER PREPARATIONS FOR HER DEFENSE? IF WE DO NOT PREPARE OURSELVES — IF LOUISVILLE IS NOT FORTIFIED, IT WILL BE TAKEN AND GIVEN UP TO CONFEDERATE PILLAGE AND MAGNAUMITY. IN GOD'S NAME, WHY DO NOT OUR PEOPLE AWAKE TO A SENSE OF THEIR DANGER?

General William "Bull" Nelson took military command of Louisville on September 19, 1862. Nelson, a massive 300-pound former Navy officer, had earned his rugged nickname by his aggressiveness and stubbornness. He desperately set about preparing Louisville for an impending assault by Confederate troops under General Braxton Bragg, while praying that Union General Don Carlos Buell would be able to reach the city before the rebels attacked. Both commanders drove their soldiers through drought-plagued central Kentucky to be the first to arrive in Louisville. After gathering a small fleet of six gunboats to patrol the river, Nelson began preparing the city as rebel forces captured the telegraph office in nearby La Grange.

SEPTEMBER 23, 1862 - CAPTAIN SHERLEY WILL HAVE TWO BOATS READY AT THE FOOT OF THIRD AND FOURTH STREETS FOR THE RECEPTION OF WOMEN AND CHILDREN.

THE PUBLIC SCHOOLS – THE CITY SCHOOLS WERE INFORMALLY SUSPENDED YESTERDAY. IT WILL BE SEEN FROM THE CARD OF THE SUPERINTENDENT AND SECRETARY, IN ANOTHER COLUMN, THAT ALL THE SCHOOLS HAVE BEEN CLOSED UNTIL FURTHER NOTICE.

THE WOMEN AND CHILDREN OF THIS CITY WILL PREPARE TO LEAVE THE CITY WITHOUT DELAY.

THE JEFFERSONVILLE FERRY WILL BE USED EXCLUSIVELY FOR MILITARY PURPOSES. PRIVATE VEHICLES WILL NOT BE ALLOWED TO GO ABOARD OF THE FERRY BOATS WITHOUT A SPECIAL PERMIT FROM THESE HEADQUARTERS. PERSONS ON FOOT WILL PASS AS USUAL. THIS ORDER WILL GO INTO EFFECT AT 12 NOON TODAY.

Mayor Delph issued his own proclamation:

ALL CITIZENS ARE HEREBY DIRECTED TO CLOSE THEIR PLACES OF BUSINESS WITHIN THE CITY. THE CITIZENS ARE CALLED UPON TO ASSEMBLE AT THE COURTHOUSE THIS DAY, AT 4 O'CLOCK P.M., FOR ORGANIZATION OF SUCH CITIZENS AS ARE WILLING TO DEFEND THE CITY.

While the city was greatly relieved when General Buell and 55,000 Union troops reached Louisville on September 24, the situation remained dire. With rebel armies advancing from the south, Louisville was being boxed into a corner with its back to the river. Evacuating the entire city on ferryboats was impossible so officials agreed upon an alternative plan, the construction of two floating pontoon bridges across the Ohio. One was placed in Portland, at almost exactly the spot which would later host the Kentucky and Indiana Terminal Railroad Bridge. The other was constructed east of town at the same location of the future Big Four Bridge. Both were made by lashing together empty coal barges and decking them over with heavy wooden planks capable of withstanding the weight of horses, wagons, carriages and terrified civilians.

The brief careers of the first two (temporary) bridges over the Ohio at Louisville are told in accounts from the *Daily Journal*:

During the Civil War, the first Galt House Hotel served as a meeting place for society ladies, as well as leading Union generals like Grant and Sherman.

October 3, 1862

THE JEFFERSONVILLE FERRY COMPANY HAS TAKEN CHARGE OF THE PONTOON BRIDGE ACROSS THE RIVER AT THIS POINT, AND HAS DISCONTINUED THE USE OF THE FERRYBOATS.

October 15, 1862

REMOVAL OF THE PONTOON-BRIDGE

WE LEARN THAT THE PONTOON BRIDGE ACROSS THE RIVER AT PORTLAND IS TO BE REMOVED BY ORDER OF GEN. BOYLE: IT BEING A HINDRANCE TO NAVIGATION.

October 29, 1862

THE PONTOON BRIDGE BETWEEN THIS CITY AND JEFFERSONVILLE IS TO BE REMOVED AT ONCE, A PORTION OF THE STRUCTURE HAVING BEEN CLEARED AWAY YESTERDAY. THE JEFFERSONVILLE FERRYBOATS HAVE RESUMED THEIR TRIPS, LANDING AT THE FOOT OF SECOND STREET AT THIS CITY.

September 25, 1862

THE PONTOON BRIDGE

THE PONTOON BRIDGE BUILDING ACROSS THE RIVER AT NEW ALBANY WAS TO HAVE BEEN COMPLETED YESTERDAY. A DOUBLE TRACK PLANK ROAD IS BEING LAID ACROSS THE SAND BAR FROM THE BRIDGE TO THE BASE OF THE HILL AT THE LOWER PORTLAND LANDING.

CAPTAIN PINK VARBLE HAS BEEN AWARDED THE CONTRACT FOR THE CONSTRUCTION OF THE PONTOON BRIDGE ACROSS THE OHIO AT TWO MILE ISLAND (TOWHEAD ISLAND), AND WAS VIGOROUSLY ENGAGED YESTERDAY IN THE CONSTRUCTION OF THE WORK.

September 27, 1862

PONTOON BRIDGE AT PORTLAND

THE PONTOON BRIDGE BETWEEN NEW ALBANY AND PORTLAND WAS COMPLETED AT FIVE O'CLOCK YESTERDAY AFTERNOON. THE BRIDGE WILL TAKE THE PLACE OF THE FERRY BOATS TODAY; THE BOATS DISCONTINUING THEIR REGULAR TRIPS. THE AMOUNT OF FERRIAGE USUALLY CHARGED ON THE BOATS WILL BE COLLECTED FROM PERSONS CROSSING THE BRIDGE.

Small dramas were played out on the Louisville waterfront daily. In early October there was a report of a rebel spy arrested at the ferry-landing trying to cross over to Indiana without a pass. So many military supplies arrived at the wharf that roustabouts and stevedores raised their pay demands to the unheard of rate of thirty cents an hour. Violent incidents between Union troops and local citizens increased dramatically.

General Buell, by force-marching his Union troops through drought-parched Kentucky, secured Louisville and began to push his adversary, General Braxton Bragg, southward. The two armies would stumble into each other while searching for water at Perryville, Kentucky. Braxton Bragg, first made famous by General Zachary Taylor's instruction at Buena Vista, "A little more grape if you please, Mr. Bragg," began his retreat from Kentucky. From this time forward, the Commonwealth was safely preserved as part of the Union.

Perryville was the only major battle waged in Kentucky. It produced some of the highest casualty rates of the Civil War, leaving thousands of wounded soldiers of both sides on the ground. Once again, emergency missions from the Louisville branch of the Sanitary Commission made a great difference as the wounded were picked up and transported to Louisville for medical care.

Steamboats were the most humane way to transport the wounded, and boats were fitted out as hospital ships or floating infirmaries. The casualties of Perryville began landing at the wharves of Portland and Louisville, disgorging their suffering passengers. Louisville was named the medical center for the western theater of the war, and eventually nineteen different hospitals were located in the city or across the river in southern Indiana. School buildings were closed and converted into hospitals, large homes of departed secessionists were seized and even the Kentucky School for the Blind was briefly commandeered.

Louisvillians continued to provide humane care to soldiers of both armies. In May 1863 the *Daily Journal* made the following announcement:

WE ARE GRATIFIED TO ANNOUNCE THAT PRESIDENT LINCOLN HAS APPOINTED THE REVEREND B. H. GOTTHELF, THE MINISTER OF THE GERMAN JEWISH CONGREGATION OF THIS CITY, AS HOSPITAL CHAPLAIN, TO BE STATIONED HERE. THE FACT THAT A VERY RESPECTABLE NUMBER OF JEWISH SOLDIERS HAVE BEEN AND STILL ARE RECEIVING MEDICAL TREATMENT AT OUR HOSPITALS, HAVING BEEN BROUGHT TO THE NOTICE OF THE HON. ROBERT MALLORY, HE MADE AN APPLICATION FOR THE APPOINTMENT OF MR.

GOTTHELF, WHICH WE TOOK PLEASURE, WITH OTHER CITIZENS, IN ENDORSING. THESE INVALIDS CAN NOW ENJOY THE INSTRUCTION AND CONSOLATION OF A MINISTER OF THEIR OWN FAITH, AND WE ARE, THEREFORE, CONVINCED THAT THE APPOINTMENT WAS AS TIMELY AS IT IS WELL MERITED.

Rabbi Gotthelf was only the second Jewish army chaplain in American history, and he joined other religious like the Sisters of Charity of Nazareth in administering to needy soldiers. The Reverend F. H. Bushnell, an inspector with the Sanitary Commission, reported on the conditions of Louisville's multiple new hospitals in February of 1863.

THE ARRANGEMENTS FOR THE CARE AND COMFORT OF SICK AND WOUNDED SOLDIERS ARE NOW FAR MORE COMPLETE THAN AT ANY OTHER TIME DURING THE WAR. THIS IS VERY APPARENT IN THE HOSPITALS OF LOUISVILLE AND VICINITY. WITHOUT ATTEMPTING TO ESTIMATE THE GREAT DIFFICULTIES IN WHICH THE BRANCH COMMISSION OF KENTUCKY BORE A LION'S SHARE, IT IS VERY EVIDENT THAT THESE PRESENT CONDITIONS FORMS A MOST PLEASING CONTRAST WITH THEIR PAST CHARACTER, NOT ONLY IN THE STYLE OF THE BUILDINGS, BUT IN MANY OTHER RESPECTS.

THE BUILDINGS NOW IN USE ARE GENERALLY THE BEST TO BE OBTAINED, THOUGH ALL ARE LESS COMPLETE AND CONVENIENT THAN IF CONSTRUCTED FOR THE PURPOSE. TEN OF THEM ARE SCHOOL-HOUSES, BUILT BUT A FEW YEARS SINCE, HAVING HIGH CEILINGS, AND WELL ARRANGED FOR VENTILATION. THEY ARE SEPARATED ON ALL SIDES FROM OTHER BUILDINGS, AND ONLY NEEDED TO MAKE THEM SATISFACTORY ADDITIONAL FRAME BUILDINGS FOR KITCHENS, WASH-ROOM, STORE-ROOM, AND DEAD-HOUSE. SOME OF THEM ARE YET UNSUPPLIED WITH THESE CONVENIENCES, AND ARE MANAGING WITH DIFFICULTY.

Three of the private houses in the outskirts of the city are elegant and costly residences, with all the appliances of modern luxury. The Griffin House, on the Newburg Road, about four miles from the city, is an unfinished building in the interior, and has much less the appearance of comfort than the others. This is the hospital for measles patients, and the greatest difficulty connected with it seems to be in the distance the sick must be transported from other hospitals or boats.

Hospital No. 7 is about two miles from the city, near Park Barracks. It is composed of frame buildings, erected by the government, and very well adapted to the purpose. This is the largest hospital in its capacity being seven hundred patients.

The cleanliness and order generally prevailing in every department, the breathing room given to each patient being not less than from 800 to 1,200 feet, and the attention given to ventilation has been so uniformly good that I have not in the past month met the odor so common even in the best of city hospitals.

The Griffin House on Newburg Road was known as the Eruptive Hospital and housed boy-soldiers suffering from measles or mumps. These two childhood diseases ravaged both armies, but especially the Confederate, because their primarily rural soldiers had never been exposed and had no immunity. This hospital was located far in the country to protect the population from infection. The Eruptive Hospital was on the grounds of today's Bellarmine University. The huge Parks Barracks hospital is also associated with a modern educational facility, and was sited on the Belknap campus of the University of Louisville.

Louisville was recognized as an important center for medical care, instruction and research. Home to the most active United States Marine Hospital, and bolstered by dozens of respected physician-professors at the University School of Medicine, Louisville's success in administering nineteen general hospitals drew national attention and admiration. The Louisville Sanitary Commission was applauded as one of the finest charities in the nation after it constructed a large Soldiers' Home at Tenth and Broadway. Their meticulous record-keeping reveals that during the four years of the war, over 420,000 Union soldiers passed through this facility.

"They have sacrificed much, endured much…"

The tensions of the time required some relief through amusement or diversion. A local daredevil drew attention in January 1864 by duplicating a scene from *Uncle Tom's Cabin*:

PERILOUS VOYAGE – A MAN COMES FROM JEFFERSONVILLE TO THIS CITY ON THE FLOATING ICE

One of the most hazardous feats ever attempted in these parts, and one which equals anything of the kind that we have ever read, or heard of, was accomplished yesterday by a citizen of our sister city, Jeffersonville, by the name of Wm. H. Harrington. This gentleman desiring to come to this city, and not wishing to take the circuitous route by New Albany, came to the conclusion that he could cross the cakes of floating ice. He accordingly commenced his perilous voyage, starting from the Indiana shore on one of the cakes of ice, and after a short but trying voyage, he reached its shore in perfect safety. The trip was made by jumping from one cake to another, Mr. H. selecting his foothold with great care. A large number of citizens who saw

A frozen Ohio River is not just an historic occurrence, as demonstrated by this photo taken in the 1990s. Severe freezes during the age of steamboats stopped all maritime traffic, including regular ferry service across the river. *(WDC photo by Michael Kimmel)*

Mr. H. start from the other shore, watched him with great anxiety, expecting every minute to see him carried over the falls and dashed to pieces by the running ice; and all were rejoiced and surprised when they saw that he had reached this side of the river in perfect safety. To accomplish this great feat it required undaunted courage, and this Mr. H. possessed to a great degree. The crossing was made without the assistance of a pole, or even a stick, and when this fact is taken into consideration, we may safely say that this is the most extraordinary feat ever accomplished in this or any other section of the country. The current at this point, owing to the suction of the falls, is very swift, and as the ice is carried over the great Falls of the Ohio, it is broken to pieces; and had Mr. H. missed his foothold, or been carried over on one of the cakes of ice, a horrible death would certainly have been his fate.

The city was also charmed by periodic visits to the Louisville stage by the young tragedian whose name would soon become infamous.

November 8, 1862

THEATER – Mr. Wilkes Booth closes his engagement this evening with *The Corsican Brothers*. His success has been marked, and he has added both to his fame and his finances. We trust he will give us another visit in the spring. Mr. Hackett will appear next week.

After the conflict at Perryville, Louisville was not in danger of invasion, but problems were growing between the citizens and the Union soldiers occupying the city. Many local people were appalled at their harsh treatment by federal troops, and Louisville resented perceived insults. A local commentator, signing himself as "Civis," wrote to the *Daily Journal* in November 1862 with an important rhetorical question, "Where Is Dixie?"

I have never had a very definite notion about the precise boundaries of the mythological land of Dixie. Can you throw any light on the subject? I have been accustomed to locate that "happy land far, far away," under the shadow of the "stars and bars," somewhere within the limits of the so-called Confederate States. But it seems different notions prevail, especially north of the Ohio, and that we in Kentucky are by no means the gainers by such notions.

I have taken some pains to ascertain the sentiments of the troops passing through this city, and I have almost unanimously found them to be, that they have arrived in "Dixie," in the land of their enemy, and are "to be let loose" to confiscate and appropriate or destroy as they please, so that they escape the censure of their officers....They have ignorantly sneered at our former "neutrality," and so often spoken lightly of our Unionism,

maintained at the expense of riven families and bleeding hearts, bitter reproaches, and often life itself, that our hard lot of being the outside row in the Union cornfields is now made harder by these reckless or vicious Union ploughmen trampling out the last vestiges of vigorous life.

I heard the Captain of a veteran company, landing at our wharf, say, "Louisville is a secesh hole." But that Captain was a German and a foreigner, and therefore his ignorance was much more excusable than that of an Ohio Colonel, who, in a neighboring county in Kentucky, recently asserted in rough language that there was no Unionism in Kentucky, and that its profession was all hypocrisy.

Do, Messrs. Editors, let our Northern friends know where "Dixie" is.

Mayor John Delph also commented on the growing tensions when he issued a statement from his office on November 20, 1862:

The people of Kentucky and especially those in the city have complained of nothing whatever that they deem necessary for the preservation and perpetuation of the Union. They have sacrificed much, endured much, and are ready, if necessary, to sacrifice and endure much more for those desirable objects....A great number of letters have been addressed to me, as Mayor of the city, by unfledged military officers, abusing the civil authorities in the coarsest and grossest style, merely because we were enforcing the laws of the Commonwealth and the city. Louisville is denounced by rebels as a den of abolitionists and Lincolnites, and by some characters who profess to be Union men, the

CITY IS GRAVELY CHARGED WITH BEING A NEST OF NEGRO THIEVES AND KIDNAPPERS, WITH KINDRED VARIATIONS OF THESE EPITHETS.

In the dying days of the Confederacy, many Louisvillians began to identify with their cause. It has often been said that Kentucky was the only state to join the Confederacy after Appomattox, and Louisville began questioning their long-term interests. The city had prospered greatly during the conflict with massive profits earned in railroad and steamboat shipping, pork-packing, quartermaster purchases and health care expansion, but the old ways were changing. Even the city's skyline was in flux.

"For years the Galt House has been associated with the name of Louisville…"

In January 1865 an unimaginable event took place when the beloved original Galt House Hotel burned to the ground.

THE GALT HOUSE IS IN RUINS! THE BEAUTIFUL STRUCTURE HAS SUCCUMBED TO THE RAVAGES OF THE DESTROYING ELEMENT. THE FIRE HAS DONE ITS WORK. THE STATELY EDIFICE, SO LONG THE PRIDE AND FAME OF OUR CITY, IS NOW A HUGE, UNSHAPELY MASS. NOTHING BUT THE NAKED, BLACKENED, CRUMBLING WALLS OF THE BUILDING REMAIN TO MARK THE SPOT, AND TOWER, SEPULCHRAL LIKE, OVER THE PILES OF RUBBISH AND THE WASTE OF RUIN. FOR YEARS THE GALT HOUSE HAS BEEN ASSOCIATED WITH THE NAME OF LOUISVILLE, AND THE ONE WAS NOT MORE WIDELY KNOWN THAN THE OTHER. WE CAN GAZE UPON THE HEAP OF RUINS ONLY WITH FEELINGS OF SADNESS.

MANY FOND ASSOCIATIONS WERE CONNECTED WITH THE BUILDING, BUT NEARLY ALL HAVE BEEN SWEPT AWAY BY THE RUTHLESS HAND OF FIRE.…THE FAMOUS MEN OF THE LAND HAVE MINGLED WITH THE THRONGS IN THE PARLORS, TROD THE HALLS WITH STATELY STEPS, AND WOOED SWEET SLEEP UPON THE DOWNY BEDS OF THE ROOMS. IN THE SPACIOUS DINING SALOON HUNDREDS OF GUESTS DAILY GATHERED AROUND THE TABLES, AND THE BUZZ OF WHITE-LIVERIED SERVANTS, THE FLASHES OF MERRIMENT, THE EXPRESSIONS OF SENTIMENT, THE SPARKLE OF BRIGHT EYES, THE WEALTH OF BEAMING SMILES, THE REFLECTION OF MIRRORS, THE GAY DECORATIONS, AND THE MURMUR OF VOICES, GAVE AN AIR OF ENCHANTMENT TO THE PLACE, AND MADE IT SEEM ALMOST LIKE A VISION FROM FAIRYLAND.

THE NEWS OF THE DESTRUCTION OF THE GALT HOUSE, AS IT SPREADS THROUGHOUT THE LAND, WILL AWAKEN FEELINGS OF REGRET AND SADNESS IN THE HEARTS OF MANY OF THE ILLUSTRIOUS SONS OF AMERICA NOW IN THE ENJOYMENT OF LIFE. IN THE HALLS OF CONGRESS THE NEWS WILL RECEIVE SOMETHING MORE THAN A PASSING THOUGHT. GEN. GRANT IN HIS CAMP ON THE JAMES, SURROUNDED BY HIS SOLDIERS, WILL REMEMBER HOW HE MOVED THROUGH THE GRAND OLD HALLS AND CLAIMED THE ADMIRATION OF THE BUSTLING CROWD. GEN. SHERMAN, AS HE GAZES OUT UPON THE PLACID BOSOM OF THE SEA FOR A FEW MOMENTS, WILL FORGET THE PRESENT, AND HOLD COMMUNION WITH THE PAST, AND AROUND THE GALT HOUSE WILL CENTRE MANY A THOUGHT.

GALT HOUSE

After being destroyed by fire in 1865, the Galt House Hotel moved one block eastward to the corner of First and Main Streets. The replacement hotel, while financially successful, never fully claimed the city's affections as had its predecessor. This site would later be replaced by the massive office and warehouse complex of Belknap Hardware.

Like the genii from the bottle, rises the smoke from Louisville's giant stacks and pulsing industry

Post-Civil War Louisville made a conversion from riverboat-based maritime commerce to heavy industrial manufacturing, especially along the waterfront. Building the Short-Line railroad trestle in the 1880s and the addition of the huge LG&E Waterside Plant changed the character of the old wharf and hindered access to the river's edge. *(University of Louisville Photographic Archives, OCL.41)*

From "Perseverando" to "Progress"

(1866-1900)

It is a source of regret that no evident progress has been made toward the acquisition of a public park, the want of which is perhaps more generally felt by all classes than that of any other improvement. There is no other city in the Union that has any enterprise but what provides for its citizens a place of this kind for healthy and innocent recreation, so much needed and sought for, particularly by the poorer and humbler classes.... The enterprise cannot be objected to on the ground of its costliness, for, as I learn from other cities, their parks are a source of revenue and profit instead of expense. For instance: Central Park, New York, cost the city over ten million dollars, and for the increased valuation of the contiguous property the city derives an income of revenue of more than $600,000, annually, above the interest on the cost of the park. I hope you will give this subject serious consideration, and place Louisville on an equal footing with her sister cities in the possession of such a park as the health and progress of the city demands.

– Mayor Philip Tomppert - 1867

Shortly before the Civil War commenced, the General Council met in 1861 and decided it was time to update Louisville's image. They replaced the original city seal with its image of a steamboat passing the wharf, to a more modern display of a locomotive under way. Louisville's motto was changed from "*Perseverando,*" meaning "by persevering," to a more mundane "*Progress.*" During the war, Louisvillians had ample opportunities to exercise their perseverance and, after the war, they would measure progress by new standards.

Louisville's second official seal, adopted in 1861, displays the transition from the original 1828 steamboat image to one reflecting the new importance of railroads. The city's motto was changed to "Progress" as more and more of the transportation duties were transferred to rail, rather than river, service.

Louisville was the only major city below the Mason-Dixon line not to suffer direct war damage. In fact, the communities on both sides of the Ohio River profited. A report in the December 10, 1865, *Daily Democrat* boasted of the prosperity of Louisville:

PROBABLY THERE WAS NEVER A TIME IN THE HISTORY OF LOUISVILLE WHEN PROGRESS WAS AS RAPID AS AT THE PRESENT, NOTWITHSTANDING THE GREAT CIVIL STRUGGLE WHICH HAS RAGED THROUGH THE COUNTRY FOR THE PAST FOUR YEARS, AND FROM WHICH WE ARE NOW EMERGING. OUR POPULATION IS RAPIDLY INCREASING — SO FAST THAT PEOPLE CAN HARDLY FIND SHELTER. THE BUSINESS OF THE CITY IS LARGER THAN EVER BEFORE, AND WE CAN SAY WITH PRIDE THAT IT IS STILL ON THE INCREASE. STREET RAILROADS ARE NOW RUNNING THROUGH SEVERAL OF THE PRINCIPAL STREETS, AND WE VENTURE THE ASSERTION THAT BEFORE ANOTHER YEAR THEY WILL CHECKER THE ENTIRE CITY SO THAT A PERSON CAN GO AND COME WHEN THEY PLEASE UPON THE STREET CARS. WHEREVER THESE ROADS EXTEND THE VALUE OF THE PROPERTY IS GREATLY ENHANCED, AND NEW HOUSES CAN BE SEEN GOING UP. THERE IS NOT A MECHANIC IN THE CITY THAT IS NOT ENGAGED AT VERY LIBERAL WAGES, AND THERE IS STILL A

DEMAND FOR MORE HANDS. THERE IS SCARCELY A STREET WHERE THE RING OF THE TROWEL OR THE SOUND OF THE HAMMER CANNOT BE HEARD.

ON MAIN STREET THERE ARE NOT LESS THAN TWENTY FINE BUSINESS HOUSES NOW BEING ERECTED, IN ADDITION TO THE NEW GALT HOUSE, WHICH WILL BE COMMENCED IN A VERY SHORT TIME. THESE HOUSES HAVE ALL ALREADY BEEN RENTED, WHICH IS A PLAIN FACT GOING TO SHOW THAT THE BUSINESS OF THE CITY IS INCREASING, AND THAT NEW FIRMS ARE DAILY BEING ESTABLISHED. ON THE DIFFERENT STREETS IN THE BACK PORTION OF THE CITY SOME OF THE MOST PALATIAL RESIDENCES ARE IN THE COURSE OF CONSTRUCTION, WHILE HUNDREDS OF OTHERS HAVE RECEIVED THE FINISHING TOUCHES FROM THE HANDS OF THE MECHANIC.

The tympanum of the City Hall's cornice displays a stone version of the new city seal. In some renderings, the powerful steam locomotive, emblazoned with Louisville's motto, is shown passing through groves of palm trees, indicating the growing importance of Southern trade.

Louisville had outgrown the narrow "stringtown" of buildings three blocks deep and forty blocks wide. Broadway was no longer considered the wilderness and a network of streetcars began to spread outward from the city into rural Jefferson County. People began to follow the interurbans out of town to cooler and quieter homes away from the river.

Many Louisvillians began to look eastward, and a suggestion printed in the *Daily Journal* urged extension of Main and other streets past the growing stockyards and into the areas known as Clifton and the Highlands.

THE WATER WORKS GROUNDS ARE CLOSE BY, AND SOME OF THE MOST DELIGHTFUL DRIVES OUR VICINITY AFFORDS ARE UP THE RIVER. WITH THE GROWTH OF THE CITY, OF COURSE THE SLAUGHTER-HOUSES WILL BE BANISHED BEYOND THE CORPORATE LIMITS, AND NO LONGER WILL THE SIGHT OR THE SMELL BE OFFENDED BY THE NECESSARILY OFFENSIVE ACCOMPLISHMENTS OF THE CITY ABATTOIRS. ALREADY THE LINE OF DWELLINGS THAT INDICATE THE CITY PROPER IS STRETCHING THAT WAY, AND IT IS CERTAINLY TO THE INTEREST OF OUR MUNICIPAL AUTHORITIES TO CONDEMN THE NECESSARY GROUND BEFORE IT INCREASES IN VALUE MUCH MORE, FOR IT CERTAINLY DOES INCREASE EVERY MONTH.

The unprecedented amount of wartime traffic exposed problems with the antiquated Louisville wharf. The 1867 Municipal Report by the city's civil engineer makes suggestions as to improving the waterfront.

AT THE CITY HARBOR, THERE IS ABOUT TWO THOUSAND FEET OF WHAT IS CALLED PAVED WHARF, EXTENDING FROM NINTH TO FIFTH STREET. THIS PART OF THE RIVERFRONT IS NOT ADAPTED TO THE RIVER TRADE; TO RENDER IT SO, AND AFFORD THAT SECTION OF THE CITY SUITABLE COMMERCIAL FACILITIES, THE BUILDINGS ALONG WATER STREET FROM A POINT EAST OF FOURTH STREET, AT LEAST AS FAR WEST AS SEVENTH STREET, SHOULD BE PURCHASED BY THE CITY. THESE BUILDINGS SHOULD BE REMOVED, AND A WHARF CONSTRUCTED IN ACCORDANCE WITH THE PLANS HERETOFORE SUBMITTED TO YOU ON THE SUBJECT. THE GRADES OF FOURTH, FIFTH, SIXTH, AND SEVENTH

STREETS CAN BE RAISED TO THE SAME ELEVATION AS THAT OF FIRST, SECOND AND THIRD STREETS, OR TO THE LEVEL OF THE ORDINARY HIGH WATER OF THE RIVER.

THE NEW WHARF EXTENDS FROM FIFTH TO FIRST STREET, A DISTANCE OF ABOUT TWO THOUSAND FEET. THE OLD BED OF BEARGRASS CREEK HAS BEEN FILLED TO A POINT EAST OF SECOND STREET.

IT WOULD BE ADVISABLE TO PURCHASE MORE OF THE WATER-FRONT, EXTENDING FROM BROOK STREET EASTWARD, FOR WHARF PURPOSES, WHILST IT CAN BE OBTAINED ON REASONABLE TERMS. THE AMOUNT EXPENDED ON WHARVES DURING THE YEAR 1867 WAS $96,524.46.

Gaming and Houses of Ill-Fame

Louisville's German-born Mayor Philip Tomppert also gave his 1867 message, and it contained an unexpectedly tolerant attitude toward vices that had grown to unparalleled local levels during the disruptive Civil War.

FOR INSTANCE: THE GAMING DENS SHOULD BE ACCESSIBLE TO EVERY ADULT, AND OPEN, ALIKE, TO THE INSPECTION OF THE POLICE AND THE CITIZENS, SO THAT THE SECRECY WHICH NOW SURROUNDS AND FOSTERS THEIR GROWTH MAY BE REMOVED, AND THE MANY CRIMES ATTENDING GAMING, HIDDEN AND SHELTERED UNDER ITS CLOAK, BE EXPOSED AND PUNISHED WHEN COMMITTED.

THE COURTESANS, HOWEVER DEEP THEIR DEGRADATION MAY BE, ARE MORE PROPER OBJECTS FOR COMMISERATION THAN FOR HARSH AND UNRELENTING PROSECUTION, AND THOUGH NO MEANS SHOULD BE LEFT UNTRIED TO EFFECT A REFORMATION, YET WHEN HARLOTRY HAS GROWN TO SUCH DIMENSIONS AS IT NOW ASSUMES IN OUR MIDST, ITSELF AFFLICTED AND SPREADING IN THE COMMUNITY THE MOST LOATHSOME DISEASES, AND FLOURISHING IN THE TEETH OF BROAD AND VINDICTIVE STATUTES, IT IS TIME, I THINK, OUR EYES WERE OPENED TO A MORE PRACTICAL AND LESS IDEAL COURSE OF ACTION THAN WE NOW FAVOR TO STAY THE DEMORALIZATION WHICH THREATENS TO OVERWHELM US — NOT BY LICENSING PROSTITUTION AND ABROGATING THE LAWS DENOUNCING IT — BUT TO THROW AROUND IT SUCH AN ADDITIONAL SYSTEM AND NETWORK OF MUNICIPAL ORDINANCES...

The city's newfound concern for public morals extended even to a long-standing tradition in Louisville, public bathing in the river. An ordinance was adopted in July 1867 to address a growing concern:

IN RELATIONSHIP TO BATHING WITHIN THE CITY LIMITS: BE IT ORDAINED BY THE GENERAL COUNCIL OF THE CITY OF LOUISVILLE, THAT IT SHALL BE UNLAWFUL FOR ANYONE, BETWEEN THE HOURS OF 4 O'CLOCK A.M. AND 9 O'CLOCK P.M. TO BATHE IN THE CANAL, IN BEARGRASS CREEK, OR IN THE OHIO RIVER AT ANY POINT BETWEEN THE EASTERN AND WESTERN BOUNDARIES OF THE CITY, OR IN ANY POND WITHIN THE CITY LIMITS. FOR A VIOLATION OF THE PROVISIONS OF THIS ORDINANCE EACH PARTY OFFENDING SHALL BE LIABLE TO ARREST, AND SHALL, FOR EACH OFFENSE, BE FINED TEN DOLLARS.

With the close of the Civil War, railroads assumed supremacy in supplying the nation's transportation needs. Vast networks of branch lines operated by dozens of separate railroad firms spread across America. Since railroads could go places not open to navigation, America began moving by rail. One major problem for railroads was that they must cross the very rivers they bypass. In 1867 Louisville was ready to span the wide Ohio over the Falls. The Pennsylvania Railroad Bridge at Fourteenth Street would be the longest bridge in

The first bridge to span the Ohio River at Louisville opened in 1870. Called many names, the Pennsylvania Railroad, the Panhandle or the Fourteenth Street Bridge, it was the longest cantilevered bridge in the world when erected. One of the original piers was placed on Corn Island and, while the bridge was replaced in 1914 by a heavier structure, the original piers are still being used.

America when completed. *Louisville Daily Courier*, August 2, 1867, reported:

> AT THREE O'CLOCK YESTERDAY AFTERNOON A GOODLY NUMBER OF PERSONS ASSEMBLED AT THE SITE OF THE MIDDLE PIER OF THE OHIO RIVER BRIDGE, ON CORN ISLAND, FOR THE PURPOSE OF WITNESSING THE DEPOSIT OF THE FIRST STONE OF THE FOUNDATION.

> THE SUPERSTRUCTURE WILL BE FINK'S PATENT IRON SUSPENSION TRUSS, CONSTRUCTED WITH A VIEW OF ADAPTATION TO CARRIAGE AND FOOT PASSAGE AS WELL AS FOR RAILROAD USE. IT WILL BE ALSO ARRANGED FOR THE CROSSING OF STREET CARS. THE THROUGH PORTION WILL CONSIST OF TWO SPANS OF 360 FEET EACH, ARRANGED RESPECTIVELY AS HIGH SPANS OVER THE MIDDLE AND INDIANA CHANNELS.

> THE BRIDGE IS TO BE CONSTRUCTED WITH BUT ONE SWINGING SPAN OR DRAW, WHICH IS OVER THE LOUISVILLE AND PORTLAND CANAL.

> THE TOTAL LENGTH OF SUPERSTRUCTURE WILL BE 5,220 FEET, AND OF GRADED APPROACHES 2,500 FEET,

At the turn of the twentieth century, local folks wishing to have a day on the river would rent skiffs or john boats from commercial operators like Jack and Andy. Their rental agency, located at the end of Shelby Street, catered to fishermen, picnickers or anyone wanting to enjoy a private day on the Ohio River. *(Filson Historical Society. BOA22)*

Rowing races, or regattas, became hugely popular in Louisville by the 1840s, often attracting tens of thousands of viewers from both shores of the river. After the Civil War, many Louisvillians began to enjoy river-related sports, with sailing and rowing regattas especially popular. In 2010, a rowing center to accommodate University of Louisville athletes was completed in the final phase of the Waterfront Master Plan.

MAKING THE TOTAL LENGTH OF BRIDGE FROM THE POINTS AT WHICH ASCENT IS COMMENCED 7,720 FEET. THE TOTAL LENGTH OF THE CONNECTION BETWEEN THE JEFFERSONVILLE RAILROAD AND THE LOUISVILLE AND NASHVILLE RAILROAD, INCLUDING BRIDGE, WILL BE ABOUT THREE AND A HALF MILES.

The bridge, anchored on the remnant of pioneer Corn Island, would take three years to complete, but with its opening in 1870, it linked north to south and reaffirmed Louisville's position as a transportation center for generations to come. A rebuilt bridge, located at the same location, was erected in 1914 to handle the heavier engines and cars of that era. The original stone pillars remain in place and are still part of the bridge supports.

**"This will certainly be the grandest
sporting event of the season."**

Louisvillians had always worked the Ohio River as commercial fishermen, shipbuilders, steamboat crews, coal barge operators, Falls pilots and ferry men. They gained an intimate understanding of the river's sandbars, eddies, freezes, floods and rapids. With its economy based on river traffic and trades, Louisville developed a deep appreciation of the river and its power.

Citizens also began to use the river for new purposes, namely recreation and relaxation. Louisville's growing middle class, and a substantial number of families made wealthy by war industries, began to embrace the Ohio River as a place to go and have fun. Louisvillians began a love affair with the river's edge which never left them. Regattas, and other contests of sailing skills or prowess with oars, were popular on both sides of the Falls, as is indicated in a *New Albany Ledger* article from August 1867:

The floating headquarters of the Louisville Boat Club, for a long time located at the end of Sixth Street, was the place for parties and entertainment on the wharf. Sited very near the mouth of the Portland Canal, recreational boaters gave way to the heavy traffic of commercial barges and packet boats of the time. *(University of Louisville Photographic Archives, P00349)*

REGATTA ON THE OHIO - BOAT RACE BETWEEN THE BRILLIANT AND THE DEXTER – EARLY REGATTA REMINISCENCES

YESTERDAY EVENING FOR THE FIRST TIME IN MANY YEARS, A REGATTA TOOK PLACE ON THE OHIO RIVER IN FRONT OF THIS CITY. THE RACE WAS BETWEEN THE ROWBOATS *BRILLIANT*, CAPTAIN JAMES MCGUIRE, AND THE *DEXTER*, CAPTAIN LEVI RIGGS, THE WINNER TO RECEIVE A HANDSOME SAIL. LONG BEFORE THE HOUR OF STARTING, THE BANK, WHARF, AND EVERY CONCEIVABLE PLACE WAS TAKEN POSSESSION OF BY ANXIOUS SPECTATORS OF THE SCENE. THE RIVER WAS FILLED WITH BOATS OF ALL KINDS, FROM THE FINEST YAWL AND ROWBOAT TO THE COMMON FLAT-BOTTOMED SKIFF, PRESENTING A VERY NOVEL AND UNUSUAL APPEARANCE.

WE REMEMBER WHEN, TWENTY-THREE YEARS AGO...

THIS WAS ONE OF THE MOST EXCITING REGATTAS

THAT HAD TAKEN PLACE WEST OF THE ALLEGHENY MOUNTAINS, AND DREW TOGETHER THE LARGEST ASSEMBLAGE OF THE KIND WE EVER WITNESSED. FULLY TWENTY THOUSAND PERSONS WERE COLLECTED ON THE POINT ABOVE BEARGRASS CREEK. THE *HENRY CLAY* ROWED BUT TEN OARS, TWO LESS THAN HER COMPLEMENT, AND THE *GREY EAGLE* HER FULL NUMBER OF EIGHT OARS. THE *GREY EAGLE*, UP TO THAT TIME, WAS CONSIDERED THE FLEETEST CRAFT AFLOAT, AND WHEN BEATEN BY THE *CLAY*, THE LOUISVILLE CLUB NOT ONLY SUBMITTED GRACEFULLY TO THEIR DEFEAT, BUT ENTERTAINED THE CHAMPIONS IN A PRINCELY MANNER.

Louisville boatmen responded in kind when the Louisville Barge Club sponsored its Anniversary Regatta:

THE REGATTA PARTY WILL START FROM THE FOOT OF SIXTH STREET, LOUISVILLE, AT 2 O'CLOCK PM, ON THE 22ND, AND PROCEED UP THE RIVER TO SILVER SPRINGS ABOVE JEFFERSONVILLE. HERE THEY WILL PARTAKE OF REFRESHMENTS; AFTER WHICH THERE WILL BE A GRAND BOAT RACE FROM THE FOOT OF TWO MILE ISLAND TO THE FERRY LANDING ON THE

Louisvillians have long had a love affair with the Ohio River. A turn-of-the-century couple prepares a picnic on Sand Island, immediately below the Falls. Similar landing places were located in Shawnee Park and were enjoyed and remembered for decades. *(Kentucky Historical Society, 3jefl.1)*

LOUISVILLE SIDE, THE DISTANCE BEING ONE MILE. A FINE AND BEAUTIFUL SILK CHAMPION FLAG WILL BE AWARDED AS A PRIZE BY THE LOUISVILLE BARGE CLUB TO THE FASTEST BOAT. THIS WILL CERTAINLY BE THE GRANDEST SPORTING EVENT OF THE SEASON.

ARRIVAL OF THE *FIRE KING*

The future arrived at the Louisville waterfront in 1867 when an entirely new type of motorized vessel landed at the wharf. Steam engines, the mechanical device that revolutionized travel, industry and daily life in the nineteenth century, depended on wood or coal as their fuel sources. Farmers all along the inland waterway systems earned cash by cutting and preparing wood yards to supply the needs

of traveling boats, and western Pennsylvania supplied mountains of coal for the steamers and gasification plants. A local reporter covering a routine story had no idea he was announcing a new era in American history when he described the arrival of the *Fire King*.

Louisville Daily Journal, September 2, 1867

THE PETROLEUM BOAT *FIRE KING* LANDED AT THE CITY WHARF YESTERDAY AFTERNOON. OUR CITIZENS WILL HAVE AMPLE OPPORTUNITY FOR INSPECTING THIS OILY-RUNNING CRAFT, AS SHE WILL REMAIN IN PORT TWO OR THREE DAYS. IT IS PROBABLE, TOO, THAT SHE WILL MAKE A TRIAL TRIP FOR THE SATISFACTION OF THOSE INTERESTED IN THE NEW FEATURE OF PETROLEUM STEAM.

For some time past, in France and England, experiments have been made under government superintendence and by private parties to introduce petroleum as a substitute for coal in ocean and river steamers, and for locomotives and other steam-engines. Thus far they have attained only a partial success, and even in this country, until lately, inventors have produced nothing of practical utility, and capable of adaptation to all the numerous machines for which coal furnishes the motive power, steam.

Yesterday a large party of gentlemen, most of them practical engineers, machinists and steamboat masters, met, by invitation of Mr. H. S. Saroni, on board the steamer *Fire King* to witness the trial of his new process of making steam by petroleum.

Mr. Saroni has fitted up a boat purchased by him with boilers arranged to be heated by naptha gas, tanks for oil, and all the apparatus required, and arrived here a day or two since from Cincinnati on its first trial trip, eminently successful as regarded the working of the machinery, but delayed by some accidents to the boat by getting aground.

Mr. Saroni uses in his operations the refuse oil from the refineries, which has as yet been wasted, owing to there being no market for it.

We confidently predict that it will be generally adopted, and will prove to be all the inventor claims for it — the greatest triumph of the age.

If petroleum can be so employed as to take the place of coal, the saving will be immense. In weight of fuel, for example, we gain 90 tons in every 100 tons, and in bulk the space saved would allow for a far greater amount of freight being carried.

Unfortunately, Saroni failed to impress investors and was unable to solve the technical problems of grease building up and seizing the boilers. The development of practical use of petroleum engines would wait a few more years.

The Short-Line is the Most Direct Line

Studying maps of Louisville from the 1870s reveals a city plan surprisingly unchanged in the ensuing decades. Most street names remain the same except for a cluster of lanes near the waterfront. Old Water Street, the first named road in Louisville, was a decrepit, winding semi-paved path which meandered along the river's edge. River Road was primarily built over the filled-in Beargrass Creek, and its parallel roadway nearer the river, Fulton Street, led from the wharf eastward through the Point. Running up the hill from the river's edge were segments of the cross-numbered streets which boasted their own identity for one short block. Bullitt Street went up from the river between Fourth and Fifth Streets. Third Street from Main down to the wharf was known as Pearl, and a small alley between Third and Fourth was known originally as Donne's Alley, and later, O'Neill's. The best known and most used route between Main and the river was Wall Street, the one-block section of Fourth Street that today ends at the wharf and the *Belle of Louisville*.

The area known as the Point also changed over the years. Originally defined as the land between the Ohio River shore and Beargrass Creek, that delineation was altered with the diversion and fill-in of the creek. The densely forested area was useful to the boat builders and sawmill operators occupying the land east of downtown. The era of the Point mansions – of the Geigers, Pagets and Barclays – had long since passed, and the Point became synonymous with woodcutters, fishermen,

A view from the steamboat *Tell City* looking up Fourth Street in 1905 indicates the constant traffic on the Louisville wharf. The Short-Line Railroad trestle, built in the early 1880s, cuts across the city's frontage and a depot appears on the left side of the photo. Roustabouts continue their endless task of loading and unloading steamboats on the riverfront. *(Kentucky Historical Society, 87ph4-061)*

boat builders and their families. This was a rough hardworking population, locally known for their willingness to drink or fight at the drop of a hat.

Increasingly, Louisville's economy turned to railroads. With a new bridge at Fourteenth Street, local businessmen sought new markets. The L&N developed the best access to a Southern market attempting to rebuild after the Civil War. William Belknap's company, a manufacturer of practical tools, harness and farm supplies, began to expand their operation southward. Working closely with the L&N, Belknap hired ex-Confederate soldiers as sales representatives and sent them into Dixie to visit every general store, mercantile and supply house in the region. By purchasing and transshipping manufactured goods from the

Northern cities, tons of tools, machine parts and other products of the Industrial Age came south into Belknap warehouses, then continued further south on L&N rails. As the railroads took passenger service away from the grand old palatial riverboats of the past, maritime traffic lost much of its charm, and the Palmy Days of Steamboats became the Practical Days of Towboats.

In 1869 the L&N completed a new link to Cincinnati, a seventy-seven-mile-long spur known almost immediately as the Short-Line. Railroad officials wanted to extend a rail line directly across the Louisville riverfront, reasoning that the shortest distance between their West End terminals and East End depots lay between the river and Main Street. C. P. Huntington, the nation's dominant railroad baron, desired to link his Southern and

Eastern lines and he was frustrated in his efforts by the stubborn resistance of Louisville businessmen wanting to preserve their access to the waterfront.

Huntington became obsessed with a plan to link his lines from New Orleans and Memphis, which ended at Fourteenth Street, and his Chesapeake & Ohio railroad terminating at Preston Street. By doing so, Huntington would control the first truly transcontinental railroad, finally allowing the same locomotive to move with no interruptions from the Atlantic seacoast to the Pacific. The Short Route Railway Transfer Company, which had existed in name only since its formation in 1873, owned rights to the passageway.

To deny Huntington's takeover of the waterfront, downtown business leaders called upon a little-known episode from Louisville's early days. James A. Pearce had married the daughter of General Jonathan Clark, the eldest of the six Clark brothers. After old Fort Nelson was razed, Pearce bought the pioneer property at Seventh and Main Streets to build a town house. Pearce left the property as a legacy to the City of Louisville, provided the city never allow any building or structure to obstruct the view of the Ohio from the donor's house, garden or vineyard. If so, the donation stipulated, the land would return to his heirs. When Huntington's C&O railroad attempted to acquire the property to build its elevated tracks along the waterfront, he was denied the right-of-way.

C. P. Huntington would not be stopped, as he purchased the Short-Line Route rights for $400,000 and paid the Pearce heirs an additional $200,000 for their legacy. After construction of the fourteen-block transfer line, Huntington spent more than a million dollars on his obsession, but within two years several other competing transcontinental routes were built across the nation.

The elevated Short-Line track was an element of Louisville's

waterfront for nearly a century. *The Courier-Journal* of March 14, 1884, provides a glimpse at the major construction project that produced the Short-Line route across the city.

THE ABUTMENT ON THE EAST SIDE OF ELEVENTH STREET WAS THE FIRST PIECE OF WORK DONE. IT IS BUILT ON A SOLID ROCK FOUNDATION, SUNK 80 FEET BELOW THE SURFACE. ON THIS ABUTMENT THE FIRST SPAN OF THE IRON STRUCTURE RESTS. THERE ARE IN ALL 484 FOUNDATION PIERS, ON WHICH REST THE IRON COLUMNS HOLDING THE BRIDGE, AND SOME OF THESE FOUNDATIONS HAVE BEEN SUNK 40 FEET BELOW THE SURFACES. THE ENTIRE TRESTLE, FROM ELEVENTH STREET TO PRESTON, IS 5,000 FEET LONG, A LITTLE OVER ONE MILE. IN THE STRUCTURE THERE ARE 572 HEAVY IRON GIRDERS AND 39 BRIDGE GIRDERS, THESE LATTER BEING 62 FEET IN LENGTH, AND SOME OF THEM WEIGHING NINE TONS.

FROM THIRD STREET TO FIRST THE STRUCTURE IS A KIND OF VIADUCT, AND RUNS THROUGH THE CENTER OF THE STREET. THE STRUCTURE IS SUFFICIENTLY HIGH HERE FOR THE LARGEST WAGONS TO PASS UNDER. THE COLUMNS ARE 30 FEET APART.

THE ONLY ALTERATION MADE IN THE STRUCTURE AFTER ITS ERECTION WAS AT THE FOOT OF THIRD STREET. THE STREET WAS REGRADED AFTER THE PLANS HAD BEEN SENT TO THE FOUNDRY, AND THIS RAISED IT NEARLY A FOOT. THE CALCULATION AS TO HEIGHT HERE HAD BEEN VERY CLOSE, AND IT WAS FOUND THAT A HIGH WAGON LOADED, SAY WITH COTTON, COULD NOT PASS UNDER THE SOUTH GIRDER CROSSING THE STREET. THIS GIRDER WAS RAISED ABOUT FIFTEEN INCHES, WHICH REMEDIED THE TROUBLE.

THE APPEARANCE OF THE RIVERFRONT IS VASTLY IMPROVED BY THE SHORT-ROUTE. INSTEAD OF THE OLD, RICKETY, DILAPIDATED, DIRTY BUILDINGS THAT ONCE

A banker's holiday in this 1905 photograph displays the thrill of going over the Falls. Young bank clerks prepare for their grand adventure of shooting the rapids, while still well-dressed for the occasion. *(Kentucky Historical Society, 3jefl40)*

These men had intimate understanding of the Ohio River at Louisville and sprang into action to rescue endangered craft. Their legend began with a March 22, 1879, event chronicled in the *Louisville Commercial.*

A RECOGNITION OF BRAVERY

William Devan, John Gillooly and John Tully, the three heroes by whose bravery a score of people have been saved from death in the breakers of the falls, did another heroic act Thursday afternoon at the time Captain Boyton made his perilous descent of the falls. In the skiff they reached in time to prevent it being dashed to pieces on the dam was the popular actor, Oliver Doud Byron, who is just now taking a little recreation, but his search after pleasure Thursday came near finding a sorrowful end. Mr. Byron and the gentlemen who were in the boat with him feel deeply grateful to the brave men who went to their rescue, and desire to give some palpable token of their esteem and appreciation.

Mr. Byron, as a further mark of gratitude, has proposed, if a number of citizens will take the matter in hand, to give Devan, Gillooly and Tully a benefit next Friday night, so that out of the proceeds they will be able to provide themselves with life-saving operations and a suitable boat. In this Mr. Byron will be seconded by all our citizens who have for several years been made familiar with the heroic conduct of those three men…Devan, Gillooly and Tully have often risked their own lives to save their fellow men, and for their bravery in the hour of peril deserve this recognition. Let them have a rousing benefit.

disgraced that part of the city, this structure gives it a metropolitan air and will do much toward making it an important business center between North and South, East and West.

Heroes of the Falls

The original 1820s Portland canal and locks remained an impediment to passage around the Falls until after the Civil War, when engineer Theodore Scowden improved the structures. By 1872, the enlargement project was completed and the impressive new structures allowed the safe passage of most vessels, but the dangers of the rocky Falls remained. Water still rushed headlong over the rapids, and God help the mariner caught in its powerful pull. Many boats, and their crews, were smashed to pieces on the treacherous Falls of the Ohio.

Three local river men would become the most admired Louisvillians of their era by their heroic volunteer efforts to save boats, crews and passengers in danger of broaching the Falls.

In 1871 the U.S. Treasury Department Revenue

A Coast Guard crew, stationed on Life-Saving Station #10, represents the only inland station in America. Founded in 1882 as part of the federal Life-Saving Service, these crews were credited with saving thousands of lives and dozens of boats from destruction on the turbulent Falls of the Ohio. *(Photo courtesy of the* Belle of Louisville*)* ,

Marine Board, the customs-collecting wing of government, established a program of rescue stations located on the nation's seacoasts and Great Lakes. Crews of trained rescuers, called surfmen, were quartered in beach installations. These coastal stations provided living quarters, a boathouse with skids to the water's edge, and a lookout tower to be manned around the clock. In 1882 Congress authorized Life-Saving Station #10 at the Falls of the Ohio. It was the only floating station ever to serve an American river, and the enabling legislation defined the problem and provided the solution for endangered mariners.

ESTABLISHMENT OF STATIONS

ANOTHER STATION, WHICH HAS BEEN ASSIGNED TO THE NINTH DISTRICT, AND DESIGNATED AS STATION NO. 10, HAS BEEN ESTABLISHED AT THE FALLS OF THE OHIO, LOUISVILLE, KENTUCKY, AND ALSO PUT IN OPERATION. THIS STATION DIFFERS MATERIALLY FROM ANY OF THE OTHERS, THE NATURE OF THE SERVICE IN THIS LOCALITY DEMANDING A PECULIAR CONSTRUCTION. IT HAS BEEN EXPLAINED IN A PREVIOUS REPORT THAT THE STRONG CHUTE, KNOWN AS THE FALLS OF THE OHIO, IS VERY DANGEROUS TO PERSONS NAVIGATING THE RIVER,

ESPECIALLY AT LOW WATER, AND A NUMBER OF LIVES AND MUCH PROPERTY HAVE BEEN LOST IN CONSEQUENCE. IT WAS, THEREFORE, FOUND DESIRABLE TO ESTABLISH A LIFE-SAVING STATION IN THIS LOCALITY, WHICH WAS DULY AUTHORIZED BY THE LAST CONGRESS, AND AS EXAMINATION DETERMINED THAT THERE WAS NO SUITABLE SITE TO BE HAD FOR IT UPON THE SHORE, IT WAS DECIDED TO MAKE IT A FLOATING STATION, CONSISTING OF A BARGE WITH A HOUSE UPON IT, TO BE MOORED WHEREVER DESIRABLE, AND FURNISHED WITH BOATS ADAPTED TO RESCUES UNDER THE EXISTING CONDITIONS, LINES FOR THE AID OF VESSELS DRAWN INTO PERIL, AND SUCH OTHER LIFE-SAVING APPLIANCES AS THE EXCEPTIONAL CHARACTER OF THE SERVICE AT THESE RAPIDS MIGHT REQUIRE. THIS SCHEME WAS ACCORDINGLY CARRIED OUT, AND THE STATION, HAVING BEEN COMPLETED AND PUT IN OPERATION, IS ALREADY MAKING A GOOD RECORD.

Captain Billy Devan was the senior member of the "heroes of the Falls." A man of massive girth and a liberal vocabulary, Devan served as the first commander of the new Life-Saving Station at Louisville. The consummate river man, Devan knew the tricky Louisville eddies and rapids as few others did. He was appointed keeper of the station at its beginning in 1882 and served until his death in 1911.

Captain Billy Devan (left), first commander of the Life-Saving Station, spent his childhood growing up on the riverfront with Pat Murphy (right). Devan was frequently decorated with gold medals celebrating his rescues, and his pal Murphy was similarly festooned by admirers in recognition of his success as a newsboy. (Kentucky Historical Society, 2jefi4)

Jack Gillooly and Billy Devan earned their livings guiding the coal barge fleets into their loading docks as they arrived from Pittsburgh. Gillooly served as second station keeper of the Lifesavers, and he continued his life-saving duties long after his retirement from the Coast Guard in 1917. "Captain Jack" did not stray far from his life's work, as he was put in charge of the lifeguards at the Crescent Hill swimming pool. When he walked to and from his home on Portland's 29th and Bank Streets, columns of neighborhood children followed their hero down the sidewalk.

John Tully, a native Irishman, made his life on the Louisville wharf. He lived at 1277 North Third Street and operated a fishing supply and chandlery, making and repairing nets for commercial fishermen. He supplemented his income by taking out fishing parties, transporting hunters to duck blinds and providing excursion outings on the Ohio River. Decorated for bravery many times over, Tully spent 55 of his 62 years rescuing people and boats in distress at the Falls of the Ohio.

The Champion Newsboy of the West

Captain Billy Devan was a product of the Louisville waterfront and, along with a childhood friend, was the most recognized person in the city for forty years. His friend was John "Pat" Murphy, referred to by many as the "Champion Newsboy of the West!" Both men possessed incredible gifts of energy and stamina, each was cocky to the point of arrogance, and each enjoyed walking around wearing vests covered with gold medals presented to them by admirers.

Devan and Murphy grew up together in the Rainbow House, a boardinghouse located at the junction of First Street and the river's edge. This famous residence for steamboat men was owned and operated by Manassa Devan, the father of young Billy. Among those living in the Rainbow House in 1854 were an Irish widow and three children who came up the river from New Orleans. The

The first of three Life-Saving Stations at Louisville is displayed during high water in 1905. Crews lived aboard the floating rescue station and were ready to respond the instant a watchman in the tower sighted a boat in danger of going over the Falls. The Life Savers were also active during floods and were sometimes transferred temporarily to other communities in crisis. *(Kentucky Historical Society, 3jefl39)*

youngest boy, Pat, was four years old and difficult to handle. He was in constant motion scurrying around the waterfront, and by age ten was known as the most energetic newsboy in town.

Pat Murphy supported his family by carrying a huge load of newspapers, all the local editions and those from other cities, which he sold night and day. He gained his reputation by running through the streets screaming out his signature call, "OH, YES!" at the top of his powerful lungs. Pat was a small child and, before reaching middle age, one of his shoulders drooped from carrying the heavy bags. Each day he started at the Louisville

wharf and met the incoming or departing steamboats; dashed to the train depot to make his sales there; ran to the Portland wharf and purchased papers from boats arriving from the Deep South; hurried back to Fourth Street to row across the river and sell more papers in Jeffersonville. During the Civil War he wrapped prohibited Confederate newspapers around his body and sold contraband papers to Hoosier Copperheads.

Murphy had a keen mathematical mind and, even though he sold dozens of newspapers to local businessmen every day, he was able to carry a running account of what each man owed him. His years of work and smart investments in real estate made Pat Murphy financially comfortable. When a local banker went bankrupt owing Murphy $750, the newsboy hectored the failed businessman who located enough money to repay Murphy in full.

The public began referring to Murphy as the "Newsboy King," and the "Champion Newsboy." Murphy became a Louisville legend, and many of his contemporaries commented on his generous handouts to tenement children. Friends began commissioning gold-plated badges and medallions to present to their hero of the streets. At a large city parade, Murphy once rented a sulky and rode down the street beneath a banner which read "The Most Enterprising Newsboy in America." One of his most memorable public moments came when the king of American journalism, Horace Greeley, was visiting Louisville on a campaign stop. As Greeley prepared to board his train, a frantic Pat Murphy came roaring through the crowd, with the newsboy proudly proclaiming, "You can't leave. You haven't met me yet!"

After Pat Murphy's death on the Fourth of July 1900, a bitter fight over his estate led to the revelation that Murphy had suffered from a mental condition which caused his compulsive behavior. Even decades after his death, aging Louisvillians would fondly recall the old days, when Pat Murphy sold his newspapers on the waterfront.

The Louisville Jubilee

When General Grant came to Louisville in 1879, following his presidency and recent trip around the world, he returned to a larger city than he knew during his Civil War days. The old Galt House where he met Sherman to plan the Georgia campaign was gone, replaced by a vastly larger facility one block east of the original. Now filling the entire Main Street block from First to Preston, the second Galt House set the standards for local accommodations. Other things had changed as well. Instead of landing at the Louisville wharf, his party now entered town by rail. As reported in the *Louisville Commercial* editions of December 1879:

TODAY WILL MARK AN EVENTFUL EPOCH IN THE HISTORY OF LOUISVILLE. THE PREPARATIONS FOR THE RECEPTION OF GENERAL GRANT WERE COMPLETED LAST NIGHT, AND THE CITY IS TODAY READY TO PAY A ROYAL TRIBUTE TO OUR DISTINGUISHED GUEST...

THE TRAIN AND LOCOMOTIVE WILL BE APPROPRIATELY DECORATED. GENERAL GRANT WILL LEAVE HERE TOMORROW MORNING, AT 8 O'CLOCK, ON A SPECIAL SHORT-LINE TRAIN FOR CINCINNATI, UNDER ESCORT OF THE COMMITTEE.

FIFTY THOUSAND PEOPLE GATHER IN THE CITY

AS THE HOUR FOR THE ARRIVAL OF THE TRAIN WHICH WAS EXPECTED TO BEAR THE DISTINGUISHED VISITOR APPROACHED, THE AVENUE LEADING TO THE J. M. & I. DEPOT BECAME THRONGED WITH PEOPLE, AND EVERY MOMENT THE THRONG INCREASED.

Another symbol of American patriotism visited the city in 1885, when the Liberty Bell was first taken down from its tower in Philadelphia for a ceremonial visit to New Orleans' Cotton Exposition, a massive trade show held to indicate that the South had returned to the American fold. The visit by the Liberty Bell was intended to symbolize the reconciliation of the nation. *The Courier-Journal* of January 24, 1885, reported on a very brief visit to Louisville by the famous relic.

PHILADELPHIA. – AT THE DEPOT THE BELL WAS TRANSFERRED TO A SPECIAL CAR, CONSTRUCTED BY THE PENNSYLVANIA RAILROAD COMPANY TO BEAR IT AND ITS GUARD OF THREE OFFICERS TO THE NEW ORLEANS EXPOSITION. THE BELL PLATFORM IN THE CAR IS PROTECTED BY BRASS RAILING, WITH POSTS DECORATED WITH GILDED BELLS. THE LARGE FRAME UPON WHICH THE BELL IS SECURED IS THE ONLY WORK UPON THE PLATFORM OF THE CAR.

LOUISVILLE – The bell of American Independence reached the city at 9 o'clock last night over the Short-Line from Cincinnati and was given a grand ovation at the river depot at the foot of First. The bell was mounted on a car specially made for it, the front half being a sleeper caboose and the other half devoted to the bell. A large crowd of ladies and gentlemen were in waiting at the depot, and as the train slowed up colored fires were lighted around the bell so that all could get a good view of it. As the fires lighted up the surroundings a loud shout of welcome was given.

The Liberty Bell rested in Louisville for only four hours. The grand torchlight celebration happened at the Water Street Station, First and Water Streets, near the old location of Devan's Rainbow House. Following the creation of the Waterfront Park years later, the site would house the Metropolitan Sewer District installation at Witherspoon and Bingham Way, about one hundred yards south of Joe's Crab Shack restaurant.

On September 12, 1882, the city held an event called "The Railroad Celebration and Grand Industrial Street Pageant," but it was better known as the Louisville Jubilee. The event celebrated the completion of three important new railroad lines entering the city. A parade featuring 1,652 wagons was held, but the highlight of the Jubilee was a grand fireworks show at the river's edge. *The Courier-Journal* reported:

> The crowd is here. Every train yesterday came in full to overflowing. The most interesting and the most novel attractions will be the illumination tonight and the display of fireworks on the river. At the request of the Executive Committee, it is understood the police will not permit any vehicle of any kind to go further north tonight than

Water Street. Every carriage or cart beyond that line would interfere with the comfort of fifty or one hundred persons. The boats and barges along the wharf will be carefully watched to prevent thoughtless or reckless persons coming to any harm. The occasion of rejoicing must not be clouded by any accident to life or limb.

Firework displays have always been an attraction to Louisville citizens. The Louisville Jubilee, held in 1882 to celebrate the arrival of three new railway companies to the city, attracted over 100,000 viewers. As they would be decades later for Thunder Over Louisville, both sides of the riverbank were lined with celebrants who were often caught in horse-and-buggy gridlock after the show was concluded.

The day after the event, the *Courier* proclaimed:

THE FIRE WORKS. A GRAND FREE SHOW ON THE RIVERFRONT WITH UNNUMBERED SPECTATORS

> There is no means of judging the size of the crowd that gathered at the river last night to see the fireworks, but there must have been fully 100,000 people gathered along the wharf from

FIRST TO TENTH STREETS. IT WAS THE GREATEST CROWD EVER SEEN ON THAT WHARF. OLD MEN AND THEIR CHILDREN AND THEIR WIVES; YOUNG GIRLS WITH THEIR LOVERS; EVERY CLASS OF SOCIETY — YOUNG AND OLD, RICH AND POOR — WAS GATHERED TOGETHER TO WITNESS THE GREATEST PYROTECHNICAL DISPLAY LOUISVILLE HAS EVER SEEN.

THE CROWNING SPLENDORS OF THE CELEBRATION WERE THE ILLUMINATIONS AND THE FIREWORKS. LONG BEFORE THE TIME FOR THE PYROTECHNIC DISPLAY THE CROWDS TEMPORARILY DESERTED THE BRILLIANTLY LIGHTED STREETS AND TOOK UP POSITIONS ON THE RIVER BANK. FOR MILES THIS NATURAL AMPHITHEATER WAS PACKED WITH PEOPLE WHO HAD SEEN THE PROCESSION, THE FAIR, THE EXPOSITION AND THE ILLUMINATIONS, AND STILL WERE NOT HAPPY. THE SCENE ALONG THE BANK WAS WEIRDLY BEAUTIFUL. CHINESE LANTERNS GLINTED FROM BOATS, BARGES AND BOATHOUSES, AND SWUNG IN GRACEFUL RADIANCE ABOVE THE DARK WATERS. IT WAS A SPLENDID AWAKENING FOR EYES THAT WERE WEARIED WITH DAY AND DUST. SHOWERS OF FIRE, PURPLE AND AMBER AND GOLDEN SHOT FROM THE ANCHORED BARGE, AND WITH ALL OF INDIANA FOR A BACKGROUND, CHARMED THE SPECTATORS. AT RAPID INTERVALS BETWEEN THE MORE EXTENDED DISPLAYS LARGE SKY ROCKETS WERE SENT CAREENING INTO SPACE. MANY OF THE PROMINENT VISITORS WERE COMFORTABLY PLACED IN THE LIFE-SAVING STATION AND IN THE CLUB'S BOAT HOUSE.

The Louisville Jubilee seems to have been a premonition of what would become the city's largest annual event, Thunder Over Louisville, the kick-off to the Kentucky Derby Festival. The Louisville riverfront is the ideal place for a large civic celebration, with the incline hill up to Main Street serving as a gigantic amphitheater and a broad open horizon. From the Indiana shore, the show is equally impressive, with the firework displays located on barges moored in the center of the river. It is the ideal place for an entire community to assemble and celebrate its fellowship.

One Island Emerges as Another Disappears

The Ohio River changes every day. The constant abrasion of moving waters, coupled with periods of flooding or low waters, reshapes and forms the land it touches, sometimes producing unexpected results. When first visited by the pioneers, Corn Island was a seventy-acre limestone outcropping rising above the river's surface. The stone island was covered with debris, sand and deposits of dirt stabilized by willow saplings. For many years the heirs of John Rowan quarried the limestone for use in construction of the early wharf, streets and paving projects in Louisville. Over time, Corn Island gradually washed away, and when navigation improvements were made by the federal government in the 1920s, all traces of Louisville's original site disappeared.

As one island departed, another emerged. Two miles upstream from the original mouth of Beargrass Creek, a new island referred to in river terms as a towhead, formed when a barge loaded with heavy millstones sank. The barge, owned by a Frankfort farmer named Cornellus Dewees, was made of oak pinned together with wooden pegs and maintained its integrity after sinking. The heavy sunken barge became the base of an island formed from driftwood, sand and gravel, often referred to as the Willow Bar on early maps. Trees and bushes grew and stabilized the new formation, soon called Towhead Island. This new addition to the Louisville riverfront appeared about one hundred yards off the shore of the Point. A shallow natural harbor was created and flat sandy beaches emerged which were perfect for swimming parties.

Being far enough away from downtown to escape close inspection, and already associated with the loose-living ways of the Point, Towhead Island gained a reputation among

Louisvillians as a racy place to play. The June 24, 1885, edition of *The Courier-Journal* provided a scandalous tale for its morning readers:

WICKEDNESS IN THE WATER

THE POLICE, ACTING UNDER INSTRUCTIONS FROM HEADQUARTERS, ARE KEEPING A SHARP LOOKOUT FOR MEN AND WOMEN WHO HAVE IN THE PAST MADE TOWHEAD ISLAND A RESORT FOR IMMORAL PURPOSES, AND SKIFF AND BOAT PARTIES GOING UP THE RIVER ARE SUBJECT TO CLOSE INSPECTION.

AT SEVERAL PLACES ON THE ISLAND THERE ARE UNUSUAL ADVANTAGES FOR BATHING. A NARROW, SMOOTH BEACH, WITH GRASS GROWING CLOSE TO THE WATER'S EDGE, AND THE COMFORTING SHADE OF TREES TO SHIELD THE TENDER SKIN FROM THE HOT AFTERNOON SUN MAKE JUST THE SPOT FROM WHICH TO ENTER THE FLOWING WATER.

YOUNG BOYS AND MEN ARE GREAT FREQUENTERS OF THE ISLAND, AND OF LATE BOAT PARTIES COMPOSED OF BOTH THE SEXES HAVE BECOME QUITE POPULAR WITH A CERTAIN CLASS. AT THE ISLAND THE MEN AND WOMEN GO IN BATHING TOGETHER, AND, ALTHOUGH THIS MAY BE THE PROPER CAPER AT FASHIONABLE SEASIDE RESORTS, THE INDULGENCE IN THE SPORT BY THE PARTICULAR CLASS WHO GO TO TOWHEAD ISLAND IS NOT THOUGHT TO BE CONDUCIVE TO GOOD MORALS.

LAST WEEK A PLEASURE PARTY UP THE RIVER COMPOSED OF HIGHLY RESPECTABLE PEOPLE WERE HORRIFIED BY THE CONDUCT OF A LOT OF MEN AND WOMEN WHO WERE IN BATHING. WITH SOME REGARD TO DECENCY THE WOMEN WORE A SEMBLANCE OF A BATHING SUIT, BUT THEIR ACTIONS AND FREEDOM OF MANNERS PLAINLY INDICATED THEY BELONGED TO THE VERY LOWEST STRATA OF SOCIETY.

THEY HAILED THE BOAT PARTY AND JEERED AND LAUGHED AT THEM, MAKING USE OF THE RUDEST AND VILEST LANGUAGE. THE BOAT HASTILY PULLED OUT OF HEARING, AND ON THEIR RETURN TOOK CARE TO COME DOWN ON THE OTHER SIDE OF THE RIVER.

ONE OF THE GENTLEMEN MADE AN IMMEDIATE COMPLAINT TO THE AUTHORITIES, AND ON LAST FRIDAY FOUR POLICEMEN IN CITIZENS' CLOTHES MADE A VISIT TO THE ISLAND, REMAINING ALL AFTERNOON, BUT WERE NOT OBLIGED TO MAKE ANY ARRESTS. THEY WARNED A LARGE NUMBER OF "REGULARS" — A GANG OF TOUGH AND HARDENED ROUSTABOUTS WHO GO SWIMMING ON THE POINT AT THE EXTREME FOOT OF THE ISLAND, AND TOLD THEM THEY WOULD HAVE TO SWIM FROM THE SHORE FACING THE INDIANA SHORE.

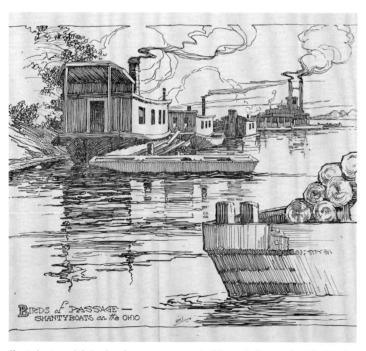

Shanty boats, and their relaxed owners, were a part of the Louisville waterfront for decades, often tying up at Towhead Island or near the piers of the Big Four Bridge. Loose and free, shantyboat families remained a part of the local river scene until the mid-1950s. *(University of Louisville Photographic Archives, OCL.15)*

Public bathing and nude swimming have been a fixture on the Louisville waterfront throughout its history. These boys take the opportunity to use the paddlewheels of the *Tell City* as their diving board while it was moored at the foot of Fourth Street. Legislation to ban nude bathing in Louisville is recorded as early as the 1820s. *(Kentucky Historical Society, 66)*

Despite the dangers inherent in the waters of the Ohio River, generations of Louisvillians tested themselves in its powerful currents. An 1889 news account warned readers to keep careful watch over their children.

WHERE THE BOYS SWIM

The good places for swimmers are the foot of the island and the "Gravel Bottoms," a shoal near the head of the island. Police try to stop this swimming because passing boats complain about the naked boys, but with little success. It is not unusual for one of the swimming parties to tearfully report that a missing boy took the cramps and drowned, or that he could not swim and got too far for his companions to help him. Then the Life-Saving Crew is notified and with a long bar from which a number of hooks dangle the river is dragged until some barbs fasten in the young body and bring up a small corpse. The coroner does his duty and one set of boys remain

too frightened to go swimming again for perhaps a week. Then the lesson is forgotten and all take to the water again.

The North Pole Exchange

Louisvillians loved to play in, and sometimes on, the river. During especially cold winters the river would sometimes freeze solid enough for skating and sleigh rides. In 1893 the river froze over for seventeen days. A kind of joyous abandon swept over the city as crowds assembled to enjoy the Ohio River in solid form. Newspaper articles capture the spontaneous festivity of that time:

Louisville Commercial, January 16, 1893:

It is estimated that ten thousand people walked across the river yesterday on the ice. From early in the morning until after dark the people crowded the riverfront, and made pathways between this city and Jeffersonville. Most of the travel was above the big gorge at the new bridge piers, where all day long a solid stream of humanity poured across. Out in front of the two Mail line wharf boats, the Life-Saving Station and the ferry-dock, from Towhead Island to the dam, the ice was crowded with skaters. All day long this merry sport was indulged in by crowds of men, women and children.

The ice varies in thickness from ten inches to twenty feet. On the big gorge great solid blocks are piled up to the latter height. In the mouth of the canal it is from ten inches to a foot and a half in thickness.

About Towhead Island the ice harvesters were busy. A splendid crop is being gathered. For the first time in years a booth was established in the middle of the river yesterday by an enterprising Jeffersonville saloon-keeper, Ed Straus. Just

At the rare times when the Ohio River froze over completely, celebrants flocked to the icy surface for skating, sleigh rides and winter fun. In 1893 the river was frozen solid for seventeen days, halting all river traffic and providing a grand holiday for people on both sides of the river. *(University of Louisville Photographic Archives P00766)*

ABOVE THE GORGE, BETWEEN TOWHEAD ISLAND AND THE INDIANA SHORE, HE CONSTRUCTED A SMALL SHANTY, AND SOLD LIQUORS AND CONDUCTED A SMALL EATING STATION. HE DID A LAND-OFFICE BUSINESS.

Louisville Commercial, January 17, 1893

YESTERDAY THERE WAS SLEIGHING ON THE RIVER. THE DAISY TRAINS ARE BRINGING THOUSANDS FROM INDIANA TO THIS SIDE TO GET A LOOK AT THE RIVER. NOT SINCE 1855 HAS THE OHIO BEEN IN SUCH A SHAPE.

Louisville Commercial, January 19, 1893

THE NORTH POLE EXCHANGE, CONDUCTED BY PADDY AHEARN AND HARRY DEBO, OF THIS CITY, WAS YESTERDAY PICKED UP BODILY BY THE PROPRIETORS AND MOVED FROM ITS LOCATION NEAR TOWHEAD ISLAND

TO THE MORE PUBLIC PATH AT THE FOOT OF SHELBY STREET. TONIGHT A DANCE WILL BE GIVEN, AND A LARGE SPACE HAS BEEN CLEARED FOR THE DANCERS, WHO ARE EXPECTED TO BE MANY. A WARMING TENT FOR LADIES AND OTHER TINY STRUCTURES MAKE THE PLACE LOOK QUITE LIKE A TINY VILLAGE.

Louisville Commercial, January 23, 1893:

A FROZEN FETE

The First Quadrille on the Ice Takes Place Successfully

Winter jollity reigned on the frozen Ohio for once in its history at last.

THE LONG EXPECTED DANCE ON THE ICE TOOK PLACE IN THE NEIGHBORHOOD OF THE NORTH POLE

The North Pole Exchange, a temporary saloon built on the frozen river near the foot of Shelby Street, served hot toddies, sausages and draft beer to celebrants. For one evening, the proprietors erected an elaborate skating rink, complete with musicians, waiters and Japanese lanterns. *(University of Louisville Photographic Archives, P00766.1)*

EXCHANGE ON THE ICE IN THE RIVER, OUT FROM THE FOOT OF SHELBY STREET. THIS WAS POSITIVELY THE FIRST EVENT OF THE KIND THAT EVER OCCURRED IN THIS CITY.

THE BAR AND THE WARMING TENT WERE GORGEOUS WITH JAPANESE LANTERNS FURNISHED BY THEIR PROPRIETORS, HARRY DEBO AND PAT AHEARN. POLES STUCK IN THE ICE IN A LARGE CIRCLE ALSO BORE LANTERNS, AND THE LIGHTS AND THE DAY COLORS REFLECTED FROM THE ICE MADE THE SPOT A SCENE OF BEAUTY. SKATERS ARRIVED EARLY. A BAND MOUNTED ON A BOARD FLOOR TO KEEP THE MUSICIANS' FEET FROM GETTING COLD DISPENSED DANCE MUSIC. A LARGE SPACE ON THE ICE HAD BEEN CLEARED OF THE SNOW TO MAKE THE SURFACE RIVAL WAXED BALL FLOORS IN SMOOTHNESS. AFTER SOME PROMISCUOUS SKATING A QUADRILLE WAS FORMED, MANY OF THE SOFTER SEX BEING PRESENT. EVERYBODY WAS ON SKATES, BUT ONLY SKILLFUL SKATERS COULD DANCE. THIS QUADRILLE WENT OFF SMOOTHLY AND WAS REPLETE WITH MOTION MORE GRACEFUL THAN VIEWED IN PERFORMANCES OF THIS KIND ON DRY EARTH. OTHER DANCES FOLLOWED

AND THE EVENING WAS MERRILY SPENT. ABOUT 400 PEOPLE WERE PRESENT.

A NEGRO, JEFF SUMMERS, ACTED AS WAITER AND SKATED ABOUT ON A PAIR OF SHERLEYS WITH A TRAY OF HOT COFFEE AND SANDWICHES FOR THE DANCERS.

Not every African-American in Louisville was fortunate enough to have a job serving sandwiches to skaters. The *Louisville Commercial* reported a different view of the effect of the winter cold:

NEGROES IN DIRE DISTRESS

THE NEGROES INHABITING TIN TOWN, THE DUMP SETTLEMENT BETWEEN THE RIVER AND THE SHORT-LINE TRACKS AND FIRST AND JACKSON STREETS, COMPOSED MAINLY OF OLD MEN, WOMEN AND CHILDREN, ARE IN THE DIREST DISTRESS AND POVERTY ATTENDING THE INCLEMENT WEATHER. MANY OF THEM ARE REALLY STARVING. OFFICER YOUNGER SAYS THAT THESE PEOPLE WORK WHEN THEY CAN, AND ARE PEACEABLE. THEY ARE QUITE AS WORTHY OF ASSISTANCE AS MOST OF THE CASES NOW BEING RELIEVED BY CHARITY.

The Cleveland, Chicago, Cincinnati & St. Louis Railroad

The east end of Louisville's riverfront began to receive more attention than just the antics of Towhead Island. In 1889 plans were being made for a new railroad bridge to cross the river to Jeffersonville. Louisville's West End already boasted two railroad bridges, the original Ohio Falls Bridge at Fourteenth, and the new Kentucky and Indiana Terminal Bridge at Thirty-Third Street. These bridges attracted investors seeking convenient shipping facilities, and factories, warehouses and switchyards sprung up in Portland. An announcement in the September 10, 1889, edition of the *Louisville Commercial* provided good news for Uptown and Butchertown.

THE BRIDGE A CERTAINTY

THE NEW LOUISVILLE BRIDGE WILL BE JUST AT THE FOOT OF THE ISLAND AND OPPOSITE THE FOOT OF SHELBY STREET, EXTENDING AT RIGHT ANGLES ACROSS THE RIVER. THE BRIDGE AND ITS APPROACHES WILL BE 9,000 FEET LONG. THE BRIDGE PROPER IS ESTIMATED TO COST ABOUT $1,250,000; THE PURCHASE OF REAL ESTATE, &C FOR THE TERMINAL WILL BRING THE TOTAL COST UP TO ABOUT $2,000,000.... THE STRUCTURE WILL BE ENTIRELY OF IRON, SAVE THE CROSS-TIES AND WALK-WAYS. IT WILL NOT BE A CANTILEVER, AND WILL CONTAIN A RAILROAD TRACK, A WAGON-WAY AND A FOOT-WAY. THE INTENTION, HOWEVER, IS TO TRANSPORT WAGONS AND OTHER VEHICLES OVER THE RAILWAY TRACK BY MEANS OF CARS ESPECIALLY MADE FOR THIS PURPOSE — SOMETHING IN THE NATURE OF A FERRYBOAT ON WHEELS.

THE EASTERN PART OF THE CITY HAS GOOD REASONS FOR REJOICING. IT HAS BEEN MORE OR LESS NEGLECTED, WHETHER ACCIDENTLY OR OTHERWISE, AND THIS IS ITS TIME TO LAUGH. THE NEW BRIDGE WILL BE WORTH MILLIONS TO THE CITY, AND WILL BE OF SPECIAL GOOD TO THE UPPER PART OF LOUISVILLE. IT IS WELL KNOWN THAT EASTERN LOUISVILLE HAS NOT KEPT PACE WITH THE WESTERN PORTION, AND THAT THE BRIDGES HAVE BEEN THE PRIME CAUSES OF THIS DIFFERENCE GOES WITHOUT SAYING. PROPERTY VALUATION WILL INCREASE AND THE GOOD EFFECT WILL BE FELT ALL THROUGH THE TOWN.

THE BRIDGE PROJECT HAS BEEN FOUGHT FROM THE START BY THE FERRY COMPANY, BUT THAT IT IS NOW GOING TO BE BUILT OR ATTEMPTED IN SPITE OF ALL OPPOSITION CAN BE ACCEPTED AS A FACT.

The bridge was called the Big Four, named for the Cleveland, Chicago, Cincinnati & St. Louis Railroad, and it seemed cursed from its first shovel of dirt. In December 1893, newspapers across the country carried the same lead story:

A BIG BRIDGE COLLAPSES
A SPAN FALLS WITH FATAL EFFECT AT LOUISVILLE

THE BRIDGE WHICH IS BEING BUILT ACROSS THE OHIO RIVER BETWEEN THIS CITY AND JEFFERSONVILLE HAS ADDED ANOTHER LONG LIST OF VICTIMS TO THE FATALITIES WHICH HAVE MARKED EVERY STEP OF ITS PROGRESS.

FORTY-FIVE MEN WERE CARRIED DOWN BY THE GIVING WAY OF THE SECOND CHANNEL SPAN AT 10:20 O'CLOCK A.M. THAT NIGHT AT 8 O'CLOCK ANOTHER SPAN FELL, BEING BLOWN DOWN BY A SHARP WIND STORM. THE NIGHT WATCHMAN AND SEVERAL WORKMEN WERE ON THE SPAN.

OF THE MEN ON THE BRIDGE WHEN IT FELL, SEVEN BODIES HAVE BEEN RECOVERED. FOURTEEN MEN WERE MORE OR LESS SERIOUSLY INJURED, FOURTEEN ARE ALMOST CERTAINLY KNOWN TO BE IN THE WATER AND TEN WHO ARE UNACCOUNTED FOR MAY BE DEAD OR MAY HAVE ESCAPED.

THE CAUSE OF THE DISASTER CANNOT BE DEFINITELY STATED, BUT THERE SEEMS LITTLE DOUBT THAT THE BRIDGE BUILDERS WERE GUILTY OF TAKING TERRIBLE RISK. WORKMEN SAY THE FALSE WORK UNDER THE SPAN HAD BEEN SETTLING FOR THREE DAYS AND THAT THE COMPANY WAS STRAINING EVERY NERVE TO COMPLETE THE SPAN BEFORE IT SHOULD FALL. THE FIRST CRASH, WHEN THE CENTRE BENT GAVE WAY WAS AT 10:25, AND THEN IT WAS THAT THE GREAT NUMBER OF FATALITIES OCCURRED. A FEW MINUTES LATER A BENT, ON WHICH THERE WAS BUT LITTLE OF THE BRIDGE PROPER, GAVE WAY ON THE INDIANA SIDE.

A FEW SUCCEEDED IN CLINGING TO PLACES OF SAFETY, AND WERE QUICKLY RESCUED BY BOATS THAT

COLLAPSE OF THE MIDDLE SPAN.

Rained in Torrents.

AT THE WRECK.

The Scene About the Fallen Spans. False Work Floated Down Stream.

SEARCHING FOR BODIES.

SCENE OF THE DISASTER.

A.—Wreckage of Middle Span and Traveler. B.—Span 3, Which Collapsed at 8:15 P. M.

MISSING.

The original Big Four Bridge earned an unenviable reputation as thirty-seven workers died during its construction. In 1893 the major collapse of a section of the bridge killed twenty-two workers and cost the bridge's owners a vast amount of money to restore.

PUT OUT FROM THE SHORE. OTHERS STRUGGLED DESPERATELY, AND WERE CARRIED OFF BY THE CURRENT TO SINK ALMOST AS RESCUE WAS AT HAND. THE WOUNDED WERE SOON REMOVED TO PLACES OF SAFETY, AND AS QUICKLY AS POSSIBLE A TUGBOAT WAS CHARTERED AND PUT TO WORK REMOVING THE DEBRIS.

THE BRIDGE WAS A CANTILEVER OF FIVE SPANS. THE SHORE SPANS, ONE ON EACH SIDE, WERE 200 FEET EACH IN LENGTH, AND ARE COMPLETED. THERE ARE THREE CHANNEL SPANS, TWO OF 550 FEET EACH AND ONE OF 553 FEET. ONE OF THE 550 FOOT SPANS HAS NOT BEEN BEGUN, AND IT WAS ONE OF THE 553 FOOT WHICH FELL DURING THE MORNING. THE OTHER FELL AT NIGHT.

THE FIRST ONE WHICH FELL WOULD HAVE BEEN COMPLETED THAT DAY. A GREAT DEAL HAS BEEN SAID ABOUT THE FALSE WORK BEING POORLY CONSTRUCTED.

This terrible accident could have been even worse. The collapsing superstructure barely missed a fully loaded ferryboat crossing the river. Other major construction accidents plagued the project and before it was completed, an estimated thirty-seven workmen – laborers, crew chiefs, mechanics and floaters – died building the Big Four Bridge.

A Flood of Fire

Bridge construction was not the only hazardous industrial undertaking in the Point. The *Louisville Commercial* of August 15, 1890, reported a bizarre scene when Beargrass Creek became a river of flames and a remarkably foul stench filled the air.

FROM BOX 94, AT 10:55 O'CLOCK YESTERDAY MORNING, THREE ALARMS, ONE AFTER THE OTHER, WERE SENT IN, CALLING THE WHOLE FIRE DEPARTMENT TO BUTCHERTOWN TO WHAT PROVED TO BE THE LARGEST FIRE THAT HAS VISITED LOUISVILLE FOR YEARS.

Before the engines could reach the spot the Beargrass Distillery, and the Great Western Pork Packing Company, were in flames, and the Old Kentucky Woolen Mills in imminent danger of destruction. Water was found to be scarce, and all the old hose at the different engine houses was sent for.

It was in the rear of the warehouse of the Kentucky Distilling Company that the fire originated. Captain H. Mathews, the storekeeper in charge of the warehouse, was engaged in watching about fifteen men as they tightened the hoops on the barrels, loosened by shrinkage. While the men were hard at work a whiskey barrel fell from the fifth tier, and crashing on the floor sent its contents flying in all directions.

Before one of the workmen who leaped for the lamp by the light of which they were working could reach it, the whisky had burst into a blaze. Seeing that nothing more could be done, the men all dashed from the building. Hardly had they left the warehouse when explosion after explosion told them the fire had gained a good start, and that it would be utterly impossible to save any of the 29,000 barrels of whisky stored in the house.

Back of the warehouse were located the stock pens of the pork house. These were soon fired by the streams of burning whisky which flowed in among the pens. All the cattle were taken out safely, but the light framework of the pens soon added fuel for the flames. The burning whisky flowed into the dirty waters of Beargrass creek.

At 1:15 o'clock the fire was completely under control, the blaze in the pork house was entirely extinguished and the fire had been confined to the warehouses where the burning whisky in the cellar still sent up a steady blaze and sickening odors, which almost overcame the firemen.

Another memorable disaster of March 1890 was the destructive tornado that devastated the West End of Louisville from Parkland to the river's edge at Seventh Street. The powerful cyclone crossed over the river to strike Jeffersonville and returned to the Kentucky shore to destroy the Water Tower on River Road. A new Central Station depot was built by the Chesapeake & Ohio Southwestern Railroad, located at Seventh Street and the waterfront. When the tornado struck the location, the original small wooden structure was blown apart, to be replaced later in the year by a larger brick building.

Over one hundred lives were lost in this unprecedented windstorm. The north side of East Main Street was destroyed, but the heavy demand for commercial property near the river caused the area to be rebuilt almost immediately.

A City's Call for Parks

A small article in the June 5, 1887, edition of *The Courier-Journal* documents one of the most significant events in Louisville's post-Civil War era. At a quiet dinner meeting between friends, a discussion was held which resulted in a movement to create a park system for Louisville. An intellectual seed was planted that evening which would produce a series of world-class public parks and parkways and transform the city and its inhabitants.

The Salmagundi Club is a society organization for mutual improvement....At one of its late meetings the subject of public parks for the city of Louisville was presented

A devastating tornado struck downtown Louisville in 1890 leveling dozens of buildings, including a temporary rail depot at Seventh Street and the river. The large mansion, built by tobacco magnate Richardson Burge, was the last of the great riverfront estates that once overlooked the waterfront and the Falls of the Ohio. *(University of Louisville Photographic Archives, 1981.37.26)*

BY CAPTAIN THOMAS SPEED, AND FULLY DISCUSSED. THE QUESTION PROVED SO INTERESTING THAT A COMMITTEE OF WHICH MAJOR WILLIAM J. DAVIE WAS MADE CHAIRMAN, WAS APPOINTED TO COLLATE THE ARGUMENT AND PRESENT IT WITH ADDITIONAL SUGGESTIONS IN THE FRONT OF A REPORT AT A FUTURE MEETING. THE COMMITTEE MADE A RÉSUMÉ OF THE DISCUSSIONS AS INSTRUCTED, AND APPOINTED COLONEL ANDREW COWAN TO WRITE OUT THE REPORT AND MR. CHARLES HERMANY TO PREPARE THE MAPS ILLUSTRATING THE LOCATION OF THE SEVERAL PARKS IT WAS THOUGHT LOUISVILLE SHOULD HAVE SOONER OR LATER.

PUBLIC PARKS FOR THE RECREATION, HEALTH AND BENEFIT OF THE PUBLIC AND FREE TO ALL FOREVER ARE RECOGNIZED AS IMPERATIVE NECESSITIES WHEREVER LARGE BODIES OF PEOPLE HAVE COME TOGETHER FOR PERMANENT RESIDENCE. IT HAS BEEN THE COMMON ASSERTION HERETOFORE WHEN THIS QUESTION HAS BEEN DISCUSSED HERE THAT WE DO NOT NEED PARKS BECAUSE OUR STREETS ARE SO BROAD AND THE GROUNDS SURROUNDING OUR HANDSOME RESIDENCES ARE SO AMPLE AND BEAUTIFUL.

BUT THE LARGEST PART OF OUR POPULATION HAS NO SUCH ADVANTAGES AND LIVES FROM YEAR-TO-YEAR IN SMALL DWELLINGS OR ROOMS OPPRESSED THROUGHOUT THE LONG SUMMER MONTHS BY EXCESSIVE HEAT, FROM WHICH THEY CANNOT ESCAPE.

THE HOT PAVEMENTS AND UNWHOLESOME GUTTERS ARE THE CHILDREN'S PLAYGROUNDS, WHILE HUNDREDS PERISH EVERY YEAR FOR LACK OF PURE AIR AND WHOLESOME RECREATION. WHEN THE HOT DAYS OF JUNE AND THE OPPRESSIVE NIGHTS OF JULY AND AUGUST PRODUCE THE USUAL EXODUS OF THE WEALTHY, AND THOSE WHO CAN AFFORD TO TRAVEL TO THE LAKES OR THE MOUNTAINS, THERE YET REMAIN ONE HUNDRED AND FIFTY THOUSAND MEN, WOMEN AND CHILDREN WHO TOIL ON AND SUFFER UNDER CONDITIONS FROM WHICH THERE IS NO RESPITE. FOR THE WORKING PEOPLE AND FOR ALL THE PEOPLE WHO MUST RESIDE WITHIN THE CONFINES OF THE CITY FROM YEAR-TO-YEAR, BECAUSE THEY CANNOT AFFORD TO GO AWAY, PUBLIC PARKS ARE IMPERATIVELY NEEDED, AND MUST BE PROVIDED.

IT MATTERS NOT WHERE THE INVESTIGATION OF THE PARK QUESTION IS CARRIED, AT HOME OR ABROAD, THE VERDICT IN ITS FAVOR IS UNIVERSAL. WHETHER WE CONSIDER THE QUESTION IN A PURELY FINANCIAL WAY OR IN THE LIGHT OF SENTIMENT AND PHILANTHROPY, IT APPEARS EMINENTLY SAFE, WISE AND IMPORTANT TO PROVIDE FREE PLEASURE GROUNDS OF THE PEOPLE. THEY INCREASE IN AN IMPORTANT SENSE THE ATTRACTIONS OF A CITY AS A DESIRABLE PLACE OF RESIDENCE.

PUBLIC PARKS CERTAINLY CONFER BENEFITS EQUAL TO ALL THAT THEY COST, AND SUCH PLEASURE GROUNDS FOR THE PEOPLE OF LOUISVILLE SHOULD BE PROVIDED WITHOUT DELAY. THE MEN OR PARTY WHO WILL ADVOCATE AND ESTABLISH A SYSTEM OF PARKS COMMENSURATE WITH THE FUTURE GROWTH OF THE CITY, IMPROVED SUFFICIENTLY TO MEET THE PRESENT NECESSITIES, WILL DESERVE AND WIN THE GRATITUDE OF ITS PEOPLE.

SURROUNDING THE CITY ON THREE SIDES ARE PICTURESQUE GROUNDS, ADMIRABLY SUITED FOR PARKS AND CAPABLE OF IMPROVEMENT, TO SATISFY PRESENT NEEDS WITHOUT A LARGE EXPENDITURE OF MONEY. AT NO FUTURE TIME IN THE HISTORY OF LOUISVILLE IS IT PROBABLE THAT THIS PROPERTY MAY BE OBTAINED AT SUCH A FAVORABLE PRICE AS AT PRESENT.

THE PARKS WILL ENHANCE THE ATTRACTIONS OF LOUISVILLE IMMENSELY, WILL INFLUENCE THOUSANDS TO MAKE THEIR HOMES HERE WHO WOULD OTHERWISE PASS US BY, WILL ADD TO THE WEALTH AND STIMULATE THE BUSINESS OF THE CITY, AND WILL SURELY REPAIR THEIR ENTIRE COST IN MANY WAYS WITHIN THE LIFETIME OF THOUSANDS WHO WITNESS THE DAY OF THEIR BEGINNING. WITHIN THE CITY LIMITS THERE IS NOW A SMALL PUBLIC PARK KNOWN AS BAXTER SQUARE, SITUATED AT JEFFERSON AND ELEVENTH STREETS. IT IS INTERESTING TO WITNESS THE CROWDS WHO FREQUENT THIS LITTLE PARK ON HOT EVENINGS AND ENJOY THE OPPORTUNITY FOR BREATHING AN ATMOSPHERE PURER AND LESS OPPRESSIVE THAN THAT AFFORDED BY THEIR SMALL ROOMS HERE.

The small park at Baxter Square had been created in 1880, one hundred years after the city's establishment, on the grounds formerly housing the first cemetery. This small plot of land and the courthouse grounds were the only public spaces in Louisville spared from the original trustees' land sale to satisfy the debt to John Campbell. The bones of Louisville's original pioneer settlers were removed from the old cemetery, and the first public park owned and maintained by the city moved in. Civic leaders, like members of the influential Salmagundi Club, started the ball in motion and sought out expert advice to plan a park system for Louisville.

The city called in America's most influential landscape architect, and Frederick Law Olmsted accepted the challenge of creating a park system for Louisville that would rank as one of the finest achievements of his long career. He knew Louisville from his time visiting as secretary general of the U.S. Sanitary Commission and, in the 1870s, had designed the grounds for Jeffersonville's Quartermaster Depot. Olmsted studied Louisville's potential as a park site and made an informal report to city leaders. In 1891 he was asked to submit a more formal document and he made powerful arguments for a systematic planning strategy. Among his observations, soon to be adopted by the City of Louisville, were the following:

WE PRESUME THAT IT WILL BE FOUND IN YOUR CITY, AS IT HAS BEEN IN OTHERS, THAT MANY GOOD PEOPLE HAVE FALLEN INTO HABITS OF CONSIDERING PROJECTS AND PLANS OF PUBLIC WORKS IN A GREAT DEGREE FROM LOCAL POINTS OF VIEW, MORE ESPECIALLY GIVING THOUGHT TO THE EFFECT THE PROPOSAL OPERATIONS MAY BE EXPECTED TO HAVE IN MAKING REAL ESTATE IN THEIR VICINITY MORE VALUABLE, RELATIVELY, TO REAL ESTATE ELSEWHERE.

THIS, UNLESS THE COMMUNITY OF LOUISVILLE IS A FORTUNATELY EXCEPTIONAL CHARACTER, WILL INVITE ATTEMPTS TO ACCOMPLISH WHAT IS DESIRED IN BEHALF OF EACH SECTION BY LOG-ROLLING COMBINATIONS AND OTHER MANEUVERS, CONCERNING WHICH IT MAY BE SAID THAT IT WOULD BE BETTER THAT THE CITY SHOULD HAVE NO PARKS AT ALL FOR THE NEXT HUNDRED YEARS THAN THAT IT SHOULD BE SADDLED

WITH SUCH WRETCHED, MAKE-SHIFT, INCOHERENT PARKS AS WOULD RESULT IF IT SHOULD BE ATTEMPTED TO MAKE THE BUSINESS OF YOUR COMMISSION, NOW OR HEREAFTER, A BUSINESS OF POLITICAL BARGAINS AND THE MARKETING OF PATRONAGE. THAT, IN PARK ADMINISTRATION, IS THE STRAIGHT WAY TO RUIN.

WE ADVISED YOU ALSO TO BE PREPARED TO STRENUOUSLY DISAPPOINT ALL NOTIONS THAT ANY MAY HAVE FORMED THAT YOU ARE TO SPEND THE PUBLIC MONEY ENTRUSTED TO YOU UPON OBJECTS OF CURIOSITY OR DECORATION; YOUR BUSINESS IS TO FORM PARKS, NOT MUSEUMS OR COLLECTIONS OF ORNAMENTS. IF GIFTS ARE OFFERED YOU OF OBJECTS SIMPLY ORNAMENTAL, BY ALL MEANS DECLINE THEM. ADMIT NOTHING TO YOUR PARKS THAT ARE NOT FITTING AND HELPFUL TO THEIR DISTINGUISHING PURPOSE.

THE OBJECT OF ACQUIRING THESE LARGE PUBLIC PROPERTIES FAR OUT IN THE ENVIRONS OF THE CITY IS TO SUPPLY SOMETHING THAT GARDENS CANNOT SUPPLY; TO SUPPLY SOMETHING RADICALLY DIFFERENT FROM, AND ANTITHETICAL TO, THAT WHICH GARDENS IN THE CITY SUPPLY. WHAT IS IT? SIMPLY THE HEALTHFULLY SOOTHING AND REFRESHING EFFECT WHICH EXPERIENCE PROVES IS EXERCISE UPON PEOPLE ESCAPING FROM THE SPLENDOR AND BUSTLE, THE CONFINEMENT AND DISTURBANCE OF TOWNS, INTO THE MIDST OF SPACIOUS NATURAL SCENERY. NOT INTO A SUCCESSION OF SCENES, BUT INTO SCENERY IN A MORE COMPREHENSIVE SENSE.

FURTHER, BUT PURSUING THE SAME LINE OF ADVICE, WE CAUTIONED YOU TO BEWARE OF YIELDING TO ANY APPARENT PUBLIC IMPATIENCE TO SEE PLEASING RESULTS OF YOUR WORK. WE HAVE KNOWN VALUABLE OPPORTUNITIES DESTROYED AND LARGE FUNDS GIVEN TO WASTE BECAUSE OF A DESIRE TO HAVE SOMETHING ACCOMPLISHED IN SHORT ORDER BY WHICH THOUGHTLESS PEOPLE MIGHT BE TRANSIENTLY PLEASED. THIS IS CHEAP POLITICS. THIS IS DEAR PARK-MAKING.

THE PRINCIPAL WORK THAT YOU HAVE TO DO IS A WORK OF PREPARATION WHEREBY NATURE WILL BE INVITED TO PRODUCE, BY GROWTH, IN THE COURSE OF YEARS, THAT WHICH IS TO BE DESIRED IN A PARK. WORK DIRECTED TO EARLY RESULTS IN PARKS IS NEARLY ALWAYS LAMENTABLE WORK; COSTLY RELATIVELY TO ITS VALUE; OBVIOUSLY ARTIFICIAL AND UNNATURAL, AND DESIGNED WITH A VIEW TO CHEAP APPLAUSE OF THOSE ON WHOM IT IMPOSES.

THE COST OF MAINTAINING PARKS IS A MATTER OF MORE IMPORTANCE IN DETERMINING PLANS FOR THEM THAN THE COST OF FORMING THEM.

THE BEST EFFECT OF SCENERY WILL BE TO PROMOTE A RESTFUL, CONTEMPLATIVE AND MUSING DISPOSITION OF MIND, AND IT IS TO BE SUITABLY ADMIRED ONLY WITH SUCH A DISPOSITION OF MIND. IT GROWS IN VALUE AS IT GIVES LESS GRATIFICATION TO CURIOSITY, AND AS ITS EFFECT IS LESS SENSATIONAL. IT GROWS IN VALUE AS IT GROWS IN AGE.

Frederick Law Olmsted, the father of American landscape architecture, met with Louisville officials to determine the future of a system of public parks for the city. During the Civil War, Olmsted served as executive secretary of the U.S. Sanitary Commission, a charitable organization especially active in Louisville. *Courtesy of the National Park Service, Frederick Law Olmsted National Historic Site*

Families on shantyboats sometimes found themselves grounded when a falling river level deposited their floating homes on the shore and many remained in place for years. Henry Dutchins and family tended a vegetable garden and raised chickens on their rent-free estate on the river's edge. *(Filson Historical Society, photo by R. C. Ballard Thruston, TC 630)*

Gateway to the South
(1901-1937)

Failure to utilize that which we have is waste. Waste does not necessarily mean to throw away something concrete – it means just as well failure to realize upon something which may have value.

That's the exact instance we have in Louisville with respect to our waterfront. We have an asset there of a value which cannot be inventoried readily. We have a river which winds about the city in a most picturesque way, and except for a few private bathing beaches out of the city limits, the river avails little save for our most stark needs.

We might have a beautiful river drive, something for which other cities have spent vast sums. We might have river beaches, by eliminating contamination. We might have a series of parks.

These are not impossibilities. They are possibilities within the means of the city.

Why should we not realize upon that which nature has given to us as a bounty?

– Louisville Civic Opinion - 1927

At the beginning of the twentieth century Louisville's prevailing economic bases, trade and transportation, were being replaced by manufacturing. Louisville's waterfront, especially the area lying east of the main landing area between Third and Sixth Streets, became home to public utilities and factories fed by coal. A *Courier-Journal* report in June 1900 reveals the impact to the waterfront by the arrival of fleets of coal barges:

COMING IN

THE CANAL AND ALMOST THE ENTIRE KENTUCKY SIDE OF THE OHIO RIVER FROM SEVENTH STREET TO AND ABOVE FIRST STREET WERE A BLACK MASS OF COAL BARGES YESTERDAY, AND FOR A FEW HOURS IT WAS ESTIMATED THAT NEARLY 3,375,000 BUSHELS OF THE BLACK DIAMONDS WERE IN THIS HARBOR.

THE COAL FLEET FROM PITTSBURGH ARRIVED YESTERDAY MORNING, AND IT WAS RESPONSIBLE FOR A LARGER DISPLAY OF COAL THAN HAS BEEN SEEN HERE FOR MANY MONTHS....EACH (TOWBOAT) TOWING FROM SIXTEEN TO TWENTY-THREE BARGES FOLLOWED. THE TOTAL NUMBER OF BARGES WAS SAID TO BE 225, EACH AVERAGING 15,000 BUSHELS, MAKING A TOTAL OF 3,375,000 BUSHELS.

The Symbol of Laziness

Perhaps as a relief from the community's growing industrialization, Louisville embraced the new park system designed by Olmsted and his firm, and families began moving to the scenic parkways linking the three major public parks on the city's edges – Shawnee, Iroquois and Cherokee. Labor-saving inventions and a gradually shortening work week for laborers caused people to seek the outdoors for recreation, exercise and relaxation.

Some folks had already achieved these noble goals – they were the people of the shantyboats. Their homes little more than simple shacks built on a floating platform, shantyboaters were free-spirited individualists who cared little for public opinion or routine jobs. Nomadic by inclination, they survived on the outside margins of society, living lives not far removed from the earliest American pioneers. They disdained wage-based labor, did not pay taxes or utility bills and reported to no census taker. The *Louisville Commercial* of September 15, 1889, provided an account.

LIFE IN A SHANTY BOAT

How the Inhabitants Make a Living and How They Live in Their Queer Domiciles

Standing on the river bank, anywhere from Floyd Street to the Cut-Off, and even to the Water Works, one can see "shanty" boats by the score, each being occupied by from four to six individuals. The inhabitants of "shanty" boats are usually a very ordinary and illiterate class, and their only visible means of support is fishing. The fish that are caught find a place in the "live box," where they are kept until a sufficient quantity has been collected, then they are marketed either in the city or to passing steamers. Fishermen who make their homes in "shanty" boats are seldom seen far from their haunts — the boats or the river very near — and it is a rare thing for any of them to visit the business portion of the city. Like the policemen, firemen, street car driver or newspaper reporter, the "shanty" boat man never knows any Sunday. He plies his vocation just the same on the day that the more religious have for rest, and his days are all days of rest, for he lounges about in a skiff watching lines or busies himself mending nets and lines, while his wife cares for the "mess" that has been made. The symbol of laziness is the "shanty" boat fisherman. He knows no hard work and such a thing as manual labor is as foreign to him as snow in midsummer.

Louisville writer Elizabeth Cherry Waltz wrote a fanciful article for *The Courier-Journal* embellishing her visit to the large shantyboat colony around Towhead Island in 1899. Miss Waltz portrayed herself as an inquiring male visitor called the "Vagrant."

But it was the water nomads that the Vagrant came to visit. He had often thought much about them in a casual way. He had read somewhere that before 1896, the people living in house-boats along the Ohio and Mississippi Rivers were estimated as being 10,000 in number. There are not nearly so many now, for a vigorous war has been waged against them as a class since then, Cincinnati and Louisville passing strong ordinances then and the river towns following their example. Many people have abandoned the life on account of the odium attached until today. It is only those who are virtually wedded to the life who survive.

The streams called them from the plow and the hoe. Afar was fortune and the river called them, afar was adventure and existence and the river was the easy and the royal way. Whole families came down the tributaries of the Allegheny and the Monongahela, entered the Ohio and floated onward month after month. What a life it was. The river teemed with fish, the wooded shores were full of game, the country was beautiful and the river a lullaby. It was easy days, easy living, and many of the weaker-minded found it more to their taste than to hew down forests and build cabins in the clearing. So began river life, so has river life lasted for generations. There are many living it who were born in it, others that would not live otherwise if they could.

Hell and High Water in Louisville

The Ohio River presented dangers and demanded respect.

Crewman Ed Farrell stands ready to launch a rescue boat from the Life-Saving Station bay. The original rescue boats were powered only by the tough crews manning oars, who were dedicated and knowledgeable of local river conditions. In later years, speed launches and other vessels took over the rescue missions. *(Photo courtesy of Michael Maloney)*

Ohio, to assist in saving lives. They loaded their rowboat on flatcars and rode the rails to where they were needed. In Dayton, Gillooly's crew was credited with saving eight hundred lives and performing heroic deeds of stamina and river skills.

Gillooly's log book on April 3, 1913, recorded conditions in Louisville.

April 3, at 8.45 a.m., 48 to 65 mile gale blowing, with heavy rain. Manned two boats and went to "Cut-Off" east of station to render assistance to a few families living on Fulton Street. One of the boats found an old man and woman in a frame dwelling that was rocking with the wind; carried them to No. 10 engine house. The other persons in this locality thought to be in need of assistance were reassured by the boatmen, and remained in their houses. Boatman Owen Curley was disabled and off duty at his home in the submerged district on this date. When the storm broke, the wall of an old building in the rear of his dwelling fell with a crash, badly frightening a number of women and children nearby. Curley, with the aid of his 16-year-old son, took the terrified persons, 14 in all, from their homes to land. While getting some of them down a ladder into his boat, he fell with a child in his arms. In trying to save the child from injury he himself was injured so badly as to require the services of a physician.

Louisville's history is filled with destructive floods which inundated the waterfront area. About every fifty years, major floods filled the streets well above the normal river level. The Flood of 1832 ravaged old Shippingport to such an extent it never really recovered its economic vitality. Louisville experienced an unprecedented three-year cycle of major flooding in 1882, 1883 and 1884, with the latter setting the local record of 46.7 feet, as recorded on the official river gauge. The waters reached twenty feet above normal flood stage and wrecked the wharf area of old Portland and destroyed most homes and buildings on the Point.

The year 1913 saw serious regional flooding in many communities on the Ohio and its tributaries. The crews of Louisville's Life-Saving Station were experts in water rescues, and Captain Jack Gillooly led a four-man crew to Dayton,

Both the lifesavers and the shantyboaters shared a love for the river, but their roles in society were vastly different. Shantyboat people, recreational boaters, amateur fishermen and weekend sailors enjoyed referring to themselves as "river rats." It was a term the lifesavers, towboat operators, packet boat crews and ferry pilots loathed. They were "rivermen" and in their minds the distinction was quite clear. Assigned the service rank of surfmen, the crews who manned the Life-Saving Station were proud and defensive about their reputations, and would not suffer the insult of being called rats.

River knowledge was demanded by utilities and others providing city services, like the Department of Sewage water gaugers measuring the depth of Beargrass Creek where it enters the Ohio River. The canalization project raised the river's level above the creek, causing backups of foul pollution upstream. *(University of Louisville Photographic Archives, MSD-47-2-13)*

Members of the Farrell and Mattingly families are shown enjoying Riverfront Park during its opening season in 1914. This tiny plot of green space and playground equipment, the only park in downtown Louisville, was later renamed the Mamie Varble Stratton Memorial Park and was located next to the old Wharfmaster's Offices until the 1970s. *(Photo courtesy of Michael Maloney)*

"...that little park at the wharf."

Louisville's waterfront slowly changed from its role as a transportation hub during the steamboat days to a more foreboding industrial landscape unrecognizable to earlier citizens. In 1919 Homer Dye, Jr., a reporter for *The Courier-Journal*, penned a nostalgic look at the end of the packet boat era on the Louisville wharf:

THE HAZE OF INDIAN SUMMER MINGLING WITH THE DEEPENING BLUE OF DISTANCE AND THE DORMANT GREEN OF WATER ABOVE THE DAM; THE CLANG OF A STEAMBOAT BELL, THE MONOTONOUS UNDERTONE OF THE OHIO FALLS, WITH AN OCCASIONAL STRAIN OF A NEGRO SONG, MAKE A VERITABLE REVERIE OF SOUND AND COLOR AT THE LOUISVILLE LEVEE.

OLD MEN GO THERE, WHERE THE LINGERING GHOSTS OF OLD RIVER GLORIES ARE BORNE TO THEM BY THE VAGRANT WHIFF OF SMOKE FROM THE BOAT AT THE DOCK, AND THE LAZY SWISH OF THE MOVING PADDLEWHEEL. YOUNGER MEN AND CHILDREN ALSO STAND ON THE COBBLESTONES THAT RUN DOWN THE EMBANKMENT TO THE WATER'S EDGE, AND FEEL THE CHARM AND ENCHANTMENT OF THE RIVER AND SHIP.

MAN WAS AMBITIOUS WHEN HE MADE THE DAM, BUT THE DREAMY, QUIET HARBOR THAT LAZILY LAPS THE COBBLESTONES OF LOUISVILLE'S WHARF HAS A VAGRANT, BEAUTIFUL, IRRESISTIBLE FASCINATION THAT AMOUNTS ALMOST TO A LURE. IT IS A BROAD, BEAUTIFUL BOSOM OF SMILING WATER, AND THAT IS WHAT MAKES IT DANGEROUS – DANGEROUS TO MAN'S AMBITION.

THERE IS ONE ADVANTAGE TO THE IRRESPONSIBLE ATTITUDE TAKEN BY THE DENIZENS OF THE LEVEE. THEY GET BY.

HOBOES OF ALL COLORS AND PERSUASIONS OF EPICUREANISM ARE ATTRACTED TO THE RIVERFRONT. THEY WOULD STAY THERE FOREVER WERE IT NOT FOR THE UNCEASING STRIFE AND AMBITION OF THE STOICS, WHO CANNOT ENDURE VAGABONDAGE, EVEN IN OTHER PEOPLE.

HENCE THE STOIC PROD OF A POLICEMAN'S CLUB, AND STERN, STOIC PROHIBITORY, "KEEP OFF THE GRASS," IN THE LITTLE PARK AT THE WHARF.

"WE KEEP THEM MOVING," SAID THE WHARF WATCHMAN.

"WE SPRINKLE THE GRASS EVERY NIGHT, AND THEY'RE NOT SO ANXIOUS ABOUT SLEEPING ON IT THEN," SAID THE SUPERINTENDANT OF WHARVES. "THE LITTLE PARK HERE IS ABOUT THE MOST POPULAR PLACE IN THE CITY. WOMEN AND CHILDREN COME HERE TO SEE THE STEAMBOATS COME IN, AND THEY WOULD NOT COME IF WE DIDN'T KEEP THE PLACE CLEARED OF LOAFERS, WHO HAVE NOTHING TO DO BUT LOOK AT THE RIVER AND LISTEN TO THE FALLS."

The "little park at the wharf" was Riverfront Park and it sat adjacent to the wharfmaster's office between Second and Third Street. A small fenced area, barely 100 feet deep and 200 feet wide, contained a grassy area and a set of swings and sliding boards for children. It was the first, and only, playground or park in downtown Louisville for decades. Constructed in 1914, it was there as the result of a group of civic-minded Louisvillians, primarily wives of wealthy industrialists, who formed the Outdoor Art League.

The league's motto, "Make the world more beautiful than you found it," expressed their charitable efforts to improve the lives of Louisvillians, young and old. The organization began at the old Galt House in 1902 as a branch of the Woman's Auxiliary of the American Park and Outdoor Art Association. The club quickly grew under the administration of Mrs. Charles W. Gheens as president, and developed further under the leadership of Mrs. Mamie Varble Stratton and Mrs. John H. Miller. By 1912 they recruited men into the group and changed the name to the Outdoor Art League, and their purpose was printed in their 1928 annual report:

BEAUTIFYING THE YARDS OF FACTORIES AND BENEVOLENT ASSOCIATIONS, THROUGH THE COOPERATION OF THE MANAGERS AND SUPERINTENDANTS, CLAIMED THE FIRST ATTENTION OF THE ORGANIZATION, ACCORDING TO THE YEARBOOK. OTHER EYESORES AROUND THE CITY WERE TACKLED WITH GRATIFYING RESULTS UNTIL THE LEAGUE COULD POINT OUT SCORES OF PARKS, GARDENS AND OTHER BEAUTY SPOTS IN LOUISVILLE, ACCORDING TO MRS. JOHN H. MILLER, PRESIDENT.

APPLICATION OF THE SEMI-ANNUAL CLEAN-UP CAMPAIGN IDEA IN LOUISVILLE AND KENTUCKY WAS FIRST BROUGHT ABOUT THROUGH THE OUTDOOR ART LEAGUE, ACCORDING TO MRS. MILLER. CLEANING UP AND THE ABATEMENT OF NUISANCES HAS BEEN ACCOMPLISHED THROUGH SOLICITATION AND COOPERATION, BUT NEVER BY SEEKING LEGISLATION, THE PRESIDENT SAID.

THE RIVER FRONT PARK, RENAMED A FEW YEARS AGO IN HONOR OF MRS. JOHN D. STRATTON, FIRST CHAIRMAN OF THE MUNICIPAL ART COMMITTEE, AND DUKE PLACE AT THE BAXTER AVENUE RAILROAD STATION ARE AMONG THE OUTSTANDING ACCOMPLISHMENTS OF THE LEAGUE IN BEAUTIFYING UNSIGHTLY SPOTS ABOUT THE CITY.

HUNDREDS OF CITY DWELLERS ENJOY THE BEAUTIES OF THE RIVERFRONT GARDEN AND THE BAXTER AVENUE PLOT HAS EVEN CAUSED TRAVELERS TO INQUIRE ABOUT THE ORIGIN OF THE GARDEN AND SEND CHECKS TO HELP IN THE WORK, MRS. MILLER DECLARES.

THE COMMENDABLE PURPOSE OF THE LEAGUE IS STATED IN THE SECOND ARTICLE OF THE LEAGUE'S CONSTITUTION, AS FOLLOWS:

ITS OBJECT SHALL BE TO PROMOTE THE CONSERVATION OF NATURAL SCENERY; TO ACQUIRE LANDS FOR PUBLIC

PARKS AND RESERVATIONS; TO ADVANCE ALL OUTDOOR ART; TO DESIGN AND FIT GROUNDS FOR PUBLIC AND PRIVATE USE AND ENJOYMENT; TO ABOLISH UNSIGHTLY BILLBOARDS; TO CULTIVATE ARTISTIC IDEALS IN THE HOME; TO ADVANCE THE COOPERATIVE INTERESTS OF PARENTS AND TEACHERS IN THE PUBLIC SCHOOLS AND TO FURTHER THE HIGHER INTERESTS OF EDUCATION.

THE FUNDS OF THE LEAGUE FOR ITS GENERAL WORK OF BEAUTIFYING THE CITY COME THROUGH THE MEMBERSHIP FEE OF $2 FROM EACH OF ITS 210 ACTIVE MEMBERS. WHEN SPECIAL PROJECTS ARE ATTEMPTED, SUFFICIENT MONEY IS RAISED BY CHARGING ADMISSION TO CARD PARTIES AND THROUGH FLOWER SALES.

THE MAMIE VARBLE STRATTON MEMORIAL PARK AT THE FOOT OF FOURTH STREET IS A CHARMING PLACE TO REST AND ENJOY THE BEAUTIFUL VIEW OF THE OHIO RIVER AS IT WINDS PAST THE KENTUCKY SHORE AND THE SILVER HILLS OF INDIANA. MANY CHILDREN FROM THE DOWNTOWN CONGESTED DISTRICTS PLAY ABOUT THIS LITTLE PARK AND TIRED TRAVELERS SIT AND REST IN THIS PLEASANT SPOT BEFORE CONTINUING THEIR JOURNEYS.

The 1931 rededication of Stratton Park was marked by ceremonies attended by Mayor William Harrison and the leadership of the Outdoor Art League. The League's president, Mrs. John Miller, dedicated a fountain and birdbath to honor Mrs. Stratton. The Outdoor Art League beautified Louisville's streets and factories, planted gardens in local schools and conducted a twice-annual city-wide cleanup campaign. *(Photo courtesy of the University of Louisville Art Library)*

The group bears a striking resemblance to a later City of Louisville effort, Operation Brightside, by organizing and promoting regular urban cleanup and beautification efforts. They also left another legacy to the Louisville riverfront, the enormous electric sign on the LG&E Waterside Station reading "LOUISVILLE – THE GATEWAY TO THE SOUTH." The electric sign was installed at the suggestion of the league's president, Mrs. John H. Miller. It served as Louisville's unofficial slogan and welcoming banner for decades, and also provided an unexpected benefit to river traffic, as told in a *Louisville Herald* article from July 7, 1924:

LOUISVILLE'S LEVEE SAFEST IN COUNTRY, SAY RIVERMEN

Louisville boasts the safest levee of any inland port in the country, in the opinion of veteran river boatmen.

It may be the extraordinary well-lighted riverfront that insures from harm visitors to the wharf. It may be the wholesale cleanup made by police on levee idlers a score of years ago that makes a trip to the boat landing devoid of danger. Despite the unusual illumination on the Louisville levee that reaches its greatest intensity along the foot of Third Street, the striking need of the landing is more light. The Louisville Gas and Electric Company's sign advertising Louisville as "The Gateway to the South" is the main factor in brightening up the Third Street sector, but even this burns only a part of the night, leaving the entire wharf in darkness in the early morning hours.

Installation of a string of high-powered lamps nearer the water's edge — tho above high-water mark — and enlargement of the lights along the front street to illuminate better the territory under the Chesapeake and Ohio Railroad trestle would remedy this deficiency in river-front safety as well as increase its attractiveness to residents and strangers, rivermen point out.

It was also appropriate that the Mamie Varble Stratton Memorial Park remembered the legacy of Captain Pinkney Varble, the most successful Falls Pilot in history. "Pink" Varble, known for taking more boats over the Falls than anyone else, was also the riverman who constructed the emergency pontoon bridge to Jeffersonville during the chaotic days of the Civil War.

Louisville's Twentieth Century Robinson Crusoe

Pinkney Varble was considered the city's most reliable riverman and once piloted eleven vessels over the Falls on the same day, earning $50 a trip. He had a carriage waiting for him at the Portland wharf, and when he successfully negotiated the passage of one boat, he hurried upstream to Louisville to board the next. If Varble was the standard of dependability, William "Ulix" McQueen was the opposite. The death of McQueen was remembered in a 1916 *Courier-Journal* weekly series called Noted Characters Memorable to Louisville, written by John W. Petrie.

MODERN ROBINSON CRUSOE

William "Ulix" McQueen passed the days and nights of his sixty-one years on Louisville's waterfront. His daring feats, his remarkable adventures and his eccentric habits branded him a river celebrity. He was Louisville's twentieth-century Robinson Crusoe.

Although McQueen little suspected he was a pioneer in a field, the importance of which medical science has discovered only recently, he was without a doubt the first man in America

TO PRACTICE HELIOTHERAPY — EXPOSURE OF THE BODY TO THE SUN FOR MEDICAL PURPOSES.... YEARS BEFORE AMERICA REALIZED THE WORTH OF THE ROLLIER SYSTEM AND ESTABLISHED THE ADAM MUNICIPAL HOSPITAL AT PERRYSVILLE, N.Y., ULIX WAS ENJOYING AND BENEFITING FROM A DAILY SUN BATH IN THE SANDS OF HIS ISLAND HOME, WHETHER THE TEMPERATURE WAS ZERO OR 98 DEGREES.

HIS ANTICS DURING THE WINTER MONTHS ATTRACTED MOST ATTENTION. GOING BACK TO NATURE IN A MOST DARING MANNER, McQUEEN CHASED THROUGH THE WHITE SHEETED FOREST AROUND HIS CABIN LIKE A NAKED BARBARIAN, STARTLING BY HIS ACTIVITY THE WINTER BIRDS, THE SQUIRRELS AND ALL HIBERNATING DENIZENS OF THE WOODS. COMBATING AND HEALING ALL AILMENTS WITH SUNSHINE AND OUTDOOR EXPOSURE, HE COMBINED THE LAST WORD IN CIVILIZATION WITH THE BARBARISM OF THE EARLIER APES. IN CONSTITUTION, HE WAS AS SHARP AS STEEL AND AS TOUGH AS SHOE LEATHER; IN SPIRITS, HE WAS LIGHT-HEARTED AS A BIRD AND AS MERRY AS A KING'S JESTER.

BORN IN THE EARLY FIFTIES IN NOAH'S ARK, A NOTORIOUS TENEMENT HOUSE ON THE RIVERFRONT AT PRESTON AND FULTON STREETS, McQUEEN GREW UP IN AN ATMOSPHERE OF RIVER LIFE FROM WHICH HE NEVER SEPARATED. ALTHOUGH HE WORKED FOR A FEW YEARS IN A ROLLING MILL, HE NEVER GOT AWAY FROM THE BANKS OF THE OHIO. THE FAME AND REPUTATION HE WON HAD THEIR FOUNDATION ON HIS EXPLOITS AS A RIVERMAN AND CAMPER.

SWIMMING WAS AS NATURAL WITH McQUEEN AS FLYING WITH A BIRD. LIKE A DUCK, HE "TOOK TO" WATER AND STAYED THERE. HE WAS ACCUSTOMED TO JOURNEY A GREAT DEAL BETWEEN CAMPS ON SIX MILE ISLAND AND

THE CAMP OF WHICH HE WAS GUARDIAN ON TOWHEAD. AND HE USUALLY TRAVELED BY WATER RATHER THAN BY LAND — SWIMMING THE DISTANCE OF FOUR MILES BETWEEN THE ISLANDS WAS MERELY A GOOD EXERCISE FOR HIM AND HIS NEVER-TIRING ARMS. PROPORTIONATELY HE DIVED AS WELL AS HE SWAM. OFTEN HE WOULD DISAPPEAR BENEATH THE SURFACE OF THE WATER — SECONDS WOULD SLIP INTO MINUTES AND JUST WHEN SIGHTSEERS WERE BEGINNING TO FEAR A SHARK MUST HAVE "JONAHED" HIM, ULIX WOULD REAPPEAR SEVERAL HUNDRED YARDS DISTANT FROM THE POINT OF HIS DISAPPEARANCE.

DESPITE HIS ALMOST BARBARIC HABITS, McQUEEN FELT DURING ONE PERIOD OF HIS LIFE THE TOUCH OF ROMANCE. CUPID AND A RED-HAIRED WOMAN TAUGHT HIM THE MEANING OF THE WORD LOVE. THOUGH IT WAS THE ONE AFFAIR OF THE HEART IN HIS LIFE, IT WAS A SERIOUS ATTACK AND ENDED ONLY WHEN DEATH ROBBED HIM OF HIS SWEETHEART. MAMIE CARNES, WHO MADE HER HOME IN A HOUSEBOAT AT THE FOOT OF CAMPBELL STREET, WAS THE ONLY WOMAN WHO EVER QUICKENED McQUEEN'S HEART. SHE WAS CALLED "RED CLOUD" BECAUSE OF HER AUBURN TRESSES AND THE "NIGHTINGALE OF THE POINT" BECAUSE OF HER WONDERFULLY CLEAR AND SWEET VOICE. PERHAPS IT WAS THE OLD STORY OF "MUSIC HATH CHARMS TO SOOTHE THE SAVAGE BREAST" THAT ANY RATE ULIX LOVED BETTER THAN ANYTHING — SAVE HIS COMMON BEER — TO SIT FOR HOURS AND HEAR HER SING FOR HIM.

ULIX NEVER LEFT TOWHEAD ISLAND, WINTER OR SUMMER, LOW WATER OR FLOOD STAGE. DURING THE FLOODS OF 1913 WATER STOOD SEVENTEEN FEET OVER TOWHEAD, COMPLETELY SUBMERGING McQUEEN'S CABIN AND THE SWIMMING CAMP. THAT DIDN'T WORRY ULIX HOWEVER — HE SLEPT IN A FLATBOAT TIED TO A TREE LIMB.

A most unusual visitor to the Louisville wharf arrived in 1917 when the *Success*, a British ship used to transport prisoners to Australia in the 1700s, landed for a promotional tour. The water in the canal was too shallow for passage and for the only time, a swiveling section of the Kentucky and Indiana Terminal Railroad Bridge was pivoted to allow passage for the tall ship to sail over the Falls. *(Filson Historical Society, BOA12)*

Kaiser Bill's Coffin

World War I had a powerful impact on Louisville's development, especially the establishment of a giant Army training center named for Zachary Taylor. Camp Taylor was built to house thousands of recruits for the war in Europe, and the U.S. Army created an extra-cantonment zone five miles around the camp to control sanitation, sewage and venereal diseases. The Army insisted that Louisville close the legendary row of brothels located on downtown's Green Street, and city officials not only complied, they changed the name of the street to Liberty to help purge the area's notorious reputation. With that move, Louisville lost the last vestige of Clark's plans for public greens. It also inspired questions in visitors' minds as to why Louisville's jail is located on Liberty.

Rumors of an armistice agreement stopping World War I swept Louisville three days prior to the actual end of the war. *The Courier-Journal* of November 7 heralded a city gone mad with joy, and a spontaneous and unorthodox ceremony at the Louisville waterfront.

CITY IN RIOT OF JOY AT REPORT
BEDLAM OF NOISE DROWNS DISCUSSION OF PEACE HOAX

WITH RUMORS OF PEACE AND PIECES OF RUMORS SPREADING LIKE WILDFIRE THROUGHOUT THE CITY YESTERDAY, LOUISVILLE AWOKE FROM THE "FLU" LETHARGY IN WHICH SHE HAD BEEN WRAPPED, AND IN COMMON WITH THE WHOLE COUNTRY BECAME A VICTIM OF THE GREAT HOAX AND THEREBY WAS CONVERTED INTO A VERITABLE MADHOUSE. EVERYONE WENT WILD, AND WILD, WILD WOMEN AND WILD, WILD MEN, TOO, PARADED THE STREETS LATE INTO THE NIGHT, CELEBRATING THE RUMORED GERMAN SURRENDER WITH A DISCORDANT MEDLEY OF BELLS, WHISTLES, AUTO SIRENS AND A THOUSAND NOISES JUMBLED FOR THE OCCASION. AFTER 1 O'CLOCK THE DOWNTOWN DISTRICTS TOOK ON A CARNIVAL APPEARANCE, WITH FLAGS WAVING, BANNERS FLYING AND CONFETTI WHIRLING THROUGH THE AIR IN SNOWY CLOUDS. IMPROMPTU FLOATS, DECORATED IN SERVICE FLAGS, PAPER STREAMERS AND BUNTING, HASTILY PROCURED, WERE ERECTED. FOURTH STREET, AS IF BY MAGIC, BECAME A SEETHING, BOILING MASS OF JOYOUS HUMANITY, WHICH SEEMED TO HAVE PRECIPITATELY FLUNG ITSELF INTO A BACCHANALIAN REVEL....

THE KAISER WAS UNDISPUTEDLY THE KNAVE OF THE CARNIVAL, AND MANY UNIQUE DEMONSTRATIONS WERE MADE OF WHAT SHOULD BE DONE WITH THIS APOSTLE OF BLOOD AND IRON, ONE OF THE MOST OUTSTANDING BEING A MOCK FUNERAL AND BURIAL OF THE HUN-KING, STAGED BY 400 EMPLOYEES OF THE KENTUCKY WAGON WORKS.

BURIED IN EFFIGY

A WOODEN CASKET, ON WHICH WAS WRITTEN "KAISER BILL'S COFFIN," WAS BORNE THROUGH THE STREETS. PRECEDING THE CASKET WERE FIFTEEN GIRLS FROM THE OFFICE. IT WAS FOLLOWED BY THE EMPLOYEES.

Before the procession wagon left the works, W. J. Colebourn made a funeral address. The parade then started from Third and K Streets, proceeding north to Broadway, west on Broadway to Fourth, north on Fourth to Market, east on Market to Third and north on Third to the river, where the coffin was "submarined" in the Ohio River. The funeral dirge emanated from hammer blows on a circular saw.

"the autoist today who does not wish to wait for the ferry…"

The closing days of the nineteenth century had quietly ushered in a dramatic change in Louisville and the rest of America. John E. Roche, president of the Louisville Carriage and Taxicab Company, purchased one of the first electric automobiles in the nation and, in 1898, it was delivered to Louisville. It was the first automobile in Kentucky and the first ever introduced south of the Ohio River. Made in the Waverly Plant in Indianapolis, the auto was powered by a 3.5-horsepower electric motor that required recharging every thirty-five miles. It had rubber tires and electric-powered lights and caused a sensation whenever Mr. Roche drove. It was a prophet of change for the Falls Cities.

Within twenty years, motorized vehicles would dominate the city's streets, and "autoists" began clamoring for better access to southern Indiana. A *Louisville Civic Opinion* article in 1921 sounded the call for a new bridge.

We have a bridge leading from Louisville to New Albany (the K&I) that is used for foot travel and for machines, but we have no bridge of this kind leading to Jeffersonville. Here, almost a stone's throw from Louisville's retail and wholesale center, lies a city of over fifteen thousand, and we do practically nothing to draw the trade from this city to ours… True, there is the interurban that goes from Louisville to Jeffersonville, and there is also the ferry. But there are many who would cross a foot bridge, and there are still more who would be only too glad to come to Louisville to do their buying in their autos if this city were only more accessible to them. As the matter stands today, the good folks of Jeffersonville who would come to Louisville in their machines, must drive down to the river, drive their machines on the ferry, and wait sometimes as much as half an hour before they can move on their way to Louisville. With a bridge for use of autos, there would be no such delays, and if the attitude taken on bridge tolls were more reasonable than the rates charged by the K&I there is little doubt that many Jeffersonville dollars would pour into Louisville pockets.

The autoist today who does not wish to wait for the ferry must cross to New Albany, and then go over the bridge to Louisville. The road between Jeffersonville and New Albany is such that no autoist in his right mind wants to drive over it, unless it is absolutely necessary.

Aside from all the benefits, there remains the benefit to those who would walk to work, and who, being spared the expense of at least ten cent trips on the interurban daily, would have just that much more to invest in this city. Aside from the benefits of a brisk walk across the bridge, it would not take these people any longer to walk across the bridge than to wait for the ferry or the car.

"the north side of Main Street could and would become a vast area of warehouses."

Since the beginning of Ohio River navigation, mariners had been frustrated by a river that was often too shallow to allow passage. The U.S. Army Corps of Engineers was charged with a massive river improvement project to provide a year-round navigation channel, of at least nine feet depth, for the entire length of the Ohio River. Through a program called canalization, made possible by the construction of new dams and locks, former sections of the river that had been mere pools were raised and made navigable. Most of the 1920s were spent on this ambitious, and very expensive, program of internal improvements that marked the return of river traffic, now dominated by towboats and barges.

The growth of industrial operations located at the river's edge caused city leaders to examine options for moving huge shipments of fuel, products and, increasingly, livestock through Louisville's streets. In 1915 engineers began to make plans for new river terminals to assist in moving heavy traffic, as detailed in a *Louisville Post* story.

THE IDEA ADVANCED AS A BASIS FOR THE PLANS INVOLVES THE CONSTRUCTION OF A SORT OF BELT LINE WHICH WILL CONNECT WITH ALL OF THE RAILROADS ENTERING THE CITY AND EXTENDING IN THE REAR OF THE HOUSES ON THE NORTH SIDE OF MAIN STREET WHERE IT IS NEAR THE RIVER AND EAST TO THE BOURBON STOCKYARDS AND NORTHEAST TO THE POINT AND NORTHWEST TO THE K & I BRIDGE. IT IS PROPOSED THE LINE SHALL BE BUILT ON A TRESTLE HIGH ENOUGH TO BE OUT OF RANGE OF THE HIGHEST POSSIBLE STAGES OF THE RIVER SO THAT THERE WILL BE NO INTERRUPTION FROM THAT CAUSE AT ANY TIME. IT IS ALSO PROPOSED THERE SHALL BE FREIGHT STATIONS DOTTED ALONG THE WAY AT FREQUENT INTERVALS WHERE SHIPPING CAN SEND AND RECEIVE FREIGHT AND THUS AVOID THE GREAT EXPENSE OF DRAYAGE. IT IS ALSO PROPOSED THAT SWITCHES SHALL BE BUILT FROM THE MAIN STEM OF THIS LINE INTO ANY BUSINESS HOUSE WHICH MIGHT REQUIRE IT. IN THIS WAY THE NORTH SIDE OF MAIN STREET COULD AND WOULD BECOME A VAST AREA OF WAREHOUSES.

THIS WOULD DO AWAY WITH A GREAT DEAL OF EXPENSE AND INCONVENIENCE AND WOULD DO MUCH TOWARD PUTTING THE TERMINAL FACILITIES OF LOUISVILLE ON A PAR WITH OTHER CITIES WITH WHICH THE MERCHANTS HERE HAVE TO COMPETE. FOR LACK OF FACILITIES OF THIS KIND, THOUSANDS OF HEAD OF LIVESTOCK ARE ANNUALLY DRIVEN EAST AND WEST ON MAIN STREET.

AS A RESULT OF THE LACK OF TERMINAL FACILITIES ALONG THE RIVERFRONT, MAIN STREET HAS GRADUALLY LOST ITS PRESTIGE AS THE LEADING WHOLESALE BUSINESS STREET OF THE CITY, AND MANY COMPANIES HAVE MOVED THEIR PLANTS TO LOCATIONS ALONG RAILROAD LINES ON FOURTEENTH STREET AND THE K&I BELT LINES. THE PROPOSED IMPROVEMENT WOULD DO MUCH TO RESTORE MAIN STREET AS A DESIRABLE LOCALITY FOR MERCHANTS AND MANUFACTURERS.

Efforts to transform the old Point area east of the Louisville wharf began to take advantage of the federal Ohio River canalization program. After a series of starts and stops, largely due to lawsuits by landowners, work on Louisville's industrial waterfront began.

Louisville Herald, April 15, 1922

WATER FRONT ASSIGNED TO NEW PROJECT

WITH THE SIGNING OF AN AGREEMENT YESTERDAY BETWEEN THE CITY OF LOUISVILLE AND THE INLAND WATERWAYS COMPANY, BY WHICH THE LATTER IS GRANTED THE PRIVILEGE OF ERECTING A RIVER

Completion of the LG&E Hydroelectric Plant on Shippingport Island in 1927 increased the number of high-powered transmission lines into the city. The Louisville waterfront, complete with the Waterside generating plant and the Short-Line Railroad trestle, began to be claimed by heavy industries and utilities. The golden days of river travel were about finished and new uses were found for the prime Louisville real estate on the river's edge. *(University of Louisville Photographic Archives, 86226)*

TERMINAL ON CITY PROPERTY EMBRACING 2,200 FEET TO THE EAST OF PRESTON STREET ON THE RIVERFRONT, THE FIRST STEP TOWARD THE COMPLETION OF THE PROJECT WHICH HAS BEEN AGITATED HERE FOR THE PAST FIFTY YEARS WAS TAKEN AND AN EPOCH MARKED IN LOUISVILLE'S ECONOMIC DEVELOPMENT.

Courier-Journal, April 15, 1922
RIVER TERMINAL SITE IS GRANTED

PLANS FOR THE DEVELOPMENT OF THE OHIO RIVER SHIPPING FACILITIES BECAME A REALITY YESTERDAY AFTERNOON WHEN C. C. STOLL, CHAIRMAN OF THE BOARD OF PUBLIC WORKS, SIGNED A LEASE GRANTING TO THE INLAND WATERWAYS COMPANY, A $1,000,000 CORPORATION, THE USE OF CITY LAND ON THE RIVERFRONT FOR THE PURPOSE OF ESTABLISHING MODERN RIVER TERMINAL DEPOTS WHERE FREIGHT MAY BE TRANSFERRED FROM BARGES TO LAND TRANSPORTATION UNITS.

SIMULTANEOUSLY WITH THE SIGNING OF THE LEASE CAME THE ANNOUNCEMENT OF GOVERNMENT ENGINEERS THAT ALL OF THE LOCKS ON THE OHIO RIVER BETWEEN LOUISVILLE AND PITTSBURGH WILL BE COMPLETED WITHIN TWO YEARS.

The economic arguments for waterfront development were compelling, as delineated by the *Louisville Civic Opinion* in 1922.

RIVER SHIPPING IS SO MUCH CHEAPER THAN RAIL SHIPPING, AND THE NATURAL ADVANTAGES ARE GREAT, TOO, IN THE COMPETITION THAT THE RIVER RATES IMPOSE ON RAILWAY RATES. THIS LATTER STATEMENT CAN BE BEST REALIZED, WHEN THE FOLLOWING COMPARISON IS SHOWN: FOR ONE DOLLAR, YOU CAN SHIP ONE TON OF FREIGHT BY HORSE AND WAGON FOUR MILES. BY ENGLISH STEEL TRUCK, YOU CAN SHIP THE SAME TON AT THE SAME COST, 20 MILES. BY UNITED STATES RAILWAY, YOU CAN SHIP A TON 133 MILES FOR A DOLLAR. ON THE ERIE CANAL, THE SAME TON WILL TRAVEL 200 MILES FOR THE SAME PRICE.

Courier-Journal, November 26, 1922
BUSINESS HUMS ON RIVERFRONT

ACTIVITY IN RIVER CIRCLES INCREASED DURING THE LAST FEW DAYS, WHEN THE INLAND WATERWAYS COMPANY, A $2,000,000 CORPORATION, STARTED THE CONSTRUCTION OF RIVER TERMINALS AT THE LEVEE BETWEEN BROOK AND CAMPBELL STREETS.

THE OHIO RIVER SAND COMPANY ALSO HAS BEGUN INSTALLATION OF A MODERN CONVEYING MACHINE AT ITS PLANT AT THE FOOT OF FIRST STREET. THE NEW STEEL STRUCTURE WILL BE CONSTRUCTED PRIMARILY FOR SAND AND GRAVEL, BUT MAY BE PUT TO OTHER USES.

Louisville Herald, April 5, 1923

A NEW PAGE IN THE HISTORY OF OHIO RIVER TRANSPORTATION WILL BE WRITTEN WITH THE COMPLETION OF THE INLAND WATERWAYS COMPANY'S EASTERN FREIGHT TERMINAL AT THE FOOT OF PRESTON STREET, WHICH IS NOW UNDER CONSTRUCTION. THE NEW PLANT WILL CONSIST OF A COMPLETELY EQUIPPED FLOATING DOCK, WITH A 500-TON DERRICK, OVERHEAD CRANE AND BELT CONVEYOR, MAKING POSSIBLE THE SPEEDY TRANSFERENCE OF FREIGHT FROM BARGES TO WAITING TRUCKS AND RAILROAD FREIGHT CARS ON THE LEVEE; A RAILROAD SWITCH ALONG THE RIVER BANK WILL BE REINFORCED BY A CONCRETE WALL THE ENTIRE LENGTH OF THE TERMINAL'S RIVERFRONT. SEVEN

FIREPROOF WAREHOUSES WILL BE ERECTED AND MORE WILL BE ADDED AS NEEDED. PREPARATIONS WILL BE MADE TO TAKE CARE OF THE RIVER BUSINESS, WHEN THE RIVER IS AT ITS LOWEST STAGE AND ALSO AT A RISE OF THIRTY FEET. THE NEW CONCERN WILL TAKE IN THE RIVER FRONTAGE FROM FLOYD STREET TO CLAY STREET. ANOTHER PROOF THAT LOUISVILLE IS TRULY THE "GATEWAY TO THE SOUTH...."

The hard-luck Big Four railroad bridge to Jeffersonville had been a deathtrap since its construction in 1895 and continued to cost lives well after completion. A January 15, 1918, story in *The Courier-Journal* described a horrifying incident involving interurban trains.

THREE KILLED, SCORE HURT IN CRASH
INTERURBAN CARS ON BRIDGE APPROACH AS CROWDED COACHES COME TOGETHER IN HEAVY SNOWSTORM

LOADED DOWN WITH HUMANITY, TWO CARS OF THE LOUISVILLE AND NORTHERN RAILWAY & LIGHTING COMPANY CRASHED TOGETHER DURING A BLINDING SNOWSTORM HIGH UPON THE APPROACH TO THE BIG FOUR BRIDGE YESTERDAY AFTERNOON AT 5:30 O'CLOCK. THERE WAS A SPLINTERING OF TIMBERS AND CRIES OF THE INJURED. SIX PERSONS FELL HEADLONG THROUGH THE TRESTLE AND INTO THE DEEP SNOWDRIFTS FIFTY-FIVE FEET BELOW ON THE LOUISVILLE & NASHVILLE TRACKS AT CAMPBELL AND GEIGER STREETS. THREE LOST THEIR LIVES AND MORE THAN A SCORE WERE INJURED, SOME PROBABLY FATALLY.

RUNNING AN HOUR AND A HALF LATE, NO. 204, THE LIMITED FROM INDIANAPOLIS, WAS GIVEN THE "CLEAR" SIGNAL AT THE JEFFERSONVILLE END OF THE BRIDGE. AS THE CAR MADE A MOMENTARY STOP ON THE NORTH APPROACH, HUNDREDS OF PERSONS CROWDED ABOUT THE CAR AND DEMANDED TRANSPORTATION. ONLY A FEW MEN MANAGED TO BOARD THE ALREADY LOADED CAR. THREE MINUTES BEFORE THE LOUISVILLE AND JEFFERSONVILLE LOCAL NO. 402 HAD GONE BY IT WAS MAKING ITS WAY SLOWLY OVER THE SNOW-COVERED TRACKS. MEN, WOMEN AND CHILDREN STOOD IN THE AISLES. THE BACK PLATFORM WAS JAMMED. UNABLE TO MOVE, THE PASSENGERS ON THE BACK PLATFORM, LOOKING OUT THROUGH THE FROSTED WINDOWS, SAW NO. 204 COMING DIRECTLY BEHIND.

NO ONE THOUGHT OF DANGER UNTIL THE HEADLIGHT'S GLARE SHOWN FULL IN THEIR FACES. THERE WAS NO SPACE AVAILABLE AND IN A MOMENT THE ENTIRE REAR PLATFORM AND VESTIBULE OF THE CAR WERE TORN AWAY. PERSONS WERE SPILLED HERE AND THERE ON THE ICE-COVERED TRESTLE. SOME FELL HEADLONG WHILE OTHERS WERE SEEN TO STRUGGLE FOR A MOMENT AND THEN SLIP.

The New Bridge inside the Old Bridge

Antiquated and poorly constructed, the original Big Four Bridge was incapable of bearing the heavy weight of modern diesel engines and their massive loads. Plans were made to upgrade the railroad bridge, but many in the community demanded a downtown automobile bridge first. In 1928 Louisville faced the necessity of building two bridges simultaneously and remarkably, the city succeeded in doing both.

Louisville Times, February 6, 1928
REBUILDING OF SPAN PLANNED
TENTATIVE PLANS FOR RECONSTRUCTION OF THE BIG

Port terminals, warehouses, scrapyards, asphalt plants and sand companies lined the riverfront east of downtown Louisville by the late 1940s. All this former industrial land was acquired, cleaned and transformed into Waterfront Park, producing a renaissance on the river's edge. *(Filson Historical Society, LAV 6)*

The interior of the original 1895 version of the Big Four Bridge featured a regulation train track, another set of rails for interurban service and two pedestrian walkways across the river. The poorly designed and constructed bridge was unable to accommodate the massive weight of diesel engines and was replaced by a new bridge in 1929. *(University of Louisville Photographic Archives, 1998.11.71)*

When the Big Four Bridge was rebuilt, its narrow single-track width fit comfortably within the structure of the original bridge. The new bridge was built upon the original piers, and when it was completed the old bridge surrounding it was torn down, allowing the entire new structure to be completed in about one year of construction. In 2010 plans were completed to convert the abandoned railroad bridge into a spectacular walking path from Kentucky to Indiana. *(Filson Historical Society, BCO4)*

FOUR BRIDGE HERE HAVE BEEN FILED WITH COLONEL GEORGE R. SPALDING, UNITED STATES DISTRICT ENGINEER FOR THE LOUISVILLE DISTRICT, IT WAS ANNOUNCED MONDAY.

THE PLANS CALL FOR THE EXPENDITURE OF BETWEEN $3,000,000 AND $4,000,000, ACCORDING TO C. A. PENNINGTON, SUPERINTENDENT OF THE LOUISVILLE & JEFFERSONVILLE BRIDGE & RAILROAD COMPANY, OWNER OF THE BRIDGE. NEW STEELWORK AND NEW APPROACHES AND RECONSTRUCTION OF PIERS ARE CONTEMPLATED IN THE PLANS.

Negotiating the financing took time, but work on the Big Four advanced quickly because of an unusual engineering solution – build a new bridge inside the old bridge.

Louisville Herald-Post, February 17, 1929
BIG FOUR BRIDGE NEARLY FINISHED
WORK ON NEW $3,500,000 STRUCTURE TO BE COMPLETED BY JUNE 1

WORK ON THE NEW $3,500,000 LOUISVILLE AND JEFFERSONVILLE BRIDGE OF THE BIG FOUR RAILROAD, BEING BUILT INSIDE THE OLD ONE AT THE FOOT OF

Campbell Street, is progressing rapidly and is expected to be ready for use by June 1.

The new bridge, being constructed on the order of the old one, will have five truss spans. The three main spans will be 547 feet each while two others will be 338 feet each and the fifth 200 feet. Approximately 24,000 rivets were driven in the main spans.

The structure is being erected on travelers which run on wheels on top of the old bridge. There is one traveler to each span. The hoisting is being done by electric engines. There are two of these engines for each traveler.

"The three large spans are being erected inside the old bridge and will be lowered into place by jacks of 500-ton capacity," Mr. McClane explained. Mr. McClane also said that the old bridge would be removed as soon as possible. Provisions are being made for railway tracks. Recently interurban service across the bridge was discontinued, but is expected to be continued when the bridge is completed.

By June 6, 1929, the Big Four Bridge had been completed in a remarkably short time and it would prove miraculously free from the bad fortune attached to the original structure. The original bridge hosted a full-size rail track next to a smaller track for interurban trains. On both sides of the tracks were six-foot-wide walking paths for pedestrians. The new Big Four was built with only a single track and it, and all the bridge's superstructure, fit neatly within the old span. When the new bridge was complete, the old bridge surrounding it was removed, and the modern Big Four Bridge emerged like a chick from an egg.

BIG FOUR BRIDGE IS IN USE AGAIN
Started 14 Months Ago

The new $3,500,000 Big Four Bridge across the Ohio River between Louisville and Jeffersonville was formally opened at 8:35 o'clock Tuesday morning as a cut of twenty loaded freight cars made the first crossing from the Louisville side. Whistles of steamboats, locomotives and factories and shouts from several hundred bridge workers sounded an acknowledgment.

Interurban cars of the Interstate Public Service Company will not begin operating over the bridge until about July 15, officials announced. Trolley wires and cables must be strung on the new span before the electric cars can operate. The interurban cars will use the same rails as the railroad cars.

"It is to be strictly a river party."

In the last week of October 1929, Louisville braced for two huge celebrations on the city's waterfront, a visit by the president of the United States and the ceremonial opening of the Municipal Bridge. The appearance by President Herbert Hoover proved to be a public relations nightmare, while the opening of the bridge was a party the city would long remember.

Louisville Herald-Post, October 20, 1929

The President is visiting Louisville to aid in celebrating the canalization of the Ohio River and the opening of the Louisville Municipal Bridge.

It is to be strictly a river party. The President will come to Louisville on the *Greenbrier*, a government light tender. Two patrol boats and the *Kentucky*, which will carry newspaper men,

President Herbert Hoover and his official party arrived in Louisville in the last week of October 1929 to dedicate the completion of the huge Corps of Engineers' project to establish a nine-foot channel for the entire length of the Ohio River. Hoover arrived in a driving rainstorm, forcing the cancellation of public activities and a major address to the nation by radio. Six days after Hoover's arrival, the stock market crashed, initiating the Great Depression. *(University of Louisville Photographic Archives, CS 105765)*

WILL MAKE UP THE FLEET OF THE PRESIDENTIAL PARTY. STRICT RIVER REGULATIONS WILL BE FOLLOWED BY THE BOATS. THEY WILL MOVE WITH A SPACE OF 400 FEET BETWEEN EACH BOAT.

Louisville Herald-Post, October 23, 1929

OWING TO BAD WEATHER CONDITIONS, PRESIDENT HOOVER'S SPEAKING PLANS HAVE BEEN CHANGED. THE PRESIDENT WILL DELIVER A HALF-HOUR ADDRESS AT THE WAR MEMORIAL AUDITORIUM AT 8:30 O'CLOCK, INSTEAD OF FROM THE STEAMER *GREENBRIER*.

AS PRESIDENT, MRS. HOOVER AND THEIR PARTY STEP FROM THE *GREENBRIER* THEY WILL BE MET BY A MOTORCADE AT THE LEVEE AND ESCORTED ACROSS THE NEW $5,000,000 MUNICIPAL BRIDGE AND THEN THROUGH APPROXIMATELY A MILE OF DOWNTOWN STREETS TO THE BROWN HOTEL, WHERE A BANQUET WILL BE GIVEN IN MR. HOOVER'S HONOR.

The plans for Hoover's reception went terribly awry, with heavy rains limiting attendance for his dramatic arrival by steamboat. A plan to address a large crowd from the boat's pilothouse later in the evening was scrubbed due to the rain.

A quick drive over and back provided the Municipal Bridge its symbolic opening event, but again weather kept people indoors. At the improvised speech at Municipal Auditorium the sound system failed and almost no one heard the President's message. On top of everything else, Kentucky's Republican U.S. Senator Fred Sackett and Governor Flem Sampson were opponents of Hoover, and they publicly snubbed him at the presentation.

An unpleasant visit to Louisville was the least of Herbert Hoover's problems. Hoover's triumphant victory tour to celebrate the completion of the great Ohio River canalization project was a disappointment, but three days later would come an even greater one. Hoover slipped out of Louisville after his dismal reception and took a train back to the White House. Six days later was October 29, 1929, Black Tuesday, the day of the stock market crash and the beginning of the Great Depression.

On that day, *The Courier-Journal* announced the formal schedule for events to celebrate the Municipal Bridge, an occasion so grand Louisville largely ignored the nation's financial crisis until after the party was over.

"A vision must inform the brain of man"

A favorite Louisville joke at the time asked: Do you know why they're building the new bridge to Indiana? No. Why? So the Hoosiers can swim over to Kentucky in the shade! The Louisville Bridge Commission decided on Second Street as the site of the new Municipal Bridge designed for vehicular traffic. Louisville's Municipal Bridge underwent a long and spirited funding debate and reached the conclusion that providing a free bridge was not an option. Succeeding where others had failed, Republican Mayor William B. Harrison negotiated a loan of $5 million from an investment firm and announced plans to collect tolls. Architect Paul Philip Gret designed an attractive and functional structure, 40 feet wide and 3,740 feet long. The contractors were Ralph Modjeska and Frank Masters. Modjeska was the son of Helene Modjeska, the popular actress who inspired Louisville's favorite caramel-and-marshmallow candy named in her honor.

Municipal Bridge's pier, adjacent to the Louisville waterfront, was near completion in the summer of 1929. In that year, both the Municipal and the re-worked Big Four Bridge were completed and ready for use. *(Filson Historical Society, BCO4)*

Two of the first cars to drive over the Municipal Bridge are poised to cross the first vehicular bridge in Louisville's history. A huge locomotive moves under the bridge on the Illinois Central trestle, emphasizing Louisville's central role in transportation in America. In 1964, the Municipal Bridge at the end of Second Street was renamed the George Rogers Clark Memorial Bridge to honor the city's founder. *(University of Louisville Photographic Archives, CS 106037)*

Oddly, the location of the Municipal Bridge was a continuation of the city's first bridge, the Second Street span over Beargrass Creek that cost $430 in 1801. The new Municipal Bridge cost $4.7 million, but it was able to pay off its loans in 1946 and has been free to the public ever since. In 1949 the city renamed the bridge to honor Louisville's founder, George Rogers Clark. It is the most significant public recognition of his legacy in the city.

PEDESTRIANS ARE FIRST
PROGRAMME OF ENTERTAINMENT PLANNED FOR FRIDAY, NOVEMBER 1.

THE HUGE HAND OF A CLOCK THAT LOOKS ACROSS THE WIDE HARBOR OF THE OHIO RIVER WILL GO LUMBERING PAST THE PHANTOM HOUR OF MIDNIGHT ON HALLOWEEN NIGHT, THURSDAY, OCTOBER 31, AND AS THE GHOSTS OF A PAST DAY GO FLEEING BEFORE THE ADVENT OF NOVEMBER 1, THE $5,000,000 LOUISVILLE MUNICIPAL BRIDGE WILL OPEN A PATH FROM NORTH TO SOUTH.

THE HOUR OF MIDNIGHT HAS BEEN SET FOR THE OPENING OF THE NEW SPAN TO VEHICULAR TRAFFIC AND DURING THE DAY OF NOVEMBER 1 A GALA PROGRAM OF ENTERTAINMENT HAS BEEN PLANNED FOR THOUSANDS WHO ARE EXPECTED TO CROSS THE BRIDGE FOR THE FIRST TIME.

THE BRIDGE WILL THEN BE THROWN OPEN TO PEDESTRIAN TRAFFIC ONLY AND UNTIL THE HOUR OF MIDNIGHT, PEDESTRIANS WILL BE GIVEN THE FREEDOM OF THE LENGTHY SPAN WITH ITS THIRTY-EIGHT-FOOT ROADWAY AND FIVE-FOOT SIDEWALKS.

Courier-Journal, October 29, 1929
WHARF IS SCENE OF FIREWORKS DISPLAY
PRESIDENT HOOVER, GEORGE ROGERS CLARK, OTHERS IN SPECTACLE.

ONE OF THE BEST FIREWORKS DISPLAYS EVER SHOWN IN LOUISVILLE HAS BEEN PROMISED BY THE FIREWORKS COMMITTEE FOR THE MUNICIPAL BRIDGE CELEBRATION, ACCORDING TO J. H. DOWNARD, CHAIRMAN OF THE COMMITTEE. THE DISPLAY WHICH MAY BE WITNESSED FROM THE RIVERFRONT, WILL BE MADE THE NIGHT OF NOVEMBER 1, AT 7:30.

THE NAVAL BOMBARDMENT OF THE *MONITOR* AND THE *MERRIMAC*, THE GRADUAL SINKING OF ONE AND ITS FINAL DESTRUCTION WILL BE REPRESENTED IN AN AQUATIC DISPLAY FIRED FROM BARGES ANCHORED OUT IN THE RIVER.

A SHELL BOMBARDMENT, PORTRAITS OF GEORGE ROGERS CLARK AND OF PRESIDENT HOOVER, FIRING OF WAR SIGNALS, A REPRESENTATION OF NIAGARA FALLS AND AN OHIO RIVER BRIDGE "BOUQUET," MADE BY THE SIMULTANEOUS FIRING OF HUNDREDS OF SHELLS, WILL BE INCLUDED IN THE DISPLAY.

BOATS WILL BE PROHIBITED FROM THE DISPLAY AREA FOR ABOUT THIRTY MINUTES OF THE PROGRAMME. PEDESTRIANS WILL NOT BE PERMITTED TO VIEW THE FIREWORKS FROM THE BRIDGE.

Events of the day called for an air show at Bowman Field, musical concerts at Municipal Auditorium and a mammoth fireworks show at the river's edge. Once again, fireworks proved irresistible to Louisvillians and more than 100,000 thronged the waterfront, after thousands had spent the afternoon jamming the bridge to claim the honor of being one of the first to cross. Even though they charged thirty-five cents for a vehicle and a nickel for pedestrians, there was little complaint about the tolls. Bicyclists were also allowed to use the bridge for five cents, but they were not allowed to ride. Instead they were required to walk their bikes across. The Municipal Bridge, toll and all, was embraced by the community and presented a dramatic new first impression to visitors to Louisville.

Tens of thousands of Louisvillians took advantage of the toll-free opening day of the Municipal Bridge. An estimated 100,000 visitors watched air shows, heard musical concerts and witnessed a massive pyrotechnic display on the river at night. Embraced by Louisvillians long ago, the tradition of extravagant fireworks displays continues on a greater scale. Thunder Over Louisville, the kick-off celebration for the annual Kentucky Derby Festival, routinely draws crowds in excess of 750,000 annually. *(University of Louisville Photographic Archives, CS-106037)*

The Bridge
by Fred Karem

And, as the people celebrated the

    Achievement of

    An engineering feat,

The old ferry slowly steamed away

    To join the

    Ever dying fleet

Of things that have served their purpose in the

    Progress of the human race.

It seemed to say that even the great

    Bridge might

    Some day be commonplace

As soon as the way was open, the

    Endless swirl of

    Motors began

Over the bridge whose every beam

    Dripped of the

    Sweat of man!

The Old and the New
by Kaufus Kurtz Gustling

The dreamed-of, far-flung steel now spans the flood,

    And cities, highways, States are joined at last.

Majestic still, the ferry thrills our blood

    Since every trip brings it nearer to the last.

A vision must inform the brain of man,

    Ere he can fashioned arch and mighty pier:

And proud are we to view the finished plan,

    To think how strong are those who persevere.

New times, new manners; this the common thought;

    But piers are built ere arches prove their power.

Since in each age, a vision must be wrought.

    Dreams from the past perfect this longed-for-hour.

The exuberant celebration at the opening of the Municipal Bridge did not seem very concerned with the collapsing national economy, which was occurring simultaneously with the Louisville ceremonies. The occasion inspired local artists and poets to create new works proclaiming a great day in Louisville history, the *Louisville Herald-Post* crowing loudest of all.

The *Froman M. Coots* was the final ferry boat to serve the Falls Cities area, ending a 122-year-old tradition of local cross-river service. The *Coots* was a large and powerful ferry boat converted to diesel power in 1925. Hundreds of people lined the shores and watched and the last automobile transfer was made on January 1, 1930. *(University of Louisville Photographic Archives, CS089489)*

"That's the last trip."

The opening of the Municipal Bridge ended a 122-year-old tradition at the Falls of the Ohio. On January 1, 1930, *The Courier-Journal* reported when the last ferry made its final voyage.

Captain N. Durand snuggled the *Froman M. Coots* into her berth at the foot of Third Street at 6:22 o'clock Tuesday, churned her into position with her starboard wheel, and lifted the pilot house controls to "stop."

With that informal gesture, a simple repetition of what had occurred every forty minutes for twenty hours a day, the veteran river ferry pilot ended 122 years of ferry service between Louisville and Jeffersonville, Indiana, and marked the suspension of business by the Falls City Transportation Company.

"Cap" secured the valise which contained his personal possessions, and dropped down from the pilot house to leave the ferry with the crowd. "There's nothing much to say. That's the last trip," was all he confided as he swung up the wharf.

"He'd have made that last trip or bust," a member of the crew said.

Down in the engine room, I. R. Perry, engineer on the *Coots* since she was equipped with diesel power in 1925, shut off the port engine, pulled his controls to conform with those of the pilot house, checked his gauges, and leaned over the sill of the engine room window to watch the crowd leave.

A crowd of approximately 500 lined the rails of the ferry as it swung into the wharf. More than twenty-five automobiles made the last run from Jeffersonville to Louisville, and hundreds of watchers stood on the Indiana shore to watch the ferry as it pulled away for the final trip.

The deck of the *Froman M. Coots* was a familiar sight to anyone needing to travel from Louisville to Jeffersonville. The only other vehicular bridge in the city was Portland's K&I, a toll bridge like the newly completed Municipal Bridge. *(University of Louisville Photographic Archives, CS128234)*

General Clark Returns to the Falls

New ideas abounded for the Louisville waterfront in this era. Congressman Maurice H. Thatcher represented the Louisville area and, in 1930, he sponsored a bill to establish a memorial to George Rogers Clark which would also serve as a lighthouse.

Louisville Herald Post, May 4, 1930

This nation owes a debt of gratitude to this illustrious soldier-patriot which it can never repay.

I have always believed that upon the site of Corn Island, or at some point adjacent thereto, the nation should erect an appropriate George Rogers Clark Memorial. Also, since I have been familiar with the navigational perils of the Ohio River in the Louisville sector, I have believed that the federal government should provide, at or near the Falls, a lighthouse as an aid to navigation.

With these general facts in mind, during the first session of the sixty-ninth Congress, that is today on February 22, 1926, I introduced a bill, known as H. R. 9644, providing for an appropriation of one hundred and fifty thousand dollars of federal funds (but without any local contribution provided), for the erection of a George Rogers Clark Memorial Lighthouse at, or near, the head of the Falls at Louisville.

My conception of this memorial lighthouse follows. The erection of a tall, substantial, and shapely tower of masonry at a point just above the outer shore point of the Louisville and Portland Canal. This is the site selected by the Bureau of Lighthouses after a survey of the Louisville situation in connection with the proposed lighthouse. This site is in the immediate vicinity of Corn Island. Superimposed on this tower there will be placed a heroic figure of General Clark, in bronze or other appropriate metal, with uplifted sword pointed

TO THE NORTHWARD, TO THE NORTHWEST TERRITORY, WHICH HE CONQUERED; AND THERE WILL BE PLACED IN THE SWORD HAND, OR IN THE OTHER HAND, A FLASHING TORCH OR LIGHT OF BRILLIANT POWER, TO WARN AND GUIDE NAVIGATION IN THE FALLS SECTION OF THE RIVER AT NIGHTTIME.

THUS, THE GEORGE ROGERS CLARK MEMORIAL LIGHTHOUSE WILL NOT ONLY SERVE AN EVEN HIGHER PURPOSE, THAT OF GIVING FORTH SPIRITUAL ILLUMINATION, IN CALLING TO MIND AND HEART AND EMULATION THE ILLUSTRIOUS DEEDS OF ONE OF THE NATION'S FOUNDERS AND GREATEST SONS, WHOSE NAME AND FAME SHALL LIVE AS LONG AS HISTORY SHALL ENDURE.

Given the economic realities of the Depression era, 1930 was no time to suggest such an expensive monument. Years later, the city would install a handsome bronze figure of George Rogers Clark on the Belvedere and, as Congressman Thatcher suggested, it points to the Northwest Territory he conquered.

The Comprehensive City Plan

A far more expensive proposition for waterfront improvements came with the 1931 public release of Louisville's first comprehensive city plan by the respected urban planning firm of Harland Bartholomew of St. Louis. Since the turn of the century, city leaders quietly worked to create such a plan. In 1901, a paper by local architect J. C. Murphy was read to the Engineers & Architects Club, suggesting the organization of a City Art Commission. In 1908 Murphy was asked to head the City Planning Committee of the Engineers & Architects group. The year 1913 saw the creation of the City Improvement Commission by Mayor William O. Head, followed fourteen years later by the first City Planning & Zoning Association. In 1929 the Bartholomew firm was hired and began their study and recommendations to present to the city.

A staff artist for the *Louisville Herald-Post* created this image of a Falls' lighthouse and heroic statue of George Rogers Clark, a project stimulated by a bill sponsored by Congressman Maurice H. Thatcher. Thatcher's passionate sponsorship was of little avail to a nation gripped by the Great Depression.

Highlights of the plan, released in April 1933, included:

RIVERFRONT DEVELOPMENT

THE PROPOSALS INCLUDE A NUMBER OF PROJECTS WHICH MAY BE EXECUTED INDEPENDENTLY OF ONE ANOTHER, EACH PROJECT, HOWEVER, BEING AN INDISPENSABLE LINK IN THE COMPREHENSIVE PLAN.

- Acquisition and development for park purposes of all lands lying between the Upper River Road and river from the Big Four Railroad bridge to Goose Creek excluding, however, the gas manufacturing plant of LG&E and the Louisville Water Company property.

- Construction of a four-lane elevated highway along the riverfront from a point in the River Road between First and Brook Streets to a point in Northwestern Parkway between Sixteenth and Seventeenth Streets.

- Depression and relocation of present Illinois Central elevated tracks from First Street to Ninth Street, these tracks to be below the elevated highway in a waterproof tunnel.

- Creation of a plaza opposite the central business section bounded by Third, Main, Seventh and the levee.

The Upper River. It is proposed that the city acquire all the river frontage from Goose Creek to the Big Four Railroad Bridge and convert the area lying between the River Road and water's edge into parks.

The Central Riverfront. The predominating feature of the plans for the central riverfront is the magnificent open plaza to be created between Main Street and the river, Third Street and Seventh Street. As an important part of this development, a connecting link to the upper and western sections is to be provided by construction of an elevated highway connecting River Road at Brook Street to Northwestern Parkway at Seventeenth Street. This elevated highway is necessary to provide a continuous uninterrupted riverfront drive.

It is further recommended that the future City Hall and Court House be built on the south side of Main Street between Fourth and Sixth Streets overlooking the Plaza and River.

It is planned to landscape this large open space with trees and shrubs, the axis of the development being on Fifth Street where it is proposed to construct a fountain. The cross axis would be terminated at Sixth and at Fourth, its extremities providing excellent locations for public monuments.

Access to the levee would be provided by ramps at Seventh and at Third Streets and it is proposed to construct an additional ramp at Third Street leading to the L&N Freight House at First and River Road.

One of the most important features of the plan is a proposed underground parking space to be provided beneath the plaza and where there will be space sufficient for the accommodation of approximately four thousand automobiles, or more than the entire street parking facilities within the area bound by Sixth, Second, Main and Broadway.

The PROPOSED
RIVER FRONT PLAZA
LOUISVILLE KENTUCKY

CITY PLANNING & ZONING COMMISSION

BARTHOLOMEW & ASSOCIATES
City Plan & Landscape Engineers
SAINT LOUIS MISSOURI

The City of Louisville hired the nationally respected urban planning firm of Harland Bartholomew of St. Louis in 1929. The firm's study was instrumental in influencing nearly all subsequent plans for renewal of the Louisville waterfront. Bartholomew's fanciful Art Deco Louisville landscape featured two towers (on the right side) which were envisioned as the new City Hall and County Court House. Other Deco masterpieces would fill in the area between the towers and the LG&E plant and the Belknap complex. The entire surface from Third to Sixth Streets was termed a plaza with 4,000 parking spaces provided beneath. *(Louisville Metro Archives)*

COST

THE COST OF THE UNDERTAKING, WHICH IS ESTIMATED AT APPROXIMATELY EIGHT AND ONE-HALF MILLION DOLLARS, WILL BE MORE THAN COMPENSATED BY THE INCREASED VALUE OF THE PROPERTY IN THE NORTH END OF THE BUSINESS DISTRICT AND, TOGETHER WITH CERTAIN MAJOR STREET IMPROVEMENTS, WOULD DISCOURAGE A FURTHER SHIFTING AND DESTRUCTION OF ESTABLISHED VALUES THROUGHOUT THE ENTIRE BUSINESS DISTRICT.

THE CITY'S APPEARANCE

AMERICAN PEOPLE HAVE LONG THOUGHT OF CIVIC BEAUTIFICATION, THE IMPROVEMENT OF THE CITY'S APPEARANCE, AS SOMETHING THAT WOULD BE DESIRABLE BUT TOO COSTLY TO OBTAIN AND ECONOMICALLY UNJUSTIFIABLE....PUBLIC OPINION HAS CHANGED IN RECENT YEARS AND STEPS TO IMPROVE THE APPEARANCE OF CITIES ARE NO LONGER VIEWED ASKANCE BY THE MAJORITY OF CITIZENS.

CIVIC PRIDE AND THE DESIRE FOR A MORE BEAUTIFUL CITY BY ITS CITIZENS IS THE MOST IMPORTANT FACTOR IN CARRYING OUT A PROGRAM OF CITY BEAUTIFICATION.

THE CIVIC CENTER

THE GROUPING OF PUBLIC BUILDINGS IN A CIVIC CENTER HAS BEEN A SUBJECT FOR PUBLIC DISCUSSION IN LOUISVILLE FOR A NUMBER OF YEARS. MANY OTHER CITIES HAVE FOUND IT DESIRABLE FROM THE STANDPOINT OF PUBLIC CONVENIENCE AND FOR ESTHETIC CONSIDERATIONS TO EXPEND LARGE SUMS OF MONEY TO CARRY OUT SUCH PROJECTS. IN THE PAST, THE TENDENCY OF AMERICAN CITIES HAS BEEN TO DISREGARD OR SLIGHT THE APPEARANCE OF THEIR PUBLIC BUILDINGS, WATER-FRONTS, AND OTHER OPEN SPACES. PUBLIC OPINION HAS CHANGED RECENTLY, HOWEVER, AND THERE IS NOW A DECIDED REACTION AGAINST THE FORMER PREVALENT POLICY OF SUBORDINATING THE ESTHETIC TO THE PURELY UTILITARIAN IN PUBLIC CONSTRUCTION.

THE LOCATION FURNISHES AN OPPORTUNITY FOR A BUILDING GROUP OF OUTSTANDING DISTINCTION. THE PROPOSED RIVERFRONT PLAZA WILL FURNISH A SETTING FOR THE CITY HALL AND COURT HOUSE THAT CANNOT BE EXCELLED. IT IS ONLY BY MEANS OF AMPLE OPEN SPACES THAT FULL ADVANTAGE CAN BE TAKEN OF ARCHITECTURAL OPPORTUNITIES. NO OTHER SITE COULD BE DEVELOPED SO SATISFACTORILY. THE TERM "CIVIC CENTER" IMPLIES THAT THE GROUP WOULD ACTUALLY BE IN THE CENTER OF PUBLIC ACTIVITY AND THE FRONT DOOR TO LOUISVILLE WHEN BUILT IN CONNECTION WITH THE RIVERFRONT. THE PRINCIPAL ENTRIES INTO THE CITY FROM THE NORTH OVER THE MUNICIPAL BRIDGE AND FROM THE NORTHEAST OVER THE RIVER ROAD WILL CONVERGE NEAR THIS CENTER.

"The city's Ugly Duckling...is to become a swan"

Efforts to implement the planning strategies suggested by

The Point had long been the home of sawmills, lumber yards and boat building firms. The lumber industry was especially important as huge rafts of tree trunks were floated downstream from the hardwood forests of eastern Kentucky and southern Ohio. The trees were hauled ashore and cut into lumber on the Point and then shipped by either convenient rail or barge services. *(University of Louisville Photographic Archives, OCL.39)*

Bartholomew began almost immediately, and they coincided with the first effort to build a vehicular highway between Louisville and Cincinnati, the road that would become Highway 42. The road was destined to become a new entrance to the city, and officials began making plans to beautify the highway and rid itself of some persistent problems along the road's path.

Louisville Herald-Post, June 1, 1932

NEW CUT-OFF SPAN, PARK PLAN SIFTED
CITY HOPES FOR BEAUTIFICATION ALONG RIVER WITH NEW HIGHWAY

LOUISVILLE, AWAITING COMPLETION OF THE NEW CINCINNATI HIGHWAY, HAS PLANNED A GATEWAY FOR THE $400,000 ROAD ALREADY. AND THE VISION IS ON PAPER.

CONSTRUCTION OF A NEW BRIDGE ACROSS BEARGRASS CREEK, TO TAKE THE PLACE OF THE BOTTLE-NECK CUT-OFF BRIDGE, IS ANTICIPATED. DEVELOPMENT OF PROPERTIES ALONG THE RIVER ROAD FOR A NEW PARK SYSTEM IS CONSIDERED ONE OF THE MOST IMPORTANT MUNICIPAL PROJECTS.

THE UNSIGHTLINESS OF THE MILE-LONG STRETCH ALONG RIVER ROAD, BETWEEN THE BIG FOUR BRIDGE AND BEARGRASS CREEK, AND THE NARROW BRIDGE ACROSS THE CREEK, CONCERNS THOUSANDS OF MOTORISTS WHO WILL ENTER LOUISVILLE AFTER COMPLETION OF THE JEFFERSON COUNTY LINK IN THE LOUISVILLE-CINCINNATI HIGHWAY.

"THIS HIGHWAY IS DESTINED TO BE ONE OF THE MOST IMPORTANT ARTERIES IN LOUISVILLE, PROVIDING A SHORT, DIRECT ROUTE TO CINCINNATI," THE COMMISSION RECOMMENDATIONS POINT OUT.

H. W. ALEXANDER, RESIDENT ENGINEER FOR BARTHOLOMEW & ASSOCIATES OF ST. LOUIS, AND AUTHOR OF THE IMPROVEMENT PLANS, SAID THE SURVEY WAS MADE WITH THE KNOWLEDGE THAT THE EXPECTED HIGHWAY FROM CINCINNATI WOULD CLOSELY FOLLOW THE PRESENT RIVER ROAD.

PARK DEVELOPMENT INCLUDED

THE NEW ROAD, AS PROPOSED BY THE PLANNING COMMISSION, WOULD LEAVE THE PRESENT ONE WEST OF THE LOUISVILLE COUNTRY CLUB ENTRANCE TO RUN PARALLEL TO THE PRESENT ROAD AND JOIN IT AT GOOSE CREEK. THE PRESENT ROADWAY WOULD BE RETAINED FOR PLEASURE AND SLOW MOVING TRAFFIC.

THE NEW ROAD, AS PROPOSED BY THE STATE BODY, WOULD LEAVE THE PRESENT HIGHWAY NEAR THE STANDARD CLUB AND RUN THROUGH THE COUNTRY CLUB PROPERTY, ALSO REJOINING IT AT GOOSE CREEK.

"…the average Louisvillian has forgotten how to play."

The technical demands of designing a new highway, complete with a replacement for the narrow Cut-Off Bridge over Beargrass Creek, were simple compared to the larger problem of life on the Point. The area had become an embarrassment, especially for those executives commuting into the city from their estates along River Road. The future of the Point, and its many substandard houses, was addressed by proposals to relocate the residents and turn the entire area into a riverside park.

It was not the first park on River Road. In 1919 a park for African-American children was donated to the city by Mrs. Charles Ballard, Mr. and Mrs. B. Thruston Ballard and R.C. Ballard Thruston. Their donation of $12,000 created Thruston Park on Caldwell Street, between Jackson and Hancock.

Louisvillians love their river, a place where everyday cares can be replaced by sheer fun. Many private boat clubs have lined the shorelines of both Kentucky and Indiana on the broad waters above the Falls, and generations of local families have spent their summers in a beloved camp like Transylvania Beach. The river meant freedom, relaxation, adventure and recreation to many Louisvillians, rich and poor. *(Kentucky Historical Society, al5jefa14)*

Louisville Herald-Post, June 19, 1935

THE POINT...UGLY DUCKLING RIVERFRONT

THE POINT, LOUISVILLE'S MOST ABUSED COMMUNITY, IS ABOUT TO BECOME A MILLION-DOLLAR PLAYGROUND. ALREADY THE CITY ADMINISTRATION HAS COMMENCED THE ESTABLISHMENT OF A SERVICE OF AN UNPARALLELED TYPE — THE CREATION OF A MUNICIPAL DOCK, BEHIND TOWHEAD ISLAND, FOR SMALL BOATS.

THE CITY'S UGLY DUCKLING, NOW HEADQUARTERS FOR SORDID SHACKS, TIN CAN-STREWN DUMPS AND RAMSHACKLE SHANTYBOATS, IS TO BECOME A SWAN. LOUISVILLE IS TO HAVE A WATERFRONT, WITH RECREATIONAL FACILITIES AND A RESIDENTIAL DISTRICT, WHICH MAY BECOME THE SHOWPLACE OF THE CITY.

BUT BEFORE THE BLUEPRINTS OF THIS LITTLE UTOPIA — WHICH HAS BEEN DRAWN UP BY MAYOR NEVILLE MILLER AND WOOSLEY M. CAYE, TECHNICAL ENGINEER FOR THE COMMISSIONERS OF SEWERAGE — CAN BE TRANSFORMED INTO A WIDE MUNICIPAL BOAT HARBOR WITH LANDSCAPED SCENERY AND PURE AIR...THERE ARE SEVERAL THINGS TO BE ACCOMPLISHED.

THE POINT HAS BEEN BEFOULED IN RECENT YEARS BY ONE NAUSEOUS SOURCE. ITS AIR HAS BEEN POLLUTED BY SICKENING STENCHES. ITS POOLS OF STAGNANT WATER HAVE BEEN THE BREEDING PLACES FOR MOSQUITOES AND GERMS WHICH ACTUALLY HAVE THREATENED HEALTH IN THE ENTIRE CITY.

THE CAUSE OF THIS DANGEROUS CONDITION HAS BEEN, MAINLY, THE FAILURE OF BEARGRASS CREEK TO CARRY OFF SEWAGE EMPTYING INTO IT. AND BEARGRASS CREEK HAS FAILED TO DRAIN PROPERLY SINCE THE RAISING OF THE RIVER LEVEL TO THE NINE-FOOT STAGE BLOCKED THE STREAM.

THIS CONDITION HAS MADE THE POINT ONE OF THE MOST UNATTRACTIVE SECTIONS OF THE CITY. AND, SINCE THE MOUTH OF BEARGRASS CREEK IS ABOVE TOWHEAD ISLAND, THE RIVER IN THAT NEIGHBORHOOD HAS BEEN A STREAM OF BILGE WATER.

BUT THINGS ARE TO BE CHANGED. THE COMMISSIONERS OF SEWERAGE PLAN TO SPEND $940,000 TO ELIMINATE STAGNATION...CONTAMINATION...FILTH... SMELL.

IN THE FIRST PLACE, THE COMMISSION PLANS TO BUILD A SEWAGE PUMPING STATION. INSTEAD OF EMPTYING INTO BEARGRASS CREEK FROM A LOW-LEVEL SEWER, AS IT DOES NOW, SEWAGE WILL BE PUMPED INTO A HIGH-LEVEL SEWER.

THE HIGH-LEVEL SEWER WILL EMPTY INTO THE RIVER BELOW THE BIG FOUR BRIDGE. SINCE NO OTHER SEWERS DISCHARGE THEIR CONTENTS ABOVE THIS POINT, THE OHIO, WHERE IT RUNS PAST TOWHEAD ISLAND, WILL BE AS CLEAN AS AT ANY PLACE IN THE VICINITY OF LOUISVILLE.

THE PUMPING STATION WILL COST $220,000 AND WILL BE LOCATED AT THE CUT-OFF BRIDGE. BUT MUNICIPAL DEVELOPMENT OF THE POINT WILL NOT STOP THERE.

THE FIRST STEP IN THE PROGRAM WAS TAKEN LAST MONDAY WHEN EVICTION OF THE PICTURESQUE BUT DIRTY SHANTYBOAT TOWN FROM ITS LAST STRONGHOLD NEAR THE PIERS OF THE BIG FOUR BRIDGE WAS STARTED. MANY OF THE SHANTYBOATERS MOVED TO TOWHEAD ISLAND, WHERE HARRY W. ALEXANDER, SECRETARY OF THE PLANNING AND ZONING COMMISSION, HOPES TO "CULTIVATE THEIR PAGEANTRY AND MARK TWAIN SETTING, WHILE KEEPING THE COLONY AT A HIGH SANITATION LEVEL."

"THE BOAT HARBOR PROJECT WILL BE SELF-LIQUIDATING," POINTED OUT THE MAYOR, "AND WILL BE PRIMARILY FOR THE USE OF PERSONS OF SMALL MEANS — STENOGRAPHERS AND CLERKS, WHO WILL BE ABLE TO RENT BOATS AND CANOES AND BUY FISHING BAIT AND SOFT DRINKS AND LUNCHES."

BOATS, TENNIS COURTS AND PAVILIONS WILL BE BUILT BY THE 300 MEN THE COMMISSION EXPECTS TO EMPLOY ON THE FIVE-ACRE STRIP OF SHORE OWNED BY THE CITY.

IN THE WORDS OF MAYOR NEVILLE MILLER, "WE HAVE FOSTERED A TRADITION THAT THE AMERICAN SURVIVES, NOT ONLY BECAUSE HE WORKS AND EATS... BUT BECAUSE HE KNOWS HOW TO PLAY. AND IN RECENT YEARS, THE AVERAGE LOUISVILLIAN HAS FORGOTTEN HOW TO PLAY — HE CAN'T AFFORD THE VACATION TRIPS HE ONCE TOOK. BUT HE'LL HAVE NO EXCUSE NEXT YEAR. ALMOST NONE OF US IS MORE THAN TWO OR THREE GENERATIONS REMOVED FROM THE FURROW, AND THERE DOUBTLESS REMAINS A GENUINE PULL OF HEREDITARY HABITS AND MEMORIES DRAWING US BACK TO THE LAND NOW.

"AND A GOOD SUBSTITUTE FOR THIS URGE WILL BE SUPPLIED BY THE CITY, WHEN THE BOAT HARBOR IS OPENED DOWN ON THE POINT...AND EVERY MAN CAN SPEND A FEW DAYS FISHING, AND THE YOUNGSTERS WILL PLAY TENNIS, SWIM, GO SURF-BOARD RIDING — ALL FOR A VERY NOMINAL FEE."

A Good Case of Pandemonium

Mayor Miller's municipal boat harbor was built by three hundred men working for the federal Works Progress Administration but, in two short years, the WPA would be involved in a project of a different nature. In January and February of 1937, the entire Ohio River Valley, but most especially the Louisville area, was struck by a natural disaster of immense proportions. Any flood setting new records for elevation is designated by the adjective "Great" to indicate it is the standard until a higher flood occurs. On the Ohio River, the term Great Flood refers to 1937.

The lowest lying areas of the river's edge always flooded first, the downtown wharf, the old towns of Portland and Shippingport and the long expanse of River Road through the Point. These locations were inundated in even moderate rises of the river, but in 1937 waters rose to nearly thirty feet above flood stage. Before the sewers backed up, Beargrass Creek went over its banks and 175,000 people were evacuated from their homes throughout the city, with residents of the Point the first to feel the impact of the rising waters.

On January 22, the first day the extent of the disaster became clear, reporter Molly Clowes of *The Courier-Journal* described the scene of chaos and rescue in the Point.

RESCUE WORK CONTINUES DESPITE RAIN

A GOOD CASE OF PANDEMONIUM IS OPEN FOR INSPECTION AT THE WHOLESALE MOVING OUT NOW IN

PROGRESS ALONG MOST OF THE STREETS BORDERING THE PARTLY INUNDATED RIVER ROAD. TRUCKS SNORT, WAGONS CREAK, PADDLING CHILDREN YELL FOR THE DOG, MOTHERS WADE BACK AFTER THE DISHPAN FLOATING OUT OF THE FRONT ROOM WINDOW.

CONFUSION CENTERS PRINCIPALLY AROUND THE CUT-OFF BRIDGE, WHERE THE DRY ROAD ENDS AT THE CITY LIMITS. THE ROAD HERE IS SOLIDLY JAMMED WITH TRUCKS, FURNITURE, SPECTATORS AND PATIENT POLICEMEN ENDLESSLY EXPLAINING THAT YOU CAN'T GO THROUGH THAT WAY.

RESCUERS NOT OPTIMISTIC

THE RESCUE CREW IS WELL CONTENT WITH ITS WORK SO FAR, BUT NOT VERY OPTIMISTIC. IF THE WATER RISES, OTHER HOUSES ON HIGHER LEVELS MUST BE ABANDONED, WHICH MEANS OTHER ALL-NIGHT SESSIONS WITH ROW BOAT AND, VERY PROBABLY, IN THE RAIN. BUT THEY ARE A CHEERFUL CROWD. SOMEBODY DASHES IN WITH THE NEWS THAT THERE'S AN OUTBOARD MOTOR ON THE WAY DOWN. SOMEBODY ELSE ANNOUNCES THAT IF IT KEEPS RAINING, SOMEBODY IS SURE TO COME ACROSS WITH CAPES AND BOOTS. THEN THERE'S A GENERAL MOVEMENT OUT INTO THE RAIN, AND TOWARDS THE SHACK OF AN OBSTINATE OLD MAN WHO REFUSES TO BE BUDGED FROM THE SECOND FLOOR OF HIS HALF SUBMERGED HOUSE FURTHER DOWN THE ROAD.

Access across the Ohio River by bridge was eliminated when high waters covered the approaches to the Municipal, Pennsylvania, K&I and Big Four bridges. The huge Waterside Plant of LG&E at Second Street, the city's main supply of electricity, was shut down while waters rushed in to drown the boilers. Unimaginable scenes of destruction became commonplace, as described in a *Courier-Journal* story:

BARN FILLED WITH HAY TIED TO PACKET NEAR WHARF ON RIVERFRONT

A HUGE RED BARN, FILLED WITH HAY, HAS BECOME AN ADJUNCT OF THE DOWNTOWN LOUISVILLE WATERFRONT, APPARENTLY FOR THE DURATION OF THE FLOOD.

IT FLOODED DOWN FROM UPRIVER AND BUMPED INTO THE PACKET, *CHRIS GREENE*, MOORED SOUTH OF WHAT USED TO BE THE WHARF. MEMBERS OF THE *CHRIS GREENE* DECIDED THE BARN MIGHT TURN INTO A FIRE HAZARD OR A NAVIGATION HAZARD IF ALLOWED TO FLOAT ON DOWN, AS THEY TIED IT UP TO THEIR BOAT'S PADDLE WHEEL.

FLOATING RAILROAD TANK CARS, BOBBING ALONG THE RIVER'S EDGE, HAVE CAUSED FURTHER TROUBLE FOR THE ONLY BOAT MOORED HERE.

The river at Louisville remained at or above flood stage for three weeks, allowing the destructive forces of moving water, melting plaster and mold to eat away at many structures. In July of 1937 one of the last wharf-side buildings of the steamboat days was destroyed, and with it many memories of times gone by.

HOTEL FAMOUS IN THE 1870S WRECKED

THOSE WHO KNEW LOUISVILLE IN THE 1870S, WHEN CHESTNUT STREET WAS YET A SUBURB, WILL BE SAD TO SEE WORKMEN DEMOLISHING THE FALLS VIEW HOTEL FRONTING 4TH AND THE RIVER.

OPEN FOR BUSINESS UNTIL JUST A FEW YEARS AGO, THE 72-YEAR-OLD STRUCTURE WAS ONE OF THE LAST PICTURESQUE REMINDERS OF "BETTER DAYS" ON THE RIVERFRONT. CYCLONES SWEEPING UP THE RIVER HAD TORN ITS ROOF AWAY NUMEROUS TIMES; EVERY FLOOD OF CONSEQUENCE HAD PERMEATED ITS STURDY WALLS — IT WITHSTOOD ALL THAT — AND NOW IT MEETS INGLORIOUS DESTRUCTION OVER THE SETTLEMENT OF A FAMILY ESTATE.

The Great Flood of 1937 poured over the Louisville waterfront on its way to inundating most of the city. The second floor windows of the Wharfmaster's office stand out of the flood, while water laps at the Short-Line rail trestle. The massive LG&E Waterside Plant, the main provider of the community's electricity, was out of commission and in danger of collapsing entirely. *(University of Louisville Photographic Archives ,R. G. Potter Collection – 501)*

For decades, a massive electric sign facing Indiana proclaimed Louisville to be the "Gateway to the South." Behind that sign, the LG&E generating plant looms over the skyline. Rail lines feed coal into the plant's yard, all located at the junction of Second Street and the Municipal Bridge. In the fall of 2010, a huge new indoor facility, the KFC Yum! Center, opened for University of Louisville basketball games and scores of musical and entertainment attractions. *(University of Louisville Photographic Archives, CS 071639)*

CATERING PRINCIPALLY TO STEAMBOAT PILOTS, THE FALLS VIEW, WITH ITS DINING HALL AND SALOON, WAS PROBABLY THE GAYEST SPOT IN LOUISVILLE. MONEY CAME EASY AND WENT EASY. IN THOSE DAYS PILOTS RECEIVED $600 FOR A ONE-MONTH'S TRIP TO MEMPHIS AND BACK; $900 TO NEW ORLEANS.

A WEEK'S LODGING IN EVEN THE BEST OF THE FALL VIEWS' ROOMS COST ONLY $1.25, PAYABLE IN ADVANCE. FURNISHINGS CONSISTED OF BED, WASHSTAND, DRESSER

AND GAS JET. ACCORDING TO GEORGE DALTON, WHO WAS CARETAKER THERE FROM 1888 TO 1934, THERE WAS A BELL-PULL IN EVERY ROOM.

ON THE MAIN FLOOR, THE PILOTS RENTED "KNOWLEDGE POINT," A PRIVATE PARLOR WHERE THEY CONGREGATED TO DISCUSS NAVIGATION PROBLEMS. "BEFORE THE PORTLAND CANAL WAS BUILT," THE OLD CARETAKER EXPLAINED, "BOATS COULD ONLY TRAVEL AS FAR DOWN AS 4TH STREET. THAT'S WHY THE FALLS VIEW had such good business. People would get off the boats, stay overnight at the hotel and continue their journey next morning from Shippingport. Freight and luggage was transported on tandem drays, one horse leading the other."

"Those days are gone forever," he said, sadly. "Even the old hotel register that I prized so highly floated away in the January flood."

"The Point has its own code."

The aftermath of the 1937 flood rang the death-knell for the Point as a residential neighborhood. The Robert Fulton elementary school, located on River Road east of Adams, had been in operation since 1865, and even it was forced to close permanently. While the waters still covered the streets and houses, city officials were making plans to remove the inhabitants and convert the waterside property into public parks. On February 9, 1937, just four days after the swollen river had dropped below flood stage, an article in *The Courier-Journal* commented on the stubbornness of residents who were proud to refer to themselves as "dirty-necked Pointers."

Heretofore when the Ohio rose, the folks nonchalantly moved out. There was no hysteria, little commotion, few rescue squads. It was just one of those things that happened every year or so and residents in shantyboats, frame cottages or tidy brick houses either "rode it out" or moved out. When the water receded they moved back.

Mrs. Rose Devine and Mrs. Matie Dabney, who live at 708 and 706 River Road, respectively, with a host of children and in-laws, were others who "carried on" the code of The Point, although they, too, were just a bit worried over possibilities.

"We want to move back just as soon as possible," explained Mrs. Devine, as she herded a bunch of "young'uns" down the River Road. "What we don't know is will they let us live there. We've been through high water before, but nothing like this. Now our neighbors say maybe the Government won't let us go back."

And Mrs. Devine and Mrs. Dabney and the "young'uns" trudged away down the muddy River Road to see what was left of their homes.

The Point has its own code – it reads in capitals, "CARRY ON."

Only one house survived the 1937 Flood on the Point. The Heigold house located on Marion Street stood alone, with a frame cottage sprawling across its side yard and a row of three wooden houses lying on their sides blocking the front entrance. The house lovingly built in 1857 by stonecarver Christian Heigold suffered little more than a thorough drenching, one broken window and two buckled floor boards.

Charles Perryman, a grandson of Heigold who was born in the old house, credited the tall trees surrounding his birthplace for saving it from destruction. After checking the fanciful decorative stone carvings on the house's façade, Perryman found nothing missing but one stone dove. "Won't hardly miss that though," he said. "Even Noah lost one dove."

A newspaper article on February 13 indicates that plans for the old Point emerged very soon after the waters had receded.

Negotiations may begin shortly for a city-county arrangement to provide Louisville with a riverside park running all the way from the Big Four Bridge to the water pumping station at Zorn Avenue.

The area contemplated would embrace the entire Point from Beargrass Creek to the river, Towhead Island and the new municipal boat harbor, and beyond the Cut-Off Bridge, all the territory between Mellwood Avenue and the river. Its eastern boundary would run from Mellwood along the boundary of the Standard Club property and the water station grounds.

Mr. Alexander, who Tuesday presented to the Mayor's flood committee plans for converting the Portland waterfront, Shippingport and Point areas into parks, pointed out that the authority of the Zoning Commission cannot be extended to territory outside the city limits. For the proposed upriver park to be under proper control, the city's limits would have to be extended around it after the land is purchased.

In the Point area within the city limits, Mr. Alexander estimated, there dwelt about 500 families before the flood. If the city takes over this property they must be reimbursed, and the cost will run considerably higher than in the sparsely settled territory just beyond the limits.

Although several residents resisted losing their property, even going so far as filing lawsuits to halt the process, land sales and condemnations loomed for the Point. A *Courier-Journal* editorial on May 5 spoke loudly and strongly for improvements.

AN OPPORTUNITY THAT MUST NOT BE LOST

Authority is to be asked of the Board of Park Commissioners to condemn property for park purposes on a portion of the Point subject to disastrous floods. There should be no doubt of the willingness of the board to grant this authority. Its object is to enable the city to make a municipal improvement in the effectuation of which the board should be glad to co-operate.

The plan proposed for the new park covers the territory from Thruston Park to the Cut-Off Bridge, adjacent to the Boat Harbor. It always suffers from floods, and suffered so seriously from the recent flood that the opportunity now presses for guarding against such suffering in the future, while at the same time converting the affected area into a valuable asset of the municipality instead of a costly liability. The plan conforms to the river and park development long ago worked out by the City Planning and Zoning Commission — a development whose desirability has never been questioned, but whose accomplishment has been obstructed by difficulties most of which have now been removed by the flood. The question at this time is whether the territory shall be rebuilt and reoccupied, subject to inevitable future river ravages, or whether it shall be converted into a park for the benefit of the citizens, instead of a plague. The opportunity to make that conversion is here now as never before, and it should not be lost, as it will be lost unless the action necessary to take advantage of it be taken promptly.

The Heigold house, survivor of every challenge, managed to be the only building in the Point to survive the 1937 flooding. Details of the intricate carvings above the door show that the stone was originally painted by Christian Heigold to emphasize his work. In 2010 the carved details survive, but few traces of the paint remain. *(University of Louisville Photographic Archives, CS 071639)*

To facilitate the city's takeover of the Point properties, Mayor Miller instituted a public fund drive to solicit money to acquire private lands. In June, *The Louisville Times* could report progress on the acquisition project.

THIRD OF POINT LAND BOUGHT

THE MAYOR'S FIGURES SHOWED THAT OF THE 11,440 FRONT-FEET IN THE POINT NEEDED FOR IMMEDIATE PARK PURPOSES, THE CITY NOW OWNS OR HAS AGREEMENTS TO PURCHASE 3,432 FEET. THE TWENTY-SEVEN PARCELS INVOLVED IN PURCHASE AGREEMENTS HAVE COST THE CITY $27,706, AND WHILE TITLE EXAMINATION WAS BEING PUSHED BY THE LAW DEPARTMENT, MAYOR MILLER CALLED ON THE PUBLIC TO HASTEN CONTRIBUTIONS TO THE POINT PURCHASE FUND, WHICH NOW TOTALS $47,440 IN DONATIONS. HE EXPECTS THE SUM TO PASS $50,000 BY THE END OF THE WEEK.

By July, the mayor could announce that $50,422, including a gift of $2,000 from Ambassador Robert W. Bingham in England, had been raised. The total estimated purchase requirement was $136,000, and he pledged $25,000 of city funds to match incoming donations. The renovation of the Point, and a firm commitment to park building on the river's edge, had begun.

By Factory and Cottage the Beargrass Winds its way to the Ohio. o o o View from the Ellison Av. Bridge

Van Leshout

Alex Van Leshout depicts a scene along Beargrass Creek as it flows through the Butchertown neighborhood. Once a pristine stream fed by natural springs in the Highlands, the Creek's reputation suffered as it served as an open sewer when the canalization project forced sewage back upstream. *(University of Louisville Photographic Archives, OCL.04)*

The lazy Louisville skyline seen from Indiana reflects a time when the city had lost a great deal of its previous spark. Characterized in a *Harper's Magazine* article as "the city of let-well-enough-alone," Louisville's economy gained a great many new jobs, thanks to World War II-related industries coming to town. *(Kentucky Historical Society ,a7jefl5)*

Turning Our Backs to the River

(1938-1972)

> As the City has grown, we have turned our backs to the Ohio. Between the downtown area and one of our top scenic attractions we have thrown walls of brick and barriers of indifference.
>
> It's time that we turned our faces to the River again. We capitalize on its utility as a transportation artery, which is the very reason for Louisville's existence in this location and is one of the prime reasons for our industrial growth.
>
> We can capitalize on the River as a civic and scenic attraction. Let's think big about it – let's develop riverfront apartments between Main Street and the River. Let's provide indoor underground parking, riverside terraces and easy access through the proposed riverfront expressway.
>
> – *Louisville Magazine* - 1956

After the water had receded Louisville emerged a changed city. Citizens who had always lived near the river's edge began moving to higher ground, with Shively and St. Matthews becoming destinations. The city adopted a system of one-way streets and built a four-lane highway, Shelbyville Road, to provide evacuation routes. The greatest change was the adoption of a Corps of Engineers plan to protect the city and county by building a comprehensive system of floodwalls and levees. The August 1955 edition of *Harper's Magazine* made the astute observation, "The flood of 1937 seems to have been the jolt that awoke Louisville. Like San Francisco's earthquake and Baltimore's fire, the flood became a local benchmark. Modern Louisville started with it."

Louisvillians were pleased with this mention in *Harper's*, but many were still angry over an article published in that magazine's September 1937 edition. Journalist George R. Leighton wrote a withering critique of the city and its leaders entitled "LOUISVILLE, KENTUCKY: An American Museum Piece." The lead paragraph of the article, and nearly every word that followed, challenged the city as never before.

LOUISVILLE, KENTUCKY IS A MUSEUM PIECE AMONG AMERICAN CITIES. THERE, AS UNDER GLASS, THE CURIOUS MAY SEE MEMORIALS OF THE "AMERICAN SYSTEM" IN ITS PUREST FORM, MONUMENTS OF INDIVIDUAL ENTERPRISE. THERE CHANGE CAME DELIBERATELY AND WHEN IT DID COME IT DISGUISED AND HID ITSELF IN THE FORMS FAMILIAR TO A TOWN WHOSE PALMY DAYS WERE DURING ITS YEARS OF GROWTH BESIDE THE FALLS OF THE OHIO, WHEN IT WAS A METROPOLIS OF THE GREAT VALLEY, A RIVAL OF CINCINNATI, THE QUEEN CITY OF THE WEST, A NERVE CENTER OF A YOUNG COUNTRY. IF YOU COME DOWN INDIANA ON A WARM MAY MORNING YOU WILL REACH THE RIVER AT LAST, THE MUDDY OHIO, AND THERE ON THE OTHER SIDE, ALL HAZY AND HEAPED UP, IS LOUISVILLE. THE TRAIN CRAWLS OUT ON THE BRIDGE. DOWN BELOW, ON THE INDIANA SHORE, ARE SOME MEN AND BOYS FISHING WITH BAMBOO POLES. THEN THE HAZE DISSOLVES AND THE CITY MATERIALIZES IN AN OLD RED-BRICK JUMBLE. THERE SHE IS ON THE RIVER BANK, LOUISVILLE, THE CITY OF LET-WELL-ENOUGH-ALONE.

Leighton's article brilliantly analyzed Louisville's slow decline from its promising frontier beginning to its status in 1937 as just another average American city. The article enraged local boosters, letter writers and editorialists who screamed their disagreement with Leighton's assertion that the city had grown complacent, and was ruled by a class of people only interested in preserving their personal wealth. One Daughter of the Confederacy had her own complaint about the article, "It's every word true, but it shouldn't have been written by a damyankee."

Others in the community, while stung by the disapproving tone of Leighton's article, quietly agreed with its conclusions. A number of younger Louisvillians, many of whom became the city's leaders during the 1960s and '70s, took the *Harper's Magazine* article to heart and began to question Louisville's status quo attitude toward new blood and new ideas.

As the Great Flood receded, oily high-water marks became visible around town and the extensive clean-up and repairs, aided by funds from the federal government and the Red Cross, helped to restore the city. Local and national officials recognized that a comprehensive system of flood controls was needed to prevent further destructive floods, and after World War II a project to build floodwalls and levees was instituted. *(University of Louisville Photographic Archives, R-50307.01)*

Cut-Off Bridge: The A-Number-One Hazard

Louisville's infrastructure suffered punishing blows during the Great Flood. Afterwards architects inspected every building, bridge and roadway before approving their use. One particular problem was the rickety bridge over Beargrass Creek at the old Cut-Off. The single-lane bridge was a bottleneck requiring

repairs at regular intervals. It was incapable of withstanding loads of more than five tons and was closed for replacement in 1941. The Cut-Off Bridge, built in 1884, was replaced by a 180-foot concrete span costing $49,002.

The Last of the Packet Boats

World War II had as much impact on Louisville life as the Civil War. The city went from product manufacturing to heavy industries as existing plants converted to production of war materials. The Hillerich & Bradsby Company switched from making baseball bats to gunstocks. Huge ammunition and gunpowder bagging factories opened in southern Indiana, while synthetic rubber and airplane plants operated nonstop in Louisville. Record numbers of women entered the work force and rural people from the South or Appalachia moved into town for good paying labor jobs.

After the war, G.I. Bill benefits allowed record numbers of families to purchase houses for the first time. Many people wanted to live away from the downtown area and closer to the Ford or Naval Ordnance plants and new roads were needed to serve these communities growing on the fringes of Louisville. The population of Jefferson County surged while the city experienced little and, eventually, no growth.

More changes followed the war's end, when the Louisville waterfront witnessed the beginning of one era and the end of another. The Municipal Bridge was renamed the George Rogers Clark Memorial Bridge, and in January 1949 it was the site of the first radar beacon to aid navigation on an American river. The Corps of Engineers installed radar beacons for the bridge as technology began to supplement the skills of river pilots. In 1946 only six boats had radar on the Ohio River, while three years later more than fifty craft used the navigation guides.

While the technology of marine traffic improved, some forms of river transportation lost out to commercial airlines, luxury

The *Gordon Greene* and the *Chris Greene* are shown tied to the wharf boat that was their dock during frequent trips to Louisville. As luxury train service, and eventually airline travel became available, passage on the commuter boats ceased entirely. The *Tom Greene* and *Chris Greene* were the last to service the Louisville port, and they left in such poor condition they had to be towed away. *(Filson Historical Society, Irma Byrd Collection)*

rail service and Americans' newfound passion, traveling across the country in station wagons. The graceful days of steamboat passage, when the great boats were thought of as floating luxury hotels, had ended on American rivers. The *Louisville Times* chronicled the departure of the last packet boats as they limped out of the Port of Louisville on April 22, 1950.

LAST OF STERN-WHEELERS
LEAVE WATERFRONT

A ROMANTIC 122-YEAR CHAPTER IN OHIO RIVER HISTORY ENDED HERE TODAY AS THE LAST OF THE DAILY STERN-WHEELER PACKET BOATS LEFT THE WATERFRONT AT THE FOOT OF SECOND STREET.

THEY ARE THE *TOM GREENE* AND *CHRIS GREENE*, BOTH OWNED BY GREENE LINES, CINCINNATI. THE COMPANY IS THE "DESCENDANT" OF THE ORIGINAL CINCINNATI PACKET LINE, STARTED IN 1828. THE ONCE PROUD FREIGHTERS SLIPPED AWAY WITHOUT FANFARE, NOT EVEN UNDER THEIR OWN POWER. THEY WERE TOWED BY THE *J. H. DUFFY*, FURNISHED BY THE OHIO RIVER SAND CO.

ALSO IN THE TOW, BOUND FOR TEMPORARY HARBOR AT TOWHEAD ISLAND, WAS THE GREENE LINE'S WHARF BOAT. THE PACKETS ACTUALLY QUIT RUNNING IN FEBRUARY, 1947, FOLLOWING A DISPUTE WITH LOCAL 89 OF THE TRUCK DRIVERS UNION. THE *TOM* AND *CHRIS* HAVE BEEN OUT OF COMMISSION SINCE THEN, TIED UP TO THE WHARFBOAT WHICH WAS USED AS A FLOATING WAREHOUSE AND DOCK.

THE GREENE PASSENGER BOATS, THE *DELTA QUEEN* AND *GORDON GREENE*, CONTINUE IN OPERATION, BUT HENCEFORTH WILL DOCK AT THE COBBLESTONES OF THE PUBLIC WHARF INSTEAD OF AT THE WHARFBOAT.

The City Dump Wars

Driving into Louisville from the East End along River Road was no bed of roses. Large dumps, both publicly and privately owned, crowded the route with the Ohio Street dump being the largest. Fires routinely began deep inside the massive refuse piles and burned for months without relief. Smoky clouds covered homes, cars and pedestrians. City officials knew they had a fight on their hands when it came to cleaning up this embarrassing situation, but they had no idea it might lead to an actual battle.

Courier-Journal accounts, beginning in May 26, 1950, detail a little known episode in Louisville's military history.

BARRAGE BY PICKERS' ARMY
ROUTES CITY-DUMP WORKERS

A SMALL ARMY OF PICKERS TOOK CONTROL OF THE OHIO STREET DUMP YESTERDAY, DRIVING CITY WORKERS INTO RETREAT WITH A BARRAGE OF BOTTLES, ROCKS, GARBAGE AND OTHER CONVENIENT MISSILES.

FOR NEARLY 2 HOURS, THE PICKERS, WHO MAKE A LIVING BY SELLING SALVAGE MATERIAL GATHERED FROM THE DUMP, HELD THE UPPER HAND WHILE THE CITY WORKERS

REMAINED OUT OF RANGE IN THE DUMP OFFICE.

NO ONE WAS INJURED, BUT ONE BULLDOZER OPERATOR WAS KNOCKED DOWN BY A PICKER DURING THE INITIAL PHASES OF THE BATTLE.

THEN AT 3 P.M., POLICE ARRIVED WITH A MESSAGE FROM CITY HALL. PICKING "MUST BE STOPPED IMMEDIATELY," SAID THE ORDER WHICH WAS READ OVER A LOUD-SPEAKER. THE PICKERS LEFT, AND THE DUMP WORKERS WENT BACK TO WORK.

"IT WAS A BATTLE ROYAL FOR A WHILE," REPORTED WORKS DIRECTOR HERMAN T. MEINERS WHOSE DEPARTMENT OPERATES THE DUMP.

IMMEDIATE CAUSE FOR THE TROUBLE, MEINERS SAID, WAS A SERIES OF NEAR ACCIDENTS IN WHICH PICKERS WERE ALMOST COVERED BY DIRT BEING PUSHED AND DUMPED ON TOP OF FRESH GARBAGE. BUT THE WORKS DIRECTOR SAID THE UNDERLYING CAUSE WAS THE PICKERS' RESENTMENT AGAINST NEW LAND-FILLING METHODS.

On April 25, 1950, the editorial voice of the *Courier-Journal* could remain silent no longer.

THE GARBAGE DUMPS
CAN'T SUPPORT SQUATTERS

THE BRIEF BATTLE BETWEEN THE PICKERS AND DUMP WORKERS ON TUESDAY WAS PROBABLY PAINFUL TO BOTH. BUT THE TRADE THAT HAS BLOWN UP AMONG THESE MOUNTAINS OF STINKING GARBAGE IS ONE THAT CANNOT EXIST ALONGSIDE A REALLY SANITARY SYSTEM OF GARBAGE DISPOSAL AND THIS LAST IS SOMETHING LOUISVILLE HAS URGENTLY NEEDED FOR A LONG TIME. PEOPLE WHO HAVE NO OTHER WAY OF MAKING A LIVING ARE, AS MR. MEINERS' MESSAGE TO THEM IMPLIED, VERY PROBABLY IN NEED OF

PUBLIC ASSISTANCE, AND THEY SHOULD BE GIVEN IT. BUT FEW MODERN CITIES TOLERATE OPEN GARBAGE DUMPS AND ARMIES OF RAG PICKERS ANY LONGER, AND THERE IS NO REASON WHY LOUISVILLE SHOULD DO SO.

Mayor Andrew Broaddus agreed, and plans were made to build city incinerators to burn combustibles. The May 1952 Grand Jury visited the Ohio Street city dump to investigate conditions and make recommendations for improvements. According to the April 11, 1952, *Courier-Journal* article, they had a memorable visit.

THE JEFFERSON COUNTY GRAND JURY GOT AN EYEFUL, AN EARFUL, AND A NOSEFUL YESTERDAY AS IT INSPECTED THE CITY'S OHIO STREET DUMP AND THE "LAST STINKING MILE" OF BEARGRASS CREEK.

THE EYEFUL WAS A HUGE MOUND OF UNCOVERED GARBAGE SEWAGE BACKED UP IN BEARGRASS CREEK, AND GARBAGE, INCLUDING DEAD FISH AND CHICKENS, DUMPED ALONGSIDE STREETS. THE EARFUL CAME FROM RESIDENTS OF THE AREA, WHOSE LETTER TO THE GRAND JURY PROMPTED THE INSPECTION TOUR. THE NOSEFUL CAME FROM THE SEWAGE IN BEARGRASS CREEK, THE ROTTING FISH, AND A BARREL OF CHICKENS SWARMING WITH MAGGOTS.

NEAR THE MOUTH OF BEARGRASS CREEK THE JURY SAW AN ACCUMULATION OF DEBRIS. SOME OF THE NEIGHBORHOOD COMPLAINANTS SAID RAW SEWAGE COLLECTED THERE, WHERE THE CREEK HAS NO CURRENT. THE CREEK, IN THE STRETCH AFTER ITS THREE BRANCHES COME TOGETHER, TO FLOW TOWARD THE OHIO RIVER, HAS BEEN THE CAUSE OF MANY COMPLAINTS IN THE PAST.

Louisville would not resolve the issue of the noxious dumps and landfills until 1957, as new city incinerators were installed to replace the smoldering dumps. A near-downtown helicopter port was suggested. City sanitation engineers estimated it would take a year to cover the rat and vermin-infested city dump, an operation that would result in sixteen city blocks being made available for other uses. The Ohio Street dump occupied a quadrangle bounded by River Road, Letterle Avenue, Story Avenue and Adams Street. The dump, the only municipal landfill, was a product of the 1937 Flood, when many of the destroyed houses from the Point were buried on the spot.

In 2009 Louisville Mayor Jerry Abramson joined a group of local volunteers announcing plans to establish a Botanical Gardens on the twenty-two-acre site of the former Ohio Street dump. Working with the Louisville Botanical Garden and Conservatory not-for-profit organization, the group's announced goal was to raise the $30 to 40 million needed to provide quality nature experiences to the south side of River Road, opposite and just past the eastern edge of Waterfront Park.

Long after the Louisville city dump wars were over, the old Ohio Street dump faces a brighter, and better smelling, future. A civic organization, Botanica, is completing plans to reclaim the former junkyard and provide quality educational and nature exhibits. Botanica's site, adjacent to the old Heigold façade, lies at the north end of Frankfort Avenue and River Road.

"…it's more history than architecture."

As in the past, only one surviving landmark remained of the glory days of the Point. Once again, the home of Christian Heigold endured and began its strange fifty-year odyssey.

Courier-Journal, April 8, 1950

DUMP LAND-FILL ALTERED TO SAVE 92-YEAR-OLD HOME

THE FUTURE OF A HOUSE WITH A PAST HAS BEEN ASSURED EVEN THOUGH IT IS LOCATED IN THE PATH OF THE OHIO STREET LAND-FILL DUMP.

AT THE REQUEST OF A SPECIAL COMMITTEE NAMED TO HELP SAVE LOUISVILLE'S LANDMARKS, THE 92-YEAR-OLD HEIGOLD HOUSE AT 264 MARION WILL NOT BE TORN DOWN AS PLANNED TO MAKE WAY FOR THE ADVANCE OF THE DUMP. THE CITY ADMINISTRATION HAS AGREED TO ROUTE LAND-FILLING OPERATIONS AROUND THE HOUSE, SAID GEORGE HENDON, JR., EXECUTIVE ASSISTANT TO THE MAYOR AND SECRETARY OF THE SPECIAL COMMITTEE.

JUST WHAT WILL BE DONE WITH THE HOUSE ULTIMATELY HAS NOT BEEN DECIDED, HENDON SAID. IT PROBABLY WILL BE LEFT INTACT TO BECOME A FOCAL POINT OF A PARK THAT IS TO BE ESTABLISHED ON THE LAND-FILL WHEN IT IS COMPLETED, HE ADDED.

FOR THE TIME BEING, HENDON SAID, IT WILL SERVE AS AN OFFICE FOR THE DUMP'S SUPERVISOR. THE OFFICIAL SAID THE DEED TO THE HOUSE WILL BE DELIVERED TO THE CITY THIS MORNING BY ITS PRESENT OWNER, ED PERRYMAN. THE PURCHASE PRICE IS $7,250.

Courier-Journal, April 11, 1953

Letter to the Editor from (preservationist) Walter L. Creese:

MANY LOUISVILLIANS HAVE HEARD OF THE HOUSE, BUT FEW SEEM TO HAVE SEEN IT. WE HOPE TO REMEDY THIS BY MOVING IT CLOSER TO THE RIVER ROAD WHERE IT COULD BECOME A PARK FEATURE IN CONJUNCTION WITH THE PAGET HOUSE AND THE WATER TOWER.

THE OTHER QUESTION, IS IT ARCHITECTURE OR MERELY AN ODDITY? REQUIRES MORE THOUGHT. WE CANNOT PROPERLY PICTURE THE CONDITIONS WHICH CAUSED MR. HEIGOLD TO CARVE THIS FAÇADE UNLESS WE THINK BACK TO THE REVOLUTION OF 1848 IN GERMANY, THE LOUISVILLE KNOW-NOTHING RIOTS AGAINST THE GERMANS AND IRISH IN 1855 AND TO THE CELEBRATION AT THE JEFFERSON COUNTY COURTHOUSE ON WASHINGTON'S BIRTHDAY, 1861. MR. HEIGOLD HAD BEEN EMPLOYED ON THE COURTHOUSE AS A STONEMASON. BUCHANAN WAS THE NOMINAL LEADER OF THE OPPOSITION TO KNOW-NOTHINGISM. THE POLITICAL ATMOSPHERE WAS TENSE, THE WAR BETWEEN NORTH AND SOUTH WAS THREATENING. MR. HEIGOLD WANTED TO TELL THE WORLD HOW HE FELT ABOUT ALL THIS. THUS, THE NAMES OF BUCHANAN, GEORGE WASHINGTON AND THE UNION APPEAR SEVERAL TIMES ON THE FAÇADE AND THUS THE STYLE OF THE SCULPTURE IS EMPHATIC AND TOUCHED UP WITH PAINTING. IT IS CERTAINLY NOT A CURIOSITY IN A HALF-HUMOROUS, HALF-TRIFLING SENSE, LIKE A TRINKET. WITHIN ITS LIMITS IT IS SINCERE AND SERIOUS.

I SHOULD PREFER TO THINK THAT THE BEST REASON FOR SAVING IT IS THAT AN OBJECT LIKE THIS CAN REAWAKEN THE PAST IMMEDIATELY AND VIVIDLY. IT IS NOT ESSENTIALLY AN ODDITY. INSTEAD, LET'S CALL IT AND MAKE IT A KEEPSAKE FOR THE COMMUNITY.

Courier-Journal, August 19, 1953

HEIGOLD-HOUSE FAÇADE, NOW IN PIECES, BEING PUT TOGETHER IN THRUSTON PARK

THE FAMOUS FAÇADE OF THE HEIGOLD HOUSE WITH ITS BUSTS OF PRESIDENT WASHINGTON AND BUCHANAN LIES IN PIECES IN THRUSTON PARK ON RIVER ROAD.

THE LARGE CHUCKS OF STONE LOOK LIKE TOMBSTONES

NOW, BUT THEY WON'T FOR LONG. YESTERDAY EMPLOYEES OF THE F. W. OWENS COMPANY, CONTRACTOR, BEGAN PUTTING THE PIECES TOGETHER, LIKE A GIANT JIGSAW PUZZLE, IN THRUSTON PARK.

IN APRIL DR. WALTER CREESE AND GEORGE A. HENDON, JR., FORMED A TWO-MAN COMMITTEE TO PRESERVE THE HOME. SOON AFTER THAT THE BOARD OF ALDERMEN APPROPRIATED $5,000 TO HAVE THE FAÇADE MOVED TO THE PARK.

LAST WEEK THE OWENS FIRM MOVED THE FAÇADE PIECE BY PIECE — A FOUR-DAY JOB. C.F. DECKER, SUPERINTENDENT FOR THE FIRM, ESTIMATED IT WILL TAKE ABOUT EIGHT DAYS TO PUT IT BACK UP. DECKER DEVISED A SYSTEM FOR NUMBERING EACH OF THE 315 STONE PIECES IN THE FAÇADE SO THEY COULD BE PUT TOGETHER AGAIN. EACH PIECE IN THE BOTTOM ROW OF STONES IS NUMBERED, FROM RIGHT TO LEFT, 1-1, 1-2, 1-3, &C THE SECOND ROW IS NUMBERED 2-1, 2-2, &C

Louisville Times, January 10, 1960

by John Fetterman

CHARLES ROWLAND PEASLEE FARNSLEY HAD THE HOUSE FRONT PRESERVED. FARNSLEY WAS MAYOR. THAT WAS BACK IN 1950 WHEN THE LAND-FILL CITY DUMP BEGAN TO GROW ALONG RIVER ROAD. THE DUMP THREATENED TO ENGULF THE HOUSE. HIS HONOR SAID THE CITY BETTER SAVE THE HOUSE. ...RECALLS FARNSLEY, "IT WAS MORE INTERESTING AS HISTORY THAN AS ARCHITECTURE. I ADMIT IT IS NOT GOING TO SAVE THE WORLD, BUT IT IS AN INTERESTING PART OF LOUISVILLE WE WERE ABLE TO PRESERVE.

ARCHITECT FRED L. MORGAN SAID PRESERVING THE HEIGOLD FRONT WAS "A SILLY THING TO DO. TO STAND THAT WALL UP THERE JARS ON MY SENSE OF THE FITNESS of things," said Morgan. "I've taken people by there and they nearly fall out of the car."

Architect Jasper Ward looked and reported back, "It has no great architectural significance, but it has tremendous local significance. I think it is a lot of fun. Certainly no architect would do it, I'm glad a carver went wild and did it. He was trying to make a statement. I'm glad somebody had the gumption to preserve it."

"It's American," Farnsley said. "It's more history than architecture."

"A good project for some dreamer"

In 1954 Liberty National Bank commissioned a useful illustrated history of the city called *Louisville Panorama*. It looked backward on Louisville's history, but it also glanced into the future:

It has been suggested by various individuals and civic organizations in recent years that the beautification of Louisville's riverfront would be a great asset to the city, particularly the bridge and river approaches. This is a good project for some dreamer, who combines vision with energy, determination and singleness of purpose. The City government last year (1953) made a good start several miles up the River Road by creating a new and attractive riverside park, with plenty of parking space for river lovers — and incidentally, just lovers...

The city once again brought in the Bartholomew & Associates firm in 1955 to prepare a detailed study of developmental potential of the land lying east of Adams Street and west of the Water Tower. Suggestions for the area included additional park land developed around Thruston

Park, acquiring Towhead Island and filling in the channel, and elimination of all substandard residential units in the Point. Like many others, most of the recommendations of this study were not implemented.

By the late 1950s dreamers were beginning to focus on riverfront development as a path to rejuvenate downtown Louisville. The May 1957 edition of *Louisville Magazine* described the beginning efforts.

NEW LIFE FOR THE CITY'S HEART

Louisvillians probably will vote on another City bond issue this November. If Louisville voters approve the bond issue, a major operation in "surgery" on the face of Louisville will begin.

Michael J. O'Dea, chairman of the Mayor's Citizens Advisory Committee on Redevelopment, has presented to Mayor Broaddus the results of weeks of volunteer work on the part of a 29-man group. Final consideration of the Mayor's committee was the Riverfront. In its report, this subcommittee cautioned against two extremes.

"A 'blue sky' visionary attitude might well result in nothing being done," said the group, "because the magnitude of the finished product could discourage the first step. On the other hand, allowing uncoordinated, piecemeal patching up could be expected to result in isolated small and other new structures inaptly related to the over-all welfare."

How this area changes, the Committee reported, will depend largely on the location of the Riverfront Expressway. Expected now

TO RUN ABOVE THE RAILROAD TRESTLE, SOME 40 FEET ABOVE THE GROUND, THE RIVERFRONT EXPRESSWAY WOULD HAVE RAMP EXITS AT SECOND, AT THIRD AND AT SEVENTH, BUT NO OTHERS IN THIS IMMEDIATE AREA.

THE SUBCOMMITTEE ON THE RIVERFRONT PROPOSED THAT THE PROGRAM BE CARRIED OUT BY PRIVATE INTERESTS, AND GOVERNMENTS MIGHT GIVE CONSIDERATION TO TAX INCENTIVES FOR PRIVATE FIRMS WHICH WOULD VENTURE INTO SUCH DEVELOPMENTS AS PARKING GARAGES.

In May 1958 engineers working on plans for the new interstate highway system made recommendations based on forecasts of local traffic needs in 1975. They agreed that two new bridges should be built to link the Indiana and Kentucky shores and facilitate transcontinental traffic through the area.

Governor A. B. Chandler of Kentucky and Governor Harold Handley of Indiana agreed that the north-south route to Jeffersonville (the future I-65) should be built just west of the Big Four railroad bridge. The Louisville and New Albany bridge, named for Justice Sherman Minton, would carry traffic on Interstate Highway 64 west to St. Louis.

Local access to the Riverfront Expressway (soon to be referred to as I-64 West) was determined by standards of the U.S. Bureau of Public Roads. They required 3,000 feet between interchanges and prohibited the introduction of local traffic into an interchange between two of the Interstate routes. The question of on- and off-ramps in the downtown area was critical, especially after a local corporation announced their bold plans for an unprecedented downtown waterfront redevelopment project.

In the 1950s large crowds visited the Louisville waterfront for periodic powerboat regattas. Boats were launched from the foot of Second Street and attracted large and enthusiastic crowds for several years. *(Kentucky Historical Society, 6jefa14)*

"…a showplace, a focal point for downtown Louisville."

The *Louisville Times* of March 14, 1961, announced a vision for the future.

RIVERFRONT APARTMENT TALKS ON

THE NEWEST DETAILS OF A PROPOSAL FOR A BIG APARTMENT PROJECT ON LOUISVILLE'S DOWNTOWN WATERFRONT WERE BROUGHT BEFORE MAYOR BRUCE HOBLITZELL AND HIS URBAN RENEWAL STAFF TODAY. THE MEETING WITH OFFICIALS OF REYNOLDS ALUMINUM SERVICE CORPORATION, PROMOTERS OF THE RIVERFRONT PROJECT, WAS CLOSED TO THE PRESS AND PUBLIC. THIS AFTERNOON, THE VISITORS WILL PUT THEIR PROPOSAL BEFORE A LARGER GROUP, INCLUDING LOUISVILLE CHAMBER OF COMMERCE OFFICIALS AND REPRESENTATIVES OF LOUISVILLE CENTRAL AREA INC.

THE SITE UNDER CONSIDERATION FOR THE RIVERFRONT PROJECT IS NORTH OF MAIN STREET AND SOMEWHERE BETWEEN THIRD AND SIXTH STREETS. THE IDEA OF THE DOWNTOWN WATERFRONT DEVELOPMENT WAS FIRST BROACHED TO THE CITY LAST JUNE. THE METALS

COMPANY SUBSIDIARY, WHICH WAS ESTABLISHED TO GO INTO URBAN REDEVELOPMENT WORK THROUGHOUT THE NATION, OFFERED TO HIRE THE WELL-KNOWN DOXIADIS FIRM TO DRAW PLANS.

AT THAT TIME THE REYNOLDS PEOPLE SAID THEY DIDN'T ANTICIPATE A NEED FOR ANY GOVERNMENT SUBSIDY OF THE PROJECT, EXCEPT THE POSSIBILITY TO ACQUIRE OPEN SPACE OR PARK SPACE AROUND THE PROJECT SITE. HOWEVER, THE MOST RECENT WORD FROM THE REYNOLDS CORPORATION WAS THAT THE PROJECT WOULD BE WORKABLE IF THE CITY COULD GIVE SOME ASSISTANCE TO ACQUISITION OF THE SITE. THE CITY HAS BEEN ENTHUSIASTIC ABOUT THE REYNOLDS PROJECT SO FAR AND IS HOPEFUL THAT THE HELP NEEDED WILL BE FINANCIALLY WITHIN THE CITY'S POCKETBOOK.

THE LOCAL GOVERNMENT AID, PRESUMABLY WOULD TAKE THIS FORM: THE CITY WOULD ACQUIRE THE LAND FOR THE PROJECT, CLEAR IT AND RESELL IT TO THE APARTMENT DEVELOPERS, TAKING ONE-THIRD OF ANY LOSS INVOLVED IN THE SALE. THE FEDERAL GOVERNMENT WOULD PAY THE OTHER TWO-THIRDS.

The next day's *Courier-Journal* provided details of the project.

THE CITY MAY TAKE ITS FIRST STEP IN A PROPOSED $24,000,000 DOWNTOWN RIVER-FRONT REDEVELOPMENT PROJECT THIS MONTH. AND CITY HALL HAS RECEIVED A FAVORABLE RESPONSE FROM STATE HIGHWAY COMMISSIONER HENRY WARD TO ITS REQUEST THAT RAMPS BE BUILT LINKING THE PROJECT SITE TO THE I-65 SUPERHIGHWAY AND THE NEW BRIDGE TO JEFFERSONVILLE, SCHEDULED FOR COMPLETION IN 1963. THE RAMPS WOULD GO UP WITH THE BRIDGE AND THE INTERCHANGE. IN EFFECT, THESE RAMPS WOULD BE THE FIRST UNIT OF THE PROPOSED RIVERSIDE EXPRESSWAY.

THE RAMPS WOULD BE OF GREAT IMPORTANCE TO THE PROJECT, WHICH IS DESIGNED TO JUT OUT LIKE A LEDGE OVER THE RIVERFRONT. IT WOULD NEED THESE LINKS TO LOUISVILLE'S ELEVATED DOWNTOWN HIGHWAYS FOR MAXIMUM ACCESSIBILITY.

THOSE AT THE AFTERNOON CONFERENCE SAW ARCHITECTS' SKETCHES AND HEARD REYNOLDS OFFICIALS DISCUSS PLANS FOR:

- THREE 14-STORY APARTMENT BUILDINGS AND ONE 25-STORY APARTMENT BUILDING AT THE SIXTH STREET END OF THE PROJECT SITE. IN ALL, THERE WOULD EVENTUALLY BE 1,000 APARTMENTS.

- A 250-UNIT MOTOR HOTEL WITH A SWIMMING POOL THAT COULD BE USED FOR ICE-SKATING IN WINTER.

- THREE RESTAURANTS, INCLUDING ONE ATOP THE TALLEST APARTMENT BUILDING.

- SWIMMING POOLS FOR EACH OF THE FOUR APARTMENT STRUCTURES.

- AN ELABORATE RESTAURANT AND NIGHT CLUB, A 48-LANE BOWLING ALLEY, AND NUMEROUS SHOPS.

- AN AUDITORIUM BIG ENOUGH TO HANDLE MAJOR THEATRICAL AND MUSICAL ATTRACTIONS — PROBABLY DEVELOPED AS A COMMUNITY OR PUBLIC PROJECT, NOT BY THE PROMOTERS OF THE APARTMENT-MOTEL COMPLEX.

- A PARK-LIKE PUBLIC SQUARE WITH A FOOTBRIDGE OVER MAIN LEADING INTO A MALL THROUGH THE CENTER OF THE BLOCK BOUNDED BY FOURTH, FIFTH, MAIN AND MARKET.

- Street-level parking space at the east end of the project between the buildings and the LG&E substation at Third near River Road.

- A marina on the river just east of Third, connected with the apartment-shopping complex by a pedestrian walkway. Reynolds doesn't propose building the marina, but thinks it is probable that others could be interested in doing so.

City Consultant Roy Owsley and Beck said the City would probably involve between $500,000 and $1,000,000. The U.S. share would run to about $20,000,000. The investment by Reynolds and any private agents they might contract with would run to about $20,000,000.

Reynolds proposed to solve the problem of the sharp slope from Main to the river by building some of its structures on fill and putting others, nearer the river, on a shelf, supported by a substructure. The effect would be of continuing the Main Street level for pedestrians to the northern-most edge of the complex of buildings — in essence, a kind of balcony overlooking the river.

There would be a public park along the southern edge of part of the project, a space now occupied by Main Street buildings. Officials said the project will have to be built in stages. Jagger said construction could begin in a year and that it would take between 18 and 24 months to finish the project's first apartment building. Other apartments would be added "as the market could absorb them."

Reynolds Metals began in Louisville in 1919 to produce tin foil and in the mid-1960s they began an ambitious national plan to showcase aluminum as a modern building material. They were involved in planning major projects in nine cities, which projected eight thousand dwelling units costing more than $283 million.

In an interview, Albert M. Cole, executive vice-president of Reynolds Aluminum Service Corporation, the aluminum firm's subsidiary handling urban renewal operations, said, "Rising like an amphitheater around a marina leading into the Ohio River, it will be a showplace, a focal point for downtown Louisville, and an exciting place to live. We believe it can be a powerful catalyst in the process of restoring the downtown as the center of community life for Louisville and Jefferson County." Reynolds hired Doxiadis Associates, an internationally known planning firm from Greece, to design the project.

Mayor William O. Cowger has pledged that the City will provide $441,615 for the extra cost of splitting the I-64 Riverside Expressway to provide the open space for the development.

The Louisville Central Area prepared a master plan by the Urban Design Committee of the West Kentucky Chapter, American Institute of Architects. The co-chairs were Jasper D. Ward and Lawrence P. Melillo.

The plan called for a promenade deck below the expressway level; extension of the wharf into the river as a quay with boat docking; amphitheater-like steps leading down to the water's edge; and an oval area for a bus turnaround in the space between and under the expressway lanes. All facilities were designed to withstand flooding.

Future generations of Louisvillians would recognize elements

Shortly after its purchase, restoration and re-naming, the *Belle of Louisville* moves up the Portland Canal toward the city of Louisville. The scene from 1964 was taken just before a great expanse of downtown building radically changed the sparse Louisville skyline. *(Collection of the Belle of Louisville)*

of the plan, many of which would appear on the future Belvedere.

Louisville Falls in Love with a Belle

Another thing Louisvillians would come to recognize, and love, was a 1962 addition to the waterfront – a listing, stripped-down shell of a tramp steamer called the *Avalon*. Its entrance to the city could not have been more inauspicious as she was towed from Cincinnati by American Commercial Barge Lines. The firm provided the free service because the old steamboat could tag along with a larger tow of coal barges.

The rusty old steamer had quite a journey to reach Louisville. Originally launched in 1914 as the *Idlewild*, she provided ferry service for livestock being transported across the Mississippi River to Memphis. In 1925 the boat was upgraded to serve as a day packet transporting passengers and cargoes all over the inland waterways. She was a popular excursion boat during the 1930s, often using the Port of Louisville to carry visitors to the upriver amusement park called Rose Island. During World War II the *Idlewild* towed oil barges during the day and was transformed into a USO boat at night.

In 1948 the boat's name was changed to *Avalon* and she began her long career as a tramp steamer. There were few American river towns not visited by the *Avalon* as she earned her living as a freelance excursion or party boat. By 1962 the boat was already forty-eight years old, an ancient vessel when compared to the average steamboat's career of three to five years on the rivers. When the boat, now stripped of nearly every architectural detail, was put up for auction, Jefferson County Judge Marlow Cook seized the opportunity to purchase it for a mere $34,000. His goal was to use the riverboat as a promotional tool for the Falls City and, with that in mind, her name was changed for a third time to the *Belle of Louisville*. Although many in the community questioned the judgment of Judge Cook, the old boat succeeded beyond anyone's expectations, but not without a great deal of hard work and determination by a group of gifted "river rats."

Maritime architect Alan Bates and C. W. Stoll, a Louisville philanthropist with a passion for steamboats, produced a plan for the immediate restoration and rehabilitation of the *Belle*. Volunteers and river-related industries contributed their efforts to paint, decorate and upgrade the vessel, with over $20,000 needed to make it safe and stable on the river. The *Belle of Louisville*, with its 157-by-36-foot hull, became an integral part of local life and, during the coming decades, hosted innumerable public cruises, teen dances, parties for social clubs, candidates for the presidency and uncounted numbers of schoolchildren. Its big annual event was "The Great Steamboat Race" when she was most often challenged by Cincinnati's *Delta Queen*, and the Wednesday evening event became one of the signature elements of the Kentucky Derby Festival.

In 1966 architect Robert L. Applegate provided his thoughts on the importance of this steamboat to the people of the city. "The *Belle of Louisville* might be considered 'floating architecture' in the gingerbread tradition of the old packets, but its real significance is as a focal point marking the beginning of the downtown corridor. The affection which the *Belle* has so quickly won from Louisville citizens shows how hungrily men need a focal point to relate to. Louisville has turned its back on the river at the area of its historic beginnings, but the very fact that the *Belle* is there shows that the city is uneasy about this rejection and would like to renew the relationship."

Remarkably, the engines of the Belle are much older than the boat itself. These powerful steam engines, the last of their kind

When many people come to Louisville the first place they want to visit is the *Belle of Louisville*, the oldest operating steam-driven sternwheeler in the world. Presidential candidate Richard M. Nixon made a campaign stop, and took a brief cruise on the Belle, in 1968. He is greeted by County Judge Marlow Cook, the man responsible for purchasing the *Belle of Louisville* for her educational and promotional value to the city. *(University of Louisville Photographic Archives, LC.6.3)*

in operation, were built in 1890 and transferred to the newly built *Idlewild* in 1914. In 1968 the curator of the Smithsonian Institution's heavy-machinery division of civil engineering wrote to Judge Cook and requested the opportunity to preserve the engines when the boat stopped operating. The Smithsonian must wait. In 2014 the *Belle of Louisville* will continue to demonstrate Louisville's original motto, "*by persevering*", when she celebrates her one hundredth birthday.

The *Belle of Louisville* fit comfortably at her new docking place at the foot of old Wall and Water Streets (today's Fourth Street and River Road). Considering the litany of unusual boats to tie up at the same location, the *Belle* seemed rather routine. At this spot in 1803 Lewis and Clark began their great journey; in 1809 a flatboat bearing an elephant landed here; and during the 1850s the marvelous circus boat *The Floating Palace* made this its temporary home.

Even stranger vessels would visit the Louisville Wharf in later years. None of the earlier oddball boats were stranger than the mission ship *Megiddo* in 1901, as remembered in a *Courier-Journal* article from December 20, 1956.

STEAMBOAT CHURCH

AN OLD STERNWHEELER ONCE BROUGHT RELIGION TO PORTS ALONG THE OHIO

IT WAS JUST ABOUT THE MOST UNUSUAL CHURCH THE OHIO VALLEY HAS EVER SEEN.

THE STEAMBOAT HAD LIVING QUARTERS FOR THE PREACHER AND MANY OF HIS FOLLOWERS, IN ADDITION TO A LARGE ROOM WHERE SERVICES WERE HELD IN RIVER TOWNS. IT PLIED THE OHIO FOR 10 YEARS BACK IN THE EARLY 1900S.

THE PASTOR WAS THE REVEREND L.L. NICHOLS, A BEARDED, ASTUTE MAN. DURING HIS YOUTH HE CLOSELY EXAMINED MANY RELIGIONS, BUT FOUND NONE TO HIS LIKING. HE FINALLY FOUNDED A SECT OF HIS OWN, AND IT BECAME KNOWN AS THE MEGIDDOS.

AT FIRST, MR. NICHOLS JOURNEYED FROM VILLAGE TO VILLAGE THROUGHOUT THE MIDWEST, PREACHING THE GOSPEL AS HE SAW IT, AND GATHERING A SMALL FLOCK OF FOLLOWERS. MANY OF THEM WERE HOMELESS. THEY WELCOMED THE OPPORTUNITY TO JOIN MR. NICHOLS, WHO PREACHED THE SECOND ADVENT OF CHRIST BEFORE THE YEAR 1941, AND PROMISED SALVATION TO ALL WHO JOINED HIM.

Screen legend John Wayne rode the *Belle of Louisville* as grand marshal of the Kentucky Derby Parade in 1976. Young deckhands were eager to pose with Wayne, including Mike Fitzgerald (back row and on right), a future captain of the vessel. Another longtime Belle employee is engineer Jim McCoy (front row on left). *(Collection of Belle of Louisville)*

ABOUT 1900, MR. NICHOLS BOUGHT A STERN-WHEEL STEAMBOAT, THEN ON THE WAYS AT THE LYONS, IOWA, SHIPYARDS. AS SOON AS THE BOAT WAS COMPLETED, HE HAD AN AUDITORIUM EQUIPPED TO SEAT MORE THAN 200 PERSONS. THE REST OF THE BOAT WAS CONVERTED INTO LIVING QUARTERS FOR HIS CONVERTS.

THE CRAFT WAS NAMED *MEGIDDO* MISSION SHIP, AND BETWEEN THE TALL SMOKESTACKS WAS A SIGN, "UNITED WE STAND."

A NEWS ITEM IN *THE WEST POINT BEACON*, ON SEPTEMBER 23, 1901, NOTED THAT THE *MEGIDDO* WAS TIED UP AT THE WHARF WITH SOME 95 FOLLOWERS LIVING ON BOARD. IT WAS A FEW DAYS AFTER THIS THAT THE *MEGIDDO* PAID ITS FIRST CALL TO LOUISVILLE, AND SERVICES WERE HELD ON THE FOURTH STREET WHARF. BUT THE MEGGIDO REMAINED MOSTLY A MISSION FOR THE SMALLER RIVER TOWNS.

The Hollywood Show Boat made occasional visits during the 1920s to revive classic American melodramas. The June 29, 1920 *Louisville Herald-Post* details a new fashion sweeping the city's smart set.

THE LURE OF THE RIVER SHOW IS STRONG

THERE WAS A STORY OF ONE OF THE LEADING SHOW BOATS OF THE FORTIES: OF THE BATTLES WITH FISTS AND CLUBS BETWEEN OWNERS, PLAYERS AND TOWN THUGS AT MANY OF THE PERFORMANCES. ONE ATTENDING A SHOW BOAT PERFORMANCE TODAY SEES IN THE AUDIENCES LADIES AND GENTLEMEN OF HIGHEST SOCIAL STANDING. SOME SAY THAT TO MAKE A WEEKLY VISIT TO THE HOLLYWOOD BOAT IS THE FAD OF THE MOMENT OF LOUISVILLE SOCIETY PEOPLE. BUT THE FAD SEEMS TO BE FAR FROM WANING, FOR ONE SEES, LARGELY, THE SAME FACES, HERE AND THERE, WITH NEW ONES, NIGHT AFTER NIGHT. THE FACT IS, IT IS A FASCINATION AND NOT A FAD. IN THE BREASTS OF THE PEOPLE OF THIS DAY THERE IS THE SAME YEARNING, THE SAME IRRESISTIBLE SOMETHING TO SEE THE SAME MANNER OF ENTERTAINMENT THAT APPEALED SO STRONGLY TO DAD AND HIS DAD.

The city's love affair with melodrama continued into the 1930s, when the Showboat came again to the Louisville waterfront to help raise funds to support a charitable cause. The boat's operator, J. W. Menke, claimed the success of Edna Ferber's novel, *Show Boat*, was the reason for their success.

Courier-Journal, September 20, 1936

MELODRAMA ON SHOWBOAT RAISES $1,000 FOR DROUGHT AID FUND

AMATEUR VILLAIN BOMBARDED WITH PEANUTS AND HISSES FROM $2 SEATS.

THE REGULAR STAFF OF ACTORS ON THE HOLLYWOOD SHOWBOAT, AT THE FOOT OF FOURTH STREET, ENJOYED A REST FRIDAY NIGHT AS A SPECIAL CAST OF LOUISVILLE AMATEURS PRESENTED A THUNDERING MELODRAMA OF THE GAY '90S. SEATS HAD BEEN BOUGHT DURING THE THREE DAY ADVANCE SALE OF TICKETS AT $2 EACH, UNDER THE DIRECTION OF MRS. BREAUX G. BALLARD. MRS. CHURCHILL HUMPHREY WAS CHAIRMAN OF THE GENERAL COMMITTEE SPONSORING THE PRESENTATION.

APPROXIMATELY $1,000 WAS REALIZED BY THE PERFORMANCE. THE MONEY WILL BE USED FOR AIDING DROUGHT-STRICKEN KENTUCKIANS THROUGH THE WINTER MONTHS.

THE PATRONS BOUGHT PEANUTS ($40 WORTH) AND THREW ALL THEY DIDN'T EAT AT THE VILLAIN, BESIDES HISSING HIM THOROUGHLY. BUT THE HERO, AH, AND THE HEROINE, AH AH! THESE TWO WERE ENCOURAGED WITH CHEERS LADEN WITH NECTAR AND WILD HONEY.

Aluminum Apartments Fade

Things were not all nectar and wild honey for the Reynolds proposal to remake the waterfront. Price estimates continued to grow and, even though the General Electric Company showed some interest in becoming a partner, the passion was fading on aluminum apartment buildings on the waterfront. The state of Kentucky deflated all the elaborate plans by refusing to fund the questionable design of a park for children surrounded by exhaust fumes and noise of an overhead Interstate highway. Energy had begun to drain away from waterfront development.

Courier-Journal, May 2, 1964

STATE WON'T PAY WHARF, PARK PLAN PUT AT $1.2 MILLION

A $1.2 MILLION PRICE TAG WAS ATTACHED YESTERDAY TO A PLAN TO BUILD A PARK AT THE FOOT of Fourth Street and enlarge the downtown wharf area. The State won't pay any part of it, Highway Commissioner Henry Ward announced.

The proposal by Louisville Central Area, Inc. called for dividing eastbound and westbound lanes of the Riverside Expressway between Third and Fifth to provide space for a two-level public park and plaza. The wharf would be extended into the Ohio River and several hundred feet of raised public parking areas would be built beneath the expressway.

Ward wrote Mayor William O. Cowger that Hazlet & Erdal, consulting engineers, estimated that the additional highway work would cost $441,615 and the park project $785,783. The commissioner said the Highway Department would cooperate in the redesign of the expressway section, "subject to the condition that the City of Louisville...will bear the increased cost resulting from the change."

Cowger, who has supported the proposal, has not received Ward's letter and will have no comment until he and his staff have studied it, a City spokesman said. Ward endorsed the redesign subject to approval of the Army Corps of Engineers and the United States Bureau of Public Roads.

He said the expressway could be divided if the

Newspaper publisher Barry Bingham, Sr. spoke to a group of executives in Baltimore in 1964 and detailed his vision of a successful Louisville. He spoke warmly of hoping the community would remember and respect its roots and celebrate its unique nature. Bingham's vision would in many ways be realized in the creation of Waterfront Park, where attractions like the Water Feature draw people back to the river's edge.

CITY PUT UP THE EXTRA $441,615 AND THE PARK AREA COULD BE BUILT LATER IF LOUISVILLE LACKED THE FULL $1,227,398.

WARD AGAIN EXPRESSED FEAR THAT THE BUREAU OF ROADS MIGHT DROP THE EXPRESSWAY FROM THE INTERSTATE HIGHWAY PLANS IF WORK IS NOT BEGUN SOON. THE FEDERAL GOVERNMENT PAYS 90 PERCENT OF THE COST OF THE INTERSTATE SYSTEM.

"...some subtle but insistent quality that makes us different from all the other cities in America"

As interest in riverfront development began to flag, Louisville's most elegant advocate, publisher Barry Bingham of *The Courier-Journal*, addressed a conference of downtown executives in Baltimore in 1964. Among his thoughtful observations were his ideas about development, and the character of Louisville.

PEOPLE ARE CREATING ENTIRELY NEW CITIES IN VACANT TRACTS OF COUNTRYSIDE THESE DAYS, AND A FASCINATING EXERCISE IT MUST BE. OTHERS ARE DEMOLISHING HUGE BLIGHTED AREAS OF OLD CITIES AND REPLACING THEM COMPLETELY WITH ACRES OF NEW TOPLESS TOWERS.

THE GREAT QUESTION IS YET TO BE ANSWERED: WILL THESE NEW CREATIONS BE LIKE WOMEN WHO ARE HANDSOME AND FLAWLESS BUT COLD? IN THEIR SHINING RAIMENT OF THE FUTURE, WILL THEY LACK THE RICH, WARM COLORS OF THE PAST?

THAT IS A QUESTION THAT AFFECTS ALL THE PLANNING WE ARE DOING IN LOUISVILLE FOR THE IMPROVEMENT OF OUR COMMUNITY.

WE KNOW THAT WE MUST PRODUCE DRAMATIC CHANGES IN THE APPEARANCE OF OUR DOWNTOWN CENTRAL CORE. BUT WE ARE DETERMINED AT THE SAME TIME TO PRESERVE THE FLAVOR OF OUR OLD RIVER TOWN.

WHEN A VISITOR WAKES UP ON HIS FIRST MORNING AND LOOKS OUT OF HIS HOTEL WINDOW, WE WANT HIM TO FEEL THAT HE IS IN LOUISVILLE, NOT IN KEOKUK OR MIAMI OR NOME, ALASKA.

TO PUT IT VERY PERSONALLY, WE WANT PEOPLE TO FALL A LITTLE IN LOVE WITH LOUISVILLE. THEY HAVE DONE THAT IN YEARS PAST. WE WANT THEM TO GO ON DOING IT, BECAUSE OF SOME SUBTLE BUT INSISTENT QUALITY THAT MAKES US DIFFERENT FROM ALL THE OTHER CITIES IN AMERICA....

ONLY A FEW YEARS AGO, THE LADY THAT'S KNOWN AS LOUISVILLE WAS LOOKING PRETTY SEEDY. SHE WAS AGING BUT NOT MELLOWING. SHE WAS SUFFERING FROM MIDDLE-AGED SPREAD, HER TRIM LINES LOST IN SUBURBAN SPRAWL....

A GOOD MANY OF OUR CITIZENS TOOK ALARM AT THIS SITUATION, I AM GLAD TO SAY. THEY BEGAN TO TURN THEIR ANXIETIES INTO ACTION. MUCH OF THE ACTIVITY HAS CONVERGED IN AN ORGANIZATION CALLED LOUISVILLE CENTRAL AREA.

WE WANT TOURISTS. WE WANT CONVENTION DELEGATES AND THEIR WIVES. WE WANT MORE DOWNTOWN OFFICE WORKERS. WE WANT REGIONAL SHOPPERS, THOSE FROM WITHIN 50 MILES OR SO, WHO ARE MORE ATTRACTED BY THE RICH VARIETY OF A DOWNTOWN DISTRICT THAN BY A SUBURBAN SHOPPING CENTER.

WE WANT MORE LOCAL CITIZENS LIVING DOWNTOWN, WITHIN WALKING DISTANCE OF SHOPS,

THEATERS AND RESTAURANTS. WE WANT OUR OWN SUBURBAN DWELLERS TREKKING DOWNTOWN, BOTH BY DAY AND NIGHT, BECAUSE SOMETHING DYNAMIC IS HAPPENING THERE TO PULL THEM IN....

THE MOST EXCITING PROJECT JUST AHEAD IS A DEVELOPMENT THAT WILL OCCUPY THREE BLOCKS OF OUR OLD RIVERFRONT. LOUISVILLE CAME INTO BEING BECAUSE OF THE OHIO RIVER, THE TRANSPORT ARTERY THAT LINKED THE EAST WITH THE MIDWEST AND SOUTH. NOW A MODERN CITY WITHIN A CITY IS DUE TO RISE ON THE WATERFRONT....HIGH-RISE APARTMENTS AND OFFICE BUILDINGS WILL BE PLACED AROUND A MARINA INTO THE RIVER.

ONE CIVIC ENDEAVOR HAS ATTRACTED MORE ATTENTION TO LOUISVILLE PER DOLLAR INVESTED THAN ANY OTHER PROJECT. IT WAS THE PURCHASE OF A STATELY OLD PADDLE-WHEEL STEAMER, RECHRISTENED THE *BELLE OF LOUISVILLE*....

THERE IS A GREAT DEAL MORE TO DO. WHAT MAKES ME HOPEFUL IS THAT THE COMMUNITY HAS BEGUN TO FOCUS AND CONCENTRATE ITS EFFORTS.

WE CAN'T AFFORD TO BUILD A NEW CITY TO REPLACE THE OLD ONE THAT GREW FROM A PIONEER STOCKADE ON THE RIVERBANK. WE WOULDN'T BUILD A BRAND NEW CITY IF WE COULD.

WHAT WE WANT IS A MODERN CITY THAT STILL REMEMBERS THE PAST, AS OLD BRICKS REMEMBER THE SUN OF MANY SUMMERS AND THE SOFT RAIN OF A HUNDRED AUTUMNS. THAT IS WHAT GIVES THEM CHARACTER AND BEAUTY.

WE DON'T WANT A NEW CITY, BUT A TRULY RENEWED

ONE THAT WILL KEEP ITS OWN SPECIAL PERSONALITY. WE DON'T WANT IT TO LOOK LIKE A PLASTER MODEL OF A METROPOLIS, WITH TINY FIGURES STANDING FORLORNLY IN FRONT OF COLD, IMPERSONAL BUILDINGS. WE WANT IT TO LOOK LIKE NO PLACE ON EARTH BUT LOUISVILLE.

The Louisville wharf slowly slipped away from the city's consciousness during the 1940s and '50s. With most shipping now performed by massive diesel towboats steering fifteen-barge tows, foot traffic on the old wharf was increasingly rare. *(Collection of the Belle of Louisville)*

"There are a lot of people who don't even know what a wharf is."

One of the last pieces of local architecture that made Louisville like no other place on earth was the old Wharfmaster's Office, located just west of the Second Street bridge on the old cobblestone landing. Originally built in the early 1880s to serve as the depot for the Louisville, Harrods Creek and Westport Railroad (a commuter train that operated only within the boundaries of Jefferson County), the depot survived floods, ice and tornadoes, but couldn't survive termites. The old Wharfmaster's office was a splendid Victorian two-story house with twin cupolas. In 1955 it was replaced by a drab, one-story twenty-by-twenty-five-foot concrete block building which provided office space and public restrooms for the small Mamie Varble Stratton Park still located next door.

With the decline of boats stopping at the waterfront, the

office saw very little business. As indicated in a June 8, 1967, article written by Ward Sinclair in *The Louisville Times*, two bored city workers unconsciously noted the nadir of local heritage – Louisvillians had forgotten their wharf.

BIGGEST JOB FOR TWO WORKERS AT WHARF-CHASING DRUNKS

"You would not believe," said O.D. Lantz, "all the work there is to do around the wharf."

What's worse, he added, "There are a lot of people who don't even know what a wharf is."

His assistant, Frank Murphy, nodded in solemn agreement.

Lantz and Murphy are city employees who keep a daily vigil over what is left of Louisville's wharf – the downtown Ohio River landing between First and Sixth Streets.

The wharf used to be a very busy place, indeed. That was where passengers and cargo were loaded and unloaded from river boats. But that was a long, long time ago. Nowadays the wharf is used mainly for parking, occasional pleasure-boat launchings and sight-seeing.

Lantz and Murphy also have another duty. They watch over a block-long strip of city park between Second and Third on the river. They say that's the hard part of their job.

"The toughest thing is keeping drunks, bums and thieves out," Lantz said. "They'll congregate in here...it's a helluva problem...you just tell'em to get out as best you know how."

"Yeah," said Murphy, "you've got to protect little kids who come here to play."

Motioning outside his office, he said, "We also have that birdbath out there...we turn that on."

"...one of the city's most treasured historic assets."

Even the wharf's pavement was no longer safe. Often referred to as "cobblestones," the actual surface was made up of rectangular granite blocks. Cobblestones are naturally rounded river stones that produce a rough walking or driving surface. Louisville historian Sam Thomas debunked a local myth that the pavement blocks were brought from Belgium as ballasts on ships. Granite blocks had been used in Louisville as early as the 1880s, but Arkansas and other southern states were the source, not far-off Belgium. Pavement of the granite waterfront started in 1910, and was later replaced with concrete. Progress on the wharf meant the old stones must go, as reflected in a May 17, 1963, article in *The Louisville Times*.

U.S. ROAD OFFICIAL CRITICIZES IDEA OF SAVING COBBLED WHARF

Plans to preserve Louisville's historic cobblestone downtown wharf after the Riverside Expressway is built have been "seriously questioned" by a representative of the Federal Bureau of Public Roads.

The cobblestone wharfage, which stretches from Second to Fifth, is one of the few public riverfront areas left inside the city limits. Most others have been leased by industries or the areas are inaccessible.

Last week a Bureau of Public Roads official

HERE TO REVIEW THE PRELIMINARY PLANS FOR THE EXPRESSWAY SAID HE COULD SEE "NO JUSTIFICATION" FOR PRESERVING THE WHARFAGE.

THE EXISTING WHARF IS TO BE DESTROYED WHEN THE ELEVATED EXPRESSWAY IS BUILT. RIVER ROAD IS TO BE WIDENED CONSIDERABLY AND RELOCATED TO SERVE AS ACCESS LANES FOR TRAFFIC GOING TO AND FROM THE EXPRESSWAY. HOWEVER, PRELIMINARY PLANS CALL FOR REBUILDING A WHARF AREA — MUCH LIKE THE PRESENT ONE — ABOUT 100 FEET FARTHER OUT IN THE RIVER. THIS WOULD BE DONE BY FILLING IN ALONG THE SHORE.

LODGE CALLED THE AREA "ONE OF THE CITY'S MOST TREASURED HISTORIC ASSETS."

LODGE ALSO SAID THAT THE AREA PROVIDES 200 FREE PUBLIC PARKING SPACES.

America's First Tribute

Work was advancing on the new Interstates that suddenly seemed to be crisscrossing Louisville. The north-south bridge on the expressway had long been scheduled for completion in late 1963. The date set for the opening was December 1, and the new Interstate 65 bridge, as yet unnamed, was eagerly anticipated by Kentuckiana drivers. On November 24, 1963, two days after the assassination of John F. Kennedy and prior to his burial, the following article appeared in the *Courier-Journal*.

RESOLUTIONS TO NAME THE NEW I-65 BRIDGE AFTER THE LATE PRESIDENT JOHN F. KENNEDY WILL BE INTRODUCED IN THE GENERAL ASSEMBLY.

THE BRIDGE BETWEEN LOUISVILLE AND JEFFERSONVILLE IS SCHEDULED TO OPEN NEXT MONTH.

The John Fitzgerald Kennedy Memorial Bridge carries the busy traffic of I-65 north and south through Louisville. Scheduled for opening in early December, 1963, the bridge was immediately named to honor the recently assassinated president. Political cooperation between parties and states made the decision nearly unanimous just two days after JFK's death.

APPARENTLY RESOLUTIONS WILL BE INTRODUCED BY BOTH REPUBLICANS AND DEMOCRATS.

THE REPUBLICANS MADE THE FIRST ANNOUNCEMENT YESTERDAY AFTER A MEETING AT CITY HALL OF MAYOR WILLIAM O. COWGER, COUNTY JUDGE MARLOW W. COOK, AND THE REPUBLICAN DELEGATION TO THE LEGISLATURE FROM JEFFERSON COUNTY.

COWGER AND COOK REQUESTED THAT THE DELEGATION INTRODUCE RESOLUTIONS IN BOTH HOUSES OF THE LEGISLATURE AS SOON AS POSSIBLE, PROBABLY

TOMORROW. THE RESOLUTIONS WILL ASK THAT THE BRIDGE BE NAMED THE "JOHN F. KENNEDY MEMORIAL BRIDGE."

LATER DEMOCRATIC SENATOR MARTIN J. DUFFY, JR., SAID THE DEMOCRATS WILL INTRODUCE SIMILAR RESOLUTIONS.

The measure quickly passed and was signed into law by Kentucky Governor Bert T. Combs. The JFK Bridge was America's first public memorial dedicated to the memory of John Kennedy.

Another change to the riverfront was the oddly utilitarian new building at the end of First Street. *Louisville Magazine's* January 1964 edition tells the origin of the building that would become home for the Waterfront Development Corporation.

The Ohio River Sand Company's corporate headquarters at the end of First Street was built in 1964 to sell sand and gravel from its adjacent yard. The unusual building was designed to stand on a tall column to prevent damage from flooding. The building took on a far different character when purchased for the Waterfront Development Corporation to serve as its headquarters. *(University of Louisville Photographic Archives, LG&E.10)*

OHIO RIVER SAND COMPANY

HAS BEGUN CONSTRUCTION ON A NEW OFFICE BUILDING OPPOSITE FIRST STREET ON THE BANK OPPOSITE THE OHIO RIVER. THE FOUR-STORY STRUCTURE WILL PROVIDE 2,000 SQUARE FEET OF AIR-CONDITIONED RENTAL SPACE ON THE THIRD FLOOR, IN ADDITION TO 2,500 SQUARE FEET ON THE OTHER FLOORS FOR THE OWNER'S USE. A LARGE PAVED PARKING LOT WILL ADJOIN THE BUILDING.

THE COMPANY'S PRESENT OFFICES AT 129 RIVER ROAD ARE INCLUDED IN LAND REQUIRED FOR THE PRESTON-TO-THIRD STREET SECTION OF THE RIVERSIDE EXPRESSWAY. A GENERAL REORGANIZATION OF THE SAND AND GRAVEL STORAGE YARD AND MATERIAL HANDLING SYSTEM IS ALSO PLANNED TO ACCOMMODATE THE LOSS OF ABOUT 25 PERCENT OF THE EXISTING YARD AREA.

THE NEW BUILDING, DESIGNED BY THE FORMER ARCHITECTURAL FIRM OF HARSTERN, LOUIS & HENRY, IS CHARACTERIZED BY THE CANTILEVERED TOP TWO STORIES WHICH EXTEND BEYOND THE SMALLER TWO-STORY BASE ON THREE SIDES. THE FOURTH SIDE CONSISTS OF A PAIR OF TOWERS ENCLOSING THE ELEVATOR AND STAIRWELL SHAFTS.

THE EXTERIOR FINISHES WILL BE A HARMONIOUS BLEND OF MATERIALS FEATURING THE COMPANY'S PRODUCTS. PRECAST CONCRETE WALL PANELS DISPLAYING EXPOSED RIVER GRAVEL WILL FORM THE WALLS OF THE THIRD AND FOURTH FLOORS. NORTH AND SOUTH WALLS OF THE BASE AND TOWERS WILL BE POURED-IN-PLACE CONCRETE WITH A ROUGH SAND-BLASTED SURFACE. OTHER WALLS WILL FEATURE EXPOSED KENLITE LIGHTWAY CONCRETE BLOCKS LAID IN AN ATTRACTIVE PATTERN WITH THE VERTICAL JOINTS "RAKED" TO CREATE SHADOW EFFECTS. INTERIOR PARTITIONS WILL ALSO BE TEXTURED KENLITE BLOCKS IN VARIOUS PATTERNS.

An Evening of Generosity

At the western end of the wharf, a change in the city's cultural landscape was taking place. The old Central Station Depot, located at Seventh Street and the river, was in for a dramatic change. In 1960 the Chesapeake & Ohio Railroad operated the last two trains to use the fine old station with its striking tower. Originally built in 1890, a temporary wooden shed housing passenger and cargo exchange was blasted apart by the cyclone of that year. In 1909, after other buildings came and went, the three-story office space, originally called Union Depot but later changed to Central Station, opened just feet above the river's normal level. In times of flooding, the Station looked like a fortress surrounded by a vast moat. Appropriately enough, Central Station was precisely on the spot originally occupied by Fort Nelson and marked the terminus of the Wilderness Road.

After the C&O closed its operation the City Urban Renewal Agency attempted to purchase the building north of the floodwall. They wanted access to land for an extension of River Road to Seventh. A possible tenant for the old depot was the Kentucky Railroad Museum, located in an outdoor lot on River Road near Beargrass Creek. A fortunate opportunity arose when a young theatrical group looking for a place to grow found Central Station.

Courier-Journal, November 5, 1965

ACTORS THEATRE SEEKS OLD IC DEPOT AS HOME

Actors Theatre of Louisville is negotiating for a lease on the old Illinois Central Railroad station at Seventh and the Ohio River, and is confident that the old depot will be its new home.

The move will give ATL all the space and facilities it lacked in its former home, an overcrowded loft at 617 ½ S. Fourth.

Central Station, located at the north end of Seventh Street, was completely isolated by the rise of the river during the Great Flood of 1937. Throughout its history, the railway depot was a frequent casualty to flooding and high waters, often curtailing rail service. *(University of Louisville Photo Archives, CS 149476)*

Although the old station may seem an unusual location, producer-director Richard Block believes it is the perfect place for the theatre's permanent home.

Plans call for using the station's main waiting room, which is 60 feet by 40 feet and two stories high, for the auditorium. The auditorium will seat approximately 250, and the main stage will occupy the southwest corner of the room. The remainder of the station will be used for offices, rehearsals, dressing rooms, scenery buildings, costumes and storage, placing all the theatre's operations under one roof. Presently, it functions at four locations.

The basic remodeling job, which includes new heating and air-conditioning systems, will cost $40,000 to $50,000. No plans have been made for the interior and exterior décor of the building.

Hard work and imagination turned the old depot into a Louisville

Actors Theatre, one of Louisville's leading arts organizations, began its successful expansion when it purchased and renovated the old Central Station at the foot of Seventh Street. A quick conversion from depot to theater in 1965 heralded a new day in the city's cultural development, and at its premiere guests arrived in a special three-car train. *(University of Louisville Photographic Archives, 1979.31.31)*

institution and a jewel of American regional theater. *The Louisville Times* of October 15, 1965, recalls a memorable opening night.

FIRST-NIGHTERS' SPECIAL TRAIN GETS ACTORS THEATRE OFF ON RIGHT TRACK

THE THREE-CAR TRAIN HALTED IN CENTRAL STATION WITH A LURCH SO GENTLE THAT HARDLY A COCKTAIL WAS SPILLED.

THE RED-CLAD WAGGENER HIGH SCHOOL BAND STRUCK UP A SNAPPY MARCH TUNE.

WOMEN IN FURS, SATINS AND VELVET AND MEN IN TUXEDOS PILED OFF THE TRAIN. AN ARMY SEARCHLIGHT CUT A WHITE FINGER THROUGH THE NIGHT AIR.

AND SO ACTORS THEATRE OF LOUISVILLE BEGAN ITS FIRST SEASON LAST NIGHT IN ITS NEW HOME, THE OLD CENTRAL STATION AT THE NORTH END OF SEVENTH STREET.

IT WAS AN EVENING OF GENEROSITY.

THE AUDIENCE – PATRONS OF THE THEATER AND CIVIC LEADERS – GAVE EAGER APPLAUSE AND LAUGHTER TO THE PLAYERS.

AND GOVERNOR EDWARD T. BREATHITT TOPPED OFF THE GENEROSITY WITH AN ANNOUNCEMENT AFTER THE PLAY THAT ACTORS THEATRE IS IN LINE FOR A SHARE OF $50,000 IN FEDERAL AID THAT WILL BE DIVIDED AMONG KENTUCKY ARTISTIC ENDEAVORS.

BUT IT IS REMARKABLE THAT THE THEATER WAS READY AT ALL. ACTORS THEATRE BEGAN FASHIONING AN AUDITORIUM IN THE OLD STATION ONLY THREE WEEKS AGO.

THAT MAY HAVE BEEN ONE REASON THE PERFORMANCE HAD SOME ROUGH EDGES. THE ACTORS HADN'T HAD A CHANCE TO RUN THROUGH THE PLAY ON THE NEW STAGE BEFORE LAST NIGHT.

The riverfront location was so successful even Louis Calta of the *New York Times* took notice.

ALL WORLD'S A STAGE, INCLUDING A RAILROAD STATION IN LOUISVILLE

THE SMELL OF THE GREASEPAINT AND THE ROAR OF THE CROWD HAS REPLACED THE ODOR OF COAL-BURNING AND THE CRY OF THE TRAIN CALLER AT AN OLD RAILROAD DEPOT IN KENTUCKY.

WHERE ONCE PASSENGERS WERE DISCHARGED AND FREIGHT WAS UNLOADED, THEATERGOERS NOW ARRIVE BY CAR, BOAT OR TRAIN. THE DEPOT IS AT SEVENTH STREET, HARD BY THE OHIO RIVER, WHERE IT SEPARATES KENTUCKY AND INDIANA.

The Dismal Drive

The new expressway system led travelers through, past and over much of the downtown area, and the new visual perspectives gained by driving over the elevated roadways were less than impressive. Industrial blight had grown in the River Road corridor and city leaders were slow to address the negative impressions gained by travelers using I-64. A *Louisville Times* article from July 10, 1968, pulled few punches.

DISMAL DRIVE – A SUPER ROAD WITH A SUPER UGLY VIEW

YOU COULD HARDLY CALL IT THE SCENIC ROUTE INTO LOUISVILLE.

MOUNDS OF SCRAP METAL TOWER UPWARD. ACRES OF JUNKED CARS SPRAWL OVER THE HILLSIDE. AND A BLOCK-LONG HEAP OF BLACK RUBBISH ASSAULTS THE EYES AND NOSE.

THAT'S THE VIEW FROM THE RIVERSIDE EXPRESSWAY – AN EASTERN APPROACH TO THE CITY THAT COULD BE RECHRISTENED "DISMAL DRIVE."

DISMAL DRIVE ISN'T VERY LONG. IT BEGINS NEAR THE KENNEDY BRIDGE, WHERE TWO SCRAP-PROCESSING YARDS FLANK THE EXPRESSWAY, AND COURSES EASTWARD FOR ROUGHLY TWO MILES PAST THE CITY LANDFILL AND TOW-IN LOT.

UP TO THAT POINT, WHERE NATURE REASSERTS HERSELF AND THE SCENERY BECOMES MORE SCENIC, THERE ARE AT LEAST 10 SEPARATE BLOTS ON THE LANDSCAPE. SOMETIMES IT'S HARD TO TELL WHERE ONE ENDS AND THE NEXT BEGINS.

BRANCHING OFF SOUTH FROM DISMAL DRIVE IS A SHORT STRIP OF INTERSTATE 64 WHERE THE VIEW

Three views show the progression of the same lot at the river's edge and First Street, originally owned by pioneer merchant Daniel Broadhead. At left, a view by Alex Van Leshout showing the Jeffersonville Wharf boat and a smoking factory reflects the site during most of the nineteenth century. *(University of Louisville Photographic Archives, OCL.22)*

The center view shows the area between the Ohio River Sand Company (on right) and the Kennedy Bridge in 1970, displaying the mountains of sand and scrap materials which formed most people's first impression of Louisville. *(University of Louisville Photographic Archives, 1979.31.16)*

The scene on the right, taken forty years later, shows the modern Waterfront Park with its headquarters and the popular restaurant Joe's Crab Shack, indicating a much more people-friendly environment.

IS MARRED BY TWO MORE EYESORES, BOTH AUTO GRAVEYARDS.

THE PROBLEM OF PROLIFERATING UGLINESS ALONG THE RIVERSIDE EXPRESSWAY WAS DISCUSSED YESTERDAY BY MAYOR KENNETH A. SCHMIED. HE TOLD REPORTERS HE WAS CONCERNED LEST THE SUPER ROAD "BE SPOILED BY OVER-FLOWING DUMPS AND PILES OF JUNK CARS." THE CITY, HE SAID, WAS LOOKING AROUND FOR OTHER LANDFILL SITES AND STUDYING THE POSSIBILITY OF LEASING PORTABLE AUTO CRUSHERS.

THE EXISTING LANDFILL OCCUPIES ABOUT 20 TO 30 ACRES ON THE NORTH SIDE OF THE EXPRESSWAY AND IS IN PLAIN VIEW OF PASSING MOTORISTS. THE LANDFILL, IN USE 15 YEARS, ONCE WAS AT LEAST 40 ACRES. WHEN THE EXPRESSWAY CUT THROUGH THE PROPERTY, THE LOGISTICS OF USING THE SOUTHERN PORTION FOR DUMPING BECAME TOO TRICKY. IT WAS CONVERTED INTO A RESTING PLACE FOR DERELICT AUTOS – THE OVERFLOW FROM THE CITY TOW-IN LOT AT EIGHTH AND MAGAZINE.

SOME OF THE MOUNDS OF SCRAP METAL AT THE WESTERN END OF DISMAL DRIVE BELONG TO THE LOUISVILLE SCRAP METAL CO., 125 N. PRESTON.

The Klempner Brothers Scrap Yard was cleared and reclaimed as the location of the Waterfront Harbor, one of the signature attractions to the Park. This was the site of filming a famous scene in the 1964 James Bond thriller *Goldfinger*, where a new Lincoln Continental is crushed into a metallic bale. (*University of Louisville Photographic Archives, 1979.31.11*)

David S. Blue, vice-president, said he was "very disturbed" by Mayor Schmied's remarks because his company has come up with an answer to the junk car problem.

Next month, he said, the final stage of the company's $500,000 auto-shredding equipment will be installed and put in operation.

"We will be able to take every car and more within 50 miles of Louisville," Blue said. "There won't be enough cars in the city to keep our operation going…we will be able to process over 300 a day."

But existing laws don't seem to provide many controls.

State law requires screening of junkyards along newer highways, but the law can't be enforced within municipalities.

In Louisville and Jefferson County, there are controls for new junkyards – but apparently not for the kind of older, established operations that dot Dismal Drive.

One of the waterfront salvage yards gained a measure of cinematic immortality in 1964, when the filming of a classic James Bond-thriller, *Goldfinger*, was shot at the Klempner Brothers facility. In a scene memorable to car lovers, the villain "Odd Job" is shown driving a shining new Lincoln Continental, with its trunk loaded with gold and a dead body, into the Klempner yard, where it was crushed and loaded into the back of a pickup truck. This cinematic action took place at almost the exact spot where Waterfront Park's Harbor, adjacent to the Great Lawn, would be built some forty years later.

"things were a mess at first…"

A new generation of post-1937 Flood Louisville leaders began stepping up to challenge the city's traditional "let-well-enough-alone" attitude and provide fresh thinking to questions of riverfront development. A key player was Archibald P. Cochran whose intelligence, energy and commitment to Louisville's future marked him as an important, non-elected, local leader.

Archie Cochran was vice-president of Reynolds Metals by age thirty-five and in 1939 founded Cochran Foil Company, a Louisville firm that later merged with Anaconda Aluminum. There were few civic organizations that did not feel the touch of Cochran's hand, and he was the crucial public advocate to draft and gain approval of a $29.8 million city bond issue in 1965. Passage of this bill provided funding for the new home of the Louisville Free Public Library, the medical-dental school complex of the University of Louisville, the Jefferson Community College, Founders Square and the new Life Sciences Building on University of Louisville's Belknap Campus. The bond money also helped finance the construction of a new General Hospital and the downtown riverfront project. At the same time, Cochran served as chairman of the University of Louisville Board of Trustees and guided the former municipal university into the state system of education.

Archie Cochran's involvement with the riverfront project began in 1964, when he served as the mayor's expediter with the Reynolds Corporation. First a member and, later, chairman of the Riverfront Commission, Cochran provided the reason for his interest in the waterfront. "You might say I'm just coming back to the river. It's where my grandfather got his start, making steamboat boilers at Tenth and Main."

Archie Cochran quickly realized his principal challenge was to re-think the early preconceived design notions of the Reynolds plan. He discovered, "things were a mess at first…with that marina idea. I knew people didn't want to keep small boats in a marina down there, with barge tows going by the entrance all the time and oil slicks and the dam too close. It took a year to get away from that idea to an office and business complex." He gained local commitments to a new approach for riverfront progress, with the addition of a 1,600-car underground garage a priority, but soaring interest rates created by the current tight bond market threatened to sidetrack the project.

Locally owned Louisville banks offered the solution by taking short-term notes for $10 million to get the project off the ground. With the banks holding the bonds until the bond market improved, the initial financing problem was solved. Cochran praised the cooperative attitude by commenting, "Detroit has its automobile industry to carry the ball, Pittsburgh its steel men, Hartford its insurance companies – and Louisville has its banks for leadership."

"What's a town without a beating heart?"

One of Archie Cochran's most valuable contributions was the recruitment of an unexpected ally, Louisville's thoroughly unorthodox builder and businessman Al J. Schneider. When the Reynolds' notion of marina and apartment complexes proved unappealing, Al Schneider came forward with the only private proposal to invigorate the riverfront development by offering to build a high rise hotel at the foot of Fourth Street. The proud old Brown Hotel at Fourth and Broadway had recently been sold to the Louisville Board of Education and Louisville's tourism industry desperately needed a large anchor hotel.

The March 1971 edition of *Louisville Magazine* ran a profile story and interview with Al Schneider providing details about the man local folks referred to as the "Great Bear." At the time of the interview, Schneider was in the process of choosing a name for what would be Louisville's largest hotel complex.

I'D KIND OF LIKE TO CALL IT THE GALT HOUSE. SEVERAL WEEKS BEFORE HIS DEATH, THE LATE ARCH

Al Schneider, a major force in building modern Louisville, was a larger-than-life character immortalized in a bronze statue in front of his two Galt House hotels. Inspired by his friendship with philanthropist Archibald Cochran, Schneider named his hotel at the river's edge after Louisville's two premier hotels of the nineteenth century.

COCHRAN SAID, PROMISE ME THREE THINGS – THAT THE HOTEL WILL BE NAMED THE GALT HOUSE, THAT THERE WILL BE A COCKTAIL AREA OR GARDEN ON THE PLAZA, AND ALSO SOME SPOT ON THE BELVEDERE WHERE PEOPLE CAN BUY A CUP OF COFFEE OR A SOFT DRINK.

ALTHOUGH I DIDN'T PROMISE, IT'S GOING TO BE HARD NOT TO CARRY THESE THINGS OUT. ARCH WAS LIKE A FATHER TO ME. A LOT OF CREDIT HAS BEEN GIVEN TO DESERVING PEOPLE, BUT IN MY ESTIMATION ARCH SURELY DESERVES 98 PERCENT. WITHOUT HIS HARD WORK DAY AND NIGHT, THE RIVERFRONT WOULD HAVE GONE DOWN THE OHIO RIVER ON SEVERAL DIFFERENT OCCASIONS.

Schneider could have been a nineteenth-century Louisvillian. A third-generation builder, he grew up in the Shively area and, after graduating from Manual High School, began his contracting career in Louisville. Like a predecessor, Mayor James S. Speed, another builder from Shively who forever changed the face of Louisville in the 1850s, Al Schneider began to remake the city. His legacy of construction projects during the middle of the twentieth century is staggering. In two decades Schneider built the Stouffer's Louisville Inn, the Portland Federal Building, the Bank of Louisville, the Executive Inn and the Medical Arts complex on Eastern Parkway. While building his new Galt House, he also was putting up the Louisville Trust Company headquarters, a twenty-four-story office tower on the northwest corner of Fourth and Main.

Schneider also built the Parkway Extended Care Center, a second 400-room motel at the Kentucky Fair & Exposition Center, Bellarmine College, the MSD building, the headquarters of Mammoth Life Insurance and the new Atherton High School.

Stubborn and opinionated, Schneider frequently annoyed some civic leaders but, from his understanding of Louisville, he emerged as an outstanding citizen with a powerful love of the city.

SUBURBAN PROMOTERS SHOOK THEIR HEADS IN LATE 1969, WHEN SCHNEIDER VOLUNTEERED TO BUILD A HUGE HOTEL AT THE FOOT OF FOURTH STREET. HE WAS UNDETERRED. "WHAT'S A TOWN WITHOUT A BEATING HEART?" HE SAID AT THE TIME. "WHAT WOULD NEW YORK OR SAN FRANCISCO BE IF YOU HAD NOTHING BUT SUBURBS?"

HIS 25-STORY, 714-ROOM HOTEL IS THE KEYSTONE OF A COMPLEX HE IS BUILDING FOR THE CITY THAT INCLUDES A PARKING GARAGE AND PUBLIC BELVEDERE-PLAZA OVERLOOKING THE RIVERSIDE EXPRESSWAY AND THE OHIO RIVER BEYOND.

"THE CITY WILL RECEIVE, ON A PERCENTAGE BASIS FROM FOOD AND GUEST ROOMS, ABOUT $200,000 A YEAR, PLUS AN ADDITIONAL $250,000 A YEAR FOR PARKING PAID

The sloping roadway on Fourth Street between Main and the river was traditionally called Wall Street in early Louisville. The narrow roadway passes between the two Galt House hotels and arrives at the stern of the *Belle of Louisville*.

BY THE HOTEL AND ITS GUESTS," SCHNEIDER EXPLAINS. "THE PARKING REVENUE WILL BE IN ADDITION TO DAYTIME PARKING BY OFFICE WORKERS AND SHOPPERS, PLUS ANOTHER $25,000 IN MISCELLANEOUS REVENUE, PRODUCING A TOTAL OF $475,000. THAT'S ONE REASON THE HOTEL HAD TO BE BUILT IN CONNECTION WITH THE GARAGE — THIS INCOME WAS NEEDED TO RETIRE THE BONDS FOR GARAGE CONSTRUCTION.

"THIS IS ONE OF THE FEW CITY PROJECTS THAT ARE SELF-SUPPORTING. THE HOTEL WILL NOT COST THE TAXPAYERS A PENNY, AND WILL BRING LIFE AND

LIGHT TO A CITY THAT'S DEAD AFTER DARK. WHEN IT'S
COMPLETED TWO YEARS FROM NOW, THE CITY WILL END
UP OWNING A $10.5 MILLION HOTEL."

CONCERNING THE WISDOM OF THE RIVERFRONT
DEVELOPMENT, SCHNEIDER WISELY OBSERVED, "WHEN
YOU STOP TO THINK OF IT, THE NEWEST SECTION OF
LOUISVILLE IS ALSO THE OLDEST — WE'RE STARTING
OVER ON THE SAME SITE."

"…the promise of Louisville's future in microcosm."

On the cusp of the decade of the 1970s, *Louisville Magazine*
trumpeted "The Promise of the New Decade."

THE RIVERFRONT PROJECT IS, OF COURSE, THE
BIG NEWS. THE BULLDOZERS AND CONCRETE MIXERS
WILL SOON BE RATTLING AWAY ON THIS COMBINATION
OF PUBLIC AND PRIVATE DEVELOPMENT THAT WILL
BRING NEW LIFE AND GLAMOUR TO THE AREA WHERE
LOUISVILLE HAS ITS ROOTS. THE KEYSTONE ELEMENT
IS THE HUGE UNDERGROUND GARAGE, TO BE BUILT BY
THE CITY, THAT WILL EXTEND FROM MAIN TO RIVER
ROAD BETWEEN FOURTH AND SIXTH. THE ROOF OF THE
GARAGE, ON THE SAME LEVEL AS MAIN STREET, WILL BE
TRANSFORMED INTO A LANDSCAPED PLAZA. EXTENDING
FROM THE RIVER SIDE OF THE PLAZA WILL BE A
BELVEDERE OVER THE RIVERSIDE PARKWAY, PERMITTING
AN OBSTRUCTED VIEW OF THE RIVER. (CONSTRUCTION
OF THIS SECTION OF THE PARKWAY IS SLATED TO BEGIN
EARLY NEXT YEAR).

ALL OF THESE PUBLIC FACILITIES WILL BE FINANCED
BY THE CITY: $2.1 MILLION FROM THE 1965 BOND
ISSUE, $1.4 MILLION FROM THE CAPITAL IMPROVEMENT
RESERVE FUND AND $10 MILLION IN SHORT-TERM NOTES
TO BE RETIRED LATER BY A REVENUE BOND ISSUE. THE
PRESENT STATE OF THE BOND MARKET, WITH RECORD

HIGH INTEREST RATES, THREATENED TO DELAY AGAIN
THE LONG-DELAYED PROJECT, BUT LOUISVILLE BANKS
CAME TO THE RESCUE, AGREEING TO TAKE THE NOTES AT
78 PERCENT, EVEN THOUGH THEY COULD EARN HIGHER
INTEREST ELSEWHERE.

PARTICIPATING IN THE FINANCING WERE CITIZENS
FIDELITY BANK & TRUST COMPANY, FIRST NATIONAL
BANK, LIBERTY NATIONAL BANK & TRUST COMPANY,
LOUISVILLE TRUST COMPANY AND BANK OF LOUISVILLE,
ALONG WITH CHEMICAL BANK OF NEW YORK.

The 1970 annual report of the Urban Renewal Agency
provided a summary of progress made.

THE RIVERFRONT REDEVELOPMENT PROJECT
BETWEEN SECOND AND SIXTH STREETS, MAIN TO THE
RIVER, AND FROM FOURTH TO FIFTH STREETS, MAIN TO
MARKET STREETS, IS NOW WELL UNDERWAY, AND EVER
INCREASING ACTIVITY IS QUITE EVIDENT. MOMENTUM
FOR THE REDEVELOPMENT OF THE PROJECT HAS BEEN
GENERATED AND WITH THE COMMITMENT FROM THE
FIRST NATIONAL BANK FOR A 40-STORY OFFICE BUILDING
ON THE SOUTH SIDE OF MAIN, BETWEEN FOURTH
AND FIFTH STREETS, THE DOWNTOWN RIVERFRONT IS
DESTINED TO BE A FOCAL POINT OF ACTIVITY.

CONSTRUCTION ALSO BEGAN LAST WINTER ON THE
INTERSTATE 64 RIVERSIDE EXPRESSWAY, AND UNDER
THE SAME CONTRACT THERE WAS INCLUDED A PORTION
OF WHARF CONSTRUCTION WHICH WILL PROVIDE
DOCKING FACILITIES FOR THE *BELLE OF LOUISVILLE*.
THE CITY IS TO CONSTRUCT THE BELVEDERE, IN
CONJUNCTION WITH THE EXPRESSWAY. ESTIMATED
COMPLETION DATES FOR THE VARIOUS SEGMENTS
OF CONSTRUCTION RANGE FROM JULY OF 1971 FOR
THE PARKING GARAGE; JULY 1972 THE RIVERSIDE

Expressway; to December 1972 for the Belvedere and Plaza. The Louisville Trust Building at Fourth and Main Streets and the Hotel should both be completed by the latter part of 1971 or early 1972, with the First National Bank building following later in 1972. The initial stage of the Wharf construction between the Coast Guard Station and Fourth Street, including mooring facilities for the *Belle of Louisville*, should be completed by mid 1972 and the balance of the Wharf between Fourth and Sixth Streets to follow approximately a year later.

The *Louisville Magazine* summed up the project in these words: "The Riverfront Project can be considered the promise of Louisville's future in microcosm."

The Louisville waterfront was the first impression made on visitors arriving over the Municipal Bridge when approaching the city. High tension lines covered utilities, train lines and other industrial operations, which dominated the city's waterfront for decades. *(Collection of Belle of Louisville)*

Rediscovering the Water's Edge
(1973-1982)

> *The fact remains that the Ohio Riverfront is everyone's front yard but no one's responsibility. It is not a neighborhood and not an incorporated area of the County. It does not have specific implementation funds set aside and it does not have a group to lobby for improvements.*
>
> *There is a great potential for future development to create a new connection to the Ohio River. The natural resource still exists even though it has been abused. The future of Louisville's riverfront is not in a plan but in the people who desire to improve conditions.*
>
> **– Report of the Riverfront Plan - 1981**

Louisville's reawakening riverfront area was more than just newer buildings. Some older structures still retained their importance to the local economy. Belknap, Inc., a fixture of downtown Louisville since William B. Belknap opened up business in 1840, could legitimately claim the title of the "Biggest Hardware Store on Earth." At their annual Belknap Dealer Market in 1972, more than 8,500 buyers and dealers from across the nation came to Louisville to inspect the unparalleled choice of hardware goods. The Belknap catalogue issued to their traveling salesmen was legendary, a valise load of 4,568 pages listing over 70,000 items. Virtually all of these items were shipped from Belknap's distribution center at the river's edge.

An article describing the annual Belknap sales event appeared in the September 1972 issue of *Louisville Magazine*. The scale of their operation is difficult to imagine.

THE FIRM SERVES MORE THAN 25,000 DEALERS IN 27 STATES FROM A COMPLEX OF BUILDINGS THAT EXTEND OVER SOME 46 ACRES NEAR THE RIVER, ONLY TWO BLOCKS FROM THE SPOT WHERE THE BUSINESS WAS FOUNDED AND HARD BY THE NEW DOWNTOWN RIVERFRONT PROJECT THAT'S BRINGING A BOLD NEW SKYLINE TO THE AREA WHERE LOUISVILLE HAD ITS BEGINNINGS.

THE FIRM EMPLOYS ABOUT 900 PEOPLE, OF WHOM MORE THAN HALF HAVE BEEN WITH BELKNAP FOR MORE THAN A DECADE. THE COMPLEX OF 17 BUILDINGS PROVIDES 1.75 MILLION SQUARE FEET OF USABLE FLOOR SPACE AND IS THE CENTRALIZED SHIPPING, RECEIVING AND STORAGE FACILITY FOR THE FIRM'S ENTIRE OPERATION. THE 11TH FLOOR OF THE MAIN BUILDING AT 111 EAST MAIN HOUSES ALL ADMINISTRATIVE OFFICES. THE HUGE 12-STORY STRUCTURE STANDS ON THE SITE OF THE THIRD OF LOUISVILLE'S FAMED GALT HOUSES. THE FOURTH, BRAND-NEW AND WITH 714 ROOMS LOUISVILLE'S LARGEST HOTEL, IS ONLY THREE BLOCKS AWAY, A REMARKABLE TESTAMENT TO THE VITALITY OF MAIN STREET WHERE BELKNAP STARTED.

TRANSPORTATION HAS BEEN ANOTHER AREA OF CHANGE, OF COURSE. WHEN THE COMPANY MOVED TO ITS PRESENT LOCATION IN THE EARLY 1900S IT WAS PARTLY TO BE NEAR THE RAILROAD SIDINGS AND FOR MANY YEARS THE RAILROAD WAS THE MAIN METHOD OF SHIPPING. BELKNAP'S GENERAL MANAGER BERSOT WILHOYTE ALSO

RECALLS THAT THERE WAS A REGULAR RIVERBOAT SERVICE BETWEEN HERE AND CINCINNATI EVEN TILL AFTER WORLD WAR II AND THE COMPANY PURCHASED TWO ADDITIONAL WAREHOUSES AT PRESTON STREET AND RIVER ROAD IN THE MID-1940S MAINLY TO GAIN A CONVENIENT LOADING AND UNLOADING DOCK FOR BARGES. AS RECENTLY AS THE LATE '50S BARGES WERE STILL USED FOR HAULING HEAVY PIPE, SHEET STEEL AND METAL ROOFING FROM UPRIVER TO THE WAREHOUSES.

"IT'S ALMOST ALL DONE BY TRUCK NOW," WILHOYTE EXPLAINS. "THE HEAVIER ITEMS ARE JUST SHIPPED IN SMALLER QUANTITIES, MORE FREQUENTLY."

WILHOYTE AND GENERAL SUPERINTENDENT J. W. EMERY ESTIMATE THAT ABOUT 12 MILLION POUNDS OF MERCHANDISE IS LOADED AND UNLOADED – ABOUT 34 INCOMING TRUCKS, 30 OUTGOING – AT THE LOUISVILLE COMPLEX IN AN AVERAGE DAY.

The Doctor-Mayor's Prescription

At this time, Louisville boosters liked to tout their hometown as the "Strategic City of the Seventies," and political and economic changes were occurring. In 1973 a young idealistic physician, who did not fit the mold of a classic Louisville politician, ran for mayor. He was a thirty-seven-year-old millionaire, from a patrician New England background, campaigning for a $26,000 a year job to affect change in his adopted community.

His name was Dr. George Harvey Ingalls Sloane and he did have one unusual local connection. His great-grandfather was Melville Ezra Ingalls, president of the Big Four Railroad, an important Louisville presence since 1895. Sloane's unorthodox style and personal energy – he campaigned by walking through nearly every Louisville neighborhood – appealed to voters. He was inaugurated as mayor of Louisville on December 1, 1973.

Those seeing Louisville, Kentucky, after the completion of Phase I of the Waterfront Park are amazed at the changes in the environment. Scenes of a declining industrial age dominated the river's edge, some of the most valuable real estate in the city, but with the establishment of Riverport in southwestern Jefferson County, several large industrial operations were able to relocate away from the downtown district.

Sloane's first term was marked by two significant challenges, a brutal tornado and a collapsing mass transit system. The tornado of 1974 cut right across Louisville and did unequalled damage. The jewel of Louisville's Olmsted park system, Cherokee Park, was splintered from a direct hit of the cyclone. The stunning destruction provided a renewed interest in the parks system and green spaces in general. During the first Sloane administration, city and volunteer efforts to re-green the community became a priority.

Dramatic declines in users of public mass transit threatened to end bus service in 1972. The private firm providing local bus service, the Louisville Transit Company, projected record financial losses and announced their intention to cease operation in 1974. Likewise, the Bridge Transit Company serving Jeffersonville, and other community bus firms, were closing. Harvey Sloane used his political popularity to convince voters to approve a controversial referendum to increase the occupational tax and underwrite a regional bus system. The Transit Authority of River City (TARC) was formed to provide affordable public transportation to local citizens. Louisville, which pioneered the first American interurban rail line between the city and Portland in 1837, rescued its public transit at the last moment, and Mayor Sloane staked a great deal of political capital to make it happen.

"The largest industrial and port development on the inland river system."

Downtown real estate, and especially that near the Ohio River shore, began to increase in value as riverfront renaissance programs began to take hold. Many of the traditional waterfront industries began relocating outside the downtown area. Creation of the Louisville & Jefferson County Riverport Authority in 1966 provided new life for the community's oldest industry, transshipping. Southwestern Jefferson County, the area west of Dixie Highway and downriver from the Rubbertown industrial complex, had

long felt ignored by the rest of Jefferson County. Residents of Shively, Pleasure Ridge Park and Valley Station had grown used to commuting to factories and jobs far from their homes, and the Ohio River shoreline remained an under-utilized economic asset.

Historian George H. Yater, writing for *Louisville Magazine* in July 1974, provided a very good picture of the continuing economic impact of transshipment of cargoes.

RIVERPORT: NEW KINGDOM FOR THE SOUTHWEST

Geographically, it's 1,740 acres of flat, flood-prone river-bottom land in southwestern Jefferson County, now used mainly for farming. Planned for industrial and port use, it stretches along Lower River Road from near Cane Run Road on the north to Johnsontown Road, some 3½ miles to the south. It's bounded by the Ohio River on the west and meandering Mill Creek on the east.

Potentially it holds immense promise not only of boosting the economy of all Louisville and Jefferson County (17,250 new jobs over the next decade in the industrial park), but also of aiding in the solution of a lot of nagging, long-standing problems in the southwestern sector of the county: flooding, water pollution, lack of sewers, poor drainage, inadequate recreation facilities, bumper-to-bumper traffic and more.

In size it will be the largest industrial and port development anywhere on the inland river system: that includes the Ohio, Mississippi, Missouri, Arkansas, Tennessee and Cumberland Rivers. Furthermore, according to a 1972 market analysis for Riverport by John Clair Thompson

ASSOCIATES OF STORRS, CONN., THERE'S NO OTHER SITE ALONG THE INLAND RIVERS THAT CAN MATCH THE LOCAL PROJECT'S UNUSUAL COMBINATION OF SIZE; RIVER, RAIL AND ROAD TRANSPORTATION; PROXIMITY TO A MAJOR METROPOLITAN CENTER WITH ALL THAT IMPLIES IN THE WAY OF A POOL OF SKILLED LABOR AND OTHER URBAN ADVANTAGES; AND ITS STRATEGIC LOCATION, PROVIDING WHAT THE ANALYSTS CALL "LINES OF FORCE TO THE SOURCES TO DEMAND," WHICH IS ANOTHER WAY OF SAYING EASY ACCESS TO MARKETS FOR MANUFACTURED GOODS IN THE MIDWEST, THE SOUTH AND THE EAST.

THE STUDY ALSO REPORTS THAT SOME 20 FIRMS EMPLOYING ABOUT 25,000 WORKERS WITH TOTAL WAGES OF $235,375,000 IN 1972 WERE LOCATED IN LOUISVILLE FOR REASONS RELATED TO WATER TRANSPORTATION. EIGHT OF THESE FIRMS MOVED TO LOUISVILLE DURING THE PAST TWO DECADES.

BACK IN THE EARLY AND MIDDLE YEARS OF THE 1960S, LOUISVILLE-AREA COMMUNITY LEADERS SAW AN ECONOMIC PROBLEM COMING INTO VIEW ON THE FAR HORIZON. THE AREA'S INDUSTRIAL GROWTH WAS SEVERELY DEPLETING THE SUPPLY OF LAND SUITABLE FOR NEW INDUSTRY. IN FACT, A CRISIS IN ECONOMIC GROWTH WAS SEEN AS AN INEVITABLE FUTURE PROBLEM UNLESS ADDITIONAL LAND SUITABLE FOR INDUSTRIAL USE WAS PRESERVED FROM ENCROACHMENT BY OTHER USES.

Better Known as the Belvedere

The 1975 annual report of the Urban Renewal Agency was unusually upbeat when counting recent accomplishments in riverfront renewal. The newly constructed area, officially called the Riverfront Plaza, but referred to by many as the Belvedere, provided good reason for civic chest-thumping.

THE RIVERFRONT PLAZA HAS BECOME A HOUSEHOLD

The Belvedere, an adaption of the original Bartholomew Plan's Plaza, stimulated interest in downtown Louisville and attracted tens of thousands to its Heritage Weekends. The Belvedere provides a sweeping view of the Falls of the Ohio from the same place where the Bullitt mansions formerly stood.

WORD THROUGHOUT LOUISVILLE AND JEFFERSON COUNTY. VISITORS CAME FROM ALL OVER THE COUNTRY TO SEE WHAT LOUISVILLE CIVIC LEADERS, PUBLIC AND PRIVATE, HAVE DONE WITH A BLIGHTED AREA OF OLD WAREHOUSES, OBSOLETE BUILDINGS AND PARKING LOTS. IMAGINATIVE DESIGN COORDINATED THE NATURAL ASSETS OF THE AREA AND COMPENSATED FOR PROBLEMS – PERIODIC FLOODINGS, A RIVERSIDE EXPRESSWAY, A RAILROAD AND A UTILITY COMPANY SUBSTATION.

TOPPING A THREE-LEVEL PARKING GARAGE, THERE IS A 6.5-ACRE TREE-STUDDED OPEN SPACE WHICH INCLUDES A SERIES OF FOUNTAINS, WATERFALLS AND POOLS. A LARGE REFLECTING POOL CONVERTS TO AN ICE SKATING RINK DURING WINTER MONTHS AND THIS YEAR THE CITY COMPLETED AND DEDICATED A PERMANENT STRUCTURE FOR SKATE RENTAL, TICKET SALES AND OFFICE FOR THE RINK.

THE PLAZA-BELVEDERE PROVIDES A PLACE FOR THE PEOPLE OF THE COMMUNITY TO ENJOY ETHNIC HERITAGE WEEKENDS, MUSICAL PRESENTATIONS AND A WIDE VARIETY OF EVENTS. THE BELVEDERE EXTENDS OVER THE HIGHWAY AND LETS US TAKE IN ONE OF THE MOST IMPRESSIVE VIEWS OF THE OHIO RIVER AND SEE THE BELLE OF LOUISVILLE

(EXCURSION STEAMER) BERTHED AT THE WHARF BELOW.

PRIVATE BUSINESSES CONTINUE TO THRIVE IN THE
RIVERFRONT DISTRICT: GALT HOUSE HOTEL, THE
LOUISVILLE TRUST BUILDING, AMERICAN LIFE AND
ACCIDENT INSURANCE COMPANY, FIRST NATIONAL
TOWER, KINGFISH RESTAURANT, FARM CREDIT BANK AND
GREATER LOUISVILLE FIRST FEDERAL SAVINGS AND LOAN
ASSOCIATION. ON THE WEST END OF THE PLAZA, THE CITY'S
INFORMATION CENTER RIVERFRONT OFFICE, POLICE SUB-
STATION AND POST OFFICE HAVE PROVED WELCOME ADDITIONS.

A series of summer events on the Belvedere, the Heritage
Weekends, featuring Louisville's international community,
proved unexpectedly popular. Tens of thousands of people left
their suburban or neighborhood homes and drove downtown
to enjoy ethnic foods and music from members of Louisville's
Greek, Irish, Arab, Japanese, Middle Eastern, Latin American,
African and other communities. The events proved so popular
the smaller ethnic populations were unable to physically
keep up with the demands for their unusual home cooking.
The Heritage Weekends on the Belvedere brought a sense of
cosmopolitan experience unfamiliar to Louisville.

Annual Bluegrass music festivals, winter skating on
frozen pools, and outdoor picnic areas for downtown workers
proved irresistible. The Belvedere, a large community platform
overlooking the Falls of the Ohio and sitting atop a large
underground parking garage, had been originally envisioned by
the Bartholomew Plan in 1931. Its popularity confirmed the fact
that people would come back to the river, if given an opportunity.

Adjacent to the Belvedere, on the block of Main Street
formerly owned by Thomas and Cuthbert Bullitt, a superb new
facility, the Kentucky Center for the Arts, opened to enthusiastic
applause in 1983. And finally, a heroic bronze memorial to
George Rogers Clark found an appropriate location. Sculptor

General George Rogers Clark, a heroic bronze by Felix de Weldon, shows Louisville's founder
pointing to the Northwest Territory he conquered. Although of a more modest scale than the
proposed GRC Lighthouse of the 1930s, the piece captures Clark's vitality.

Felix de Weldon's tribute shows Louisville's founder pointing
northwestward toward the territories he conquered during the
American Revolution.

To Merge, or Not to Merge

Local officials and community leaders had long realized
that the balance of power had shifted since the end of World
War II, with the dramatic growth of rural Jefferson County
and numerous small cities scattered away from the downtown
area. For decades, political leaders had pressed for some kind of
unified local government. The earliest plan started in 1956 and
was referred to as the Mallon Plan. A study group led by John

Mallon sought to consolidate Louisville and twenty-eight small cities located within two or three miles of the city limits. Viewed by many as a takeover by city government, the referendum passed in the city but failed in the rest of the county.

In 1970 the Morton-Wyatt Plan, led by former U.S. Senator Thurston B. Morton and former Lieutenant Governor Wilson W. Wyatt, Sr., called for a merger of the two major governments under the city's administration. Drafted and endorsed by the Louisville Area Chamber of Commerce, it called for enabling legislation to prepare a charter to be publicly affirmed. Louisville Mayor Frank Burke was an advocate, but County Judge Todd Hollenbach withdrew his support, citing concerns it would seriously diminish the political powers of county residents.

Efforts by the Louisville Area Chamber of Commerce in 1972 requested the General Assembly to create a study committee on local government, with staff work to be financed by city and county governments. A lack of unity among the Jefferson County legislative delegation doomed the proposal.

When the Lexington and Fayette County governments merged in 1978, an effort to permit merger of first-class cities was attempted. Louisville, the state's only such city, failed to generate sufficient support among local legislators.

The January 1980 issue of *Louisville Magazine* detailed the most current effort to achieve a unified local government.

A NON-PARTISAN GROUP OF CITIZENS AND LOCAL OFFICIALS, APPOINTED TO A 30-MEMBER LOCAL GOVERNMENT REORGANIZATION COMMITTEE BY THE MAYOR AND THE COUNTY JUDGE, HAS PROPOSED LEGISLATION THAT WOULD PERMIT THE APPOINTMENT OF A LOCAL COMMISSION TO DRAFT THE CHARTER FOR A LOCAL REFERENDUM. HOPING TO ENHANCE THE POSSIBILITIES FOR CHANGE, JUDGE MITCH MCCONNELL ALSO HAS PROPOSED A CONSTITUTIONAL AMENDMENT WHICH WOULD LET KENTUCKY VOTERS DECIDE WHETHER THE COUNTY SHOULD BE THE PRINCIPAL LOCAL GOVERNMENT. IN EITHER CASE, LOCAL-GOVERNMENT REORGANIZATION WOULD NOT TAKE EFFECT UNTIL 1985 OR 1986.

JEFFERSON COUNTY CURRENTLY CONTAINS 87 SEPARATE GOVERNMENTS: COUNTY GOVERNMENT, A FIRST-CLASS CITY GOVERNMENT AND 85 INCORPORATED CITIES. IN ADDITION, THERE ARE MORE THAN 100 SPECIAL LOCAL-GOVERNMENT ENTITIES SUCH AS SPECIAL DISTRICTS AND INDEPENDENT AGENCIES, MANY OF THEM SPONSORED BY THE CITY OF LOUISVILLE AND JEFFERSON COUNTY.

WYATT NOTED THAT AS PUBLIC EXPECTATIONS MOUNT, UNDER THE PRESENT SYSTEM GOVERNMENT COSTS ESCALATE WHILE THE QUALITY OF SERVICES DETERIORATES, A SITUATION WITH RUINOUS POTENTIAL FOR FINANCIALLY PRESSED CITY GOVERNMENT.

THE CITY'S INCOME HAS CONTINUED TO DECLINE BECAUSE OF FLIGHT TO THE SUBURBS IN THE PAST 20 YEARS, CAUSING DRAMATIC CHANGES IN PROPERTY VALUES. BEFORE THE MID-1960S LOUISVILLE'S TOTAL PROPERTY ASSESSMENTS EXCEEDED THAT OF THE REST OF THE COUNTY. BY 1969, HOWEVER THE COUNTY'S ASSESSMENT TOTAL ($1.99 BILLION) HAD SURPASSED THAT OF THE CITY ($1.71 BILLION). TODAY THE DISPARITY IS EVEN MORE PRONOUNCED - $4.85 BILLION IN THE COUNTY AS COMPARED TO $2.62 BILLION IN THE CITY.

FACED WITH RECURRING BUDGET DIFFICULTIES THAT WOULD HAVE BEEN SEVERE EVEN WITHOUT SPIRALING INFLATION, THE CITY HAS BEEN TRYING, SO FAR WITHOUT MUCH SUCCESS IN THE COURTS, TO BROADEN ITS TAX AND POPULATION BASES BY ANNEXING LUCRATIVE LAND AREAS IN THE COUNTY.

Merged government, a hot local political topic for years, had finally reached the community's front burner. The economic realities of urban sprawl and a demand for greater levels of service in the county put pressure on political leaders to find a middle ground. As the decade of the 1980s began, Louisvillians were looking seriously into their future, and to the future of the riverfront.

The future site of the Great Lawn demonstrates the challenges, both esthetic and engineering, faced by Waterfront Development officials and designers. A bleak landscape on the area formerly known as the Point had suffered flooding, pollution and industrial blight for generations.

Everybody's Front Yard

A 1981 study called the Riverfront Plan was prepared by the staff of the Louisville and Jefferson County Planning Commission under contract with the City of Louisville Community Development Cabinet. The Commission worked closely with the Riverfront Plan Task Force to set priorities for Jefferson County's thirty-seven-mile border shared with the Ohio River.

The Plan covered the area of the riverfront between Shawnee Golf Course and the Louisville Water Company Pumping Station. The purpose of the study was to identify needs and recommend actions to enhance budgetary, zoning and other planning requirements.

The Plan's introduction proclaimed its intentions.

"IN LOUISVILLE THE REHABILITATION AND REUSE OF EXISTING BUILDINGS IS VERY EVIDENT. RENOVATION OF OLDER STRUCTURES IS OFTEN THE RULE RATHER THAN THE EXCEPTION. NEW CONSTRUCTION AND REINVESTMENT IN THE DOWNTOWN AREA IS ALSO A REALITY. PROPOSED HOUSING AND AN EXPANDING MEDICAL COMPLEX CLOSE TO THE DOWNTOWN SHOW POSITIVE ACTIONS.

BUT LITTLE USE HAS BEEN MADE OF THE RIVERFRONT FOR PUBLIC PURPOSES. IT HAS BECOME SEPARATED FROM MOST RESIDENTS OF THE CITY. HERE ARE FEW DEVELOPMENTS TAKING ADVANTAGE OF A RIVER LOCATION. THERE HAS BEEN LITTLE PLANNING OR DISCUSSION ABOUT RIVERFRONT FACILITIES, NEW DEVELOPMENT OR FUTURE USES THAT ARE ORIENTED TOWARD THE OHIO.

The Plan identified a crucial weakness in past efforts to rehabilitate Louisville's waterfront, the question of who was to lead efforts to improve conditions at the river's edge. "The fact remains that the Ohio Riverfront is everyone's front yard but no one's responsibility. It is not a neighborhood and not an incorporated area of the County. It does not have specific implementation funds set aside and its does not have a group to lobby for improvements."

The Plan's Summary pointed out some important considerations. In the 7.5 miles of riverfront in the study area, there were only six publicly accessible areas, providing almost no space for pedestrians. They agreed that the marginal heavy industrial installations on the Louisville waterfront were "visually unpleasant and ugly." This industrial blight was seen as having an adverse effect on surrounding properties. They made strong recommendations to increase pedestrian and bike paths along the river's edge; develop the Louisville wharf for maximum public access and utilization; study traffic patterns; pursue and encourage major development of the Big Four Bridge; develop facilities for the upriver Eva Bandman Park and prepare major new plans for the riverfront between the Clark and Kennedy Bridges.

Early visitors to pioneer Louisville routinely commented on hearing the low steady rumble of sound emanating from the Falls of the Ohio, and they stated it was a background noise of which they were continually aware. In the early 1980s a similar low murmur concerning waterfront development was being heard and that sound was growing. In the two hundred years since Louisville received its original town charter, questions as to proper use of the Louisville waterfront had confounded each subsequent generation. But a consensus was growing. It was now time to seize the opportunity and bring new life, and a new vision, to Louisville's waterfront.

One of the last transshipping operations on the Louisville wharf was the transport of Ford automobiles on gigantic barges. In the 1950s cars were brought from the Louisville Ford Plant and parked on the wharf until they were loaded on barges and sent to Cincinnati. In Cincinnati the barges were unloaded and restocked with Chevrolets for transport to Louisville. The industrial packet runs were efficient and cost-effective. *(Filson Historical Society, BOA 43)*

A Strategy Emerges
(1983-1986)

Waterfronts don't have to be designed as something special. They already are, by their very nature, something special. If they are to be successfully revitalized and made part of an enduring legacy, they must be designed and built sensibly, with an eye to practicality and proven appeal.

– New York University Conference on Waterfront Development - 1985

The Kentucky Center for the Arts, the state's official performing arts center, was completed in 1983 after a decade of planning, fundraising and construction. The impressive modern arts complex, located on the north side of Main Street between Fifth and Sixth, occupied the same location as Thomas Bullitt's terraced estate of the 1820s. This historically prime piece of downtown real estate served as the center of a gradually re-emerging Main Street, replete with authentic Victorian-era commercial buildings boasting impressive façades of locally made cast iron work. In an earlier era, several of the foundries and forges that produced Louisville's cast and wrought iron had lined the river bank between the Center and the Ohio River.

The Center was made possible by an arrangement between state, city, county and private donors. Through innovative new cooperative agreements between government and the private sector, large-scale projects requiring long-term planning and substantial financial investments were stoking the efforts to revitalize Louisville's downtown. For decades the center of commerce, transportation and accommodations, Main Street's glory days had faded. During the early part of the twentieth century, the center of Louisville's business, professional and entertainment section had moved ten blocks south to Broadway. Following the construction of the Brown Hotel in the 1920s, coupled with lavish movie palaces like the Rialto and the United

Artists, the locus of Fourth and Broadway became known as Louisville's "Magic Corner."

When Louisville turned its back to the river, it did so literally. In the Steamboat Era, most buildings on the north side of Main Street faced toward the Ohio and its Falls. Over time, buildings shifted their front doors to the southern side, leaving the back of Main Street buildings as the first impression visitors got of Louisville when arriving from Indiana or the Ohio River. Complete with a blackened elevated railroad track, masses of electrical power lines and a worn stone levee, the city's welcome mat presented a drab collection of back doors, dull brick, loading docks, sheds and fences. The front door of Louisville was in dire need of a fix up, and some people in the community were quietly working to see some of the waterfront's grandeur restored.

"Our government is inefficient, duplicatory, and is not one that the citizens of this community can respect."

The year 1983 heard political rumblings in Louisville. The City of Louisville and the County of Jefferson had become increasingly separated as much of the downtown population moved to suburbs, enjoyed their new malls and shopping centers, and left behind time-honored associations of old neighborhood clubs, churches, bowling leagues, lodge nights, schools and corner taverns. The movie palaces on Fourth folded as a massive multiplex center opened on suburban Bardstown Road, and the regular hordes of Fourth Street strollers and cruisers stayed home and watched television.

A growing number of people thought that it was time to consolidate city and county governments to increase efficiency and trim expensive duplication of services. In 1980 the first of several groups formed to address issues of merger of government. A thirty-member nonpartisan group, the Local Government Reorganization panel, was named by the County Judge and Mayor to propose legislation to establish a local commission charged with drafting a local referendum charter. County Judge/Executive Mitch McConnell proposed a constitutional amendment to let Kentucky voters decide if the county should be the principal local government entity.

A pro-merger vote was defeated in 1983, with the margin of defeat only 1,452 out of 180,000 ballots. Efforts to convince people to vote pro-merger were led by professional engineer Joe Corradino, the campaign's chairman. *Louisville Magazine* in its October 1983 edition profiled this non-politician emerging into Louisville political process.

So how and why did a relative newcomer to Louisville come to be the big man at the big moment? In short, Corradino was selected because Mayor Harvey Sloane and County Judge/Executive Mitch McConnell liked the facts that he was a member of last year's Charter Commission, that he's a *bona fide* political independent, that his work has allowed him to understand some of the intricacies of government, and that he had well-established leadership abilities.

Others who are working on the merger issue point out that Corradino is doing for merger what he's done daily since he went into business almost 20 years ago: presenting a professional document that will sell to both politicians and the public, be it a bid for a multi-million-dollar transportation system or a set of plans for Louisville's Broadway Project.

Corradino says. "I took the job because the status quo of our government is inefficient, duplicatory, and is not one that the citizens of this community can respect."

"I've always envied people with a cause."

One of Main Street's anchors, Belknap Hardware, was in danger of pulling up stakes and leaving the street they had occupied, and in many ways dominated, since 1840. Severe business declines led Belknap, "the world's largest independent hardware wholesaler," to consider seeking new ownership and move to Chicago. A most remarkable Louisvillian, David A. Jones, stepped up with alternative plans to incorporate the good of Louisville into the equation.

A Chicago investor offered $22 a share for control of the wavering giant, and Jones surprised everyone by upping the bid to $24. With the enthusiastic support of the board of directors, David Jones became the owner of the largest complex of buildings north of Main Street. The jobs of five-hundred workers in the massive warren of warehouses, shipping yards and administrative offices were saved. David A. Jones, of Louisville's Parkland neighborhood, had risen to the top of the local economic totem pole through his creation, with partner Wendell Cherry, of Humana, Inc., another essential Main Street presence.

David Jones thrived on community involvement and difficult challenges. In 1969 he was quoted as saying: "I've always envied people with a cause. Well, building a business can be a cause, I've found, or a good substitute." Jones invested $35 million to acquire Belknap and planning its future became his new focus. David Jones' genuine care for his hometown is evident in his words. "Anything that can be done anywhere can be done in Louisville," Jones stated. "Many young people want to come back here, and organizations that provide good jobs can give them the opportunity."

Shortly after the acquisition Jones announced his plans to move the entire operation to the new Riverport facilities in southwest Jefferson County. Moving out of the Main Street complex freed up a seventeen-acre property, and imaginations began to quicken at the potential for redevelopment. Historian George H. Yater, in *Louisville Magazine* of October 1984, believed the Belknap move sparked new movement in the "Between the Bridges" plan proposed in the 1981 Planning Commission study suggesting a "major new development between Clark and Kennedy bridges." Mayor Harvey I. Sloane and his task force, working with a joint endeavor of the City and Louisville Central Area, Inc., retained the Philadelphia urban planning firm of Wallace, Roberts & Todd as consultants, along with local firm Bickel-Gibson & Associates Architects.

THE THREE PLANS ALL HAVE THE SAME THEME: PARKLAND ACCESS TO THE RIVER, INCLUDING A BOARDWALK ALONG THE WATER'S EDGE AND AN OBSERVATION TOWER FOR A CROW'S-NEST VIEW OF RIVER TRAFFIC; AN AMPHITHEATRE; A MARINA; RESIDENTIAL TOWERS PLUS OFFICE AND COMMERCIAL BUILDINGS AND LIGHT INDUSTRY EAST OF PRESTON STREET; AND – GOOD NEWS FOR PRESERVATIONISTS – RENOVATION OF THE VICTORIAN COMMERCIAL STRUCTURES BETWEEN SECOND AND BROOK TO MATCH THE RENAISSANCE ON WEST MAIN. ONE PLAN INCLUDES A HOTEL ON THE RIVER SHORE.

"THE IDEA," EXPLAINS LOUISVILLE CENTRAL AREA PRESIDENT ROBERT W. BIVENS, "WOULD BE TO INTEREST A DEVELOPER AND GET THE PROJECT GOING WITH A COMBINATION OF PUBLIC AND PRIVATE COMMITMENT IN THE SAME WAY THAT THE GALLERIA AND THE BROADWAY PROJECT GOT GOING." BUT TO INTEREST DEVELOPERS IN THE PROFIT POTENTIAL, AND TO PROVIDE FACTS FOR PUBLIC OFFICIALS, A COST-BENEFIT ANALYSIS AND FEASIBILITY STUDY NEEDS TO BE MADE. NOW THE CITY HAS AGREED TO ALLOCATE $45,000 FOR THIS CRITICAL STEP.

A LOT OF PROPERTY INVOLVED IS ALSO COVERED BY RAILROAD TRACKS OWNED BY THE SEABOARD SYSTEM RAILROAD. SEABOARD IS PART OF THE CSX CORPORATION AND THE CHAIRMAN OF CSX IS LOUISVILLE-NATIVE HAYS WATKINS. JONES HAS DISCUSSED THE RIVERFRONT PROPERTY WITH WATKINS AND FINDS THAT HE, TOO, IS ENTHUSIASTIC ABOUT THE PROJECT. BOB BIVENS REPORTS THAT THE RAILROAD HAD PREVIOUSLY AGREED IN WRITING TO REMOVE THE TRACKS. MAYOR SLOANE ALSO IS TAKING A PERSONAL INTEREST IN THE PROPOSED REDEVELOPMENT AND HAS HELD DISCUSSIONS WITH JONES. THE CITY OWNS 50 ACRES OF THE SITE.

THE HUMANA CHAIRMAN CAUTIONS THAT "NONE OF THIS PROJECT MAY COME TO PASS, BUT SIGNS STRONGLY POINT TO SOME KIND OF REDEVELOPMENT. IT'S NOT TOO EARLY TO START MOVING NOW," BIVENS NOTES. "FOR A PROJECT OF THIS SCOPE, WE'RE TALKING ABOUT 25 YEARS."

WHATEVER THE FUTURE HOLDS, THE POTENTIAL OF THE RIVER IS SUMMED UP BY SHARON WILBERT: "WATER IS CALMING. PEOPLE WANT TO BE BY IT. WE'VE GOT IT."

"Is 'another study' really necessary?"

By the end of 1984, Louisville faced essential decisions on the future of the city's inert riverfront. Since the initial 1931 study completed for the city by Harland Bartholomew and Associates, and a subsequent report made by the firm in 1955, eleven studies of the riverfront were made, including those by the Louisville and Jefferson County Planning Commission and a study commissioned by the City of Louisville and the Louisville

Central Area Riverfront Task Force in 1983.

Louisville writer Ronni Lundy, in *Around Downtown* magazine, surveyed local political and opinion leaders to gauge opinions and options made possible with the relocation of Belknap from the heart of the waterfront area.

Over the years various agencies, urban planning firms and commissions had studied and re-studied the renewal of the Louisville waterfront. A quiet rediscovery of the downtown waterfront area was spurred by successful night clubs and a budding art scene during the mid-1970s.

LOUISVILLE FACES A QUESTION…WHAT TO DO WITH THE DOWNTOWN RIVERFRONT?

THE POSSIBLE SOLUTIONS RANGE FROM LEAVING THE RIVERFRONT AS IT IS — A MIX OF BUSINESS AND HEAVY INDUSTRY — TO SWEEPING IT CLEAN AND BUILDING A "NEW" RIVERFRONT, ONE THAT FEATURES RESIDENCES, SHOPS, ENTERTAINMENT AND PUBLIC BEAUTY.

THE REAL-LIFE ANSWER PROBABLY WILL BE FOUND SOMEWHERE BETWEEN THESE POLAR EXTREMES.

LEE SMITH AND VIPEN HOON ARE TWO PEOPLE WHO BELIEVE THAT LOUISVILLE'S RIVERFRONT IMAGE COULD USE A REFURBISHING.

"IT'S MORE THAN SKIN-DEEP," SAID SMITH,

EXECUTIVE DIRECTOR OF RIVER FIELDS, A LOCAL CITIZENS' GROUP CONCERNED WITH RIVER USE. "MAKE-UP AND APPEARANCE CAN AFFECT THE WAY PEOPLE SEE YOU. ARE WE PUTTING OUR BEST FOOT FORWARD WITH THE EXISTING RIVERFRONT?"

"I THINK THERE IS DEFINITE ROOM FOR IMPROVEMENT."

HOON, VICE PRESIDENT OF THE LOUISVILLE CENTRAL AREA INC., SAID THAT LOUISVILLE IS NOT THE ONLY CITY CONSIDERING CHANGING ITS WATERFRONT IMAGE. REDEVELOPMENT ALONG THE RIVER IS HAPPENING IN TOWNS SUCH AS BOSTON, TORONTO, PHILADELPHIA, SAN DIEGO AND BALTIMORE.

THIS DEVELOPMENT REFLECTS A GROWING CHANGE IN THE NATIONAL ECONOMY — THE MOVE FROM AN INDUSTRIAL BASE TO A SERVICE BASE, HOON SAID. THE IMAGE A CITY PROJECTS AT ITS FRONT DOOR CAN HAVE CONSIDERABLE IMPACT ON WHICH BUSINESSES CHOOSE TO ENTER.

"WE LOOK AT THAT AREA AS HIGHLY VISIBLE, AND IT REALLY IS CRITICAL," HOON SAID. AS YOU COME SOUTH FROM THE NORTH, THAT (THE RIVERFRONT) IS THE FIRST THING YOU SEE IN KENTUCKY. "I THINK IT GIVES THE IMPRESSION THAT WE ARE AN OLD MANUFACTURING TOWN."

THE FUTURE OF LOUISVILLE'S RIVERFRONT PROBABLY WILL LIE SOMEWHERE IN THE MIDDLE — SOMEWHERE BETWEEN SWEEPING THE AREA CLEAN AND HAVING THE RIVERFRONT AS IT IS, SAID JOE CORRADINO, CHAIRMAN OF MAYOR HARVEY SLOANE'S ECONOMIC DEVELOPMENT ADVISORY COMMITTEE.

SLOANE HAS ASKED CORRADINO TO SUPERVISE A STUDY OF POSSIBLE RIVERFRONT DEVELOPMENT AND TO COME

UP WITH A COMPREHENSIVE PLAN FOR THE LOUISVILLE RIVERFRONT, FROM CHICKASAW PARK TO ZORN AVENUE. IN NOVEMBER, CORRADINO BEGAN GATHERING INFORMATION ON POSSIBLE PROBLEMS AND SOLUTIONS.

THE INTENT IS TO OUTLINE BROAD GOALS FOR DEVELOPING THE RIVERFRONT, BUT TO REMAIN FLEXIBLE ENOUGH TO ADAPT TO THE CHANGING MARKET. SLOANE MENTIONED THE POSSIBILITY OF A RIVERFRONT AUTHORITY TO BE ESTABLISHED THROUGH THE 1986 STATE LEGISLATURE AS THE TOOL FOR IMPLEMENTING THE RIVERFRONT PLAN.

THE SIZE OF THE BELKNAP PROPERTY, ITS CRUCIAL LOCATION BETWEEN THE RIVERFRONT AND MAIN STREET, AND JONES' PERCEIVED STATUS AS A MOVER AND SHAKER IN THE COMMUNITY, HAVE REVIVED ONCE-DORMANT SPECULATIONS ABOUT WHAT MIGHT HAPPEN ON THE LOUISVILLE RIVERFRONT AND MAIN STREET.

DAVID JONES SAID THAT AFTER BELKNAP MOVES, HE WOULD BE INTERESTED IN SEEING THE BELKNAP SITE DEVELOPED.

"THE CAUTION I WOULD GIVE IS THAT I SEE THIS AS A LONG-TERM RATHER THAN A SHORT-TERM PROPOSITION... PROBABLY 10 YEARS INSTEAD OF TWO OR THREE. YOU CAN'T ABSORB 1,500,000 SQUARE FEET IN AN ECONOMY THE SIZE OF LOUISVILLE OVERNIGHT."

LOUIS FREDERICK, OWNER OF THREE BUILDINGS IN THE 100 BLOCK OF WEST MAIN STREET, JUST WEST OF BELKNAP'S HEADQUARTERS AND IN FRONT OF SEVERAL OF BELKNAP'S WASHINGTON STREET WAREHOUSES, THINKS JONES' ACQUISITION OF BELKNAP IS THE KEY IN THE REDEVELOPMENT OF THAT AREA.

"THE BELKNAP MOVE IS THE MOST IMPORTANT MOVE IN THE MAIN STREET AREA SINCE AL SCHNEIDER DECIDED TO TAKE THOSE VACANT LOTS AND MAKE THE GALT HOUSE OF THEM," FREDERICK SAID.

THE AREA IS OCCUPIED BY INDUSTRY — SAND COMPANIES, SCRAP METAL PROCESSORS, BARGE LINES, RAIL YARDS AND WAREHOUSES. MUCH OF THE LAND IS OWNED AND LEASED TO THOSE BUSINESSES BY THE CITY.

CSX CORP., A BARGE AND RAIL OPERATION, CONTROLS SEVERAL PARCELS OF RIVERFRONT LAND. (SOME OF ITS BUSINESSES ARE ON PROPERTY LEASED FROM THE CITY, AND CSX ITSELF OWNS A 31-ACRE RAIL YARD IN THE HEART OF THE RIVERFRONT.)

THE COMPLEXITY OF THE RIVERFRONT SITUATION PROMPTED SLOANE TO INITIATE THE LATEST DEVELOPMENT STUDY. BUT THE STUDY HAS MET WITH SOME CRITICISM.

"A MASTER PLAN FROM ZORN AVENUE TO 14TH STREET IS STUPID," FRANK METTS SAID.

BOTH METTS AND FREDERICK, WHOSE THREE BUILDINGS ON MAIN INCLUDE TWO NIGHTCLUBS AND AN OFFICE BUILDING, SAID THAT THE CITY COULD MAKE BETTER USE OF ITS MONEY BY TAKING CARE OF AMENITIES SUCH AS LIGHTING, TRASH PICKUP, SIDEWALK REPAIRS AND INCREASED POLICE PROTECTION IN THOSE AREAS SURROUNDING THE RIVERFRONT WHERE SOME DEVELOPMENT HAS ALREADY TAKEN PLACE.

"WE REALLY DON'T NEED ANOTHER COMMITTEE," FREDERICK SAID. "WHAT WE NEED IS A CZAR — SOMEONE WHO HAS THE POWER AND AUTHORITY TO TALK TO THE METROPOLITAN SEWER DISTRICT, LOUISVILLE GAS & ELECTRIC AND PROPERTY OWNERS AND GET THINGS DONE."

METTS SAID ENOUGH STUDIES OF THE RIVERFRONT ALREADY EXIST. "IF YOU LOOK INTO THE HISTORY OF

STUDIES OF THE RIVERFRONT, YOU'LL FIND OUT JUST HOW MUCH TIME, MONEY AND FALSE HOPES HAVE BEEN WASTED, HOW MUCH B.S. HAS BEEN PUT OUT ABOUT THIS DEAL," METTS SAID.

"THIS OBVIOUSLY MAKES YOU WONDER. ARE WE INTO THE 1985 STAGE OF A 1931 DEAL? THAT'S A FAIR QUESTION. AFTER SOMEBODY'S BEEN SAYING THEY'RE GOING TO DO SOMETHING FOR 50 YEARS, YOU'VE GOT A RIGHT TO SAY, "I DON'T BELIEVE IT."

LAST YEAR CSX, A RAILROAD COMPANY, COMPLETED A MERGER WITH AMERICAN BARGE LINES, MAKING IT ONE OF THE LARGEST TRANSPORTATION CORPORATIONS IN THE COUNTRY. THAT MERGER WAS ACCOMPLISHED WITH ENDORSEMENT FROM BOTH CITY AND COUNTY GOVERNMENTS. THE MERGER MEANS THAT CSX NOW OWNS AN EXTENSIVE COMPLEX ALONG LOUISVILLE'S RIVERFRONT, INCLUDING PORTS, RAIL YARDS AND TRUCKING FACILITIES THAT EXTEND FROM NEAR ZORN AVENUE TO THE HEART OF THE DOWNTOWN DEVELOPMENT AREA.

AND DAVID JONES, WHO CAN VIEW THE RIVERFRONT FROM THE WINDOW OF HIS OFFICE ON THE 18TH FLOOR OF THE FIRST NATIONAL TOWER, SAID THIS.

"SITTING HERE RIGHT NOW LOOKING AT THE RIVER, I WOULD SAY THAT IT LOOKS VITAL ALREADY. IT'S ALL INDUSTRY THERE NOW, BUT IT'S VITAL.

"AT THE SAME TIME, I'M LOOKING AT ZURICH AND GENEVA IN MY MIND'S EYE. AND I REALIZE THAT WATERFRONT DEVELOPMENT IN MANY CITIES CAN BE QUITE BEAUTIFUL.

"I FEEL THAT LAND PROBABLY HAS BETTER USE THAN SAND PILES…

"I CAN MAKE THAT CASE BY TURNING MY GAZE 90 DEGREES TO THE WEST AND SEEING THE BELVEDERE. THERE ARE PEOPLE THERE EVERY NOON HOUR HAVING LUNCH, SKATING. AND I WONDER IF WE DON'T HAVE A BETTER USE FOR THAT LAND ALONG THE RIVER, A PEOPLE USE."

"Can't you just see it with people living here?"

A quiet revival had begun in the mid-1970s as entrepreneurs began renovating the largely empty commercial buildings on old Washington Street, the narrow avenue north of Main. Jack Trawick, executive director of the Louisville Community Design Center, stated, "The block of 100 West Main Street is one of the most important, if not the most important, in the downtown. If there's to be any riverfront development, this block and the Belknap area around it are the key." Louis Frederick, the owner of three buildings on the block, echoed Trawick's view. "Can't you just see it with people living here? These are all very interesting historic buildings. It is a cohesive block. Its proximity to the river makes it an exciting possibility."

For a brief period, nightclubs on the ground level of Washington Street flourished and, as artists began moving their studios into the buildings' upper floors, a growing cadre of creative young people embraced the 100 block of West Main, the site of the original Galt House. Many were excited about the potential of renovating the tall-ceiling nineteenth-century commercial buildings into residential units. Wayne Lord and his partners Larry Jones and Henry Potter purchased four of the adjoining buildings and created the Artists' Main Exchange, opening a series of shops, art galleries and food outlets called the Festive Trading Galleries.

Lord hoped that other developers would see the possibilities and return to the area north of Main Street.

"My own feeling is that the more things are going on, the more opportunities are being played out in the city, the better off we are. You have people coming back downtown because they feel it is the most exciting place to be in the city, the center of it all. No shopping mall or suburb can ever equal that."

"I ask your help in this effort."

Individual developers and promoters were making a difference, but to successfully address the challenges and potential of waterfront development, a more systematic effort was required. In 1985 Mayor Sloane wrote an open letter to the public to advocate a new plan, called the Waterfront Redevelopment Strategy, to be the master blueprint for the city's return to its river roots.

Dear Citizens:

This thought expresses the theme of the work on the Waterfront Redevelopment Strategy and Implementation Program. Observation of waterfront plans nationwide has led me to the conclusion that the most successful and appropriate projects, whatever their size, follow sensible guidelines; learn from what exists; integrate; and design in achievable increments.

In examining this document, then, the key word to keep in mind is "evolve," not invent. This is just what was done in establishing a strategy for the next ten to fifteen years to be followed in redeveloping the City's waterfront. For example, a key element in this program was put into place on June 22, 1985, when I completed an agreement, along with Governor Collins, the CSX Corporation, Jefferson County Government and the Riverport Authority, to relocate the rail-to-barge coal transfer activities from Upper River Road to Riverport. This agreement allows the transfer to government of an eight-acre area vacated by the CSX Corporation and the use of that land for industrial purposes, in keeping with the community's objectives. Additionally, this agreement provides us with the opportunity to buy up to eighty additional acres of CSX-owned land at fair market value as it becomes available in the area near Zorn Avenue. Then, within fifteen years, the land not yet in our ownership will be sold to us at fair market value.

In the West End of our community, the program calls for increased access to the waterfront, the development of housing, and the near-term application of adequate maintenance procedures to eliminate debris from the river's edge. In downtown, my strategy is aimed at establishing a mixed-use redevelopment pattern in the area between the Clark and Kennedy Bridges, with relocation of heavy industrial uses which are not compatible with this intent. And, east of downtown, the strategy calls for eventual conversion of the land to a mixed use from the Kennedy Bridge to Adams Street and for a mixture of parks and river-oriented industrial uses from Adams Street to Zorn Avenue.

In every segment of the waterfront, a course of action has been designed that is pragmatic and sensible. Those that will remain along the river will be encouraged to join the "development team;" those that will be asked to relocate will be kept financially "whole" through government support.

The implementation program that accompanies this strategy will also be sensible. It will continue the public-private partnership that has been so successful in revitalizing downtown Louisville. This approach calls for incorporating City, State and County governments into a management organization, along with those in the private sector who have shown a commitment to the integrity of the waterfront.

It will take several years to complete the program. To meet this challenge, I propose the development of a unique financing approach which will be able to respond to and withstand the increasing pressures placed upon local government.

So, as you will see by this "Waterfront Redevelopment Strategy," a realistic and achievable plan is now available to improve the City's waterfront. With your cooperation, each day will allow us to move another step closer to the most productive and complete enjoyment of this important area. I ask your help in this effort.

Respectfully,
Harvey I. Sloane

An aerial view looking downstream from Towhead Island indicates the problems, and potential, of reclaiming the Ohio River shoreline in Louisville. Thousands of people relocated to the suburbs or adjacent counties, often following industries like the General Electric Plant, away from downtown. As downtown residencies declined, so did the upkeep and vitality of the city.

An End to the Age of the Lame Duck

The Strategy, created by the firm of Joe Corradino, with the able assistance of Marie Abrams and Marlene Grissom, formed the basis for planning, discussion and implementation of waterfront redevelopment. Its understanding and acceptance by the public was the crucial first step in reclaiming Louisville's waterfront. But poised to take dramatic steps to implement the Strategy, the city faced one additional hurdle in achieving its goals. Knowing that a successful campaign to redevelop Louisville's waterfront would be measured in decades, rather than years, a nagging 104-year-old amendment to the Kentucky constitution needed changing.

In 1888 Kentucky's popular state treasurer for twenty years, the ironically named "Honest" Dick Tate, disappeared, taking a quarter million dollars of state funds with him. A furious state legislature passed an amendment prohibiting holders of major state offices and the mayors of the nine largest cities from succeeding themselves. With Louisville's mayors being limited to one four-year term, they became lame ducks on the day they were elected. A candidate could be elected again after a four-year interval, but all sense of continuity and policy development was thwarted.

The Courier-Journal of August 15, 1985, described the political process for passing a mayoral succession amendment.

It was a balanced team from all sections of Kentucky when the Kentuckians Supporting Mayoral Succession Committee introduced its lineup in Frankfort on August 13.

Supporters of the constitutional amendment say that's natural. They depict the amendment as a critical statewide economic issue, as well as an issue of governmental equity.

"When new business and developers come to Kentucky and find they can't deal with stable leadership, they just throw up their hands," said Rep. Ken Harper (R) of Crestview Hills in a recent interview. He cited Lexington as an example of a city that "has just taken off," partially due to its political climate. Harper co-chairs the committee along with Louisville's Sen. David Karem (D). Karem cites Louisville's Riverfront development as the type of project that demands some continuity in political leadership. It's estimated that redevelopment there will take 15 to 20 years, even without the interruptions and delays caused by the political musical chairs of changing mayors every four years.

In November 1985 Kentuckians voted to change the constitution to allow mayors of larger cities to serve up to three consecutive terms. This allowed the chief executive of Louisville to operate in a more stable and predictable manner, permitting long-term economic development plans to grow. Term limits were still in place, as every four years the incumbent must again become a candidate for office and subject to the public's endorsement, but a new era in political sophistication now became possible.

With all elements now in place, a formal structure for waterfront development was at hand. In early February 1986 an historic agreement was announced that created the mechanism needed to make decades of planning a reality. The Waterfront Development Corporation Interlocal Cooperation Agreement declared:

This AGREEMENT made and entered into this 21ST day of February, 1986 by, between and among the Commonwealth of Kentucky, the City of Louisville, and Jefferson County, hereinafter referred to as "Parties";

WHEREAS, THE KENTUCKY INTERLOCAL COOPERATION ACT (KRS 65.210 ET SEQ.) PERMITS THE JOINT EXERCISE OF POWER BY STATE AGENCIES WITH OTHER PUBLIC AGENCIES TO MAKE THE MOST EFFICIENT USE OF THEIR POWERS; AND

WHEREAS, KRS 58.180 ALLOWS THE CREATION OF A NON-PROFIT CORPORATION TO ACT AS AN INSTRUMENTALITY OF GOVERNMENTAL AGENCIES IN THE ACQUISITION AND FINANCING OF PUBLIC PROJECTS; AND

WHEREAS, THE OHIO RIVER IS A VALUABLE RESOURCE TO THE LOUISVILLE AREA AND THE COMMONWEALTH OF KENTUCKY; AND

WHEREAS, THE REDEVELOPMENT OF THE LOUISVILLE WATERFRONT REQUIRES A COMPREHENSIVE STRATEGY AND IMPLEMENTATION PROGRAM; AND

WHEREAS, CENTRALIZING THE EFFORTS OF THE STATE, THE COUNTY, THE CITY AND PRIVATE ENTITIES WOULD ELIMINATE FRAGMENTATION AND WOULD PROMOTE EFFECTIVE REDEVELOPMENT OF THE LOUISVILLE WATERFRONT;

NOW, THEREFORE, THE PARTIES AGREE AS FOLLOWS:

Purpose:

THE PARTIES SHALL PARTICIPATE JOINTLY IN THE INCORPORATION OF A NON-PROFIT CORPORATION NAMED "WATERFRONT DEVELOPMENT CORPORATION" FOR THE PURPOSE OF COORDINATING CITY, STATE AND COUNTY GOVERNMENTS ALONG WITH THE PRIVATE SECTOR IN THEIR EFFORTS TO IMPLEMENT A REDEVELOPMENT STRATEGY FOR THE LOUISVILLE WATERFRONT.

The Waterfront Development Corporation has adopted two different logos during its existence, the earliest (above) a result of an artist competition made possible by a local sponsor. The newer version (below) is the familiar blue and green device that appears on Park vehicles, letterhead, uniforms and other publications.

The Louisville business community, led by local bankers, began to aggressively develop downtown, especially old Main Street. This important avenue had long hosted Louisville's luxury hotels, banks and commission merchants, and its distinctive cast-iron front façades made it a prime case for historic preservation. A blend of old and new architecture began in the 1970s as Main Street staged a comeback.

Setting Priorities – The People Speak

(1987-1990)

The forums provided an ideal opportunity to gather a wide range of answers for the question: "What are the community's hopes for its waterfront?" Although the variety of answers to this question reflects the diversity of opinions and interests in people who participated, there emerged several consistent themes. It will be these common threads that will facilitate the planning to link community expectations to the future reality that will be Louisville's dynamic waterfront.

– Public Forum Report on Waterfront Development Corporation - 1988

The Louisville Waterfront Strategy states its case concisely in precise engineering terms. The report warned readers that waterfront development would be a long-term project and the key word to remember was "evolve," not invent.

The goal of the Strategy was to provide balanced utilization of the riverfront by providing areas for recreation, open space and public access to the river while preserving areas for industrial and transportation uses which benefit from riverfront access. The plan encompassed a collection of Louisville neighborhoods, starting at Gibson Lane in southwestern Jefferson County and sweeping clockwise past Shawnee, Portland, Shippingport, Downtown, Butchertown and the now-abandoned Point. The development plan continued past the Beargrass Creek Cut-Off and extended along River Road to Zorn Avenue.

The plan's highest priority was the waterfront "between the bridges," from the George Rogers Clark Bridge to the John F. Kennedy Bridge, the area known in nineteenth-century Louisville as Strader's Wharf, home to innumerable grog shops, boatmen's inns, shipyards, sawmills and slaughterhouses.

Dollars and cents issues shaped the project, and the Strategy clearly indicated the challenges that lay ahead. The forward-looking document made strong recommendations for the coming efforts, and spoke in clear language.

IN ADOPTING LOUISVILLE'S WATERFRONT STRATEGY IN 1985, PUBLIC SECTOR INVESTMENT OF $19 MILLION WAS COMBINED WITH A PRIVATE SECTOR COMMITMENT OF $14 MILLION ($4 MILLION FOR CONSTRUCTION PLUS $10 MILLION FOR OPERATIONS) TO RELOCATE AN ENVIRONMENTALLY UNACCEPTABLE COAL DUMPING FACILITY FROM AN AREA CLOSE TO THE WATER TOWER HISTORICAL LANDMARK (ON RIVER ROAD AT ZORN AVENUE) TO THE RIVERPORT, THE 1,600-ACRE INDUSTRIAL ZONE IN SOUTHWEST JEFFERSON COUNTY. THIS INVESTMENT WILL ALLOW THE LONG-AWAITED PORT TO BE BUILT AT RIVERPORT, THEREBY COMPLETING A PROJECT INITIATED OVER TWENTY YEARS AGO AND INVOLVING PREVIOUS GOVERNMENT COMMITMENTS THAT TOTAL $100 MILLION. IN ADDITION TO ALLOWING THE RIVERPORT PROJECT TO REACH COMPLETION, THIS EARLY INVESTMENT WILL FACILITATE REDEVELOPMENT OF OTHER SEGMENTS OF THE WATERFRONT, PARTICULARLY THE AREA NEAR DOWNTOWN LOUISVILLE.

THE INVESTMENTS CREATING ACCESS TO ATTRACTIONS ALONG THE WATERFRONT IN DOWNTOWN LOUISVILLE OVER THE PAST QUARTER OF A CENTURY HAVE ALSO BEEN IMPRESSIVE. IN 1962, JEFFERSON COUNTY GOVERNMENT SPENT $34,000 TO PURCHASE THE *BELLE OF LOUISVILLE*, WHICH DOCKS AT THE FOURTH AVENUE WHARF. TWENTY-

FIVE YEARS LATER THE *BELLE* HAS AN ANNUAL GROSS INCOME IN EXCESS OF $750,000. IN 1973, GOVERNMENT SPENT $13.5 MILLION TO CREATE THE BELVEDERE AND ADJOINING GARAGE BETWEEN FOURTH AVENUE AND FIFTH STREET. IN TURN, THE PRIVATE SECTOR BUILT THE $20.5 MILLION RIVERFRONT PLAZA COMPLEX. IN 1977, THE MUSEUM OF HISTORY AND SCIENCE WAS CREATED AT A LOCATION BETWEEN SIXTH AND SEVENTH STREETS ON MAIN; THIS REPRESENTED A $2.5 MILLION PUBLIC INVESTMENT. NOW, THE CIVIC-MINDED ALL-VOLUNTEER BOARD OF THE MUSEUM HAS RAISED $4 MILLION IN CONTRIBUTIONS TO FUND THE NEXT PHASE OF THE MASTER PLAN. CURRENTLY, THE CITY OF LOUISVILLE INTENDS TO INVEST OVER $1.2 MILLION TO BRING THE ATTRACTION KNOWN AS THE ISLANDS TO THE FOURTH AVENUE WHARF. THE ISLANDS WILL BRING 250 JOBS TO THE CITY AND CONSTITUTE A YEAR-ROUND ATTRACTION ALONG THE WATERFRONT.

OVERALL, THE COMMUNITY'S PUBLIC AND PRIVATE SECTORS HAVE RAISED AND/OR INVESTED OVER THE LAST 25 YEARS A TOTAL OF $163 MILLION ALONG THE WATERFRONT.

NOW, THE NEXT PHASE OF DEVELOPMENT – CONSIDERED BY MANY TO BE THE MOST IMPORTANT – MUST BEGIN. HOWEVER, TIMES HAVE CHANGED. NO LONGER IS GOVERNMENT AS WELL EQUIPPED TO MAKE MAJOR CAPITAL INVESTMENTS. AS A MATTER OF FACT, THE ELIMINATION OF FEDERAL REVENUE SHARING AND SIGNIFICANT CURTAILMENT OF MANY OTHER PROGRAMS HAS CAUSED LOCAL GOVERNMENTS TO STRUGGLE TO PROVIDE DAILY SERVICES SUCH AS POLICE AND FIRE PROTECTION, LIBRARIES AND THE LIKE. YET, NEVER BEFORE HAS COMPETITION AMONG COMMUNITIES BEEN MORE FIERCE IN SUCCESSFULLY ATTRACTING PRIVATE SECTOR INVESTMENTS. GOVERNMENT HAS AND MUST PLAY A ROLE. PUBLIC SECTOR FINANCING IS CRITICAL TO STARTING A MAJOR URBAN REVITALIZATION EFFORT. THIS

IS EQUALLY TRUE FOR THE NEXT PHASE OF LOUISVILLE'S WATERFRONT REDEVELOPMENT.

TO DEAL WITH THIS SITUATION AT A LOCAL LEVEL, THE KENTUCKY GENERAL ASSEMBLY IN 1986 PASSED A "TAX INCREMENT FINANCING" LAW. IT WILL ALLOW LOCAL GOVERNMENTS TO ALLOCATE THOSE INCREASED TAX REVENUES FROM NEW DEVELOPMENT TO PAY FOR A PORTION OF THE PUBLIC SECTOR COSTS. HOWEVER, MANY IMPROVEMENTS FOR WHICH THE PUBLIC SECTOR IS RESPONSIBLE ARE "UP FRONT" IN THEIR COST IMPACT. TAX INCREMENT FINANCING DOES NOT ADEQUATELY DEAL WITH THESE EARLY COSTS. SOME OTHER PUBLIC SUPPORT IS NEEDED, PARTICULARLY IF THE INCREMENT OF NEW TAXES IS TO BE USED TO SUSTAIN LATER PHASES OF DEVELOPMENT.

TRANSLATING THE PRELIMINARY DEVELOPMENT CONCEPT TO A QUANTITATIVE RESPONSE TO THE QUESTION "WHAT DO WE GET IN RETURN?" YIELDS THE FOLLOWING. THE NEXT TWO PHASES OF PUBLIC INVESTMENT ($61 MILLION) IN THE AREA IN THE DOWNTOWN COULD LIKELY BEGIN A FIFTEEN YEAR CONSTRUCTION PROGRAM TOTALING $467 MILLION, MOST OF WHICH WILL BE ACCOMPLISHED BY THE PRIVATE SECTOR. THIS COULD CREATE OVER 9,000 PERSON YEARS OF EMPLOYMENT IN THE CONSTRUCTION AND RELATED INDUSTRIES, WHICH ALONE WOULD YIELD OVER $2.0 MILLION IN INCREASED OCCUPATIONAL TAXES. WITH THE PROJECT COMPLETE, THE LAND IN DOWNTOWN WOULD BE WORTH $495 MILLION, WITH ANNUAL PROPERTY TAXES TOTALING $7.0 MILLION, COMPARED TO $0.4 MILLION TODAY. LIKEWISE, WHEN THE OFFICES AND SHOPS ARE FILLED, ANNUAL OCCUPATIONAL TAXES WILL TOTAL $6.0 MILLION; OCCUPATIONAL TAXES FROM JOBS IN THIS AREA TODAY ARE LESS THAN $0.5 MILLION. THIS NEW TAX REVENUE CAN BE USED TO STIMULATE OTHER PHASES OF WATERFRONT REVITALIZATION THROUGHOUT THE COMMUNITY.

David K. Karem, a skilled political leader with a background in design, has piloted the Waterfront Development Corporation from its inception. Widely respected for his mastery of political process, fundraising and landscape design, Karem assembled a core staff of dedicated individuals who shared his vision of Waterfront Park. *(© Courier-Journal)*

"I'm just a Louisville kid."

The Strategy was well-crafted, ambitious and comprehensive and all it needed was a qualified, dedicated and savvy leader to champion its cause. For such a sweeping and long-range plan, the project required what the *Louisville Panorama* had called for in 1954, "This is a good project for some dreamer, who combines vision with energy, determination and singleness of purpose."

At a quiet dinner held at Myra's Restaurant in the Highlands, three acquaintances, each deeply engaged in local governmental issues, sat together to discuss current projects. Shortly after helping lead the successful campaign for the mayoral succession amendment, skilled political expert Terry Feathers, the government relations specialist for the Louisville Chamber of Commerce, was dining with Joe Corradino, just in the process of completing the Waterfront Redevelopment Strategy. Joining them at the table was State Senator David K. Karem of Louisville.

David Karem had served four years in the Kentucky General Assembly as a Representative, and then began a long career in the State Senate. Armed with an engaging charm and disarming sense of humor, the Louisville Democrat was blessed with the communication skills necessary to reach both rural and urban delegates in the General Assembly. Karem rose to several of the key party leadership positions, serving first as Caucus Chairman and later Majority Floor Leader. He served in the General Assembly for thirty-three years, becoming one of the longest, if not the longest, serving legislator in the Commonwealth's history. Karem had co-sponsored the mayoral succession amendment and was instrumental in its passage, securing the essential support from rural delegates from across the state. Virtually all questions concerning legislation impacting Kentucky's urban governments passed through Karem's hands, and both Feathers and Corradino had worked closely with him on several projects impacting the city's future.

Their dinner discussion came around to the topic of Mayor Harvey Sloane's second term, 1982-1985, and what might become the signature accomplishment of his administration. During his first term, Sloane had successfully worked to secure the reorganization and creation of the Transit Authority of River City (TARC). Twenty-five years after the event, David Karem recalled the outcome of that informal dinner discussion.

JOE AND I HAD RUN INTO EACH OTHER A LOT, AND TERRY FEATHERS AND I WORKED TOGETHER VERY CLOSELY IN FRANKFORT. MY RECOLLECTION IS NOW WE HAD THIS STRATEGY AND THE QUESTION WAS HOW DO WE BRING THIS THING TO REALITY? THERE WAS A FAIRLY SMALL GROUP OF US WHO WERE TALKING ABOUT WHAT WAS THE NEXT STEP. AND THE NEXT STEP WAS THE IDEA THAT YOU WOULD CREATE THIS INDEPENDENT CORPORATION THAT GOVERNMENT WAS ALLOWED TO SPIN OFF, THIS TYPE OF DEVELOPMENT CORPORATION. AND BOLDLY WE SAID THAT SINCE THIS WAS THE FRONT DOOR OF THE STATE, WE NEEDED TO HAVE THE STATE INVOLVED, THE CITY INVOLVED AND THE COUNTY INVOLVED. THE SUGGESTION CAME OUT THAT YOU NEEDED TO CREATE THIS CORPORATION WITH FIFTEEN DIRECTORS – FIVE STATE, FIVE COUNTY AND FIVE CITY. THIS WAS COMING RIGHT AT THE END OF HARVEY'S SECOND ADMINISTRATION AS MAYOR AND THE BEGINNING OF JERRY ABRAMSON'S FIRST TERM, SO THE ACTUAL INCORPORATION WAS SIGNED BY JERRY AS MAYOR, HARVEY AS COUNTY JUDGE AND MARTHA LAYNE COLLINS AS GOVERNOR. I GOT INVOLVED BECAUSE THE PHONE RANG IN MY LAW OFFICE ONE DAY, AND IT WAS A CALL TO MEET WITH JERRY AND HARVEY. THE THREE OF US SAT DOWN IN THE MAYOR'S OFFICE, AND THEY ASKED ME TO SERVE AS THE FIRST CHAIR OF THIS COMMITTEE. I HAD BEEN SO INVOLVED AND WAS IN THE LEGISLATURE, AND THE QUESTION CAME, WOULD YOU SERVE AS FIRST CHAIRMAN? I OBVIOUSLY AGREED TO THAT.

David Karem was uniquely qualified to serve. A native Louisvillian from a respected Lebanese-American family, both his parents and a brother were successful lawyers. After graduating from St. Xavier High School, Karem decided to attend the University of Cincinnati College of Design, Architecture, Art & Planning and studied Interior Design. Following a family tradition, Karem enrolled in the University of Louisville Law School and after graduation in 1969 joined the family law firm. The unusual combination of advanced design training and legal experience was soon joined by another family tradition, involvement in local Democratic party politics.

At a home where lively dinner conversations frequently centered on Louisville's political environment, David Karem was a willing learner. His father, Fred Karem, was a successful attorney and had been a well-known amateur actor and playwright in his younger days. A poet of some skill, Fred Karem had penned the ode "The Bridge" to celebrate the opening of Louisville's Municipal Bridge in 1929.

Upon David Karem's return to Louisville following his graduation from the University of Cincinnati, his mother announced she was retiring her position as precinct captain and was turning the job over to David. Two years later, while still a law student, Karem ran in a three-person Democratic primary race, coming in second to Wilson Wyatt, Jr. In the next election cycle, Karem won the nomination and election to serve as State Representative from Louisville.

The decision to renew Louisville's waterfront required a strong consensus of local leaders to push forward to its successful mission. When the first board of directors adopted its official mission statement there was no mention of building a park on the site. The mission was defined as "the development of projects that will enhance the usefulness, economic value and attractiveness of Louisville's waterfront."

But perhaps the most enduring gift from his family was spending summers at a camp on the Ohio River. Karem recalled the warm, lazy days of growing up watching the river roll past. "My folks owned a cabin on the Ohio River...On the day school was out we moved to the cabin, and when school started we moved back into the city. The cabin was on Transylvania Beach. We were little river rats. We could identify certain vessels by their whistles, so if you heard the *Avalon*, you knew it was the *Avalon* from the whistle.

"I'm just a Louisville kid."

Work on implementation of the Waterfront Redevelopment Strategy began in a donated office with Angela Murray, on loan from the Economic Development office, assisting during the organizational period. When they agreed to the Interlocal Agreement, the state, city and county pledged $100,000 each for yearly operational costs. River Fields, a local land conservation advocacy group, donated $1,000 to fund a logo competition. The winning entry, from Carol Kamenish, was a simple graphic symbol uniting land and water imagery. The City of Louisville agreed to serve as the fiscal agent, and work continued in Karem's law office. His deep involvement with the Waterfront project,

and his leadership position in the State Senate, left Karem with diminishing billable hours from private clients. In 2010 David Karem reflected upon the earliest days of the Waterfront Development Corporation (WDC).

I JUST BECAME FASCINATED BY THE WHOLE CONCEPT OF THIS THING AND ENDED UP HAVING A DISCUSSION WITH HARVEY AND JERRY, AND I SAID I WOULD LIKE TO DO THIS FULL TIME. I ASKED WHY WE CAN'T GET SOMEBODY WITH A REALLY HIGH PROFILE TO SERVE AS CHAIR. I THEN RESIGNED MY POSITION AS CHAIR, AND STEVE MILES, WHO WAS THEN PRESIDENT OF THE OLD FIRST NATIONAL BANK, AGREED TO SERVE AS THE NEXT CHAIRMAN OF THE ORGANIZATION. WE CREATED THE OFFICE OF PRESIDENT AS A FULL-TIME POSITION, AND THE REST OF THE STORY IS THAT I'M STILL HERE.

"...enhance the usefulness, economic value and attractiveness of Louisville's waterfront."

A fifteen member board of directors, appointed by city, county and state governments, formed the trustees of the Waterfront Development Corporation. Each group had represented five members on the Board. The Mayor represents the City of Louisville along with the president of the Board of Aldermen or his/her designee, and three at-large appointees. The county judge/executive represented Jefferson County along with one Fiscal Court commissioner, and three at-large appointees. The state had four at-large appointees with the governor appointing his own representative from his staff.

The state appointments were A. Stevens Miles, Chair; C'Allen Chauvin; Michael Davidson, Vice Chair; Orson Oliver and Michael Ruehling.

Appointees representing Jefferson County included Judge/Executive David Armstrong; Oliver Barber, Jr.; Chris Gorman; James W. Stites, Jr., and Joseph Warren, secretary.

The City of Louisville appointments were Mayor Jerry Abramson; Paul Bather; Phillip Bond; Creighton Mershon, and Marcia Roth, treasurer.

It was a board of directors any not-for-profit organization would yearn for. Its first meeting was held in the Court Room at the Galt House East on November 12, 1986.

After the original organization paperwork, by the time of the initial meeting there had been several changes in board personnel. Several new additions, including Al. J. Schneider, Mary Helen Miller, Leonard Lyles, Steve Bing and Bill Wilson, were present to meet and agree upon a common intent.

MISSION

THE PURPOSE OF THE WATERFRONT DEVELOPMENT CORPORATION IS TO PLAN, COORDINATE AND CAUSE THE DEVELOPMENT OF PROJECTS THAT WILL ENHANCE THE USEFULNESS, ECONOMIC VALUE AND ATTRACTIVENESS OF LOUISVILLE'S WATERFRONT. THE CORPORATION IS THE SOLE AGENCY, DERIVING ITS AUTHORITY FROM KRS 58.180, REPRESENTING THE CITY OF LOUISVILLE, JEFFERSON COUNTY AND THE COMMONWEALTH OF KENTUCKY IN WATERFRONT DEVELOPMENT ALONG THE OHIO RIVER (THE AREA FROM SHAWNEE PARK TO COX'S PARK).

To gauge the success or failure of other cities' attempts at waterfront rehabilitation, a group of Louisvillians, including David Karem, Creighton Mershon, Marcia Roth and Melissa Mershon, toured Toledo, St. Paul, Detroit and Minneapolis. They came back with definite ideas on setting priorities, including a policy of opening a dialogue with the community to explore its thoughts, sponsoring riverfront activities as soon as possible and exploring David Jones' plans for the renovated Belknap properties. They also received negative reports about the operation of "festival marketplaces" – the groupings of small shops and trendy restaurants – to attract visitors, but not

During Public Forums held during 1988 and 1989, people repeatedly called for green space, a park, to be created at the river's edge. Louisvillians, long accustomed to the presence of landscape masterpieces created by Olmsted, enjoyed a tradition of outstanding urban parks, but none in the downtown area.

necessarily locals, to the river's edge. In no case were any of the marketplaces visited by the Louisville group proving financially successful, and in several instances, millions of dollars were lost in the civic experiments.

"…we had a park tradition. We love our parks."

Nowhere in the original Mission Statement is there mention of a park. The goal of the project was revitalization of the waterfront and a commitment to facilitate improved access to the river's edge. Since there were no textbooks on the subject of waterfront development, David Karem recalled the opportunity to clear the table and explore fresh thoughts on Louisville's premier asset, its waterfront.

One of the things that I always thought was wonderful about the organization was that there was no road map, which sounds kind of strange to say, and so you got to kind of free think. There wasn't any hidden document. At this same time there was a lot of criticism about the meeting of the Air Board where they came out of a single meeting and said we've unfolded a huge plan for the redevelopment of the airport. It created some ill feelings that took a while to heal. So we decided that it should be as open a process as it was humanly possible to do. In fact, I'm predisposed to openness. I think people are suspicious of government because we sometimes think things should be done behind closed doors. So with no game plan, we decided to make up our own.

If there was a national model, Baltimore was doing something like what we were talking about. There were other national models, but they were not working. We decided that there was a big chunk of land down here and we wanted to know what does the public want to do with it? So we came up with this brainstorm of having a series of public forums that anybody could attend. There were ten of these over the summer. We did this series over the summer of '88, once a week for a ten-week period of time. We sent some invitations, but it was very much open to the public. They were very well attended and we had 20-25 at most of the meetings.

At each meeting we laid out the Corradino plan, called the Waterfront Development Strategy. We said here is this document and asked what do you people want down here? Some said, just pave the whole damned thing

and use it as free public parking and that might revitalize the downtown. And downtown wasn't very vital at the time. Or we could underwrite the building of an outlet mall, 10-15 stores and ample parking. But 85-90 percent of the people, without being coached, said we want downtown green space, there is no downtown park space. We don't consider Central Park a downtown park, it was always a neighborhood park. And you heard people say, without coaching, we had this Olmsted tradition in Louisville, we had a park tradition. We love our parks. If you look at the housing stock around Shawnee Park, or Cherokee Park, it appears that the housing stock stays in the best preservation. They are better maintained and hold their values better. And we want park lands. There is no public gathering space, if we want to do something, where do we gather? So armed with that – it was parkland and that pretty much focused the mission for us to do a park.

Some of the suggestions coming out of the public forums bordered on the bizarre. Ideas included installing an educational submarine in the Ohio River; tunneling under the river to Indiana; building skating rinks; or paving the entire area and having weekend flea markets on the site. Most of the suggestions were sound and well-reasoned, and many were incorporated into the eventual plans for the area. Solid suggestions included the creation of a riverside walking and jogging path; building a stairway link between the overhead Belvedere to the wharf below; turning River Road into a parkway; and, perhaps most importantly, making Louisville's waterfront unique and indigenous to Louisville.

But the public's overwhelming sentiment was for green space and access to their river. A call for parks has long sounded in Louisville, Kentucky. In the public forums of 1988, echoes of the past resonated. A May 13, 1853, article in the *Louisville Daily Courier*, made an oddly similar plea:

THE ATTENTION OF OUR CITIZENS HAS BEEN REPEATEDLY CALLED TO THE PROPRIETY OF ESTABLISHING A SHADE GROUNDS IN LOUISVILLE, THROUGH THE COLUMNS OF THE *COURIER*, WITHIN A FEW MONTHS PAST; - BUT THIS IS ONE OF THOSE SUBJECTS WHICH REQUIRE FREQUENT MENTION, IN ORDER TO FILL THE PUBLIC MIND WITH THEM, AND HENCE WE SHALL FROM TIME TO TIME RECUR TO IT, IN THE HOPE OF DOING GOOD AT LAST.

ONE OF THE FIRST THINGS THAT ARE NECESSARY IN LARGE CITIES, YET ONE OF THE LAST THAT ARE SUPPLIED, ARE BREATHING-SPOTS FOR THE MASSES OF THE PEOPLE. – THOUGH MANIFESTLY CHEAPER AND BETTER THAN THE DOCTOR, YET SUCH SPOTS ARE NEGLECTED, AND THE DOCTOR SENT FOR. THOUGH BEYOND ANY QUESTION WHOLESOMER THAN THE FOETED STREET, YET THE STREET, FILLED WITH DUST AND EMITTING NAUSEATING STENCH, IS OCCUPIED, AND THE BREATHING-SPOT IS A THING ONLY DREAMED OF. INSTEAD OF HAVING SHADED ALLEYS FOR THE PROMENADES OF ADULTS, AND GRASS-SPEARS AND CLOVER-BLOSSOMS FOR THE PLAY-THING OF CHILDREN, THE YOUNG ONES ARE LEFT TO SWELTER IN THE HOUSE OR PLAY WITH PIGS IN THE GUTTERS, AND THEIR SENIORS BURN THEIR FEET ON HOT PAVEMENTS AND HAVE THEIR NOSES SINGED BY MIDSUMMER AND MIDDAY REFLECTIONS FROM HOT BRICK WALLS.

Twenty-Seven Shades of Pink

While the questionable pleasure of playing with pigs in the gutter had been eliminated, many waterfront conditions were the same as when Beargrass Creek flowed out into the river at Third Street in the 1850s. The only two playgrounds in the city's business district were at Baxter Square on Jefferson and the tiny Mamie Varble Stratton Park adjacent to the Wharfmaster's office.

Splash nightclub and its companion The Islands restaurant brought new life and a colorful presence to the Louisville wharf in 1987. Although the upper-scale restaurant eventually saw its business decline, the floating restaurant/night club attracted younger people down to the waterfront for fun and entertainment in the evenings.

While public opinion crystallized around the idea of a riverfront park, other plans were being made to bring some light and life to the Louisville wharf.

Louisville's new young mayor was Jerry E. Abramson, a font of energy, effort and enthusiasm. Often referred to as "Louisville's greatest cheerleader," Abramson embraced his new job with an eagerness to get things moving. One of his mentors was Al Schneider, builder and owner of the Galt House Hotel, the first important private development on the waterfront for generations. Early on, Abramson and Schneider, two strong-willed personalities, met weekly for lunch to talk about their shared dream of revitalizing Louisville. This closeness ended when the mayor described a new attraction moving to the Louisville wharf just below the Galt House. A huge 500-foot floating double-barge, housing The Islands restaurant and Splash nightclub, had agreed to relocate from the Newport, Kentucky, waterfront. In March 1987 the city awarded a five-year franchise to Schilling Enterprises Inc., and promised to spend $2.5 million to extend the wharf and add a riverfront walkway. The Islands/Splash received a $1 million dollar upgrade, including a fresh coat of paint on its signature twenty-seven shades of pink exterior.

The new dawn greets a renovated Belknap complex, renewed as Humana Waterside and the Presbyterian Center. The vision of Louisville businessman David A. Jones was realized when he purchased the old Belknap Hardware property and tastefully converted parts of the 1.5 million-square-foot complex into office buildings, bringing thousands back to work in downtown Louisville. *(WDC photo by Rick Bell)*

Schneider was outraged. Instead of the small dinner boat he anticipated resting at the river's edge, he saw The Islands as a bright and brassy distraction to the Galt House and he resented what he considered a poor investment by the city. He believed The Islands would have a negative impact on downtown and attract unsavory people. Schneider filed suit to stop the agreement and threatened to scuttle his new hundred-unit riverfront apartment complex next to the Galt House East.

Schneider, a member of the Waterfront Development Corporation Board, voted against The Islands proposal at the January 1987 meeting, and his friendship with the new mayor was broken. The lawsuit would later be dropped, and The Islands moved to Louisville.

Predestined for Louisville

The Islands was not the only new tenant on the waterfront. In 1987 the newly united Presbyterian Church chose Louisville as its national headquarters, pending the merger of the New York and Atlanta offices of the denomination, divided since before the Civil War. Presbyterians had always had an important presence in Louisville, even before the antebellum period when Reverend Alex Cowan was sending boatloads of freed slaves for their journeys to Liberia from the city wharf. In 1974 the General Assemblies of the northern and southern Presbyterians met in Louisville and began discussions which led to their eventual reunion. Both bodies had jointly supported the Louisville Presbyterian Seminary since 1901, the only seminary in the nation to represent both wings.

Perhaps more importantly, Louisville was also the home of David A. Jones, an active Presbyterian with a huge empty office building on Main Street. With his offer to help renovate part of the old Belknap property as their national headquarters, the merged Presbyterian Church surprised many by announcing Louisville as its new home. With the influx of hundreds of new downtown office workers, a new parking garage would be needed for their use. Louisville's waterfront, so dormant for so long, suddenly seemed to be coming back to life.

August 1, 1987, marked a quiet start of what would become a local tradition when the Dream Factory's "Hands Across the Water" fundraising event became the first charitable organization to use the waterfront. The group raised money by sponsoring a march from the City Hall to Court Avenue in Jeffersonville, via the Clark Memorial Bridge. It was the first of what would be many not-for-profit organizations to find a friend in Waterfront Park.

A new organization such as the Waterfront Development Corporation needed friends and attention. In an early 1987 letter to Mayor Abramson, David Karem presented an idea that would take root and grow:

IT OCCURRED TO ME WHILE THINKING OF CREATIVE AND INTERESTING THINGS ALONG LOUISVILLE'S WATERFRONT THAT A REAL EFFORT COULD BE MADE TO DO SOMETHING CREATIVE FOR THE 1988 DERBY FESTIVAL OR AT LEAST THE 1989 DERBY FESTIVAL. WHILE I AM AWARE THAT THERE IS A BOAT RACE CENTERING ON THE WATERFRONT THAT REALLY IS FOR ALL PRACTICAL PURPOSES THE ONLY EVENT, IT SEEMS LIKE IT MIGHT BE OF INTEREST EVEN TO CONSIDER SOMETHING LIKE THE CHOW WAGON BEING PLACED IN AN APPROPRIATE SPOT IF ONE COULD BE FOUND.

IN ANY EVENT AS THE WATERFRONT BEGINS TO OPEN UP AGAIN WITH THINGS LIKE THE FLOATING RESTAURANT

IT WOULD CERTAINLY BE FUN TO TAKE ADVANTAGE OF SOMETHING ELSE RELATED TO THE DERBY FESTIVAL.

CERTAINLY THE WATERFRONT DEVELOPMENT CORPORATION WOULD BE EAGER TO ASSIST IN SOME WAY.

Doing Due Diligence

Louisville's waterfront presented special challenges to any design intended to provide public access and flexibility of purpose. Famously prone to flooding throughout its history, after World War II the city and county worked with the U.S. Army Corps of Engineers to plan, construct and maintain a flood control system of levees and floodwalls stretching over twenty miles. In any consideration of building on the riverfront, maintaining the integrity of the flood protection system was paramount. Most access to the river in the area "between the bridges" was severely limited by I-64 passing overhead. Access to the river's edge was limited to going over or under the expressway. Building a protective floodwall beneath the interstate would defeat the goal of Waterfront development efforts.

With the Presbyterian Center needing a parking garage, it was determined to make it a part of the flood control system. An installation for flood gates to seal the aperture was provided between the proposed parking garage and the Metropolitan Sewer District pumping station at Bingham Way, just north of Witherspoon Street. This was the same site as the old Water Street Station, the old train depot that hosted the Liberty Bell very briefly in 1885.

To reflect its new status as future public park land, the waterfront area was governed by a special zoning regulation called the "Waterfront Development Review Overlay District," more commonly referred to as the WRO District. All land use in this special zoning district required a two-phase approval process involving two agencies: the Louisville and Jefferson County Planning Commission and the Louisville Waterfront

Development Corporation. Anyone considering construction or exterior changes to a building or structure within the WRO District needed permission to alter its business identification signs, change the use of property or construct public parking. Any demolition project also required WRO review. The area, essentially the land north of Main Street between Tenth Street and Zorn Avenue, was subject to review and required undergoing a stringent application process.

"What is Best for Louisville?"

The project to restore Louisville's waterfront stimulated the imagination of community leaders, financiers, urban planners, entrepreneurs, politicians and philanthropists. When David Karem and Deputy Mayor Joan Riehm appeared one evening on a popular WHAS radio call-in show hosted by Milton Metz, the response was overwhelming. The talk show host later declared it was one of the most successful shows ever and the WHAS switchboard was jammed with people wanting to share their comments. The public began to embrace the park before plans were ever put on paper.

In its July 1988 edition, *Louisville Magazine* interviewed local leaders on the subject, "What's Best for Louisville?" Those interviewed agreed that waterfront development was the most important action to assist the economic development of the area. Jim Roberson, then-president of the Louisville Chamber of Commerce observed:

I WOULD AGREE THAT IT'S ONE OF MANY IMPORTANT THINGS THAT WILL BE GOING ON IN THE NEXT SEVERAL YEARS. I THINK THE REASON THAT READERS PUT IT SO HIGH, AND THE REASON IT WOULD BE DIFFICULT TO OVERSTATE ITS IMPORTANCE, IS BECAUSE OF ITS VISIBILITY. WHAT HAPPENS ON THE WATERFRONT IS SOMETHING THAT IS GOING TO BE SEEN MUCH EASIER THAN, SAY, THE LOCATION OF AN INDUSTRIAL PLANT IN AN INDUSTRIAL PARK SOMEWHERE. PEOPLE ARE GOING TO SEE IT AND THEY'RE GOING TO FORM OPINIONS ABOUT WHAT'S

HAPPENING TO LOUISVILLE. I SUSPECT THERE ARE A LOT OF PEOPLE, AND MAYBE ALL OF US ARE AMONG THEM, WHO ARE IMPATIENT ABOUT SEEING THE WATERFRONT DEVELOPED. BUT IT CERTAINLY SHOULD BE DONE WITH THE LONGEST POSSIBLE VIEW IN MIND, SO THAT IT REALLY SETS A TONE, A TENOR, IF YOU WILL, FOR PEOPLE'S ATTITUDES. IF YOU LOOK AT THE FOUNTAIN...AND ITS POTENTIAL AS A SYMBOL OF WATERFRONT DEVELOPMENT THAT IS ACCESSIBLE TO THE PUBLIC — ESPECIALLY BECAUSE THE INTERSTATES COME TOGETHER THERE — IT WOULD BE REALLY DIFFICULT TO OVERSTATE ITS IMPORTANCE.

The Louisville Falls Fountain, loved by some and scorned by others, was the generous gift of Barry and Mary Bingham to the people of Louisville. When the fountain was able to resist buffeting by the Ohio River currents, the lighted spray of water forming a fleur-de-lis was a delight to viewers from the shore or on board excursion boats.

The "fountain" referred to a proposal made by Barry and Mary Bingham. Their dream was to provide a dramatic floating fountain in the Ohio River to spout a gigantic water feature depicting a *fleur-de-lis,* the symbol of Louisville. Mayor Jerry Abramson, one of the most consistent supporters of Waterfront Park, shared his point of view:

ANOTHER DIMENSION OF ECONOMIC DEVELOPMENT IN THIS COMMUNITY IS PRIDE. PEOPLE HAVE TO CARE ENOUGH ABOUT THE PRODUCT TO SELL IT. AND EVERYTHING THAT WE DO TO ENHANCE THE QUALITY OF THE COMMUNITY, THE EXCITEMENT ABOUT THE

COMMUNITY, THE AURA OF THE COMMUNITY, ARE ALL IMPORTANT. AND TO HAVE THE LARGEST FLOATING FOUNTAIN ANYWHERE IN THE WORLD IN THE SHAPE OF A *FLEUR-DE-LIS* ENDS UP BEING THE SIGNATURE FOR THE COMMUNITY, IN ADDITION TO THE TWIN SPIRES AT CHURCHILL DOWNS. I THINK IT ADDS TO THE EXCITEMENT AND THE PRIDE THAT WE HAVE RECENTLY BEGUN TO FEEL ABOUT OURSELVES AND OUR COMMUNITY.

I FEEL VERY STRONGLY THAT THE WATERFRONT ITSELF OUGHT TO BE AS OPEN AND ACCESSIBLE TO THE PUBLIC AS POSSIBLE. IN ADDITION, I THINK THERE ARE AREAS ON THE WATERFRONT WHERE HOUSING WOULD BE APPROPRIATE, BE IT APARTMENTS OR CONDOMINIUMS, AND WHERE ENTERTAINMENT FACILITIES, CONTIGUOUS TO OR BUILT ON THE WATERFRONT, PLAY A ROLE IN TERMS OF THAT PUBLIC ACCESS TO THE RIVER. SO I SEE IT AS A MOSAIC. I SEE A POTENTIAL FOR BUSINESS OFFICE AND ECONOMIC DEVELOPMENT ACTIVITIES SOUTH OF RIVER ROAD. AND I THINK THE OPPORTUNITY TO KEEP ECONOMIC DEVELOPMENT ON THE SOUTH SIDE OF THE ROAD AND KEEP THE WATERFRONT OPEN TO THE PEOPLE IS AVAILABLE THERE, ALL THE WAY FROM EVA BANDMAN PARK AROUND TO SHAWNEE AND CHICKASAW PARK. I SEE LOTS OF INTERESTS PLAYING A ROLE IN THE DEVELOPMENT OF THE WATERFRONT.

Mayor Abramson's views echoed one of his predecessors in office. As Mayor James S. Speed, in his 1853 message to the Common Council, had stated:

THE MAYOR IS OF THE OPINION THAT THE PROSPECTS OF LOUISVILLE WERE NEVER BEFORE SO BRIGHT AND ENCOURAGING AS THEY ARE AT THIS TIME, AND IN ORDER THAT THOSE PROSPECTS MAY NOT BE BLIGHTED, HE RECOMMENDS A LIBERAL POLICY IN THE MATTER OF APPROPRIATIONS OF MONEY FOR OBJECTS OF UNDOUBTED PUBLIC UTILITY.

A Tradition of Generosity

The Bingham family has been a pillar of philanthropy in Louisville. Their ownership of the *Courier-Journal* & *Louisville Times* newspapers, WHAS radio and television and Standard Gravure printing made them both wealthy and public-spirited. Engraved in the lobby of the *Courier-Journal* building, the creed of Judge Robert W. Bingham proclaimed his belief that his newspapers were a "public trust," and his heirs took that charge seriously. Barry Bingham, Sr., the son of the judge, ran the newspapers in the perilous days of 1937, while his father was serving as Roosevelt's Ambassador to Great Britain. During the Great Flood of 1937 Barry Bingham turned over the assets of his company and WHAS radio became the voice of rescue and relief with its familiar announcement "Send a Boat!" The clear-channel station operated around the clock for 187 consecutive hours providing information, directions, comfort and reassurance to the 175,000 evacuees and those who stayed behind in upstairs rooms. This was the first time in broadcast history a station operated on a round-the-clock basis, and the powerful 50,000-watt clear channel station spread descriptions of Louisville's plight to a worldwide audience.

After the flood, the Bingham family sponsored a huge free radio program to thank the people outside of Louisville who had welcomed refugees into their homes during the crisis. In the early days of television, Barry Bingham inaugurated an annual telethon which closely resembled the flood tribute show. The "Crusade for Children" became a cherished Louisville tradition, providing millions of dollars to serve issues of child health and welfare.

Barry Bingham and his elegant wife, Mary, had shared bountifully of their wealth in a number of worthy causes, including education, fine arts, historic preservation and public welfare. Late in their lives, they took a special interest in redeeming the city's riverfront.

The Louisville skyline, brightened by the red lights on the Falls Fountain, displays a downtown awakening after a long slumber. The world-famous Humana Building, and creations by other great architects, began to establish Louisville as a progressive place to live and work.

The Largest Floating Fountain in the World

The Louisville Falls Fountain, imagined and sponsored by Barry and Mary Bingham, was an ambitious enterprise requiring highly specialized technical considerations to create a floating fountain capable of providing dependable and entertaining light and water spray shows. All this in the middle of a powerful river with abundant heavy river traffic from the nearly constant flow of coal, petroleum, salt, salvage and chemical barges pushed by diesel towboats. As shipping had since 1830, each massive tow was required to thread its way down the Portland Canal and pass into the lower river below the McAlpine Lock and Dam. Public reaction to the spectacular fountain was mixed, to say the least. Michel Marriott, in a 1992 *New York Times* article, examined questions concerning the maritime installation.

LOUISVILLE, KY. – FOR MORE THAN 200 YEARS, THIS CITY HAS HUGGED A HAIRPIN TURN OF THE OHIO RIVER. AND ALTHOUGH PADDLE WHEELERS DON'T CHURN THE WATERS THE WAY THEY ONCE DID, THIS FORMER FRONTIER TOWN PROUDLY REMAINS A CITY OF THE RIVER.

SO IT DIDN'T SURPRISE MANY FOLKS AROUND HERE WHEN WORD SURFACED SOME FIVE YEARS AGO THAT LOUISVILLE WAS TO GET A NEW PUBLIC SYMBOL: A 400-FOOT-HIGH GEYSER OF RIVER WATER SPEWING FROM THE OHIO ITSELF. IT WOULD BE THE LARGEST FLOATING FOUNTAIN IN THE WORLD. BETTER YET, IT WOULD CREATE A SPRAY IN THE SHAPE OF A GIANT *FLEUR-DE-LIS*, IN HOMAGE TO THE CITY'S NAMESAKE, LOUIS XVI OF FRANCE.

But ever since the $2.1 million Louisville Falls Fountain was unveiled in 1988, a gift of Mary and Barry Bingham Sr., it has surprised and troubled many of Louisville's 269,000 people because of its clunkiness and its penchant for problems.

The fountain's machinery is housed in a 20-foot-high, octagonal steel platform that stands on the water, 1,650 feet from shore, like an abandoned oil rig. Every 15 minutes 41 jets spray almost 240,000 gallons of water into the air, and for four minutes a central nozzle propels water at 125 miles an hour to form the *fleur-de-lis*. It is illuminated at night and operates from May 1 to Nov. 30.

Follow the Red Brick Dust Road

An opportunity arose in 1987 to acquire the distinctive Martin Marietta building on the waterfront at the north end of First Street. The three-story cantilevered building was the former headquarters of Ohio River Sand Company and still contained a thick bank vault to handle the cash-only transactions of supplying loads of sand and gravel for construction purposes. Like a stork on one leg, the flood-proof Martin Marietta building and 1.2 acres of land were sold to the Waterfront Development Corporation, the purchase made possible by Barry and Mary Bingham. Now that the fledgling waterfront authority had a home and a small presence on the river's edge, it was time to begin offering public access. When an additional seven adjacent acres were offered, they were purchased and added to the public space.

At the earliest possible moment, the fledgling Waterfront Development Corporation paved a few acres of property next to its headquarters and built a short 800-foot walking path using railroad ties and crushed red brick. After borrowing a few picnic tables, the staff was pleased to discover the downtown lunch crowd had immediately discovered the site. Although it would soon be replaced, the paved area created program opportunities and kept the new Park in the public's mind.

With a limited budget provided by the annual $300,000 contribution from state, city and county governments, David Karem and his small staff made their first improvements to the park when they placed railroad ties along a wide path created on the river's edge. An 800-foot-long walking surface of crushed red brick filled the pathway leading from First Street and extending eastward several hundred yards. A few picnic tables were secured and placed on the pathway, and almost immediately these minor improvements were recognized and embraced. Before public announcements were made, people began exercising on the path within hours of its completion, and the next day people were sitting at the picnic tables enjoying their lunches outdoors.

Waterfront officials and the Kentucky Derby Festival agreed to work jointly on a plan to consolidate many of the annual spring festivities in one place, and to make that place Waterfront Park. In March 1989 Waterfront matched a grant of $18,000 by the Kentucky Derby Festival and began preparing a black-topped surface with electricity to serve as one of the sites of the popular Chow Wagon program.

Despite a chilly and rainy pre-Derby season in 1989, response to the waterfront location was positive. The food fairs were offered in several community locations in that era, and 148,000 turned out at Waterfront Park, 70,500 at Dixie Manor Shopping Center and an additional 60,000 at the Outlets Limited Mall. The food court raised $25,000 more than the previous year's total and demonstrated that the public would come to the river's edge if given an opportunity, or even an excuse.

In the summer of 1989, the Waterfront Development Corporation received its first earned income by hosting a public event called City Fair. Just before that, a new support group of civic-minded younger professionals from around the city created the Friends of the Waterfront (FOTW). The group was established to channel an outpouring of support from the community and created a network of involved individuals donating their skills

and dollars for the growth of the Park. The volunteers helped plan and staff events like the Wharf dedication, Falls Fountain dedication and were instrumental in moving the Chow Wagon to its riverfront location. FOTW held its first meeting in August 1989 with twenty-five people in attendance. Seemingly within months, the group had grown to three hundred members who raised in excess of $50,000.

Gathering Land and Experience

At the same time that simple early programming was taking place, the board of the Waterfront Development Corporation was grappling with one of its major duties, the acquisition of waterfront land for park use. At its May 1989 meeting, the board was updated by city law Department attorney David Morris on the status of what was known as the "CSX Agreement."

MR. MORRIS STATED THAT JUST AFTER THE WATERFRONT DEVELOPMENT CORPORATION WAS FORMED, AND BEFORE A BOARD WAS APPOINTED, THE CITY OF LOUISVILLE, JEFFERSON COUNTY, AND STATE OF KENTUCKY AND CSX CORPORATION ENTERED INTO AN AGREEMENT REGARDING A PIECE OF PROPERTY, KNOWN AS THE AMERICAN COMMERCIAL TERMINAL, LOCATED ON RIVER ROAD. THIS AGREEMENT STATED THAT THE WATERFRONT DEVELOPMENT CORPORATION WOULD PURCHASE THE PROPERTY, OWNED BY CSX, FOR $2 MILLION; AND WOULD THEN LEASE THE PROPERTY BACK TO CSX FOR $1 PER YEAR. CSX WOULD, IN RETURN, CONTRIBUTE $2 MILLION TO THE WATERFRONT DEVELOPMENT CORPORATION, WHICH WOULD BE USED TO BUILD CERTAIN TRACKAGE AT RIVERPORT. CSX WOULD AT THE SAME TIME CONSTRUCT A TERMINAL AT RIVERPORT AND WOULD EVENTUALLY MOVE TO RIVERPORT, WHERE THE NEWLY INSTALLED TRACKAGE WOULD ENABLE CSX TO OPERATE. THE AGREEMENT STATED THAT THE WATERFRONT DEVELOPMENT CORPORATION WOULD HOLD THE $2 MILLION UNTIL THE IMPROVEMENTS AT

RIVERPORT WERE COMPLETED, AT WHICH TIME THE $2 MILLION WOULD BE TURNED OVER TO RIVERPORT TO PAY FOR THE IMPROVEMENTS. IF THE IMPROVEMENTS WERE NOT COMPLETED, THE WATERFRONT DEVELOPMENT CORPORATION WOULD BE OBLIGATED TO RETURN THE $2 MILLION CONTRIBUTION TO CSX AND THE PROPERTY WOULD REVERT BACK TO THE AMERICAN COMMERCIAL TERMINAL.

MR. MORRIS STATED THAT RIVERPORT AND JEFFERSON COUNTY HAVE REQUESTED THAT THE $2 MILLION BEING HELD BY THE WATERFRONT DEVELOPMENT CORP. (WDC) BE TURNED OVER TO RIVERPORT. SINCE WDC HAS A FIDUCIARY DUTY TO PROTECT THE INTERESTS OF THE CITY AND PRIVATE DONORS WHO CONTRIBUTED THE $2 MILLION, IT WAS DETERMINED THAT WDC WOULD NOT TRANSFER THE FUNDS UNTIL IT COULD BE ASSURED THAT IT COULD NOT BE REQUIRED TO REFUND THE $2 MILLION TO CSX. RIVERPORT, HOWEVER, HAS STATED A NEED FOR THE MONEY SO THAT THE IMPROVEMENTS CAN BE MADE. MR. MILES, MR. MORRIS AND DAVID KAREM MET TO DISCUSS THIS SUBJECT; AS A RESULT, A NEW AGREEMENT HAS BEEN DRAFTED THAT WILL: TRANSFER THE $2 MILLION TO RIVERPORT; HAVE CSX ACKNOWLEDGE THE WATERFRONT DEVELOPMENT CORPORATION'S PAYMENT TO RIVERPORT AND RELEASE THE WDC FOR ANY LIABILITY SHOULD THE IMPROVEMENTS NOT BE COMPLETED; HAVE THE COUNTY AND RIVERPORT AGREE TO ASSUME ANY AND ALL OBLIGATIONS OR LIABILITY SHOULD THE TERMS OF THE AGREEMENT NOT BE MET AND THE PROPERTY REVERT BACK TO CSX. MR. MORRIS STATED THAT THE BOARD NEEDS TO APPROVE A RESOLUTION REFLECTING THIS NEW AGREEMENT. AS A RESULT OF THE NEW AGREEMENT, THE WATERFRONT DEVELOPMENT CORPORATION'S INVOLVEMENT IN THIS TRANSACTION WOULD BE LIMITED, AS AGREED TO BY CSX, THE COUNTY, AND RIVERPORT.

CREIGHTON MERSHON ASKED WHY RIVERPORT FELT IT HAD TO HAVE THE MONEY IN HAND TO GET THE WORK AT RIVERPORT DONE, SINCE A FORMAL AGREEMENT HAD BEEN DRAWN UP AND THE OBLIGATION TO PAY WAS THERE. MR. MILES RESPONDED THAT THERE WAS A MISUNDERSTANDING ON THE PART OF RIVERPORT, WHO FELT THAT THE WDC COULD RELEASE THE FUNDS AT ANY TIME; THE WDC FELT THAT UNDER THE AGREEMENT, IT HAD TO HOLD THE MONEY UNTIL SUCH TIME THAT THE IMPROVEMENTS WERE COMPLETED. MR. KAREM STATED THAT THERE IS THE MATTER OF INTEREST ON THE $2 MILLION; IF THE WDC HELD THE MONEY UNTIL THE IMPROVEMENTS WERE COMPLETED, BETWEEN $150,000 - $175,000 IN INTEREST WOULD HAVE BEEN EARNED ON THE MONEY. OLIVER BARBER MADE THE MOTION THAT THE RESOLUTION BE ADOPTED; CHRIS GORMAN SECONDED THE MOTION. THE RESOLUTION PASSED UNANIMOUSLY.

To accomplish the myriad tasks needed to plan and implement the work of the WDC, David Karem began to carefully hand pick a highly specialized staff of professionals. In 1987 Phyllis Williams joined the staff as Financial Officer to navigate the complex accounting requirements of separate funding streams from state, city, county and private donations. In the following year Marlene Grissom came on board as a $1-a-year volunteer to serve as Director of Special Projects, focusing on public relations, art programs and fundraising. In 1989 Karem hired Terry Feathers' former assistant Margaret Walker as graphic designer, computer expert and general assistant. Michael Kimmel, an urban planner with special emphasis on environmental studies, was a veteran of the Kentucky Natural Resources Cabinet with an exceptional understanding of water-related issues, engineering and governmental regulations. He would serve as Deputy Director of the Corporation and supervisor of the WRO District. Each of the original staff continued serving twenty-plus years, and formed the core of the Waterfront Development Corporation from its earliest days through the completion of the park's final

An early success was the project to light the Clark Bridge, led by WDC staff member Marlene Grissom. The splashes of purple light, officially known as Gypsy Lavender, bring an emphasis to the bridge's presence and drama to the approach to Louisville from Indiana.

phases. Collectively, their fingerprints are etched into the fabric, function and face of Waterfront Park.

The staff plunged into work with Marlene Grissom in charge of Project BridgeLight, a program to provide lighting on the Clark and Kennedy bridges and create a series of kinetic sculptures for daytime enjoyment. Grissom, with a background of owning and operating the successful Byck Gallery in downtown Louisville, gathered the information and volunteers needed to study the special needs of the project and to secure funding.

One of the earliest suggestions as an anchor attraction for the Waterfront Park was the addition of a major regional aquarium on the site. A subcommittee was formed and consultants engaged to gauge the viability of the plan to make one of the Park's attractions a permanent, large and very expensive installation of fresh- and salt-water aquatic life. The aquarium plan was later dropped as too costly, and was deemed inappropriate to the emerging vision of Waterfront Park.

A Grid Pattern Gone Mad

Even prior to the assembly of the Waterfront Strategy, most city planners agreed that the road system around the waterfront was in need of major rethinking if the twin goals of accessibility to the shore and flood protection were to be achieved. The old tangle of small narrow streets and alleys that connected Main Street and the Louisville waterfront had long formed a maze of poor traffic circulation. Gone were the streets of the nineteenth century – Water Street and Fulton Streets, lying north of the bed of old Beargrass Creek were abandoned, but not officially closed, as River Road provided the major east-west route along the river's edge. Gone also were Wall, Pearl and Bullitt Streets, as well as Donne and O'Neill's Alleys.

Twentieth century additions, especially the I-64 expressway with its east-bound entrance ramp at First Street, greatly complicated the chance to gain meaningful extensions of land between the Ohio River and Main Street. River Road, a major feeder into downtown Louisville from the east, was frequently jammed as traffic negotiated the narrow downtown streets.

The Waterfront Strategy described the crucial need for changes in the street patterns. In the first section of their report, Public Sector Costs, the highest priority was road improvements for the revitalization of the Louisville waterfront.

The announcement of plans to block and re-route River Road would become a local controversy lasting several years, especially with area businessmen who believed it would negatively impact their sales, services or employees. The *Courier-Journal* editorial board entered the discussion on August 27, 1997.

ROADWAYS - $10 million. The roadway system is most in need of improvement in the Phase II redevelopment area. The interior street system in the area between the Clark and Kennedy Bridges will cost $3.8 million to repair/recreate. This includes improvements to First, Second, Brook, Floyd, Preston, and Jackson Streets. Likewise, Washington and Water Streets, in the east-west direction, will be repaired. River Road, from Preston to Clay Street (2,600 feet) would be reconstructed to a four-lane facility at a cost of $700,000. Additionally, about $3 million will be needed to relocate the I-64 ramps at Third and First Streets. When these roads in downtown are redone, River Road should be improved outside the downtown to make the downtown roadway system function property. To "fix" River Road from Beargrass Creek to Zorn Avenue (5,400 feet) will cost $2.5 million.

The permanent closing of a short stretch of River Road last Friday to make way for the waterfront's "Great Lawn" is a necessary step. There are few projects that promise more for this community, as a whole, than the Waterfront Development.

However, it is up to the city – through its police and sanitation forces – to see that the re-routing of traffic onto existing roadways goes smoothly. That is what was promised five years ago, when the original plans to block River Road were announced.

There is much work to be done. For starters, the suggested new route south from the river is along Clay Street, but those who follow it are dumped into the gridlock on Main Street, which has grown worse with the closing of River Road.

Then there's Preston Street. It's a mess.

While it is not just the scrap metal yard between River Road and Main Street that causes the problem, it is a major impediment to safety and traffic flow. Louisville Scrap Metal seems to regard Preston as a private driveway for loading and unloading. If any other business or industry in downtown Louisville blocked a street in this manner, not to mention littering it with debris, the town would be in an uproar.

The ultimate plan is for Louisville Scrap Metal to move, but that is not going to happen soon. As on other main downtown arteries, stopping – much less parking – cannot be tolerated on Preston Street during rush hour.

Everyone is pleased to see progress at the waterfront, but if the result is lost time at rush hour, the thrill and goodwill of strolling along the Great Lawn will diminish – rapidly. It's time for the Mayor and his police chief to send the forces.

Clean up the street. Clear out the trucks at rush hour.

And stay on top of it.

FallsHarbor

The Waterfront Strategy envisioned development in the West End and the area east of "between the bridges" and Zorn Avenue, not just the old city wharf area. The riverfront acres north of River Road, the heart of the old Point neighborhood where the Geiger and Paget mansions once entertained boat captains and visiting French writers, provided prime river views upstream and downstream. The small channel between Towhead Island and the Municipal Boat Harbor of the 1930s was an appealing location crying out for development. In June 1989 the Waterfront Development Corporation issued a call for proposals to developers interested in the area. As reported by Sheldon Shafer in *The Courier-Journal* of August 28, 1989, the call got a spirited response:

LOUISVILLE'S SEARCH FOR A WORKABLE PLAN TO DEVELOP 108 ACRES SURROUNDING ITS OHIO RIVER BOAT HARBOR NEAR TOWHEAD ISLAND HAS NARROWED TO THREE, EACH PROPOSING MORE THAN $300 MILLION IN APARTMENT HOUSING PLUS PLACES TO EAT AND SHOP, BOAT SLIPS AND PARKS.

ALL THREE PLANS OFFERED HUNDREDS OF APARTMENTS CLUSTERED ALONG THE HARBOR'S EDGE, WITH EXTENSIVE PARK LAND REMAINING SOUTH OF RIVER ROAD. ALL THREE CALL FOR FAIRLY HEAVY GOVERNMENT INVESTMENT.

THE PROJECT, WHICH IS NEAR THRUSTON AND EVA BANDMAN PARKS JUST UPSTREAM FROM THE BIG FOUR BRIDGE, MAY SET THE TREND FOR EVENTUAL DEVELOPMENT OF THE ENTIRE RIVERBANK FROM THE HARBOR TO THE DOWNTOWN WHARF, ACCORDING TO OFFICIALS OF THE WATERFRONT DEVELOPMENT CORPORATION.

MAYOR JERRY ABRAMSON HAS NAMED A NINE-MEMBER

In 1989 an ambitious proposal to build FallsHarbor, a condominium and apartment complex on the shoreline opposite historic Towhead Island, attracted attention to the need for downtown residences. The City of Louisville provided $4 million to improve infrastructure and access around the development. Extensive work on the CSX rail lines and River Road was required to make the project feasible.

COMMITTEE, HEADED BY STATE ADJUTANT GENERAL MICHAEL DAVIDSON, TO REVIEW THE PROPOSALS.

DURING THE PAST 10 DAYS, THE COMMITTEE HAS HEARD PRESENTATIONS FROM ALL THREE GROUPS: BELLE-ILE, WHICH INCLUDES THE KADEN COMPANIES AND SCHIMPLER-CORRADINO & ASSOCIATES PROPERTIES; FALLSHARBOR, COMPOSED OF HFH INC. AND LOUIS & HENRY GROUP; AND TOWHEAD MARINE CENTER, MADE UP OF EIGHT LOCAL INVESTORS AND ARCHITECT K. NORMAN BERRY ASSOCIATES.

KAREM SAID THE COMMITTEE WILL STUDY THE GROUPS' FINANCIAL CAPABILITIES AND EACH PROJECT'S WORTH AND MAKE RECOMMENDATIONS TO THE MAYOR AND ALDERMEN THIS FALL.

About eighteen months later, *The Courier-Journal* would report on June, 26, 1991, on the formal arrangements between Louisville and promoters of a development to be called FallsHarbor.

THE CITY OF LOUISVILLE HAS AGREED TO PAY FOR $4 MILLION IN CAPITAL IMPROVEMENTS TO MAKE WAY FOR THE FIRST PHASE OF THE FALLSHARBOR PROJECT JUST UPRIVER FROM THE BIG FOUR BRIDGE, MAYOR JERRY ABRAMSON SAID YESTERDAY.

THE $20 MILLION DOLLAR DEVELOPMENT IS PROPOSED BY THE HFH INC. DEVELOPMENT FIRM AND THE LOUIS & HENRY GROUP DESIGN FIRM.

THE FIRST PHASE IS TO FEATURE A 200-SLIP MARINA, 200 APARTMENTS, AT LEAST ONE RESTAURANT, A PROMENADE ALONG THE RIVER AND RECREATION FACILITIES. CONSTRUCTION WILL START IN ABOUT A YEAR.

WORK MUST WAIT FOR COMPLETION OF THE CITY-FINANCED RELOCATION OF THE CSX RAIL LINE RUNNING THROUGH THE PROJECT SITE, KNOWN AS THE LOUISVILLE MUNICIPAL BOAT HARBOR. THE RAILROAD IS BEING MOVED SOUTH OF RIVER ROAD.

CONSTRUCTION OF FALLSHARBOR'S FIRST PHASE WILL THEN TAKE ABOUT TWO YEARS.

AT A NEWS CONFERENCE AT THE SITE YESTERDAY, ABRAMSON SAID FALLSHARBOR WILL "LAUNCH THE REDEVELOPMENT OF THE CITY'S GREATEST TREASURE — THE OHIO RIVER."

THE PROJECT IS ENVISIONED AS AN EASTERN ANCHOR IN THE PROPOSED $50 MILLION MASTER PLAN TO REDEVELOP THE LAND ALONG THE OHIO DOWN TO THE DOWNTOWN WATERFRONT.

MOST OF THE CITY'S FUNDS WILL GO FOR THE RAILROAD'S RELOCATION; THE MONEY HAS ALREADY BEEN BUDGETED. THE CITY ALSO IS TO CONDUCT ENVIRONMENTAL AND ARCHAEOLOGICAL STUDIES OF THE SITE.

AS FEDERAL AND STATE FUNDS BECOME AVAILABLE, THE CITY ALSO WILL RELOCATE AND WIDEN RIVER ROAD NEAR THE SITE, MOVING IT ABOUT 250 FEET TO THE SOUTH. THAT PROJECT PROBABLY WILL BE COMPLETED IN THREE TO SIX YEARS, OFFICIALS SAID.

LOUIS & HENRY SPOKESMAN BILL WEYLAND SAID WORK ON PHASE ONE DOESN'T HAVE TO WAIT UNTIL RIVER ROAD IS RELOCATED.

WITH MUCH OF THRUSTON PARK IN THE PROJECT AREA, THE AGREEMENT CALLS FOR THE DEVELOPERS TO BUILD SOFTBALL FIELDS AND BASKETBALL AND TENNIS COURTS.

IT ALSO CALLS FOR THE CITY TO LEASE THE LAND TO FALLSHARBOR INC. FOR 99 YEARS. UNDER THE LEASE, THE CITY IS TO INITIALLY GET 5 PERCENT OF THE RESTAURANT INCOME AND 2.5 PERCENT FROM THE REST OF THE PROJECT EACH YEAR.

THE DEVELOPERS ARE TO APPLY TO THE ARMY CORPS OF ENGINEERS FOR A PERMIT TO ENLARGE THE EXISTING MARINA AND TO CONSTRUCT THE BUILDINGS.

THE DEVELOPERS ALSO WILL PAY TO CONVERT THE EXISTING RAILROAD BRIDGE ACROSS BEARGRASS CREEK TO EVA BANDMAN PARK TO A PEDESTRIAN BRIDGE.

PHASE ONE IS TO FEATURE AN EIGHT-STORY BUILDING AND THREE SMALLER BUILDINGS. MOST OF THE PARKING WILL BE UNDER THE APARTMENTS, TO ELEVATE THEM ABOVE THE FLOOD PLAIN. THE GROUND FLOOR OF THE TALLER BUILDING WILL HAVE ABOUT 23,000 SQUARE FEET OF COMMERCIAL SPACE.

Each apartment is to have a balcony and a river view, overlooking a large central fountain. The apartments will rent for $600 to $1,500 a month and eventually be converted to condominiums, HFH officials said. The boat slips also will be rented.

The main restaurant will be to the west, just off the harbor, with outside dining and a pier. Another restaurant or two could end up being incorporated into phase one, Weyland said.

Users of the existing harbor will be offered a chance at some of the 200 new marina slips. Some of the new slips will be reserved for transient boat operators.

The site plan for phase one also calls for nature trails, landscaping and other amenities, as well as rehabilitation of an historic house,

probably into a river-related museum, Weyland said.

HFH Inc. president Bill Hinton said no attempt has been made yet to get financing. He said the developers hope the restrictive lending market will be relaxed in the next year.

Two additional phases of development at FallsHarbor are planned but uncertain. The concept is eventually for about $90 million of development at the 100-acre site, including 200 more boat slips and 400 more apartments.

"When all else fails in the process, use common sense."

By late 1988, many people were beginning to pay attention to Louisville's riverfront revitalization project. Locally, David Karem was awarded the Kentucky Society of Architect's Citizen Laureate Award for his innovative leadership of the project. He was also becoming a growing national voice in what was

The original FallsHarbor design concepts called for upscale riverfront residences combined with an attractive marina to replace the old Municipal Boat Harbor. Over time, a declining economy and changes in local real estate doomed the FallsHarbor plans, but the city's infrastructure improvements opened other opportunities.

becoming a national and international movement to recognize and restore the urban asset of waterfront access. At the "Urban Waterfronts '88" national conference, David Karem shared his experience with other communities preparing similar civic improvements. Speaking on "Getting Waterfront Renewal Organized," Karem remarked:

> I DON'T CARE WHAT ENTITY YOU USE — A HARBOR COMMISSION, A CITIZENS' COMMISSION, AN INTERNAL POLITICAL ENTITY, WEALTHY PEOPLE WHO PUT TOGETHER A DO-GOODER ORGANIZATION — IT IS VITAL TO GET SOMETHING STARTED, TO GET AN INFINITESIMAL TOE IN THE WATER."

AMONG THE PEOPLE ESSENTIAL TO THAT PROCESS, ACCORDING TO MR. KAREM, ARE "A GOOD MAYOR AND A GOOD CITY COUNCIL," BOTH OF WHICH ARE PRESENT IN LOUISVILLE AND RESPONSIBLE FOR MUCH OF THAT CITY'S SUCCESS IN WATERFRONT RENEWAL. "THE MAYOR IS ENTHUSIASTIC ABOUT WHAT WE'RE DOING ON THE WATERFRONT AND THAT'S A BIG HELP," MR. KAREM SAID.

GOOD STAFF AND VOLUNTEERS ARE ALSO CRUCIAL. "YOU DON'T NEED PEOPLE WHO ARE JUST GOING TO SIT AROUND TALKING ABOUT IT," SAID MR. KAREM.

GETTING INVOLVED IN THE POLITICAL PROCESS ALSO IS VITAL TO THE SUCCESS OF WATERFRONT RENEWAL ACTIVITIES, MR. KAREM SAID. "YOU NEED TO SOIL YOUR HANDS POLITICALLY. DON'T BE AFRAID TO GET INVOLVED IN THE POLITICAL PROCESS. GET SOMETHING GOING POLITICALLY."

"DON'T TRY TO BE SOMETHING YOUR COMMUNITY IS NOT," MR. KAREM SAID. "I CAN'T IMAGINE ANYTHING DUMBER, FOR INSTANCE, THAN LOUISVILLE SPENDING SEVERAL MILLION DOLLARS ON TRYING TO CREATE A CALIFORNIA-STYLE, WEST-COAST MARINA. IN LOUISVILLE, IT MAKES SENSE TO CAPITALIZE ON OUR RIVER HISTORY. THE WATERFRONT IS OUR DOWNTOWN FRONT DOOR."

WHILE LONG-TERM PLANNING CLEARLY IS IMPORTANT TO RENEWAL EFFORTS, MR. KAREM ALSO STRESSED THE NEED FOR SHORT-AND MID-TERM PLANNING, EACH OF WHICH REQUIRES A DIFFERENT FOCUS. "THE MOST MISUNDERSTOOD OF ALL AND MOST NEEDED IS SHORT-TERM PLANNING," HE SAID. "YOU MUST HAVE THE SHORT-TERM 'HITS,' DOING LITTLE THINGS THAT KEPT PEOPLE INTERESTED AND INVOLVED AND GET YOU MEDIA COVERAGE, WHETHER IT'S EVENTS, SIGNAGE, A GARDEN CLUB COMING DOWN AND DOING SOME PLANTING. IF YOU DO NOTHING BETWEEN BEGINNING YOUR 10-YEAR PLAN AND COMPLETING THE PLAN, THE PUBLIC WILL YAWN AND LOSE INTEREST."

REALISM IN PLANNING IS A KEY ELEMENT, ACCORDING TO MR. KAREM. HE URGED WATERFRONT ACTIVISTS TO FOCUS ON BUILDING ATTENTION AND INVOLVEMENT IN RENEWAL OVER TIME. "EVEN THOUGH WE DON'T HAVE ANY FABULOUS THINGS ON THE WATERFRONT YET, WE WANT TO ACQUAINT THE PUBLIC WITH THE IDEA THAT THERE IS A WATERFRONT THERE, SO WE'VE HELD EVENTS ON LAND THAT IS ONLY MARGINALLY ATTRACTIVE," HE SAID. "BRING THE PUBLIC DOWN THERE AND BEGIN TO SENSITIZE THEM TO THE FACT THAT THERE IS A WATERFRONT THERE. JUST GET SOME THINGS GOING."

UNDERLYING ALL RENEWAL EFFORTS IS ONE ESSENTIAL REALITY, ACCORDING TO MR. KAREM. "WHEN ALL ELSE FAILS IN THE PROCESS, USE COMMON SENSE. COMMON SENSE TELLS YOU THAT THE PUBLIC WANTS TO GET BACK TO THE WATER AND WE NEED TO CREATE ACCESS SO THEY CAN DO SO."

Other speakers, including Peter Brink, executive director of the Galveston Historical Foundation, cautioned against one currently popular waterfront strategy, adoption of the so-called "festival marketplace," and he gave strong warnings of its limitations.

"The danger of some waterfront developments, with their emphasis on specialty retail and restaurants, is that they become simply picturesque shopping malls. Interpretation of the history of the waterfront...provides depth and substance as well as enjoyment to the public's experience on the waterfront.

The role of special waterfront features is to help each waterfront preserve its unique character," Mr. Brink concluded. "Without these special features, we simply have 'malled the waterfront' in the same way that we have 'malled' or strip-developed much of the suburban land in our country. Our waterfronts deserve better and the public who ultimately owns them deserves to experience the specialness which is, after all, what draws us to the waterfront in the first place."

As almost a counterpoint, at that same time the nation's largest and splashiest festival marketplace, Mud Island in Memphis, locked its doors. It began to become apparent that people were not searching for new shopping options, they sought green space, parkland, a "breathing-hole for the masses of the people."

The End of a Louisville Institution

Physical change became obvious when David Jones began a major renovation of the Belknap properties. The old hardware distributer was a victim of rapidly evolving new distribution systems, emerging super-sized hardware stores and a changing manufacturing environment. With the development of computer-controlled inventory systems, Belknap was as modern as the buggy whips they once made and sold. The firm declared bankruptcy, and a Louisville institution faded from memory, but its 1.5 million-square-foot headquarters still towered over the waterfront development zone. A *Courier-Journal* article on February 22, 1989, told of positive changes to the riverfront.

Two huge warehouses long leased to Belknap Hardware will be torn down later this year, and the land they occupy near River Road and the Kennedy Bridge will be held for development.

One reason for demolishing the corrugated metal buildings, which date to World War II, is to provide a clear view of the Ohio River, said David Karem, president of the Waterfront Development Corporation.

Karem said the city estimates that removing asbestos from the buildings before demolition begins this summer will cost $250,000 and that the razing and cleanup will cost another $250,000 or so. The city expects to recover about $150,000 from Belknap assets in bankruptcy proceedings. The rest of the cost will be paid by about $100,000 from the city's general fund and about $250,000 pledged from anonymous sources.

The property is part of more than 30 acres that the city hopes to set aside for public use and development north of River Road between the Clark and Kennedy bridges. The western portion of the property between the bridges is targeted for a riverfront park; federal money will be sought to develop it.

THE PORT OF LOUISVILLE, AMERICAN BUILDER'S SUPPLY CO. AND KLEMPNER BROS. SCRAP OCCUPY OTHER LAND IN THE AREA OWNED AND LEASED BY THE CITY. KAREM SAID THAT THOSE LEASES EXPIRE IN MID-1993, AND THAT THE COMPANIES MAY BE RELOCATED.

KENTUCKY DERBY FESTIVAL OFFICIALS HAVE BEEN TOLD BY THE CITY THAT THE WAREHOUSES WILL STILL BE AVAILABLE THIS SPRING FOR ASSEMBLY OF PEGASUS PARADE FLOATS.

"To truly understand the river you have to go there."

One element of the Strategy got a jump start when a local architectural firm, Presnell Associates Inc. (PAI) volunteered to design a riverside walkway tying the Shawnee and Portland neighborhoods to downtown. The May/June issue of the *AIA-CKC Architect Newsletter*, provides an overview of the project.

TO TRULY UNDERSTAND THE RIVER YOU HAVE TO GO THERE. WHAT TWO HUNDRED YEARS AGO WAS BOTH AN EASY MATTER AND A REQUISITE OF DAILY LIFE IN LOUISVILLE HAS BECOME SOMETHING OF AN ADVENTUROUS FEAT ALONG MANY STRETCHES OF THE OHIO, ESPECIALLY THOSE STRETCHES WEST OF DOWNTOWN LOUISVILLE.

WHILE THE NEED TO HALT LOUISVILLE'S RETREAT FROM THE RIVER HAS BEEN DISCUSSED FOR YEARS, IT WAS NOT UNTIL THE EARLY 1970S – WITH THE COMPLETION OF THE RIVERFRONT PLAZA/BELVEDERE – THAT THE OHIO RIVER BECAME THE "FOCUS OF LOUISVILLE'S REVITALIZATION."

PEDESTRIAN ACCESS, WATERFRONT RECREATION ACCESS, SCENIC OVERLOOKS, AND LINKAGE BETWEEN SCENIC AREAS ALONG THE WATERFRONT WESTWARD FROM DOWNTOWN LOUISVILLE ARE AMONG THE RECOMMENDATIONS FEATURED IN THE PLANNING DOCUMENT, LOUISVILLE WATERFRONT STRATEGY. THESE RECOMMENDATIONS WERE A DIRECT RESPONSE TO LONG-STANDING PUBLIC INTEREST IN AND REQUEST FOR SUCH ACCESS – MORE SPECIFICALLY, ACCESS VIA A TRAIL SYSTEM ALONG THE RIVERBANK.

THE SIX-MILE RIVERWALK, EXTENDING FROM THE LOUISVILLE WHARF AND BELVEDERE TO CHICKASAW PARK, IS INTENDED FOR MULTIPLE USE AS AN URBAN TRAIL SERVING THE NEEDS OF MANY INTEREST GROUPS, FROM TOURISTS TO NATURALISTS, FROM NEIGHBORHOOD RESIDENTS TO SCHOOL CHILDREN ON FIELD TRIPS.

THE ROUTE OF RIVERWALK TRACES THE RIVER'S EDGE, AND IS LOCATED, WHERE POSSIBLE, CLOSE TO THE TOP OF THE BANK THROUGHOUT THE TRAIL'S LENGTH. AT POINTS THE TRAIL DEPARTS FROM THE RIVER BANK OWING TO DIFFICULT NATURAL CONDITIONS OR LAND OWNERSHIP CONSIDERATIONS. IT IS PROPOSED TO BE A CONTINUOUS TRAIL, ALTHOUGH ITS DEVELOPMENT MAY BE PHASED IN CONSTRUCTION.

WITH THE ENDORSEMENT OF MAYOR JERRY ABRAMSON, AND ASSISTANCE FROM CITY PUBLIC WORKS DEPARTMENT DIRECTOR BILL HERRON AND WATERFRONT DEVELOPMENT CORPORATION EXECUTIVE DIRECTOR DAVID KAREM, WE BEGAN THE PLANNING PROCESS. THE RESULTING "PRELIMINARY CONCEPT: RIVERWALK" REPORT INCLUDES A MAP SHOWING THE PREFERRED ROUTE ALIGNMENT, SITE DEVELOPMENT FEATURES, AND SKETCHES OF VIEWS ALONG RIVERWALK. COST ESTIMATES FOR THE FINAL DESIGN AND CONSTRUCTION WERE ALSO PREPARED.

OUR RESEARCH PRECEDING THE SELECTION OF A ROUTE AND SITE FEATURES UNCOVERED TWO EXCITING COINCIDENCES: FIRST, 1989 MARKED THE ONE-HUNDREDTH ANNIVERSARY OF THE CITY PARK ACT, WHICH GAVE BIRTH TO THE SYSTEM WE HAVE TODAY. MORE EXCITING STILL, ONE HUNDRED YEARS AGO FREDERICK LAW OLMSTED WAS HIRED TO DEVELOP THAT SYSTEM, BEGINNING WITH IROQUOIS, CHEROKEE AND SHAWNEE PARKS. CHICKASAW, ANOTHER OF LOUISVILLE'S OLMSTED-DESIGNED PARKS, IS ALSO INCLUDED IN RIVERWALK.

The Louisville RiverWalk provides a pleasant path along more than six miles of Ohio River waterfront. Beginning at the eastern end near Tumbleweed Restaurant, to downstream Chickasaw Park, the RiverWalk unites Louisvillians from the East End to the West End. Most travelers on the RiverWalk find their way through Waterfront Park at some stage of their journey.

IT SEEMS FITTING THAT, ONE CENTURY LATER, WE ARE ABLE TO PRESENT A PLAN THAT WILL LINK SHAWNEE AND CHICKASAW PARKS WITH THE CITY OF LOUISVILLE, AND WITH ALL THE HISTORY THAT LIES BETWEEN.

In October 1990 Humana, Inc. announced that the main Belknap building would be converted into a modern office complex housing 2,500 employees. Life was returning to West Main Street, and progress was becoming obvious. The WDC Board of Directors recommended the removal of billboards from the park's proximity, and efforts began to purchase and eliminate existing signage visible from the Park property. With everything seeming to move together in the same direction, it was the time to make one of the most important decisions in the history of Waterfront Park, the selection of the designer to bring together the vision of what could, and should, be built. This architect, or architectural firm, would create the blueprint and planning document for all design and build activities in the park, the Waterfront Master Plan.

The Three Angels

Louisvillians have a long tradition of helping their neighbors. Perhaps it was due to the persistent memory of floods past, when everyone became their brother's keeper, but organized charities were established at an early era in the community. Numerous benevolent institutions, financed by various denominations and ethnic groups, were a mainstay of local life. The building of the Louisville Marine Hospital in 1822, and the city's response during the Civil War with its support of the U.S. Sanitary Commission, underscored the charitable nature of Louisvillians.

"Make the World More Beautiful Than You Found It," was the motto of the Outdoor Art League of Louisville which, since its founding in 1902, had worked to beautify the city and improve the lives of its citizens. The organization was composed of wealthy ladies of society, normally the wives of successful businessmen, who gathered together to affect change in their home town. Although they were privy to lives

of comfort and relaxation, they chose to expend considerable effort and financial resources to improve conditions for others. By organizing programs that established gardens at neighborhood schools, planted flowers around their husbands factories, organized an annual city-wide clean up or created the Mamie Varble Stratton Park for the children of the Louisville waterfront, these wealthy dowagers were motivated by the highest goals. Charitable efforts of ladies like Mrs. John Miller, Mrs. Breaux Ballard and others set high standards of behavior, comportment and responsibility, and they were widely admired and respected. Their generosity and commitment made Louisville a much better place to live.

At a most critical stage in the future of the Waterfront Park, two such modern-day ladies of wealth stepped primly forward. Mrs. W. L. Lyons (Sally) Brown and Mrs. Barry (Mary) Bingham opened their purses and their minds and, in doing so, enabled the waterfront revitalization movement to advance. Long known for their philanthropic work, each had gained valuable insight into solid management practices by their service on not-for-profit boards and as charity trustees. Sally Brown and Mary Bingham added their influential weight to the Park effort, and in doing so made success possible.

Barry and Mary Bingham had sponsored the Falls Fountain to draw attention to Louisville's waterfront, and they donated $500,000 for the purchase of the Martin Marietta building to be WDC headquarters. That helped establish a beachhead for actual programming on the river's edge. Sally Brown, matriarch of the Louisville's Brown-Forman distilling empire, was a renowned environmental advocate active in many organizations.

What was needed at this particular time was a process for locating and hiring a world-class landscape architect to mastermind the design process. Mrs. Bingham and Mrs. Brown each gave $150,000 to help fund the development of the Master Plan. David Jones, already responsible for a huge investment in saving and renovating the Belknap buildings and creating the new Presbyterian Center, again opened his wallet and donated an additional $150,000.

With $450,000 in hand, the Waterfront Development Corporation was ready to begin the process of selecting its designer.

David Karem vividly remembers the doors opened by the generosity of these lead donors.

…THAT WAS A REALLY CRITICAL PIECE OF THE THING, BECAUSE HAVING THAT PRIVATE MONEY GAVE YOU AN ENORMOUS AMOUNT OF FREEDOM TO HIRE – YOU WERE FREE FROM POLITICAL CONCERNS SO SOMEONE DIDN'T GO OUT AND HIRE THEIR BEST FRIEND TO DO THE JOB. AND IT WAS VERY TRANSPARENT, AND ARMED WITH THAT MONEY, WE HAD THE FREEDOM TO MAKE IT UP.

WE CAME UP WITH THIS MADCAP SCHEME TO DEVELOP A REQUEST FOR QUALIFICATIONS, TO RUN AN AD IN THE *NY TIMES*, ARCHITECTURE MAGAZINES AND *COURIER-JOURNAL*. JIM WALTERS, OF BRAVURA, HAD BEEN UNDERWRITTEN BY DAVID JONES TO DO THE GRAY BOOK, SORT OF LIKE A ROAD-MAP TO THE BACKGROUND OF SITE INFORMATION, OTHER INFORMATION. AT THIS POINT WE KNEW WHAT WE WERE ASKING FOR WAS A PARK. WE HAD A HUGE RESPONSE FROM THE SERIES OF ADS WE RAN. WE HAD WELL OVER 100, CLOSE TO 125 DIFFERENT FIRMS RESPOND. BY THIS POINT THERE WAS GETTING TO BE A BUZZ AROUND THE COUNTRY THAT LOUISVILLE WAS GOING TO DO SOMETHING.

The Selection Committee for the choice of the Master Plan designer was as blue-ribbon as Louisville has ever produced. Chaired by David Karem, the group included Mayor Jerry Abramson, Alderman Paul Bather, Mrs. Barry Bingham, Sr., Phil Bond of the Metro United Way, Mrs. W. L. Lyons Brown, Grady Clay, architect Alvin Cox, David A. Jones, WDC board chair A. Stevens Miles and developer Bill Weyland.

Of this elite group, the addition of Grady Clay would prove invaluable. Clay, a nationally respected Louisville writer, speaker and urban-affairs specialist, was the founding editor of the influential publication, *Landscape Architect* magazine. As one of the most respected voices of intelligent architectural design, Grady Clay brought a lifetime of experience and an exacting demand for accurate data and technical proficiency to the project before he would recommend any designer. Again, David Karem recalls that time.

GRADY CLAY – AFTER AGREEING – CAME DOWN AND SPENT ENDLESS HOURS IN THIS BUILDING. HE AND ROWLAND MILLER, AN ARCHITECT, REALLY SPENT A LOT OF TIME. WE GOT THESE 100-PLUS PROPOSALS, AND THE FIRST PASS WAS EASY. ABOUT 50 WERE INAPPROPRIATE. WHEN WE GOT DOWN TO 15, THAT'S WHEN GRADY HAD OUR STAFF CALL AND FERRET OUT WHY THEY (THE CANDIDATE) DID SUCH-AND-SUCH, AND IF IT WASN'T SOMETHING GRADY LIKED, THEY WERE OUT. WE GOT DOWN TO FOUR FINALISTS. WE DECIDED TO TAKE A TWO WEEK PERIOD OF TIME AND GET EACH FIRM HERE FOR A DAY, AND ON THE FIFTH DAY WE MADE THE SELECTION. DAVID JONES LOANED US THE TOP FLOOR OF THE HUMANA BUILDING. IN THE MORNINGS WE WENT OVER THEIR CREDENTIALS AND THEY WENT OVER THEIR PROJECTS. WE WEREN'T ASKING THEM TO DESIGN ANYTHING, BUT WANTED TO KNOW THEIR THOUGHTS. WE OFFERED EACH OF THEM $3,500, ENOUGH FOR OUT OF POCKET TRAVEL EXPENSES, AND THAT LENT AN AIR OF SINCERITY TO THE THING.

THE SELECTION MEETING ON THE FIFTH DAY TOOK ABOUT FOUR MINUTES AND IT WAS INSTANTLY AGREED THAT IT WAS TO BE HARGREAVES ASSOCIATES, EVERYBODY WAS COMPLETELY CAPTIVATED WITH THEM. AND THAT FIRM WAS SELECTED.

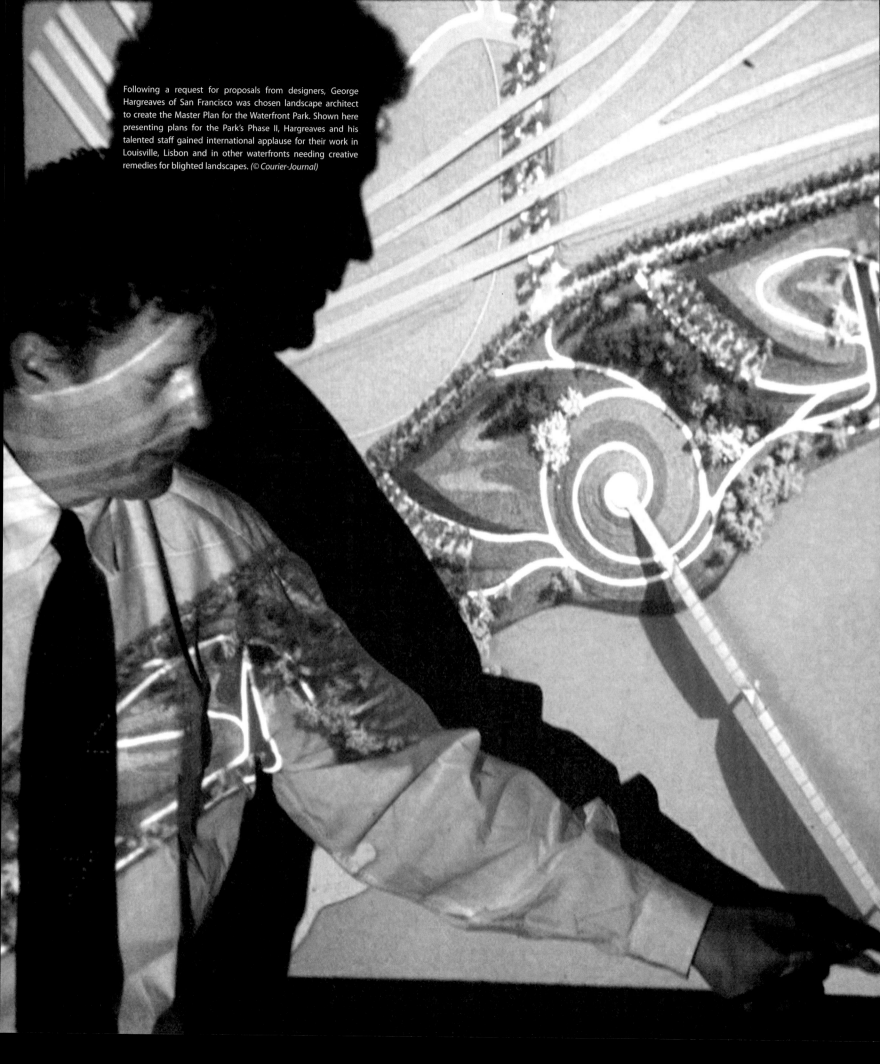

Following a request for proposals from designers, George Hargreaves of San Francisco was chosen landscape architect to create the Master Plan for the Waterfront Park. Shown here presenting plans for the Park's Phase II, Hargreaves and his talented staff gained international applause for their work in Louisville, Lisbon and in other waterfronts needing creative remedies for blighted landscapes. (© Courier-Journal)

A Master Plan and its Creative Source

(1990)

The Waterfront Master Plan is not conceived as a generic waterfront development project that merely facilitates activities next to the river. Rather, it is seen as an opportunity to respect the history and character of Louisville; to create a place where nature and the city meet in a way that is unique to this time and place.

— Waterfront Development Corporation - 1988

Of the four applicants making the Master Plan final cut, Hargreaves Associates of San Francisco was immediately recognized as the most imaginative. The New York firm of Cooper Robertson offered a rather generic turnkey proposal; EDAW, of San Francisco and London, provided a little more involvement and originality, and M. Paul Friedberg presented a strong, but rather orthodox vision of the Park. The young firm of George Hargreaves Associates, an emerging landscape architectural design company from San Francisco, had already garnered attention and applause for their waterside improvements to Candlestick Park and their imaginative treatment of Fiddler's Green in Colorado.

Unbeknownst to the Waterfront Development Corporation George Hargreaves had quietly visited the Louisville site and walked most of the river corridor prior to submitting his plan. While the three other competing firms had well-established professional reputations and signature looks to their work, Hargreaves specifically addressed the needs of the Louisville project, rejecting transplanted ideas from other models.

Aided by an engaging personality and imposing physical presence, Hargreaves confidently combined a mastery of design principles with a gift for creating special features. He had demonstrated an appreciation of event spaces with his "powerful earthscape when no one is in the amphitheatre" at his award-winning Fiddler's Green Amphitheatre, a project combining simple design solutions with reasonably priced construction methods. The Hargreaves firm believed in incorporating historical research of a site and was especially aware of environmental conditions.

Following his selection as the designer of Louisville's Waterfront Park and the acceptance of his Master Plan proposal, George Hargreaves' national and international reputation soared. A profile in the December 1995 edition of *Landscape Architecture* magazine by John Beardsley, written just five years after becoming the Louisville park designer, examined the dynamic design force that is George Hargreaves. In the article, Hargreaves was hailed as the "Poet of Landscape Process."

SOMETIMES IT SEEMS AS IF GEORGE HARGREAVES HAS NEVER ENCOUNTERED A PIECE OF DERELICT LAND THAT HE COULDN'T LEARN TO LOVE. FROM THE TATTERED WATERFRONTS OF LISBON AND LOUISVILLE TO THE LANDFILLS OF SAN FRANCISCO BAY, HARGREAVES PERFORMS A KIND OF ALCHEMY IN WHICH THE DROSS OF

THE POSTINDUSTRIAL LANDSCAPE IS TRANSFORMED INTO SOMETHING APPROXIMATING GOLD. IN THE PROCESS, HE IS BEGINNING TO TRANSMUTE THE PROFESSION ITSELF, COMBINING A STRONG SCULPTURAL LANGUAGE WITH A SENSITIVITY TO BOTH ENVIRONMENTAL PROCESS AND SOCIAL HISTORY AND CREATING A NEW TYPE OF PUBLIC SPACE — ONE RICH IN SYMBOLIC AND METAPHORICAL ASSOCIATES.

The article detailed George Hargreaves' training at the School of Environmental Design at the University of Georgia where he earned his BLA in 1977. He then went on to Harvard's Graduate School of Design. After receiving his MLA in 1979, he joined the SWA Group of Sausalito, California, where he impressed his co-workers at the beginning of his working career.

HE HAD A BROAD INTELLIGENCE AND A COMPREHENSIVE TALENT THAT ENCOMPASSED BOTH DESIGN AND BUSINESS SKILLS. SWA PUT HIM ON AN ACCELERATED TRACK AND MADE HIM A PRINCIPAL AFTER JUST TWO YEARS. IN RETURN HARGREAVES BROUGHT THE FIRM CONSIDERABLE VISIBILITY. HIS DESIGN FOR HARLEQUIN PLAZA IN AN OFFICE PARK IN ENGLEWOOD, COLORADO, ATTRACTED MEDIA ATTENTION IN BOTH ART AND ARCHITECTURE PUBLICATIONS; IT WON AWARDS — THE FIRST OF DOZENS THAT HARGREAVES WOULD GARNER OVER THE NEXT FEW YEARS.

IN EARLY 1983 HARGREAVES LEFT THE SWA GROUP TO START HIS OWN FIRM, AND LANDED A SERIES OF PUBLIC PROJECTS IN THE BAY AREA THAT FINALLY ESTABLISHED HIM. THESE PROJECTS ALL INVOLVED ENVIRONMENTAL REMEDIATION.

ALL THESE PROJECTS SHARE ANOTHER QUALITY: THEY USE STRONG SCULPTURAL FORMS TO CREATE WHAT HARGREAVES CALLS "A THEATER OF THE ENVIRONMENT." HE HAS CREATED A CONTEXT IN WHICH WE INTERACT WITH THE ELEMENTS — EARTH, WIND, AND WATER. THIS

RESULTS IN A LANDSCAPE THAT IS NATURAL, BUT, AS HARGREAVES PARADOXICALLY ACKNOWLEDGES, "NOT NATURAL-LOOKING."

AS COMPELLING AS HARGREAVES'S BUILT WORKS ARE, HE MAY JUST BE HITTING HIS STRIDE. THE TRAJECTORY IN HIS WORK IS MOVING TOWARD EVER MORE COMPLEX AND EXPRESSIVE PROJECTS EVEN AS HE MAINTAINS HIS COMMITMENT TO THE RESTORATION OF THE BLIGHTED PUBLIC LANDSCAPE. PLANS SUGGEST THAT HE IS WEAVING TOGETHER THE SCULPTURAL, SOCIAL, ENVIRONMENTAL, AND PRACTICAL THREADS OF HIS WORK WITH INCREASING SOPHISTICATION AND DEFTNESS; HIS REACH IS BECOMING MORE LIKE THAT OF FREDERICK LAW OLMSTED, FROM WHOSE WORK HE DRAWS INSPIRATION. LOUISVILLE RESIDENT GRADY CLAY, A FORMER EDITOR OF *LANDSCAPE ARCHITECTURE* AND A LONGTIME ADMIRER OF HARGREAVES'S WORK, HAS BEEN MONITORING THE PROGRESS OF THE PARK; HE CALLS IT "THE MOST EXCITING PIECE OF LANDSCAPE IN THIS PART OF THE COUNTRY. YOU'LL EXPERIENCE THE RIVER IN A WAY YOU NEVER COULD BEFORE, WITH A MORE-THAN-ONE-HUNDRED-EIGHTY-DEGREE BURST OF VISIBILITY."

DENNIS RUBBA PUTS IT SUCCINCTLY: "IT'S AMAZING HE GETS THESE THINGS BUILT." TO SOME DEGREE HIS SUCCESS MAY REFLECT THE ENORMITY OF THE PROBLEMS CONFRONTING THE PUBLIC SECTOR AND THE CORRESPONDING NEED FOR COMPREHENSIVE SOLUTIONS. BUT IT MAY ALSO HAVE SOMETHING TO DO WITH HARGREAVES'S MASTERY OF THE POLITICAL PROCESS AND HIS ABILITY TO PRESENT HIS IDEAS IN THE PUBLIC FORUM. CLAY REPORTS THAT HARGREAVES'S CLIENT IN LOUISVILLE, THE WATERFRONT DEVELOPMENT CORPORATION, "HAS BEEN VERY ASSIDUOUS ABOUT PROTECTING HIS DESIGN. GEORGE IS AN ELOQUENT AND PRECISE EXPLAINER OF HIS WORK. THIS GIVES HIS PLAN CONSIDERABLE POLITICAL BACKING."

HARGREAVES RECOGNIZES THE SAME ECUMENICAL SKILLS IN THE OTHER LONG-TIME PRINCIPALS IN HIS FIRM, GLENN ALLEN AND MARY MARGARET JONES. "I LOOK FOR PEOPLE WHO CAN DRAW, DESIGN, AND MANAGE AT THE SAME TIME," HARGREAVES EXPLAINS, "RATHER THAN SEPARATING PROJECT DESIGN AND PROJECT MANAGEMENT."

George Hargreaves was more than a gifted designer, he also became a central figure in building public excitement and raising the considerable private funding needed to build Waterfront Park. "We trolled him out as bait for donations, and we teased him, we don't mind taking him out to help raise money," said David Karem, noting Hargreaves six-foot-three height and good looks. "In another life, he would have been a wonderful fixture in Hollywood."

Following the successful implementation of his master plan, George Hargreaves became a major force in international landscape design projects. David Karem reflected that at the time of their selection for Louisville's Waterfront Park, Hargreaves' company "was a very young firm, one office in San Francisco. Now they have an office in New York, Cambridge, London and San Francisco. They designed all the spaces at the Sydney Olympics and are now planning the grounds for the 2012 London Olympics. A lot of people are saying, and it's not an overreach to say, he is the Olmsted of today."

"...an unparalleled urban waterfront that is distinctively Louisville."

After the selection of Hargreaves, and a period of contract negotiations on fees, philosophy and scheduling, the Waterfront Development Corporation announced details of its Master Plan. With the strong support of the WDC board chair, Charles McCarty, the foundation document of Louisville's Waterfront Park was ready for public presentation and reaction. It is a sweeping vision of lofty intent coupled with practical considerations, and although not all of the ideas ended up being built, the Master Plan delineated the future of Waterfront Park.

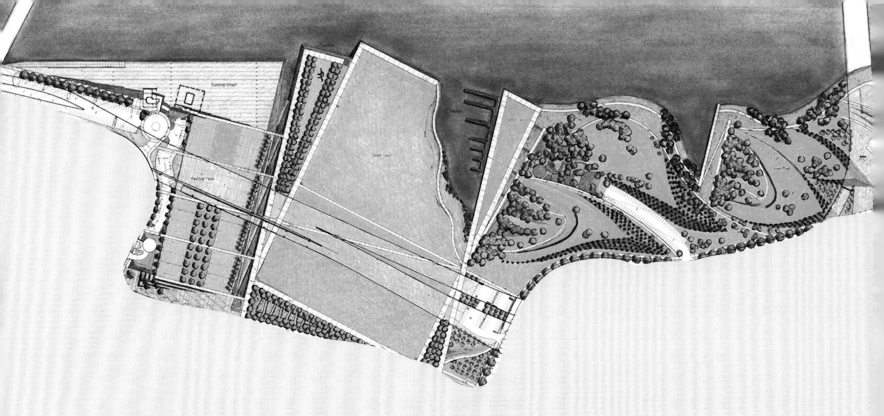

The Master Plan Purpose:

For the people of Louisville and the surrounding community, the Ohio River is a unique and powerful force in daily life. The city's history is inseparably intertwined with commerce and industry on the river, and the collective image of the city – held in the minds of Louisvillians today – is that of the riverfront. The people of Louisville see in this Master Plan the opportunity to reclaim their riverfront heritage.

The Waterfront Master Plan is not conceived as a generic waterfront development project that merely facilitates activities next to the river. Rather, it is seen as an opportunity to respect the history and character of Louisville; to create a place where nature and the city meet in a way that is unique to this time and place.

Louisville, at the end of the twentieth century, has outgrown its dependence on its wharf and industrial waterfront. Most of the land has long since been abandoned. The Master Plan envisions a new kind of interaction between people and the Ohio, with some of the natural character of the river – as the original source of life for the city – recaptured, and use of the waterfront turned over to the people of Louisville.

Through an open and interactive design process, a flexible and powerful master plan concept was developed; a concept that can be realized over time – while responding to infrastructure improvements – to guide and control new development. Its goal is to achieve a waterfront and park truly unique to Louisville, embodying those qualities of site and life that are special to the inhabitants of the region.

The Master Plan responds to the community's desires and aspirations:

- Let the river be a river.

- Let the people of Louisville have green space by the river.

- Let the Waterfront design come from the natural ecology of the river's shore, and find its way into the city.

- Let the city edge be redesigned to preserve, enhance and

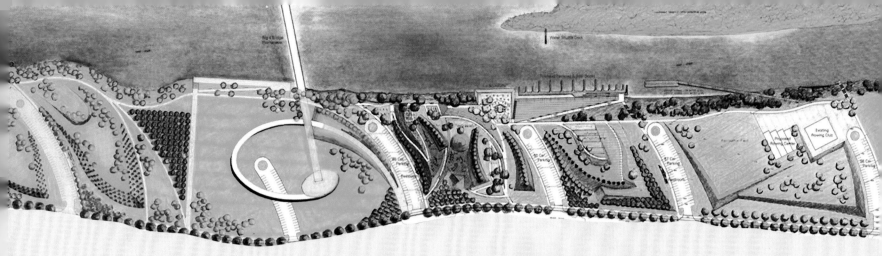

respect the classic grid pattern and density established in the early years of the city as it grew out of the wilderness.

- Let the urban force on the one side meet the natural continuum of the Ohio River on the other, in a people-oriented place that attracts active participation.

- Let the evolution of Louisville meld the natural setting of the Waterfront with the development needs of a large city.

The resulting master plan must also be flexible and buildable, and must allow for phasing that can respond to funding opportunities as they arise.

The Louisville Waterfront Master Plan reinforces a romantic image of the city's culture, vitality and history, as held in the minds of the people who live there. The creation of this important civic open space will lead to residential and commercial revitalization, resulting in an unparalleled urban waterfront that is distinctively Louisville.

Overview of Design Process:

The design process leading to the creation of the Waterfront Master Plan has been an open and interactive investigation, probing the desires and objectives of the citizens of Louisville and the region. Emphasizing public input in the planning and design process, the WDC sponsored a series of public forums in an effort to assemble community ideas for incorporation into the master plan program design. Additionally, input was offered by

private individuals, and Louisville's state and local agencies.

The dominant theme of public input into this process can be characterized as a desire to rejoin public activity with the river and its natural systems. Throughout the process the word "green" was heard over and over again. However, there was also a strong desire for public activities along the waterfront that would require hard paved surfaces. Due to the size of the waterfront area, these two public goals are not mutually exclusive.

Site Conditions:

The land between River Road and the river's edge is roughly low-lying and level, sloping steeply from the top of the bank at (plus or minus) 440' elevation to the river's normal pool elevation of (plus or minus) 420' above sea level. The bank is mostly stabilized with large rocks and sparse riparian vegetation. Land gently slopes upward between the riverbank and River Road with minimal elevation change. South of River Road the topography continues sloping upward to Main Street, where elevations are typically (plus or minus) 463'.

Since the 1937 flood, the Flood Control System along the Ohio has been improved by the U.S. Army Corps of Engineers and their construction requirements for flood protection. Today, the river profile anticipates a 100-year flood level of +450'. An additional one foot of free-board above the 100-year level results in a recommended flood protection level of +451.0'. This is the elevation considered in the planning of all waterfront development.

The sprawling "Spaghetti Junction" where three interstate highways merge and attempt to cross the same bridge presented one of the greatest design challenges for Waterfront Park planners. Tens of thousands of vehicles, directly overhead of many of the main park attractions, passed through the planned heart of Waterfront Park.

Master Plan Concept:

The Master Plan concept is also about connections:

• Primeval connections between human beings and ecological process.

• Historical connections between the abandoned industrial waterfront and its legacy as a flourishing commercial center.

• Geographic connections between communities east and west of the downtown waterfront.

• Recreational connections allowing pedestrians and bicyclists barrier-free access along the entire river frontage.

• Real physical connections between downtown and the river.

• And lastly, a connection between Louisville (the city, the river and the people) and the future.

Handicapped Accessibility:

All components within the Master Plan will be fully accessible to the handicapped, the elderly and users with special mobility considerations (such as baby strollers). Ramps will be constructed wherever necessary to conform with public safety specification and local and federal handicapped access codes.

Bicycles:

Proposed bicycle routes through the project site have the potential to connect existing paths in adjacent parks and open spaces, creating a bicycle path network throughout the city. Thruston Park, to the east of the site, connects via a path along River Road. A Chickasaw Park connector to the west (for which a bike path extension has already been recommended) establishes the path network from Thruston Park to Shawnee Park along the river's edge.

Service and Emergency Access:

Service and emergency access are crucial to the successful functioning of any master plan. Various components of the Waterfront Master Plan, while primarily pedestrian zones, have been designated to accommodate service and emergency vehicles in all locations. Service and emergency access ways are provided within the Waterfront Plaza, Great Lawn and Harbor, and Linear Park.

The design of these access ways, while pedestrian in appearance, will accommodate service and emergency vehicles with the appropriate paving support, truck turning radii, access width and length, and lighting.

Grading:

Existing flood-walls protect only the western portion of the planning area, and from between Floyd and Preston out to the east. The grading scheme for the waterfront development area of the Master Plan raises the elevation of Witherspoon, from approximately Brook to I-65, to 451', closing the gap between the existing flood walls. Finished floor elevations throughout the Waterfront are held above 451.5'. Together with proposed flood wall improvements, including gates across Second Street and Bingham Way, and a pumping station at Bingham Way, this completes the flood protection system for the Waterfront area.

Waterfront Plaza:

As the hard urban wharf area of the Waterfront Park and planning area, the Waterfront Plaza serves as a major downtown public open space, accommodating festivals, celebrations and special events year-round. The plaza, a 2.5-acre, hard-surface area, is designed to hold crowds as large as 15,000 persons, such as those that congregate for the Kentucky Derby Festival Chow Wagon. Within the plaza, a bosque of shade trees provides protection from summer sun and heat, and creates smaller spaces for intimate social gatherings.

The Waterfront Plaza, beneath Interstate 64, is designed to accommodate portable food stands and entertainment venues. Built-in utility access, proximity to restrooms and a stain-resistant crushed rock ground covering allowed for the practical considerations of feeding thousands of people at the annual Derby Chow Wagon and other events.

Chow Wagon and Seasonal Events:

Since its beginning in 1972, the Chow Wagon has become one of the most popular events of the Kentucky Derby Festival. Live music, food and drink and other activities attract crowds in excess of 30,000 daily, and 15,000 people at one time.

Greg January, a member of the maintenance crew of Waterfront Park, mows some of the forty-five acres of lawn on the grounds. Special lawn-keeping techniques, and constant year-round care, keep the Park fresh and ready for use. During the busy months following the Kentucky Derby Festival, tens of thousands of visitors gather to enjoy the Independence Festival, Waterfront Wednesday concerts and untold numbers of family picnics and parties.

The Great Lawn:

The Great Lawn is the centerpiece of the Downtown Waterfront Master Plan. Viewed from tall buildings, I-64, the river, or from street level, the Great Lawn will be the waterfront's most distinctive open space – "the public civic room" at the water. The Great Lawn is a frame magnifying the relationship between river and people.

The 14-acre lawn provides a transition between the shoreline and the downtown environment. Conceptually, the Great Lawn is an emblematic reenactment of the European settlement of Louisville's mainland – of westward expansion and colonization – of creating a clearing in the woods.

The tilted green plane of the Great Lawn touches the river's edge and extends to Witherspoon Street, rising a total of 28 feet. The sidewalk along the river edge of the lawn maintains a minimum height of 3' above normal pool elevation. The tilt of the lawn and its lowered elevation as it slips under Interstate 64 reduces the psychological and visual impact of the interstate passing overhead. Lowering the land under the interstate passing overhead opens expansive views of the river and Indiana shore.

Harbor Inlet:

Pulling the river in toward the city, the Harbor Inlet represents the outlet of Beargrass Creek, and the return of river traffic into the city – re-establishing the core's historic connection to wharf commerce.

Linear Park:

Linear Park is a place where natural and cultural phenomena meet at the river's edge; where the natural character of the Ohio

River penetrates the urban environment of downtown Louisville. Running along the river's edge north of River Road from the eastern edge of the Great Lawn to Towhead Island, Linear Park is a 3000' long area of approximately 50 acres, varying in width from 500' to 800'. Designed as a pedestrian space, Linear Park reclaims the industrial riverfront for nature and for the enjoyment of the entire community.

The plan creates Upland Play Meadows, Lowland Meadows, Inlets and Islands with landforms, vegetation and the water's edge. *(Plans for creating new inlets and islands were later dropped from the Master Plan due to anticipation of maintenance difficulties.)* The exposed upland "plinths" and protected lowland valleys recall the historic natural landscape of the Ohio Valley, while providing places of prospect and refuge – for outdoor activities and environmental interaction.

Security:

Designed within the National Crime Prevention Institute guidelines for natural surveillance, the landforms of Linear Park are situated so that all portions of the park are visible from the parking lots placed at 750' intervals along the length of the park. The path system is lighted by 8' high pedestrian fixtures at 60' intervals, providing safe, easy access from the river's edge to River Road throughout the park.

Maintenance:

For continuity and quality of maintenance, and for an ongoing presence in the park, it is suggested that the Waterfront Development Corporation provide a level of service beyond traditional park maintenance. This will address the need for unique maintenance requirements and will add visible security.

Upland Play Meadows:

Upland play areas, or Activity Plinths, are exposed landforms rising out of Linear Park. Resembling man-made objects while reflecting the dendritic drainage patterns of the Ohio Basin, the raised nature of these areas provides for "prospect" – spectacular views up and down river. The plinths gently slope toward the river, giving prospect to other components of the park and providing abundant space for recreational play. Upland areas are sparsely vegetated, forming large turf areas of active recreational play.

Lowland Play Meadows:

Inspired by the flow of river water, the landforms create lowland meadow areas suitable for active or passive uses.

Children's Play Area:

The Children's Play Area is an active recreation and imaginative play zone. While the entire Waterfront Park is designed to be kid-oriented, this area gives children their own place within which to experience the natural wonders and processes of the Ohio River. Children will play in a secured area with restroom facilities provided. The play area is tucked between sculpted earth forms planted with a variety of vegetation that recall land-forming processes specific to the waterfront site. The play area will provide children with a special environment to experience the outdoors and learn from their surroundings.

Concluding Remarks:

In broad philosophic strokes, the Master Plan seeks to pull into the 21st century the cultural waterfront heritage of the 18th and 19th centuries, to interpret and restore the ecology of the river as it was before western civilization, and to extend downtown Louisville to the river – and conversely, magnify the presence of the river and extend the river into downtown. In so doing the Waterfront can become a vessel for public activities, with the natural systems of the Ohio Valley generating its structure and power. However, it is the spirit of the people who will fill this space that adds the final dynamic.

The Waterfront Plan should be seen as a continuum – downstream to upstream; where a river-city embraces its river downstream, and the Ohio embraces its own natural systems upstream. Across this continuum a broad range of public activities are available.

Louisville's Waterfront, as delineated here, draws heavily upon the Ohio River and the Falls for inspiration and subject. As the mighty river pursues its course along the Louisville bank, this Master Plan seeks to rejoin the public of the region to its source – in a bond that is readily apparent and permanent. However, the Plan is just a beginning. Only by its implementation can the vision begin to be realized, and when done, the citizens of the present will be presenting to future generations a legacy that has no equal.

Building Guidelines - General Objectives:

The creation of a new, green open space at the river's edge in downtown will create development opportunities on bordering land. The new park will be of such importance not only to downtown, but to the entire region, that the pattern of building development must be guided to assure that the City's objectives for its waterfront are met.

Therefore, it is essential to support the goals of the Downtown Plan that apply specifically to this area:

- First, it is extremely important to develop residential uses adjacent to the park, to create continuous public activity, and to create a constituency for the park that will protect it and be sure that it is cared for. There must be a sufficient density, therefore, to create a true neighborhood, which is part of both downtown and the new waterfront.

- Second, retail and offices should be included in areas adjacent to the neighborhood to further reinforce the day-long and weekend use of the park and surrounding streets.

- Third, the building forms which edge the park must contain large open areas and be of such architectural interest that they create a "sense of place" that is unique to Louisville. The buildings along New York's Central Park and the Boston Common do just that for their open spaces.

- Fourth, it is important that the park be strongly linked to downtown. Therefore, the north-south streets which connect Main Street to the Great Lawn must be wide, landscaped places that create gracious auto and pedestrian gateways. Also, it is necessary that specific buildings along the Park be tall, unique forms that are visible from other parts of downtown; they must be evident symbols that the park and river are "here," offering a sense of destination for the waterfront and connection to downtown.

- Finally, views of the river must be created and preserved as development takes place. Louisville loves to see its river and its parks, as well as to use them; therefore, one development cannot take place at the expense of another's view.

Design Principles:

New buildings should reflect the character of the existing. East Main Street, especially, can in the future be seen as a part of historic West Main Street if new buildings are appropriately designed.

With a designer in hand, and the Master Plan published for scrutiny and review, the next step of the process of park-making was implementation. It was time to build a park at the river's edge.

The site of the Great Lawn prior to construction indicates an urban landscape devoid of vegetation and filled with reminders of its industrial past. The huge Belknap complex of warehouses, loading docks and rail lines dominated the waterfront and blocked access to the Ohio River.

Acquiring the Assets
(1991-1994)

With the public release of the Master Plan, people around the community became aware of the scope and potential of a major parkland installation on Louisville's waterfront. The idea excited imaginations, and public discussion of the project became commonplace. Executive Director David Karem realized that the public must be engaged as soon as possible. Karem's words recall that optimistic time.

THE REACTION WAS SOMEWHAT ENERGIZED — WE WERE WONDERFULLY NAÏVE. IF YOU WEREN'T NAÏVE YOU WOULD LET YOURSELF BE STIFLED AT EVERY CORNER. WE STARTED GETTING PUBLIC REACTION. EVERY PLACE WE COULD GO AND TALK ABOUT IT, WE WENT. ABOUT 100 PRESENTATIONS A YEAR FOR THREE YEARS, ANYONE WHO WANTED TO HEAR US TALK, WE WENT THERE. GARDEN CLUBS, SENIOR CITIZENS' LUNCHES, NEIGHBORHOOD GROUPS, ROTARY CLUB, EVERYTHING — DOING THOSE PRESENTATIONS AND GETTING PEOPLE EXCITED. WE CAME IN AND DID A COUPLE OF THINGS. WE HAD THE CHOW WAGON, SO WE SPENT A LITTLE MONEY TO DO SOME BLACKTOPPING. THE OLD MARTIN MARIETTA PIER WAS STILL THERE, SO WE PUT IN A PATH TO IT — A CRUSHED BRICK SURFACE BETWEEN RAILROAD TIES — AND PEOPLE STARTED USING IT FOR EXERCISE. WE WERE JUST DOING THINGS TO KEEP THE PUBLIC'S ATTENTION.

THE OTHER STRATEGIC THING WAS I ASKED EVERYONE ON STAFF TO DO PRESENTATIONS, SO THAT AS MANY PEOPLE

Rather than divide the park into permanent sports installations like tennis courts or ball fields, the Waterfront Park design accommodates less-structured recreation, where participants bring their own equipment and make up their own games. Touch football, kite-flying or tossing a Frisbee are the most commonly seen activities on the Great Lawn.

AS POSSIBLE COULD GO OUT AND DO A TALK ON IT. WE HAD A SELF-GENERATING GROUP CALLED THE FRIENDS OF THE WATERFRONT AND THEY WENT OUT AND ENERGIZED THE COMMUNITY.

We expected it to take years and years. It's part of the openness of truth, to tell people it's a long-term project that will take years to do, and when it's done, it will never be complete. There will always be something to retrofit or repair, the park will never be finished.

Take the sports thing. We have had many people over the years ask, Where are the tennis courts? Where are the basketball courts? We said it's an 85-acre park and we aren't going to do something that is dedicated to one particular sport. If somebody wants to come on the Great Lawn, they can play Frisbee or football or fly kites. Here you have eighty-five acres that need to be available to everybody — it works best to leave it as flexible as possible.

Mountains of Paper

To make those eighty-five acres available, small mountains of studies, estimates, planning documents, reports and more reports were required. The WDC retained the Louisville architectural firm of Bravura, led by its chief, Jim Walters, to prepare an Implementation Strategy for Hargreaves' Master Plan. In the document's executive summary, the following points were reported.

- All tasks necessary for the Master Plan Implementation were identified.

- Four areas were defined as Pre-Development Activities: 1) Master Plan Refinement, 2) U.S. Army Corps of Engineers' Permitting Process, 3) The Site Survey/Collection of Technical Data, and 4) Project Coordination Activities.

- For scheduling and cost estimating purposes, seventeen Development Packages were identified.

As the Waterfront Development Corporation acquired land for the park, ownership of many of the numerous gigantic billboards lining I-64 was secured by Waterfront Park. A program of eliminating the unsightly signage and improving the approach to the city was instituted.

- The best case schedule for implementation of the Waterfront Plan was projected to take place from December 1991 to May 1997.

- The Louisville Waterfront Development Corporation could use the scheduling computer data to modify the schedule and sequence of Development Packages.

- The estimated total cost to implement the plan, excluding land acquisition, but including Pre-Development Activities, infrastructure cost and fees/expenses, was set at $90,328,900 in current 1992 dollars, or $101,378,000 if inflated as 1999 dollars.

A serious document for a serious project, the Implementation Strategy set in motion the planning mechanism, which in turn quickly presented the financial realities of the park project. As details were sharpened, a true understanding of the funding challenges became clear. The WDC staff's commitment to appearing before any and every community gathering paid dividends when the board of directors asked the community for a great deal of support.

Comings and Goings at the Louisville Wharf

As the small asphalt-covered clearing at the former Martin Marietta building succeeded in drawing daily crowds of walkers, lunch-time visitors and river-gazers, another waterfront attraction was ending its run at the Louisville wharf. The August 30, 1991, edition of *The Courier-Journal* reported a change in the riverfront menu.

ISLANDS, SPLASH LEAVING DOWNTOWN RIVERFRONT AS BUSINESS DECLINES

THE ISLANDS RESTAURANT AND SPLASH NIGHTCLUB ARE LEAVING LOUISVILLE'S RIVERFRONT, WHERE THEY HAVE BEEN MOORED SINCE LATE 1987, MAYOR JERRY ABRAMSON SAID YESTERDAY. BUT HE EXPRESSED OPTIMISM THAT SOMETHING AS GOOD OR BETTER WILL TAKE THEIR PLACE.

THE FRANCHISE AGREEMENT BETWEEN THE BARGE'S OWNERS AND THE CITY LAPSES JULY 31. SCHILLING ENTERPRISES WILL PAY THE CITY ALL LEASE OBLIGATIONS THROUGH THAT DATE, EVEN IF THE BARGES LEAVE BEFORE THEN, ABRAMSON SAID.

ABRAMSON SAID THE CITY WILL ADVERTISE, PROBABLY IN SEVERAL MONTHS, FOR COMPETITIVE PROPOSALS FOR USING THE 500 FEET OF DOWNTOWN WHARF SPACE BEING VACATED BY THE TWIN BARGES.

HE SAID ANY NEW OPERATION PROBABLY WILL INCLUDE A MORE CASUAL RESTAURANT. BUT HE SAID THE CITY DOESN'T WANT TO RULE OUT INCORPORATING OTHER TYPES OF ENTERTAINMENT.

ABRAMSON SAID SPLASH AND THE ISLANDS, WHICH CONVERTED FROM A PUBLIC RESTAURANT TO PRIVATELY CATERED AFFAIRS, WERE PIONEERS AND PROVED THAT PEOPLE ARE INTERESTED IN COMING TO THE WATERFRONT. THE BARGES' REVENUES, HOWEVER, DROPPED FROM $5.7 MILLION IN 1988 TO $2.4 MILLION LAST YEAR.

ABRAMSON SAID THE ISLANDS' EFFORTS AS A FINE-DINING RESTAURANT "PROVED TO BE THE WRONG KIND OF RESTAURANT IN THAT LOCATION." HE SAID THE FAILURE OF WHITE-TABLECLOTH RESTAURANTS HAS BEEN A TREND IN THE RESTAURANT INDUSTRY.

ABRAMSON SAID SEVERAL LOCAL AND OUT-OF-TOWN RESTAURANT OPERATORS HAD EXPRESSED INTEREST IN LOUISVILLE'S WATERFRONT. ABRAMSON SAID RECENT RIVERFRONT DEVELOPMENT SHOULD SPARK SUBSTANTIAL INTEREST IN THE DOCK SPACE.

GENE JOHNSON, A CO-OWNER OF THE *STAR OF LOUISVILLE* DINNER CRUISE SHIP, SAID HE AND HIS PARTNERS MIGHT CONSIDER PROPOSING A RESTAURANT WHEN THE CITY SEEKS BIDS FOR THE DOCK SPACE.

MEANWHILE, DEVELOPER AL SCHNEIDER SAID "NATURALLY, I'M HAPPY" ABOUT THE MOVING OF SPLASH AND THE ISLANDS. SCHNEIDER, WHO OWNS THE RIVERFRONT GALT HOUSE HOTELS, HAS BEEN A CRITIC OF THE TWO BARGES.

As one barge left the wharf, another took its place, although briefly. A museum exhibition barge, equipped with displays of river heritage, arrived for a brief, one-week stay. "Always a River: The Ohio

A multi-state humanities project, "Always a River," spent ten days in Louisville in 1991. A museum on a floating barge, the project stopped at river towns downriver from Pittsburgh providing educational exhibits, special folk-life demonstrations and heritage discussions. Over 175,000 people visited the floating museum in the course of one summer's voyage.

River and the American Experience," a joint project of humanities councils from the river states, spent the summer of 1991 tramping the length of the Ohio. Its 5,000 feet of exhibit space was enjoyed by over 175,000 people as it worked its way downstream from Pittsburgh to Cairo, stopping at many of the smaller river towns for a day, and extending their stay in larger population centers. The large crowds attending the attraction indicated a craving among the public for heritage-related activities at the water's edge.

One element of waterfront heritage finally officially ended about this time. The *Frankfort State Journal* of September 21, 1992, documented the last trace of old Corn Island and the legacy of Judge John Rowan's ownership of the Louisville waterfront.

TITLE TO CORN ISLAND – AS WELL AS HUNDREDS OF OTHER ACRES NOW SUBMERGED – PASSED FROM KING GEORGE III TO HENRY CLAY TO JUDGE JOHN ROWAN, A PIONEER SETTLER OF LOUISVILLE WHO LIVED AT FEDERAL HILL IN BARDSTOWN, THE HOUSE IMMORTALIZED IN "MY OLD KENTUCKY HOME."

BUT THE COLORFUL STORIES HAVEN'T ENDED YET. AS RECENTLY AS 1987, ROWAN'S GREAT-GREAT-GRANDDAUGHTER, ALICE JAMES OF LOUISVILLE, PAID $35 A YEAR FOR 600 ACRES, SUBMERGED LAND – INCLUDING CORN ISLAND.

MS. JAMES SAID SHE DID SO OUT OF SENTIMENTAL REASONS AND TO KEEP ALIVE HER FAMILY'S CLAIM ON THE PROPERTY WHILE IT FOUGHT THE CONDEMNATION OF THE LAND IN COURT. THE FAMILY OPPOSED THE FLOODING OF CORN ISLAND IN LAWSUITS THAT STEMMED FIVE DECADES.

ALTHOUGH MS. JAMES STOPPED PAYING TAXES ON CORN ISLAND WHEN THE FAMILY LOST A LAWSUIT IN 1987, THE JEFFERSON COUNTY TAX COMPUTER IS STILL SENDING HER BILLS.

"I WAS TOLD THEY CAN'T GET (THE SUBMERGED ACREAGE) OUT OF THE COMPUTER."

Moving the Tracks and Attracting Attention

Before final plans could be made, acquisition of the land for the future Waterfront Park had to be completed. To clear the park of railroad tracks running parallel to River Road on the north side of the street, a plan was made to shift these still-viable rails to the south side. In November 1991 Deputy Director Mike Kimmel reported to Mayor Abramson on the progress of negotiations.

RAIL RELOCATION

Appraisals have been conducted on each piece of property on which the new rail will be constructed except for the parcel under the expressway at Clay Street which is controlled by the State Transportation Cabinet and the Federal Highway Administration. We are currently working out an arrangement with them and an appraisal will follow.

Luckily, over 30 parcels impacted by the rail relocation are in the hands of only fourteen owners. We have purchased one property: Ohio Street Auto Parts. Negotiations are currently underway with seven of the eight owners along River Road. The negotiations range from a contract in hand for the Shell property easement to preliminary price discussions for the Bollinger parcel. The final parcel on River Road is owned by the Waterfront Development Corporation. While "negotiations" have not yet begun, it is anticipated that an easement will be purchased at market rates.

Property on Campbell Street is also being negotiated with substantial agreement between us and the primary land owner Mr. Millard. We are also seeing continued progress with another. It appears that the remaining three parcels on Campbell Street must be condemned in order to acquire, as ownership is uncertain owing to deeds that date to the 1800s.

CSX APPROVAL

All plans for relocation of CSX rail lines must be approved by CSX engineers in Jacksonville, Florida. Following a two-month period where our plans were waiting to be reviewed, preliminary conditional approval was given for everything except the bridge. The conditions are currently being resolved. We expect resolution and final drawings to be completed in December.

RIVER ROAD RELOCATION

Kentucky's Transportation Cabinet's "Six-year Plan" includes two projects that will reconstruct River Road between Clay Street and Zorn Avenue as "Parkway." Preliminary designs have been drafted by District 5 and reviewed by both Hargreaves and Bravura.

The CSX Corporation controlled much of the rail and barge services still active on the Louisville waterfront. The corporation and City of Louisville worked closely to accommodate the railroad's current needs and the long-term plans for Park development.

Many eyes were on Louisville and the Waterfront Park plans. In February 1991 Mike Kimmel was invited to participate in the prestigious Wakayama International Conference on Public Spaces Design in Japan, where he shared his expertise in the environmental aspects of riverfront park design. The following year the Master Plan was honored with the National Urban Planning Merit Award from the American Society of Landscape Architects. The Master Plan was saluted for its success in its mission "to reunite the people of Louisville with the city's source and reason for being: the Ohio."

The Check Was Good

While all the technical planning and decision-making by designers, environmental experts, governmental agencies,

David A. Jones (left) was greeted by Mayor Jerry Abramson at the official dedication of the Great Lawn. On right of photo, Kentucky Governor Paul Patton joined in the celebration, where souvenir Frisbees were given out to the audience.

construction managers and urban planners were proceeding, the other essential element – fundraising – was advancing as well. Directed by Board Chair Charles McCarty and David Karem, quiet conversations were held between people and organizations capable of providing generous assistance, and once again David A. Jones was at the center of these efforts. In early December 1992 *The Courier-Journal* provided details on the park's finances.

CALLING REDEVELOPMENT OF THE WATERFRONT "THE MOST SIGNIFICANT CIVIC PROJECT IN LOUISVILLE IN MY LIFETIME," HUMANA INC. CHAIRMAN DAVID JONES EXPRESSED CONFIDENCE YESTERDAY THAT $14 MILLION IN PRIVATE MONEY CAN BE RAISED FOR THE EFFORT.

JONES SAID THAT SOME COMBINATION OF HIMSELF, THE HUMANA FOUNDATION AND HUMANA INC. WILL MATCH A $3 MILLION GIFT PLEDGED TO THE WATERFRONT FUND DRIVE BY THE J. GRAHAM BROWN FOUNDATION.

JONES ANNOUNCED THAT WITH THE HUMANA AND BROWN FOUNDATION PLEDGES, $9.3 MILLION HAS BEEN RAISED TOWARD THE $14 MILLION GOAL. THE MONEY IS SOUGHT IN MATCHING FUNDS TO RELEASE $12.5 MILLION IN STATE AID TO GO TOWARD THE REDEVELOPMENT'S $58 MILLION PHASE I. THE EXTRA $1.5 MILLION IS SOUGHT AS A CUSHION. ADDITIONAL FUNDING FOR PHASE I WILL COME FROM FEDERAL, CITY, COUNTY AND OTHER PRIVATE MONEY.

CIVIC LEADERS HAVE UNTIL JUNE 30 TO MATCH THE STATE MONEY, AS RECOMMENDED BY GOVERNOR BRERETON JONES AND APPROVED BY THE 1992 GENERAL ASSEMBLY.

CIVIC LEADER MARY BINGHAM AND BUSINESSMAN GENE SMITH EACH PLEDGED $1 MILLION TO THE PROJECT. AN ANONYMOUS DONOR GAVE $250,000 AND CITIZENS FIDELITY CORP. $200,000.

PLEDGES OF $100,000 CAME FROM CARL POLLARD, HUMANA'S PRESIDENT; THE LAW FIRM OF WYATT TARRANT & COMBS; AND STEWART COBB AND HIS FAMILY, WHICH IS AFFILIATED WITH THE COBB GROUP. VENCOR INC. PLEDGED $80,000 WHILE GIFTS OF $75,000 CAME FROM CHARLES AND ANN MCCARTY, THE JUNIOR LEAGUE OF LOUISVILLE AND THORNTON OIL.

PLEDGING $50,000 WERE DAVID AND MARLENE GRISSOM, MAREA GARDNER AND HILLIARD LYONS INC.

DAVID JONES SAID SEVERAL BANKS AND OTHER LOCAL CORPORATIONS ARE CONSIDERING GIVING. HE AND CHARLES MCCARTY, WATERFRONT DEVELOPMENT CORP. CHAIRMAN, SAID THE PUBLIC PROBABLY WILL BE ASKED TO CONTRIBUTE WHEN PLEDGES REACH PERHAPS $12 MILLION.

Shortly after this event the Brown-Forman Corporation, one of Louisville's leading industries and a generous supporter of local activities, added an additional pledge of $3 million. A beautiful amphitheater at the extreme east end of the park, opposite "Ulix" McQueen's beloved Towhead Island, was named after the company to honor their support of Waterfront Park.

The story behind the news account is much more interesting than the published facts. The episode became a legendary tale among the Louisville not-for-profit community and everyone present recalled the remarkable moment. Around a large board table, the prime donor candidates sat while campaign chairman David Jones laid out plans for the fundraising campaign. At that time he promised to equal any pledge made before the June 30 state deadline for matching funds.

Mrs. Bingham quietly reached into her purse and took out her checkbook. She sat at the table and wrote a personal check for $1 million, which she passed down to the momentarily-stunned Mr. Jones. In a moment the campaign fund was doubled from Jones' initial challenge and Mrs. Bingham's response. Immediately, the project had $2 million to begin work. Within a very short time, the J. Graham Brown Foundation upped the ante when they pledged $3 million to the project. Jones' one million dollar commitment became three and a total of seven million was now committed. In fundraising nothing succeeds like success, and others in the community stepped forward to join the list of supporters.

WDC Financial Officer Phyllis Williams attended the meeting and remembers being handed Mrs. Bingham's check to deposit. She noticed that she and Mrs. Bingham used the same bank, and their personal checks were of the same pattern. "She wrote a personal check for $1 million while I had to stop and think about writing one for a hundred dollars." The legendary Bingham philanthropy reached an entirely new level.

In June Mayor Abramson presented special Awards of Thanks to Jones, Brown and Bingham for their leadership and generosity. The Friends of the Waterfront presented the trio its Silver Anchor Award in 1993 to echo that appreciation.

Gathering to celebrate the Great Lawn's dedication are (left to right) David K. Karem and Marlene Grissom of the Waterfront Development Corporation staff, with Ina Brown Bond, a member of the board of directors. She is with her mother, Mrs. Sally Brown (on far right), one of Louisville's most active champions of environmental issues and a master gardener in her own right.

In the front row at the Great Lawn dedication, Congressman Romano Mazzoli and Mrs. Mary Bingham join others on the program to officially open the civic commons and to welcome everyone to Louisville's party. Mr. and Mrs. Barry Bingham, Sr. were among the earliest and most active supporters of waterfront renewal, by having first sponsored the Falls Fountain and then providing the funding to acquire the former Ohio River Sand Company to serve as WDC's headquarters.

Another community donor, the Junior League of Louisville, had received the first Silver Anchor award from the Friends of the Waterfront the previous year for their sponsorship of equipment for the Children's Playground.

As the project progressed, other individuals, corporations and foundations stepped up to share in supporting the Park's development. The James Graham Brown Foundation alone donated more than $14 million, in four separate grants, over the life of the project. Eventually, private donations for the Waterfront Development Corporation funded nearly 40 percent of the entire project.

A Thunderous Good Time

The year 1992 would see the establishment of a Louisville institution which would dwarf, for sheer scale, every other public Louisville event. "Thunder Over Louisville," the kick-off event of the annual Kentucky Derby Festival, began rather modestly with a fireworks display, air show and social gathering at the river's edge. The first event in 1992 drew an estimated 70,000 participants, but within a few years, as its reputation as the "nation's largest fireworks display" grew, massive numbers of viewers on both the Indiana and Kentucky shores multiplied. Eventually, crowds of 750,000 people began assembling for the annual event, routinely attracting five times the number of visitors as attended the Derby itself.

While people complained about massive traffic jams following the explosive event at the Waterfront Park, they continued to come each year in increasing numbers, and this was not a new phenomenon at the Louisville waterfront. The June 3, 1900, edition of the *Courier-Journal* had told of a similar event when the national reunion of Confederate veterans met in Louisville and invited the whole town to their party.

PYROTECHNIC DISPLAY FOR THE VETERANS - LIGHTS BLAZE

BETWEEN 40,000 AND 50,000 PERSONS LINED THE RIVERFRONT FROM FIRST STREET TO SIXTH STREET LAST NIGHT TO WITNESS THE FIREWORKS DISPLAY GIVEN IN HONOR OF THE CONFEDERATE VETERANS. THE CROWD BEGAN TO ASSEMBLE AT 7 O'CLOCK AND BY 8 O'CLOCK EVERY AVAILABLE SPACE FROM MAIN STREET TO THE RIVER AND AS FAR AS THE EYE COULD REACH TO THE EAST AND TO THE WEST WAS TAKEN. THE ROOFS OF ALL THE BUILDINGS ON MAIN STREET WERE PACKED WITH PEOPLE, AND HUNDREDS OF OTHERS PERCHED ON THE BIG FOUR BRIDGE, OVERLOOKING THE THOUSANDS ON THE LEVEE BELOW. TO THE EAST, THE BANKS OF THE RIVER WERE ALIVE WITH PEOPLE, AND TO THE WEST WERE AS MANY MORE, STANDING, SITTING OR CROUCHING ON HOUSETOPS AND ON BOATS IN THE RIVER....THE INDIANA SIDE OF THE RIVER, TOO, WAS FILLED WITH PEOPLE, THE CROWDS STRETCHING OUT IN LONG LINES FROM THE BIG FOUR BRIDGE TO A POINT FAR BELOW THE FERRY DOCK....THE RIVER FROM A FEW HUNDRED YARDS ABOVE THE FALLS TO THE BIG FOUR BRIDGE WAS FILLED WITH CRAFT OF ALL DESCRIPTION, AND ALL WERE IN GALA DRESS.

The public's embrace of Thunder Over Louisville caused Kentucky Derby Festival officials to offer more of their growing list of activities in Waterfront Park. What in the past had been a relatively simple run-up to Derby Day, the Great Steamboat Race and Derby Parade, evolved into a two-week festival featuring dozens of diverse events. The Chow Wagon found its permanent home on the grounds and began opening a week earlier to coincide with "Thunder." To support this increased involvement at Waterfront Park, the Derby Festival contributed $100,000 for physical improvements to the grounds.

Other Louisvillians found ways to assist in the Park's development. The Doe-Anderson advertising firm donated graphic design services for promotional brochures to give WDC publications a more professional presentation. In addition,

When the Confederate Veterans came to Louisville for their annual convention in 1900 they produced a free fireworks display enjoyed by an estimated 100,000 on the Louisville waterfront. The large crowds were thrilled by elaborate pyrotechnic displays originating on barges moored in the middle of the river.

One hundred years later the crowds would be eight times greater, and Thunder Over Louisville would attract the public as no other event in the city.

the advertising agency gave seven oil paintings by the beloved Kentucky painter and shantyboatman Harlan Hubbard. The series depicts the history of Ohio River transportation from the age of the flatboat to the towboat, a collection that hangs in the second floor of the WDC headquarters building.

"Clearing a major hurdle."

Behind the scenes, work was quietly progressing on the nuts-and-bolts issues of park building. Mike Kimmel focused on the required Environmental Impact Statement (EIS), a three-year application process for the U.S. Army Corps of Engineers. Working with Bravura, Kimmel negotiated the bureaucratic obstacle course of required data related to archaeology, traffic, environmental protection, water quality and navigational issues. He participated in a seemingly endless series of public hearings, negotiations and technical planning sessions. One aspect that made the paperwork project especially challenging was the Corps' requirement that the Park and the FallsHarbor residential development be combined.

To add another layer of reporting, the U.S. Coast Guard demanded a voice in the planning process. The Coast Guard, successor to the old Life-Saving Service, had been a part of the Louisville waterfront since before its founding in 1915. Issues concerning river safety were their prime directive. Finally, reporter Sheldon Shafer was able to file a September 24, 1994, story in *The Courier-Journal* of a successful conclusion to the EIS process.

COAST GUARD SHIFTS COURSE, BACKS HARBOR

THE U.S. COAST GUARD, REVERSING AN EARLIER POSITION, HAS ENDORSED WATERFRONT OFFICIALS' PLANS TO CARVE A HARBOR INTO THE DOWNTOWN SHORELINE.

HOWEVER, THE WATERFRONT DEVELOPMENT CORP. STILL HAS NO PLANS TO TRY TO PERSUADE FEDERAL OFFICIALS TO OPEN THE HARBOR TO OHIO RIVER PLEASURE BOATERS. THE HARBOR WOULD BE LIMITED, AS PLANNED, TO THE JEFFERSON COUNTY RIVER PATROL AND WATER TAXIS.

The U.S. Coast Guard has been part of the Louisville waterfront since its inception in 1915. Park officials and designers worked closely with the Coast Guard and the U.S. Army Corps of Engineers to coordinate plans and gain the necessary permits to build so near the active commercial maritime channel hugging the southern shore of the Ohio River.

THE ARMY CORPS OF ENGINEERS, WHICH IS NOW CONSIDERING APPROVAL OF A PERMIT FOR THE DEVELOPMENT, HAS THE FINAL SAY ON THE $58 MILLION DOLLAR MASTER PLAN. BUT THE CORPS PROBABLY WOULD NOT APPROVE THE HARBOR PROJECT WITHOUT THE COAST GUARD'S CLEARANCE, SAID DAN EVANS, CHIEF OF THE CORPS' PERMITS SECTION REVIEWING THE WATERFRONT PROJECT.

DAVID KAREM, PRESIDENT OF THE WATERFRONT CORPORATION, VIEWED THE COAST GUARD'S ENDORSEMENT AS "CLEARING A MAJOR HURDLE."

THE COAST GUARD INITIALLY OPPOSED ANY DOWNTOWN HARBOR, FEARING IT MIGHT DRAW MORE PLEASURE CRAFT TO THE WHARF AREA AND CREATE NEW HAZARDS FOR BARGES THAT MUST COME CLOSE TO THE KENTUCKY SHORE TO ENTER THE McALPINE LOCKS.

THE CORPORATION, RIVER PATROL AND COAST

GUARD HAVE AGREED ON SAFETY PROVISIONS NEAR THE HARBOR, INCLUDING A HEAVY PRESENCE BY RIVER POLICE. SGT. TOM OLYMPIA, HEAD OF THE RIVER PATROL, SAID IT WILL BE ON DUTY 20 OR MORE HOURS A DAY DURING BOATING SEASON.

OLYMPIA SAID THE RIVER PATROL HOPES TO BE STATIONED IN A NEW OFFICE AND SUPPORT AREA AT THE DOWNTOWN HARBOR AS EARLY AS FALL 1995. ITS BASE IS NOW UPRIVER, NEAR HARRODS CREEK.

THE CORPS IS CONSIDERING A PERMIT FOR NOT ONLY THE MASTER-PLAN DEVELOPMENT, WHICH INCLUDES THE GREAT LAWN, A FESTIVAL PLAZA AND UPRIVER PARK, BUT ALSO FOR FALLSHARBOR, A 200-UNIT CONDOMINIUM PROJECT NEAR TOWHEAD ISLAND. WATERFRONT SPOKESMAN MIKE KIMMEL SAID THE CORPORATION HOPES THE CORPS WILL APPROVE THE PERMIT BY LATE FALL.

DEMOLITION OF THE OLD PORT OF LOUISVILLE FACILITY NEAR THE KENNEDY BRIDGE, WHICH CLEARS OUT THE TARGET AREA, IS ALMOST COMPLETE. SOME HEAVY GRADING CAN BEGIN SOON, EVEN BEFORE THE CORPS ISSUES THE PERMIT.

A FEW LOOSE ENDS RELATED TO THE PERMIT REMAIN.

WHOLESALE RIVERFRONT ROAD IMPROVEMENTS – AT LEAST AS NOW DESIGNED – ALSO CAN'T ADVANCE TOO FAR WITHOUT RESOLUTION OF THE RIGHT-OF-WAY DISPUTE WITH LOUISVILLE SCRAP MATERIAL COMPANY. THE CITY NEEDS THE RIGHT OF WAY UNENCUMBERED BECAUSE THE WITHERSPOON STREET EXTENSION IS TO RUN OVER IT – IN THE HEART OF THE MASTER-PLAN AREA.

Often frustrated with slow responses and processing concerns in offices far away, Kimmel doggedly steered the Environmental Impact Statement process to its successful conclusion. But even as the permitting process reached completion, a contentious issue remained before the Park could blossom. A resolution to a long-standing disagreement with Louisville Scrap Materials was needed, and soon, if the Park was to advance.

"The Project, as proposed, will be of little benefit to the general public..."

The Master Plan envisioned a waterfront free from the tangle of industrial blight – the mountains of sand and gravel, railroad tracks, riverfront terminals, electrical lines, billboards, dumps and heavy metal scrapyards – which had characterized the area for much of its history. Around the turn of the twentieth century, new riverside industries and port terminals were hailed as signs of great progress; but a hundred years later, Louisville was committed to a program of developments to meet current needs.

Perhaps the most serious challenge to the realization of Hargreaves' Master Plan was the large industrial salvage operation, Louisville Scrap Material Company, located along Washington Street between Floyd and Hancock Streets. The firm, founded in 1913, was headed by David Blue, the fourth generation to head the firm. The company had 150 employees with an annual payroll of $4.7 million, with their prime operation being to cut up and dispose of old railroad cars. Accessibility to rail lines was critical to their operation.

Supporters of Louisville Scrap Material and backers of the Waterfront development plans were diametrically opposed on the question of the heavy industrial site in the center of the Park's planned Great Lawn feature. The Corps of Engineers, charged with administering environmental impact requirements, asked for public comment on the controversial issue and received response letters from advocates of both sides:

June 10, 1994

We have reviewed the above-captioned application and wish to raise the following objections to the Project, as submitted:

The proposed Witherspoon Street extension as shown in Figure 4 incorporates private property owned by Louisville Scrap Material Co., Inc., which is used for railroad ingress and egress.

The project's proposed redirection of River Road traffic southbound into the already congested Main Street, stop-and-go traffic pattern is ill-conceived and will create significant additional downtown traffic congestion and related hazards. This additional congestion will also add to the downtown air pollution generation.

The proposed riverfront development plan, incorporating the expansive "Great Lawn" – extending on both sides of I-64 (and under the overhead roadway) – is disproportional to the City's needs and results in a gross misuse of public funds at a time when many worthwhile social projects remain in dire need. The Project, as proposed, will be of little benefit to the general public and whatever benefit does accrue to the public will be more than offset by the long-term financial burden being placed upon all of the taxpayers of the community.

Your serious review of the above matters of concern will be appreciated.

Thank you.
Douglas C. Smith
Vice President, Louisville Scrap Material Co., Inc.

As she had consistently done, Mary Bingham championed the cause of the Waterfront Park in her written response to the Corps' invitation for comments.

June 23, 1994

Thank you for sending me the Corps of Engineers' notice of the application for a permit by the Louisville Waterfront Development Corporation.

I wish to support as vigorously as I possibly can the issuance of a permit to allow the Waterfront Master Plan to be implemented.

The Plan was created by the nationally distinguished waterfront designer, George Hargreaves. It has been the subject of innumerable public meetings; necessary land for its realization has been acquired up and down the Riverfront; it has the unqualified support of the public and the political structure of the City and County.

The 19th century properties within the Waterfront's boundaries will be renovated and properly integrated into the Hargreaves scheme.

The deliverance of the Louisville Waterfront from the forbidding industrial development along the river will make the Ohio in all its beauty and recreational value accessible to the general public. It has not been this accessible for generations. The Hargreaves design assures us of adding to Louisville's Olmsted inheritance another park with all the advantages of its splendid river views and ambience.

Sincerely yours,
Mrs. Barry Bingham, Sr.

Two such dramatically opposite positions were not resolved by negotiations, but entered a stage of disagreement and litigation. A July 8, 1994, article in *The Courier-Journal* details what would be a confusing legal judgment that was unsatisfactory to both sides of the issue.

COURT RULING COULD DELAY RIVERFRONT PROJECT

A Jefferson Circuit Court ruling could delay the start of work on the $58 million first phase of the downtown riverfront's redevelopment, city and waterfront officials fear.

Although less likely, the ruling also could mean that most of the road system for the riverfront master plan would need redesigning.

The uncertainty stems from Judge Thomas Wine's ruling June 27 that Louisville Scrap Material Company, which owns property near the river, can use a three-block-long railroad right of way north of Main Street.

It was uncertain whether the city or Louisville Scrap would appeal the ruling by the late July deadline. If it stands, the city and Louisville Scrap are supposed to agree on some rail access for the company.

A central portion of the waterfront master plan involves tearing up the rail line and extending Witherspoon east along the right of way to connect with the existing River Road, near Clay Street.

Waterfront Development Corp. President David Karem said the master plan's road system depends on the extension — which can't occur, as designed, if Louisville Scrap must use the existing railroad.

The city sued last year to clarify rights related to the railroad property. The city claimed ownership under an 1873 condemnation. Louisville Scrap fought it because CSX granted the company a quit-claim deed on the 100-foot-wide strip of land seven years ago.

Wine ruled the city owned the railroad. He also said a long-defunct public way, Water Street, parallels the railroad. But he said Louisville Scrap has the right to use the existing railroad, as it has for years — as long as the use is "in the least obtrusive manner."

James Williamson, an attorney for the law firm of Stites & Harbison, PLLC, representing the City of Louisville and the Waterfront Development Corporation, stated that Judge Wine had not defined "least obtrusive manner," but also held that a railroad, and its successor, Louisville Scrap Materials, having the right to use public rights of way without the city's consent, was not supported by Kentucky law and should be appealed.

Discussions concerning the "least obtrusive manner" produced a stalemate, and the City of Louisville filed an additional suit, one contesting the firm's right to run rail spurs across Preston, Floyd and Jackson Streets. The City argued Louisville Scrap had no authorization to cross public streets, while the company answered they had used the spur for years and they were absolutely necessary for operations. The scrap company argued that Phase I could be redesigned, with their operation remaining in the center of the Park, but discretely screened from view. Of this tense situation, David Karem recalls the City's decisive advantage, and it involved the oldest street in Louisville.

Removing the bleak industrial landscape between the Clark Memorial and Kennedy bridges was a high priority for WDC officials. Decades of hard usage had left the land scarred and polluted, and before the Waterfront Park renovations could begin, removal of the mountains of scrap iron, sand and gravel piles and asphalt plants was necessary.

LOUISVILLE SCRAP MATERIALS ASKED FOR $40 MILLION TO RELOCATE AND WE GOT INTO SOME LITIGATION. OUR COUNSEL DISCOVERED THEY WERE OPERATING ON AN OLD STREET CALLED WATER STREET, WHICH WAS THE FIRST STREET IN LOUISVILLE. IT HAD NEVER BEEN CLOSED AND YOU CAN'T ADVERSELY POSSESS AGAINST A MUNICIPALITY. THEY HAD BOUGHT PROPERTY FROM CSX AND GOT A QUIT-CLAIM DEED. IT TURNED OUT THAT THAT CSX WAS A SUCCESSOR TO SEVERAL OTHER RAIL COMPANIES THAT GOT THE ORIGINAL PUBLIC RAILROAD EASEMENT FROM THE CITY IN THE 1800S, AND THAT IF THE RAILROAD COMPANY EVER ABANDONED THE RAIL LINE, THE EASEMENT REVERTED TO THE CITY OF LOUISVILLE. THERE WAS A SERIOUS FEDERAL LAW SUIT THAT WE WON AT EVERY TURN TO RECAPTURE WATER STREET AND THIS RAIL LINE. WE HAD A BETTER MEETING OF THE MINDS AND GOT WHAT WE NEEDED, THEY GOT SOME MONEY, NOT FOR THE WATER STREET RIGHT OF WAY, BUT FOR OTHER LAND INTERESTS TRANSFERRED TO THE CITY BY LOUISVILLE SCRAP MATERIALS.

The key event that led the parties to serious settlement discussions was the near unanimous ruling of the Kentucky Supreme Court reversing Judge Wine's "least obtrusive manner" decision. The Supreme Court was unambiguous in its holding that Louisville Scrap had no right to use Water Street or any other public right of way for railroad access to its facilities without the City's consent. That decision in the summer of 1996, more than any other, provided the impetus for the City to stop the flow of rail traffic in and out of Louisville Scrap Materials yard. At that point, the city works department actually barricaded the tracks on the east side of Jackson Street, preventing all rail access to and from the scrap yard, a dagger in the heart of Louisville Scrap's ability to remain in operation on the waterfront.

In the summer of 1995 an agreement was reached with Louisville Scrap Materials being paid five million dollars for the disputed land. A *Business First* editorial of September 9, 1995, highlighted the positive development.

SUMMER PLAYS OUT ON A POSITIVE NOTE

AFTER A LONG, HOT SUMMER — EVEN BY LOUISVILLE STANDARDS — SOME PRETTY COOL THINGS HAVE HAPPENED IN THE LAST WEEK OR SO.

COOL HEADS FINALLY PREVAILED WHEN OFFICIALS OF THE LOUISVILLE SCRAP MATERIALS CO. INC. AND THE WATERFRONT DEVELOPMENT CORP. OFFICIALLY SIGNED OFF ON A PROPERTY SETTLEMENT THAT WILL ALLOW THE RIVERFRONT REDEVELOPMENT EFFORT TO PROCEED WITHOUT COSTLY AND TIME-CONSUMING LITIGATION.

ALTHOUGH THE AGREEMENT ADDS $5 MILLION TO THE COST OF REVAMPING THE DOWNTOWN SHORELINE, THE BEST INTERESTS OF A LONGTIME BUSINESS AND THE COMMUNITY ARE BEING SERVED.

A joint press release from both Louisville Scrap Materials and the Waterfront Development Corporation provided details.

DOUGLAS C. SMITH, SENIOR VICE PRESIDENT OF LOUISVILLE SCRAP MATERIALS CO., INC., AND DAVID K. KAREM, EXECUTIVE DIRECTOR OF THE WATERFRONT DEVELOPMENT CORPORATION, ANNOUNCED TODAY THAT PARTIES FROM LSM AND WDC HAVE BEEN WORKING TOWARD AN AGREEMENT THAT WOULD MAKE IT POSSIBLE FOR WATERFRONT DEVELOPMENT PLANS TO PROCEED WHILE AT THE SAME TIME ALLOWING LOUISVILLE SCRAP MATERIAL TO REMAIN IN BUSINESS IN THE AREA WHERE IT HAS OPERATED FOR OVER 80 YEARS. THE AGREEMENT WOULD SETTLE THE CITY'S LITIGATION WITH LSM; PERMIT WDC TO OBTAIN A SECOND MAJOR DEVELOPMENT BLOCK; AND SECURE A MORE EASTERLY SITE FOR LSM, WITH THE ASSURANCE THAT SUCH SITE WOULD BE A PERMANENT HOME FOR THEIR OPERATION.

UNDER THE PROPOSED ACCORD, AN EXCHANGE OF

As property was acquired by the Waterfront Development Corporation, signs were put up to stir the public's interest in the Park project. The successful resolution of the Louisville Scrap Materials land acquisition allowed plans for the Park's Phase I to advance.

CERTAIN PROPERTIES WOULD TAKE PLACE THAT WOULD ALLOW LSM TO EXPAND TO THE EAST, BETWEEN ITS CURRENT SITE AND I-65, TO PROPERTY CURRENTLY OWNED BY LG&E. LSM WOULD CONVEY TO WDC THE BLOCK BOUNDED BY FLOYD, PRESTON AND WASHINGTON STREETS TO USE AS A SECOND MAJOR DEVELOPMENT BLOCK IN ACCORDANCE WITH THE WATERFRONT MASTER PLAN. NEW RAIL ACCESS TO LSM WOULD BE DEVELOPED FROM THE CSX MAIN LINE EAST OF I-65, CONNECTING TO THE SOUTHEAST PORTION OF THE RECONFIGURED LSM SITE. LSM WOULD ABANDON CLAIM TO THREE STRIP TRACTS NORTH OF THEIR PROPERTY THAT ARE CURRENTLY USED FOR RAIL ACCESS TO LSM PROPERTY. THESE THREE TRACTS WILL BE USED FOR THE EXTENSION OF WITHERSPOON STREET EAST TO CLAY STREET AND THE BURIAL OF LG&E TRANSMISSION LINES. WDC WOULD PAY FOR AND CONSTRUCT THE NEW RAIL ACCESS AND BE RESPONSIBLE FOR OBTAINING ALL PROPERTY

Forgotten by the march of history, Louisville's oldest road, Water Street, held the key to resolving access issues concerning land ownership near the old city wharf. A detail from an 1852 map of Louisville reveals the warren of small streets and alleys that once dotted the waterfront area. *(Published by I.H. Colton & Co. No. 172 William St New York)*

NECESSARY FOR SUCH ACCESS. THE AGREEMENT WOULD SEEK TO CLOSE A PORTION OF JACKSON STREET WITHIN THE PROPERTY AREA.

AS PART OF THE PROPERTY EXCHANGE, LSM WOULD ALSO AGREE TO CONVEY TO WDC SMALL PARCELS AT THE NORTHEAST CORNER OF JACKSON AND MAIN STREETS AND ON THE SOUTHWEST CORNER OF PRESTON STREET AND RIVER ROAD. MAYOR JERRY ABRAMSON IS WORKING WITH LG&E REGARDING THE FEASIBILITY OF OBTAINING ITS PROPERTY FOR EXCHANGE UNDER THE PROPOSED AGREEMENT.

THE SETTLEMENT BETWEEN THE WATERFRONT DEVELOPMENT CORPORATION AND LOUISVILLE SCRAP IS CONTINGENT UPON THE EXECUTION OF A DEFINITIVE AGREEMENT. NEGOTIATIONS ARE ONGOING, AND ATTORNEYS FOR THE TWO PARTIES ARE DRAFTING THE AGREEMENT.

Louisville's old Water Street had been described in 1852 by a writer in the *Louisville Daily Democrat:*

SUPPOSE WE LEAVE THE MAIL BOAT TELEGRAPH NO. 2, ON WHICH YOU STAYED ALL NIGHT. AS WE STAND ON THE FORWARD GUARD AND THE SUN IS JUST RISING, WE LOOK OUT UPON THE "FALLS CITY!" – PRECIOUS LITTLE WE CAN SEE FROM THIS POINT; WHAT WE CAN SEE GIVES ANY OTHER IDEA THAN THAT OF A GREAT CITY BEHIND THE IRREGULAR ROW OF OLD BRICKS, ON A CROOKED APOLOGY FOR A STREET, WHICH OUR FOREFATHERS CALLED WATER. NEVER MIND; WHEN WE GET UP INTO "TOWN," WE'LL SHOW YOU SOME THINGS YOU WOULD NOT EXPECT TO FIND. WE ARE SORRY TO BE COMPELLED TO ACKNOWLEDGE THAT OUR CITY PRESENTS A VERY UNINVITING ASPECT FROM THE RIVER, BUT SO IT IS. WE HOPE ONE DAY TO SEE THIS WATER STREET MADE STRAIGHT, WITH A BETTER APPEARANCE FROM THE RIVER.

Crooked old Water Street, with portions covered by the fill-in of the original Beargrass Creek bed and other stretches covered by the elevated Short-Line Railroad trestle, was the only named Louisville street prior to 1812. It had been forgotten, abused and abandoned, but never officially declared closed by the municipal government. The eighteenth century roadway was the key to resolving a twentieth century dispute.

Making the Connection

At the same time, other developments in the Waterfront Overlay District were also moving toward positive accomplishments. In March 1993 the Hard Dock Café, a floating restaurant, moved into position on the Louisville wharf. A lower-priced vendor than its predecessor, The Islands, the casual restaurant served sandwiches and lighter fare on a boat rocked continuously by the nearby barge traffic proceeding through the navigation channel. Two months later, the Louisville Ballet announced its acquisition of a space on East Main Street to build an innovative complex of office space and dance practice area. All EIS investigations were performed by WDC Deputy Director Mike Kimmel, and, when completed, the ballet building was a powerful new downtown building that served the dance company and the waterfront neighborhood very well.

The Belvedere, originally suggested in the 1931 Bartholomew Report, had always been envisioned as being joined to the wharf area. After several attempts, U.S. Representative Romano Mazzoli obtained funding to build a connecting set of stairs and elevators to link the upper deck of the Belvedere and the riverside wharf. In appreciation for his continual support, the connector was named in Mazzoli's honor. Ground was broken on the project in July 1993 and, on February 17, 1995, *The Courier-Journal* could report a successful outcome.

Although the Belvedere was very popular, it was extremely difficult to travel between the high-rise plaza and the Fourth Street wharf. Congressman Romano Mazzoli was instrumental in obtaining funds to build the Belvedere Connector, the series of stairs and landings that were named in his honor. *(Photo courtesy of the Belle of Louisville)*

BELVEDERE CONNECTOR OFFERS NEW VISTA AN IN-YOUR-FACE VIEW OF THE OHIO

ON A COLD, WINDY DAY, CITY OFFICIALS YESTERDAY GAVE THE MEDIA THE FIRST WALK-THROUGH OF THE $4.7 MILLION SET OF STEPS AND RAMPS THAT ALLOW PEDESTRIANS TO MOVE FROM THE DOWNTOWN WHARF TO THE BELVEDERE 65 FEET ABOVE.

THE CONNECTION WAS PLANNED AS PART OF THE ORIGINAL RIVERFRONT PLAZA/BELVEDERE PROJECT MORE THAN 20 YEARS AGO. BUT THE LINK WAS DROPPED TO KEEP COSTS WITHIN BUDGET.

WORK ON THE CONNECTOR BEGAN IN AUGUST 1993 AND SHOULD BE FINISHED BY APRIL 22 FOR THUNDER OVER LOUISVILLE.

SOME ADDITIONAL WORK — LANDSCAPING, A SECOND ELEVATOR AND RESTROOM FIXTURES THAT WERE FUNDED SEPARATELY — WILL BE COMPLETED BY FALL. THE TOTAL PROJECT BUDGET WAS $4.7 MILLION, NEARLY ALL IN FEDERAL MONEY.

THE CONNECTOR HAS 75 STEPS THAT ANGLE SHARPLY AT SOME POINTS OUT TOWARD THE RIVER. THE ENTIRE SYSTEM IS ACCESSIBLE TO THE DISABLED; ELEVATORS WILL CARRY PASSENGERS BETWEEN THE BELVEDERE AND WHARF AND STOP AT MIDLEVEL. BUT ONLY THE MIDLEVEL IS ACCESSIBLE BY RAMP, AND ONLY FROM FOURTH STREET SOUTH OF I-64.

Mayor Jerry Abramson (in trench coat) inspected the Belvedere Connector during its construction. This connector helped link Main Street to the waterfront as part of major improvements to upgrade the old Louisville wharf, home of the *Belle of Louisville.*

THE MIDLEVEL OFFERS A LONG PROMENADE OVERLOOKING THE OHIO. IT WILL FEATURE HUGE PLANTERS AND AN ARBOR BUILT FROM LARGE COLUMNS.

THE STEPS WILL HAVE A 3½-FOOT-HIGH RAILING, WITH VERTICAL RODS BETWEEN THE CONCRETE AND THE RAIL.

THE CONNECTOR IS A KEY ELEMENT OF THE WATERFRONT PLAN BECAUSE IT PROVIDES ACCESS TO THE RIVERWALK TO THE WEST AND THE SOON-TO-BE-DEVELOPED WATERFRONT PARK JUST UPRIVER.

SULLIVAN & COZART IS THE GENERAL CONTRACTOR ON THE PROJECT, AND SENLER-CAMPBELL & ASSOCIATES THE ARCHITECT. MAYOR JERRY ABRAMSON SAID THE CITY WILL BEGIN COMPANION WORK SOON ON REBUILDING THE RIVERFRONT PLAZA/BELVEDERE.

"Admit nothing to your park that is not fitting and helpful..."

Along with other signs of progress, the Waterfront Development Corporation was growing in professionalism and had already put into place underlying operational policies to govern the Park when completed. In January 1994 a detailed maintenance plan was written to address all aspects of care, including mechanical, horticultural, cleaning and conservation. This progressive Park Maintenance Plan, established before the area had been developed, was the first such in the United States. WDC officials sensed echoes of Frederick Law Olmsted in his first 1891 communication with the Louisville Parks Board, "The cost of maintaining parks is a matter of more importance in determining plans for them than the cost of forming them."

More Olmstedian wisdom from the same communication was also incorporated into the vision of Waterfront Park. "We advised you also to be prepared to strenuously disappoint all notions that any may have formed that you are to spend the public money entrusted to you upon objects of curiosity or decoration; your business is to form parks, not museums or collections of ornaments. If gifts are offered you of objects simply ornamental, by all means decline them. Admit nothing to your park that is not fitting and helpful to their distinguishing purpose."

Guided by art-savvy Marlene Grissom, a policy governing gifts of art was proposed and adopted. Only a handful of pieces of outstanding merit would become part of the Park's fabric. "Gracehoper," by Tony Smith, was placed on the Overlook. The massive black sculptural masterpiece is on permanent loan from the Kentucky Center for the Arts. Originally donated to the Center by Humana Inc. to honor co-founder Wendell Cherry,

A graceful piece of contemporary sculpture, "Tetra," by Charles O. Perry, was donated to the park by four of Sally Brown's grandchildren, in tribute to her contributions to the city and Waterfront Park. Placed at the park's entrance off Witherspoon Street, its sweeping circular design seems to welcome visitors to the grounds.

Marvin Finn, a self-taught Louisville artist known for his colorful wooden chickens, provided the inspiration for one of the most popular features in the Park, the "Flock of Finns." Fabricated from metal and brightly painted, the "Flock of Finns" provide a whimsical background for family photos, and are a delight to children.

the piece was moved to Waterfront Park prior to an extension of the Arts Center toward the Belvedere. "Tetra," an engaging metallic oval with see-through segments, created by Charles O. Perry, was a gift from the four grandchildren of Sally Brown to honor her lifelong commitment to Louisville and her legacy to Waterfront Park.

Easily the most whimsical and colorful of the selective art installations in Waterfront Park is the "Flock of Finns." Mayor David Armstrong and the Mayor's Advisory Council on Public Amenities arranged for dozens of brightly painted

fantasy birds fabricated from sheet metal to be built. The sculptures were enlarged replicas of the painted wooden chickens made famous by Louisville folk artist Marvin Finn. Engaging and affectionate, the "Flock of Finns" would be enjoyed by visitors of all ages after reaching their final destination in Waterfront Park in 2001. Despite their easily accessible location, these tempting targets are rarely vandalized. The Flock seems protected by a commonly held attitude of affection and respect for Waterfront Park.

One last piece of the park puzzle was resolution of the

The Overlook provides a dramatic stage for a Tony Smith sculpture named "Gracehoper." Originally located on the grounds of the Kentucky Center for the Arts, the grand piece was presented to the Center by Humana, Inc., in honor of co-founder Wendell Cherry. When an expansion of the Center for the Arts crowded the piece in its original location, the piece was loaned to Waterfront Park. The Friends of the Waterfront helped raise the funds necessary for the difficult move of this impressive piece of art.

problem of the myriad high-powered electrical lines running from the LG&E Waterside station located at Second Street and the river. While no one wanted a curtain of power lines and transmission towers to dominate the waterside landscape, resolving the issue of overhead lines would prove a troublesome and expensive proposition, as indicated in an August 19, 1994, article in *The Courier-Journal*:

RIVERFRONT POWER-LINE
BURIAL IS SOUGHT

THE PRETTY MODELS AND SKETCHES OF LOUISVILLE'S

PROPOSED WATERFRONT PARK SHOW A SHORELINE OF GRASS AND TREES, MARINAS, WATERFALLS, OPEN-AIR PLAZAS AND HIGH-RISE APARTMENT BUILDINGS.

WHAT THEY DON'T SHOW ARE THE STEEL TOWERS THAT NOW CARRY HIGH-VOLTAGE ELECTRICAL LINES EASTWARD ALONG RIVER ROAD FROM AN OLD LOUISVILLE GAS & ELECTRIC CO. GENERATING PLANT AT THE FOOT OF THIRD STREET.

BACKERS OF THE WATERFRONT PLAN WANT TO SEE THE POWER LINES – PART OF THE UTILITY'S LOAD-DISTRIBUTION

SYSTEM — MOVED UNDERGROUND, AND THEY'VE COME UP WITH A PLAN THAT COULD MAKE LG&E'S CUSTOMERS PAY THE MULTIMILLION-DOLLAR BILL.

THE LINES HAVE TO BE MOVED FOR THE WATERFRONT PLAN TO SUCCEED, SAID DAVID KAREM, PRESIDENT OF THE WATERFRONT DEVELOPMENT CORP. "YOU CAN'T BUILD A HIGH-RISE APARTMENT BUILDING NEXT TO POWER LINES."

LG&E, WHICH HAS BURIED HIGH-VOLTAGE LINES BEFORE, SAYS IT WILL COST ABOUT $9 MILLION TO PUT THE LINES UNDERGROUND BETWEEN THIRD STREET AND THE KENNEDY BRIDGE.

LG&E SPOKESWOMAN KATHY CAMPBELL SAID THE UTILITY CAN'T MAKE WHAT SHE CALLED A COSMETIC RELOCATION WITHOUT A SPECIFIC ORDER FROM A GOVERNMENTAL AGENCY AND CONSULTATION WITH THE PUBLIC SERVICE COMMISSION.

"WE WILL COMPLY WITH AN ORDER IF ONE IS ISSUED FROM A GOVERNMENT AGENCY," SHE SAID. "SINCE THE COST WOULD BE PASSED ALONG TO OUR CUSTOMER GROUPS, THAT'S NOT A DECISION WE COULD MAKE ON OUR OWN."

LOUISVILLE ALDERMAN BARBARA GREGG, WHO SERVES ON THE BOARD OF THE WATERFRONT DEVELOPMENT CORP., SAID CITY OFFICIALS WILL TRY AN ORDINANCE REQUIRING DOWNTOWN-AREA UTILITIES TO BE BURIED TO APPLY TO THE WATERFRONT AREA.

"THAT MAKES SENSE BECAUSE SO MUCH OF THE WATERFRONT IS NOW BECOMING WHAT WE CALL THE DOWNTOWN AREA," GREGG SAID.

CAMPBELL SAID THE POWER LINES, WHICH NOW

PASS OVER THE WITHERSPOON PARKING GARAGE AND TRAFFIC LANES ON THE CLARK MEMORIAL BRIDGE, ARE PART OF A POWER GRID THAT FEEDS DOWNTOWN LOUISVILLE, INCLUDING THE CITY'S OFFICE TOWERS.

A DIFFERENT SECTION OF THE SAME POWER LINE SEGMENT WAS RELOCATED IN THE 1960S WHEN THE GALT HOUSE AND THE RIVERFRONT PLAZA/BELVEDERE WERE BUILT.

"WE DIDN'T WANT THEM HANGING OVER THE BELVEDERE, SO THEY'RE BURIED UNDER THE PARKING GARAGE," SAID LAWRENCE MELLILO, ONE OF THE ARCHITECTS FOR THE PROJECT.

MELLILO SAID THE LINES WERE ENCASED IN CUSTOM-BUILT STEEL TUBES AND COVERED IN OIL TO KEEP THEM COOL.

JOHN WALKER MOORE, WHO DIRECTED THE BELVEDERE DEVELOPMENT PROJECT IN THE 1960S, SAID MUCH OF THE COST OF THE POWER LINE RELOCATION WAS PAID FOR IN A $10 MILLION BOND ISSUE THAT FINANCED THE BELVEDERE. HE SAID SOME FEDERAL GRANT FUNDS WERE ALSO USED.

"LG&E DIDN'T PAY A DIME. I KNOW THAT," HE SAID.

MATT RHODY, A SPOKESMAN FOR THE KENTUCKY PUBLIC SERVICE COMMISSION, SAID UTILITIES SUCH AS LG&E TYPICALLY BEAR THE COST OF RELOCATIONS IF THEIR LINES ARE LOCATED ON PUBLIC RIGHTS-OF-WAY, SUCH AS THE SHOULDER OF A HIGHWAY.

IN CASES WHERE THE UTILITY HAS AN EASEMENT OVER PRIVATE PROPERTY, AS THE LG&E DOES ALONG THE

RIVER, GOVERNMENT OR PRIVATE DEVELOPERS PAY.

KAREM SAID THAT PASSING THE RELOCATION COST ON TO LG&E AND ITS CUSTOMERS IS ONE OF THE FEW OPTIONS AVAILABLE TO PAY FOR THE PROJECT. HE SAID NO FEDERAL GRANTS OR BOND ISSUE MONEY IS AVAILABLE, AS WAS THE CASE FOR THE BELVEDERE.

THE WATERFRONT DEVELOPMENT CORP., WHICH IS FUNDED BY DONATIONS — INCLUDING A $150,000 PLEDGE FROM LG&E — PLANS TO SPEND $58 MILLION OVER THE NEXT TWO YEARS TO CREATE A PLAZA, THE GREAT LAWN, A HARBOR AND A PARK.

"DONORS ARE NOT GOING TO GIVE MONEY TO BURY UTILITY LINES," KAREM SAID. "THAT MONEY WAS RAISED AND BUDGETED FOR PHYSICAL CONSTRUCTION."

AND GREGG SAID THE CITY DOESN'T HAVE MONEY FOR THE RELOCATION, EITHER.

"THIS IS NOT A GOVERNMENT PUBLIC WORKS PROJECT," SHE SAID.

SHE SAID SHE HOPES LG&E SPOKESMAN CLAY RYCE INDICATED THAT THAT'S THE ROUTE THE UTILITY WILL TAKE.

"IF THE ALDERMEN SAY THIS PROJECT MUST BE DONE, THEN SOMETHING ELSE WILL BE PUT ASIDE," HE SAID. "IF WE HAVE TO DO IT, IT WILL BE DONE AND IT WILL BE PAID FOR, LIKE ALL OUR CAPITAL CONSTRUCTION PROJECTS, BY OUR RATEPAYERS.

HE ESTIMATED THAT THE $9 MILLION PROJECT WOULD COST CONSUMERS ABOUT 10 CENTS A MONTH ON

THEIR UTILITY BILLS. ALTHOUGH RYCE WOULDN'T RULE OUT A RATE INCREASE TO COVER THE COSTS, HE SAID LG&E WOULD PREFER NOT TO DO THAT.

GREGG SUGGESTED THAT LG&E MIGHT WANT TO PAY AT LEAST SOME OF THE RELOCATION COST AS A CONTRIBUTION TO THE WATERFRONT PROJECT.

BUT RYCE INDICATED THAT THAT'S VERY UNLIKELY.

"A $9 MILLION DONATION FOR ANY PROJECT IS EXPENSIVE," HE SAID. "WHO ELSE IS MAKING THAT KIND OF DONATION?"

Officials of the Louisville Gas & Electric Company, a fixture on the Louisville waterfront since its incorporation in 1839, worked with city and park officials to extend the area served from underground lines in the downtown area. A rate increase would not be required, as the utility discovered creative ways to accomplish the mission of burying the lines at a minimum of expense. Installed while streets and expressway ramps were being relocated, the new subterranean power grid accomplished the goal of clearing the riverfront's view shed.

By Thanksgiving 1994 *The Courier-Journal* was able to report this welcome story:

THE TRANSFORMATION OF LOUISVILLE'S DOWNTOWN RIVERFRONT HAS BEGUN.

HUGE TRACK HOES SCOOP UP DIRT, WHICH IS DUMPED IN TRUCKS AND CARTED AWAY. PANSCRAPERS AND BULLDOZERS RUMBLE AND SNORT — BACKWARD, FORWARD; LEVELING HERE, ELEVATING THERE — AS THEY CARVE OUT A NEW LANDSCAPE THAT NOW RESEMBLES A CRATERED MOON SURFACE.

Large pilings that were part of the recently razed Port of Louisville warehouse protrude from the earth, awaiting removal.

By mid-1997 this land along the Ohio River between the Clark and Kennedy bridges will be a newborn gateway to the city.

Louisville urban affairs author Grady Clay watches the work with a bit of wonder. The shoreline has been stripped of vegetation and buildings.

"Part of the northern coast of Kentucky has been cleared of the last remnants of the industrial revolution," Clay said. "A jewel awaits us."

With many of the legal and design issues settled, work began on transforming the rugged industrial wasteland into a beautiful and accessible public park. In 1994, after nearly six years of planning, people began to see daily progress at the foot of Third Street. Not since the relocation of Beargrass Creek from this same location in the 1850s would the Louisville waterfront experience such a radical improvement in its condition.

Construction of the improved wharf facility, located just north of the WDC office building, required stabilization of the riverbank and small coffer dams to allow for work to proceed. A heavy crane, mounted on a floating barge, provided the power necessary to complete this portion of Phase I.

The City Builds a New Front Yard
(1995-1999)

The Ohio River is to Louisville, Kentucky, what the Grand Canal is to Venice…. It is a quintessential American riverfront city. The streets of its central core are laid out in a gridiron pattern, and in the 19th and early 20th centuries its riverfront was given over almost exclusively to industry related first to river and later to railroad transportation. Such industry was crucial to the city's prosperity, but its citizens paid a price. Layer upon layer of steel, asphalt and concrete infrastructure divided the city and the river, making it almost impossible to use the riverfront for recreation or civic events.

By the late 20th century Louisville's post-industrial economy was no longer dependent on riverfront industries. Its riverfront, like that of many American cities, became a bleak zone of abandoned industrial buildings interspersed with scrap metal yards, oil storage tanks, dilapidated warehouses and a gravel pit. Layered with a collage of unused railroad tracks and walled off from the central city by an elevated superhighway (Interstate 64) stretching along the river's edge like a giant concrete centipede, the riverfront's problems were compounded by the Ohio's frequent floods.

– AQUAPOLIS - 1998

Waterfront Development officials knew the park could not be built in one smooth, continuous flow of funding and construction. An early decision to divide the project into segments was the most realistic option for the park's final completion. Construction estimates for Phase I, placed at $58 million, focused on the western-most area of the project, beginning at the original Louisville wharf. The main design elements, beginning at the west and continuing eastward fifty-five acres, were as follows:

- AN EXTENDED AND IMPROVED PUBLIC WHARF, WITH FACILITIES AND DOCKING SPACE FOR LARGE VISITING EXCURSION BOATS LIKE THE *DELTA QUEEN*, *STAR OF LOUISVILLE* AND THE MASSIVE FLOATING BARGE HOTEL, THE *MISSISSIPPI QUEEN*;

- A TWO-LEVEL RESTAURANT WITH ENCIRCLING RAMPS AND A 60-FOOT HIGH OBSERVATION DECK, BUILT ON STILTS TO SAFELY POSITION THE SERVICE AREA ABOVE THE 451-FOOT-ABOVE-SEA LEVEL MEASUREMENT THAT WOULD KEEP IT SAFE IN EVEN A 100-YEAR FLOOD;

- A SERIES OF CASCADING FOUNTAIN POOLS, CALLED THE WATER FEATURE, EXTENDING FROM WITHERSPOON STREET DOWN TO THE RIVER;

- A FIVE-ACRE FESTIVAL PLAZA, WITH INFRASTRUCTURE FOR FOOD VENDORS AND ENTERTAINMENT, TO SERVE AS A STAGING AREA FOR THE LARGE SCALE EVENTS LIKE THUNDER OVER LOUISVILLE, THE CHOW WAGON AND THE INDEPENDENCE FESTIVAL;

- THE OVERLOOK, A TREE-LINED ELEVATED OBSERVATION AREA EXTENDING OUT INTO THE OHIO RIVER, COMPLETE WITH BENCHES AND THE "GRACEHOPER" SCULPTURE;

- THE GREAT LAWN, A 13-ACRE MULTI-USE GREEN SPACE THAT WOULD FORM THE CORE OF THE

ENTERTAINMENT, RECREATIONAL AND PROGRAMMING
FUNCTIONS OF WATERFRONT PARK;

- THE HARBOR, AN INLET ADJACENT TO THE GREAT LAWN,
  WITH DOCKING FACILITIES FOR VISITING PLEASURE
  CRAFT, WATER TAXIS AND RIVER PATROL BOATS;

- THE LINEAR PARK, WITH BIKE AND JOGGING TRAILS, A
  CHILDREN'S PLAYGROUND, AN INLET AND SCULPTURED
  HILLS THAT PROVIDE AREAS FOR PRIVACY, RECREATION
  AND PERSONAL SPACE.

A vastly improved wharf was extended from the Belvedere Connector to the Great Lawn. Great touring boats like the *Delta Queen* and *Mississippi Queen* found dock space at the new Louisville wharf, recalling the glory days of the great packet boats. The newly paved dockside infrastructure provided flexible space for a variety of passenger vessels, landing thousands of tourists seeking local attractions in Louisville.

The Palmy Days Revisited

The improved wharf docking area was designed to handle the increasing volume of touring paddlewheel excursion boats then plying the inland river system, providing authentic river heritage experiences as well as comfortable overnight accommodations and food service. This addition brought back to life Louisville's tradition as a destination port, recalling the glory days of steamboating. Arrival of the modern "floating palaces" reawakened a familiar pattern at the waterfront, with hundreds of tourists disembarking to board buses for day-long tours of Louisville's attractions like Churchill Downs or the Louisville Slugger baseball bat factory, a powerful enhancement to the city's important and profitable tourism industry.

Collectively, the area between the Festival Plaza and Brook Street lying north of Witherspoon Street was termed the Bingham Way. A hard-surfaced plaza replaced the original small patch of asphalt adjacent to the old Martin Marietta building, now known as the WDC offices, and served as a location for food carts and other vendors during public events. The plaza is paved with decomposed granite, a soft and cool material, allowing easy clean-up in case of grease spills during food preparation. The paving is embedded with concrete bands, lighting standards and utilities for vendors. The area was designed for practical considerations of accessibility, ease of clean-up and sanitary control. The space easily accommodates 15,000 at one time and, during the largest events, this capacity can be stretched to its limits.

Cleverly concealed utility hook-ups, access to city water and public restrooms were part of the practical operational "backstage" of the Park. The elevated two-story restaurant, soon to house the seafood-themed Joe's Crab Shack, was near the river's edge where diners could sit on the outdoor porch and enjoy an expansive view of the Ohio, the bridges and skyline of Louisville.

While Waterfront Park is designed to accommodate tens of thousands of visitors, Hargreaves' design created private spaces where individuals, or intimate groups, could find privacy in the areas produced by the distinctive earthen forms called plinths. Private spaces abound in the Linear Park section of the Park.

A Water Feature, a design that would dramatically change from the original Master Plan, was intended to bring moving waters into the park for the visitors' enjoyment. Other early ideas, such as a high-rise boathouse and memorial to the 1937 Flood, would morph into alternative features as plans were studied and modified in an ongoing process of reappraisal.

"…the rich, fresh greensward – the honest grass – upon which we could sit down with comfort"

The Great Lawn, an expansive thirteen-acre stretch of open land between Brook and Preston Streets is the soul of Waterfront Park. Running from Witherspoon Street, under I-64 expressway, and sloping downward to the river's edge, the Lawn serves as auditorium, amphitheater, sports field, festival grounds, staging area for charitable fundraising events and an ideal urban space for flying kites or playing Frisbee. The open field was tilted from its highest entry point on Witherspoon, and descends twenty-eight feet in elevation to meet the river. Hargreaves' inspired design solved multiple problems by negating the visual obstruction of the expressway and also

functions as an integral segment of the flood-protection system.

Stadium lights are placed around the lawn, allowing the grounds to be used for recreational purposes until the park's closing at 11 p.m. The Great Lawn was designed to drain quickly and be usable the day after a flood. The lawn has an extensive under drain system, reinforcement, irrigation system and soil that is a mix of 90 percent sand and 10 percent Michigan peat.

The Great Lawn, and its companion boat harbor inlet and adjacent Harbor Lawn, would become the most conspicuous and popular area in Waterfront Park. Able to accommodate tens of thousands of concert-goers or pyrotechnic enthusiasts during huge fireworks shows, the Great Lawn provides an expansive open skyline and creates a grand viewing area for public spectacles like Thunder Over Louisville and its daytime air show. Nowhere else in Louisville is there such an expanse of open sky combined with a river view.

George Hargreaves, in the Master Plan, referred to the area as being symbolic of the first European settlers' efforts to cut down the forests and open the fields for cultivation. The Great Lawn is much more than mere symbolism. For the first time since the original town trustees were forced to sell off the lands at the riverfront to satisfy the debt owed to Colonel John Campbell, Louisville finally had a town common. These open places for community get-togethers are staple elements of towns and, with the construction of the Great Lawn, Louisvillians had a central place to come together as a community. Located in the heart of Louisville's waterfront, the area was equally accessible to people from the West End, East End, central city and suburbs. It was the realization of Olmsted's lofty goal of producing parks that represent the best traditions of American democracy by bringing people together.

The Great Lawn served individuals or throngs of people equally. Its central placement indicates its importance to

Convenient parking lots, referred to as fingers, reach into the park and help provide security and visibility to the grounds. Sculpted earthen mounds, or plinths, break the Park into smaller spaces between upland meadows and wooded areas. The crisply edged grassy knolls provide intimate spaces in a park that can accommodate tens of thousands but also provide quiet and private areas.

Waterfront Park, and the place vividly re-creates an earlier Louisville, as described by British Navy Captain Basil Hall during his visit to the Falls in 1828.

NOTHING DELIGHTED US MORE AT THIS BEAUTIFUL SPOT THAN THE RICH, FRESH GREENSWARD — THE HONEST GRASS — UPON WHICH WE COULD SIT DOWN WITH COMFORT. THE TREES ALSO ABOUT THE TOWN WERE INCOMPARABLY FINER THAN ANY WE HAD SEEN ELSEWHERE. THEY WERE NOT ONLY TALLER, BUT, HAVING PLENTY OF SPACE TO SPREAD OUT THEIR BRANCHES, THEY HAD GROWN UP WITH SINGULAR BEAUTY AND EFFECT. THE VARIOUS BENDS AND REACHES, ALSO, OF THE MAGNIFICENT OHIO, JUST AT THIS SPOT, COVERED OVER WITH STEAMBOATS AND RAFTS, AND FRINGED WITH NOBLE FORESTS AND NUMBERLESS GAY VILLAS, ADDED GREATLY TO THE ENCHANTMENT OF THE SCENERY AT THIS MOST INTERESTING STATION OF ALL THE BACK-WOODS.

As work on Phase I progressed, new opportunities for programming began to open on the waterfront. In 1997 the first annual Independence Day celebration brought people to the river's edge to celebrate the Fourth of July holiday. The program became a signature event at the park and would expand into a two-day affair because of its great popularity. In 2010 over 160,000 people flocked to the Great Lawn for fireworks, food, music and community celebration. When John James Audubon described a similar event on the same site in 1808, he recalled the festivities with great affection, "…although more than twenty years have elapsed since I joined a Kentucky Barbecue, my spirit is refreshed every 4th of July by the recollection of that day's merriment."

"Condensed Picturesque"

The final element in Phase I plans was the creation of the Linear Park. This segment differs from the Waterfront Plaza and Great Lawn sections lying to the west. They featured hard-surfaced areas to serve as commercial wharf, restaurant, festival

Extravagant joy, as that of Uncle Sam on stilts, is unleashed by celebrants at the annual Waterfront Independence Day Festival. As documented by John James Audubon, Louisvillians had long enjoyed the nation's birthday, and have gathered on the waterfront area for more than two centuries.

accommodations and open-air theater. Designed to serve masses of people, they were the most public sections of Waterfront Park.

Linear Park was Hargreaves' vision of a new urban park, incorporating traditional elements of bucolic green space, groves of trees, play areas for children and leafy walking, running and bike paths. Picnic tables, grills and swings provide facilities for families or small groups to gather and enjoy quiet activities by the river's edge. This segment of the park supplies the green space so often requested in the public forums in the early days of WDC.

The Great Lawn hosts the largest public gatherings to be held in Waterfront Park. Events like Thunder Over Louisville, the annual Independence Festival and summertime Waterfront Wednesdays bring large crowds to enjoy the natural amphitheater running down to the Ohio River. While the Harbor recalls Louisville's days as a busy inland port, it is enjoyed by contemporary boaters who tie up to enjoy concerts and other activities.

A complex and imaginative design, the Linear Park brings the country into the city, and rethinks traditional park designs that approximate natural space and atmosphere. Especially when superimposed on the former blighted industrial wasteland at the river's edge, Linear Park establishes new national standards for innovative park design.

George Hargreaves characterizes the Linear Park as Condensed Picturesque. An idealized vision of nature, Hargreaves created sculptural land masses, called plinths, to approximate the river's flow and drainage patterns. Arranged purposely throughout Linear Park, the sharply delineated small plateaus divide the area into open meadows, picnic areas, playgrounds and private groves. A lower walking path alongside the river, typically flooded at high river levels, features an area of native riverbank vegetation.

"…the freeway helped to carry workers out of downtown to their suburban homes, rendering downtown a ghost town after 6:00 p.m."

No feature of the Louisville waterfront area presented a greater design challenge than the presence of I-64 expressway passing immediately overhead. Meg Calkins, a writer for *Landscape Architecture* magazine, wrote a perceptive analysis of the Park's first phase in the publication's July 2001 issue.

The Master Plan was fully cognizant of the concrete interstate highways rising above, and through the Waterfront Park. The Plan's designs opens new corridors to the river along the entire length of the Park.

Over the years, as river conveyance diminished and other forms of transport took over, the riverfront, as in so many other waterfront cities across the United States, was severed from downtown by the railroad, roads, industrial uses, and finally the construction of the elevated Interstate 64 in 1972. As in so many other cities, the freeway helped to carry workers out of downtown to their suburban homes, rendering downtown a ghost town after 6:00 p.m.

Almost as soon as the freeway was completed, people started talking about reconnecting the city with the river. Cities across the country were discovering their waterfronts as assets, not liabilities — assets that could bring people back to largely deserted downtowns. Louisville was no different. But Louisville could not remove its freeway to reconnect to the waterfront, as such cities as Baltimore, San Francisco, and Portland, Oregon, have done. Interstate 64 is a through freeway, not just a means of access to downtown, and would be prohibitively expensive to relocate.

The Hargreaves Associates design solves that conundrum by sliding the sloping plane of lawns under the freeway, opening views from downtown to the river. Earlier in the process, design director George Hargreaves felt that the psychological barrier of the elevated freeway could be overcome if the high-speed River Road underneath were rerouted into downtown and an on-ramp moved one block west, freeing up views under the freeway. He was right. The freeway overhead is hardly noticed as the sunlight on the lawn, the cascading water

of the adjacent linear fountain, and the clear view to the river pull one forward to the Ohio. Before, "standing at the Humana building near the edge of the site," explains Glenn Allen of Hargreaves Associates, "one could only see the north bank of the Ohio — not the river itself. By carving the bank back and giving the lawn a tilt, the view from the city to the river is open, and one psychologically slides right under the freeway to the water."

Invisible Challenges

Waterfront Park's design, ambitious and imaginative, looked beautiful in the colorful architectural renderings and scale models. After imagining the Park, the next task was to surmount the technical aspects of its construction, maintenance and public use. An April 10, 1995, article in Louisville's *Business First*, written by Kate Dalton, provides an idea of the challenges awaiting park developers in Phase I of the project.

After eight years, Waterfront Park in downtown Louisville seems to be coming together. The park is about three years away from completion of its first phase, said Mike Kimmel, deputy director of the Waterfront Development Corporation.

The project already has faced many challenges and has several ahead... Nevertheless, demands such as building out into the Ohio River, or constructing a water's edge that can withstand the waves made by barge traffic, have taken a great deal of planning and thought.

But Kimmel said moving roads and ramps is not technically hard to do. The real technical

CHALLENGES FALL WITHIN THE PARK ITSELF — AND OFTEN IN ITS UNDERLYING STRUCTURES, WHICH FEW LOUISVILLIANS WILL EVER SEE.

THE PIER

IN HARGREAVES' DESIGN, TWO MAIN FEATURES OF THE PARK — THE OVERLOOK AND GREAT LAWN — EXTEND BEYOND THE EXISTING RIVER'S EDGE INTO THE OHIO. "WHAT WE HAD HOPED TO DO IS JUST DROP SHEET PILING INTO THE WATER TO MAKE THAT FORM AND THEN BACKFILL IT," KIMMEL SAID.

THAT WAS NOT FEASIBLE FOR TWO REASONS: THE RIVER BED DROPS OFF SUDDENLY, WHICH MEANS IT WOULD TAKE A LOT OF FILL, AND NEW FILL WOULD HAVE CHANGED THE CURRENT NEAR THE BANK IN HIGH WATER.

MOFFATT & NICHOL ENGINEERS, WATERFRONT PARK'S MARINE CONSULTANT, HAS BEEN CLOSELY INVOLVED IN WORK ALONG THE RIVER'S EDGE. McCOY BUTLER, CHIEF STRUCTURAL ENGINEER IN THE FIRM'S RALEIGH, N.C., OFFICE, SAID BARGE COMPANIES EXPRESSED CONCERN ABOUT BEING PULLED OFF COURSE WHILE LINING UP ALONG THE OHIO'S SOUTHERN BANK TOWARD THE PORTLAND CANAL. IN HIGH WATER, THE RIVER FLOWS OVER THE DAM TO THE NORTH. THIS CREATES A PULL TOWARD INDIANA THAT COULD MAKE TROUBLE FOR A BARGE TRYING TO HUG THE SOUTH SHORE.

THE SOLUTION: TO BUILD THE EDGES OF THE OVERLOOK AND GREAT LAWN ON A PIER MADE OF PIPE PILINGS DRIVEN INTO THE RIVER BED. THE PILINGS SUPPORT A DECK THAT WILL BECOME THE BASE FOR THE CONCRETE OVERLOOK AND THE TOPSOIL AND GRASS OF THE GREAT LAWN, WHICH WILL SIT A FEW FEET ABOVE THE NORMAL WATERLINE. THE PIER IS OPEN UNDERNEATH TO LET THE RIVER FLOW THROUGH.

THE DESIGN WILL "MINIMIZE THE IMPACT ON THE CURRENT," BUTLER SAID, AND ALLOW THE WATER TO "FOLLOW ITS NATURAL PATH UNDERNEATH THE STRUCTURE." BECAUSE BARGES COME ALONG THE RIVER'S SOUTHERN EDGE AND BECAUSE THE PIERS WILL EXTEND INTO THE CHANNEL 115 FEET FURTHER THAN THE EXISTING RIVER BANK, THE PIERS NEED PROTECTION. WHAT THEY WILL GET ARE MARINE FENDERS.

SHOULD A RUNAWAY BARGE HIT THE GREAT LAWN, A HUGE CAP OF CONCRETE (SET ON ANGLE, LIKE THE SIDE OF A HILL) WILL TAKE THE BRUNT OF THE BLOW AND BREAK OFF INTO THE RIVER. BEHIND THE CAP ARE MARINE FENDERS ABOUT 4 FEET THICK, SAID DAN DEYOUNG, DIRECTOR OF PROJECT SERVICES AT BRAVURA. THE FENDERS WILL BE MADE WITH A RUBBER MATERIAL THAT WILL COMPRESS TO ABSORB MORE SHOCK, AND BEHIND THEM ARE MORE CONCRETE AND FILL.

THE IDEA IS TO SAVE THE PIERS FROM DAMAGE, SINCE REPLACING THE CONCRETE CAP IS MUCH LESS EXPENSIVE THAN REPLACING THE PIERS. THIS KIND OF CONSTRUCTION IS USUALLY USED FOR BIG DOCKING PIERS SUITABLE FOR SHIPS.

THE WATER'S EDGE

THE ENGINEERING CHALLENGE OF CREATING THE LINEAR PARK'S RIVER EDGE IS AS MUCH AESTHETIC AS TECHNICAL. WHAT THE WATERFRONT DEVELOPMENT CORP. ORIGINALLY WANTED, KIMMEL SAID, WAS A NICE GRASSY SLOPE DISAPPEARING INTO THE RIVER. BUT BECAUSE OF THE WAVES CREATED BY WIND AND BARGE TRAFFIC, THAT IS NOT POSSIBLE. TWO-FOOT WAVES TRANSLATE INTO A 9-FOOT-WIDE EDGE WHERE VEGETATION WILL NOT GROW AND WHERE UNPROTECTED GROUND WOULD GRADUALLY BECOME ERODED.

THE MOST LIKELY POSSIBILITY IS A SEMISOFT EDGE. GABIONS – WIRE-MESH BASKETS TILLED WITH ROCK – AT THE WATER'S EDGE WOULD TAKE THE BRUNT OF THE SCOURING. ABOVE THEM, GEOTECHNIC MATS – A SYNTHETIC MESH FOR HOLDING EARTH – SECURED WITH MORE ROCK WOULD TRAP SILT AND GIVE A FOUNDATION ON WHICH SOME HARDY RIVER PLANTS COULD GROW, BUTLER SAID. ABOVE THAT, DEPENDING ON WHERE ONE IS WITHIN THE PARK, WOULD BE COBBLESTONES, PATHS OR LAWN.

DURING EXCAVATIONS, FEDERAL AND STATE ENVIRONMENTAL REGULATIONS REQUIRE THAT TOPSOIL BE RETAINED. WHILE SOME CONTAMINATED DIRT WAS HAULED AWAY TO LANDFILLS, MOST SOIL WAS KEPT ON SITE, TO BE REUSED AS TOPSOIL AND TO CREATE THE HILLS PLANNED FOR THE LINEAR PARK AREA.

GEOTECHNIC MATS COVERED WITH TOPSOIL AND PLANTINGS SHOULD SECURE THE FINAL SHAPE OF THE PARK'S HILLS, AND STABILIZE THE SOIL DURING FLOODS. "WE NEED TO MAKE SURE THAT IF WE DESIGN A HILL, THE HILL STAYS THERE, AND EROSION DOESN'T TAKE IT DOWN TO PADUCAH," KIMMEL SAID.

THE HARBOR

ACCORDING TO THE WATERFRONT DEVELOPMENT CORPORATION, BRAVURA AND MARINE CONSULTANT BUTLER, CUTTING THE RELATIVELY SHALLOW HARBOR (ABOUT 13 FEET DEEP) WILL NOT BE DIFFICULT. THE DOCKS

A graceful harbor welcomes boaters to the edge of the Great Lawn and its many events and activities. Reminiscent of when Louisville hosted thousands of riverboats every year, the Harbor's docks are designed to rise up tall towers in case of unusually high water.

WILL HAVE SOME INTERESTING FEATURES, HOWEVER, TO ENABLE THEM TO RISE AND FALL WITH THE RIVER.

TO COPE WITH THE CHANGING FLOOD LEVELS, THE DOCKS WILL BE BUILT ON TELESCOPING PILES, ONE INSIDE ANOTHER. THE DOCKS THEN CAN RISE AND FALL AS THE RIVER RISES AND FALLS. UNLIKE A FIXED DOCK, THE FLOATING DOCK WON'T BE FLOODED IN HIGH WATER OR STICK OUT MANY FEET IN THE AIR DURING LOW WATER.

THE DOCK PILES CAN TELESCOPE UP TO A FEW FEET OVER 100-YEAR FLOOD LEVELS, OR 451 FEET ABOVE SEA LEVEL (THE NORMAL LEVEL OF THE RIVER IS 421 FEET). DESIGNING FOR 100-YEAR FLOOD LEVELS IS THE STANDARD PRACTICE, BUTLER SAID. IF WATER RISES HIGHER THAN THAT, HOWEVER, THE DOCK WILL FLOAT OUT OF ITS PILINGS AND DRIFT AWAY.

THE WHARF, POOLS, RESTAURANT AND FLOOD PROTECTION

TO PREVENT SILT FROM COLLECTING BELOW THE LOWEST CASCADING POOL, THE POOL WILL HAVE A PUMPING SYSTEM THAT DRIVES A SMALL CURRENT OF WATER OUT INTO THE RIVER. WITH THIS FLUSHING SYSTEM, BY THE TIME A PIECE OF SILT IS "READY TO SETTLE OUT, IT'S BACK IN THE RIVER," BUTLER SAID.

AS FOR THE RESTAURANT, THE MAIN ISSUE IS TO MAKE SURE THE OCCUPIED SPACE IS ABOVE THE 100-YEAR FLOOD LINE, SAID JIM WALTERS, PRESIDENT OF BRAVURA. AS THE BUILDING IS CURRENTLY BEING DESIGNED BY WALTERS' FIRM, IT WILL REST ON STILTS, AND THE LOWER LEVEL WILL CONTAIN ONLY SOME DOORS, ELEVATORS AND THE BEGINNING OF THE ENCIRCLING RAMPS, WHICH WILL ALLOW VISITORS TO CLIMB TO THE OBSERVATION DECK.

THE FINAL ISSUE BEING ADDRESSED IS FLOOD CONTROL. "IN ANY DEVELOPMENT, A GOOD USE OF RIVER-EDGE PROPERTY IS A PARK, BECAUSE YOU CAN GET IT FLOODED WITHOUT INCONVENIENCING PEOPLE," SAID WATERFRONT DEVELOPMENT'S KIMMEL.

The Water Feature, originally conceived as running parallel to the Ohio River, just east of the Clark Bridge at Second Street, was changed from its original design as too expensive to build and operate. The replacement design was a long horizontal fountain, running north to south from Witherspoon Street down to the Ohio River, linking the Festival Plaza with the Great Lawn via a series of walking bridges. At nine hundred feet in length and thirty feet of width, the feature contains five sequentially-joined pools where water from the top flowed down through each subsequent chamber, much like the design of the original Lock system of the 1830 Portland Canal. A series of water cannons added bursts of spray jets of water in fifteen-foot-high arches.

The $3 million water feature is entirely original to Waterfront Park. Hargreaves' elongated fountain was reminiscent of old Beargrass Creek before it was relocated two miles upstream in the 1850s. Like Beargrass Creek, it is crossed by five bridges. The design features five descending pools, with water flowing from fissures in limestone walls at the top of each. The water, only eighteen inches deep, cascades over a series of stair steps, greatly resembling the early descriptions of the river rapids that came to be called the Falls of the Ohio. When the water reaches the lowest pool adjacent to the river, it appears to empty directly into the Ohio, but it is actually captured and re-circulated back up to the highest point by a sophisticated system of pumps and pipes. Computers control the water cannons, flow rate and mist from the fissures. The entire operating system is entirely unseen by visitors, and the visual effect is of a natural stream flowing as a tributary into the great Ohio River. WDC chairman Charles McCarty believed the fountain "will bring activity and excitement to the riverfront" and "have a major impact on the area."

Although it was near the Falls Fountain out in the river, it provided an entirely new and original presentation of the arresting qualities of moving water.

The Water Feature, one of the most complex designs in Waterfront Park, is meant to recall the time when Beargrass Creek entered the river in downtown Louisville. Gigantic fountains, called water cannons, periodically spray streams of water horizontally into stair-stepped chambers that are reminiscent of the chambers of the original Louisville-Portland Canal. Park officials continually remind the public the Water Feature is not a swimming pool, but its lure during summer months is nearly irresistible.

The Power of Continuity

A project with the complexity and sophistication of Louisville's Waterfront Park demanded a long germination period. Originally envisioned as a project requiring twenty-five years to complete, it took thirteen years from the founding of WDC in 1986 until Phase I could be publicly dedicated and celebrated in 1999. Jim Walters, president of Bravura Corporation, the project managers for Phase I, stated that consistency and political ability made the project feasible. "Master plans are only as good as the institutional memory creating them. Mayors and aldermen come and go, but the Waterfront Development Corporation and David Karem, the president/executive director, were there from the beginning and are still working toward phases II and III of the Hargreaves master plan."

Farewell to the Fountain

The Louisville Falls Fountain, one of the earliest attempts to draw attention back to the waterfront, was gradually showing the effect of being buffeted by strong currents, floating debris and mechanical failures. Repeated attempts to make the huge floating installation look less industrial ugly were unsuccessful. Ideas included painting the base in a variety of *trompe l'oeil* techniques, adjusting colored lighting or covering the surface with mirrors. To enhance the visual effect of the fountain, it was moved closer to the Kentucky shore, but to little avail.

Scheduled to begin operating on Memorial Day, the Falls Fountain seemed to suffer from annual bouts of stage fright. WDC spokesperson Marlene Grissom routinely made an announcement each year concerning the water jets' status. In 1995 operations were delayed by high water and current too strong for divers to reconnect the mooring cables. The following year, high water again prevented moving the floating machine from its winter home in Utica, Indiana. In 1998 a news account in *The Courier-Journal* reported the declining status of the Falls Fountain.

FRAYED CABLES DELAY
FALLS FOUNTAIN'S RETURN

THE 12-YEAR-OLD LOUISVILLE FALLS FOUNTAIN IS SHOWING ITS AGE.

THE 40-FOOT-LONG STEEL CABLES THAT HOLD THE FOUNTAIN IN PLACE IN THE OHIO RIVER ARE FRAYED AND NEED TO BE REPLACED.

REPLACING THE CABLES WILL COST THE LOUISVILLE WATER COMPANY ABOUT $7,000 AND DELAY THE FOUNTAIN'S SCHEDULED RETURN ON MEMORIAL DAY WEEKEND AT LEAST A FEW DAYS.

"WE DIDN'T WANT IT TO GET LOOSE ON US," SAID CARL FAUTZ, THE WATER COMPANY'S PLANT-MAINTENANCE MANAGER, WHO TENDS THE FOUNTAIN.

THE FOUNTAIN COST ABOUT $90,000 TO OPERATE AND MAINTAIN LAST YEAR, BUT IT'S GETTING MORE UNRELIABLE AND COSTING MORE TO KEEP UP EACH YEAR, FAUTZ SAID.

EACH CABLE HAS SIX WOVEN STRANDS OF STEEL WIRE ABOUT 1 ¼ INCH IN DIAMETER. AT LEAST A STRAND OF EACH CABLE WAS BROKEN, AND ONE OR MORE STRANDS WERE FRAYED. ALL FOUR CABLES WERE THE ORIGINALS.

THE CITY, IN EFFECT, PAYS FOR MAINTENANCE OF THE FOUNTAIN; IT OWNS ALL THE STOCK IN THE WATER COMPANY, WHICH DEDUCTS THE COST OF REPAIRS, MAINTENANCE AND ELECTRICAL POWER FOR THE FOUNTAIN FROM THE ROUGHLY $10 MILLION A YEAR DIVIDEND IT PAYS THE CITY.

Finally, the expense of replacing the frayed cables, coupled with the disclosure that the main propulsion engine needed replacement, sounded the death knell to the fountain. With no one willing to step forward to pay for repairs, the Louisville Falls Fountain was quietly retired in 1998. Always a daunting technical challenge, more than anything else it was the Ohio River that defeated the floating appliance. As from time immemorial, the river will have its way, and all the planning on earth cannot tame its power when the Ohio River decides to roar.

Louisville's Old Adversary Returns

And the river decided to roar once again in March 1997. A recurring heavy rain pattern deluged the Ohio River Valley, and the worst flood since 1964 struck Louisville. Measuring fifty-five feet at the Lower McAlpine Lock gauge, the rising waters closed the Portland Canal and Interstates 64 and 65. Over 50,000 Louisville homes were affected and the event caused an estimated $200 million in damages.

Waterfront Park was facing its first major natural disaster, and

the first target of the high water was the WDC headquarters in the former Martin Marietta building. Designed for such a catastrophe, the building's first floor took on river water to a depth of 6 ½ feet deep. The staff attempted to sandbag the entrance, but to no avail. Offices on the second and third floors were unaffected, but the WDC staff was forced to relocate its operations to donated hotel rooms on Zorn Avenue. The headquarters building was designed and hardened for such a predictable event as an Ohio River flood, but the new park, still under construction, had never before been so tested.

High water in March 1997 once again brought home the reality that periodic flooding on the Ohio River is inevitable, and the original design of the WDC headquarters was of sound practical sense. The river rose 6 ½ feet in the entrance lobby of the building.

A *Courier-Journal* article investigated conditions at the waterfront after the Flood of '97.

FLOOD VICTIMS MAY INCLUDE PARK TREES

AS THE OHIO RIVER ROSE INTO LOUISVILLE'S RIVERFRONT PARK LAST WEEK, NEWLY PLANTED EVERGREEN TREES LOOKED AS IF THEY WERE SCRAMBLING FOR HIGHER GROUND ON THE PARK'S ARTIFICIAL HILLS.

BUT MANY OF THE TREES WERE COVERED OR PARTLY COVERED BY THE OHIO'S SILT-LADEN WATER.

WHETHER THE HEMLOCKS, PINES AND SPRUCES SURVIVED THE EXPERIENCE WON'T BE KNOWN FOR A MONTH OR TWO. BUT SOME TREE EXPERTS QUESTIONED THE WISDOM OF PLANTING EVERGREENS, WHICH DON'T TOLERATE FLOODING, WITHIN THE RIVER'S REACH.

DEPUTY DIRECTOR MIKE KIMMEL ACKNOWLEDGED SOME OF THE TREES MIGHT DIE, BUT HE DEFENDED THE DECISION TO PLANT THEM.

THE LIKELIHOOD OF FLOODING "WAS A BIG FACTOR" IN DESIGNING LANDSCAPING FOR THE PARK, HE SAID. WATER-TOLERANT TREES, SUCH AS RIVER BIRCHES AND SYCAMORES, WERE PLANTED CLOSER TO THE WATER, WITH EVERGREENS RESTRICTED TO THE PARK'S HIGHER REACHES, KIMMEL SAID.

IN ANY CASE, IT WILL BE THE CONTRACTORS FOR THE PROJECT, NOT THE WATERFRONT DEVELOPMENT AGENCY, WHO WILL HAVE TO PAY TO REPLACE ANY TREES THAT DON'T SURVIVE, KIMMEL SAID.

KIMMEL SAID THAT SOME TREES SUFFERED PHYSICAL DAMAGE BUT THAT "IT'S NOT AS BAD AS WE THOUGHT IT WOULD BE." IN GENERAL, THE PARK CAME THROUGH THE FLOODING QUITE WELL, HE SAID.

MATTING LAID DOWN TO PREVENT EROSION "HELD BEAUTIFULLY," KIMMEL SAID. WHERE EROSION OCCURRED, SOME RECONTOURING MAY BE DONE TO PREVENT IT IN THE FUTURE, HE SAID.

"Flood debris is our main nemesis."

The impact of the flood was felt most by the newest member of the WDC staff. Gary Pepper was recruited and hired in June 1996 to fill the essential role of Landscape Manager. A landscape architect with years of practical experience in a commercial nursery, Pepper became the Park's first line of defense against horticultural disasters, eroding riverbanks, overfull garbage containers, damaged park benches and untold other threats to the

Deputy Director Mike Kimmel climbed a ladder to enter the sand-bagged entrance of the Waterfront Development Corporation headquarters. Despite all efforts, access to the building was impossible, and although the upper offices remained high and dry, the staff was forced to relocate for about ten days until the river receded.

Gary Pepper, the WDC staff person in charge of park maintenance and care, devised a system of pushing driftwood and other river-born debris after the 1997 Flood. The park, and especially the Great Lawn feature, was designed to withstand flooding. When the debris is removed, the entire surface can be washed with fire hoses and be operational again in a few days.

new park, filled with fresh plantings and eager visitors wanting to enjoy the space.

In a 2009 interview in *TURF* magazine, a trade publication for the lawn-care industry, Gary Pepper revealed some parts of his job that required considerable innovation.

WHILE THE WATERFRONT LOCATION IS A LARGE PART OF WHAT ATTRACTS VISITORS (SOME 1.5 MILLION A YEAR BY THE LATEST COUNTS) TO THE GRAND PARK, THE RIVER ALSO PRESENTS SIGNIFICANT LANDSCAPE MAINTENANCE CHALLENGES. "THE PARK IS SET IN A FLOOD PLAIN," SAYS PEPPER. "A GOOD PORTION OF THE GREAT LAWN GETS WHAT IS CALLED 'NUISANCE FLOODING.'" FOR PEPPER AND HIS STAFF, THE FLOODS ARE MORE THAN A NUISANCE, THOUGH. THEY'RE A ROUTINE PART OF THE WORKDAY. THE FLOODING EVENTS CAN BE 4 TO 10 FEET, AND OCCUR AS MANY AS 12 TIMES PER YEAR. "ROUGHLY 20 TO 30 PERCENT OF THE GREAT LAWN CAN BE FLOODED IN THE SPRING," HE SAYS.

THEREFORE, THE GREAT LAWN WAS BUILT ON A 12-INCH SAND BASE. "THE SAND IS BLENDED WITH PEAT MOSS AND A SHREDDED GEOTEXTILE MATERIAL CALLED NETLON," EXPLAINS PEPPER. "THAT MATERIAL WAS ROLLED AND GRADED, AND HAS GRASS GROWING ON IT." THE UNUSUAL CONSTRUCTION HELPS THE LARGE, OPEN TURFED AREA WITHSTAND COMPACTION FROM THE LARGE NUMBER OF VISITORS (150,000 ON THE FOURTH OF JULY ALONE) BUT, MORE IMPORTANTLY, HELPS THE GREAT LAWN RAPIDLY DRAIN AND RECOVER FROM FLOODING.

TO HELP CLEAN UP AFTER FLOODING, PEPPER HAS DEVISED A SYSTEM FEATURING TWO RATHER UNUSUAL PIECES OF TURFGRASS MAINTENANCE EQUIPMENT: SNOWPLOWS AND A PONTOON BOAT. "FLOOD DEBRIS IS OUR MAIN NEMESIS. WE USE JOHN DEERE GATORS WITH PLOWS ON THE FRONT TO PUSH ALL THE MUD AND DEBRIS OFF. (HE SAYS KEEPING THE PLOW FACING STRAIGHT AHEAD RATHER THAN ANGLED HELPS TO MINIMIZE THE TEARING OF TURF.) THE GATORS HAVE HEATED CABS, SO EVEN ON COLD WINTER DAYS WE CAN USE THEM. THEN, WE HAVE FIRE HOSE CONNECTIONS THROUGHOUT THE ENTIRE PARK SO WE CAN HOSE EVERYTHING DOWN WITH FRESH WATER," SAYS PEPPER. "THE NETLON IS AN ENGINEERING TURF; THE ROOT INTERWEAVES THROUGH THE TEXTILE FABRIC AND CREATES A VERY STABLE BASE SO THE PLANT DOESN'T GET WASHED OUT." ON THE HARDSCAPE AREAS, A PICKUP TRUCK AND SNOWPLOW ARE USED TO CLEAR DEBRIS MORE QUICKLY.

TO ASSIST IN CLEANUPS, INCLUDING THE REMOVAL OF LARGE LOGS AND OTHER DEBRIS THAT FLOAT INTO THE HARBOR AREA AND ALONG THE SHORE OF THE PARK, PEPPER BOUGHT AN OLD PONTOON BOAT. "WE DISASSEMBLED THE WHOLE THING, PUT THE STEERING COLUMN IN THE MIDDLE AND MOUNTED A GIANT BOOM ON THE FRONT OF THE BOAT WITH A WINCH," PEPPER EXPLAINS. FROM THE BOOM HANGS A "RAKE-TYPE" DEVICE THAT WAS BUILT TO ALLOW THE PONTOON BOAT TO PUSH THE FLOATING DEBRIS BACK OUT INTO THE RIVER. BY LAW, ANY DEBRIS THAT HAS COME COMPLETELY OUT OF THE RIVER AND ONTO SHORE MUST BE COLLECTED, PLACED INTO DUMPSTERS AND DISPOSED OF.

Gary Pepper had a much more enjoyable duty in 1997 when the park dedicated a new section of trees to a longtime television personality, Fred Wiche, who turned his amateur interest in horticulture into a regular, and very popular, WHAS-TV feature called "The Weekend Gardener." Mayor Jerry Abramson and Operation Brightside, the citywide clean-up and beautification initiative, honored Wiche for his contributions to the community, and especially to Waterfront Park.

A grove of trees for the Linear Park had been purchased through an innovative recycling scrap paper program joined by 130 local businesses and organizations. Proceeds from the organized paper drive were used to buy trees for the park – not just new saplings, but trees that were substantially larger than provided for in the park's budget. Planting trees with five- to six-inch diameters allows them to stabilize and grow far better than the typical one- to six-inch planting.

"To think that my name is associated with a project like this is beyond my wildest expectations," Wiche declared. "It's just a wonderful thing to watch the development of the waterfront."

Mayor Abramson was delighted to recognize Wiche's generous spirit. "He has helped spread the word about Operation Brightside from the beginning," Abramson said. "He has such credibility.…when Fred Wiche says it's good, it's good." The mayor also presented a community-service award to David Wilkins, the president of Doe-Anderson Advertising, who originated the recycling plan, which in less than two years had collected and recycled more than one hundred tons of paper.

In the spring of 1998, the Waterfront Development Corporation announced a new program which encouraged donations of trees and plants to the park.

WHERE IN DOWNTOWN LOUISVILLE CAN YOU FIND RED MAPLE, AMERICAN BEECH, GREEN MOUNTAIN SUGAR MAPLE, BLACKGUM, VERNAL WITCHHAZEL, FRAGRANT SUMAC AND BOTTLEBRUSH BUCKEYE ENHANCING THE CITYSCAPE? YOU DON'T HAVE TO TRAVEL FAR – JUST HEAD OVER TO THE NEW WATERFRONT PARK.

AND WHAT DOES THE PARK HAVE TO DO WITH THE WATERFRONT TREE EXCHANGE (WTE) AND YOU? IT WAS YOUR PARTICIPATION IN WTE WHICH HELPED TO PLANT A GROVE OF TREES IN PHASE ONE OF THE PARK'S DEVELOPMENT. AND ADDITIONAL TREES WILL BE PLANTED DURING 1998 AS PART OF PHASE II. THE AREA HAS BEEN DESIGNATED AS THE WATERFRONT TREE EXCHANGE GROVE. AS THE DEVELOPMENT OF THE PARK CONTINUES, THERE WILL ULTIMATELY BE ATTRACTIVE SIGNAGE NOTIFYING ALL WHO VISIT THIS SECTION OF THE PARK OF YOUR GENEROUS CONTRIBUTION TO CREATING THIS PEACEFUL, SHADY PLACE.

Back to the River for Food and Fun

Boating is still a popular activity up and down the Ohio River. Whether their purpose is industrial, recreational or educational, water craft are integral to the character of Louisville and Jefferson County. In 1995 then-County Judge/Executive Dave Armstrong negotiated the purchase of an additional riverboat. As his predecessor, Judge Marlow Cook, had done when he purchased the *Belle of Louisville* in 1962, Armstrong got a very good bargain on a St. Louis-based boat called the *Huck Finn.* Jefferson County government spent $395,000 to buy the diesel-powered excursion boat to be moored at the Farnsley-Moremen Landing below the McAlpine Locks and Dam. This location allowed river-borne tours to visit Otter Creek Park, West Point and festivals in Shawnee Park for citizens of the southwestern section of the county, without the need of negotiating the Portland Canal.

The excursion craft was decorated to look like the steamboats of old. Mike Fitzgerald, captain of the *Belle*, promised to give the craft the decorative details of a steamboat, even though two of the four smokestacks were merely ornamental.

Judge Armstrong sponsored a contest to rename the vessel, and Chuck Parrish, historian of the Corps of Engineers, came up with the winning entry, the *Spirit of Jefferson.* The boat picked up nearly one hundred small charters annually that the *Belle* was unable to handle. Ideal for smaller groups like wedding parties, corporate receptions or regional tours, the

In 1995 County Judge Executive Dave Armstrong negotiated the purchase of the *Huck Finn*, a smaller excursion boat, to be headquartered at the Farnsley-Moremen Landing in southwestern Jefferson County. The boat, renamed the *Spirit of Jefferson*, was later moved to the Fourth Street wharf and is a popular attraction for weddings and other events too small for the *Belle of Louisville*. A series of smaller floating eating places replaced the original Islands restaurant on the rapidly improving public landing between Fifth and Second Streets. *(Photo courtesy of the Belle of Louisville)*

Spirit moved to the improved Louisville wharf after the park improvements were made.

Another waterfront attraction arrived in 1997 as a floating restaurant, Towboat Annie's, replacing the former Hard Dock Café at the Fourth Street wharf. A few years later its replacement, Port O'Call, lasted only one year before closing. The casual dining craft serving day visitors to the waterfront was swamped with the opening of the very large new restaurant, Joe's Crab Shack, on the Festival Plaza grounds.

Early in the planning process, WDC officials invited local restaurant operators to discuss locating in the Park. The response was negative, with each explaining that there would not be enough customers to justify the expense of setting up, but they would be willing to discuss moving there if the Waterfront Development Corporation would pay all construction costs and an operational fee to underwrite their business.

KingFish Restaurant, a popular Louisville seafood chain for decades, proposed to officials their willingness to buy outright a prime waterfront location and offered to pay a total of $10,000 for a fifty-year contract. The firm asked for tax incentives, insisted the Park pay for raising the site above the flood plain, and that they have the exclusive rights to sell seafood in the park. Officials rejected the rather one-sided offer and opened a bidding process seeking a restaurant operator.

Landry's Seafood, a national chain of upscale restaurants, recognized the potential of the waterfront location and agreed to place one of their popular attractions called Joe's Crab Shack next to the WDC office building. While sometimes criticized for its high-concept commercial architecture, this location would become one of the most successful locations in the nation. For Thunder Over Louisville, this Joe's Crab Shack location becomes the single highest-producing Landry property in America. Constructed by the restaurant chain, the restaurant became a very popular attraction, making the waterfront a destination

A popular seafood theme restaurant, Joe's Crab Shack, rises on stilts to avoid periods of Ohio River high water. This design replaced a series of failed floating restaurants and was able to claim the chain's most successful single-day operation during annual Thunder Over Louisville celebrations.

FEATURES OF THE PARK ARE THE GEOMETRIC LANDSCAPE SCULPTURES. THE DEGREE OF DIFFICULTY OF THE PROJECT CENTERS AROUND TWO MAJOR EVOLUTIONS: THE PRECISION GRADING OF THE SITE DUE TO THE LIGHT TOLERANCE REQUIREMENTS OF THE GEOMETRIC LAND FORMS AND SCULPTURES, AND THE RECONSTRUCTION OF THE SITE AFTER THE MARCH 1997 HISTORIC FLOOD WHICH SUBMERGED THE ENTIRE SITE FOR TEN DAYS.

How May We Help You?

The rapidly developing Park attracted the attention of many individuals and organizations eager to hold their activities on the grounds. Ashley Cox, a recent graduate of the University of Kentucky School of Communications, began her first full-time job as an assistant to Marlene Grissom helping plan and coordinate events. Beginning her new job in June 1998, Cox immediately plunged into a swirl of activity, helping plan the first Independence Day festival using the new and improved park grounds. On October 19 a large dedication ceremony was held to officially open the Great Lawn. Typical of a rather low-key approach to self-promotion, WDC officials passed out commemorative Frisbees to an appreciative audience.

dining location and generating over $130,000 annually to help support and maintain operation of the Waterfront Park.

"The degree of difficulty…"

As Phase I of the project emerged from its construction period, the Park began gathering public accolades and awards. In presenting the 1998 "Building America" Construction Award of Excellence, the Associated Builders and Contractors of Kentuckiana recognized WDC with an Award of Honor. Named in the award presentation was the contractor, MAC Construction & Excavating, and the project manager, the Bravura Corporation. The honor, given by the local building trades, saluted the Park's success at solving design and building problems, by stating:

THE PARK WAS OFFICIALLY NAMED LINEAR PARK BECAUSE OF THE UNIQUE GEOMETRIC LANDSCAPE THAT MARKS THE PROJECT. SITUATED ALONG THE OHIO RIVER, IT HAS 1800 LINEAR FEET OF FRONTAGE, OVER 80,000 SQUARE YARDS OF LANDSCAPED AREA, AND 9,000 LINEAR FEET OF LIGHTED SIDEWALKS. THE MOST NOTABLE

As the park developed, so did Cox's job responsibilities, and she was soon named Marketing and Events Manager. George Hargreaves observed that the modern urban park differed from the traditional Olmsted bucolic model in that the newer facilities hosted far greater numbers of events and activities. Cox began her career by assisting with the arrival of visiting excursion boats to the improved wharf, but soon began coordinating the numerous requests for weddings, parties, corporate events and, increasingly, the desire of local charities to hold fundraisers on the grounds. Her efforts were largely responsible for making events run smoothly, professionally and without harm to the park or its visitors.

"After the smoke cleared…"

Having served the maximum-allowed three terms made

possible by the mayoral succession amendment, Jerry E. Abramson's role as the city's chief executive came to a close, at least for a while, and former County Judge/Executive David Armstrong was elected Mayor. Armstrong and David Karem had attended U of L Law School together and had worked closely together during Karem's years in leadership in the Kentucky State Senate. Armstrong, a strong advocate of downtown development, made one of his signature initiatives in office the establishment of the downtown Extreme Park. The facility just south of Waterfront Park on Witherspoon Street provided smoothly paved ramps, jumps and obstacle courses needed for the wildly popular new sport of skateboarding. Waterfront Park assisted by donating a small segment of land to complete the Extreme Park facility and Mike Kimmel helped with the required Environmental Impact Statement.

"Rockin' at Riverpoints" was one of the first series of outdoor concerts made possible by the completion of the Great Lawn. Events Manager Ashley Cox created several of the most popular regular entertainment offerings in the park and helped establish the area as an attraction to younger audiences wishing to enjoy waterfront concerts in the evenings.

In 1999 the WDC Board squarely faced a lingering question. The plans for a large residential development of apartments and condos, called FallsHarbor, had stalled due to financing issues. The ambitious development, located at the end of Frankfort Avenue and River Road, faced Towhead Island and would be the Park's nearest east side neighbor and part of the Waterfront Overlay District. Mayor Armstrong asked the Board to review revised design plans for the project to see if they were acceptable to WDC officials. The developers of FallsHarbor had won a three-entry competition in 1989 to develop the land, and in 1991 the City had spent $4 million to help prepare the grounds and relocate rail lines from the development's property. Even after a decade, little progress had been made. At the July 1999 board of director's meeting, the WDC received a full review of the current status of the project, and board members were less than pleased.

Mr. Karem quoted from a letter written by the Mayor to FallsHarbor which stated that "It is critical that the design of the project enhance the waterfront and the surrounding areas. FallsHarbor was selected because of the quality of the original design and it is important that the high standards that characterized the original design be maintained." Karem stated that FallsHarbor would make a presentation concerning the design and at the close of that presentation, the board should vote on the design.

Steve Gouletas, with INVSCO Group Limited, briefed the board on the history of his company and introduced Harold Leifer to make the presentation concerning the project....He stated that currently there was no market for luxury units and that mid-rise and high-rise buildings are not salable but there was a market for middle-income families of $100,000-$200,000 units....He stated that FallsHarbor had commitments from five financial partners but noted that the first phase of the project by itself is not financially feasible, but the total project, which would be

OVER 600 UNITS AND INCLUDE MID-RISE AND, LAST, A LUXURY HIGH-RISE BUILDING, WAS WHAT MADE THE PROJECT FINANCIALLY FEASIBLE.

Bill Weyland, a Louisville developer with well-earned respect from preservationists and city planners because of his record of quality rehabilitation of older buildings, worked with the FallsHarbor group. He gave as reasons for the slow progress a lack of home buyers moving into urban developments. He also expressed concern about archaeological reservations on the property, requirement for public art installations, the stigma of downtown housing and concern for security. Weyland also cited the requirement for the developer to pay the City a fee of $4,000 for each unit sold, a stipulation that was part of the original 1989 agreement.

A series of sharp questions from board members resulted when it became obvious that the project had deteriorated in the past decade, and the board was not pleased with the answers.

JUDGE REBECCA JACKSON ASKED IF RESIDENTS IN THE FIRST PHASE COULD SEE THE RIVER FROM THEIR FIRST FLOOR. MR. WEYLAND REPLIED YES. THE JUDGE FURTHER ASKED IF THE BUILDING MATERIALS WOULD BE DIFFERENT MEDIA. MR. WEYLAND REPLIED YES, BUT PRIMARILY THE MATERIALS WOULD BE VINYL SIDING. CREIGHTON MERSHON OBJECTED TO THE CHARACTERIZATION OF THE SITE AS BEING POOR. MR. WEYLAND REPLIED THAT COST WAS THE MAJOR PROBLEM, NOT THE SITE. MR. MERSHON EXPRESSED CONCERN THAT THE BOARD HAD TO ACCEPT, AT FACE VALUE, FALLSHARBOR'S ASSERTION THAT THE MARKET WOULD NOT SUPPORT MORE EXPENSIVE HOUSING.

MS. INA BOND STATED THAT SHE BELIEVED THE PROPOSAL WAS A MAJOR CHANGE FROM THE EARLIER PROPOSAL AND STATED THAT SHE WAS CONCERNED ABOUT THE VINYL SIDING AND BELIEVED THAT PHASE I WOULD SET THE TONE FOR THE ENTIRE PROJECT. SHE BELIEVED THAT THE CURRENT DESIGN WAS A GIANT STEP DOWN IN QUALITY.

OLLIE BARBER STATED THAT HE BELIEVES THAT THE BOARD HAD ORIGINALLY PURCHASED A CADILLAC AND IS NOW BEING TOLD IT CAN ONLY AFFORD A WINDSTAR... CHARLES MCCARTY FELT THAT THE PROJECT LOOKED LIKE SUBURBAN APARTMENTS WITH A MASS OF VINYL SIDING. MR. MERSHON EXPRESSED CONCERN THAT THE BUILDINGS DID NOT HAVE MORE BALCONIES, WINDOWS AND BETTER VIEWS....BOB ALLISON STATED THAT HE WAS CONFUSED ABOUT THE PROJECT BECAUSE THE PRICE LEVEL OF THE CONDOS WAS MUCH LOWER THAN EXPECTED AND THE PROPOSAL DID NOT HAVE THE FEEL OF A RIVERFRONT DEVELOPMENT....CREIGHTON MERSHON STATED THAT THE DESIGN HAD CHANGED SO MUCH FROM WHAT WAS ORIGINALLY PROPOSED THAT THE BOARD MIGHT JUST WANT TO ISSUE ANOTHER RFP FOR NEW PROPOSALS.

David Karem noted that the FallsHarbor group was selected pursuant to a Request for Proposals and they had been selected because of the design they had proposed and that, therefore, the criteria which had originally been set out by FallsHarbor in their proposal was the criteria by which the project needed to be judged. Charles McCarty presented a question to the board: Does the plan submitted by FallsHarbor reflect WDC's vision of the project and does the board approve of the design? The board, by a show of hands, unanimously voted no.

When the smoke cleared, it was obvious that while the FallsHarbor project had no future, the idea of a housing development remained a good one. The WDC board remained committed to bringing people back to live at the river's edge, but times and economic realities would need to change before residents could stroll out on their balconies and enjoy the sunsets over Louisville.

With the Clark Memorial Bridge lights providing emphasis, the skyline of Louisville had grown in size and sophistication during the 1970s and '80s expansion of the Main Street corridor. Grand new buildings, most dramatically lit at night, provided an exciting first impression to people arriving in Louisville over the Kennedy interstate bridge.

"Louisville almost felt like a real city…"

As the construction of Phase I neared completion, it became clear that something special was being created on the Louisville waterfront, and critiques were published that gushed with praise and admiration. Covington's *Kentucky Post* of August 9, 1997, filed this report.

LOUISVILLE – IT WAS AS IF THE CITY HAD BEEN ROBBED OF ITS SOUL.

THE OHIO RIVER, ONCE SO VITAL, WAS FOR MANY LOUISVILLIANS SOMETHING THAT EXISTED IN THE PAGES OF A HISTORY BOOK, NOT SOMETHING THAT COULD ACTUALLY BE EXPERIENCED.

THE CITY THAT WAS BORN BY THE RIVER HAD BECOME SEPARATED FROM THE RIVER OVER THE YEARS BY A COMPLEX MAZE OF INTERSTATE HIGHWAYS, WAREHOUSES, INDUSTRY AND OVERGROWN WEEDS.

IN MANY SPOTS, YOU COULD DRIVE ALONG THE RIVER AND NEVER EVEN SEE IT, MUCH LESS GET DOWN TO THE WATER'S EDGE.

LIKE ITS NEIGHBORS TO THE NORTH – COVINGTON, NEWPORT AND CINCINNATI – LOUISVILLE HAS SLOWLY BEGUN TO RECLAIM ITS LOST HERITAGE.

"OUR GOAL IS TO CREATE ENERGY, TO CREATE EXCITEMENT, TO CREATE A DESTINATION LOCATION," MAYOR JERRY ABRAMSON SAID.

LAST WEEK, ABRAMSON ANNOUNCED PLANS FOR A WATERFRONT BASEBALL STADIUM THAT COULD SEND THOUSANDS OF PEOPLE FLOCKING TO THE RIVER. LOUISVILLE SLUGGER FIELD WILL BE A 12,000-SEAT, $34 MILLION BALLPARK THAT WILL BE HOME TO THE LOUISVILLE REDBIRDS, THE CITY'S TRIPLE-A MINOR-LEAGUE TEAM WHICH WILL PLAY MORE THAN 70 GAMES THERE PER SEASON.

THE VIEW FROM WHAT EVENTUALLY WILL BECOME WATERFRONT PARK IS SPECTACULAR.

"THE RIVER IS THE MOST MAJESTIC, REMARKABLE NATURAL RESOURCE THAT WE HAVE IN THIS COMMUNITY," MS. (MEME SWEETS) RUNYON SAID, "IT MAKES ME FEEL, AS A HUMAN BEING, CONNECTED TO CREATION. WHEN YOU WALK OR DRIVE BY, IT REALLY DOES RESTORE YOUR SOUL IF YOU ALLOW IT TO."

BESIDES GIVING LOUISVILLE A FRESH NEW FACE, THE REDEVELOPED RIVERFRONT WILL BE THE FIRST THING THAT OUT-OF-STATE VISITORS SEE WHEN THEY CROSS THE RIVER INTO KENTUCKY.

"WE REALLY DO THINK YOU CAN MARKET IT AS A NEW FRONT DOOR FOR THE WHOLE STATE OF KENTUCKY," SAID DAVID KAREM, A STATE SENATOR AND PRESIDENT OF THE WATERFRONT DEVELOPMENT CORP., THE NON-PROFIT AGENCY IN CHARGE OF RIVERFRONT DEVELOPMENT.

KAREM SAID CITY LEADERS NEVER LOOKED AT THE RIVERFRONT RENAISSANCE AS AN ECONOMIC DEVELOPMENT TOOL.

"WHAT WE SAW US DOING WERE QUALITY-OF-LIFE ISSUES THAT WOULD MAKE PEOPLE WANT TO COME TO THE AREA," HE SAID.

IN OTHER WORDS, THEY SAW IT AS A WAY TO GET MORE PEOPLE DOWNTOWN, WHERE THE STREETS ARE OFTEN DESERTED AFTER DARK.

A Cosmopolitan Salute

One of the most perceptive reviews of Waterfront Park came in 1998 via *AQUAPOLIS*, a sophisticated Italian publication specializing in waterfront and landscape architecture worldwide. Excerpts from the lengthy article make clear the international significance of the Louisville park, and began by comparing the importance of the Ohio River to Louisville as the Grand Canal is to Venice.

THE ENTIRE EFFORT IS SUPERVISED BY THE LOUISVILLE WATERFRONT DEVELOPMENT CORPORATION, WHICH WILL CONTINUE AS A SEPARATE AGENCY TO OPERATE AND MAINTAIN THE PARK ONCE IT IS COMPLETED. THIS PARK IS A TRUE "PUBLIC" PARK FUNDED BY PUBLIC TAXES AND REVENUES. THIS DISTINGUISHES IT FROM THE MANY WATERFRONT DEVELOPMENTS IN THE UNITED STATES — OFTEN CALLED "FESTIVAL MARKETPLACES" — FUNDED AND OWNED BY PRIVATE DEVELOPERS GUIDED PRIMARILY BY PROFIT MOTIVES.

ALTHOUGH LOUISVILLE DISPLAYS FEATURES COMMON TO MANY AMERICAN RIVERFRONT CITIES, THE SITE OF ITS NEW PARK HAS MANY DISTINCTIVE QUALITIES AND THE CIVIC EVENTS FOR WHICH THE PARK WILL PROVIDE THE SETTING ARE UNIQUE TO THE CITY. THE WATERFRONT DEVELOPMENT CORPORATION WORKING WITH THE DESIGN TEAM OF HARGREAVES ASSOCIATES AND BRAVURA DEVELOPED A MASTER PLAN WHICH AIMED "TO ACHIEVE A WATERFRONT PARK TRULY UNIQUE TO LOUISVILLE, EMBODYING THOSE QUALITIES OF SITE AND LIFE THAT ARE SPECIAL TO THE INHABITANTS OF THE REGION."

THE PARK'S DESIGN ATTEMPTS TO MEET THESE CRITERIA BY COMBINING STRAIGHTFORWARD FUNCTIONAL EFFICIENCY WITH ELEGANT, SOPHISTICATED ARCHITECTURAL EXPRESSION AND IMAGINATIVE PROGRAMMING. FOUR ASPECTS OF ITS DESIGN ARE NOTEWORTHY: ITS WELL-DEFINED AND CLEARLY LINKED SPACES FOR CIVIC EVENTS AND RECREATION; ITS USE OF SYMBOLIC TOPOGRAPHY TO RECALL THE CULTURAL HISTORY OF THE CITY AND TO EXPRESS THE LANDFORMS AND VEGETATION OF ITS SURROUNDING REGIONS; ITS STRONG VISUAL AND PHYSICAL CONNECTIONS TO THE CENTRE OF THE CITY; AND, FINALLY, ITS INNOVATIVE ENGINEERING STRATEGIES.

ADJACENT TO THE FESTIVAL PLAZA TO THE EAST IS A 900-FOOT-LONG FOUNTAIN COMPOSED OF SIX RECTANGULAR POOLS STEPPING DOWN TO THE RIVER, CONNECTED BY CASCADES AND ENORMOUS HORIZONTAL WATER JETS DRAMATICALLY ILLUMINATED AT NIGHT. IN THE TERMINOLOGY OF HARGREAVES ASSOCIATES, THIS LARGE WATER DISPLAY PROVIDES "PHYSICALITY" AND "NARRATIVE." "PHYSICALITY" IS THE IMMEDIATE SENSUAL QUALITY OF THE WATER WHICH REFRESHES AND DELIGHTS. "NARRATIVE" IS THE STORY THE WATER TELLS ABOUT THE HISTORY OF LOUISVILLE. THIS COMBINATION OF SENSUAL AND DIDACTIC ELEMENTS CHARACTERIZES MANY ELEMENTS IN THE PARK. ONE IS REMINDED OF THE ALLEGORICAL FOUNTAINS OF THE GREAT ITALIAN RENAISSANCE GARDENS, WHICH SERVED SIMILAR PURPOSES.

THE FOUNTAIN IS BRIDGED IN A NUMBER OF PLACES TO LINK THE FESTIVAL PLAZA TO THE CENTERPIECE OF THE PARK, THE GREAT LAWN, DESIGNED TO BE LOUISVILLE'S GREAT "CIVIC ROOM," EQUIVALENT TO THE PIAZZA SAN MARCO OF VENICE. IT JUTS OUT BOLDLY INTO THE RIVER ON A BED OF CONCEALED PILINGS, A POWERFUL FIGURATIVE SPACE WHOSE SCALE AND SLIGHT ROTATION FROM THE CITY'S GRID PROCLAIM ITS CENTRALITY. ITS 14-ACRE TURF PLANE SLOPING GENTLY DOWN TO THE RIVER IS A *TABULA RASA* CAPABLE OF SUPPORTING A WIDE RANGE OF ACTIVITIES, FROM A SMALL GAME OF TOUCH FOOTBALL

The crisp fold of a plinth in Linear Park provides a sculptural aspect to the landscape that has been described as "un-natural" nature. These design elements were envisioned as symbolic topography representing landforms in the Ohio Valley, but they also provide a mechanism of breaking space into more intimate areas. The sharply contoured plinths require special care and treatment while performing grass-cutting and other maintenance chores.

INLETS CAUSED BY THE CREEKS ARE FUNCTIONAL. THEY ARE EITHER SAND SUNBATHING BEACHES OR ARE DESIGNED TO SILT UP IN A FEW YEARS TO FORM WETLAND HABITAT FOR WILDLIFE. THIS PORTION OF THE PARK PROVIDES MORE THAN SYMBOLIC TOPOGRAPHY, HOWEVER. HARGREAVES ASSOCIATES HAS SKILLFULLY SITED PLAYGROUNDS AND PICNIC AREAS IN THE RIDGES AND VALLEYS, ALONG WITH A SERIES OF LINEAR PARKING LOTS THAT GENTLY ARCH INTO THE VALLEYS. THE STRUCTURES OF THE PARKING LOT RESTROOMS ARE INTENDED TO EXPRESS LIGHTHEARTED FANTASY. PERHAPS THEY SUCCEED, BUT THEY BORDER ON THE BIZARRE.

THE PARK'S SPATIAL SEQUENCE PROGRESSES FROM THE LARGER AREAS FOR CIVIC EVENTS IN THE WEST TO THE MORE HEAVILY PLANTED AREAS FOR "PASSIVE" RECREATION IN THE CENTER TO A SOMEWHAT MORE ACTIVE AREA TO THE EAST IN PHASE TWO. PHASE II PRESENT PLAN CALLS FOR SOME SMALL RESTAURANTS, A LARGE ADVENTURE PLAYGROUND, AN EARTHWORK AMPHITHEATRE, SUNBATHING BEACHES, AND A LARGE ELLIPTICAL MOUND WITH A SPIRAL WALK LEADING TO AN ABANDONED RAILROAD BRIDGE, REFURBISHED AS A DRAMATIC PEDESTRIAN PROMENADE ACROSS THE RIVER TO THE FAR SHORE, IN THE NEIGHBORING STATE OF INDIANA. HERE AN INDUSTRIAL ARTIFACT HAS BEEN PRESERVED AND PUT TO GOOD USE. IT IS TO THE DESIGNERS' CREDIT THAT IN BOTH PHASE I AND PHASE II THEY HAVE AVOIDED A FACILE COPY OF 19TH-CENTURY PASTORAL PARKS OR THE NOSTALGIC CLICHÉS OF 19TH-CENTURY REVIVAL ARCHITECTURAL ELEMENTS, SUCH AS FAKE GASLIGHTS, ORNATE CAST IRON PLANTERS AND BENCHES, AND MANNERED BRICKWORK, AN ALL-TOO-COMMON STRATEGY IN AMERICAN RIVERFRONT DEVELOPMENTS. INSTEAD, THE ARCHITECTURAL ELEMENTS OF THE PARK ARE FUNCTIONAL, ELEGANT AND STURDY, WHILE AVOIDING STYLISTIC REVIVAL.

TO LARGE OPEN-AIR CONCERTS AND THEATRICAL PERFORMANCES. ITS ILLUMINATION AT NIGHT IS WORTHY OF A WORLD CUP FOOTBALL STADIUM.

HERE (THE LINEAR PARK) THE LAND IS SCULPTED INTO A SERIES OF INLETS AND WEDGE-SHAPED HILLS RISING ABRUPTLY ABOVE THE RIVER AND HOLLOWED OUT ON THE SIDE. THE INLET AND HILLS ARE SYMBOLIC MINIATURIZED EXPRESSIONS OF THE TOPOGRAPHY OF THE REGION, LIMESTONE RIDGES WITH FLAT TOPS, BISECTED BY VALLEYS FORMED BY SMALL RIVERS AND CREEKS FLOWING INTO THE OHIO RIVER. HARGREAVES ASSOCIATES' VERSIONS OF THE

If phase two proceeds as planned, Louisville's Waterfront Park should emerge as one of the most innovative and successful urban parks in the United States. It is designed to do what urban parks should do. It renews the psyche through contact with processes of the natural world. It celebrates the cultural and natural history of the region. It rehabilitates natural ecosystems previously degraded by industrial development. It enriches civic life by providing places for festivals and commemoration. It protects the city from floods. It strengthens the city's economy by creating jobs, fostering tourism, and drawing new real estate development to its borders.

This park is certain to have its problems, as do all urban projects of its complexity and magnitude. It is simply too early to know what they will be and how serious. However the intelligence and sound engineering embodied in its design and quality of its construction bode well for its future. Whether or not this new park will achieve its promise will be mostly up to the people who sponsored it, the citizens of Louisville and its surrounding area. Drawing upon their inventiveness and commitment to civic life, they may discover ways to use it that transcend the most optimistic and far reaching intentions of the designers, whose flexible, multi-use spaces invite such discovery and experimentation.

"Tonight, the people have come to the city."

A *Courier-Journal* editorial of November 26, 1998, looked backward and forward at the Park's goals and accomplishments.

WATERFRONT COMES TO LIFE

A friend of ours — a man who is committed to Louisville, but also loves Boston, New York and other larger, more vital cities — made an exciting find here last weekend. His family spent Sunday touring Market Street art galleries, then wandered down to the river and the new waterfront park.

"Louisville almost felt like a real city," he exclaimed. Couples were out walking; families were out playing. Downtown areas and activities flowed together in a way that they hadn't before.

That didn't happen by chance. A lot of folks have spent a lot of years working to bring life and personality back to downtown. This fall, the opening of the Great Lawn and the use of the Festival Plaza for Strassenfest have demonstrated what a dramatic difference the work along Louisville's waterfront is making.

Many Louisvillians thought the creation of a park to connect the city to its riverfront couldn't be done. Undoubtedly, they are now thrilled to have been proved so wrong.

The Waterfront Development Corp.'s history goes back 11 years. It has involved many stages of dreaming (of what could replace those acres of scrap yards, industrial storage tanks, warehouses and sand piles) and scheming (about how to make it happen).

Then the landscape actually started to change.

(Left) WDC officials insisted that swings and park benches be an integral part of the Waterfront Park experience. While many of the seating arrangements face the river, others are turned inward so that people can monitor their children's play in the meadows or recreational areas. One of the final areas to be developed in the park, the Swing Garden, is adjacent to the Lincoln Memorial and provides areas for personal reflection and rest.

(Below) The Adventure Playground, located in the eastern section of the park, was designed to be four times larger than the original playground in the Linear Park. The early playground in the Linear Park section proved so popular it was greatly expanded and water features were added to the second installation. Fanciful fountains, many topped by whimsical fish figures, spray cooling water on the large crowds attracted to the area that is divided into age-appropriate segments.

Childhood is celebrated in two of Waterfront Park's most popular attractions. A delighted boy is king-of-the-hill in the Adventure Playground in the Park's eastern section. Children, and many adults, cool off in the Dancing Waters feature in the Park's Phase I area. Innovative thinking led to the design and construction of play areas that were flexible, durable and lively throughout Waterfront Park.

"I REMEMBER WHEN THE MASS EXCAVATION BEGAN," SAYS DAVID KAREM, THE WATERFRONT DEVELOPMENT CORP.'S PRESIDENT AND EXECUTIVE DIRECTOR, "WHEN THE BULLDOZERS BEGAN CLEARING, SHAPING, SCULPTING THE BASIC OUTLINES, AND WE STARTED TO SEE A SHAPE THAT WAS GOING TO BE A HARBOR, A GREAT LAWN, A PLAZA."

NOW, ALL BUT THE FINISHING TOUCHES OF THE $58 MILLION PHASE I ARE DONE. AND SO THE DREAMING AND SCHEMING FOR THE NEXT PHASE HAS BEGUN.

PHASE II WILL INCLUDE THE SCULPTING AND SHAPING OF ANOTHER 23 ACRES, BUT ALSO WHAT MR. KAREM SAYS MAY BE "THE NEATEST PART" OF THE WHOLE WATERFRONT PROJECT: TURNING THE RAILROAD BRIDGE INTO A BIKING/WALKING/JOGGING PATH BETWEEN KENTUCKY AND INDIANA.

THE PHASE II COST HAS BEEN SET AT $27 MILLION — A HUGE INVESTMENT, BUT ONE THAT FEDERAL, STATE AND LOCAL GOVERNMENTS SHOULD NOT BE HESITANT TO MAKE. AFTER ALL, THIS TIME THERE IS NO NEED TO TAKE ANYTHING ON FAITH: WHERE SCRAP YARDS ONCE WERE, A FANTASTIC, CREATIVE PARK NOW EXISTS; THE BENEFITS TO THE COMMUNITY ARE CLEAR AND DRAMATIC.

THE AIM OF THE SECOND STAGE IS TO DO MORE UNITING. IT WILL TIE TOGETHER MORE ELEMENTS OF THE COMMUNITY — THE PROPOSED CONDOMINIUMS AT FALLS HARBOR AND THE NEW SLUGGER FIELD.

BUT IT WILL ALSO UNITE LOUISVILLIANS AND THEIR NEIGHBORS IN SOUTHERN INDIANA. SOME DAY, ON A LAZY SUNDAY AFTERNOON, WE WILL WALK NOT JUST FROM LOUISVILLE'S ART GALLERIES TO THE RIVER. WE WILL CROSS TO INDIANA AS WELL.

More recognition came in 1999 when the Waterfront Development Corporation received the Centennial Medallion Award from the American Society of Landscape Architects. The most important praise, however, was visited by the people who came and loved their new park by the river. On the Fourth of July 1999 Waterfront Park was officially dedicated, and great crowds attended the afternoon's Opening Ceremonies and stayed through the evening's fireworks display. Mayor Dave Armstrong welcomed the celebrants and proclaimed, "Tonight, the people have come to the city."

Hundreds of thousands of revelers come to Waterfront Park for the annual Thunder Over Louisville celebration. With the downtown rising dramatically in the background, musical concerts entertain the crowd until the massive fireworks display, often called the largest show in America, blasts off after dark.

Louisville, past and present, is represented by its signature ambassador, the *Belle of Louisville*, steaming past the Fourth Street wharf, the scene of so many exciting events in the community's history. With an urban profile undreamed of by its pioneering founders, the waterfront, Louisville's oldest neighborhood, became its newest with the rediscovery of Main Street and the beginning of Waterfront Park. *(Photo courtesy of the Belle of Louisville)*

A New Millennium – A New Park

(2000-2004)

The final days of the twentieth century marked the end of Waterfront Park's Phase I and the beginning of Phase II. The public's embrace of the park's first sections spurred momentum to complete the Master Plan. The obvious path for Phase II would have been to start at the edge of Linear Park and proceed gradually eastward, moving incrementally upriver. WDC Project Manager Margaret Walker recalled an unorthodox shift in strategy. "David Karem came up with a creative solution for completing the whole park. He believed if we just kept advancing, there would be a time when some people might say we had done enough, let's stop where we are and spend that money on other projects. David reasoned that the extreme east end of the Park should be completed next, potentially leaving a gap between the first phase and the second. He reasoned it would be unthinkable to leave the center of the Park uncompleted, and that by finishing both ends, people would demand that the middle be finished."

Intense study and re-evaluation of the original Master Plan caused some early ideas to be either modified or eliminated. Building on lessons learned in Phase I and observing the public's pattern of use in the existing Park, Hargreaves and WDC staff updated plans. Clinton Deckard, owner of Construction Solutions, a project management firm,

Phase II of the Waterfront Master Plan leapfrogged from the original installation, which stopped in the Linear Park near the Kennedy Bridge. By moving to the extreme eastern end of the park property and working on the area beyond the Big Four Bridge, a center section of the property was delayed until the project's end. With work commencing on the eastern border of the park, the full extent of the project became clear to the public and spurred demand for the entire park to be completed.

was hired to serve as project manager for Phase II. Deckard had previously worked as vice president of operations for American Contracting & Services Inc. on the project's first phase. Recognized for his exacting standards and attention to minute details of construction, Clinton Deckard would continue to supervise future construction projects in Waterfront Park.

In February 2000 a draft document detailing Phase II was prepared and released to the public by Hargreaves and the Waterfront Development Corporation. Included in their recommendations were the following:

THIS DOCUMENT IS INTENDED TO OUTLINE THE SCHEMATIC DESIGN FOR PHASE II OF THE LOUISVILLE WATERFRONT PARK. IT WILL DEMONSTRATE HOW THOSE ISSUES OUTLINED IN THE 1991 MASTER PLAN AND THE IMPLEMENTATION OF PHASE I OF THE PARK CONTINUE TO FORM A SOLID FOUNDATION FOR PHASE II DEVELOPMENT. IT WILL ALSO OUTLINE A SERIES OF NEW ISSUES, INCLUDING NEW PROGRAM ELEMENTS AND A RECOGNITION OF THE SITE'S INDUSTRIAL PAST, THAT HAVE ENRICHED AND EXPANDED THE SCOPE OF THE PHASE II WORK. THE PLAN WAS DEVELOPED DURING A TWO-YEAR PERIOD FROM EARLY 1998 THROUGH EARLY 2000.

THE PLAN CONTINUES TO REINFORCE CONNECTIONS TO THE RIVER; PROVIDES A SERIES OF RIVER-RELATED SPACES FOR PLAY AND FOR CASUAL AND PASSIVE RECREATION; ACCOMMODATES AND SLOWS FLOOD WATERS; AND RE-ESTABLISHES LUSH RIVERSIDE PLANTINGS DRAWN ON A PLANT PALETTE OF SPECIES NATIVE TO KENTUCKY. THE PLAN ALSO CAPITALIZES ON SOME OF THE MOST SUCCESSFUL PIECES OF PHASE I, IN PARTICULAR THE PLAYGROUND, AND PROVIDES SIMILAR BUT LARGER SPACES TO ACCOMMODATE OVERWHELMING DEMAND ON EXISTING SPACES. PHASE II ALSO RETAINS AND DEVELOPS

In the original design of the walking approach to the Big Four Bridge, designers envisioned an earthen mound with a graduated walkway spiraling up to a large round staging area adjacent to the bridge entrance. When advanced geological studies revealed the subsurface would be unable to sustain the great weight, a more elegant solution, the free-standing ramp, was adopted.

A SPIRAL HILL AT AND ACCESS TO THE BIG FOUR BRIDGE, PUSHING ONE OF THE MOST POPULAR AND ICONIC ELEMENTS OF THE MASTER PLAN CLOSER TO FRUITION.

PHASE II RECOGNIZES MORE DIRECTLY THE ROLE INDUSTRY HAS PLAYED IN LOUISVILLE'S HISTORY AND THE PLACE IT HAS OCCUPIED ON THE WATERFRONT. AS THE MASTER PLAN OUTLINED, THE BIG FOUR BRIDGE HAS BEEN INCORPORATED INTO THE PARK DESIGN. A LARGE SPIRAL HILL PROVIDES PEDESTRIAN AND BRIDGE ACCESS TO IT, AS WELL AS PLACES TO SIT AND ENJOY VIEWS OF AND FROM IT. THE BRIDGE WILL SERVE AS A SIGNATURE PROMENADE BETWEEN THE KENTUCKY AND INDIANA SHORES.

THE PLAN ALSO RETAINS EXISTING SITE FEATURES, SUCH AS A SHEET METAL WALL, A RUBBLE SLOPE, AND EXISTING VEGETATION, IN ORDER TO PROVIDE DIRECT LINKS TO THE PAST AND PALPABLE CONNECTIONS TO THE SITE. ALSO, RAILROAD LINES AND SPURS ARE RECALLED AND ABSTRACTED IN A NEW SERIES OF LINEAR PLANTINGS, AND THE MATERIAL PALETTE HAS BEEN EXPANDED TO INCLUDE ELEMENTS SUCH AS GABION SLOPES THAT SPEAK DIRECTLY TO THE PARK'S CONSTRUCTED NATURE.

WATERFRONT PARK PHASE II ENCOMPASSES APPROXIMATELY 34 ACRES OF PUBLIC PARKLAND ALONG THE OHIO RIVER IN DOWNTOWN LOUISVILLE, AND INCLUDES THESE KEY COMPONENTS:

- BIG FOUR PEDESTRIAN WALKWAY, THE CENTERPIECE OF PHASE II, IS A PEDESTRIAN CONNECTION TO THE BIG FOUR BRIDGE WHICH WILL HELP COMPLETE A LOOP ALONG LOUISVILLE'S WATERFRONT AND INDIANA'S PLANNED GREENWAY PROJECT. CONNECTION TO THE BRIDGE IS BY WAY OF A WALKWAY THAT SPIRALS UP A HUGE, GRASSY MOUND, WHICH ALSO PROVIDES AREAS FOR PICNICS, RELAXING, AND ENJOYING A PANORAMIC VIEW OF THE PARK AND RIVER.

- CHILDREN'S PLAY AREA, A MUCH LARGER AREA FOR PLAY THAT SUPPLEMENTS THE PLAY AREA IN THE FIRST PHASE OF THE PARK. THE PHASE II PLAY AREA WILL INCLUDE A LARGE AREA FOR WATER PLAY.

- A SMALL CAFÉ LOCATED AT THE RIVER'S EDGE BETWEEN THE CHILDREN'S PLAY AREA AND THE AMPHITHEATER

- AN INFORMAL AMPHITHEATER

- A ROWING FACILITY FOR THE USE OF COMMUNITY AND SCHOOL ROWING ORGANIZATIONS

- TOWHEAD ISLAND MAINTAINED AS A NATURE PRESERVE

- FOUR ADDITIONAL PARKING "FINGERS" OFF OF RIVER ROAD

- A CONTINUATION OF THE WALKING PATHS THAT WIND THROUGH THE FIRST PHASE OF THE PARK

- ADDITIONAL PICNIC AREAS, MEADOWS, TREE GROVES, AND NATIVE PLANTINGS

A Period of Reappraisal and Renewal

George Hargreaves presented to a special board meeting the plans for the next phase. After updating the board on the accomplishments of Phase I, he laid out his concepts and listened to comments by the board.

Hargreaves spoke specifically of how he planned to incorporate the Big Four Bridge. The bridge's approach ramps had been removed in 1969 after the bridge was abandoned by the railroads. The towering structure, built in 1929 to replace the nineteenth-century original, stood as a mute testimony to the city's industrial past. For the Park's purpose, plans were made to tear up the bridge's old track and pave the Big Four as a walking promenade to Jeffersonville. A spiraling ramp would provide running, skating and walking access up to the bridge's entrance. Mayor Dave Armstrong discussed his interest in accommodating the needs of runners. Chairman McCarty asked Hargreaves if plans for a perimeter jogging path around the park had been considered and Hargreaves assured the board there would be more running space allotted in Phase II than in Phase I but there was not a fully connected perimeter path included. A question was asked about the connection of the Big Four Bridge to southern Indiana and David Karem added that WDC staff has met, on several occasions, with the mayor and others from Jeffersonville who were studying ways to connect the

Big Four Bridge to Indiana. Their plans included a possible elevator and stairs on the Indiana side.

Also included in Phase II were a much larger playground; a seasonal café; a boathouse for the University of Louisville rowing program, and the Louisville Rowing Club; an informal amphitheater in a natural setting and, potentially, access to Towhead Island as a nature preserve.

One of the things learned from the completion of Phase I was the need for more gently curving parking lots, referred to as "fingers" in the Phase II design. The playground in Phase II, nearly five times larger than the original area in the Linear Park section, was designed with earthen forms for a more adventure-type "adolescent" play area consisting of approximately 3.2 acres.

David Karem stated that a budget of $40.75 million for Phase II had been adopted by the board. The projected budget included: $12.5 million from the state, $10.5 million from the city, $4 million from the county and $13.75 million from private funding. The purchase of Towhead Island from its owner, Nugent Sand Company, was not included in the budget figure.

Chairman McCarty commented that the Towhead Island property provided an excellent element for children. Mayor Armstrong expressed a strong interest in turning the island into a nature preserve, and Executive Director Karem added that the idea ties in with other projects, such as the Jefferson County Schools curriculum material on the park, currently being prepared.

A Refined Second Phase

Certain refinements were made to the original Master Plan, now over ten years old and thoroughly tested by crowds and nature. Modifications to the original plan included an addition of seven acres to the eastern border, allowing the potential to add a connection to Towhead Island in the event it became an

The Big Four railway bridge was taken out of service in the late 1960s and the old approaches were removed, leaving just the superstructure and piers crossing the river. Very early in the design process, a vision of turning the old bridge into a pedestrian walkway between Louisville and Jeffersonville emerged. The Big Four Bridge is the most obvious reminder of Louisville's industrial past still standing in the Waterfront Park.

interpretive educational site. Early ideas of adding additional inlets and man-made islands near the shore were dropped to prevent possible exposure to industrial hazards left in the ground by previous manufacturing and transportation activities.

While one of the original goals of the Master Plan was to extend Louisville's classic grid pattern all the way to the river's edge, during the design phase the Great Lawn was shifted slightly off-kilter to line up parallel to the nearby bridges. The shift eased pedestrian access to the Great Lawn at times when large crowds moved into the park for special attractions.

At Phase II's westernmost edge, the plan extended from the vicinity of the Kennedy Bridge, adding an additional 8.8 acres to Linear Park. Lawns sloping to the river, wandering pathways and native plants allowed more quiet private space for individuals or small groups. There were none of the large public celebration spots that had been included in the first stage of the Park. A curved fifty-nine-space parking lot was added, as was the Little Lawn, reaching down to the Ohio.

The initial design for the Big Four Bridge approach, called the Spiral, was for a conical hillside to be created rising fifty-four

Few things are as joyous on a hot summer day as a splash in the Adventure Playground. Shaded seating areas line the attraction so that parents can watch their kids enjoy the refreshing spray. On many occasions, the parents have been known to join in the cooling waters themselves.

feet above River Road and seventy-six feet above normal river level. The earthen mound would include Sunning Slopes on the northwest side providing a place for picnics and sunbathing. A sixty-foot paved deck at the top allowed for small social gatherings and provided a turnaround space for emergency vehicles serving the bridge's visitors. Access to the top was provided by a gently rising quarter-mile paved path, or a very steep 700-foot staircase providing strenuous exercise for hardy step-climbers.

As events would unfold, dramatic changes would be made after geological studies were completed, and well before any construction activities began on the Big Four approach.

The Adventure Playground, a new 3.5-acre play landscape, proved to be the most joyous spot in Waterfront Park. Far larger than the initial playground in Phase I, the new grounds abounded with imaginative installations, including a seasonal water feature. The playground provided fantasy areas of landforms – a cone, pyramid slide and sky ramps – to enclose spaces for age-appropriate play for toddlers (1-2 years old), preschoolers (2-5 years) and grade schoolers (5-12 years old). Seating walls bordered a play fountain, allowing parents to sit under shading trees and watch their children splashing through the surging jets of water or being sprayed by lamppost-tall fountains topped by spouts and colorful sculpted fish. Designed for hard use, the Adventure Playground greatly expanded the park's area for individual play and youthful exercise.

The first area to be constructed was the East End, the land opposite Towhead Island and adjacent to the original Depression-

Public access to the river's edge was greatly enhanced by a project sponsored by Mayor Neville Miller in 1935. The Municipal Boat Harbor, lying at the channel between the shore and Towhead Island, hired three hundred WPA workers to provide jobs during the Great Depression and to create an affordable riverside recreational place for the community. *(University of Louisville Photographic Archives, CS 182032)*

era boat docks. This area, the most remote in the park from both Interstate 64 and 65, provided two additional new parking areas for school buses and other visitors.

A hard-surface installation called the Lookout was envisioned as an elevated promontory jutting into the river near the western end of Towhead Island. Its extension northward over the river provides unrestricted views of the island and westward toward the Louisville bridges. Originally designed as a location for a small seasonal café, plans would greatly expand when discussions began about locating a major food-service facility in the park's east end.

New boat docks, built to replace the old Municipal Boat Harbor constructed in 1935 by the WPA, provided temporary tie-ups for recreational boaters. The entire docking area again utilized telescoping attachments to secure the landing during times of floods, and was framed by concrete and lawn terraces

allowing space for quiet viewing of the boats and island. Serious discussions about the interpretive use of Towhead Island were still continuing.

The Event Slope, soon to be renamed the Brown-Forman Amphitheater to salute the local distilling firm's support of Waterfront Park, was created to allow small- to medium-sized events or performances. A series of descending terraces formed a bowl looking north to a small staging area, with the island as a backdrop.

The Rowing Center and Little Wharf were seen as the easternmost elements of Waterfront Park. Abutting the proposed FallsHarbor development, or its successor, the location would become the new home of the University of Louisville crew teams and the recreational Louisville Rowing Club. Located on an area previously owned by Shell Oil, an existing building used by the petroleum company was converted into a storage

In the summer of 2010, construction began on a modern rowing center for University of Louisville athletes at the extreme eastern point of Waterfront Park. An adjacent converted Shell Oil building houses the long sculls and equipment used by community rowing clubs. On quiet mornings, the river's surface around Towhead Island comes alive with rowers enjoying a vigorous workout on the Ohio.

facility for the long and narrow sculls and rowing equipment. The quiet river channel between the shore and Towhead Island allowed a safe place to launch and land rowboats entering the river. Rowing regattas, an activity popular with Louisvillians in the 1820s, finally found a permanent home at the eastern end of the Louisville waterfront.

Live, Work and Play

With the obvious improvement to real estate values near the river's edge, made possible by the completion of Phase I, other elements of the WDC's pre-park mission of redeveloping the Louisville waterfront came into play. A stated goal in nearly all of the dozen previous riverfront redevelopment plans was to provide living space near the river. The successful commission merchants of the 1820s – the Bullitts, Galt, Lacassagne and Burge – recognized that the Ohio River overview from Main Street was the most desirable place in Louisville to live. In 2000 discussions began on "creating an environment where residents could live, as well as work and play." Mayor Dave Armstrong had secured a $6 million, low interest loan pool with half of the money being from the city and half from private sources. With the mayor's strong support of downtown redevelopment,

A major goal of the waterfront redevelopment plan was to enhance Louisville's reputation as a place to "live, work and play." Waterfront Park Place, a high-rise apartment and condominium building developed by Bravura, Inc., brings residential living back to the area north of Main Street. It is joined by the dramatic Preston Pointe, a combination office and residential building. Such facilities, along with Humana Waterside and the Presbyterian Center, helped stimulate thousands of jobs in downtown Louisville. (WDC photo by Rick Bell)

coupled with the new financial incentives, the third phase of the waterfront strategy began.

Following a request for proposals, five firms submitted formal design concepts for an apartment and condominium complex. Bravura Corporation, the project manager for the first phase of Waterfront Park, was selected to design and develop a property called Waterfront Park Place, located at the corner of Floyd and Witherspoon streets on property belonging to the WDC. Jim Walters, president of the development company that headed the investment group planning the complex project, was encouraged by the initial public response to the winning design.

Throughout most of the city's history, access to the Ohio River was severely limited by wharves, industries and utilities. Waterfront Park, the latest incarnation of Louisville's riverfront, allows full public access to the water's edge. The Festival Plaza enhances the Kentucky shoreline with active water features, recreational attractions, concert space and an unparalleled view of the river and the Indiana shore. *(Photo by John Gollings, courtesy of Hargreaves Associates)*

Bravura's winning proposal featured a twenty-three-story building, with great expanses of exterior glass, to house 122 apartments and condominiums. The high-line residences were expected to sell from $200,000 to a half-million dollars for penthouse space. The total cost, $34.5 million, received a boost when in January 2000, very shortly after the public announcement, nearly half of the condos were tentatively reserved.

Viewers looking out the building's north-facing windows and balconies see a sweeping view of the silver knobs of Indiana descending into the cluster of lights of Jeffersonville and Clarksville at the river's northern edge. At night the darkened river is delineated by the Clark Bridge, newly lit a sprightly colored purple by the successful conclusion of Marlene Grissom's planning and fundraising efforts for Project BridgeLight. The viewer's scan registers the presence of the expressway just before the building, but eyes rise and are attracted to the lighted green pasture of the Great Lawn, occupied by musical concerts, impromptu football games and strolling couples. But even when crowded, it is a peaceful open refuge for city-dwellers, a demographic group lacking at Louisville's waterfront for too long. The words of urban pioneer Al Schneider reverberate, "What's a town without a beating heart?"

A Trade Not Made

Mayor Armstrong's strong interest in the educational opportunities offered by a nature center on Towhead Island led officials to discuss acquiring the property. The owner was Nugent Investments, a part of the large Nugent Sand Company, the long-time Louisville maritime sand and gravel operation. They earned about $100,000 a year renting the northern shore of Towhead Island to barge companies wishing to store their floating containers. When a task force, named to study the potential of wildlife programs along Beargrass Creek, recommended the city acquire the island, discussions were opened between the city and Nugent.

In early 2002 the city proposed trading ten acres of waterfront property opposite the island in exchange for Towhead. After the demise of the FallsHarbor project, Nugent officials considered developing a low-density single-family housing venture along the waterfront acreage. An appraisal performed by the Louisville Development Authority placed the value of the island at $796,000, and the land offered in trade at $789,000. When the proposal reached the Board of Aldermen, it was rejected by a vote of nine of the twelve voters. Board president Denise Bentley believed the trade would have been "a bad deal for the city. We spent a lot of time and money developing the waterfront. To do a land swap for an eroding island doesn't make sense."

The Waterfront Development Corporation never officially took a position on the swap, but David Karem stated that the board of directors had long held that it "is not terribly advisable to give up a riverfront land already in public hands."

Towhead Island, one of the most recently formed natural islands at the Falls of the Ohio, remained in the hands of Nugent Sand, and barges continued to line its northern shoreline. In many ways, nothing could be more appropriate than the presence of these mammoth floating reminders of when Louisville made its living on the waters of the Ohio. Towhead Island, once the home of "wicked women" frolicking on the beach, survived and remained for future generations of dreamers to realize its potential.

Together at Last

The question of merging the governments of Louisville and Jefferson County had simmered since the last defeat of a referendum in the early 1980s. Many community leaders still felt that joining the two governments would streamline services and reduce costs and redundancies in offices, bureaus, departments and public security agencies. On Election Day in November 2000, voters finally affirmed the Louisville-Jefferson County Compact, setting in motion a review and plan for blending together two different governments. The date set for the new government, called Louisville Metro, to begin operations was January 6, 2003, and a great amount of work was needed to make the transition as smooth as possible. Shortly afterward, Jerry Abramson announced his candidacy to serve as the first mayor and chief executive of the new Louisville Metro government.

At the same time that Waterfront Park was expanding, its constituency was growing as well. The City of Louisville was home to 256,000 citizens at the time of merger, but in January 2003 Louisville Metro claimed a population of over 721,000. This was the first large American city to merge governments in more than three decades and officials of other communities began to beat a path to Louisville to see how it could be done. Other officials of other organizations were making visits to Louisville for other reasons, primarily to witness the success of Waterfront Park and to seek the advice of WDC officials on developing their own waterside properties.

Shuffle Off to Buffalo

Executive Director David Karem became a popular resource for other communities facing a waterfront development challenge. Mayor Anthony M. Masiello of Buffalo, New York, invited Karem to speak to his city's local planning conference on waterfront development. Karem was able to look back and report on the lessons learned at WDC, as recorded in this conference article.

NEARLY TWENTY YEARS AGO, LOUISVILLE, KENTUCKY HAD AN URBAN WATERFRONT, UNDERUTILIZED AND SCARRED BY INDUSTRY. THEY HAD A PUBLIC FRUSTRATED WITH INACTION AND SKEPTICAL OF PROMISES. AND THEY HAD A FEW PEOPLE WITH A VISION FOR THE WATERFRONT THAT TO OTHERS SEEMED ALMOST LUNATIC.

SOUND FAMILIAR?

TODAY THE LOUISVILLE WATERFRONT DEVELOPMENT CORPORATION IS BASKING IN THE GLOW OF LOCAL PUBLIC ACCLAIM AND NATIONAL KUDOS FOR ITS 55-ACRE WATERFRONT PARK AND BUILDING A 34-ACRE PHASE II ON THE BANKS OF THE MAJESTIC OHIO RIVER.

DAVID K. KAREM, SPEARHEAD OF THE PROJECT AND EXECUTIVE DIRECTOR OF THE CORPORATION, IS SCHEDULED TO TELL THE STORY OF THE PARK AT THE BUFFALO WATERFRONT CONFERENCE THIS SATURDAY, MAY 17.

KAREM'S TAKEAWAY LESSONS FROM THE LOUISVILLE WATERFRONT PARK ARE SIMPLE. CHANGING AN URBAN WATERFRONT REQUIRES BROAD BASED PUBLIC SUPPORT AND PARTICIPATION, THE CONTINUITY OF A STRONG IMPLEMENTING ORGANIZATION, AND A LARGE DOSE OF PATIENCE AND DETERMINATION.

IN 2001, THE PARK WON AN AWARD FROM THE AMERICAN SOCIETY OF LANDSCAPE ARCHITECTS FOR DESIGN. LAST YEAR IT WON THE PHOENIX AWARD GRAND PRIZE FOR "BROWNFIELD" REDEVELOPMENT. MOST IMPORTANTLY, THE PARK HAS WON THE HEARTS OF THE CITIZENS OF LOUISVILLE.

SINCE ITS DEDICATION IN 1999, WATERFRONT PARK HAS DRAWN MORE THAN A MILLION USERS PER YEAR. PARENTS BRING THEIR CHILDREN TO THE PLAY AREA ALL DAY LONG. TEENAGERS COME DOWN TO TAKE THEIR PROM AND GRADUATION PHOTOS. PEOPLE WALK, RUN, BIKE, PLAY FRISBEE AND FLY KITES. WATERFRONT PARK, KAREM SAYS, HAS BECOME THE CENTRAL CIVIC SPACE THAT LOUISVILLE HAS LONG LACKED.

THE PARK IS ALSO FILLED WITH EVENTS — ABOUT 120 A YEAR — THANKS TO HEAVY PROGRAMMING BY THE CORPORATION. THERE ARE BOAT SHOWS, FESTIVALS, FREE

Louisville's Waterfront Park has garnered national and international recognition for its excellence. It was awarded the U.S. Environmental Protection Agency's Phoenix Award in 2002, the nation's highest honor for facilities that remediate and redevelop brownfield areas. Delegations from communities around the world routinely visit Louisville to consult with WDC officials on how to create such improvements in other waterfront cities. *(WDC photo by Rick Bell)*

CONCERTS, WEDDINGS — ALMOST ANYTHING YOU CAN THINK OF.

"WE HAVEN'T HAD A VIKING FUNERAL YET," KAREM QUIPS. "BUT I'M SURE WE WILL."

LOUISVILLE'S WATERFRONT PARK WAS NO OVERNIGHT SUCCESS — ONLY DECADES IN THE MAKING. THE WATERFRONT DEVELOPMENT CORPORATION WAS CREATED BY AN ACT OF THE STATE LEGISLATURE IN 1986. FROM THERE IT WAS ONLY 13 YEARS TO THE OPENING OF PHASE I. BUT THEY ARE STILL NOT DONE.

"IT WAS GOING TO TAKE TWENTY YEARS," KAREM SAYS. THAT'S WHY LINKING AN INDEPENDENT PUBLIC CORPORATION WITH AN ACTIVE PUBLIC AND GIRDING FOR THE LONG HAUL WAS SO CRITICAL. "PEOPLE WHO THINK IN TWO- OR FOUR-YEAR ELECTION BITES CAN'T GET IT DONE."

KAREM IS ENTITLED TO HIS SWIPE AT POLITICIANS. HE IS ONE. FIRST ELECTED TO THE KENTUCKY HOUSE OF REPRESENTATIVES IN 1972, HE HAS SERVED IN THE STATE SENATE CONTINUOUSLY SINCE 1976 AND IS NOW THAT BODY'S MOST SENIOR MEMBER.

Growing the vision and building support for the park also required a staunch commitment to citizen participation. In the corporation's first year of existence they held weekly workshops to help develop the concept for reuse of this piece of riverfront marred by scrapyards, asphalt plants, and other industrial ruins.

"This is a blank slate," they told citizens. "We have no secret design. You get to say whatever you want. But you have to come and participate."

"The downtown screamed for green space," Karem said. "People said 'We want parkland.' So, we made it parkland."

Yet the effort had to overcome a sense of public disbelief of almost "biblical proportions." Citizens didn't think anything could be done. In fact, they believed that nothing good had ever been done — despite the presence of a beautiful Frederick Law Olmsted-designed park on the waterfront at the other end of town.

Buffalo has the same kind of assets and the same kind of civic resources Louisville had, Karem says. It has the same kind of hang-ups and faces all the same obstacles. If Buffalo can marshal the same kind of participation, organization and perseverance, Karem concludes, "You can do something great on your waterfront, too."

Honors Abound

As a result of Karem's "slow simmer" approach to riverside development, Louisville Waterfront Park garnered attention and awards. Beginning in 1989, David Karem received the Citizen Laureate Award from the Kentucky Society of Architects; in 1992 George Hargreaves won *Landscape Architecture* magazine's Merit Award for his Master Plan; and an Honors Award from the U.S. Army Corps of Engineers was received in 1996 for the Design and Environmental Program for the Romano L. Mazzoli Belvedere Connector. In that same year, the Louisville Central Area, Inc., presented WDC its Cornerstone Award.

In 1997 the Waterfront Development Corporation was presented the Graphic Design: USA's American Graphic Design Award, and also received the Centennial Medallion Award from the Society of Landscape Architects. In 1999 both the President's Award from the Kentucky Chapter of American Planning Associates and the Metro Disability Coalition's Breaking Barriers Award were earned.

The highest recognition given by the American Society of Landscape Architects, its Honor Award, was presented in 2001. This was matched the following year when the U.S. Environmental Protection Agency's Phoenix Award was presented. This award, the nation's greatest recognition for organizations that remediate and redevelop brownfield sites, honors efforts to rehabilitate locations so impacted by industrial pollution that they were thought irretrievable. The Phoenix Awards Institute, a collaborative partnership of sponsors and conservation advocates, cited the WDC for its innovative solutions to transform a blighted site into a new and significant community asset.

In 2004, the park received the best of Top 10 Lawns for Family Fun honors by Briggs and Stratton. Locally the park won the BKD President's Award from the Kentuckiana Associated Builders and Contractors Association.

Put Your Name Up in Lights

As bulldozers and land-moving equipment worked on the eastern edge of Phase II, events in the older sections of Waterfront Park went on apace. In 2001 the floating restaurant moored at the foot of Third Street, Towboat Annie's, was bankrupt and went out of business. The KingFish Restaurant at Seventh and River Road was demolished to be the site of the new Muhammad Ali Center, on grounds that were part of the original Fort Nelson compound during the Revolutionary War.

Also at this time, an idea was floated to place the name LOUISVILLE in seven-foot-high letters along the shoreline to be visible by vehicles driving into Kentucky on the I-65 Kennedy Bridge. The idea received so many negative comments from local citizens it was soon shelved permanently.

Before any work could start on the Waterfront Development Corporation plans to turn the Big Four Bridge into a trans-river walkway, a serious legal challenge emerged. A local charity, Bridge the Gap, had purchased the bridge in 1987 at a sheriff's auction. An FM radio station, WLRS, used the bridge to string bright lights during the holiday season to promote their charitable toy drive for children. That year, after illuminating a huge "LRS 102" sign installation, an electrical short caused a fire in the old railroad bridge's wooden cross-ties.

Ownership of the Big Four Bridge was an integral part of the Master Plan and, since the first mention, people had looked forward to someday walking over to Indiana via the old railroad bridge. Negotiations to purchase the bridge began between Louisville, the Bridge the Gap charity and a Jeffersonville development firm, Martingale LLC. Martingale announced its intention to build a twenty-story condominium development to be joined to the bridge as it entered into Jeffersonville.

The WDC made an agreement in October 2001 to lease the Indiana end of the bridge from the City of Jeffersonville for one dollar a year. In exchange, the development corporation pledged $25,000 to assist in defraying the cost of designing access to the bridge from Indiana. When WDC officials, Martingale and Bridge the Gap charity could not agree on a mutually acceptable offer for the "bridge to nowhere," the City of Louisville, acting

on behalf of the WDC, filed a condemnation suit on the property. The charity argued the city could not take possession of the Big Four Bridge because it had been used in interstate commerce. They maintained the charity owned a perpetual franchise given by both the Indiana and Kentucky legislatures to operate the bridge. Their contention was that the bridge was still a part of federally protected commerce and ineligible for condemnation by a municipality.

The city's attorneys countered that the bridge was no longer part of interstate commerce since it has no approaches and it had been decommissioned by a federal agency in 1969. They argued that the charity owned the stone and steel, which the city had every right to condemn. J. David Morris, an attorney representing Louisville, said that the city desired for the public to have free and unrestricted access to the bridge 365 days a year.

The last major legal hurdle to completion of the Master Plan was overcome in Februrary 2005 when attorney James R. Williamson, of the city's law firm Stites & Harbison, reported the outcome of the litigation concerning rightful ownership of the Big Four Bridge.

The Interlocutory Judgment was entered by the Court on December 11, 2002, and provides as follows with respect to possession of the Big Four Bridge:

> "THE CITY IS AUTHORIZED TO TAKE IMMEDIATE POSSESSION OF THE ABOVE DESCRIBED PROPERTY FOR THE PUBLIC PURPOSES SET FORTH IN THE COMPLAINT UPON THE PAYMENT OF ALL COURT COSTS IN THIS ACTION AND PAYMENT OF THE AMOUNT AWARDED BY THE REPORT OF COMMISSIONERS TO THE CLERK OF THE JEFFERSON CIRCUIT COURT (THE "CLERK"), PURSUANT TO KRS 416.640. THE CLERK SHALL HANDLE THE FUNDS IN ACCORDANCE WITH THE LOCAL RULES OF THE JEFFERSON COUNTY COURT."

A dispute with the owners of the Big Four Bridge, used by a local charity to promote its annual Christmas toy drive, was resolved by a lawsuit, allowing for plans to be finalized on the design of the ramp entrance to the walkway. Funding to pave the pedestrian walkway was provided by the Kentucky General Assembly in 2010 and officials hope to complete the walking bridge within two years.

THE INTERLOCUTORY JUDGMENT WAS UPHELD BY THE KENTUCKY SUPREME COURT BY ORDER ENTERED JANUARY 12, 2005.

THE COURT-APPOINTED COMMISSIONERS AWARDED THE PROPERTY OWNERS THE SUM OF $80,000 PURSUANT TO REPORT OF COMMISSIONERS DATED AUGUST 22, 2001. THE SUM OF $80,000 WAS PAID TO THE CLERK OF THE COURT CONFIRMED BY ORDER ENTERED BY THE COURT DATED JANUARY 26, 2005, THEREBY DIVESTING THE RECORD OWNER(S) OF TITLE AND POSSESSION.

ACCORDINGLY, PURSUANT TO KRS 416.610 (2)(C) AND THE INTERLOCUTORY JUDGMENT, THE LOUISVILLE/JEFFERSON COUNTY METRO GOVERNMENT (SUCCESSOR IN INTEREST TO THE CITY OF LOUISVILLE) BY AND THROUGH ITS DULY CONSTITUTED AGENT, WATERFRONT DEVELOPMENT CORPORATION, A KENTUCKY NON-STOCK CORPORATION, FORMED BY THE CITY OF LOUISVILLE, COUNTY OF JEFFERSON, AND COMMONWEALTH OF KENTUCKY, IS THE ONLY PERSON AND/OR ENTITY ENTITLED TO LAWFUL POSSESSION OF THE BIG FOUR BRIDGE.

Heigold – Rest In Peace

With plans in hand and legal ownership rights secured, the next great step was securing the $40 million needed to complete Phase II. Democrats Jerry Abramson and David Karem credited Republican Anne Northup, U.S. Representative from Kentucky's Third District, as being instrumental in securing major portions of funding for the park through her position on the House Appropriations Committee. In 2003 she secured an earmark providing $300,000 for the Frankfort Avenue Historical Entryway and, in doing so, provided a final resting place for the Heigold House.

From the Clifton neighborhood, old Ohio Street wandered down from Story Avenue to River Road through junkyards, car wreckers and past the notorious former Ohio Street Dump. Safely covered by layers of soil, the former dump's worth was increased with the improvements along the River Road corridor and the potential for a new housing development adjacent to Towhead Island on the north side of the street. WDC Deputy Director Mike Kimmel gave a presentation to the Clifton Avenue neighborhood and suggested that Ohio Street might be designated the continuation of Frankfort Avenue, providing an opportunity to improve the image and accessibility of the community to the river.

A federal transportation grant allowed a circular island to be built with the newly named extension of Frankfort Avenue flowing around the base of an unusual monument. The façade of the Heigold house, an immigrant's 1857 salute to American democracy, was slated to move from its location north of River Road to the raised Frankfort Avenue traffic island. After being transported across River Road and installed, it stands as a victory for Mayor Farnsley and others who fought to save the patriotic tribute of Christian Heigold. Fittingly, the house-front is next to the Ohio Street Dump, now designated the future site of Botanica, an urban horticultural educational facility. The home's original location on Marion Street had been buried under a growing urban dump in the 1950s. The ornate façade, the only building to survive the 1937 Flood on the Point, would continue to stand witness to changes along the Louisville waterfront.

Return of the Explorers

The Lewis & Clark Bicentennial celebration in 2003 was a national salute to the resourceful explorers who opened Americans' understanding of the land between the Atlantic and Pacific oceans. Assembling on the Great Lawn and the Harbor, just yards from the actual location, the national Bicentennial organizing group designated a thirteen-day commemoration of the meeting of Lewis and Clark at Louisville to be one of its signature events. Arriving on

The Heigold façade finally reached its last home when it was moved from the north to the south side of River Road. Sited on a small traffic island where Frankfort Avenue meets River Road, the unique architectural testimony to Louisville's past has proved to be a popular stopping-place for tourists and has served as a backdrop for photographs.

October 14, 2003, exactly two hundred years after the actual date, re-enactors in detailed period costumes arrived in a keelboat at the former mouth of Beargrass Creek and location of Meriwether Lewis' union with his co-leader William Clark.

The Great Lawn hosted an animated thirteen-day festival featuring encampments, period artisan demonstrations and exhibits in the Expo Tent. Native American groups raised teepees, and educational lectures, evening programs and musical presentations enlivened the waterfront, attracting thousands of visitors, especially large groups of schoolchildren.

The friendly and open staff of the Waterfront Development Corporation are well represented by the dogs they bring to the office. Gladly welcoming every visitor to the headquarters' third-floor offices, the canines represent a long tradition of dogs on the Louisville waterfront, going all the way back to Captain Meriwether Lewis' great Newfoundland who accompanied the trip to the Pacific Ocean and back in 1803-06.

Watch Dogs of the Waterfront

Accompanying the Lewis & Clark re-enactors was a black Newfoundland dog, reprising the role of Seaman, Captain Lewis' pet and companion. The original Seaman is the first dog documented to have visited the Louisville waterfront, but canines have long been a part of wharf life, especially in the offices of the Waterfront Development Corporation. A predecessor of the "staff dogs" of the WDC was recorded in the October 17, 1853, *Louisville Daily Courier*.

YESTERDAY MORNING ABOUT 2 O'CLOCK, WHEN

THE MAIL BOAT LANDED AT HER WHARF, AT THE FOOT OF THIRD STREET, "WATCH" WAS FOUND AT HIS USUAL PLACE AT THE STAGE PLANK, NOT READY TO WATCH THE MAIL BAGS AS HAD BEEN HIS WONT FOR SEVERAL YEARS, BUT STONE DEAD. LIKE A FAITHFUL SENTINEL HE WAS AT HIS POST, WHEN DEATH, THE REMORSELESS DESTROYER, SEIZED UPON HIM.

AT THE TIME OF THE DECEASE OF THIS VALUABLE DOG HE WAS IN HIS 14TH YEAR, HAVING LIVED TO A GOOD OLD AGE, AND AS THE OBITUARY NOTICES SAY "RESPECTED AND BELOVED BY ALL WHO KNEW HIM" – A MISERABLE SET OF RATS, MICE AND THIEVES OF LOW DEGREE ALONE EXCEPTED. THE GOVERNMENT SHOULD NOT OMIT THE USUAL TOKENS OF RESPECT IN HONOR OF HIS DEMISE. BUT DEATH IS NO JEST, EVEN TO A POOR DOG, AND IN THIS INSTANCE THERE HAVE BEEN MANY HEARTS REALLY SADDENED BY HIS DEPARTURE TO THE REALMS OF DISENTHRALLED CANINE SPECIES, FOR WE FEEL SURE THAT *WATCH* HAS GONE WHERE ALL GOOD *BULL TERRIERS* GO WHEN THEY SHAKE OFF MORTALITY.

Pet dogs as mascots were always a part of the life on board Life-Saving Station #10, with some favorite dogs even riding along in the boats on rescue missions. This tradition was revived in the WDC offices at 129 River Road. Often during office hours, when the elevator opens into the third floor reception area, one or more dogs, usually golden retrievers, hurry to offer their welcome. In early days of the WDC, Landscape Manager Gary Pepper occasionally brought his dog Buck to work with him and co-workers in the office looked forward to the friendly visits. Later, when Ashley Cox began bringing her dog Gracie to work, a WDC tradition was established. Gracie became so well known to the visitors, she was featured on the cover of a local publication. The presence of the office dogs speaks volumes about the relaxed and collegial staff of the Waterfront Development Corporation. The longevity of service among senior staff members has developed unusual depths of respect, and a spirit of comradeship evident to even casual visitors. Fittingly, in 2010 it is not unusual to see Gary Pepper's current dog Gunnar, a massive black Newfoundland, represent the original Seaman and all the other faithful waterfront dogs, when he visits the office.

An Iconic Proposal for Living Space

Plans for a residential community opposite Towhead Island had languished since the demise of FallsHarbor but, in 2004, the old idea developed new life. A new partnership, Icon/River Partners LLC agreed to invest $20 million to build 200 condos and apartments and a large marina along the Ohio River shoreline. The partnership, in their agreement with Louisville Metro, agreed that the development, to be called River Park Place, would be substantially completed by December 2006. Metro government leased the twenty-acre site, with Icon agreeing to pay four percent of proceeds from condo sales, apartment rentals and marina boat slips.

Steve Poe, a leading partner in Icon, cited the development's proximity to downtown and the interstate system as factors, but credited Waterfront Park as the driving force in plans. The Icon partners included Poe, Nolen Allen, Clyde Ensor, William Hysinger and Mike Ehrler, all local businessmen. K. Norman Berry was named project architect. The partners agreed to restore the historic old Paget House to serve as a community room or sales office for the project. They also agreed to meet U.S. Army Corps of Engineers' requirements for floodplain construction.

Condos were projected to sell in the $170,000 to $500,000 range, with developers and Metro officials hoping to create 600 units over time. Rosy hopes to be open by 2006 proved victim to the severe national recession that roiled financial markets, delaying the project until more favorable economic conditions prevailed.

The final phase of fundraising for the entire park was also in the works. Nearly $4.5 million was secured in new federal funding, primarily dedicated to the conversion of the Big Four Bridge into the walkway to Indiana. Mayor Jerry Abramson said of recent advances in the project, that "Waterfront Park is truly becoming the regional park we envisioned." A large portion of the private dollars required to complete the project came from a grant of $3.5 million from the J. Graham Brown Foundation, allowing funding for final acquisition of land, including the last three acres near the bridge, owned by the Lafarge Corporation.

A number of restaurant operations expressed an interest in securing the area of Phase II originally called the seasonal café. In 2001 architect Norman Berry began preparing plans for another restaurant on stilts to provide full-service dining at the eastern end of Waterfront Park. A Louisville-based firm, the owners of Tumbleweed southwestern-style restaurant, submitted a winning application in 2004 to become the newest vendor in the Park and, following its opening, it became the highest-grossing location in their chain.

The Tumbleweed restaurant, located in Phase II of the Park, replaced the original concept of a small seasonal café to be placed on the grounds. The extreme popularity of the southwestern-themed eating place, and its prime location overlooking the Ohio River, often cause both adjacent parking areas to fill with cars that also spill out onto River Road.

"…a renaissance of development in downtown."

The economic impact made possible by Waterfront Park had a dramatic effect on downtown development, especially in bringing workers to the area north of Main Street, all of whom paid occupational taxes to Louisville Metro. Prior to the project's beginning in 1986, an estimated 350 people worked in the Waterfront Overlay District. The largest number, 105, worked for Tommy Borders Restaurant Services on Floyd Street, with 80 more employed at the Kurfees Paint Company on East Main Street. The *Belle of Louisville*, during cruising season, hired between thirty and forty individuals.

In 2003 an economic impact study revealed that over 5,300 people worked in the area since the opening of Waterfront Park.

Humana Inc., after renovating a large part of the old Belknap properties, housed 3,500 office workers, with an additional 700 employees of the Bank of America located in the Humana Riverside Building. The Louisville Ballet employed nineteen administrative workers and twenty-five dancers in their distinctive Main Street studio and office complex. The Presbyterian Center, one of the earliest anchors to waterfront development, brought 575 additional staff members to the Park's border.

An imaginative seven-story building, Preston Pointe, designed by Potter & Cox, housed a bank and residences in its Main and Preston Street location, brightened by its silver surface rising to a dramatic punctuation point at the top. Waterfront Park Place, with 20,000 feet of retail space, added workers and residents to

Louisville's downtown skyline, a far cry from its sparse profile at the end of the 1960s, displays a vibrant presence from the northern end of the Clark Bridge. In October 2010, a new arena (on extreme left side of photo), the KFC Yum! Center, was opened to provide a major sports and entertainment venue to the city. The arena replaced aging Freedom Hall as the basketball home for the University of Louisville.

the downtown mix. The conversion of the old Brinly-Hardy plow factory into Louisville Slugger Field brought tens of thousands of visitors during baseball season to enjoy the games, ballpark menus and community spirit. Parking, vending, maintenance and salaries for the Louisville Bats team and management also added to the downtown prosperity.

Louisville Metro and WDC officials rediscovered a lesson learned in New York City after Olmsted's creation of Central Park in the 1850s, when land values for property adjoining the park soared and attracted new buildings and people to downtown. As writer Meg Calkins noted in *Landscape Architecture* magazine, "Waterfront Park...creates a dialogue between city and river processes, heals a wound in

the city fabric, and has sparked a renaissance of development in downtown."

Popular local columnist Bob Hill summarized the feeling of many Louisvillians in his May 7, 2002, *Courier-Journal* column.

RIVERFRONT WANDERER
TAKES PULSE OF THE CITY

The emerging face of Louisville also was evident on the nearby Great Lawn. I've walked it many times, but not with the new Slugger Field fully in place, an art, museum and restaurant boom nearby, a huge construction crane dangling above riverfront condos. All of its signs of growth and

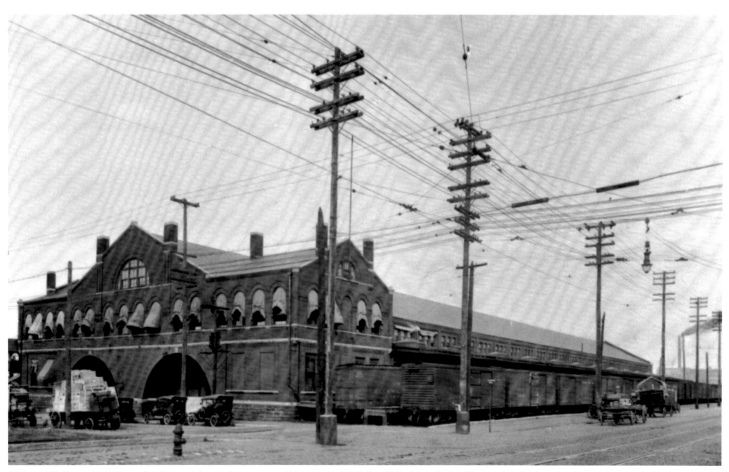

The Louisville Slugger Field, located at Main and Preston Streets, was a skilfull renovation of the old Brinly-Hardy plow factory. Where rail lines once edged between the factory and Main Street, devoted crowds of baseball fans enjoy a comfortable and affordable sports venue with surprisingly good stadium food. *(University of Louisville Photographic Archives, CS 059301)*

CHANGE IN A CITY NOT NATURALLY GIVEN TO EITHER.

AT GLOWING SUNSET, THE GREAT LAWN DWARFS AND ENERGIZES. THERE IS NO OTHER PLACE IN LOUISVILLE WHERE THE SKY IS SO BROAD, WHERE YOU CAN STAND ON ACRES OF GREEN AND WATCH THE RIVER SILVER UP, BECOME ETCHED WITH PALE-YELLOW EDDIES, AND FADE TO BLUE DARKNESS.

WHERE TENS OF THOUSANDS SAT FOR THUNDER OVER LOUISVILLE FIREWORKS, A YOUNG MAN AND WOMAN LEANED DANGEROUSLY INTO ONE ANOTHER, EXCHANGING A LONG KISS. TWO YOUNG MEN, ONE FROM HONDURAS, THE OTHER FROM MEXICO, KICKED A SOCCER BALL TO ONE ANOTHER. A TALL PRETTY WOMAN POSED FOR A FASHION SHOOT NEAR A LARGE, BLACK METAL SCULPTURE.

Beautiful in all seasons, Waterfront Park is especially attractive in the autumn, as leaves turn color and fall to uncover enhanced views through the bare trees. The initial goal of increasing access to the river's edge has been achieved, as an estimated 1.5 million visitors annually come to Waterfront Park, each with their own purpose. *(WDC photo by Gary Pepper)*

On a terrace above the Great Lawn, Wen-Jian Wu and his wife, Su-Ping Wu, natives of China, flew a kite, a swooping bird barely visible in the dimming light. Near them, across an inlet choked with debris and driftwood, dozens of adults and children — black, brown and white — laughed and played on swings and slides, or sat talking.

The consensus among them is that Waterfront Park has become a people magnet: broad, welcoming, accessible, well-lighted, safe and diverse.

It's not New York's Central Park, but a work in progress, a place where, on some nights, Louisville is slowly becoming a city.

Final components of Waterfront Park's Master Plan come together with the statue of President Abraham Lincoln adjacent to the renovated Big Four Bridge. Louisville's past and future join in remembrance of the important contribution the waterfront has made to American history and the potential of a new pathway linking Kentucky and Indiana. *(WDC photo by Rick Bell)*

Mr. Lincoln Returns and Prepares to Cross a Bridge

(2005-2010)

From the first day the design for Waterfront Park was completed, the renovation of the Big Four Bridge as a pedestrian/ bicycle bridge has been one of the most anticipated features of the park and the most asked about by the public. Every day of ramp construction you could see people standing outside the fence or sitting in their cars in the parking lot, watching….Excitement for Louisville's newest landmark seems to be the talk of the town.

As a project, the Big Four Bridge is that wonderful combination of practical and fun. It will be a perfect place to stand and dream and look out over the river, watch the barges and pleasure boats pass underneath you, listen to the Belle of Louisville's *calliope as she steams majestically up the river. It will also provide a healthy, friendly and convenient connection between Louisville and Southern Indiana cyclists and pedestrians, away from the traffic, noise, exhaust and difficult access to the planned downtown Ohio River bridge and the Second Street Bridge.*

— **David Karem,** *Courier-Journal* **Forum - 2010**

With work progressing on the extreme eastern end of Phase II, planning for the final elements of the Park, dubbed Phase III by some staff members, began in earnest. Filling the midsection, left temporarily vacant by leapfrogging the area between the Kennedy and Big Four Bridges, would unite the two segments by creating continuous parkland from the old Louisville Wharf to the 1500 block of River Road. Federal funding for the Park's completion was advanced by the continuing efforts of Congresswoman Anne Northup in her powerful position on the House Appropriations Committee.

"Since the opening of Waterfront Park, many wonderful memories have been created…"

In 2003 the Friends of the Waterfront presented Congresswoman Northup the Silver Anchor Award for securing over $10.4 million in federal support of Waterfront Park. In response, she wrote to FOTW president Dale Josey, extending her thanks for the award and regrets for missing the presentation ceremony. In her letter, Congresswoman Northup reflected on the efforts to create the park and her pride in watching it grow.

WHILE AT HOME IN LOUISVILLE, I CONSIDER MYSELF A FOLLOWER OF SOME OF THE BEST LEADERS WHO TIRELESSLY WORK TO IMPROVE OUR COMMUNITY. DAVID KAREM EPITOMIZES SUCH A LEADER. THROUGH HIS LEADERSHIP, THE WATERFRONT DEVELOPMENT CORPORATION HAS MAGNIFICENTLY TRANSFORMED A BROWNFIELD AND EYESORE AT THE BANKS OF THE OHIO RIVER IN DOWNTOWN LOUISVILLE INTO A BEAUTIFUL PARK THAT INVITES FAMILIES TO RETURN TO THE WATER'S EDGE FOR ENTERTAINMENT, EXERCISE, AND THOUGHTFUL REFLECTION. AND LOUISVILLIANS ARE NOT THE ONLY ONES WHO RECOGNIZE AND APPRECIATE THE TRANSFORMATION. THE WATERFRONT PROJECT HAS RECEIVED NATIONAL AND INTERNATIONAL ATTENTION FOR ITS OUTSTANDING LANDSCAPE ARCHITECTURAL DESIGN AND ITS BROWNFIELD REDEVELOPMENT. WINNING PROJECTS SUCH AS THIS DESERVE ACCOLADES, AND I AM PLEASED TO HAVE SECURED FEDERAL FUNDING THAT BOOSTED THIS INNOVATIVE PROJECT FORWARD.

JUST YESTERDAY, THOUSANDS OF SCHOOLCHILDREN

A volunteer support group, Friends of the Waterfront, arranged to have Waterfront Park become one of the nation's largest outdoor sites to receive wireless Internet service. The group provides community support for fundraising and volunteers for special activities and projects.

PICNICKED ON THE GREAT LAWN WHILE WATCHING A REENACTMENT OF THE HISTORIC MEETING OF EXPLORERS MERIWETHER LEWIS AND WILLIAM CLARK ON LOUISVILLE'S WATERFRONT. AS THESE CHILDREN GROW OLDER, THEY WILL FONDLY REMEMBER THEIR EXPERIENCE AT THIS NATIONAL CELEBRATION. SINCE THE OPENING OF WATERFRONT PARK, MANY WONDERFUL MEMORIES HAVE BEEN CREATED — CHILDREN RUNNING THROUGH THE WATERFALLS (MUCH TO DAVID'S CHAGRIN) ON A WARM SUMMER DAY; BOATERS HUMMING OLD ROCK-N-ROLL TUNES DURING A WEEKEND CONCERT; AND SENIORS STROLLING HAND-IN-HAND ALONG THE RIVER'S EDGE. THANKS TO ALL OF YOU AT THE WATERFRONT DEVELOPMENT CORPORATION AND THE FRIENDS OF THE WATERFRONT FOR MAKING IT ALL POSSIBLE.

THANK YOU FOR HONORING ME WITH THE SILVER ANCHOR AWARD. I AM TRULY TOUCHED.

"...crazier than a loon."

Northup was not the only person to take the time to salute David Karem's leadership of the long campaign to redevelop Louisville's waterfront. David A. Jones, one of the prime catalysts in the project, was integral in the eventual success, having secured and rehabilitated the Belknap properties, led the initial Capital Campaign and contributed generously of his own wealth. In 2004 David Jones wrote a note of appreciation to

Karem complimenting him, the WDC staff and Board for their successful efforts.

> Dear David,
>
> Driving to work past our beautiful waterfront this morning prompted me to reflect on the recent history of the site, and the key role the Waterfront Development Corporation has played in the revitalization of the adjacent area.
>
> The appealing, mixed-use combination of urban parkland alongside repurposed historic structures (Presbyterian headquarters, Humana Waterside, Business First, etc.) would not have been possible had not the Corporation spearheaded the vision, coalition-building and execution of an imaginative redevelopment plan. At a time when most Louisvillians saw only massive piles of sand, you and your team saw a vibrant commercial and recreational center, attractive and productive at once."
>
> – David A. Jones

Other less well-known Louisvillians also voiced their appreciation. After a very cold February tour and discussion in 2004, several U of L Liberal Studies students reflected on their visit and lessons learned from a seminar with David Karem.

> After meeting with you I really do feel that Louisville Waterfront Park is my own park, a park I should be proud of and should help maintain for future generations. Speaking with you gave me a sense of community in Louisville, I understood how important it is to work together with others to get something accomplished. Most importantly, I found a real life example of a person who is a leader because he empowers those who work for him.
>
> – Mariya Chernyavksaya

> Yet the Waterfront is not a singular vision, but in great part to you, one shared by the citizens of Louisville. The fact that the public was repeatedly consulted is a testament to the project's visionaries. It is a public space not to be imposed on people. I think this happens all too often with public spaces, the city manipulates a space and the result is many dissatisfied citizens. The Waterfront is a point of pride for all Louisvillians.
>
> – Leesa Wilson

> It was amazing for me to see pictures of the waterfront before the renovations began. I am not a Louisville native and have only lived here for two years. One of the reasons I moved here was because this city is so beautiful. If it had looked like it did twenty years ago, I don't know if I would have made the move to Kentucky.
>
> – Karen L. Bishop

Perhaps the most unorthodox tribute to Karem came from a most dignified source, an editorial in the March 10, 2002, issue of *The Courier-Journal*. Written with the greatest respect, the piece is a remarkable left-handed compliment to the persistence of Karem's vision for the Waterfront Park.

CRAZY ABOUT THE WATERFRONT

Back in the '80s, when Louisville's riverfront was full of scrapyards, abandoned rail lines, empty warehouses and other unsightly gunk, a few people had a vision for reclaiming it. One was State Sen. David Karem, who eventually became president of the Waterfront Development Corp.

He remembers consulting with former *Courier-Journal* publisher George Gill about the viability of such a project. Mr. Gill told Sen. Karem he was utterly insane.

A decade and a half later, both men have been proved right. It was insane to think that what has been accomplished ever could be.

The public has gained not just access to the river, but a park worthy of the city's Olmsted tradition. Parcel by parcel, land has been acquired; more than $80 million has been raised. Now, another phase is beginning and there is or will be something for everyone: acres to roam, docks and boathouses, children's play areas, an amphitheater – even a way to walk to Indiana.

As with any mammoth undertaking, a lot of people deserve credit. They include private donors, foundations, elected officials – and Waterfront Development board members and staff who have given heart and soul.

But one man has shepherded the effort from the start. That, of course, is David Karem, who has demonstrated he is crazier than a loon.

Measures of Respect

Other principals in the project also gained respect and recognition for their work on Waterfront Park. Hargreaves Associates had started as a one-office operation in San Francisco when first awarded the WDC design contract in 1990. By 2005 George Hargreaves had served as chairman of Harvard University's Graduate School of Design's landscape architecture department and his firm had opened offices in Cambridge, Massachusetts, New York and London. The firm's successful design submission to develop the Brooklyn Bridge Park, coupled with creating the grounds plans for both the Sydney and London Olympic Games, marked Hargreaves as the most recognized landscape architect of his generation. Glenn Allen was also recognized when named to an endowed chair at the landscape architecture program at Louisiana State University.

Following the successful merger of local governments, Jerry Abramson was elected to his fourth of five terms as Louisville mayor, and the first under the new Louisville Metro system. Like his 1850s predecessor, James S. Speed, Abramson was sometimes called "Mayor for Life" because of his continuity in office. Abramson continued to be re-elected because of his lengthy list of civic accomplishments and great local popularity as chief spokesperson for America's sixteenth largest city.

As a mark of respect for their administrative competency, Abramson asked the Waterfront Development Corporation to take over programming and scheduling responsibilities for the Belvedere. Events Manager Ashley Cox took on additional duties to set into place rental agreements and a new fee structure for usage, and to coordinate programming for the elevated platform over the wharf at Fifth Street.

In 2005 the mayor asked WDC officials to assume management of the premier attraction to the Louisville Wharf, the *Belle of Louisville*. Laboring under an unsatisfactory contract with an independent operator, the *Belle* suffered from sub-par attendance, low crew morale and poor visibility. Linda Harris, an experienced hospitality industry professional, was hired as CEO and consultant to re-energize the excursion boat, soon to be the last true steam-powered sternwheeler in America when the *Delta Queen* ceased operation. Mark Doty, a riverman with twenty-five years experience, was named Captain and Master of the Fleet, and Edward O'Connell named Alternate Captain.

Along with the *Belle* came control of *Life-Saving Station #10*, sometimes called the Mayor Andrew Broaddus, which serves as ticket and administrative offices for the adjacent steamboat. These floating reminders of Louisville's maritime past are two of the city's eight structures officially named National Historic Landmarks.

Friends Indeed

As Waterfront Park looked backward to its paddlewheel past, it also looked forward at forms of communications unimaginable in a location more identified with telegraphs than computers. Rapid development of personal computing equipment made many people expect instant electronic messaging wherever they went. In 2005 the Friends of the Waterfront took on a project to provide Wi-Fi (for "wireless fidelity") service for park visitors. "We happen to have a lot of technology people on the Friends board," said Ashley Cox. "They had a vision for wireless at Waterfront Park so they just kind of ran with it." Louisville's *Business First* weekly of April 8, 2005, recorded this innovative offering from the Park.

WATERFRONT PARK GOES HIGH-TECH WITH WIRELESS INTERNET

As spring nears, people often look for an

"Catfish Louie", the mascot of the Friends of the Waterfront group, appears at nearly all public events held in the park. Visitors, especially children, love to have their photograph taken with the un-characteristically active catfish.

opportunity to escape the office and enjoy the outdoors.

And Louisville Waterfront Development Corp. is taking steps to make it easier to soak up the sunshine while e-mailing sales prospects, paying bills online or simply surfing the Web.

The organization, which oversees waterfront development along the Louisville side of the Ohio River, plans to launch wireless Internet access, known as Wi-Fi, in Waterfront Park later this month.

Encompassing more than 80 acres that make up the first two phases of Waterfront Park, the Tumbleweed Free Wireless Internet Network will be the largest free hot spot in Louisville.

David Karem, president of the Waterfront Development Corp., said that while the community already enjoys the park, Wi-Fi will add a dimension to the experience.

In addition, he said, access to free wireless Internet throughout such a broad area will help enhance Louisville's reputation as a city. "We're very excited about it," Karem said. "Our understanding is that this is probably the largest park in the country so far to go wireless…That sends a message that we're forward thinking. It says Louisville understands technology." The free Internet access proved immediately popular, with over 33,000 people logging on in the first two weeks of availability.

The $168,000 Waterfront Park Wi-Fi project materialized primarily with the help of in-kind donations from technology partners.

Kevin Dowdy, who is president of the Lexington-based NetGain Technologies Inc., volunteered the services of his company, contributing about $65,000 in labor costs for the design, installation and testing of the network.

San Jose, California-based Cisco Systems Inc., a provider of Internet equipment and services, donated about $58,000 of equipment.

Also US LEC Corp., a Charlotte, N.C.–based telecommunications carrier, has agreed to provide the Internet connection free of charge for the next three years. The contribution is valued at about $30,000.

Louisville-based Tumbleweed, Inc., which is building an 11,000-square-foot Tumbleweed Southwest Grill restaurant in Waterfront Park, recently signed on as the naming sponsor for the Wi-Fi network.

Terry Smith, Tumbleweed president and CEO, said the company committed to the $10,000 naming sponsorship to support the restaurant's "prominent position" in the park.

Along with Tumbleweed, Fifth Third Bank (Louisville) and the Galt House Hotel & Suites have also agreed to sponsorships, Dowdy said.

"It will be a perfect place to stand and dream and look out over the river…"

With the opening of the Tumbleweed Restaurant, the extreme eastern section of Waterfront Park was rounding into form. A most unexpected change in plans came when it was discovered that the design of the mammoth mound of earth supporting the ramp up to the Big Four Bridge was unworkable. Mike Kimmel recalled the incident well.

It was one of those things that should have been caught in design development, it was in the conceptual plan. We were thinking that here we have a simple land form and we were using that to get up to the bridge in such a beautiful way. We loved it until the geotech folks went and made surveys and calculated compaction.

You go down 20 feet and you've got a twenty-foot sponge. This stuff is really unstable, so we had a problem. It could have heaved River Road and disconnected with the bridge. It would have created so many problems that we couldn't do it.

That whole plan had to be rethought. All the stabilization options were way too costly. Then we thought, if we made an inclined ramp, we could create some pretty cool spaces. And when you're walking on the ramp the views will be even more outrageous, plus only a small portion of the grass-cutting nightmare that would have been the mound. We couldn't use switchbacks because we needed to get emergency vehicles up there and they need a place to turn around.

The bridge ramp is built in three parts, each individual and each self-supporting. It is entirely custom-made. The ramp angle must comply with ADA (Americans with Disabilities Act) standards. It leads up to a spectacular stage on the disk at the top. That's easy enough.

In January 2005, when the Kentucky Supreme Court refused to overturn lower court rulings, Louisville Metro was allowed to condemn the Big Four Bridge and work began in earnest to solve the remaining engineering and design challenges. The ramp, made

The ramp to Big Four approach will be the only ramp in the world that is an ellipse that curves in on itself. The ramp is designed to accommodate wheelchairs, bicycles and strollers, and its pitch is well within ADA guidelines. The ramp was constructed in three independent sections and gracefully joined at the top with a large sixty-foot disk.

wide enough for emergency vehicles to drive to the top, leads up to a sixty-foot circular paved disk joining the ramp to the entryway of the bridge. An ADA-compliant grade of 4.83 percent provides a gradual rise from River Road level and prevents the ramp from being a hazard to skaters and others descending from the top.

In 2010 the Kentucky General Assembly provided $12.5 million to complete the paving across the Big Four Bridge to the Indiana shore. After Clinton Deckard assisted Jeffersonville officials in planning an innovative approach from the Indiana city, only securing a funding source for the Indiana side remained unfinished. WDC officials plan to start the final stage of decking in 2011 and, if necessary, the northern end of the Big Four Bridge will be blocked until the long, sloping ramp into Jeffersonville is funded and built.

As designed, the spiraling approach to the Big Four Bridge will be the only ramp in the world that is an ellipse that curves in on itself. Tampa Steel was the low bidder to fabricate the 1,700-foot-long ramp, costing $4.4 million. When the entire project is completed, the Big Four Bridge and its approach, measuring three-quarters of a mile in length, will be the longest pedestrian bridge in the United States.

The circular paved disk area at the top of the ramp provides a spectacular overview of the entire Falls area, with sweeping views of the Ohio River upstream and down. The Louisville skyline, never before so richly embellished with high-rise architecture, dominates the western perspective, but the most memorable sights are down in Waterfront Park itself. Displayed like an artist's rendering, the green pastures, land forms, pathways, groves of trees and maritime elements look like a scale model of urban park perfection. Looking eastward up River Road, viewers realize the impact of the time-consuming projects to widen that parkway, relocate rail lines and eliminate the industrial blight that covered the old Point area for two centuries. Design elements screened from ground view become gleaming upland meadows

when viewed from the top of the Big Four Ramp. In addition to providing incomparable overviews, the disk area will allow a small assembly space. WDC officials expect that the Big Four Bridge, when completed, will become one of the most popular elements in Waterfront Park.

Where once heavy locomotives pulled huge loads of freight across the river, the Big Four Bridge will soon provide a smooth pathway for pedestrians. Rebuilt in 1929 to replace the original structure, the new Big Four Bridge provides recreation and exercise opportunities, as well as unprecedented views of the Louisville waterfront and its park.

"…it has to look great for every visitor who comes here."

Deputy Director Kimmel was correct to be concerned about the added amount of precision grass-cutting that the great earthen mound would have demanded. Gary Pepper, or some member of his seven-person maintenance crew, is on the Waterfront Park grounds 365 days a year. The crew, six landscape employees and one plumber, all work on salaries with no overtime, and through concentrated work and tight scheduling they perform their tasks during their allotted time. The finished Park requires the mowing of forty-five acres, much of it on the exacting landforms of Linear Park. "They're incredible," Gary Pepper says of the forms, "but

(Above) Looking eastward from the ramp's deck, the overlook provides previously unseen details of Phase II of Waterfront Park's plan. River Road, widened and renewed, presents a vastly different impression than when it was lined with dumps and scrap yards of the recent past. Upland meadows, invisible from road-level, are revealed as inviting green pastures in the middle of the city.

(Left) Sailboats gather for a late-summer regatta near the Kennedy Bridge. The new ramp is a wide and comfortable walkway up to the elevated vantage point, where photographers and others will enjoy an unrestricted view of river life and urban landscape. (Photo courtesy of Clinton Deckard).

they also present their own maintenance challenges. Some are circles, some are triangles, some are long sweeping shapes. The edges have to be mowed in the same patterns, or you'll lose the crispness of the shapes."

The crew's most time-consuming task is the collection of garbage. With Waterfront Park drawing over 1.5 million visitors a year, small mountains of trash are generated at every public event and garbage cans require almost constant emptying. An outside firm is contracted to clean and supply the restrooms and a security staff patrols the park after hours, but the WDC maintenance crew has other responsibilities, including serving as guides, greeters and ambassadors to the

waves of visitors wandering the pathways. The quiet pride felt by the maintenance crew for *their* park is evident by their attentive care of the grounds. "Our goal is to be sure the park looks great every day, whether flooding has just occurred, or there was a big event the night before, it doesn't matter," says Pepper. "The park is in a very visible location, and it has to look great for every visitor who comes here."

During summer months the crew is greatly aided by the Clean Team project, started in 2007. This program provides summer jobs for a dozen or so high school students to assist in garbage and litter pickup and other light maintenance chores. The Team was sponsored by Kindred Healthcare and Aegon

Urban parks, especially one as heavily used as Waterfront, demand a rigorous schedule of planned maintenance. WDC staff is in the park every day picking up garbage, maintaining lawn care duties and repairing minor damage. They also have many opportunities to interact with visitors, routinely answering questions and providing directions. *(WDC photo by Gary Pepper)*

from 2006 through 2009, with the Friends of the Waterfront joining the effort. In 2010 WDC Board Chairman Matt Thornton offered a challenge for others to match Thornton Oil in providing the service for three additional years, and Construction Solutions agreed to provide funding for the program in 2011. Members of the Clean Team, working in four-hour shifts, provide a needed service while learning stewardship skills for their futures.

A Park Called Riverview

In 2006 Metro officials asked WDC to take on yet another park design and construction project, this time in rural southwest Jefferson County off Cane Run Road. Riverview Park, on the river side of the floodwall at the terminus of Greenwood Road, is an eighty-seven-acre installation complete with a children's water feature playground and a boat ramp. The Ohio River at this location narrows considerably from its expanse above the Falls, and on the nearby Indiana shore a knob rises dramatically, providing a sense of protection and intimacy to the park's site.

Louisville Metro officials asked the Waterfront Development Corporation to plan and supervise renovations and improvements for Riverview Park in southwestern Jefferson County. When completed, the park, located over the floodwall where Greenwood Road meets Cane Run Road, will provide many of the same features as the Waterfront Park, including a children's playground with water spray fountains.

Clinton Deckard served as the contractor for the $2.2 million-dollar first phase, which boasts a 3,000-square-foot water splash park, restrooms, parking area and playground. A walking trail

on the elevated earthen mound brings the old flood-controlling levee into the park and creates a natural amphitheatre. Most of the construction was completed in the fall of 2010.

A longtime Louisville tradition, purchasing Christmas trees at the old Jefferson Street Haymarket, has been restored at the corner of Witherspoon and Preston Streets. Every holiday season former Haymarket vendors set up their temporary displays of trees and other decorations, often mingling their presence with the nearby "Flock of Finns" art installation.

A Touch of the Old Haymarket

One of the objectives of the original Master Plan stated that the Park provided an opportunity to respect the history and character of Louisville. To most Louisvillians growing up during the 1950s, one of the highlights of each year was going to the old Haymarket on Jefferson Street to pick out the family's Christmas tree. When the Haymarket finally closed in 2003, the WDC staff decided to resurrect that community tradition by opening up Christmas Tree Lane at the corner of Witherspoon and Preston Streets.

Shortly before Thanksgiving each year, vendors Gary Jecker and Tommy Thompson set up their outdoor stands of trees, greenery and holiday decorations, just as their families had done for decades in the Haymarket. The Jecker family had operated a tree business for over thirty years, and Thompson's was the largest vendor in the entire outdoor market. Reminiscent of the old merchant stands that lined Market Street when hackney cabs and dray carts ruled Louisville's boulevards, Christmas Tree Lane restores some of the sights and smells that are elemental parts of the holiday season.

"I always knew we had 'history' but I don't think I truly felt it until now."

Honoring Abraham Lincoln, Kentucky's most famous son, was the subject of discussions in 2006 when a national project was planned to celebrate the bicentennial of the Great Emancipator's birth. State Senator Dan Kelly of Springfield, Kentucky, believed the Commonwealth should be an active participant in celebrations scheduled to begin in February 2009. The County Court House in Kelly's hometown still holds the original wedding license of Thomas and Nancy Lincoln, and the family's roots in Kentucky can be traced back to President Lincoln's pioneer grandfather and namesake, slain by Indians in eastern Jefferson County. Lincoln's wife, Mary Todd, was the daughter of a prominent Lexington family and was related to several other prominent Commonwealth families.

Senator Kelly approached WDC officials about locating a memorial near the riverfront to serve as an appropriate reminder of Lincoln's Kentucky roots. He met several times with David Karem and Marlene Grissom to discuss creating a large bust of the sixteenth president and installing it on the Belvedere. Somehow a mere bust seemed inadequate, and the idea emerged to create a bold sculptural presentation and to prominently place it in an amphitheater setting in the final Phase III segment of Waterfront Park.

Karem argued persuasively that Waterfront Park, as the front door of the Commonwealth attracting 1.5 million visitors annually, was the ideal location for the tribute. Working with Glenn Allen, the principal liaison between the WDC and Hargreaves Associates, an appropriate spot just east of the Kennedy Bridge was selected, and a small plaza with elevated grassy tiers was designed to provide a semi-circular amphitheater for public activities.

The site was especially appropriate, for just six city blocks to the west was the place where, in 1841, Abraham Lincoln witnessed chained slaves being driven through the Louisville streets to be sent south by steamboat. It was a jarring sight to the young attorney, returning to his home in Springfield, Illinois after an

Mike Kimmel (left) joins sculptor Ed Hamilton and David Karem to inspect work on one of the grand bronze *bas-relief* scenes, prior to its being installed in the Lincoln Memorial. The four bronze scenes from Lincoln's life were cast at the nearby Bright Studio in the Clifton neighborhood of Louisville.

extended visit to the Speed family at Farmington. Although born in a slave-holding state as the son of a yeoman farmer, Lincoln had little exposure to slavery prior to moving to Indiana as a seven-year-old child. Growing up in Indiana and later Illinois, Lincoln's most revealing glimpses of slavery occurred on visits to his wife's Lexington family, or when he traveled on the inland maritime highways, the Ohio or the Mississippi Rivers. As he would write in later years, "That sight was a constant torment to me; and I see something like it every time I touch the Ohio."

Very early in the planning stages for a Lincoln Memorial at Waterfront Park, a consensus choice for sculptor emerged. WDC officials sought Ed Hamilton, a native Louisvillian and nationally recognized artist with a growing list of important heroic bronze commemorative pieces to his credit. He created the Spirit of Freedom Memorial in Washington D.C., honoring the African-American troops who fought for the Union, and a striking full-length treatment of York, the Louisville slave who proved an integral member of the Lewis & Clark expedition. Hamilton's statue of York stands on the Louisville Belvedere, facing the setting sun.

Several elements aligned to create a special memorial to Abraham Lincoln in Waterfront Park. Senator Kelly sponsored a successful $2 million legislative bill, the Waterfront Development Corporation provided a prominent and appropriate location for the memorial, Glenn Allen of Hargreaves Associates designed the elegant landscaping of the site, and Ed Hamilton agreed to create what would be one of the only permanent and tangible reminders of the 2009 Lincoln Bicentennial Celebration in America.

The Lincoln Memorial, dedicated in 2009, is one of the few permanent memorials in America to result from the 200th celebration of Abraham Lincoln's birth in Kentucky in 1809. A sweeping amphitheater provides a stage for a powerful large statue of a young Abe Lincoln, accompanied by four panels of *bas-relief* bronzes depicting aspects of Lincoln's life and legacy.

Ed Hamilton explains his thinking in his own words:

When the Waterfront Development Corporation began discussing the Lincoln Memorial, we talked about the fact that most Lincoln statues show a regal and distinguished figure, sitting as if he was on a throne, or standing tall above the crowd, untouchable. We decided that the Lincoln Memorial in Louisville, Kentucky should be approachable. Lincoln was a rail-splitter, therefore this memorial depicts him as a welcoming figure who invites you to sit with him and look out over the Ohio River and talk about everyday life.

My personal journey to this Lincoln Memorial began when I was a young child, about 8-10 years old. I would visit the public library on York Street. There is a statue of Lincoln out front. He captured my imagination, he seemed huge to me, straight and tall, much larger than life.

Our Lincoln depicts the man whose lifelong ties to Kentucky helped shape his life and his presidency. We wanted this Lincoln Memorial to tell of those ties. As you approach the welcoming Lincoln, you pass through chapters of his life.

Therefore, along with the figure of Lincoln sitting on a sculpted rock, I created four *bas-reliefs* to weave in stories from his life:

- His boyhood love of books and learning while working hard on the family farm;

- The maturing of his professional life and growth into society with his wife, Mary Todd Lincoln;

- The terrible years of war that tore this nation and Lincoln's own family apart;

- The impact of the horrible institution of slavery on both his personal life and his presidency.

My journey while completing the Lincoln Memorial led me to an understanding of the humble man behind the larger-than-life portrayal he is often given. I hope your journey does the same.

Louisvillian Ed Hamilton was the overwhelming choice to create a new tribute to Abraham Lincoln in Waterfront Park. An artist of national reputation, Hamilton depicts a friendly and approachable young lawyer as he might have appeared during his important 1841 visit to Louisville to visit his friends at Farmington. Lincoln later wrote of the emotional impact caused by witnessing slaves being shackled and driven onto riverboats at the Louisville wharf. *(WDC photo by Margaret Walker)*

Ed Hamilton created a Lincoln twice the size of life. His twelve-foot frame seated on a flat rock with his books around him, Lincoln seems to beckon and invite companionship. Children, and more than a few adults, scramble up to embrace him and have their photos taken. The memorial site perfectly frames and complements the rugged bronze statue and the four elegant granite flats holding the four *bas-relief* panels. The memorial's amphitheater settles back into a Hargreaves' designed landform with maximum low-level views of the adjacent Ohio River. The area serves as a classroom for field trips and small presentations. Selected tree plantings, representing some of Lincoln's personal favorites, soften the striking granite semi-circle seating tiers. Four

famous Lincoln quotes are carved deeply into the stone: "With malice toward none, with charity for all;" "A house divided against itself cannot stand;" "As I would not be a slave, so I would not be a master;" and "I, too, am a Kentuckian."

After securing a $2 million allocation in the state budget, an additional $350,000 was needed to complete the project. The high cost of granite drove the price above the original estimate, but the family of late Louisville businessman Harry Frazier pledged $250,000 for the memorial and, along with additional funding from the Kentucky Historical Society/ Kentucky Abraham Lincoln Bicentennial Commission and the Waterfront Development Corporation, the goal was reached. The state historical society provided research, historical context and background materials during the design phase of the project. Hamilton was ably assisted in three of the *bas-relief* panels by artist Juliet Ehrlich, while the fourth panel "Slavery and Emancipation," was his sole creation.

Shortly after the Lincoln Memorial was officially unveiled on June 4, 2009, a summer workshop for Kentucky teachers toured the site. Camie Stevens, a participant in the workshop, wrote back to WDC officials and described her reaction to the Lincoln site, "I now realize history matters to Kentucky. What a rich and varied history we have! As a Kentuckian I should be embracing my state and reflecting our history to my students. I always knew we had 'history' but I don't think I truly felt it until now."

Taking the Plunge

By 2010, as the park matured and neared its completion, WDC officials recognized an unforeseen demand. Almost immediately upon opening the small blacktopped surface in 1989, people found their way to the river's edge and quickly asked for more programs, more events and more opportunities to visit Waterfront Park. Given the flexibility of the grounds, people came up with their own uses including numerous weddings or photo shoot backdrops. An early concert series, Rockin' at Riverpoints, consistently attracted crowds to enjoy the diverse combination of musical acts and styles. The annual civic rites of Thunder Over Louisville and the Independence Festival drew unparalleled audiences, and seemed to increase every year. By 2010, more than 120 different events were hosted in Waterfront Park each year.

WDC staff was encouraged to suggest and create new attractions to the Park. David Karem recalled when a staff member came to him with a fresh idea.

ASHLEY COX, ONE OF OUR YOUNGER EMPLOYEES, HAS ALREADY BEEN HERE MORE THAN 12 YEARS NOW. SHE OVERSEES ALL THE EVENTS IN THE PARK. SHE CAME IN ONE DAY AND HAD A BRAINSTORM AND WANTED TO DO A THING CALLED WATERFRONT WEDNESDAYS. BRIGHT GUY THAT I AM, I SAID, NOBODY WILL REMEMBER THESE EVENTS HAPPEN ON THE LAST WEDNESDAY OF THE MONTH. BUT I REALLY BELIEVE THAT PEOPLE NEED TO BE EMPOWERED TO MAKE DECISIONS AND BE CREATIVE, SO I SAID WE'LL FIND SEED MONEY AND SEE IF YOU CAN MAKE IT WORK. NOW EVERYBODY CALLS UP AND WANTS TO KNOW WHO ARE THE BANDS. VERY ECLECTIC BANDS AND THEY GET FIVE TO EIGHT THOUSAND PEOPLE TO EVERY EVENT. IT'S VERY SUCCESSFUL. SHE ALSO MANAGES THE WATERFRONT INDEPENDENCE FESTIVAL THAT UNDER HER DIRECTION HAS GROWN FROM A ONE-DAY TO A TWO-DAY EVENT.

The public had no problem remembering the alliterative Waterfront Wednesdays, but the name did not spring from some elaborate marketing study or audience testing. Cox had enrolled at the University of Louisville for a master's degree in business, and she was in classes all day Tuesdays and Thursdays. Wednesdays were her free day, so that was when she was able to supervise the once-monthly evening events. Thanks to corporate sponsorships, a close partnership with the local public radio station and vendor fees, the Waterfront Wednesdays, a concert

series free to the public, turns a small annual profit for the WDC.

A far greater profit for the entire Louisville community resulted from the realization that the convenient and attractive Waterfront Park was the ideal site to host charitable fundraising events, especially the "health walks" that cost little to produce and have proven profitable to not-for-profit organizations. It is not unusual for the park to host several charitable walks on the same weekend, when charities solicit pledges for individuals to come together and walk or run to earn donations.

As local charities realized the popularity of Waterfront Park, many began holding fundraising events like health walks and mini-marathons on the park's grounds. In 2010 the Friends of the Waterfront initiated their own park walk to raise funds and awareness of the riverfront facilities. *(Photo courtesy of Sandra Farmer Runyon)*

One of the most unusual and profitable annual events takes advantage of the park's direct access to the Ohio River. In late February, the Louisville Polar Plunge is held at the docks near the Tumbleweed Restaurant to benefit Special Olympics-Kentucky. Corporate teams, schools and law enforcement divisions solicit donations for their willingness to jump into the usually frigid river water. In 2010 the morning event attracted 1,300 participants and raised a staggering $340,000 in donations.

This was not the only charity to benefit from holding its events at the waterfront. In 2009 over $2.7 million was raised

After twenty-five years of work, the original Master Plan for Waterfront Park is nearly completed, creating what has been called a "jewel at the river's edge." The Waterfront Park will never be finished, as new ideas and opportunities present themselves, and visitors discover new ways to enjoy their park at the river's edge. *(WDC photo by Rick Bell)*

by non-profit organizations and agencies, including: Walk MS; Michael Quinlan Brain Tumor Foundation Walk; Lung Walk; Cruisin' for the Crusade; Liver Life Walk; Alzheimer's Walk; Champions 4 Her Walk, the Kidney Walk; Conquer Chiari; the Hunger Walk; Kentuckians Start!; Diabetes Walk; Komen Race for the Cure; Aveda Walk for Water; Making Strides for Breast Cancer; Heart Association; Down Syndrome Run/Walk and dozens of others. In 2010 the Friends of the Waterfront got into the act with a fundraising walk of their own to benefit Park programs and maintenance.

Nowhere in the enabling documents of the Master Plan or Mission Statement is there mention of the park's impact on local philanthropy. Waterfront Park, the beneficiary of generous donations, provides many civic groups a place that is convenient, safe, clean, centrally located and available for their solicitation events.

"...creating a public place for all citizens"

Providing access to every visitor was an early and emphasized part of Waterfront Park's Master Plan. In 1999, even with only a portion of the facilities completed, Dr. James O. Chatham, chair of the Human Rights Commission, wrote to WDC officials and told of his group's satisfaction with the Park's sensitive design in 1999.

ON BEHALF OF THE LOUISVILLE AND JEFFERSON COUNTY HUMAN RELATIONS COMMISSION, I WISH TO EXTEND A HEARTFELT THANK YOU FOR THE EXCEPTIONAL JOB THE WATERFRONT DEVELOPMENT CORPORATION HAS DONE IN CREATING A PUBLIC PLACE THAT ALL CITIZENS, INCLUDING THE DISABLED, CAN MAKE FULL USE OF AND ENJOY. YOUR INTENT TO CREATE A WELCOMING PLACE TO ALL INDIVIDUALS WAS APPARENT IN THE INITIAL PLANNING STAGES, WHEN YOU INVITED REPRESENTATIVES OF THIS COMMISSION, AS WELL AS MEMBERS OF THE DISABLED COMMUNITY, TO MEET WITH

The staff of the Waterfront Development Corporation is an unusually unified team that has planned, built and maintained the park. Most of the senior staff members have been present since the early days of the Waterfront project, providing a strong sense of continuity and commitment to the mission of the park to restore Louisville's riverfront and make it open to the public.

THE ARCHITECTS AND DEVELOPERS OF THE PARK.

THE ACCESS BOARD, THE REGULATING BODY OF THE AMERICANS WITH DISABILITIES ACT, HAS RECENTLY STARTED HOLDING HEARINGS ON OUTDOOR FACILITIES SUCH AS THE WATERFRONT PARK. THE WATERFRONT DEVELOPMENT CORPORATION'S GUIDANCE IN DEVELOPING A PARK INCLUSIVE TO ALL PEOPLE WILL MOST LIKELY BE A MODEL EXAMPLE OF WHAT CAN BE ACCOMPLISHED.

– DR. JAMES O. CHATHAM

That commitment to service is subtly evident in building ramps on sidewalks, controlling the pitch of grades and providing hard-paved wheelchair access to nearly all areas of the park. In 2010 a new program incorporating a Universal Signage System was inaugurated by creating a prototype of an outdoor Braille information sign. The signage system, created by an emerging Louisville firm, DeLeon & Primmer Architecture Workshop, was made possible by a grant from the Keeney Foundation. The first installation is on the pathway leading to the Lincoln Memorial and features Braille lettering on a one-piece stainless steel exhibit stand. Sidewalk footings are made with paving blocks to aid in detection of the wayfinding signs for sightless visitors. The initial installation proved successful enough to become the model for additional signage throughout the park.

Blown Away

Providing "a model of what can be accomplished" becomes more and more evident with the passage of time and the completion of the park project. Writer Joan Pauley, in a 2007 edition of *Smart Growth* magazine, describes her reaction to returning to Louisville and talking to local experts about her positive experience.

BLOWN AWAY. THAT'S MY DESCRIPTION FOR LOUISVILLE, KENTUCKY'S DOWNTOWN RENAISSANCE.

THE CITY THAT GIVES THE WORLD THE GREATEST TWO MINUTES IN SPORTS HAS SHOWN ME THE GREATEST TWO YEARS IN SMART GROWTH DEVELOPMENT.

I LEFT LOUISVILLE IN 2005 AND MADE MY WAY HOME TO ATLANTA. BY SHEER CHANCE, I LANDED WITH A GROUP OF SMART GROWTH URBAN PLANNERS AND JOINED THE CHARETTE CIRCUS.

WE PLANNED CITIES USING SMART GROWTH PRINCIPLES. THAT'S CALLED A PLANNING CHARETTE, AND THE GOALS ARE LOFTY: CREATE WALKABLE COMMUNITIES TO HELP REDUCE OUR ALMOST COMPLETE DEPENDENCY ON THE AUTOMOBILE, RECYCLE OLD BUILDINGS AND LAND FOR MIXED USES, AND FOCUS GROWTH IN DEVELOPED AREAS TAKING FULL ADVANTAGE OF EXISTING INFRASTRUCTURE AND ACCESS TO PUBLIC TRANSPORTATION.

WITH NEW EYES AND A SHARPENED SENSITIVITY FOR THE BUILT ENVIRONMENT, I RETURNED TO LOUISVILLE. I WALKED MAIN AND MARKET STREETS AND STROLLED WATERFRONT PARK. LOUISVILLE WAS FILLING IN, SPRUCING UP AND PAYING VISIBLE HOMAGE TO ITS ARCHITECTURAL ROOTS. IT WAS SMART GROWTH ON ORGANIC STEROIDS. AND, IT WAS COOL. I WOULD NOT HAVE DESCRIBED DOWNTOWN LOUISVILLE AS COOL BACK IN 2005.

I WONDERED WHAT HAPPENED. COULD LOUISVILLE'S DOWNTOWN BURST SOMEHOW POINT THE WAY FOR OTHER CITIES? DID EARLY RISK-TAKING DEVELOPERS EVEN CARE ABOUT SMART GROWTH? OR WAS IT A NATURAL BY-PRODUCT TO SOMETHING ELSE?

I WAS DETERMINED TO UNDERSTAND WHAT WENT RIGHT THROUGH THE EYES OF THESE DOWNTOWN DEVELOPERS.

BILL WEYLAND, MANAGING DIRECTOR, CITY PROPERTIES GROUP, LLC

"I DON'T KNOW ABOUT OTHER CITIES, BUT A LOT OF OUR DOWNTOWN DEVELOPMENT HAS BEEN DRIVEN BY ARCHITECTS WHO MORPHED INTO DEVELOPERS," WEYLAND SAID. "IN MY OPINION, THAT'S UNIQUE."

THIRTY YEARS AGO, HE SAID, DOWNTOWN WAS LIKE A GIANT FACTORY: WINDOWLESS BUILDINGS, INDUSTRIAL SITES, TREE-FREE STREETSCAPES. THE GOAL AFTER WORK WAS A FAST ESCAPE TO SUBURBIA. "NOW WE'RE BUILDING FROM THE HUMAN STANDPOINT."

LOUISVILLE ALSO DID NOT FALL VICTIM TO THE SILVER BULLET MENTALITY. A GOOD URBAN MASTER PLAN, EXPANSION OF THE UNIVERSITY OF LOUISVILLE'S MEDICAL DISTRICT AND PRIVATE DEVELOPMENT WERE ALL CONTRIBUTING FACTORS.

ULTIMATELY, SMART GROWTH IS PERSONAL TO WEYLAND. "I LOVE OLD BUILDINGS AND THEIR STORIES. THAT'S WHAT YOU LOSE WHEN YOU TEAR DOWN A BUILDING," HE SAID. "PEOPLE STOP ME ON THE STREET AND SHARE THEIR PERSONAL CONNECTIONS TO THESE BUILDINGS. THAT'S JUST FABULOUS."

STEVE POE, DEVELOPER, MUSEUM PLAZA

ASK STEVE POE WHAT ACCOUNTS FOR LOUISVILLE'S DOWNTOWN REDEVELOPMENT SUCCESS, AND HE IMMEDIATELY POINTS TO PUBLIC POLICY AND PRIORITIES SET MANY YEARS AGO STARTING WITH THE WATERFRONT PARK IN THE LATE 1980S.

"WATERFRONT PARK IS A VISIBLE SIGN OF POLICY AND INVESTMENT MATCHING UP," POE SAID. THE CITY MADE THE INVESTMENT TO GIVE BACK TO THE COMMUNITY OPEN, COMMON SPACE. SOME PEOPLE QUESTIONED THAT DECISION. WHY BUY UP LAND, WHEN WE'VE GOT A WORLD-RENOWNED OLMSTED PARK SYSTEM? THAT'S ALL CHANGED NOW, BUT GOVERNMENT IS THE ONLY INSTITUTION THAT CAN TAKE THE LEAD AND SET THOSE PRIORITIES."

POE BELIEVES PUBLIC OFFICIALS AND GOVERNMENT ARE LOOKING AT NEW PRIORITIES. "IT SEEMS THE PUBLIC IS COMING BACK DOWNTOWN," HE SAID, NOTING THE DEMOGRAPHIC SHIFT UNDER WAY. EMPTY NESTERS AND YOUNG PEOPLE JUST ENTERING HOMEOWNERSHIP ARE GROWING IN NUMBERS. BOTH GROUPS LOOK FOR AMENITIES FOUND IN SMART GROWTH AREAS.

Renaissance at the River's Edge

And people have returned to the Louisville waterfront, the birthplace of the city. Each person comes for a different reason, each seeking his/her own riverside experience. In the twenty-five-year history of the Waterfront Development Corporation, a renaissance at the river's edge has re-animated and inspired the city, and the park serves as a successful model for communities worldwide to emulate.

When David Karem was asked if the Park reflects the character of Louisville, he replied with a studied and perceptive opinion.

IT MEANS MANY THINGS, IT REFLECTS UPON THE PEOPLE, THE DIVERSITY. THE FACT THAT EVERY CORNER OF THE COMMUNITY IS WELCOME HERE, AND SEES THIS AS A SOURCE OF PRIDE. THEY SEE THE OHIO AS THE MOTHER RIVER, AS THE SOURCE OF OUR LIVES. PEOPLE IN LOUISVILLE UNDERSTAND THAT WHEN THEY TURN THE FAUCET ON IN THEIR HOUSE, THE SUSTENANCE IS THE RIVER. THEY SEE THAT RIVER WATER FLOWING BY AND THEY REALIZE AT SOME LEVEL IT IS A LIFE-GIVING FLUID THAT THIS TOWN IS LUCKY TO HAVE.

THAT LOUISVILLE REFLECTS THE LOVE OF THE RIVER, REFLECTS THE FACT THAT THE RIVER GIVES US LIFE. WE'RE RICH AND POOR, WE'RE BLACK AND WHITE AND HISPANIC, WE'RE EVERY RELIGION YOU CAN THINK OF, AND WE ALL COME DOWN TO THIS PLACE. AND THAT'S NOT POETIC OR HIGH-THINKING, THAT IS JUST REALITY. THEY COME DOWN TO THIS PLACE BECAUSE IT IS A JOYOUS PLACE TO BE. IT DOES REFLECT PEOPLE WANTING TO BE A COMMUNITY, WANTING TO BE A COMMUNITY IN A POSITIVE WAY.

LONG-TIME BOARD MEMBER OLLIE BARBER ALWAYS SAYS, "WHAT I LOVE ABOUT THIS PARK IS THAT SOMEBODY FROM EVERY PART OF THIS COMMUNITY IS HERE AND THEY'RE ENJOYING THEMSELVES, AND THEY ARE AT PEACE WITH EACH OTHER IN A WONDERFUL SETTING." AND I THINK THAT'S WHAT IT'S ALL ABOUT, IF THERE'S ANY SUCCESS OF THE PLACE, IT'S THAT PEOPLE LOVE IT AND CARE FOR IT, AND THAT IT'S HERE FOR THEM. I THINK PEOPLE ARE RESPECTFUL OF THE PARK. IT GOES ALL THE WAY BACK TO THE BEGINNING, THAT WE HAD NO CENTRAL GATHERING PLACE. NOW WE HAVE THAT CENTRAL GATHERING PLACE, AND THAT CENTRAL GATHERING PLACE IS OPEN TO EVERYBODY. AND THAT'S WHAT IT'S ALL ABOUT.